The FEAST *of* CORPUS CHRISTI

The
FEAST
of
CORPUS CHRISTI

Barbara R. Walters

Vincent Corrigan

Peter T. Ricketts

The Pennsylvania State University Press
University Park, Pennsylvania

Library of Congress Cataloging-in-Publication Data

Walters, Barbara R.
The Feast of Corpus Christi / by Barbara R. Walters, Vincent
Corrigan, Peter T. Ricketts.
p. cm.
Includes bibliographical references and indexes.
ISBN 0–271–02924–2 (clothbound : alk. paper)
1. Corpus Christi Festival. I. Corrigan, Vincent J. (Vincent
Justus), 1946- II. Ricketts, Peter T. III. Title.
BV63.W35 2006
263'.97--dc22
2006008926

The Pennsylvania State University Press is a member of the
Association of American University Presses.

CONTENTS

LIST OF TABLES AND INDICES

ACKNOWLEDGMENTS

A project that spans the efforts of close to two decades requires sustaining support from many people. In this case, the debt of gratitude is magnified by the special circumstances under which the book took shape, and I cannot hope to thank and acknowledge by name each person who helped. *The Feast of Corpus Christi* began over sixteen years ago, when somewhat naively I embarked on a research project for a short sociological essay on the integration of a feast day into the liturgical year. The feast of Corpus Christi came forth as an obvious choice. However, medieval studies, never an easy field, is all the more daunting when approached late in life as an outsider without the requisite skills—skills more easily acquired at a younger age. Therefore, this project stretched out and took shape across many years.

The fledgling project was initially facilitated by a temporary appointment as a Visiting Scholar at the State University of New York at Stony Brook in 1990. In their library, I discovered Juliana of Mont Cornillon through an article in *Scriptorium* by L. M. J. Delaissé. Perhaps the only intuition of the obvious over the past sixteen years concerned her authorship of the initial liturgy for the office called *Animarum cibus*. When I soon thereafter discovered the thirteenth-century Mosan Psalters at a book exhibit, the connection between these two forms of prayer from the same community importuned more systematic examination than available in existing scholarly sources. A graduate seminar in fourteenth-century musicology brought me into contact with medieval musicologist Sarah Fuller, who served as mentor and guide through the world of medieval music over the next four years. I thank her and Patrick Heelan, S.J., for support and advice during the formative stage of the project and for their assistance in engineering a post-doctoral re-admission to Stony Brook, so that I could matriculate in the Department of Music. I also thank the Department of Philosophy at Stony Brook, where I completed a number of graduate seminars germane to the topic, and in particular Richard Kramer, then Dean of Arts and Humanities at Stony Brook, who helped navigate this project through the surrounding tumult of academic disciplinary boundaries and politics. I am grateful for a small award for supplies from the Department of Music and to Daniel Kinney, Associate Director for Libraries at SUNY–Stony Brook, who provided invaluable assistance in assembling the initial collection of microfilms, microfiches and photocopies for the study of the Feast of Corpus Christi. It would be impossible to thank each of the numerous other librarians at our home institutions and at the institutions used in the research who assisted in the acquisition and appropriate referencing for facsimiles of original documents and secondary sources, but I am most appreciative of their assistance in bringing this book to fruition. The image on the front cover, from The Pierpont Morgan Library, MS M563.4, is reproduced with the kind permission of The Pierpont Morgan Library.

Cynthia Cyrus, Chair of the Music Department of Vanderbilt University, introduced me to the International Congress of Medieval Studies, and Musicology at Kalamazoo, in 1994, as I continued working toward completion of a second M.A. in Musicology, awarded in 1996. Without Musicology at Kalamazoo, this project would have faltered at the outset, and I am extremely grateful to her and the many accomplished musicological colleagues who have offered hospitality to an outsider in their intellectual home. Especially the late Ingrid Brainard secured a place for me at the Congress, prepared me for four days of dormitory life at Western Michigan University, and initiated me into the academic etiquette that characterizes this special academic environment. As the magnitude of the project unfolded before me, Ann Buckley took me under her wing, helped me navigate through the Congress and the politics of Musicology, writing often by e-mail in support of my work. It was our good fortune to encounter Peter T. Ricketts together, quite by chance, at a dormitory lunch in 1997, where he was drawn into the task of translating the poems from the Mosan Psalters. Peter has been a superb collaborator, mentor, and friend, and I thank both him and his wife, Monica, for their patience, support, time, and energy over the past ten years—and, of course, Peter, for his splendid critical edition of the poems, which is part of this volume.

In 1998, I presented a paper on Paris, Bibliothèque nationale de France, lat. 1143 (BNF 1143) at a Musicology in Kalamazoo session, which Vincent Corrigan attended. We met the next morning for a dormitory breakfast, and Vince, filled with excitement, shared and explained features of the marginalia in the manuscript that I had not yet fully understood. Shortly thereafter I sent to him my collection of microfilms, and he began the long task of patiently, carefully, and diligently transcribing the seven musical manuscripts, which are in Part II of this book. Like Peter Ricketts, Vince has been a collaborator, mentor, and friend over the past eight years, and I thank him for his kindness and generosity of spirit. I also thank both him and his wife, Ann, for their sacrifice of personal time. I am especially grateful to Vince for the transcriptions of manuscripts, which appear here for the first time with musical notation and English translations. His work will serve Corpus Christi scholars for many, many years.

Kingsborough Community College of the City University of New York has provided as supportive an environment as is possible for an interdisciplinary scholar-in-transition—on the border between social science and the humanities—learning a new academic field while working toward tenure. I thank my many colleagues and friends, not least my department chair, William Burger, and our Academic Vice-President and Provost, Stuart Suss, for their support for this intellectual work. I also thank the college for travel funds to attend the International Congress of Medieval Studies each year since 2000. And, I thank the City University of New York for three PSC–CUNY Research Awards, which have provided some release time from teaching.

The Association for the Sociology of Religion (ASR) also has provided a home over the past eight years, and I thank numerous colleagues who have welcomed, reviewed, and commented on early papers. Especially Lutz Kaelber, Patricia Wittberg, William Swatos, and six anonymous reviewers have provided invaluable insights on related articles published over the past five years. I am particularly grateful to Joseph A. Komonchak, mentor, advisor, and friend, plus three outside reviewers who provided invaluable critical comments and suggestions on the book manuscript. Thanks also to Peter S. Peek, who provided crucial help in the Latin translations, and to Carl W. Hoegerl, C.S.S.R., for his translation of the Saint Thomas Aquinas sermon on Luke 14. And, I would like to express my appreciation to Barbara Newman, who most graciously responded to my first phone call in 1990 and has given permission for the extensive quotations from her translation of Juliana's vita.

Through a special ASR session, I met our editor, Peter J. Potter, Associate Director and Editor-in-Chief of Pennsylvania State University Press (since moved to Cornell University Press), who has nurtured and encouraged this book since 2001. I thank him for his patience, support, and gentle guidance in bringing the disparate pieces together into a single coherent book. Peter has been an invaluable resource in keeping us posted on medieval publications of interest across the wide range of discipline fields relevant to this book. Juleen Audrey Eichinger, of Eichinger Communications, LLC, began working on this manuscript in 2004, and we thank her for her conscientious and diligent editorial work, including her careful reading and insightful organizational comments on earlier versions.

My parents, Eugene and Juanita Walters, now in their eighties, provided much of the childhood formation that was pivotal in conceptualizing this work. I thank them for this and their beneficence, which in part made possible this mid-life scholarly transition. My husband, Steven Doehrman, has been a sustaining force behind the project, providing the resources of warmth, friendship, and encouragement over the years. I thank him, not least, for climbing the spiral staircase with me to the top of the highest tower of the Basilica of Saint Martin's in Liège and for sharing with me all of the other signal moments in the creation of this book.

Finally, Vince Corrigan, Peter Ricketts, and I express our deepest appreciation to Saints Juliana of Mont Cornillon and Thomas Aquinas, to whom this book is dedicated, for the resources and inspiration.

Barbara R. Walters
Bay Ridge, Brooklyn
March 1, 2006

ABBREVIATIONS

CHURCH OFFICES

A	Antiphon
Ag	Agnus Dei
All	Alleluia
Ant	Antiphon
Bene	Benedictus
Cant	Canticle
Com	Communion
H	Hymn
Int	Introit
Inv	Invitatory
K	Kyrie
Gl	Gloria
Grad	Gradual
Mag	Magnificat
ND	Nunc dimittis
Noct	Nocturn
Off	Offertory
Ps	Psalm
R	Responsory
Rb	Short Responsory
San	Sanctus
Seq	Sequence
Vers	Versicle
Vesp	Vespers

MANUSCRIPTS

10770	Rome, Biblioteca Apostolica Vaticana, Vat. lat. 10770
10772	Rome, Biblioteca Apostolica Vaticana, Vat. lat. 10772
Barb	Rome Biblioteca Apostolica Vaticana, Barb. BBB. 1 1 [Dominican breviary, 1481]
BL Add. 21114	London, British Library, Add. 21114
BL Stowe	London, British Library, Stowe 17
BNF 755	Paris, Bibliothèque nationale de France, latin 755
BNF 1051	Paris, Bibliothèque nationale de France, latin 1051
BNF 1077	Paris, Bibliothèque nationale de France, latin 1077
BNF 1143	Paris, Bibliothèque nationale de France, latin 1143
BNF 1235	Paris, Bibliothèque nationale de France n.a., latin 1235
BR 139	Brussels, Bibliothèque royale, 139
BR IV—36	Brussels, Bibliothèque royale, IV–36
BR IV—1013	Brussels, Bibliothèque royale, IV–1013
BR IV—1066	Brussels, Bibliothèque royale, IV–1066
BYU	Brigham Young University, Harold B. Lee Library, Special Collections, Vault 091 263 1343
Chigi	Rome, Biblioteca Apostolica Vaticana, Chigi C V 138
EU	Edinburgh, University Library MS 211.iv
's-Heerenberg, S. H. B. 35	's-Heerenberg, Stichting Huis Bergh, 35 (225)
Fitzwilliam	Cambridge, Fitwilliam Museum, 288
Graz 134	Graz, Universitätsbibliothek, MS 134
KB 70.E.4	The Hague, National Library of the Netherlands, MS 70.E.4
KB 76.G.17	The Hague, National Library of the Netherlands, 76.G.17
Lat VI–133	Rome, Biblioteca Apostolica Vaticana, Codex Reg. Lat. V1–133 [Dominican breviary, 1480s]
Liège 431	Liège, Bibliothèque de l'Université, 431
M440	New York, Pierpont Morgan Library, 440
Melbourne	Melbourne, State Library of Victoria, *096/R66
Morgan 183	New York, Pierpont Morgan Library, 183
Rochester	Rochester, Memorial Art Gallery, 53.68
Strahov	Prague, Abbey of Strahov, MS D.E.I.7

TEXTS

AH   Dreves, Guido M., and Clemens Blume, eds. *Analecta Hymnica medii aevi.* 55 vols. Leipzig, 1886–1922.

AS   Frere, Walter Howard. *Antiphonale Sarisburiense.* London: Plainsong and Mediaeval Music Society, 1901–25. Repr. Farnborough, Hants., Eng.: Gregg Press, 1966.

CAO   Hesbert, Rene-Jean. *Corpus antiphonalium officii.* 5 vols. Rome: Herder, 1963–75.

GS   Frere, Walter Howard. *Graduale Sarisburiense*. London: Plainsong and Mediaeval Music Society, 1894. Repr. Farnborough, Hants., Eng.: Gregg Press, 1966.

Jones   Jones, C. W. *The Saint Nicholas Liturgy and its Literary Relationships*. Berkeley: University of California Press, 1963.

LMLO   Hughes, Andrew. *Late Medieval Liturgical Offices*. Toronto: Pontifical Institute of Mediaeval Studies, 1994.

LR   *Liber responsorialis juxta ritum monasticum*. Solesmis: Typographeo Sancti Petri, 1895.

LU   *Liber usualis, with Introduction and Rubrics in English*. Tournai: Desclée, 1963.

ODO   *Ordo divini officii Beati Jacobi Apostoli Maioris, patroni ecclesie parrochialis eiusdem sancti Hacobi de Carnificeria*. Paris, 1581.

Ox   *Oxford: Bodleian Library MS. Lat. Liturg. B. 5*. Ed. David Hiley. Publications of Mediaeval Musical Manuscripts No. 20. Ottawa: The Institute of Mediaeval Music, 1995.

Pat   *Antiphonale Pataviense (Wien 1519)*. Ed. Karlheinz Schlager. *Das Erbe deutscher Musik*. Vol. 88. Kassel: Bärenreiter, 1985.

PL   *Patrologia cursus completus: Series latina*, ed. J.-P. Migne, 221 vols. Paris, 1841–64.

Pm   *Processional monasticum*. Solesmis: Typographeo Sancti Petri, 1893.

RH   Chevalier, Ulysse. *Repertorium hymnologicum*. Brussels: Société Bollandistes, 1920–21.

ST   Stäblein, Bruno. *Die Hymnen. Monumenta monodica medii aevi* Bd. 1. Kassel: Bärenreiter, 1956.

Syg   *Le Codex 903 de la Bibliothèque Nationale de Paris (XIe siècle): Graduel de Saint-Yrieix. Paléographie musicale XIII*. Berne: Editions Herbert Lang et Cie, 1971.

Ut   *Utrecht: Bibliotheek der Rijksuniversiteit, Ms 406 (3.J.7)*. Intro. Ike de Loos, index by Charles Downey, ed. Ruth Steiner. Ottawa: The Institute of Medieval Music, 1997.

WA   *Antiphonaire monastique XIIIe siècle: Codex F. 160 de la Bibliothèque de la Cathédrale de Worcester. Paléographie musicale XII*. Berne: Editions Herbert Lang et Cie, 1971.

Wales   *National Library of Wales MS 20541 E: The Penpoint Antiphonal*. Intro. and indices by Owain Tudor Edwards. Ottawa: The Institute of Medieval Music, 1997.

PREFACE

The feast of Corpus Christi, added to the liturgical calendar in 1264, represents the only addition to the *Temporale* in the thirteenth century. It celebrates the sacrament of the Eucharist, believed by Catholics to have been initiated by Jesus at the Last Supper on the Passover Thursday preceding his crucifixion. The feast day and its octave were added to the calendar in the wake of philosophical-theological debates about the Real Presence and during a historical period in which religious rituals and their interpretations achieved a center stage position. The Fourth Lateran Council in 1215 established the doctrine of transubstantiation, with the intention of reconciling several divergent strains of thought that had produced controversy regarding the nature of the Eucharist during the twelfth century. The controversy was both amplified and ultimately resolved by the reception and absorption of Aristotelian thought into the domain of Neo-Platonist Christian theology during the thirteenth century. The official version of the office and Mass for the new feast, generally accepted as the work of Saint Thomas Aquinas and composed sometime after 1261, integrated the seemingly contradictory ideas of a literal physical presence and a spiritual presence reflected in the debates among the literate celebrants. Its famous homily provides a definitive statement regarding the meaning of transubstantiation; however, the liturgical office and Mass, like all works of artistic genius, resists simplistic discursive synopsis.

The intellectual context shaped by the reception of Aristotle and the accompanying new ideas about God, humans, and nature only partially explain the excitement and controversy that surrounded the development and institution of the new feast of Corpus Christi. Debates in philosophical theology during the twelfth and thirteenth centuries emerged in tandem with an official emphasis on rituals for elevating and reserving the Host. This official thrust from the Church hierarchy was echoed in a groundswell of popular piety, often expressed as miraculous visions of the presence of Jesus in the Eucharist. Because the new feast of Corpus Christi celebrated this sacrament, it galvanized and channeled widespread and popular religious emotions, providing focus in the broader contest for symbolic power and meaning. It struck a resonant chord as the emblem of a religious movement led by Juliana of Mont Cornillon, a religious woman in Liège, in a socio-historical context that gave rise to religious seekers. Within the diocese, numerous individuals, dislocated in social space by rapid changes, embarked on searches for structure, meaning, and identities that transcended their ordinary, disheveled, and prosaic pursuits, thereby fueling the human source of reception for Juliana's religious vision. The Eucharist emerged as the central symbol of faith and provided a ritual of iconic unity for a Church seeking to organize the increasingly urban and pluralist congregations into a centralized and hierocratic temporal domain.

The context of the feast provides the constituting exemplar for what Max Weber referred to as the ideal-typical Church, with its characteristic convergence of political, moral, and religious authority that emerged in tandem with a professional priesthood. This western European medieval hierocracy was simultaneously disembedded and engaged in the mundane world. According to S. N. Eisenstadt, as part of its characteristic features, political, military, and economic activities in the mundane world were by logical necessity reconstructed in accordance with other-worldly orientations and values, and these provided legitimation for the authority of religious and political elites. The requisite emphasis on the other-worldly coincided with the creation of a vast system of symbols, for which the Eucharist served as the perfect centerpiece. Specifically in reference to the feast of Corpus Christi, Miri Rubin defined religious rituals, language, and symbols as the central tools of the High Middle Ages, used to explain how the natural and supernatural were intertwined with human action in a paradigm of sacramentality, with the Eucharist at its heart. By the thirteenth century, the rich univocal power nexus and symbolic system of the Church was, in the words of Jacques Le Goff, "running out of steam." The Church and its power thereafter faced increasingly vociferous challenges to its religious authority and symbolic capital, and these repeated challenges both provoked and amplified prosecutorial reactions.

The feast of Corpus Christi arose in the midst of the legitimacy crisis and ecclesiastic reaction. Particularly in Liège, a rising stratum of urban bourgeoisie had begun to encroach on privileges that were the preserve of an already established patriciate, the prince-bishops, and the nobility. The bourgeoisie of Liège had been among the first to achieve political representation through a commune, and Liège was perhaps the first site of urban conflict. New political rivalries emerged with this growing urban political force and dominated Liège politics throughout the thirteenth century—exacerbated by Liège's situation in the broader context of conflict between the Guelphs (the party of the papacy) and the Ghibellines (the party of the Holy Roman Emperor, Frederick II). Beginning early in the thirteenth century with Bishop Hugh of Pierpont, the Liège prelates turned away from the party of the emperor and toward the papacy, while successive popes allied with France. The local turmoil was further amplified by internecine quarrels among the lower nobility in Flanders, as well as by complex but subtle rivalries among various religious stations and orders. Marginalized unmarried women and widows, whose experience with political machinations and violence was most likely entirely negative, were especially vulnerable, and it is therefore no surprise that the new feast of Corpus Christi emerged from the center of their community.

Brian Stock, with distinguished empirical fluency in medieval history, has noted both the weaknesses and strengths of the ubiquitous Weberian church-sect typology and has commented on Weber's somewhat schematic view of the medieval mentality. More important, in tandem with sociologist Norbert Elias, Stock has noted the significance of literacy and texts in understanding and interpreting the increasing rationality, diversity, and transformation that characterized the High Medieval period, factors overlooked by Weber and many later sociological interpreters. Literacy paradoxically both enabled the fissures that rent apart the old feudal order and at the same time facilitated the emerging bonds between urban patricians and the literate hierocratic Church authorities. Literacy, texts, and their face-to-face communities—as was the case for defining the Eucharist in the twelfth century—constituted the core of the movement to institutionalize the feast of Corpus Christi. The new literacy and new texts fueled what Pierre Bourdieu refers to as distinctions between genuine "literati" in Church Latin and the proliferating ranks of oral preachers and religious texts in vernacular dialects, which became contenders in the struggle for recognition, status, and legitimation. These pivotal trends are central in the movement to establish the feast of Corpus Christi and are central to this book.

All liturgical materials used in the authorized version of the office and Mass for the feast of Corpus Christi up to the time of Vatican II were generated or centonated between 1236 and 1311 as part of the initial enthusiasm surrounding the adoption of the new feast day. These include universal melodic favorites, which were given new texts, such as *Cibavit eos*, *Lauda Syon*, and *Pange lingua*; authorship of these traditionally has been attributed to Saint Thomas Aquinas. The liturgical materials also include the less well-known texts and melodies from earlier and multiple versions of the new office and Mass. The official Church doctrine of transubstantiation, first expressed in the famous homily by Saint Thomas, remains unchanged to the present day.

Equally important to this study of the feast of Corpus Christi is a primitive version of the liturgy from an oral music-textual tradition attributed to Juliana of Mont Cornillon, as well as psalters, or Books of Hours, used by religious laity in her community in imitation of clerical office hours. While these examples in Popular Latin and a regional dialect of Old French recede into the background in a study of great literature, they provide invaluable sociological information regarding the interface between popular piety and the literary religious authority. This book, therefore, through its inclusion of these more popular cultural artifacts, provides the first comprehensive presentation of source materials germane to the institution and recognition of the feast of Corpus Christi in the thirteenth and early fourteenth centuries.

The authors of this volume have drawn materials from two different kinds of manuscript sources germane to the topic: liturgical books from the thirteenth century in Latin, used by clerics or monks in their daily rounds of office prayers and the Mass, such as breviaries, antiphonals, and missals; and more decorative manuscripts in the Liège dialect of Old French known as the Mosan Psalters. These two sets of resources taken together provide both diachronic evidence on the official liturgical history of the feast and synchronic evidence regarding the problematic interface between literate elites and the regional and oral dialects of the emerging commercial classes, but especially women. Women's speech and writing betray an endorsement of the very system of intellectual, social, and moral evaluation that excluded, marginalized, and otherwise worked against their individual recognition in historical time, but that simultaneously appropriated and preserved their works for human history.

Part I of this volume includes an introduction to the feast and its founder, Juliana Mont Cornillon. It employs an interdisciplinary approach, using some basic concepts and insights from the social sciences to describe and analyze the initiation and reception of the new feast of Corpus Christi. It aims to provide the reader with a context for the critical editions of liturgical manuscripts and of vernacular poems in Old French from the psalters, executed by Vincent Corrigan and Peter T. Ricketts in Parts II and III respectively. Especially important to the introduction are the many new publications on related topics, general studies on the thirteenth century realized over the past decade by scholars from all disciplines, and the recent publications of other source documents, such as critical editions of Juliana's *vita* with translations into French and English.

Part II consists of a brief introduction by Barbara Walters and critical editions by Vincent Corrigan of seven late thirteenth- and early fourteenth-century manuscripts from the period 1269–1320, which are regarded as the central musical sources for the Corpus Christi office. These transmit a record of three major offices. The first is *Animarum cibus* and perhaps represents the "original" office composed for the initial celebration of the feast in Liège in 1246. It is preserved in The Hague, National Library of the Netherlands, MS 70.E.4 (KB 70.E.4). The second, *Sapiencia edificavit,* is preserved in Prague, Abbey of Strahov, MS D.E.I.7 (Strahov). It is roughly contemporaneous with, and shares items with, *Sacerdos in eternum,* first recorded in BNF 1143. The latter is the Roman service often attributed to Thomas Aquinas and forms the basis of the version in contemporary liturgical books. Two other central musical sources contain all or part of *Sacerdos in eternum,* but they differ from the version in BNF 1143. Graz, Universitätsbibliothek, MS 134 (Graz 134) contains the entire service in monastic format, but in staffless unheighted notation. The solo portions of the BNF 1143 responsories are transmitted in Brussels, Bibliothèque royale, 139 (BR 139), which also records an alternative set of responsories based on the office for Saint Dominic. Also important for the early history of the feast are two manuscripts more recently been identified by Thomas Mathiesen and Isobel Woods: Brigham Young University, Harold B. Lee Library, Special Collections, *Regimen animarum* (BYU); and Edinburgh University Library, MS 211.iv, the Inchcolm Antiphonary (EU). Both of these contain versions of *Sacerdos in eternum,* but they differ from each other and from the central sources in informative ways. The critical editions of the manuscripts are accompanied by indices that record each musical item from all seven manuscripts by incipit, classify each musical item by genre and manuscript, provide musical incipits for each chant, identify the mode, and identify all concordances between manuscripts. An index is provided for each manuscript in the order of the service, and for all manuscripts using an alphabetical ordering for the musical items.

Part III consists of a brief introduction by Barbara Walters and a critical edition of twenty Old French poems in Liège dialect by Peter T. Ricketts. The critical edition is based on readings found in fourteen manuscripts dated roughly from between 1230 and 1330: New York, Pierpont Morgan Library, 440; BNF 1077; Liège, Bibliothèque de l'Université, 431; The Hague, National Library of the Netherlands, 76.G.17; Melbourne, State Library of Victoria, *096/R66; London, British Library, Add. 21114; 's-Heerenberg, Stichting Huis Bergh, 35 (225); New York, Pierpont Morgan Library, 183; Cambridge, Fitzwilliam Museum, 288; Brussels, Bibliothèque royale, IV–1066; Brussels, Bibliothèque royale, IV–1013; Brussels, Bibliothèque royale, IV–36; London, British Library, Stowe 17; and Rochester, Memorial Art Gallery, 53.68. The critical edition of the poems is accompanied by a critical apparatus and is abridged with extensive commentary and notes by Peter T. Ricketts.

PART I

INTRODUCTION

THE FEAST AND ITS FOUNDER

Barbara R. Walters

THE *VITA* OF JULIANA OF MONT CORNILLON

HAGIOGRAPHIC *VITAE* AND JULIANA'S BIOGRAPHY

Juliana of Mont Cornillon, a religious leader and prophetess from thirteenth-century Liège, was the undisputed leader of the movement to establish the feast of Corpus Christi. The principal source of information about Juliana comes from her *vita* (ca. 1280).[1] The author of the *vita* is unknown; however, he cites an earlier *vita* written in Old French, authored by a "personne fort religieuse" and approved by John of Lausanne, canon of the church of Saint-Martin in Liège. The "personne fort religieuse" is widely believed to be Juliana's friend, Eve of Saint-Martin, who most likely wrote the Old French version immediately upon Juliana's death in 1258.[2] A friend of Canon John is the most probable candidate for the Latin translation, which was executed sometime between 1261 and 1264.

Hagiographic *vitae* served as a popular form of devotional expression during the thirteenth century and earlier. These typically were authored by monks in religious orders and, as a genre, differ significantly from critical biographies.[3] The authors of *vitae* drew together facts and myths about an exemplar to present religious ideals to the faithful and to expand the cult of the saint. Because of the shared ideals in a given reli-

[1] Godefridus Henschenius and Daniel Papebrochius, eds., Vita Julianae, *Acta Sanctorum* April t. 1 (1866), 435–75. Jean-Pierre Delville, ed., *Vie de Sainte Julienne de Cornillo*n, Critical Edition, vol. 2 of *Fête-Dieu (1246–1996)* (Louvain-la-Neuve: Institut d'Études Médiévales de l'Université Catholique de Louvain, 1999), v, cites an earlier version published in Anvers in 1675. The seventeenth-century authors consulted three fifteenth-century manuscripts: one from the Hospice de Saint-Mattieu à la Chaîne à Liège, one from the Chartreux à Liège, and one from the *Hagiologium Brabantinorum* by Jean Gielemans. Delville also notes that in 1946 Cyrille Lambot found a fourth Latin manuscript dated ca. 1280, Bibliothèque de l'Arsenal à Paris (BN 1168A), in which folios 1–56v are titled *Vita venerabilis Iuliannae de Corelion*. Delville's analysis of the manuscripts and their stemmatic filiation can be found in the above-cited Introduction to the critical edition, pp. v–xv. His edition of the *vita* with its translation into French and critical apparatus provides the Latin text source used throughout this introduction to the feast and its founder.

[2] Joseph Demarteau, *La première auteur Wallonne: la bienheureuse Eve de Saint-Martin* (Liège: Demarteau, 1896).

[3] See Catherine M. Mooney, ed., *Gendered Voices: Medieval Saints and their Interpreters* (Philadelphia: University of Pennsylvania Press, 1999).

gious order, which were always situated in a historical life world, there is a great deal of similarity between individuals selected and portrayed in a given time and place. That is, the historically specific saintly prototypes depicted in *vitae* often were constituted at the expense of the vivid biographical details that might provide more accurate descriptions of actual persons. Roisin in 1947 noted this "halo effect" tendency, which resulted from the joining of religious ideals with living people to function as meaningful exemplars to the co-temporal readers of *vitae*.[4] The resulting religious archetypes typically engaged both the psychic-ideal needs and the material interests of their receptive audiences.[5] They shaped and were shaped by real human interaction, attribution, and projection in specific historical contexts. The *vitae* thus are neither literary fiction nor history, but rather are akin to myth. Roisin writes:

> Mais encore fallait-il, pour que ce moyen fût réellement efficace, présenter des modèles incarnant, au jugement des supérieurs, un véritable idéal de sainteté selon l'esprit de leur ordre. Il était tout aussi désirable que cet idéal de sainteté répondît aux aspirations du public auquel il était proposé.[6]

> [But still it was necessary, in order that this vehicle (saintly exemplars) might be really effective, to present living models incarnating, in the judgment of the superiors, a true ideal of sanctity in accordance with the spirit of their order. It was just as desirable for this ideal of sanctity to match the aspirations of the public to whom it was proposed.]

The information in Juliana's *vita* must be interpreted in the context of the hagiographic genre. She was one of a number of thirteenth-century women from the diocese of Liège who appear in the popular Cistercian *vitae*, most of whom, like Juliana, had few formal connections to the Cistercian order.[7] The women portrayed in the genre were nearly always from the educated, urban bourgeoisie. Their stories typically recount a renunciation of wealth and/or marriage combined with an attraction to penitence and contemplation.[8] Sometimes the renunciation was part of a family conflict in which the mother encouraged religious devotion in opposition to a father who applied pressure for an advantageous marriage. But the exemplar message was nearly always the same: an interior movement away from acquisitiveness, pride, and vanity toward humility and purification of the heart in imitation of the human sufferings of Jesus.

The saintly prototype developed in the *vitae* of the Liège women corresponds to a more general transformation in religious ideals during the historical context of their creation and reception, a context in which penitence and sacramental devotion received special emphasis.[9] Church authorities encouraged lay participation in overt religious

---

[4] Simone Roisin, I.E.J., *L'Hagiographie cistercienne dans le diocèse de Liège* (Louvain: Bibliothèque de L'Université, 1947), 80.

[5] Cf. H. H. Gerth and C. Wright Mills, eds. and trans., *From Max Weber: Essays in Sociology* (New York: Oxford University Press, 1946), 62–63.

[6] Roisin, *L'Hagiographie cistercienne dans le diocèse de Liège*, 80.

[7] Ibid.; While Juliana was not a Cistercian, she eventually was buried in their cemetery at Villers.

[8] See Caroline Walker Bynum, *Jesus as Mother: Studies in the Spirituality of the High Middle Ages* (Berkeley: University of California Press, 1982), 1–21.

[9] Roisin, *L'Hagiographie cistercienne dans le diocèse de Liège*; André Vauchez, *Sainthood in the Later Middle Ages*, trans. Jean Birrell (Cambridge: Cambridge University Press, 1997).

rituals celebrating the sacraments. These rituals, such as the Eucharist, confession, and devotion to the elevated Host, symbolized and celebrated the unity of the entire Church. They replaced and supplanted in importance the consecration of military heroics and relics, which in earlier times had enriched and distinguished individual and local monasteries.[10] Women, and especially women in the cultural-religious region of Lotharingia, led this spiritual turn.[11] Thus, Juliana represents the quintessential exemplar of the new religious age. Her *vita* depicts her as capable of inward progress toward Cistercian perfection and highlights her preternatural visions of the Eucharist, which increasingly confirmed the perceived link between spiritual progress and allegiance to the sacerdotal authority of the Church.[12] Moreover, Juliana combined gifts believed to be divinely inspired with the sacramental penitence requisite "to raising those who had fallen."[13] The population of those perceived to have fallen was no doubt numerous and growing in the context of incessant warfare, the crusades, the Inquisition, temporal rivalries, new urban wealth, and bitter envy. Her *vita* needs to be read in this social context, which celebrated withdrawal and inward spiritual progress through penitence and prayers for others alongside the Eucharist as an outward symbol of allegiance to Church unity, while the Church herself increased in temporal wealth and power.

BIOGRAPHICAL SUMMARY OF JULIANA'S LIFE

Juliana was born ca. 1192–93 at Retinne, a small village near Liège, the younger of two daughters born to wealthy but non-aristocratic parents. Although their identity is unknown, Mulder-Bakker astutely asserts the plausibility that Juliana's natural parents were related to the Abbess Imena of Loon or her stepbrother, the archbishop of Cologne, Conrad of Hochstaden, both of whom demonstrated a special and particular protectiveness toward Juliana in her later and more troubled years.[14] These natural parents of Juliana, in their advancing years, prayed for descendents.[15] Their prayers were answered by the birth of two daughters, Agnes and Juliana, according to the *vita*:

> Benignus autem et misericors deus qui preces ad se clamantium precipue ubi efficatiam orationis manus adjuvat pie operationis solitus est exaudire, decrevit gemine prolis exibitione fidelium suorum preces et opera petitionis munere non privare. Procreate sunt namque ex eis due filie. . . .[16]
>
> [The gracious and merciful God, who is accustomed to grant the prayers of those who cry to him—especially when works of kindness make the prayer more effective—

---

[10] Vauchez, *Sainthood in the Later Middle Ages*.

[11] Cf. Bernard McGinn, *The Flowering of Mysticism: Men and Women in the New Mysticism—1200–1350*, vol. 3 of *The Presence of God: A History of Western Christian Mysticism* (New York: Crossroad, 1998); Anneke B. Mulder-Bakker, *Lives of the Anchoresses: The Rise of the Urban Recluse in Medieval Europe*, trans. Myra Heerspink Scholz (Philadelphia: University of Pennsylvania Press, 2005).

[12] Bynum, *Jesus as Mother*.

[13] Roisin, *L'Hagiographie cistercienne dans le diocèse de Liège*, 79, 82.

[14] Mulder-Bakker, *Lives of the Anchoresses*, 84.

[15] A frequent biblical topos, e.g., Sarah and Abraham; Zacharias and Elizabeth.

[16] Delville, *Vie de Sainte Julienne de Cornillon*, 12.

decided to reward the prayers and works of his faithful servants by granting their plea. Thus two daughters were born to them. . . .][17]

The two girls were orphaned at a young age in 1197 and were placed by friends of the family in a newly founded (1176) hospice at Mont Cornillon, along with a gift of approximately 250 hectares of land.[18] Mont Cornillon was located outside Liège, along the route to Aix-la-Chapelle (Aachen) at the foot of a hill where the Premonstratensians had an abbey. The house functioned as a *leprosarium* with four types of residents: men and women suffering from leprosy, and healthy men and women entrusted with various duties in the care of those afflicted. The men and women who provided care were celibate and celebrated the divine office, but were not under religious rule until 1242, when the bishop placed the house under the Rule of Saint Augustine.[19] Because the citizens of Liège had founded the house, two or three provisional lay representatives were appointed to administer the secular business of the monastery, a manifestation of the conflict between the spiritual and civil sides of the institution.[20] When Agnes and Juliana were placed at Mont Cornillon, they were immediately moved to an adjacent farm under the care of Sister Sapientia, prioress of the house.

Juliana was a precocious child, mature and gifted in her studies. She mastered French and Latin at an early age and had by adolescence memorized the Psalms, the Song of Songs, and twenty of Saint Bernard's sermons. Moreover, she routinely displayed the characteristic asceticism, obedience, humility, piety, charity, and eucharistic devotion that typified the religious prototype in the Cistercian *vitae* of the epoch.[21] Juliana was also a prophetic and mystical visionary. In 1210, at age eighteen, her hallmark vision of a full moon with a small fraction missing began.[22] Through constant prayer she came to interpret this vision as a revelation from Christ. The moon symbolized the Church, and the missing quarter symbolized the absence of a feast day that Christ wanted his faithful to celebrate: "institutio sacramenti corporis et sanguinis sui quolibet anno semel sollempnius ac specialius recoleretur quam in cena, quando circa lotionem pedem et memoriam passionis sue ecclesia generaliter occupatur"[23] [once every year the institution of the Sacrament of his Body and Blood should be celebrated

[17] *The Life of Juliana of Mont Cornillon*, trans. Barbara Newman (Toronto: Peregrina, 1988), 26. Newman's translation of the *vita* into English is used for all translations from Latin. The corresponding page number(s) for Newman follow each Delville reference for exact quotations.

[18] Émile Denis, *Sainte Julienne et Cornillon* (Liège: Printing Co., 1927), 49.

[19] R. Hankart, "L'hospice de Cornillon à Liège," *La Vie wallonne* 40 (1966), 5–49, 93–135; *La Vie wallonne* 41 (1967), 79–112; see also Delville, *Vie de Sainte Julienne de Cornillon*, 15.

[20] Delville, *Vie de Sainte Julienne de Cornillon*, 106–11.

[21] Roisin, *L'Hagiographie cistercienne dans le diocèse de Liège*.

[22] Delville, *Vie de Sainte Julienne de Cornillon*, 120–23. This is one of the most famous episodes in Juliana's life. A historiated initial in her *vita* as it appears in Paris, Bibliothèque de l'Arsenal, MS 945, fol. 2, shows her kneeling before an altar with David emerging from a cloud holding a defective moon. Coincidentally, perhaps, the reported vision coincides roughly with the date when Liège was sacked by Henry I, duke of Brabant (3–5 May 1212): see Jacques de Vitry, *The Life*, trans. Margot H. King, in *Two Lives of Marie D'Oignies*, 4th ed. (Toronto: Peregrina, 1998), 146 n 14.

[23] Delville, *Vie de Sainte Julienne de Cornillon*, 122; see also Diplôme of Hugh of Saint-Cher, 29 December 1252, in E. Schoolmeesters, "Le Diplôme de Hughes de Saint-Cher instituant la Fête-Dieu," *Leodium* 5 (1906), 42–43.

more solemnly and specifically than it was at the Last Supper, when the Church was generally preoccupied with the washing of the feet and the remembrance of his passion].[24] After long years of prayers, protest, and revelations from Christ, Juliana embraced as her divinely inspired vocation the task of initiating and promoting the new feast, which should "deinceps per personas humiles promoveri"[25] [from then on be promoted by humble people].

In 1230, after the death of Sapientia, Juliana became prioress, serving under Prior Godfrey, in the episcopacy of the Liège prince-bishop, John of Eppes.[26] She began to confide her vision for the new feast day to her close circle of friends: Eve, an anchoress and recluse at Saint-Martin's, the collegiate church in Liège; Isabella, a béguine from Huy; and John of Lausanne, the canon at Saint-Martin, who knew the many French theologians and Dominican professors in Liège.[27] She requested of Canon Dom John that he set her visions of the new feast before his distinguished acquaintances without disclosing her identity. And thus the idea of the new feast day was explained to Jacques of Troyes, archdeacon of Liège, later bishop of the church of Verdun, then Patriarch of Jerusalem, and finally, pope, under the name of Urban IV. Her idea also was put forward before Hugh of Saint-Cher, Prior Provincial of the Order of the Dominicans, who was later promoted to cardinal of the Church of Rome, and before the most reverend Father Guiard, bishop of Cambrai. Additionally, these matters were shown to the chancellor of Paris, to the friars Gilles, John, and Gerard, who were lectors to the Dominican preachers in Liège, and to many others.[28] All of these luminaries were of one mind and spirit and could find no reason in divine law that might prohibit the institution of a special feast day celebrating the Sacrament.[29]

Juliana was elated by the approbation. However, she had no erudite or distinguished scholars on whom she could depend to compose the office and Mass for the new feast, and so she chose a young and innocent brother, John, "(q)uem licet in litterarum scientia nosceret imperitum"[30] [although she knew him to be inexperienced in literary matters]. The *vita* reports that John centonated the office, that is, he employed a process in between rote reproduction from memory and extemporization, which was characteristic of oral transmission,[31] through "the miraculous intervention of the Holy Spirit" while Juliana prayed. When their work was shown to the learned theologians in Liège, it was found theologically perfect and aesthetically pleasing. "Hec autem omnia tante suavitatis et

[24] Newman, *Life of Juliana of Mont Cornillon*, 80.

[25] Delville, *Vie de Sainte Julienne de Cornillon*, 124; Newman, *Life of Juliana of Mont Cornillon*, 81.

[26] Jean d'Eppes served as prince-bishop from 1229 to 1238. See Jean-Louis Kupper, "La cité de Liège au temps de Julienne de Cornillon," in *Actes du colloque de Liège*, vol. 1 of *Fête-Dieu (1246–1996)*, ed. André Haquin (Louvain-la-Neuve: Institut d'Études Médiévales de l'Université Catholique de Louvain, 1999), 20.

[27] Jean Cottiaux and Jean-Pierre Delville, "La Fête-Dieu: Eve, Julienne et la Fête-Dieu à Saint-Martin," in *Saint-Martin, Mémoire de Liège* (Liège: Éditions du Perron, 1990), 31–53.

[28] Delville, *Vie de Sainte Julienne de Cornillon*, 125–31.

[29] Ibid., 125–31.

[30] Ibid., 136.

[31] See Peter Jeffery, *Re-Envisioning Past Musical Cultures: Ethnomusicology in the Study of Gregorian Chant* (Chicago: University of Chicago Press, 1992), 14.

dulcedinis sunt in littera et in cantu, ut etiam a lapideis cordibus devotionem merito debeant extorquere"[32] [And all of the texts and melodies are of such beauty and sweetness that they should be able to wring devotion even from hearts of stone].

Not everyone in Juliana's world shared in the approbation and enthusiasm for the new feast of Corpus Christi. Especially the canons and high clergy at the cathedral of Saint Lambert expressed vehement opposition to the new feast day. "Qui priores in promotione debuerant existere, priores facti sunt in impugnatione"[33] [Those who should have been first to promote became the first to impugn it]. They thought it ridiculous and redundant, since Mass was celebrated each day, and they spared no mercy in their attacks on Juliana. This opposition likely stemmed from local political turmoil that emerged in the wake of the death of Bishop John of Eppes in 1238 and the subsequent contested election of the new bishop, rather than from real opposition to the new feast.[34] Whatever its source, Juliana resolved to "look toward heaven" for help and departed for a pilgrimage to Cologne, Notre Dame at Tongres, and Saint Servais.

After the death of Bishop John of Eppes, the bishopric remained vacant for two years, ultimately resolved by pontifical arbitration in 1240. In the meantime, Prior Godfrey of Mont Cornillon died and was replaced by a Prior [Roger].[35] The new prior was an enemy of Juliana who allegedly obtained his office through simony, pandered to the bourgeoisie, and befriended those brothers and sisters in the house opposed to her strict enforcement of the religious rule. He further took advantage of the opportunity afforded by the transition of authority in the bishopric to incite the citizens of Liège to riot by accusing Juliana and several nuns of stealing the charters of the house and diverting funds to bribe the bishop for the institution of the new feast. The townspeople assaulted the monastery and destroyed Juliana's oratory but did not find the charters, which the nuns had carefully hidden. Juliana fled to the cell of the recluse, Eve of Saint-Martin, but actually was received into Canon John's larger residence adjacent to the basilica.

Bishop Robert of Thourette was named successor to John of Eppes by a pontifical council in 1240 but never received the then-customary investiture from Emperor Frederick II.[36] He initiated an inquest at Mont Cornillon and in 1242 deposed the simoniac Prior Roger, ordering him to the *leprosarium* at Huy. He installed the young and naïve brother John as prior at Mont Cornillon. Bishop Robert then reinstated Juliana as prioress, had her oratory rebuilt, reconfirmed the religious Rule of Saint Augustine, and excluded the lay citizens of Liège from further participation in the governance of the house. Following these events, Bishop Robert was introduced to the new feast of Corpus Christi. "[V]iri venerabiles et religiosi sollempnitatis ordinem et processum exposuerunt reverendo patri domino roberto leodiensi episcopo et eidem ut divine munus

---

[32] Delville, *Vie de Sainte Julienne de Cornillon*, 138–40; Newman, *Life of Juliana of Mont Cornillon*, 88.

[33] Delville, *Vie de Sainte Julienne de Cornillon*, 140; Newman, *Life of Juliana of Mont Cornillon*, 89.

[34] Schoolmeesters, "Le Diplôme de Hughes de Saint-Cher " and "Les actes du cardinal-légat Hughes de Saint-Cher en Belgique, durant les années de sa légation, 1251–53," *Leodium* 6 (1907), 150–66, 172–76.

[35] Newman, *Life of Juliana of Mont Cornillon*, 11, indicates that a Prior Roger was appointed in 1237, upon the death of Godfrey. Delville, *Vie de Sainte Julienne de Cornillon*, 179, indicates that Prior Godfrey died in 1240 and an anonymous prior was appointed at that time, perhaps also named John.

[36] Delville, *Vie de Sainte Julienne de Cornillon*, 151, n 222; Schoolmeesters, "Les actes du cardinal-légat," 482–85.

gratie agnosceret et exaltaret verbis efficacibus suggesserunt"[37] [Venerable religious men set the order and progress of the feast before the reverend father Dom Robert, Bishop of Liège, and effectively persuaded him to acknowledge and exalt the gift of divine grace].

Bishop Robert died at Fosses on 16 October 1246.[38] On his deathbed, in a letter to all clergy,[39] he established the feast for the diocese of Liège on the Thursday after Trinity Sunday.[40] The letter notes two reasons for instituting the new feast. The first, "to counteract the madness of heretics,"[41] was a rationale later repeated in nearly exact wording by both Hugh of Saint-Cher and Urban IV. The second reason was explained by reference to the saints, whom the Church commemorates every day and yet still honors individually in a yearly feast on their death date. Robert exhorted those around him to love and promote the feast and had them celebrate the new office immediately before his last breath.[42] He concluded his letter with a quote from Matthew 28: 20: "And behold I am with you always, to the end of time."[43]

The narrative in the *vita* describing the initial institution of the feast of Corpus Christi receives corroboration from other documents. However, these documents, especially those pertaining to dates during which Church dignitaries held the offices mentioned in the *vita* and the dates during which they were known to have visited or been in Liège, suggest a slightly different chronology. Relying on these independent sources, Delville[44] indicates that Juliana most likely confided in Eve and John of Lausanne in 1230, the year she was named prioress. Canon John most likely first consulted Gilles, John, and Gerard after 1232, when the Dominican house in Liège was founded. Guiard, bishop of Cambrai, was sent to Liège by the pope in 1238 to resolve the problem of the election of the new bishop after the death of John of Eppes. Jacques of Troyes was archdeacon of Liège between 1243 and 1249, and most likely he approved of the new feast between those two dates. Therefore, he may have been the last person to be con-

---

[37] Delville, *Vie de Sainte Julienne de Cornillon*, 150; Newman, *Life of Juliana of Mont Cornillon*, 93.

[38] E. Schoolmeesters, "Regestes de Robert de Thourette," *Bulletin de la Societé d'art et d'histoire du diocèse de Liège* 15 (1905), 1–126.

[39] Schoolmeesters, "Regestes de Robert de Thourette," 84. The entry indicates that between October 13 and October 16 he reproduced twenty copies of the office composed by the cleric John and distributed them in the diocese. He died on October 16.

[40] The Office of the Trinity dates back to Alcuin, who compiled a version. Authorship of the later rhymed numerical version (a classic Liège style in which antiphons and responsories are arranged in ascending modal order, most typically with rhyming lines that correspond to musical phrases) has been debated; perhaps Hucbald de Saint-Amand composed the text and Etienne of Liège the music. The office, originally a Sunday votive mass for preachers, has been in uninterrupted use since the tenth century. The early use prepared the way for its inception into the liturgical cycle. Etienne (bishop from 901 to 920) adopted it for Liège for the Sunday after Pentecost. It was officially recognized in 1334 by Pope John XXII. See Ritva Jonsson, *Historia: Études sur la genèse des offices versifiés* (Stockholm: Almqvist and Wiksell, 1968), 164–65.

[41] See Peter Browe, *Textus antiqui de festo Corporis Christi*, Opuscula et textus, series liturgica IV (Münster: Aschendorff, 1934), 21–26.

[42] Delville, *Vie de Sainte Julienne de Cornillon*, 192.

[43] See Browe, *Textus antiqui de festo Corporis Christi*, 21.

[44] Delville, *Vie de Sainte Julienne de Cornillon*, 30–33.

sulted rather than the first. John and Juliana composed the feast before John was appointed prior in 1242, most likely between 1236 and 1240. They must have consulted Hugh of Saint-Cher in 1240, when he had visited the new Dominican convent, founded in Liège eight years earlier in 1232.[45]

The young Henry of Gueldre, cousin to Count William of Holland and nephew of Duke Henry of Brabant, replaced Bishop Robert of Thourette in 1247, following the death of the latter. Bishop Henry was appointed with the encouragement of the papacy as part of its efforts to secure political support and a suitable successor to Frederick II, Holy Roman Emperor, upon his deposition in 1245. As bishop, Henry initiated a statute reconfirming the rights of the bourgeoisie in the administration of the house at Mont Cornillon, deposed the young prior John, and brought back the simoniac Roger, who had earlier been sent to Huy by Bishop Robert. The citizens again invaded the monastery and destroyed Juliana's oratory.

In 1247, Juliana fled Mont Cornillon for a second time with sisters Agnes, Isabella, and Ozile and found refuge in the Cistercian monasteries at Robermont, Val-Benoît, and Val-Notre-Dame. However, the new bishop, Henry, pursued the women, and at each place through cunning machinations prevented their benefactor from extending their stay.[46] The women departed for Namur, where they initially found shelter among the poor. Their situation came to the attention of Abbess Imène, sister of the most reverend Conrad, archbishop of Cologne, who contacted the reverend John, archdeacon of Liège. The archdeacon procured a house for the women close to the church of Saint Aubain.[47] Abbess Imène also used her connections to obtain annuities from Mont Cornillon commensurate with the considerable inheritances that each had bestowed upon the monastery and took the women under the protection of the monastery. "Que de consilio peritorum et religiosorum virorum maxime autem reverendi patris Guiardi cameracensis episcopi subiectioni et protectioni prefate abbatisse se quamdiu viverent subdiderunt, ne absque superiore sed solo proprie voluntatis arbitrio vivere dicerentur"[48] [On the advice of experienced religious, especially the reverend father Guiard, Bishop of Cambrai, they submitted to the obedience and protection of the abbess for as long as they lived, lest anyone should say they were living merely at their own whim without a superior].

After the deaths of Agnes and Ozile between 1248 and 1252, Isabella, no doubt influenced by the abbess, persuaded Juliana to move to the larger abbey at Salzinnes; this came under the protection of Cardinal Hugh of Saint-Cher around 1252. After the death of Isabella, Sister Ermentrude from Mont Cornillon later was persuaded to join her there. But the house at Salzinnes was dispersed in 1256, after a furious revolt on the

---

[45] Schoolmeesters, "Le Diplôme de Hughes de Saint-Cher."

[46] Delville, *Vie de Sainte Julienne de Cornillon*, 206–07.

[47] The church was the repository of a number of important relics, including the wood of the Sacred Cross and the Sacred Blood, which were transported to Namur from Constantinople in 1205. See Delville *Vie de Sainte Julienne de Cornillon*, 215 n 333.

[48] Delville *Vie de Sainte Julienne de Cornillon*, 216; Newman, *Life of Juliana of Mont Cornillon*, 121.

part of the townspeople of Namur against a certain Empress Marie,[49] who managed the county of Namur in the absence of her husband between 1253 and 1256. Already unpopular, she incensed the local population by ordering the destruction of the house of a cleric, which was located near the abbey and used as a brothel. Juliana earlier had warned Abbess Imène that it would be wise to avoid familiarity with Marie, but without result. Upon the dispersal of the abbey at Salzinnes, the abbess took Juliana to the house of a cantor at the Cisterican abbey at Fosses. The cantor provided Juliana with a cell, initially built for a recluse who had recently died. Juliana remained there until her death on 5 April 1258.

On her deathbed she asked for her confessor, John of Lausanne, the canon at Saint-Martin's. "Desiderabat autem illum ea specialiter ut creditur intentione, ut secreta sua que tantopere in vita celaverat eidem vel in vite sue termino revelaret"[50] [I believe she wanted him specifically so that at the end of her life, she could reveal the secrets she had hidden so long]. Neither he nor any of her friends from Liège came, and so these secrets, perhaps concerning her work on the feast, remain unknown. The cantor of Fosses administered the last rites to her immediately before her death, and a sacrifice for the dead was offered the next day in the Fosses church. Then, in accordance with Juliana's wishes, her friend, the monk Gobert d'Aspremont, moved her body by carriage to the Cistercian monastery at Villers.[51] On the following Sunday, an unknown priest arrived and gave an eloquent sermon on the Sacrament, after which Juliana was buried in the section of the cemetery at Villers reserved for saints.[52] Her cult developed immediately, although it did not receive official recognition until 1869, under Pius IX.[53]

REALIZING JULIANA OF MONT CORNILLON'S VISION

Juliana's vision for the new feast of Corpus Christi was realized slowly after she left Liège and did not obtain full recognition until the first quarter of the fourteenth century. Between 14 October and 9 November 1251, Cardinal-Legate Hugh of Saint-Cher traveled to Liège and noted that the late Bishop Robert of Thourette's order for celebration of the feast of Corpus Christi was not being observed. He re-instated the new feast and celebrated its Mass at the collegiate church of Saint-Martin sometime during this visit.[54] Juliana's *vita* indicates that Cardinal Hugh used the version of the liturgy that

---

[49] Empress Marie was most likely the wife of Baldwin of Courtenay, Count of Namur, who became the second emperor of the Latin Orient in 1239. She was also most likely the younger daughter of John of Brienne, by a second marriage, and thus the step-sister of Isabella, wife of Frederick II. Her political ties were the only plausible reason for Juliana's warning, since surely both she and Empress Marie opposed the brothel.

[50] Delville, *Vie de Sainte Julienne de Cornillon*, 240; Newman, *Life of Juliana of Mont Cornillon*, 133.

[51] Vauchez, *Sainthood in the Later Middle Ages*, 198. Gobert d'Aspremont participated in the crusade against the Albigensians in 1226 and then served as a lay brother in the Cistercian abbey at Villers.

[52] G. Lambert, "Sainte Julienne de Liège dans le Brabant: Considérations sur ses Reliques," *Le Folklore Brabaçon* 16 (1936).

[53] H. Schuermans, *Les reliques de la B. Julienne de Cornillon* (Nivelles: Ch. Guignarde, 1899); *La chasse des XXXVI saints à Anvers—Julienne de Cornillon* (Brussels: Vive de Backer, 1900); *L'Église de l'abbaye de Villers* (Brussels: Van Langendonck, 1904).

[54] Schoolmeester, "Le Diplôme de Hughes de Saint-Cher," 150–66.

she and Prior John had compiled and that he had reviewed while Prior Provincial of the Liège Dominicans between 1232 and 1238. For the 1251 celebration he perhaps added a sermon to the Mass, or may have composed some new material. Deeply moved by the Mass, an elderly canon named Stephen of Châlons bequeathed a stipend for the perpetual celebration of the new feast at Saint-Martin.[55] At the exhortation of Cardinal Hugh, the canons of the cathedral of Saint-Lambert celebrated the feast "cum officio plenario"[56] [with the full office] while the cardinal was present in the region. The reception by the canons apparently stemmed from a desire to please the cardinal rather than from genuine persuasion, since the leaders of the cathedral banned the feast before the year ended and spoke of it with derision.

In a brief dated 26 April 1252 at the abbey of Villers-en-Brabant, Cardinal Hugh established an indulgence for the faithful who celebrated the feast of Corpus Christi in the abbey church.[57] In October of the same year he took the abbey of Salzinnes, where Juliana found refuge, under his protection. And on 29 December 1252, he established the feast for the Thursday after the octave of the Trinity with an indulgence for all penitents in his jurisdiction (Germany, Dacia, Bohemia, and Moravia) who confessed and attended church on a date and in a place where it was celebrated.[58] The diploma echoes the initial rationale of Bishop Robert Thourette, stating that "sane licet hoc venerabile sacramentum in cotidiana memoria cum devotione debita recolatur; dignum tamen est ad confutandam quorumdam hereticorum insaniam, ut vel semel in anno specialius ac sollempnius . . ."[59] [It is fitting, to repress the madness of certain heretics, that once a year it (the venerable Sacrament) be recalled to mind more specifically and solemnly . . .]. The Cardinal-Legate established additional indulgences for all who visited the collegial church of Saint-Martin on the feast day of its patron saint, demonstrating his special interest in the collegiate church in Liège as well as the possible influence of Eve and Canon John on the 1252 diploma. Cardinal Peter Capocci in Liège confirmed the diploma two years later.[60]

On 11 August 1264, Urban IV promulgated the bull known as *Transiturus de hoc mundo*,[61] which established the feast for the universal Church on the Thursday after Pente-

[55] Charter of November, 1251, Archives de l'État de Liège, Collégiale Saint-Martin, charte n 56; see Delville, *Vie de Sainte Julienne de Cornillon*, 164–67. See also J. Bertholet, *Histoire de l'Institution de la Fête-Dieu: avec la Vie des bienheureuses Julienne et Eve qui furent les premières promulgatrices*, 3rd ed. (Liège: Barchon et Jacob, 1746; Liège: Jacques-Antoine Gerlachm, 1781; and Liège: F. Oudart, 1846); reproduced in *Saint-Martin, Mémoire de Liège*, 47.

[56] Delville, *Vie de Sainte Julienne de Cornillon*, 156.

[57] Schuermans, *Les reliques de la B. Julienne de Cornillon*, 62–63.

[58] Schoolmeester, "Le Diplôme de Hughes de Saint-Cher," 42–43.

[59] Delville, *Vie de Sainte Julienne de Cornillon*, 162; Newman, *Life of Juliana of Mont Cornillon*, 97.

[60] Schoolmeesters, "Le Diplôme de Hughes de Saint-Cher," 152.

[61] Published by J. Bertholet, *Histoire de l'Institution de la Fête-Dieu, avec la vie des bienheureuses Julienne et Eve, toutes deux originaires de Liège*, translated into French and republished by F. Baix and Cyrille Lambot, *La dévotion à l'eucharistie et le VIIe centenaire de la Fête-Dieu* (Gembloux-Namur: J. Ducolot, 1946), 136–38. For a discussion of the three important redactions of *Transiturus*, including one found in the Clementines and edited by Ezio Franceschini, "Origine e stile della bolla 'Transiturus'," *Aevum* 39 (1965), 218–43, see Pierre-Marie Gy, "L'Office du Corpus Christi et S. Thomas d'Aquin: état d'une recherche," *Revue des sciences philosophiques et théologiques* 64 (1980), 494–95, notes 13–17. Gy also cites the work of Tulllio Bertamini, "La bolla 'Transiturus'

cost.[62] He sent this to the Patriarch of Jerusalem along with a new Roman liturgy for the office and Mass. In September he sent copies of the *Transiturus* accompanied by copies of a Roman liturgy to all of the bishops. On 7 September he wrote to the bishop of Liège, Henry of Gueldre, exhorting him to inaugurate the feast without delay in his diocese, and he attached a copy of the bull.[63] On the next day he wrote a letter to Eve, the recluse at Saint-Martin and friend to Juliana,[64] mentioning Eve's desire to see the feast established and indicating that the pope had recently celebrated the feast with his cardinals, bishops, and other prelates. The letter also mentions that the pope had enclosed under his seal a quire with the new office for the feast. The new office mentioned most likely was a different version from the one included in the letter of Bishop Robert Thourette in 1246, since one of the three versions of the *Transiturus* clearly states: "Once when we held a lesser office."[65] The attached version most likely was *Sapiencia [a]edificavit sibi domum*, but was perhaps *Sacerdos in [a]eternum,* a version most definitively composed by Thomas Aquinas.

While popular enthusiasm remained strong, it was clearly local. Official interest in the new feast waned, except in Liège, where it was again instituted by Jean de Dampierre of Flanders,[66] bishop of Liège from 1282 to 1291. His synod does not mention Urban IV or the *Transiturus* but, rather, cites Robert Thourette and Henry of Gueldre.[67] In the universal Church, until 1312 the official status of the feast was retained nominally under the the bull *Transiturus*, but the feast day failed to gain widespread acceptance. At the Council of Vienne in 1312, Pope Clement V included it as part of his efforts to bring together in a Constitution laws that had been enacted but not codified in a volume known as the Clementines. As a consequence of Clement V's premature death, John XXII promulgated the Constitution in 1317 and formally instituted the feast of Corpus Christi for the universal Church.[68]

The various chapters of the Dominican order began to adopt the new feast early in the fourteenth century. The chapters of Lyon in 1318, of Rouen in 1320, and of Florence

---

di papa Urbano IV e l'uffizio del 'Corpus Christi' secondo il codice di S. Lorenzo di bognanco," *Aevum* 42 (1968), 29–58, in his analysis and detailed set of references. The topic is taken up at great length by Ronald Zawilla, *The Biblical Sources of the Historia Corporis Christi Attributed to Thomas Aquinas: A Theological Study to Determine their Authenticity* (Ph.D. diss. University of Toronto, 1985), 25–74.

[62] The octave of the Trinity had been established only in Liège at that time.

[63] Bull of Pope Urban IV to the bishop of Liège, Henri de Gueldre, 7 Septembre 1264, Paris, Bibliothèque nationale de France, lat. 9298.

[64] Cyrille Lambot, "La bulle d'Urbaine IV à Eve of Saint-Martin sur l'institution de la Fête-Dieu," *Scriptorium* 2 (1948), 69–77, repr. in *Revue bénédictine* 79 (1969), 215–22; the letter is reproduced in Newman, *Life of Juliana of Mont Cornillon*, 147–48.

[65] Tulllio Bertamini, "La bolla 'Transiturus' di papa Urbano IV e l'uffizio del 'Corpus Christi' secondo il codice di S. Lorenzo di bognanco," *Aevum* 42 (1968), 47. Cf. Zawilla, *Biblical Sources of the Historia Corporis Christi*, 41. Refer to note 61 above.

[66] Jean of Dampierre was the son of Guy of Dampierre, the grandson of Margaret, and the great-grandson of Count Baldwin IX.

[67] Cyrille Lambot, "L'Office de la Fête-Dieu: Aperçu nouveaux sur ses origines," *Revue bénédictine* 54 (1942), 61–123; Cyrille Lambot and Irenée Fransen, *L'Office de la Fête-Dieu primitive: Textes et mélodies retrouvés* (Maredsous: Editions de Maredsous, 1946), 13–14; Zawilla, *Biblical Sources of the Historia Corporis Christi*, 43.

[68] Browe, *Textus antiqui de festo Corporis Christi.*

in 1321 each communicated to the Master-General of the order that they wished to adopt the new feast day and needed an office. The adoption by the chapters of Rouen and Florence was approved in 1322 at Vienne. The requisite third approbation came up in Barcelona in 1323, and the Roman office, perhaps the one that had been enclosed with the letter from Urban IV was selected, this time because, *ut asseritur*, their brother Saint Thomas Aquinas had composed it.[69]

The fuller mystical and more personal vision of Juliana regarding the role of women in the Church has to date remained largely unrealized; it is revealed in the last anecdote in her *vita*. During the vigil of the feast of Corpus Christi, a venerable person who had been a close friend of Juliana was very ill and desired wine and food. Juliana visited her in a dream and told her to prepare for the grace that God would give her the next day.

> Que cum ipsa sollempnitatis die tempore misse orationi insisteret, in excessum mentis subito est effecta. Et vidit; et ecce dominus Ihesus indutus sacerdotalibus reverendissime celebrabat, cui anchilla sua iuliana virgineis manibus ministrabat. Videbatur autem ei que sic excesserat quod ipsa ad altare accedebat, et summus ille sacerdos assistente sibi sua virgine ad calicem pulcherrimum et optimum sibi poculum propinabat.[70]

> [While she was praying at Mass on the feast day, she was suddenly rapt into ecstasy. And she saw a vision, and behold! The Lord Jesus, dressed in priestly vestments, was celebrating Mass with great reverence, and his handmaid Juliana was serving him with virgin hands. It seemed in her ecstasy that she approached the altar and the great High Priest, assisted by his virgin, offered her the splendid and beautiful chalice.]

The anecdote provides an example of a religious-mystical apparition characteristic of thirteenth-century religious women and a type of devotional expression for which Juliana shaped the saintly prototype. Bynum[71] indicates that women often expressed visions of themselves in priestly roles, projecting themselves onto the role more than undercutting its priestly authority. Likewise, Wogan-Browne and Henneau note that Juliana "represented the desire of many women: the exclusion of women from the priesthood left women in any kind of religious institution dependent on male ecclesiastic control of this sacrament, and visions in which the priesthood is bypassed and Christ himself offers the Sacrament are relatively frequent."[72] The visions reinforced rather than challenged the already growing prestige and power of the male ecclesiastical hierarchy through their shared conception of a corporate identity for women within the Church as priestesses and Christ's handmaidens in direct communication with God. The Eucharist, but especially the reserved Host, functioned to preserve women's reli-

[69] James A. Weisheipl, *Friar Thomas D'Aquino: His Life, Thought and Works* (Garden City, NY: Doubleday & Co., 1974), 176–85.

[70] Delville, *Vie de Sainte Julienne de Cornillon*, 266 (Delville transcribed this as *anchilla*); Newman, *Life of Juliana of Mont Cornillon*, 146.

[71] Bynum, *Jesus as Mother*, 184–85.

[72] Jocelyn Wogan-Browne and Marie-Élisabeth Henneau, "Liège, the Medieval 'Woman Question,' and the Question of Medieval Women," in *New Trends in Feminine Spirituality: The Holy Women of Liège and Their Impact*, ed. Juliette Dor, Lesley Johnson, and Jocelyn Wogan-Browne (Turnhout: Brepols, 1999), 13.

gious authority through the real presence of Jesus in the corporeal absence of the priest as *persona Christi*, without challenging the existing hierocratic power and authority.[73]

JULIANA OF MONT CORNILLON AS PROPHETESS

Juliana of Mont Cornillon was one of a number of medieval women who exercised considerable religious influence and authority, although outside the official hierarchy of the priesthood.[74] Her intense devotion to establishing the new feast and the widely accepted belief that her mission was divinely inspired suggest a pattern typical of charismatic leaders.[75] Recent scholars, including Mulder-Bakker and Robert Moore, have noted the "community forming" power of such women leaders under the rubric of medieval prophetess.[76] In Juliana's case, her charisma and this power were constituted by distinctive features that form a *topos* in the hagiographic *vitae*: (1) special gifts such as prophecies, miracles, and teaching; (2) a divine "calling"; (3) recruiting disciples through networks; (4) provoking hatred as well as devotion; and (5) non-remuneration for services.[77] Juliana's musical gifts are added as an analytic element that enhanced her charisma, especially in the face-to-face interactions that characterized the initiation of the movement.

INTELLIGENCE

In keeping with the representational style of the thirteenth-century hagiographic vitae, Juliana is characterized by personal qualities common to most individuals in the literary genre: obedience, discipline, contrition, asceticism, humility, detachment from the material world, para-mystical experiences, and extreme devotion.[78] In addition to these saintly virtues, which might describe all thirteenth-century female saintly exemplars, three loom large in the life of Juliana: her intelligence, the gift of prophecy, and her devotion to the Eucharist. The first two characteristics are not typical of the hagiographic genre for women within her historical context. Intelligence, in fact, is rarely mentioned in the vitae of women. Weinstein and Bell enumerate only 29 prophets out of 360 female saints.[79] But devotion to the Eucharist is a trait for which descriptions abound. This was perhaps the hallmark of the Liège community of women[80] and can be found as a topic in nearly all hagiographic vitae for

[73] Cf. Mulder-Bakker, *Lives of the Anchoresses*, 106–07.

[74] Mulder-Bakker, *Lives of the Anchoresses*, 82.

[75] See Max Weber, *Economy and Society*, vols. 1 and 2, trans. Ephraim Fischoff, Hans Gerth, A. .M. Henderson, Ferdinand Kolegar, C. Wright Mills, Talcott Parsons, Max Rheinstein, Guenther Roth, Edward Shils, Claus Wittich; ed. Guenther Roth and Claus Wittich (Berkeley: University of California Press, 1978), 216–17; 241–45; 1111–48.

[76] Mulder-Bakker, *Lives of the Anchoresses*; R. I. Moore, *The Formation of a Persecuting Society: Power and Deviance in Western Europe, 950–1250* (Oxford: Oxford University Press, 1990).

[77] See Barbara R. Walters, "Church-Sect Dynamics and the Feast of Corpus Christi," *Sociology of Religion* 65 (2004), 285–301; see also Jack T. Sanders, *Charisma, Converts, Competitors: Societal and Sociological Factors in the Success of Early Christianity* (London: SCM Press, 2000).

[78] Roisin, *L'Hagiographie cistercienne*.

[79] Donald Weinstein and Rudolf Bell, *Saints and Society: The Two Worlds of Western Christendom, 1000–1700* (Chicago and London: University of Chicago Press, 1982), 229.

[80] Cf. Caroline Walker Bynum, *Holy Feast and Holy Fast: The Religious Significance of Food to Medieval Women* (Berkeley: University of California Press, 1987), and her *Jesus as Mother*.

women during this period.[81] Juliana, however, was singular in the intensity, nature, and frequency of miracles centered on her eucharistic devotion. She is the group exemplar. This special gift, or virtue, was part of her divine calling.

Juliana's *vita* also places atypical emphasis on her intelligence, expressed through references to her capacious memory. Memory shaped virtue in the medieval world, and the term often was employed by writers to address the moral character of the creative genius,[82] although it was typically reserved for male saints. In contrast to modern geniuses who are described as having "creative imagination, which they express in intricate reasoning and original discovery, in earlier times they were said to have richly retentive memories, which they expressed in intricate reasoning and original discovery."[83] *Memoria*, to the medieval mind, was based on texts within the "firm tradition of verified ancient sources" and formed the basis of claims to *auctoritas*.[84] Such textual memory distinguished moral rectitude from vulgar self-seeking popularizations by individuals who garnered attention from "the profane multitude" through unreliable novelty, *rusticitas.*

Juliana's *vita* notes the combination of capacious memory, discipline, and prodigious intellect that defined her creative genius and surfaced early in her childhood. Her prodigy was observed first by her foster mother and teacher, Sapientia. "Erat quippe corpore juvencula, sed animo cana"[85] [In body she was a little girl, but in mind a grey-haired old lady]. By virtue of her intelligence and other character traits, such as humility and discipline, Juliana's knowledge of literature and biblical writings flourished. The *vita* reports of her childhood: "Et factum est in brevi tempore ut non solum psalterium legere sciret, sed etiam cordetenus retineret. Dederat enim ei deus et intellectum capacem et memoriam tenacem"[86] [In a short while she not only knew how to read the Psalter but had also learned it by heart. For God had given her both a capable understanding and a retentive memory].

By adolescence, Juliana combined service work, reading, and prayer. Again, unusual or atypical for *vitae* of religious women are references to her creative genius as educated memory, always combined with frequent, vivid, and more gender-typical descriptions of her ascetic self-discipline and acts of humility. The emphasis on her memory facilitates understanding as well as reinterpretation of her role and contribution to the development of the new feast of Corpus Christi.

> Cum autem ab opere sibi vacaret; continuo se ad studia spiritualia convertebat, et aut orabat aut legebat aut meditationi inserviebat. Mire enim meditativa semper fuit. Que cum jam omnem scripturam latinam et gallicam libere legere didicisset; libros beati augustini multo affectu legebat, ipsumque sanctum plurimum diligebat. Verum quoniam

[81] See Roisin, *L'Hagiographie cistercienne.*

[82] Mary Carruthers, *The Book of Memory: A Study of Memory in Medieval Culture* (Cambridge: Cambridge University Press, 1990).

[83] Ibid., 13.

[84] See Brian Stock, *The Implications of Literacy: Written Language and Models of Interpretation in the Eleventh and Twelfth Centuries* (Princeton: Princeton University Press, 1983), 245.

[85] Delville, *Vie de Sainte Julienne de Cornillon*, 16–17; Newman, *Life of Juliana of Mont Cornillon*, 27.

[86] Delville, *Vie de Sainte Julienne de Cornillon*, 16; Newman, *Life of Juliana of Mont Cornillon*, 27.

scripta beatissimi bernardi vehementer ignita sibi visa sunt et dulciora super mel et favum; ea legebat et amplectabatur devotione multa valde, ipsumque sanctum immense
dilectionis privilegio honorabat. Dedit igitur animum suum ad eloquia eius; et plus-
quam viginti sermones extreme partis editos ab eodem super cantica canticorum in
quibus ipse beatissimus humanam scientiam visus est excessisse studiose cordetenus
didicit, et firme memorie commendavit.[87]

[But when she had leisure from work, she devoted herself constantly to spiritual efforts
and either prayed, read, or meditated—for she was always wonderfully given to meditation. As she had already learned to read anything written in Latin or French with ease,
she used to read St. Augustine's books with great sympathy, and she had a special love
for that saint. Yet the writings of the most blessed Bernard seemed to her ablaze with
fire and sweeter than honey and the honeycomb [Ps 18: 11], so she read and embraced
them with the most fervent devotion and honoured that saint with the privilege of a
boundless love. Therefore she yielded her mind to his eloquence and learned by heart
more than twenty sermons from the last part of his work on the Song of Songs, in which
the blessed saint seemed to transcend human knowledge.]

PROPHECY

Juliana's *vita* makes specific reference to her gifts of *karismata*[88] and offers numerous
examples of prophecy as one of these. The term *karismata* as used in the *vita* refers specifically to the biblical reference (1 Cor 12) and the "gifts of the Holy Spirit." This biblical description of the charismatic gifts appears in the context of a discussion of the division of labor and the hierarchy of the early Church.[89] Nonetheless, the emphasis on
prophecy in Juliana's *vita* highlights the rejection of a subaltern or subordinate role in
the Church, replaced by one of active leadership on the part of thirteenth-century
women in Liège.[90] Execution of their gifts obviously required delicate manners,[91] since
the office of the priesthood was closed to women and leadership agency could easily
have been interpreted as heretical usurpation.

Juliana's *vita* makes specific mention of the gift of prophecy and provides a precise
definition:

---

[87] Delville, *Vie de Sainte Julienne de Cornillon*, 20–22; Newman, *Life of Juliana of Mont Cornillon*, 30.

[88] Delville, *Vie de Sainte Julienne de Cornillon*, 62–63.

[89] The *Corinthians* reading follows Paul's discussion of divisions in the community at Corinth and the Last
Supper. Paul uses the human body as an analogy for the Christian society, the *Corpus Christi*, and explains
the way in which the Holy Spirit provides different gifts to each person for the betterment of the entire community. The gifts mentioned include wisdom, knowledge, faith, healing, working miracles, prophecy, and
the interpretation of tongues. At the end Chapter 12, Paul specifies a hierarchical ordering, placing the apostles first, prophets second, teachers third, then miracle workers, healers, helpers, governments, and interpreters of tongues.

[90] Cf. Cottiaux and Delville, "La Fête-Dieu," 44–45.

[91] See Olivier Quenardel, *La Communion Eucharistique dans "Le Héraut de L'Amour Divin" de Sainte Gertrude
D'Helfta* (Abbaye de Bellefontaine: Brepols, 1997), 10–11; see also Erving Goffman, *The Presentation of Self in
Everyday Life* (New York: Doubleday, 1959), and his *Interaction Ritual* (New York: Pantheon Books, 1967).
Sociologist Goffman provides concepts for analysis of face-to-face interaction, "facework," which are put to
imaginative use by Quenardel in his analysis of Gertrude of Helfta.

Secundum ethimologiam nominis dicitur prophetia quia predicit futura et secundum hoc tantummodo temporis est futuri. Verum sicut evidenter probat beatus gregorius in expositione iezechielis prophete in prima videlicet omilia, preteritum presens et futurum tempus continet prophetia. Ut igitur expositio huius nominis prophetia, tribus hijs temporibus valeat convenire, recte dicitur prophetia: non quia dicit furura sed quia prodit occulta.[92]

[Etymologically, prophecy is so called because it predicts things to come, and accordingly it deals with the future. But as St. Gregory clearly proves in his exposition of the prophet Ezekiel, in the first homily, prophecy includes past, present, and future tenses. Since the meanings of the word can refer to these three tenses, then, prophecy is rightly so called not because it predicts the future, but rather because it reveals the hidden.]

Further elaborations in the *vita* make clear that the term *prophecy* is employed to describe psychic phenomena such as foreknowledge of future events, discernment of the unspoken feelings of others, knowledge of events that have taken place but that the prophetess has not seen or heard about, clairvoyance, and telepathy.

The *vita* cites numerous specific examples of Juliana's gift of prophecy. Four vignettes, taken together, reflect her character as perceived by others and the unique pattern of analytic elements that define the perceived prophetic component of her identity: visions, telepathy, clairvoyance, telekinesis, and foreknowledge. The first vignette is representative of many visions centered on devotion to the Eucharist. Juliana went to visit her friend Eve, a recluse at Mont Saint-Martin in Liège and, although perhaps ten to fifteen years younger than Juliana, a close friend. After Juliana completed her prayers she said to her friend: "Corpus domini reclusa post missam in hac ecclesia non servatur, quod tamen in alijs ecclesijs fieri consuevit"[93] [The Lord's Body is not kept in this church after Mass, recluse, as the custom is in other churches]. After a later visit she remarked, "Revera reclusa solito nunc opulentior est vestra ecclesia, quoniam corpore christi quod in ipsa ante missam et post continue"[94] [Truly, recluse, your church is richer than before, for it has been endowed with the Body of Christ that remains in it continually before and after Mass]. Here Juliana was able to intuit the presence or absence of the reserved Host at Saint-Martin. This gift of clairvoyance, or telepathy with the hidden Christ, is subsumed by the definition of prophecy in the *vita*. Mulder-Bakker comments on this anecdote, seeing the intuition as a "means of direct access to the godhead" for women spiritual leaders.[95]

Juliana's gift of prophecy also included the ability to discern telepathically the thoughts and feelings of other persons in her social world. She once asked her friend Eve to reveal her secret emotions. When Eve demurred, Juliana said: "Quid est inquit o reclusa: putas te michi celare abscondita cordis tui? Scio inquit scio tam bene tuum per omnia cogitatum, ac si in palma mea ducebat autem digitum super palmam viderem oculis corporalibus quid cogitas litteris exartum"[96] ['Why do you think you can hide

[92] Delville, *Vie de Sainte Julienne de Cornillon*, 62–64; Newman, *Life of Juliana of Mont Cornillon*, 52.

[93] Delville, *Vie de Sainte Julienne de Cornillon*, 68; Newman, *Life of Juliana of Mont Cornillon*, 54,

[94] Delville, *Vie de Sainte Julienne de Cornillon*, 68; Newman, *Life of Juliana of Mont Cornillon*, 54.

[95] Mulder-Bakker, *Lives of the Anchoresses*, 112–13.

[96] Delville, *Vie de Sainte Julienne de Cornillon*, 68–70; Newman, *Life of Juliana of Mont Cornillon*, 54–55.

the secrets of your heart from me, recluse? I know your thoughts about everything as well as if I saw what you are thinking with my own eyes, written in letters on my palm (and she traced a finger over her hand)]. Juliana then proclaimed exactly what Eve was thinking. Other sections of the *vita* report, in the pious language of the thirteenth century, Juliana's special ability to apprehend exactly what was troubling others.

Perhaps the most interesting anecdote regarding Juliana's prophetic gift suggests an allegory of the Eucharist. The episode also provides an excellent exemplar of the prophetess and her followers in the context of the popular feminine piety characteristic of their period. A young woman came to visit at Mont Cornillon and was told by the other sisters that Juliana had been lying in bed for three days with a grave illness. The young woman persisted and was shown in at Juliana's request. The two women greeted each other, after which Juliana suggested that they begin with a prayer to the Holy Spirit. After their prayer the visitor experienced an intimate and sweet presence, which she interpreted to be the result of Juliana's prayer. Juliana revealed to her an astonishing knowledge of the death of a friend of the young woman without having been told of it. In response to a query as to how she knew of the death, Juliana described the unbearable pain, which she experienced every time a friend of hers passed from life. When the woman departed, Juliana gave her an apple. The woman later ate part of the apple and found it to be amazingly sweet. To be sure that this was not just her imagination, the woman shared part of it with her companions who reported the same experience. The young women believed that the apple had somehow increased in sweetness through Juliana's special merits, or gifts from God. The vignette is particularly noteworthy because it highlights a theological image of the Eucharist as reversing the expulsion of Adam and Eve from the Garden of Eden for tasting fruit of the forbidden apple tree. The apple was to the medieval mind the fruit of the Tree of Life through the flower of his mother, Mary. "Accrevisse dixerim ad cognoscendum quanta dulcedinis suavitate electam et dilectam suam christus perfunderet in interiori homine, qui etiam gratia ipsius tantum dulcorem fecisset in pomo visibili considere"[97] [I would say it was infused to show how much sweetness of delight Christ pours into the inner self of his chosen and beloved, when by his grace he had made such sweetness dwell even in a visible fruit].

Finally, in ca. 1248, Juliana was living in a Cistercian nunnery in Salzinnes at Namur, under the direction of Abbess Imène, who frequently told guests of Juliana's gift of prophecy. On one occasion the women were discussing the legend of Ursula and the 11,000 virgins.[98] Juliana told the abbess that she and her sister, the abbess of Saint Walburgis, would honor the martyred women. The two abbesses later obtained permission to excavate in a cemetery at Cologne, where they found the remains of 500 or more bodies. The relics were transported to Flanders and received by Margaret of Constantinople, Countess of Flanders from 1244 to 1263.[99] The vignette illustrates the na-

---

[97] Delville, *Vie de Sainte Julienne de Cornillon*, 76; Newman, *Life of Juliana of Mont Cornillon*, 58.

[98] According to a ninth-century legend, Ursula and her companions were returning to the Rhineland when they were attacked by Huns and martyred.

[99] Delville, *Vie de Sainte Julienne de Cornillon*, 219 n 342; see also Wim Blockmans, "Flanders," in *The New Cambridge Medieval History V: c.1198–c.1300*, ed. David Abulafia (Cambridge: Cambridge University Press, 1999), 405–16, who dates her reign from 1214 to 1278. The actual historic source of the legend of Ursula is most

ture of Juliana's prophecies and the religious culture of an ever-widening group of women for whom the tales had meaning. Moreover, it introduces empirical evidence of a connection between Juliana and the heirs of Count Baldwin IX (Baldwin I of Constantinople), through interpersonal networks that included his younger daughter, Countess Margaret.

DIVINE CALLING

Juliana's revelations and prophecies about the feast of Corpus Christi were so frequent as to constitute a divine calling. And she, if most reluctantly, believed herself to be called by God to establish a new feast day celebrating the sacrament of the Body and Blood of Jesus. Her most famous vision began in ca. 1210, when she was about eighteen, and recurred whenever she prayed. In this vision she saw the moon with a piece missing and was unable to interpret its meaning. "Tunc revelavit ei christus in luna presentem ecclesiam; in lune autem fractione defectum unius sollempnitatis in ecclesia figurari, quam adhuc volebat in terris a suis fidelibus celebrari"[100] [Then Christ revealed to her that the moon was the present Church, while the breach in the moon symbolized the absence of a feast, which he still desired his faithful upon earth to celebrate]. As noted earlier, he wished for a feast that celebrated the sacrament of his Body and Blood once a year at a time more special and solemn than during Holy Week. Moreover, the *vita* reports that Christ revealed to Juliana that he wished her to initiate the feast and announce it to the world. The two visions are perhaps best known through their visual representation in miniatures that precede Books I and II of the *vita*.[101] The first, on fol. 2v of Arsenal 945, represents Juliana kneeling before an altar. Above the altar is the head of Christ, turned to present a three-quarter profile and suspended within an oval over a chalice placed on the altar. The second, on fol. 24, represents Juliana kneeling and presenting a book of the feast of Corpus Christi.[102]

For twenty years Juliana prayed that Christ would find someone else to initiate the new feast, prayers to which the *vita* reports Christ responding with admonishments that she alone was entrusted with this divine calling. Juliana always responded to this calling in the same way:

Domine dimitte me, et quod michi iniungis iniunge potius magnis clericis lumine scientie fulgentibus, qui sciant et possint tantum negotium promovere. Nam quomodo id possem? Non sum ego domine digna nuntiare mundo rem tam arduam; tam excelsam, nec ipsam scirem nec possem aliquatenus adimplere.[103]

[Lord, release me, and give the task you have assigned me to great scholars shining with the light of knowledge, who would know how to promote such a great affair. For

likely a church dedicated to eleven (11) virgins martyred in the fifth century. A poor reading of the inscription transformed the 11 into 11,000. The bones discovered by Saint Walburgis were actually part of a Roman cemetery.

[100] Delville, *Vie de Sainte Julienne de Cornillon*, 122; Newman, *Life of Juliana of Mont Cornillon*, 80.

[101] Paris, Bibliothèque de l'Arsenal, MS 945, fols. 2v and 24, reproduced in *Saint-Martin, Mémoire de Liège*, 33, 57.

[102] See Delville, *Vie de Sainte Julienne de Cornillon*, viii.

[103] Ibid., 122–24.

how could I do it? I am not worthy, Lord, to tell the world about something so noble and exalted. I could not understand it, nor could I fulfill it.]

Christ always responded with an affirmation that Juliana should be the one to initiate the new feast and that humble people would thereafter promote the feast of Corpus Christi. This became Juliana's central and divine calling. Mulder-Bakker speculates that at age forty, it became more acceptable for women to embrace a more active social role and that this might explain the lengthy delay.[104] Also important was the length of time it must have taken her to organize the theological texts and compose the music.[105]

MUSICAL GIFTS

While liturgical and other scholars have been unanimous in crediting Juliana with promoting the new feast of Corpus Christi, especially among the Dominicans in Liège, they say little, if anything, about Juliana's musical gifts. Here, critical examination of details previously overlooked in the *vita*, including the description of the scene in which the composition of the new office and Mass took place, provides strong support for the thesis that Juliana was the "composer" of the original version of the office. Mulder-Bakker most recently notes: "Even if the hagiographer suggests here that John wrote the actual text, he allows no room for doubt that Juliana is the intellectual author."[106]

After receiving the requisite approbations from Church officials, Juliana chose the young and innocent John, then a monk at Mont Cornillon, [although she knew him to be inexperienced in literary matters], to compose the new feast. In the following quote from the *vita* describing the scene in which the composition occurred, I have placed emphases on the application of the term *auctoritate virginis*, which might be strictly translated as source or authorship. The term *auctoritas* was used in the thirteenth century to refer to authoritative quotations, and persons who produced them were called *auctores*,[107] meaning author or originator. The authorship of Juliana is further emphasized in the passage by John's requests for edits and corrections and his attributions to Juliana's prayers.

> Quem licet in litterarum scientia nosceret imperitum; sciens tamen dei virtutem et sapientiam cuius opus fieri volebat digna posse dicere per indoctum, ipsum de inquirendo et componendo nove festivitatis officio studuit exhortatoriis sermonibus convenire. . . . Ipse licet ingenii et scientie sue mensuram excerdere non ambigeret opus tantum; modice quippe litterature erat, victus tamen precibus et **auctoritate virginis** cuius optime noverat sanctitatem, inquirere et ordinare predictum officium est aggressus. Aggressus inquam de illius persuasus confidere adiutorio qui dicit per prophetam, *Aperi os tuum et ego implebo illud.* Sique frater ille iuvenis et christi virgo condixerant; ut cum ille pergeret ad scribendum illa similiter accederet ad orandum, ut alter alterius labore iu-

[104] Mulder-Bakker, *Lives of the Anchoresses*, 88.

[105] See Jean Cottiaux, "L'Office liégeois de la Fête-Dieu, sa valeur et son destin," *Revue d'histoire ecclésiastique* 58 (1963), 5–81, 405–59, and his *Sainte Julienne de Cornillon, promotrice de la Fête-Dieu: Son pays, son temps, son message* (Liège: Carmel de Cornillon, 1991), 183.

[106] Mulder-Bakker, *Lives of the Anchoresses*, 91.

[107] R. J. Henle, ed., *St. Thomas Aquinas Summa Theologiae I–II; qq. 90–97: The Treatise On Law* (Notre Dame: University of Notre Dame Press, 1993), 94.

varetur et sic ad invicem consolarentur. Percurrens igitur ille multorum sanctorum libros sicut apis prudentissima divinarum sententiarnum flores legebat; sacramenti corporis et sanguinis christi dulcedinem sapientes, ex quibus intra semetipsum antiphonarum responsoriorum hymnorum et aliorum que ad ipsum officium pertinent mella conficiens ea in tabularum alveario recondebat; ceris sua mella restituens, profecto prioribus dulciora. . . . Et cum aliquid ad predictum officium pertinens composuerat, hoc ipsum ad illam afferens aiebat. **Hoc domina mea vobis mittitur de supernis; videte et examinate si quid sit in cantu vel littera corrigendum.** Quod illa per permirabilem scientiam sibi infusam tanta subtilitate et perspicacitate cum id exposceret necessitas faciebat, ut post ipsius examinationem et correctionem numquam necesse fuerit limam etiam summorum accedere magistrorum. Et quod christi virgo probaverat hoc ille retentabat, quod virgo ipsa dignum correctione iudicaverat aut ipsa corrigebat aut illius correctioni relinquebat. Sicque factum est, ut totum officium nove solempnitatis nocturnum et diurnum in hymnis antiphonis responsoriis lectionibus caputlis collectis et aliis omnibus proprie proprijs christi virgine orante iuvene fratre componente.[108]

[Although she was aware that he lacked literary knowledge, she knew that the power and wisdom of God, whose work she wanted to accomplish, could speak worthily through an uneducated person. So she zealously encouraged him to assemble and compose an Office for the new feast. . . . Though he had no doubt that such a task exceeded the measure of his talent and knowledge—for he was indeed of very modest learning— he was overcome by the prayers and **authority of the virgin**, whose sanctity he well knew. So he set out to compose and arrange an Office. He set out, I say, trusting in the help of him who says through the prophet, 'Open your mouth and I will fill it' [Ps 80: 11]. The young brother and Christ's virgin agreed that when he began to write, she would begin to pray; in this way each would be helped by the other for their mutual comfort. Thus the brother, perusing the books of many saints like a clever bee, culled the flowers of divine quotations that were fragrant with the sweetness of the Sacrament of Christ's Body and Blood. From these he inwardly confected a honey of antiphons, responsories, hymns, and other items pertaining to the Office and stored it in the hive of his wax tablets. In these honeycombs he made the confection sweeter than before . . . but he ascribed his success to the prayer of Christ's virgin rather than his own industry or labour, and when he had composed any part of the Office he would bring it to her and say, **'This is sent to you from on high, my lady. Look and see whether anything needs to be corrected in the chant or in the text.'** With the wondrous knowledge infused in her, she did this with such shrewdness and subtlety when the need arose that, after her examination and correction, even the greatest masters did not need to polish it any further. And what Christ's virgin had approved, he retained or submitted to her correction. So it happened that the whole Office for the new feast—the Night Office and the daytime Hours, with the hymns, antiphons, responsorial readings, chapters, collects, and all the other propers—was completed, while Christ's virgin prayed, the young brother composed . . .].[109]

The description of their work together on the office and Mass lends itself to interpretation as a scene in which Juliana sings or prays, while John functions as the scribe. This interpretation is perhaps corroborated by the description of the death scene in the *vita*, in which Juliana asks for a scribe to whom she can make known the secrets of her

---

[108] Delville, *Vie de Sainte Julienne de Cornillon*, 136–38.

[109] Newman, *Life of Juliana of Mont Cornillon*, 86–88, emphasis added.

heart. Clearly, she understood the function of a scribe and expressed the desire for something to which she felt entitled. And her humility was prudent. The thesis of Juliana's authorship is further corroborated in passages in her *vita* that make direct reference to her musical gifts. There are many references to specific chants, which Juliana is able to recall and recite from memory as appropriate for the liturgical occasion: the Magnificat, *Vexilla Regis prodeunt*, *Nunc dimittis*, the office of the Ascension, the office of Saint Lambert, and *Christum regum Regem adoremus Dominum*, the Matins invitatory of the office for the feast of Corpus Christi. There are numerous mentions of her responses to her favorite chants. She especially loved the Magnificat and once spoke to the abbess of Salzinnes about "dulcedine huius cantici"[110] [the sweetness of this canticle]. When the abbess urged "ut illa eam quam super hoc sentiebat mellitam dulcedinem aliquatenus eructaret; iuliana repente veluti inebriata non tamen vino sed spiritu"[111] [her to impart some of that honeyed sweetness she felt in it, Juliana suddenly burst out as if she were drunk, not with wine but with the Spirit (Eph 5: 18)]. Juliana wished this canticle be rapidly diffused everywhere, especially among the convents and béguines.[112]

The *vita* makes specific mention of her knowledge of the feasts and seasons of the liturgical year and her daily repetition of the office and the proper. "Cum autem aliquid eiusmodi sancta ecclesia congruo tempore recolebat, iuliana se tempori per omnia conformabat"[113] [When the holy Church commemorated any event at the proper time, Juliana conformed herself entirely to the season]. Other descriptions make it clear that Juliana had committed much of this to memory, and this memorization was not limited to text alone: she heard and replayed both the music and text of the offices and Mass in her imagination. For example, when Prior John died, Juliana heard the first words from the Matins invitatory of the office for the feast of Corpus Christi as part of a religious vision. "Audiebat etiam et recognoscebat vocem fratris iohannis inter choros psallentis multitudinis"[114] [She also heard and recognized the voice of Brother John among the vast choirs singing praises].

The *vita* makes specific mention of Juliana singing. Especially interesting is the description of her singing from the Song of Songs.

> Et vide an digne canere potuerit illud cantici canticorum, "Fasciculus myrre dilectus meus michi, inter ubera mea commorabitur." Et revera digne. Ex omnibus enim dilecti anxietatibus et amaritudinibus que per myrram designantur veluti ex ramusculis myrre odorifere sibi fasciculum colligaverat; collectumque inter ubera sua collocaverat; amara illa sed salutifera que in salutem mundi salvator noster dignatus est pati; in principali sui pectoris reponendo, patientisque et morientis christi memorialia memorie sue arctius commendando.[115]

---

[110] Delville, *Vie de Sainte Julienne de Cornillon*, 50.

[111] Delville, *Vie de Sainte Julienne de Cornillon*, 50; Newman, *Life of Juliana of Mont Cornillon*, 45. See Peter T. Ricketts, Poem XX, line 55, in Part III this volume, whose work suggests the term *proclaim* rather than *impart*.

[112] Delville, *Vie de Sainte Julienne de Cornillon*, 52.

[113] Delville, *Vie de Sainte Julienne de Cornillon*, 54; Newman, *Life of Juliana of Mont Cornillon*, 47.

[114] Delville, *Vie de Sainte Julienne de Cornillon*, 234; Newman, *Life of Juliana of Mont Cornillon*, 129.

[115] Delville, *Vie de Sainte Julienne de Cornillon*, 56; Newman, *Life of Juliana of Mont Cornillon*, 48.

[Now see whether she could worthily sing that verse from the Song of Songs: "My be-loved is to me a bag of myrrh that shall lie between my breasts' [Song 1:12]. Worthily indeed! From all the anguish and bitter sufferings of her beloved, which are designated by myrrh, she gathered for herself a little bundle as if from sprigs of fragrant myrrh and laid it between her breasts, setting in the core of her heart that saving bitterness which our Saviour deigned to suffer for the salvation of the world, and strictly committing to memory the memorials of the suffering and dying Christ.]

The description corresponds with another important reference to Juliana's musical gifts: her performance of the office of the Ascension. On this feast day she typically was unable to remain indoors but, rather, had to go outside where she always had visions of the human Christ ascending and piercing the heavens. The *vita*, in its characteristic style, reports that she went to visit a friend on this feast day. Especially crucial to the incident here is the parallel reported between the words by Juliana, "Recessit dominus meus," and the words of Psalm 47, "Ascendit deus in iubilatione." The term *iubilus*, or song of joy, according to Cassiodorus (ca. 485–580), referred in its origins more specifi-cally to an extended melisma, a vocal melodic phrase on one syllable, which followed the singing of the Alleluia in medieval performance practice. Later, a text, usually from the Psalms, was added to the Alleluia.[116] The Psalm in the *vita* that provides the parallel phrase to Juliana's words makes reference to the ascension of the Lord with the sound of a trumpet, followed by a command to sing praises.

Unde cum in die sollempnitatis memorate ad quandam dilectam sibi personam visi-tandi gratia divertisset, sic repleta et referta gratie fuit ut plenitudinem eius angusto corpore capere non valente illa ad quam iuliana venerat plurimum timeret, ne disrupto corporis vasculo sua visitatrix per medium scinderetur. Illa autem que sic affecte presto erat mirabile dictu vocem iuliane audiebat, quam sine oris apertione sed solo pectore proferebat. Pro captanda vero aliquantula evaporatione ardoris, quem intra se patieba-tur ut vocem inclusam emitteret admonuit, neminem hanc asserens auditurum. At illa exclamavit et dixit. Recessit dominus meus. Nonne tibi videtur dixisse: ascendit deus in iubilatione? Sic autem veluti ascensionis peracto officio cum ad se foret reversa sic sibi erat per quandam mestitie gravitatem. . . .[117]

[Once when she had gone to visit a close friend on this feast day, she was so filled and overflowing with grace that her narrow body could not contain its fullness, and her hostess was afraid that Juliana's body would burst and split down the middle. She was ready to help the afflicted one when she heard Juliana's voice proceeding from her chest alone, strange to say, while her mouth remained closed. To let some of the painful inner heat escape, her friend urged her to let out a cry, saying that no one would hear it. And Juliana cried out and said, "My Lord has departed!" Is it not as if she had said, "God has gone up with a shout of joy" (Ps 46: 6). When she had finished the office of the As-cension, as it were, she returned to herself with a heavy sadness. . . .]

These excerpts provide strong evidence that Juliana was a musician, a singer, and quite knowledgeable in the liturgy. They corroborate the thesis that it was Juliana, not John, who led in the composition of the music for the "original version" of the new

[116] Cf. Willi Apel, *Gregorian Chant* (Bloomington: Indiana University Press, 1990), 41, 185, 496–99).

[117] Delville, *Vie de Sainte Julienne de Cornillon*, 58; Newman, *Life of Juliana of Mont Cornillon*, 49.

feast of Corpus Christi.[118] She was a musical and theological "insider,"[119] familiar with the musico-liturgical culture of the thirteenth-century world. Specific mention of her familiarity with the office of Saint Lambert and of the Trinity, both composed by Stephen, bishop of Liège (850–920), in particular provides evidence of her familiarity with the rhymed numerical office, a characteristic compositional style also manifest in the office for the feast of Corpus Christi. Because of the medieval and Neo-Platonic interpretation of music as connecting the human body to the soul [*anima*] and therefore to God through harmonic proportions, the musical gifts provide further insight into the widespread image of Juliana as a divine vessel for the voice of God. Moreover, whereas women were not permitted to preach, they were permitted to sing, which provided for them an important venue through which to express homiletic agency. Viewing Juliana as a singer explains the immediate emotional appeal of the feast during her lifetime among face-to-face audiences, as well as the impulse to transform the liturgy from an oral into a literate form when she was no longer the exclusive performer.

DIFFUSION OF THE FEAST THROUGH SOCIAL NETWORKS

Religious rituals and shared symbols in a shared physical, liturgical, and social space are central to understanding the significance of Juliana's role in the initiation and acceptance for the new feast of Corpus Christi. Recognition of her special gifts and her consequent influence began at the small group level among intimate friends and then spread through face-to-face networks into the formal and impersonal space of the larger institution of the thirteenth-century Church. The empirical details of the diffusion process emphasize the importance of friendships and social networks in the initiation, performance, and appreciation for religious ideas as expressed through new liturgy.[120] Friendships and emotional energy both fortified and were fortified by liturgical rituals, while novelty added a level of intellectual excitement and engagement, an effect especially pronounced in the pre-modern world.

Delville[121] notes that Juliana's interpersonal relationships began with religious women, then spanned out through networks to French members of the religious community, and finally embraced the Holy See. These highlight a social network in which Juliana's allies were woven together, typically as part of the Church hierarchy and papal party. Her friends, even when marginal, were connected through her to immediate sources of dynastic and official Church power as the Church turned increasingly toward

---

[118] In 1475, a *glossateur* inserted a note into the *vita* of Juliana indicating that the liturgy for the new office was preserved at church at Tongres and elsewhere and that the first antiphon began with the incipit "Animarum cibus." "Hoc officium incipit, Animarum cibus; et reperitur plenum in Ecclesia Tungrensi et aliis locis. Deinde Urbanus IV; officium quod ubique cantatur, instituit." C. Lambot in 1946 found a version of an office that begins with this incipit in a composite manuscript catalogued as KB 70.E.4.

[119] Jeffery, *Re-Envisioning Past Musical Cultures*, 54.

[120] See Stark and Bainbridge, "Networks of Faith: Interpersonal Bonds and Recruitment to Sects and Cults," *American Journal of Sociology* 85, (1980), 1376–95; see also Lutz Kaelber, *Schools of Asceticism: Ideology and Organization in Medieval Religious Communities* (University Park: Pennsylvania State University Press, 1998), 175–224, and his description of the mid-twelfth to thirteenth-century Cathars, especially 223.

[121] Jean-Pierre Delville, "Julienne de Cornillon à la lumière de son biographe," in *Fête-Dieu (1246–1996)*, vol. 1, 27–53.

France. Interesting exceptions in the socio-organizational landscape were the status occupants of the bishopric and the priory, who displayed favorable attitudes toward her and the new feast under John of Eppes, Robert Thourette, Godfrey, and John, but hostile ones under Henry of Gueldre and Roger. Close examination of the religious, social, and political orientation among these ties—those favoring and those opposing the feast of Corpus Christi—reveals interesting contours in human groups. The networks around Juliana betray the fault lines of a larger-scale political fragmentation and conflict.[122]

THE CLOSE CIRCLE OF WOMEN FRIENDS

Most of Juliana's friendships were with women and ranged from close, personal relationships to more distant acquaintances. The *vita* describes twenty-eight encounters with women and twenty-three with men.[123] The encounters differed not only in number but also in content and substance. Juliana's relationships to women most often were intimate, affective, and expressive. Those with men, by contrast, were more formal, based on specific role expectations within the organizational framework. These proceeded more closely along hierarchical lines, and their content was directed largely to specific tasks.

The first person to whom Juliana revealed her vision of the moon with its missing quarter was her friend Eve, the recluse at Saint-Martin's. Juliana visited Eve, who regarded her as strangely preoccupied, asked what was troubling her, and offered to share her burden. Juliana responded:

> Meditationes inquit cordis mei, causam sumunt ex quadam sollempnitate sacramenti. Hec a longo tempore usque ad diem hanc in corde meo continuo versata est, nec unquam alicui demonstravi nec verbis aliquibus explicare possem quid ex hac sentire michi divinitus est concessum. Attamen quod potero dicam vobis, quandoquidem qualecumque illud est scire cupitis. Hec sollempnitas, semper fuit in secreto trinitatis.[124]

> [The meditations of my heart have to do with a certain feast of the Sacrament. This thought has been in my heart continually for a long time, even to this day, and I have never revealed it to anyone. Nor could I express in words what God has granted me to sense. Yet I will tell you what I can, since you want to know whatever it may be. This feast has always existed in the mystery of the Trinity.]

Juliana then revealed to Eve the entire story of her vision of the moon and the revelations by God. Eve begged Juliana to pray that she, Eve, might feel the same about the new feast. Juliana responded that this would not be a good thing because it would cause her to experience more torture than her frail body could bear. God would grant to her and other friends a share of affect about the new feast as useful, measured out in proportions to each in accordance to strength. Thereafter, as Eve increasingly shared in Juliana's love for the feast, her pain increased with each delay in its implementation.[125]

---

[122] See Walters, "Church-Sect Dynamics and the Feast of Corpus Christi," 285–301.

[123] Ibid., 288; see also Delville, "Julienne de Cornillon à la lumière de son biographe," 37.

[124] Delville, *Vie de Sainte Julienne de Cornillon*, 174; Newman, *Life of Juliana of Mont Cornillon*, 103.

[125] Delville, *Vie de Sainte Julienne de Cornillon*, 174–75.

This encounter between Juliana and Eve underscores the affective nature of the friendship and Eve's supportive role in the institution of the new feast. Cottiaux and Delville[126] have noted four basic features of their "indissolubili vinculo caritatis"[127] [unbreakable chain of charity]. Eve was the protégée, the spiritual daughter, of Juliana. However, Juliana shared many of her ecstatic spiritual experiences with Eve, such as the absence of the Blessed Sacrament at Saint-Martin's, and in this sense was her equal and friend. In other instances Eve was Juliana's confidante and protector. She was the first person with whom Juliana shared her vision of the new feast honoring the Sacrament and the person with whom Juliana initially stayed when she fled Mont Cornillon after the death of Prior Godfrey.[128] When the townspeople attacked the monastery and destroyed Juliana's oratory, Eve financed its reconstruction.[129] And finally, Eve was a liaison between Juliana and the higher clergy in Liège: when Urban IV embraced the feast of Corpus Christi in 1264, he wrote a congratulatory letter to Eve, who survived Juliana by eight years.

Juliana formed another significant personal friendship with Isabella of Huy, a béguine. Shortly after Juliana received official approbation for the new feast day, she arranged for the highly esteemed Isabella to be received as a sister at Mont Cornillon. During one of their many conversations [in the language of the *vita*], Juliana, wishing to know if God had shown Isabella any of the great mysteries regarding the feast of Corpus Christi, asked her what she would think of a new feast day celebrating the Sacrament. Isabella's response clearly indicated that she had no knowledge or understanding of the feast that Juliana mentioned; it paraphrases from the prophecy of Simeon: "Tunc soror iuliana ex illius responsione percipiens de cognitione archani sibi revelati necdum illi quippiam revelatum, non aliter se habuit quam si gladio ancipiti cor eius transverberatum fuisset"[130] [Then Sister Juliana, perceiving from this response that the secret revealed to her had not yet been imparted to Isabella, behaved as if her heart had been pierced by a two-edged sword (Lk 2: 35)]. When Sister Isabella saw the pain and disappointment in Juliana's face, she prayed and asked the other sisters to pray that God would open her eyes to understanding. This enlightenment occurred when Isabella visited Eve at the church of Saint-Martin where she, too, had a vision of the new feast of Corpus Christi. Isabella became Juliana's lifelong friend. She fled Mont Cornillon with her, Agnes, and Ozile in 1247, and died at Salzinnes in Namur, the last of the monasteries in which Juliana and her companions found refuge.[131]

Juliana's more distant face-to-face friendships with women articulate the political, social, and interpersonal connections among the people in her networks even while the contents of the interactions remain more personal than those with men. The abbess of

---

[126] Cottiaux and Delville, "La Fête-Dieu," 35.

[127] Delville, *Vie de Sainte Julienne de Cornillon*, 66; Newman, *Life of Juliana of Mont Cornillon*, 53; see also Cor 3:14.

[128] Delville, *Vie de Sainte Julienne de Cornillon*, 182.

[129] Delville, *Vie de Sainte Julienne de Cornillon*, 186.

[130]Delville, *Vie de Sainte Julienne de Cornillon*, 132–34; Newman, *Life of Juliana of Mont Cornillon*, 85.

[131] Although esteemed, as a béguine, Isabella must have come from a lower social stratum than Eve or Juliana, who were placed in official church and monastic settings, enriching them with their respective dowries.

Salzinnes, Imène, was born in 1218 and thus was much younger than Juliana. She was the half-sister of Conrad of Hochstaden, the archbishop of Cologne. Imène became abbess at Salzinnes in 1239, and in 1248 learned of Juliana's plight at Namur. She was in touch with John, archdeacon of Liège, who had constructed a hospice for the béguines and then provided Juliana and her companions with land adjacent to the hospice on which they were permitted to build themselves a small house. Imène was persuasive in getting a pension for the women from Mont Cornillon, and she was in touch with Guiard, the bishop of Cambrai, who advised the women to submit to the authority of the abbess of Salzinnes for their own protection. In 1252, Imène received the women into the abbey of Salzinnes and in the same year was able to obtain from Cardinal Hugh of Saint-Cher a charter of protection for the abbey. In April of the next year she obtained a similar charter from Archbishop Conrad, her half-brother, and then a bull of papal protection from Alexander IV in 1256. She obtained from the abbess of Saint Machabees the bones of the eleven thousand virgins in 1256. When the abbey was dispersed, Abbess Imène found a place for Juliana at the Cistercian monastery at Fosses.

The remarkable and striking feature of Juliana's network of women friends was its breadth. The network spanned all types of religious organizations, from cloistered Cistercian nuns, to Dominican nurses and teachers, and finally to béguines, religious women living outside of orders. The networks also reflect the full spectrum of socioeconomic status in thirteenth-century Belgium, ranging from the extremely wealthy and landed aristocracy to impoverished and often homeless widows, and encompassing in between the established urban and commercial patriciate, as well as the newer merchant strata. The geographic span is equally expansive, extending throughout the archdiocese and including bordering territories in Flanders. Their breadth and depth contribute to a deeper understanding of women's issues and the issue of women during the thirteenth century.

The contents of the interactions, but especially those centered on the Eucharist, reveal much about the way in which the women of Liège achieved emotional energy, solidarity, and reinforcement so as to produce a contagious effect that spread to other groups. Metaphors for the Eucharist, such as the anecdote of the apple that became sweeter, reveal the charismatic religious authority of the prophetess, Juliana of Mont Cornillon, in producing good will. Mulder-Bakker quite remarkably highlights the way in which parts of the liturgy composed by Juliana for the feast of Corpus Christi interpret the Eucharist so as to maximize the emotional energy generated face-to-face among friends. "With Paul, she emphasizes the banquet character of the Eucharist celebration, its communal dimension and eschatological perspective. In doing so she could fall back on the Church Fathers who had added a Neoplatonic twist by presenting the Eucharist as the visible, earthly realization of the invisible, heavenly type and by declaring that believers could, in the here and now, take part in the heavenly banquet."[132] Juliana's understanding enabled her to capture and communicate a direct, unmediated relationship to the triune God, who was truly present as refreshment for the journey on earth: "Panis vite panis angelorum, Ihesu Christe vera mundi vita qui semper nos refi-

---

[132] Mulder-Bakker, *Lives of the Anchoresses*, 109.

cis et vite nunquam deficis ab omni sana languore ut te nostro viatico in terra recreati te ore plenissimo manducemus in eternum"[133] [Bread of life, bread of angels, Jesus Christ, true life of the world, you who perpetually restores us and never fails us; guard us from all languor so that recreated by you through the food for our journey on earth we might partake of you most fully in heaven].

FORMAL AND COLLEGIAL RELATIONSHIPS TO MEN

Even Juliana's closest personal relationships with men were more formal and task-oriented than those with women. Prior Godfrey is mentioned only as a prior with a venerable life, who provided Juliana with much comfort during her trials and tribulations. Brother John, who became prior at Mont Cornillon in 1242, must have been the first male to whom Juliana spoke regarding her vision for the new feast. She mentioned him to Eve in a prophecy as "iuvenis et innocens"[134] [young and innocent], but nonetheless one who would support her during difficult times. John's life unfolded in tandem with that of Juliana: he was made prior at the same time she was restored as prioress and was deposed when she left. They worked together as co-administrators at Mont Cornillon. John was also a singer, and the two worked together on the office and Mass for the new feast. He visited Juliana during her exile at Salzinnes, and predeceased her by three years. The relationship to John is the only relationship between Juliana and a male that is described as collegial. In all others, the language of the *vita* suggests deference, humility, and requests for approbation on the part of Juliana in an ordered sequence that follows the hierarchical organization.

John of Lausanne, the canon at the church of Saint-Martin, was Juliana's confessor. Through this formal role relationship they developed a friendship that was close, intimate, and personal. Canon John offered Juliana his house at Saint-Martin when she fled Mont Cornillon. And he shared the expense of rebuilding her oratory with Eve, paying from his own funds. Juliana asked for Dom John, her confessor, on her deathbed so that she could make known the secrets of her heart. The canon was well known by most of the local priests and religious persons and thus was acquainted with the great Dominican teachers and theologians in Liège. For this reason Juliana requested that he submit her idea of the feast for scrutiny to the theological and religious luminaries among his acquaintances without disclosing her identity, in order to see how they might respond. Canon John therefore served as a bridge between the formal and informal social and organizational worlds, a conduit between the intimate and highly personal friendships in the community of women and the more formal role relationships among men within the official Church hierarchy, between the oral traditions and the literate world of philosophical theology. He was her "interpreter." Like Eve of Saint-Martin and the Abbess Imène, John stood among the "circle of followers comprising those who support[ed her] with lodging, money, and services and who expect[ed] to obtain their salvation through [her] mission."[135]

---

[133] Juliana of Mont Cornillon. *Animarum cibus*. Benedictus antiphon: see the Benediction antiphon for lauds in the Corrigan edition of KB 70.E.4.

[134] Delville, *Vie de Sainte Julienne de Cornillon*, 120.

[135] Weber, *Economy and Society*, 452.

COMMUNICATION WITHIN THE OFFICIAL CHURCH HIERARCHY

Juliana's role in spreading the feast of Corpus Christi among the women in Liège was mirrored, actually anchored, in the official and formal Church authority and personage of Hugh of Saint-Cher, who apparently stepped into the breach created by the contested bishopric in Liège in 1238. His networks were formidable, encompassing the most distinguished and influential theologians of the historical period, such as Albertus Magnus and Saint Thomas Aquinas, as well as the most humble of women, who served as nurses and teachers in the new Dominican convents. Hugh served directly and worked closely with three popes: Innocent IV, Alexander IV, and Urban IV. His power, authority, and influence were formalized and official through a succession of increasingly important appointments, and his career developed alongside and through the institution of the new feast. It became the emblem of the textual *auctoritas* of the Dominicans as the order moved from the margins to the center of ecclesiastic power.

Hugh's contributions to the feast of Corpus Christi include: (1) approval of the idea of the new feast in 1240; (2) presentation of the idea to the cardinal and to the bishop of Cambrai; (3) approbation of the office and Mass composed by Juliana and John; (4) celebration of the new feast for the first time at Saint-Martin, perhaps adding a sermon; (5) accordance of indulgences at Saint-Martin, Villers, and eventually for all his legation; (6) active support for the initiative among men within the official hierarchy of the Church, including bishops and popes; and (7) spreading its celebration among lay people within his jurisdiction by preaching and granting of indulgences. Moreover, Zawilla, through painstaking analysis, has demonstrated the extent to which versions of the office and Mass subsequent to the one centonated by Juliana and John, versions referred to as *Sapiencia [a]edificavit sibi* and *Sacerdos in [a]eternum*, relied directly upon Hugh's biblical commentaries.[136] Thus while his actual role in the authorship remains an open question,[137] Zawilla notes with respect to *Sapiencia [a]edificavit sibi*: the evidence "indicates that Hugh could be considered as likely a candidate for the composer of the *historia*, that is, of the biblical parts of the office, as Thomas."[138] Moreover, in sacramental theology, Hugh "was the first theologian to discern a matter and a form in all the sacraments and to understand these principles in the Aristotelian sense of determinable and determining elements."[139] Without doubt, Hugh, "author of the most influential *Sentences* commentary of his time and leader of an *équipe* of biblical commentators,"[140] played a central role in the official institution of the new feast and in providing protection for Juliana.

Hugh was born in Saint-Cher in ca. 1195, a town near Vienne in southeastern France, and achieved early recognition for his intellectual prowess. He completed the baccalaureate in philosophy and theology at the University of Paris, as well as a Master

---

[136] See Tables 3 and 4 in the "Introduction to the Liturgical Manuscripts."

[137] Cf. Zawilla, *Biblical Sources of the Historia Corporis Christi*, 205–06 and 334–37.

[138] Ibid., 206.

[139] Walter H. Principe, *Hugh of Saint-Cher's Theology of the Hypostatic Union* (Toronto: Pontifical Institute of Mediaeval Studies, 1970), 19.

[140] Miri Rubin, *Corpus Christi: The Eucharist in Late Medieval Culture* (Cambridge: Cambridge University Press, 1991), 174.

of Law in 1224.[141] In February 1225, he entered the Dominican order. Between 1227 and 1230 he served as the provincial of the Dominicans in France, then as regent master of theology at the University of Paris in 1230. In ca. 1236, he was named provincial a second time and visited the new Dominican monastery in Liège sometime between then and 1240, while Juliana and John were at work on the office and Mass. The *vita* notes that Juliana's idea for the feast of Corpus Christi was approved by "fratri hugoni tunc priori provinciali ordinis fratrum predicatorum"[142] [Friar Hugh, then Prior Provincial of the Dominicans]; Hugh became Vicar General of the order in 1240, thus his title was then different. He must also have been acquainted with Bishop Guiard, in the adjacent diocese of Cambrai, who served the papal envoy that resolved the contested election of the Liège bishop in 1238 and who consecrated the Dominican church in 1242.

Hugh was appointed Cardinal-Legate in April 1244 and then to a diplomatic post under Innocent IV.[143] At the Council of Lyon in 1245, the venue of the deposition of Frederick II by Innocent IV, he encountered both the Liège bishop, Robert Thourette, and Archbishop Conrad, also participants in the council.[144] He overlapped with theological luminaries Albertus Magnus and Saint Thomas Aquinas in Cologne between 1251 and 1252, where Aquinas was working as a *baccalarius biblicus* under Albert.[145] Albert had been sent to Cologne in 1248 to preside over the first Dominican *studium* at Heilige Kreuz.[146] In 1252 Cardinal Hugh wrote a letter, at the request of Albert, in support of the dispensation permitting Thomas to begin studies for the mastership in theology at the University of Paris at the age of twenty-seven.[147]

As Cardinal-Legate, Hugh traveled extensively and widely, acquiring a reputation for diplomatic skills, which no doubt helped immensely in the spread of the feast of Corpus Christi. His support for Juliana and her work was not atypical; he was well known for his interest and support of women's communities. Grundmann writes:

> He was the man best suited to reorder the relations between the order and women's houses. Himself a Dominican by origin, he had been active as cardinal (since 1244) in promoting Dominican interests, and he could serve as guarantor of the order in the College of Cardinals. On the other hand, during his legation in Germany he had passionately defended the women's religious movement, supporting women's houses and communities to the best of his strength. He had come to understand the importance of and needs of the women's religious movement as had few others.[148]

Cardinal Hugh of Saint-Cher returned to Rome in 1254 and died on 19 March 1263 at Orvieto, in the company of Pope Urban IV. There he must have encountered Saint Tho-

---

[141] Cottiaux and Delville, "La Fête-Dieu"; Delville, *Vie de Sainte Julienne de Cornillon*, 129 n 183.

[142] Delville, *Vie de Sainte Julienne de Cornillon*, 128; Newman, *Life of Juliana of Mont Cornillon*, 83.

[143] Delville, *Vie de Sainte Julienne de Cornillon*, 129 n 183.

[144] Ibid., 151 n 222, 213 n 328.

[145] Zawilla, *Biblical Sources of the Historia Corporis Christi*, 334–35.

[146] Weisheipl, *Friar Thomas D'Aquino*, 41.

[147] Ibid., 51.

[148] Herbert Grundmann, *Religious Movements in the Middle Ages*, trans. Steven Rowan (Notre Dame: University of Notre Dame Press, 1995; first published in 1935 as *Religiöse Bewegungen im Mittelalter*), 126.

mas Aquinas, perhaps for the second time. Aquinas was then in Orvieto as a Master theologian, completing the *Catena aurea*, which he dedicated to his friend Pope Urban IV. Aquinas very likely was working on the second or third version of the liturgy for the feast of Corpus Christi.[149] Both Hugh and Urban IV recognized and admired the religious devotion of women, especially those who channeled their energies into eucharistic devotion and the movement to establish a new feast celebrating the Sacrament.

Pope Urban IV officially established the feast of Corpus Christi for the universal Church by papal bull. He was personally unknown to Juliana of Mont Cornillon but was among those theologians and Church dignitaries who were in Liège and to whom her idea of the feast was initially proposed. His involvement therefore marks a decisive shift away from an informal and expressive diffusion among friends and acquaintances toward formal institutionalization of a new feast.

Born Jacques Pantaléon in Troyes (ca. 1190–1264), Urban IV came from a poor but honest family[150] and thus had a great deal in common with and a great deal of sympathy for the impoverished béguines. He was ordained in 1215 and in 1220 advanced to doctor of theology in Paris, becoming canon at Laon in the same year. In 1243 he was appointed archdeacon of Liège, remaining in that position until 1249. Here he learned of the visions of Juliana and her idea for the new feast of Corpus Christi. He approved of the new feast and influenced its adoption through his support for the initial decree of institution on the part of Bishop Robert. Jacques was named Bishop of Verdun in 1254 and then Patriarch of Jerusalem in 1255. On 29 August 1261, he was named Pope and took the name Urban IV.

Legend has it that Pope Urban IV did not act on promoting the new feast of Corpus Christi until the people of Italy were inspired by their own miracle, the Miracle of Bolsena. This legend tells of a German priest, deeply disturbed by doubts about transubstantiation, who was on pilgrimage to Rome. While celebrating Mass in the church of Santa Cristina in the Umbrian town of Bolsena, he saw blood emerge from the consecrated morsel and drench the host. Rumor quickly spread through the village and a procession formed, which took the bloodstained host to Urban IV in Orvieto, a short distance away. The miraculous host was enshrined and placed in a reliquary at the church of Santa Cristina, where it remains to this day. Raphael immortalized the event in a painting that now hangs in the Vatican. Contemporary scholars have questioned whether this event in fact inspired Urban IV to establish the new feast.[151] Miri Rubin notes the disjunction in time between the alleged miracle, with its tradition that began in the fourteenth century, and the interests of Pope Urban IV, which began in Liège in the 1240s. She suggests that the attempt to link the foundation directly to the alleged miracle "seems, therefore, to be perhaps misplaced."[152]

---

[149] Weisheipl, *Friar Thomas D'Aquino*, 171–72; Jean-Pierre Torrell, *Saint Thomas Aquinas*, vol. 1, trans. Robert Royal (Washington, D.C.: Catholic University Press, 1996), 129–41.

[150] Robert Brentano, *Rome before Avignon: A Social History of Thirteenth-Century Rome* (New York: Basic Books, 1974), 148.

[151] Cf. Zawilla, *Biblical Sources of the Historia Corporis Christi*, 47–49.

[152] Rubin, *Corpus Christi*, 176.

On 11 August 1264, Urban IV promulgated the bull known as *Transiturus*,[153] which established the feast for the universal Church on the Thursday after Pentecost.[154] He sent it, along with a copy of the new Roman liturgy for the office and Mass, to the Patriarch of Jerusalem.[155] He also wrote to the bishop of Liège, Henry of Gueldre, on 7 September, exhorting him to inaugurate the feast without delay in his diocese, and attached a copy of the bull.[156] In this second version of the *Transiturus*, sent to Henry of Gueldre and the bishops, Urban IV echoes the language of Robert Thourette and Hugh of Saint-Cher:

> Therefore, although this sacramental memorial is observed daily in the solemnities of the mass, we judge it proper and fitting that once a year a more solemn and special memorial of it should be held, especially to counteract the madness and faithlessness of heretics.[157]

On the next day he wrote a letter to Eve, the recluse at Saint-Martin, mentioning her desire to see the feast established and indicating that he had recently celebrated the feast with his cardinals, bishops, and other prelates at the curia.[158] The letter mentioned enclosing under his seal a quire with a copy of a Roman office and Mass for the feast, which contemporary scholars believe to be a third version of the liturgy, *Sacerdos in [a]eternum.*

SAINT THOMAS AQUINAS AND THE FEAST OF CORPUS CHRISTI

Saint Thomas Aquinas had no direct acquaintance with Juliana of Mont Cornillon, although they shared numerous indirect connections.[159] Yet it is he rather than she whose name typically is associated with the feast of Corpus Christi. Saint Thomas Aquinas, born ca. 1224, was separated from Juliana, Hugh of Saint-Cher, and Urban IV by a generation. Like Juliana, at the age of five, he was placed in a monastery, although not as an orphan. His parents placed him as an oblate in the ancient Benedictine abbey of Monte Cassino, where he made his monastic profession ten years later. In 1244 he joined the Dominicans, having completed the basic medieval curriculum for boys at the

[153] Published by Bertholet in 1746, *Histoire de l'Institution de la Fête-Dieu*; translated into French by Baix and Lambot, *La dévotion à l'eucharistie*; also see Zawilla, *Biblical Sources of the Historia Corporis Christi;*" Ezio Franceschini, "Origine e stile della bolla 'Transiturus,'" *Aevum* 39 (1965), 218–43; Bertamini, "La bolla 'Transiturus' di papa Urbano IV."

[154] The octaves of Pentecost and Trinity Sunday had been established only in Liège at that time.

[155] The topic of the three versions of the *Transiturus*, T-1, T-2, and T-3, is discussed in Part II of this volume.. Scholars now believe the attached liturgy to be either a second or third version of the office.

[156] Bull of Pope Urban IV to the bishop of Liège, Henri de Gueldre, 7 Septembre 1264, Paris, Bibliothèque nationale de France, lat. 9298.

[157] Ibid.; see also Zawilla, *Biblical Sources of the Historia Corporis Christi*, 38 (translation); Franceschini, "Origine e stile della bolla 'Transiturus'; Bertamini, "La bolla 'Transiturus' di papa Urbano IV."

[158] Bull of Pope Urban IV to Eve of Saint-Martin, 8 September 1264, Liège, Bibliothèque du Séminaire 6. L. 21; see also Lambot, "La Bulle d'Urban IV à Eve de Saint-Martin," 261–70.

[159] In addition to those mentioned, Saint Thomas corresponded with Countess Margaret in 1271 regarding the proper treatment of her Jewish subjects. See John Y. B. Hood, *Aquinas and the Jews* (Philadelphia: University of Pennsylvania Press, 1995), 37; see also Torrell, *Saint Thomas Aquinas*, 219.

studium generale at Naples. His formative education was enhanced further by an early exposure to Aristotle through five years of study at the university in Naples, at a time when such study was forbidden at the University of Paris. He studied with Saint Albert Magnus and served as a bachelor and master of theology at the University of Paris, and as a master theologian to Pope Urban IV. Saint Thomas remained in the Dominican order until his death in 1273. His canonization process began in 1319 and was finalized by Pope John XXII in 1323.[160]

It is widely accepted that Saint Thomas Aquinas composed the liturgy for an office and Mass for the feast of Corpus Christi between 1261 and 1263, during his stay at Orvieto. However, modern scholarly corroboration of this fact is somewhat new. Lambot noted that when the feast of Corpus Christi was reaffirmed in 1311 by Pope Clement V, there was no specific attribution of authorship to Saint Thomas, nor was there any such consensus, even among the Dominicans.[161] However, in 1324, when the Dominicans adopted the office, authorship of the liturgy was attributed to Saint Thomas. The attribution remained uncontested until the seventh-centenary celebration, when the Thomist authenticity became the focus of modern critical research by Lambot and Delaissé.[162]

Lambot, whose 1942 research examined the attribution problem, cited the oldest biography of Saint Thomas Aquinas, written by Peter Calo between 1318 and 1323. Calo was mute on the subject of Saint Thomas' authorship of the Corpus Christi liturgy.[163] Likewise, there is no mention of the Thomist attribution in the acts of canonization.[164] And there is no mention of the feast of Corpus Christi in the official catalogue of works by Saint Thomas Aquinas, compiled by Reginald of Piperno and copied by Bartholomew of Capua for the canonization inquiry.[165] The Dominican Tolomeo of Lucca was first to mention the Aquinas authorship in his *Historia ecclesiastica nova*,[166] published between December 1312 and September 1317.

> By order of the same pope, Friar Thomas also composed the Office for Corpus Christi — the second commission from the pope to which I referred above. The Corpus Christi Office Thomas composed in full, including the lessons and all the parts to be recited by day or night; the Mass, too, and whatever has to be sung on that day. An attentive reader will see that it comprises nearly all the symbolic figures from the Old Testament, clearly and appropriately relating them to the sacrament of the Eucharist.[167]

The Tolomeo attribution may have been the source for two later attributions, found in the biographies by Dominicans William of Tocco, ca. 1322, and Bernard Guidonis, ca.

[160] See Torrell, *Saint Thomas Aquinas*; Weishepl, *Friar Thomas D'Aquino*.

[161] Lambot, "L'Office de la Fête-Dieu."

[162] Cf. Torrell, *Saint Thomas Aquinas*, 129–41.

[163] *Vita sancti Thomae Aquinatis*, auctore Petro Calo, unedited documents published by *Revue Thomiste* (Toulouse, 1911), cited by Weisheipl, *Friar Thomas D'Aquino*.

[164] Paris, Bibliothèque nationale de France, lat. 3112.

[165] P. Mandonnet, ed. *Des écrits authentiques de saint Thomas d'Aquin*, 2nd ed. (Fribourg en suisse: Imprimerie de l'œuvre de Saint-Paul, 1910); see also Weisheipl, *Friar Thomas D'Aquino*, 177.

[166] Michael Bucchingerus, *Historia ecclésiastica nova qva brevi compendio* (Antwerp: Widow S. Sasseni, 1560), Book 22, c.21, col. 1154; see also Weisheipl, *Friar Thomas D'Aquino*, 177; Lambot, "L'Office de la Fête-Dieu."

[167] Translation by Weisheipl, *Friar Thomas D'Aquino*, 177.

1323.[168] However, as time passed, the attribution to Aquinas became more frequent and widespread, often attached to legends such as the Miracle of Bolsena. Inserted into the Breviary of Pius V, at the head of the lessons for the second nocturn, are the words: *Sermo sancti Thomae Aquinatis*.[169]

Lambot observed that the witness of Tolomeo coincided with the adoption of the feast by the Dominican order, between 1318 and 1323, more than half a century later than the papal bull *Transiturus*.[170] At this time, various Dominican chapters were occupied with the adoption of the new feast and several versions of the liturgy were available. The chapter of Lyon in 1318, of Rouen in 1320, and of Florence in 1321, each communicated to the Master General of the order that they wished to adopt the new feast day and needed to select an office. Lambot noted that if the various chapters had been certain that the Roman office was the work of their illustrious brother, they would not have expressed this hesitation. The adoption of the feast for the chapters of Rouen and Florence was approved in 1322 at Vienne. However, when the requisite third approbation came up in Barcelona, in 1323, the question of office revealed a change of opinion. The Roman office was again selected, but this time, because, *ut asseritur*, their brother, Saint Thomas Aquinas, had composed it.

> Cum ordo noster debeat se sancte romane ecclesie, inquantum est possibile, in divino officio conformare, et precipue quod per nostrum ordinem de mandato apostolico est confectum, volumus quod officium de corpore Christi per venerabilem doctorem fratrem Thomam de Aquino editum, ut asseritur, per totum ordinem fiat v feria post festum Trinitatis usque ad octavas inclusive.[171]

> [Since our order ought to conform in the divine office to the Holy Roman Church, in so far as possible, and particularly in an office which is a product of our Order by apostolic command, we now wish that the office of Corpus Christi, composed, as it is said, by the venerable doctor Thomas d'Aquino, be observed throughout the entire Order on the Thursday after the feast of Trinity and throughout its octave inclusive.][172]

Lambot, after examining the manuscript evidence, concluded that Saint Thomas hastily composed a provisional version while in Orvieto, *Sapientia [a]edificavit*, which was first celebrated in the papal chapel for an extraordinary celebration. This office was, most likely, sent along with the bull *Transiturus* to the Patriarch of Jerusalem in August 1264, and then to the bishops in September. He further proposed that after the death of Urban IV, Saint Thomas revised this version to create *Sacerdos in [a]eternum*, which was the version institutionalized by Pope Clement V and transmitted across the generations. Gy, and later Zawilla, modified the thesis to show the relationship be-

---

[168] Lambot, "L'Office de la Fête-Dieu."

[169] Ibid.

[170] Browe, *Textus antiqui de festo Corporis Christi*, 107–43; see also Lambot, "L'Office de la Fête-Dieu"; Weisheipl, *Friar Thomas D'Aquino*.

[171] *Acta Capitulorum Generalium Ordinis Praedicatorum* 2, ed. B. M. Reichert, *Monumenta Ordinis Fratrum Praedicatorum historica* 3–4 (Rome, 1899), 109; see also Weisheipl, *Friar Thomas D'Aquino*, 183–84; Pierre-Marie Gy, "L'Office du Corpus Christi et s. Thomas d'Aquin: état d'une recherche," *Revue des sciences philosophiques et théologiques* 64 (1980), 492; Zawilla, *Biblical Sources of the Historia Corporis Christi*, 79.

[172] Weisheipl, *Friar Thomas D'Aquino*, 183–84.

tween the two texts to the early and later works of Saint Thomas.[173] Torrell, faithful to the Leonine tradition, writes: ". . . since the labors of Father Pierre-Marie Gy, attribution to Saint Thomas can no longer reasonably be placed in doubt."[174] Clearly these intellectual debates, centered on concordances among versions and the later writings of Thomas, belong to a different phase and a second generation of the movement, a topic taken up at greater length in the discussion of the manuscripts and concluding remarks. That Saint Thomas composed the version known as *Sacerdos in eternum* can scarcely be doubted; when he did so remains open to further scholarly investigation.

THIRTEENTH-CENTURY LIÈGE

FRAGMENTATION

Religious prophets or prophetesses have typically appeared in historical contexts of fragmentation and crisis, in situations or among groups in which the traditional patterns or routines of life for large numbers of people have been disrupted or destroyed. Thirteenth-century Europe, and especially the diocese of Liège, presented exactly such a societal condition. The autonomy and centralization of ecclesiastical authority that resulted from the reforms of Gregory VII in the eleventh century had been transformed by the end of the twelfth century into a compulsory government under a royal priesthood. The outcome was a consolidation and expansion of Church authority, manifest in a vast system of canon law, binding upon all members of society and superseding every other law and legal system in Europe.[175] This unification revitalized tension between the mystical body of Christ as the trans-historical community of believers and the *Corpus Christi Juridicum* in historical time.[176] Through active participation in battles for power and territory in the temporal world, the atemporal goals of the Church became increasingly intertwined with the compromise and violence of political realities.[177] Thus, the hybrid organization of the Church-State, while presenting a veneer of unity "under the canopy of a Christian symbolic universe,"[178] simultaneously kindled a kind of pluralism in this world that inflamed rather than consoled temporal rivalries and local factions.

[173] Gy, "L'Office du Corpus Christi," 491–507, and his "Office liégeois et office romain de la Fête-Dieu," in *Fête-Dieu (1246–1996)*, vol. 1, 117–26; see also Zawilla, *Biblical Sources of the Historia Corporis Christi*, 323–37.

[174] Torrell, *Saint Thomas Aquinas*, 130.

[175] See Walter Ullmann, *The Growth of Papal Government in the Middle Ages* (London: Methuen & Co., Ltd, 1965); John A. Watt, *The Theory of Papal Monarchy in the Thirteenth Century* (London: Burns & Oates, 1965); Otto Gierke, *Political Theories of the Middle Ages*, trans. Frederic William Maitland (Cambridge: Cambridge University Press, 1913); *Popes, Teachers, and Canon Law in the Middle Ages*, ed. James Ross Sweeney and Stanley Chodorow (Ithaca, NY: Cornell University Press, 1989).

[176] Cf. Ernst H. Kantorowicz, *The King's Two Bodies: A Study in Mediaeval Political Theology* (1957; repr., Princeton: Princeton University Press, 1997), 197.

[177] Ernst Troeltstch, *The Social Teachings of the Christian Churches*, trans. O. Wyon (1931; repr. New York: Harper Torchbooks, 1960); see also Wolfgang Schluchter, *Paradoxes of Modernity: Culture and Conduct in the Theory of Max Weber*, trans. Neil Solomon (Stanford: Stanford University Press, 1996), 209.

[178] Schluchter, *Paradoxes of Modernity*, 210.

The new term *corpus mysticum*, hallowing, as it were, simultaneously the *Corpus Christi Juridicum*, that is, the gigantic legal and economic management on which the *Ecclesia militans* rested, linked the building of the visible Church organism with the former liturgical sphere; but at the same time, it placed the Church as a body politic, or as a political and legal organism, on a level with the secular bodies politic which were then beginning to assert themselves as self-sufficient entities.[179]

Liège was at the vortex of the temporal storm. Founded as an episcopal see in the eighth century, the *ville* of Liège was an old and venerable city at the heart of the archdiocese of Cologne, in the bishopric of Liège. The diocesan territory was heir to the Lotharingians, geographically between nascent France and Germany; it covered half of modern-day Belgium. As part of the Holy Roman Empire up to the thirteenth century, Liège shared in the cultural dominance of the empire and functioned as a crossroads in international trade. Aachen, constructed by Charlemagne and the site of the coronation of all Holy Roman Emperors after 962, was less than fifty miles from the old city of Liège. By the eleventh century, Liège boasted seven collegiate churches as well as two great monasteries, which surrounded the cathedral and bishop's palace. These imparted to the city its essential clerical character. The laity served largely as knights and ministers to the bishops: a coterie of artisans served the needs of the clergy,[180] and strata of craftsmen as well as influential administrators and merchants emerged early in the city's history. In the thirteenth century, Liège was a declining cultural and intellectual center, slowly giving way to the new magnet of Paris and the growing political power of the French.

Liège was ruled by prince-bishops who from the tenth century forward set up a strong central government, organized revenues, and established defense systems[181] such as the "divinité-porte" constructed by Notger at the church at Saint-Martin on Publémont.[182] The autocratic system of territorial bishops functioning simultaneously as ecclesiastics and landed proprietors may have worked well during the early period when the population was largely rural, but with economic growth and vast movement of people

---

[179] Kantorowicz, *The King's Two Bodies*, 197.

[180] Henri Pirenne, *Early Democracies in the Low Countries: Urban Society and Political Conflict in the Middle Ages and the Renaissance*, trans. J. V. Saunders (1915; repr. New York: Harper and Row, 1963), 59–61; F. Vercauteren, *Luttes sociales à Liège* (Brussels: La Renaissance du Livre, 1946), 13–14.

[181] Pirenne, *Early Democracies in the Low Countries*.

[182] Bishop Notger (972–1008) constructed an immense cathedral on the original site of Saint Lambert in the valley below Publémont hill and dedicated it to Saint Martin. This dedication was especially appropriate for the church in Liège. Located on the west periphery of the city inside the wall, it formed a citadel that was incorporated into the medieval defense system associated with the protection of a "porte;" it was a "sacred fortress." "Gardienne, désormais, de l'issue qui s'ouvrait sur la route de Huy, l'église Saint-Martin exprimait, on ne peut mieux, cette association 'divinité-porte' qui se trouve dans toutes les civilisations et qui revêt une importance appréciable dans la mentalité religieuse et guerrière du Moyen Age" [As guardian henceforward of the exit that opened up onto the road from Huy, the church of Saint-Martin expressed—it could not be better—this association of a "divinité-porte," which is found in all civilizations and which took on considerable importance in the religious and warlike mentality of the Middle Ages] (Jean-Louis Kupper, "Les Origines de la Collegiale Saint-Martin," in *Saint-Martin, Mémoire de Liège*, 20).

into cities throughout the twelfth century, the system was challenged and transformed.[183] After 1200, the institutional structures within the diocese were further modified by new commercial activities and the appearance of a strong political force in the urban bourgeoisie, which increasingly pushed for representation in the affairs of the city.

Bishop Albert de Cuyck between 1196 and 1200 granted to the bourgeoisie a collection of customs, rights, and liberties in the "Charter of Albert de Cuyck."[184] The first commune was established in Liège in 1230 and provided elected representation for the bourgeoisie; it functioned as an expression of municipal autonomy. The prince-bishops thereafter continued to exercise power, "but they were elected, in the name of the clergy and the people, by the cathedral chapter of St Lambert, their election had to be confirmed by the pope, their regalia was supposed to be conferred by the emperor."[185] Additionally, the "increasingly effective and significant commune of Liège . . . claimed its share of power. Elections often were highly contested, and seven thirteenth-century bishops (five of whom were designated by the pope) were foreigners, oriented to the French sphere of influence."[186]

Liège's central position in the Mosan trading orbit also declined during the thirteenth century compared to the earlier period, as commerce in the empire moved to the Cologne–Louvain–Bruges line.[187] Nonetheless, a new rising stratum of bourgeoisie amassed monetary wealth in new forms of commerce: through wool, wine, and money trade, as well as through coal mining. Two woolen cloth markets emerged in Liège during the first quarter of the thirteenth century. In monetary and banking development, Pope Innocent IV himself deposited 15.000 marks in Liège in 1246 to support the forces of Henri Raspe, adversary of Frederick II. The prosperity of Liège also increased through smaller local trade, crafts, and light manufacturing.[188] These economic developments resulted in shifting political alliances among new strata of *grande* and *petite* bourgeoisie.

The economic shifts in Liège and consequent political pressure from rising strata were perhaps most evident in the territorial expansion of the town, as the population seeking protection literally pushed against the *enceinte* that had been constructed in the tenth century for the city's fortification. Accommodating the newer groups necessitated the construction of a new fortification wall for the city, the first such modification for security purposes since the tenth century. The construction was funded by a special tax, the *fermeté*, whose collection was resisted by both lay people and the clergy of the cathedral chapters. This kind of taxation issue heightened political tensions in Liège throughout the thirteenth and fourteenth centuries.[189]

[183] See Walter Simons, *Cities of Ladies: Beguine Communities in the Medieval Low Countries, 1200–1565* (Philadelphia: University of Pennsylvania Press, 2001), 1–7, for an especially informative introduction to the sources of tensions in the Low Countries during the thirteenth century.

[184] Kupper, "La cité de Liège au temps de Julienne de Cornillon," 19–26.

[185] Wogan-Browne and Hennau, "Liège, the Medieval 'Woman Question,'" 9.

[186] Ibid.

[187] Rubin, *Corpus Christi*, 4.

[188] Kupper, "La cité de Liège," 21–22; Rubin, *Corpus Christi*, 164–65; Wogan-Browne and Henneau, "Liège, the Medieval 'Woman Question,'" 8–9.

[189] Kupper, "La cité de Liège," 19–26.

Perhaps most significant in defining the character of the political climate in thir-teenth-century Liège was the uprising led by Henry Dinant in 1253. Dinant was a patri-cian, from a family of wealthy bankers who, by legendary accounts, organized the cop-persmiths of Dinant to shake off the power of the *échevins*, or local courts, and consti-tute themselves as a "self-governing corporation."[190] The population was divided, with the manual workers or "lesser folk" favoring the recognition of the guild and the patri-cians or "greater folk" opposed. Vercauten accurately noted that the difference in line-age among the new wealthy bourgeoisie, the established patricians, and the nobility, was not a distinction often made by the artisans, or little folk.[191] The strife continued throughout the late thirteenth century, with Saint Lambert's cathedral initially the ally of the "lesser folk" and the church at Saint-Martin the refuge of the *grands lignages*.[192]

Pirenne[193] held that the Dinant uprising in 1253 resulted in a constitutional extension of rights won in the twelfth century by sworn councillors, jurés, who were elected by the townspeople and participated in municipal government. Kupper,[194] in contrast, views the uprising as a quarrel between opposing clans, both patriciates, two grand lignages of the bourgeoisie. Delville notes still another irony in the feast of Corpus Christi:

> Il est curieux de constater que la fête du Saint-Sacrement est née dans une situation d'opposition entre Julienne et la commune, alors que cette même fête deviendra au siècle suivant le lieu par excellence de la représentation des pouvoirs de la ville, hiérar-chiquement ordonnés dans les processions du Saint-Sacrement.[195]

> [It is curious to note that the feast of the Blessed Sacrament was born in a situation of opposition between Juliana and the commune, while this same feast became in the fol-lowing century the place *par excellence* of the representation of the power of the city, hi-erarchically ordered in the processions of the Blessed Sacrament.]

Most important perhaps in the shifting commercial and political allegiances in Liège was the reorientation of the prince-bishops away from the party of Emperor Frederick II, the Ghibellines, and toward the party of the papacy, the Guelphs, during the early thir-teenth century.[196] In the abstract, the two parties symbolized the spiritual and temporal spheres, the respective domains of the papacy and emperor, which to the medieval mind ideally might function in a harmonious alliance. However, during the thirteenth century, as the Church increasingly became a corporeal and political presence, these names came to stand for temporal and factionalist strife, which reached its apogee in the excommuni-cation of Frederick II by Innocent IV at the Council of Lyon in 1245. The Guelph name came to stand for the republican and commercial burghers who supported the papacy, while the Ghibellines symbolized the princes of the house of Hohenstaufen and their

---

[190] Pirenne, *Early Democracies in the Low Countries*, 135.

[191] Vercauteren, *Luttes sociales à Liège*, 27.

[192] In 1312, the *lignages* united but were overpowered by the sheer number of artisans and took refuge at the Church at Saint-Martin. The church was set on fire and the noble refuges were burned.

[193] Pirenne, *Early Democracies in the Low Countries*, 134–42.

[194] Kupper, "La cité de Liège," 23.

[195] Delville, "Julienne de Cornillon à la lumière de son biographe," 37.

[196] Kupper, "La cité de Liège," 19.

40   The Feast of Corpus Christi

constant opposition to the papacy. The struggles between the two factions divided the Italian cities by civil war for most of the later medieval period, as the papacy engaged in bitter conflict to wrest Sicily from Hohenstaufen control.

Beginning with the French-born bishop Hugh of Pierrepont, 1200–29, the Liège prelates shifted allegiance away from the emperor and toward the papacy, while succsssive popes nourished their ties with France.[197] Liège between 1238 and 1278 became a Guelph citadel,[198] in part through papal intervention in local political affairs and in part as a consequence of successive French appointments. Robert Thourette was appointed after papal intervention in the contested election of 1238, through the influence of Bishop Guiard of Cambrai. Bishops Guiard and Robert, as well as Hugh of Saint-Cher and Archbishop Conrad, were present at the Council of Lyon in 1245. Henry of Guelders was appointed to succeed Robert Thourette in 1247 as part of papal efforts to secure the succession of his uncle, William of Holland, to the imperial throne.

Local conflicts in Liège were amplified further by the dynastic fragmentation among the heirs of Count Baldwin IX of neighboring Flanders, which stemmed from disaccord between the count's dynastic heirs. Count Baldwin had participated in the Fourth Crusade and in 1204 had been elected Emperor of Constantinople. He was captured in 1205 and died, leaving two daughters, Joan and Margaret, under the regency of Philip of Namur.[199] In 1212 Joan married Ferrand of Portugal in exchange of relief for 50,000 *livres parisis* and the castellanies of Saint-Omer and Aire, which were lost to the Artois.[200] The size of the relief provoked revolts from two Flemish nobles and in the city of Ghent.[201] In 1237, now a widow, Joan married Thomas of Savoy, the uncle of Margaret of Savoy, who was the wife of Louis IX and uncle to Beatrice of Savoy, who was married to Charles of Anjou.[202] Joan remained childless, and thus the succession went to her younger sister, Countess Margaret, noted in one of the visions of Juliana for her reception of the relics of the eleven thousand virgins.

In 1212, at the age of ten, Margaret had married Bouchard d'Avesnes, but the marriage had been annulled because Bouchard was a member of the clergy. However, Margaret gave birth to two sons by Bouchard and remained his loyal wife, even after his excommunication. Only when her sister insisted that she obey the injunctions of the Church did Margaret in 1222 marry William of Dampierre, by whom she had two sons, William and Guy. She later shared her title as Countess with William and then, after William's death, Guy. Pope Gregory IX declared the children from her first marriage to be bastards; Emperor Frederick II recognized them as legitimate.[203] The competition between the heirs from the two fathers resulted in arbitration through Louis IX and Innocent IV in 1246,

---

[197] Kupper, "La cité de Liège," 20.

[198] Ruben, *Corpus Christi*, 172.

[199] Blockmans, "Flanders," 406.

[200] Ibid.

[201] Ibid.

[202] Eugene Cox, "The Kingdom of Burgundy, the Lands of the House of Savoy and Adjacent Territories," in *The New Cambridge Medieval History V: c.1198–c.1300*, ed. David Abulafia (Cambridge: Cambridge University Press, 1999), 366; see also Henri Pirenne, *Histoire de Belgique* Book 1, 5th ed. (Brussels: Maurice Lamertine, 1929), 254.

[203] Pirenne, *Histoire de Belgique*, 255.

which awarded Hainault to the Avesnes and Flanders to the Dampierre.[204] A ten-year conflict ensued without much effect. From May to December of 1254, the principality of Liège was desolated by a civil war that resulted from the refusal of Henry Dinant to bring troops to the assistance of Bishop Henry Guelders, who wished to come to the aid of John of Avesnes against his mother, Margaret of Flanders.[205]

John of Flanders, one of sixteen sons of Guy of Dampierre, succeeded Henry of Gueldre as bishop of Liège.[206] In February 1288, he confirmed the feast of Corpus Christi in the synodal statutes of Liège. In the legislation, Bishop John makes no mention of Urban IV or the *Transiturus*, but rather mentions the earlier decrees by bishops Robert Thourette and Henry of Gueldre.[207] Likewise, the date mentioned for the feast is the Thursday after Trinity, as would be the proper time in Liège, rather than the Thursday after Pentecost.

A related conflict in Liège resulted from the imperial claims of a certain "Empress Marie," most likely the second daughter by a second marriage of John of Brienne. John of Brienne had inherited the title "king of Jerusalem," through his first marriage to Maria, the daughter from the second marriage of Isabella (daughter of King Amaury (1163–74) to Conrad of Montferrat. From his marriage with Maria, who died in 1212, John of Brienne sired Isabella, who later married Frederick II and bore him a son, Conrad IV. Conrad was Frederick's heir as Holy Roman Emperor but was defeated in his imperial ambitions through military force and the coronation of William of Holland at Aachen. Marie, most likely a later daughter, married the brother of Count Baldwin IX, Robert of Courtenay, through whom she became the pretender Empress. In 1263 Empress Marie sold her rights as Countess of Namur to Guy of Dampierre.[208]

THE POLITICS OF HERESY

The context of fragmentation produced religious seekers whose vast numbers exceeded what could be absorbed by established orders. In earlier centuries, religious *virtuosi* were sons and daughters of a powerful aristocracy who entered well-endowed monasteries both for religious reasons and because the regular rituals of contemplative life offered a sharp contrast to the brute force and chaotic peril of the secular world.[209] Entrance to an established religious order was typically accompanied by gifts of land, which forged alliances between the nobility and the Cluniacs, as well as the later Cistercian monks and nuns, who also embraced the Rule of Saint Benedict.[210] *Virtuosi* were

---

[204] Blockmans, "Flanders," 407; Pirenne, *Histoire de Belgique*, 255.

[205] Delville, *Vie de Sainte Julienne de Cornillon*, 34.

[206] Blockmans, "Flanders," 407.

[207] Lambot and Fransen, *L'Office de la Fête-Dieu primitive*, 13–14; see also Zawilla, *Biblical Sources of the Historia Corporis Christi*, 43.

[208] Delville, *Vie de Sainte Julienne de Cornillon*, 221 n 249. Juliana, while at Salzinnes, had warned the Abbess Imène against her friendship with Empress Marie, who was very unpopular with the citizens of Namur.

[209] Barbara H. Rosenwein, *To Be the Neighbor of Saint Peter: The Social Meaning of Cluny's Property, 909–1049* (Ithaca: Cornell University Press, 1989); Constance Hoffman Berman, *The Cistercian Evolution: The Invention of Religious Order in Twelfth-Century Europe* (Philadelphia: University of Pennsylvania Press, 2000).

[210] Note that Juliana and Agnes endowed Mont Cornillon with land.

cloistered and removed from the struggles of a temporal world, for which they prayed. This pattern of exchange between landed nobility and cloistered orders changed in the twelfth and thirteenth centuries with the emergence of cities and the new rising urban strata that emerged in the transformation of a barter system to a monetary economy. Sons and daughters among the rising strata of merchants in the urban context often were drawn to the newer mendicant orders, such as the Dominicans or Franciscans, who embraced the sacraments, endorsed the authority of the ecclesia, and sought papal recognition. Grundmann was first to note that the proliferation of religiosity and religious movements was "not a protest of the 'poor and oppressed' against the accumulation of wealth and luxury, and the beginnings of capitalism and 'exploitation,'" which were characteristic of the thirteenth century. "On the contrary, the religious protest against these developments came from the same circles originating the development and profiting from it."[211]

Likewise, the religious practices that came to be defined as heresies, for the most part, grew from problematic heterodoxies within the Church fold, generally from those which pressed religious beliefs and practices to an extreme.[212] The apostolic imitation of the life of Jesus shaped the core of lay religious movements in the twelfth century, often shaping up as direct opposition to the power and opulence of the official Church. The problematic heterodoxy typically was apprehended and defined as heretical when its practitioners avoided Church authorities, preached in the vernacular, and engaged in "non-neighborly" conduct, such as the failure to attend church.[213] Simons, following on the work of Moore, points to the local parish as the "meeting point" between "two opposing concepts of community: one locally shaped by its lay members expressing themselves in the vernacular, another defined as the lowest level of a vertical hierarchy, administered from above by the higher clergy using Latin as the vehicle of communication."[214] Catharism in particular pitted the laity and lower clergy against those in higher levels of authority within the Church during the twelfth century. The Cathar theology of a radical dualism in the universe and the inherent evil of the visible and material world, but more especially the rejection of the Eucharist and other Church sacraments, brought the group into direct conflict with the Church. The extent of their influence in Liège is unclear, but by the thirteenth century, they had gone underground.[215]

It was perhaps the strength and tenacity of other independent strands of the evangelical poverty movement that forced papal efforts to incorporate the unlicensed and proliferating apostolic preachers into the Church fold. Thus, when Innocent III as-

---

[211] Grundmann, *Religious Movements*, 87.

[212] Gordon Leff, *Heresy in the Later Middle Ages: The Religion of Heterodoxy to Dissent, c. 1250–1450* (Manchester: Manchester University Press, 1967), 2; see also Edward Peters, *Inquisition* (New York: The Free Press, 1988), 40–74.

[213] Augustine Thompson, O.P., *Cities of God: The Religion of the Italian Communes, 1125–1325* (University Park: Pennsylvania State University Press, 2005), 235; see also Simons, *Cities of Ladies*, 17.

[214] Simons, *Cities of Ladies*, 15; see also R. I. Moore, "Heresy, Repression, and Social Change in the Age of Gregorian Reform," in *Christendom and its Discontents: Exclusion, Persecution, and Rebellion, 1000–1500*, ed. Scott L. Waugh and Peter D. Diehl (Cambridge: Cambridge University Press, 1996), 19–46.

[215] Simons, *Cities of Ladies*, 16–19; For a more general discussion of the Cathars, see Malcolm Lambert, "The Cathars," in his *Medieval Heresy: Popular Movements from the Gregorian Reform to the Reformation*, 3rd ed. (Oxford, UK, and Malden, MA: Blackwell Publishing, 2002), 115–57.

sumed the papacy in 1198, he wielded a double-edged sword.[216] He acceded to the demands for recognition by apostolic preachers and devotees to apostolic imitation of Christ, so long as they displayed appropriate reverence for the sacerdotal hierarchy and orthodox doctrine. At the same time, he prosecuted heretics to the fullest. Thereafter, sectarian movements that transformed religious impulses into ideologies with an explicitly anti-sacerdotal character did not achieve ecclesiastic recognition and were defined as heretical.[217] In 1215, the Fourth Lateran Council took a decisive stand. It proclaimed the primacy of the pope, called for annual confession of sins, and mandated participation in communion. It established a definitive formulation of the real presence of the body and blood of Christ in the Eucharist in the vaguely defined doctrine of transubstantiation.[218] The creation of new religious orders was forbidden; thereafter, persons wishing to embrace the apostolic life as monks or nuns had to do so under one of the approved rules, and new houses had to be incorporated by charter with one of the existing associations.[219] Canon 3 of the Fourth Lateran Council decreed that heretics be excommunicated and handed over to secular authorities, who were ordered to confiscate their property and execute punishment as they saw fit.[220] In 1227, Gregory IX, opponent of Frederick II and successor to Innocent III, began to delegate the work of the Inquisition to the Dominicans and Franciscans who, as professional theologians, were deemed qualified to identify heresies.[221]

THE COMMUNITY OF WOMEN

The rising power and vulnerability of women in the context of the medieval city received initial recognition through the work of Herbert Grundmann, who in 1935 published his classic volume on religious movements in the High Medieval period. His analysis of women in the ascetic movements of the twelfth and thirteenth centuries inspired many subsequent and even more penetrating assessments of medieval gendering and religious power. Both Bynum and Oliver acknowledge his importance and influence on their work, as do later scholars working within this framework.[222] A number of themes

---

[216] Grundmann, *Religious Movements*.

[217] Leff, *Heresy in the Later Middle Ages*; Schluchter, *Paradoxes of Modernity*, 212–13.

[218] Gary Macy, *Treasures from the Storehouse: Medieval Religion and the Eucharist* (Collegeville, MN: The Liturgical Press, 1999), 81.

[219] The Augustinian Rule was especially useful because it provided the flexibility required by the missions of the newer urban orders. It was embraced by the Victorine canons in 1113, the Dominicans in 1216, and the Franciscans in 1226.

[220] Bernard Hamilton, "The Albigensian Crusade and Heresy," in *The New Cambridge Medieval History V: c.1198–c.1300*, ed. David Abulafia (Cambridge: Cambridge University Press, 1999), 164–81.

[221] Ibid.; see also Peters, *Inquisition*, 40–74.

[222] Bynum, *Jesus as Mother*; Judith Oliver, *Gothic Manuscript Illumination in the Diocese of Liège (c.1250–c.1330)*, 2 vols. (Leuven: Peeters, 1988); see also Wogan-Browne and Henneau, "Liège, the Medieval 'Woman Question'"; Brenda Bolton, "Thirteenth-Century Religious Women: Further Reflections on the Low Countries as a 'Special Case,'" in *New Trends in Feminine Spirituality: The Holy Women of Liège and Their Impact*, ed. Juliette Dor, Lesley Johnson, and Jocelyn Wogan-Browne (Turnhout: Brepols, 1999), 129–57; Barbara Newman, *From Virile Woman to WomanChrist: Studies in Medieval Religion and Literature* (Philadelphia: University of Pennsyl-

emerged in Grundmann's work, which were later developed by McDonnell,[223] and then further refined by medievalists over the past two decades. Most important were: (1) a demographic imbalance in the ratio of marriageable males to females that was especially pronounced in urban areas; (2) an abundance of high-born and rising middle class women seeking to fulfill religious vocations, especially in Liège; (3) a higher level of literacy in general, a trend that included women; (4) the emergence of *courtoisie* and the court tradition in poetry; and (5) new religious and secular writings in the vernacular in a context of linguistic diversity. Close analyses of these trends taken together have disclosed an extraordinary transformation in the power and influence of women in thirteenth-century society and in the regard with which women were held.

Beginning in the twelfth century—possibly due to wars, the crusades, and accidents—the ratio of marriageable males to females declined.[224] Laws establishing primogeniture as the means through which property and authority were transmitted, at least in France, may have amplified this imbalance.[225] These laws were central to internal pacification in France and to the early consolidation of Capetian dynastic power. Especially in the tenth and eleventh centuries, the family model of the territorial prince through which one son, typically the eldest, inherited an indivisible kingdom had become the dominant pattern. The internal stability of France followed from increased normative acceptance of this pattern of primogeniture and the "gradual spreading among all levels of aristocratic society of a lineage-oriented family structure that was modeled upon the royal example."[226] The establishment of this patrimony in property inheritance resulted in an excess of second-born sons, deprived of ancestral inheritance and excluded thereby from prospects of marriage, creating an abundance of unmarried women.

The increasing number of women in Liège was no doubt related to the broader trend and the resulting imbalance in the sex ratio in the general population. However, Liège had a special attraction for women. Scholars such as Bolton continue to find support for the thesis that the Low Countries more generally should be regarded as a "special case" of religious women.[227] This thesis is borne out by demographic data. Overall in Europe, there were seven hundred Cistercian communities of men during the early thirteenth century, and nine hundred communities of women. In the Low Countries the trend was accelerated such that, "in a country as small as Maine, the Cistercians at one time had fifteen communities of men and sixty-six of women."[228]

---

vania Press, 1995), and her *God and the Goddesses: Vision, Poetry, and Belief in the Middle Ages* (Philadelphia: University of Pennsylvania Press, 2003); Simons, *Cities of Ladies.*

[223] Ernest McDonnell, *The Beguines and Beghards in Medieval Culture with Special Emphasis on the Belgian Scene* (New Brunswick, NJ: Rutgers University Press, 1954).

[224] Georges Duby, *Medieval Marriage: Two Models from Twelfth-Century France*, trans. Elborg Forster (Baltimore: The Johns Hopkins University Press, 1978), 10–11.

[225] Ibid.

[226] Ibid., 10.

[227] Bolton, "Thirteenth-Century Religious Women," 131; Bolton traces the development of the béguines in the thirteenth century, compares the Low Countries to England, and shows how the application of the Special Case works less well later in the thirteenth century.

[228] R. De Ganck, "The Cistercian Nuns of Belgium in the Thirteenth Century," *Cistercian Studies* 5 (1970), 169; see also Simons, *Cities of Ladies*, 8–9; Bolton, "Thirteenth-Century Religious Women," 136.

Recent scholars, such as Simons, have argued that the excess of women in the Low Countries was part of a broader migration pattern in pre-industrial societies. Women in Flanders could inherit property from their parents, which favored the continuity of small businesses and other enterprise. Women also left the countryside and moved to cities—especially to the larger cities and service centers—in greater numbers than men because they could more easily find work there in a large array of trades and industries, or as domestic servants and maids.[229] Liège, an emerging center for the textile industry, was especially attractive.

These multiple causes led to a growing population of women in cities that far exceeded the capacity of the established religious orders to either absorb their numbers or provide effective religious guidance and counsel. Thus, the newly arrived, unmarried, and unsupervised women from the countryside may have been easy targets in the anomic urban context, becoming convenient scapegoats for a wide variety of social ills.[230] Moreover, high-born women may have been disproportionately drawn into the urban, anti-clerical, and heretical movements of the thirteenth century. However, in Liège, women became noted more for their orthodox piety than their heterodoxy, and more for their power and influence than their vulnerability, at least until the Council of Vienne in 1311–12. Bynum observes:

> A focus on women as oppressed or as outsiders obscures the extent to which women—particularly in the late Middle Ages—were the actual creators of some of the distinctive features of mainstream Christian piety. . . . Herbert Grundmann in the thirties . . . pointed out that, if women were overrepresented in heterodox movements, they were overrepresented in orthodox ones as well, and that the women (like the men) often came from the privileged classes. . . . The most creative and thoughtful scholarship on women in religion is based more on Grundmann's sense that women's piety was at the center of late medieval developments than on Weber's . . . sense of women as outsiders or disprivileged.[231]

The tradition of orthodox piety and religious influence on the part of Liège women began with Marie d'Oignies (1117–1213), "initiator of the new beguine *religio*" in Nivelles.[232] By the end of the twelfth century, Marie and the women known as béguines had already achieved widespread recognition and fame. Saint Francis himself began a pilgrimage to Liège in 1217 to visit their community, seven years after Juliana's famous vision for the feast of Corpus Christi.[233] Jacques de Vitry also was drawn to the region by the reputation of Marie d'Oignies. Jacques interrupted his studies in Paris to join the community of Augustinian canons in the Liège diocese, and after a brief return to Paris, returned to Liège to celebrate his first Mass in the church of St. Nicholas in her pres-

[229] Simons, *Cities of Ladies*, 8–9.

[230] See René Girard, *The Scapegoat*, trans. Yvonne Freccero (Baltimore: The Johns Hopkins University Press, 1986), 12–23.

[231] Caroline Bynum, *Fragmentation and Redemption: Essays on Gender and the Human Body in Medieval Religion*, (New York: Zone Books, 1991), 57.

[232] Simons, *Cities of Ladies*, 47.

[233] Margot H. King, "General Introduction" in Jacques de Vitry, *The Life*, trans. Margot H. King, *Two Lives of Marie D'Oignies*, 4th ed. (Toronto: Peregrina, 1998), 10.

ence. He was deeply inspired by her: "Although he was Marie's confessor, he confesses that in the spiritual sphere she was the master and he disciple."[234] She helped him in the preparation of sermons and served as a source of inspiration.[235] In 1216 Jacques obtained special permission from Pope Honorius III for her and the Liège women to live in communal houses without formal affiliation with a religious order, three years after he was commissioned by the papal legate to preach against the Albergensians in France and German-speaking Lotharingia.[236] Jacques had nothing but praise for the virtues of the Liège women:

> But since it is written "By their fruits shall you know them" (Mt 7:16), it is sufficiently demonstrated that they truly clung to the Lord during the destruction of the city of Liège. Those who could not flee to the churches threw themselves into the river and chose to die rather than to incur harm to their chastity. Some jumped into dung-filled sewers and preferred to be snuffed out in the stinking manure than to be despoiled of their virginity. Despite all this, the merciful Bridegroom so deigned to look after his brides that not a single one in such a great multitude was found who suffered either death to her body or harm to her chastity."[237]

The term *béguine* itself is highly controversial. Scholars for years associated it with Lambert le Bègue, an ordained priest from a modest Liège family who lived during the third quarter of the twelfth century. Lambert was active in Liège during the 1170s as a preacher and translator as well as the author of pious essays in Old French.[238] The perceived link between the term *béguine* as applied to the Liège women, and the earlier community that formed around Lambert was propagated in the mid-thirteenth century and revived during the modern age.[239] This myth gained in credibility thorough an Easter calendar for a group of Psalters used by the béguines, through a portrait that appears in one of them, and through mention of the office of tenth-century Saint Lambert, patron saint of Liège, in the *vitae* of women, including Juliana's.[240] Simons has adeptly reviewed the problematic nature of the attribution and the many plausible sources of what was most likely a pejorative term for "single women" and their efforts to live "a righteous life" under conditions of "exposure to the spectacles of the city."[241]

---

[234] Ibid., 10.

[235] Bolton, "Thirteenth-Century Religious Women," 138.

[236] Marco Bartoli, "Les femmes et l'Église au 13e siècle," in *Fête-Dieu (1246–1996)*, vol. I, 73.

[237] Jacques de Vitry, *The Life of Marie D'Oignies*, 41.

[238] Lambert sought to combat the worldliness that he found rampant in the new urban context of Liège through his sermons and example, but in 1175 he was accused of heresy and was imprisoned for preaching against the excesses of the clergy and for exhorting the laity to the contemplative life. Pope Calixtus III took Lambert under his protection against the accusations of the bishop and clergy. Lambert owned, or was at least familiar with, a psalter in vernacular French, which has been linked to the group of Mosan Psalters that appears in Part III of this book. However, Oliver, *Gothic Manuscript Illumination*, 1: 112, emphatically states that any attribution of authorship to Lambert is absolutely groundless.

[239] Simons, *Cities of Ladies*, 30.

[240] Simons, *Cities of Ladies*, 32; see also Delville, *Vie de Sainte Julienne de Cornillon*, 196; Newman, *Life of Juliana of Mont Cornillon*, 114–15.

[241] Simons, *Cities of Ladies*, 24–34, 121–23.

The béguines were most noted for a lifestyle that combined spiritual piety with hard work. They did not beg in the streets but, rather, were gainfully employed in a wide variety of settings. Their exemplum combined active service in the world through charity, manual labor, and teaching, with public worship and private devotion.[242] They set in place new initiatives in education for the poor that may have inspired the fifteenth-century pattern, which under the guidance of the *Devotio Moderna* created remarkable gains in literacy among urban children.[243] In 1253, Robert Grosseteste preached a sermon at Oxford to the Franciscans, extolling the virtues of the béguines. He proclaimed that they occupied a "higher rung" on the spiritual ladder than the Franciscans, because they "earned their living with their own hands" and did not "make burdensome demands on the world."[244]

Roisin and Grundmann[245] were first to comment on the upper-class origins of the Liège women and the spirit of their religiosity as part of a rebellion against the opulence of the preceding generation. Grundmann specifically noted that the religious movements of the thirteenth century were not, in general, movements of the poor and oppressed, who were outside the economic and cultural trends, but rather were rooted in the very circles that participated in the expansion of wealth and prosperity.[246] Nonetheless, while upper-class and literate women no doubt shaped the religious leadership and provided charitable care for béguines, "that these aristocratic women were representative of the early béguine movement as a whole may be doubted."[247] Many women who moved from the country to the cities worked in the large textile centers such as Liège, at menial jobs such as weavers, spinsters, and other roles associated with the preparation of raw materials, such as wool, and in finishing the cloth.[248] Béguine communities, especially court beguinages like those sponsored by the countesses Joan and Margaret of Flanders and Hainaut, provided shelter, charitable care, and other social services to impoverished women, as well as vocational employment for educated and pious women from a wide range of backgrounds. These latter served in the emerging professions of nursing, social work, and teaching, as well as in book production and the literary and musical arts and crafts.[249] They often provided spiritual guidance and stepped into the breach filled by the shortage of priests. They both led and were led by the new urban preaching orders such as the Dominicans and Franciscans.

The hagiographic *vitae*, inspired by individual women—béguines and nuns—and typically authored by male admirers, provide evidence for extraordinary friendships be-

---

[242] Ibid., 35, 61, 115.

[243] Ibid., 6; see also Oliver, *Gothic Manuscript Illumination*, 1: 207. The similarities to the later *Devotio Moderna* lifestyle are tantalizing, even if they call for generalizations well beyond the scope of this book and project. See especially Anne Winston-Allen, *Convent Chronicles: Women Writing about Women and Reform in the Late Middle Ages* (University Park: The Pennsylvania State University Press, 2004), 81.

[244] Simons, *Cities of Ladies*, 35; Bolton, "Thirteenth-Century Religious Women," 138.

[245] Roisin, *L'Hagiographie cistercienne*; Grundmann, *Religious Movements*.

[246] Grundmann, *Religious Movements*, 86–87.

[247] Simons, *Cities of Ladies*, 92.

[248] Ibid., 115.

[249] Simons, *Cities of Ladies*; Oliver, *Gothic Manuscript Illumination*, 1: 206.

tween men and women,[250] not entirely unlike the *fin'amor* tradition that emerged in the aristocratic courts. However, these friendships avoid any mention of unrequited love or unfulfilled sexual longing. Rather, they conform more closely to an earlier Cistercian ideal of human relationships through mutual love for God, rooted perhaps in the work of Aelred of Rievaulx, *De spiritali amicitia* [*On Spiritual Friendship*], which emphasized disinterested friendship as described in Cicero's *De Amicitia.*[251] Etienne Gilson took great pains to articulate the distinction between Saint Bernard's disinterested friendships based on spiritual love and the courtly expressions of the troubadours, which more explicitly expressed unfulfilled carnal longings: *agape contra eros.* Rubin makes note of the extraordinary friendships between men and women, such as the one between Marie D'Oignies and Jacques de Vitry and those between Juliana and her male friends/colleagues in Liège, which were central in disseminating her written ideas.[252] Mulder-Bakker, in corroboration, notes the significance of this solidarity between priests and women in networks of interdependence and mutual support in other settings.

Friendships between men and women who were supposed to be celibate largely occurred among members of the aristocracy or patrician stratum, within which women leaders were able to exercise considerable power and influence. The upper-class origins and elite status of the women are betrayed both by their literacy and by their reputations for *pietas* and *courtoisie*, virtues most frequently associated with cloisters and courts.[253] Male-female relationships in these strata were pivotal to the new liturgical office of the feast of Corpus Christi, to other Latin *historia*, and to a wide variety of new genres in the vernacular, including the devotional poetry from the Mosan Psalters, found in Part III of this book. The latter, translated here into English for the first time, are far more significant as evidence regarding popular piety and devotion than as innovative forms of higher cultural literature or theological interpretations of the Eucharist. They provided text-image sources for lay women, and possibly men, which prompted interior contemplation on scenes from the life of Jesus on Mary.[254] These are simple and pious Bible stories, intersecting literate and oral culture with vernacular recitations and prompting, perhaps, a newer and more popular form of mystical infusion.[255]

Marie d'Oignies is thought to have initiated a new mysticism.[256] McGinn, in summarizing Marie's *Life*, notes the unique combination of asceticism and "ecstatic rap-

---

[250] See J. Coakley, "Friars as Confidants of Holy Women in Medieval Dominican Hagiography, in *Images of Sainthood in Medieval Europe*, ed. R. Blumenfeld-Kosinski and T. Szell (Ithaca and London: Cornell University Press, 1991), 222–46; Mooney, *Gendered Voices*.

[251] Etienne Gilson, *The Mystical Theology of Saint Bernard*, trans. A. H. C. Downes (London: Sheed and Ward, 1940).

[252] Rubin, *Corpus Christi*, 169–71; see also Bolton, "Thirteenth-Century Religious Women," 138.

[253] While these two terms pose difficulties for translators because of the many connotations associated with them, Quenardel, *La Communion Eucharistique*, 19–20, through extensive textual analysis provides a constellation of adjectives that surround *pietas* in the later work of Saint Gertrude: *divina, gratuita, incontinens, supereffluens, benigna, liberalis, dulcis, largiflua* [divinely inspired, voluntary, intemperate, overflowing, kind-hearted, courteous, delightful, gushing].

[254] Cf. Thompson, *Cities of God*, 357–64.

[255] See Stock, *The Implications of Literacy*, 6–8.

[256] Jacques de Vitry in *The Life* describes especially her visions of the Presentation during the Candlemas procession. See also Wogan-Browne and Henneau, "Liège, the Medieval 'Woman Question'"; Carolyne Larring-

ture," combined with visions and devotion to the Eucharist, characteristic of her per-
formances and of the women in her liturgical community. Jacques de Vitry described
her devotional practices in detail in her *vita*, dated 1226, paying special attention to her
virtuosity as a singer.[257] McGinn remarks in particular on the *iubilus*, which she allegedly performed for three days:

> The connection between mystical states of consciousness and singing—whether liturgi-
> cal song or personal outbursts of melody—has yet to receive adequate attention, either
> in Christianity or in other mystical traditions. But prior references to the role of a song
> of jubilation (*iubilum* and later *iubilus*) in the history of Christian mystical literature do
> not prepare us for Jacques de Vitry's extended description of Mary's singing. . . .[258]

Jacques de Vitry's description of Marie's musical virtuosity at her death anticipates language later used to describe Juliana in her *vita*: "It seemed to her that one of the Seraphim was stretching his wings over her breast and with this help and sweet assistance,
she was inspired to sing without any difficulty."[259] According to the *vita*, Marie
D'Oignies sang in the vernacular verses that paraphrased stories from the Old and
New Testaments. The organization of Book 2 of Marie's *vita* into the seven gifts of the
Holy Spirit shows a close relationship between its author and the Old French poems in
the Psalters, Poem II in particular.[260]

Barbara Newman has provided an extensive analysis of other literary genres that
appeared in the thirteenth century, genres that conjoined two prevailing if contradictory themes in the constitution of a "mystique courtoise." Most notably, the Cistercian
abbot of Val-Saint-Lambert, Gérard of Liège, in 1250 created a new idiom that "blended
not only two languages, but the diverse thought-worlds they represented: the Latinate
realm of monastic bridal mysticism, known to Gérard primarily through Augustine
and Bernard, and the vernacular realm of *courtoisie* represented by his French lyrics,"[261]
fin'amor. Newman argues that his *Quinque incitamenta ad deum amandum ardenter* [*Five
Incitements to the Ardent Love of God*] led in a direct line of development to the didactic
text, the *Règle des Fins Amans*, written by a friend of the béguines, a French priest, at the
end of the thirteenth century,[262] fifty years after Hadewijch (perhaps the most important female exponent of love mysticism in vernacular lyrics). Newman indicates that
the French priest "wrote them a rule, not so much to legislate as to articulate the ideals

ton, "The Candlemas Vision and Marie D'Oignie's Role in Its Dissemination," in *New Trends in Feminine Spirituality: The Holy Women of Liège and Their Impact*, ed. Juliette Dor, Lesley Johnson, and Jocelyn Wogan-Browne
(Turnhout: Brepols, 1999), 195–214; Bynum, *Holy Feast and Holy Fast*, 115–29. McGinn, *The Flowering of Mysticism*, 37 applies the term *new mysticism*.

[257] Bernard McGinn, *The Flowering of Mysticism*, 37; see also Jacques de Vitry, *The Life*.

[258] McGinn, *The Flowering of Mysticism*, 39.

[259] Jacques de Vitry, *The Life*, 128.

[260] Barbara R. Walters, "*O verge de droiture ki de Jessé eissis* from the Mosan Psalters," in *Études de langue et de
litterature médiévales offertes à Peter T. Ricketts à l'occasion de son 70ème anniversaire*, ed. A. Buckley and D. Billy
(Turnhout: Brepols, 2005).

[261] Newman, *God and the Goddesses*, 155.

[262] Ibid., 155.

of their community."[263] Within these "rules" the contradictory ideas of mystical union with the Beloved Christ and the flirtatious *fin'amor* of the aristocracy were wed in an ethos that perhaps provided a psychological cloister for unmarried women workers outside the walls, confronted with the dangers and spectacles of city life.

> [The] complex of attitudes—loyalty to the Beloved at any cost, intimate friendship with the circle of *fin amans,* and contempt for the uncomprehending masses—is discernible in all the extant beguine texts. Their striking elitism is part of a simple transposition of the courtly ethos into religious terms. But more important, it sets a limit to the democratization of mystical piety that beguines themselves were promoting. Without the physical and symbolic protection of the cloister, these women were left painfully vulnerable to their enemies, and their attitude of lofty disdain can be seen as a cultural barrier raised to compensate for the lost privilege afforded by monastery walls.[264]

Newman's thesis, to a certain extent, is corroborated by the exemption of the béguines from the parishes and parish churches of Tongeren in 1245 initiated to protect them as much as possible from the dangers arising from the crowds in the marketplace, squares, streets, and inns.[265] She nonetheless has acknowledged that this ethos and its accompanying "crossover" texts—literary works that used monastic bridal mysticism as a metaphor for *fin'amor* and texts that represented monastic life through *fin'amor*—worked better, pragmatically speaking, in the courts and cloisters than on the streets. The "crossover" texts in particular provided an important expressive venue for celibates but were confusing when written and propagated by lay men and women "who were, or at any rate wished to be, sexually active."[266] The difference in contexts may partially explain the very different consequences for proclaiming a mystical love union with the Godhead for Gertrude of Helfta, cloistered in a well-endowed Cistercian monastery, and Margaret Porette, in the generation after Juliana.[267] Moreover, the prototype Cistercian text by Gerard marked a different path and a different textual thread than the textual community constituted by Marie d'Oignies and further developed by Juliana of Mont Cornillon. Theirs was a community centered on public liturgy and the Eucharist or, in private, on Psalters, which functioned as breviaries for béguines who wished to participate in or imitate the Divine Office.

TEXTUAL COMMUNITIES AND TEXTS

Two types of texts follow this Introduction as Part II and Part III of this book. They facilitate a more discerning and profound understanding of the many groups of women that gathered in Liège during the thirteenth century, but especially the community of women that formed around Juliana of Mont Cornillon and her friend Eve, the anchoress at the church of Saint-Martin. The texts provide insight into their religious beliefs

---

[263] Newman, "The Order of *fin amans,*" in her *From Virile Woman to WomanChrist,* 139.

[264] Ibid., 142.

[265] Simons, *Cities of Ladies,* 113–14.

[266] Newman, *From Virile Woman to WomanChrist,* 156.

[267] See Barbara R. Walters, "Women Religious *Virtuosae* from the Middle Ages: A Case Pattern and Analytic Model of Types," *Sociology of Religion* 63/1 (2002), 69–89.

and devotional practices and highlight the intellectual exchange between them and the highly literate theologians in the newly formed Dominican order. The contents of the texts are discussed and analyzed in detail in the introductory materials that precede each set of critical editions. These introductory materials strive only to connect the historical narrative and the critical editions of texts; to highlight the significance of the latter in shaping what Brian Stock has called a textual community:

> Wherever texts are read aloud or silently, there are groups of listeners who potentially can profit from them. A natural process of education takes place within the group, and, if the force of the word is strong enough, it can supersede the differing economic and social backgrounds of the participants, welding them, for a time at least, into a unit. In other words, the people who enter the group are not precisely the same as those who come out. Something has happened, and this experience affects their relations both with other members and with those outside of the group. Among the members, solidarity prevails; with outsiders, separation. The members may disperse, but they also can institutionalize their new relations, for instance by forming a religious order or a sectarian movement that meets on regular occasions. If they take this course, the community acquires the ability to perpetuate itself.[268]

LITURGICAL MANUSCRIPTS

The first set of texts are Latin liturgical versions of the office and Mass for the feast of Corpus Christi, transcribed from manuscripts and insertions to manuscripts dating from the late thirteenth to the early fourteenth centuries. The introductory material preceding the critical editions should acquaint the reader with modern research on the manuscripts. Most important, both for manuscript studies and for examination and analysis of the textual community formed by the new liturgy, are the three distinct versions widely recognized among medieval liturgical scholars. The first, found in The Hague, National Library of the Netherlands 70.E.4 (KB 70.E.4), *Animarum cibus*, is the work of Juliana of Mont Cornillon, assisted by the young prior John. The second version, from Strahov, *Sapiencia [a]edificavit*, may have been the work of Saint Thomas Aquinas during his years in Orvieto; it relies extensively on the biblical exegesis of Hugh of Saint-Cher. The third version, *Sacerdos in [a]eternum*, is widely regarded by modern scholars to be the work of Saint Thomas, executed during the last years of his life and theological career.

During the years in which Juliana compiled the texts and composed the music for *Animarum cibus*, the twelfth-century debates regarding the real presence of Christ in the Eucharist—debates among theologians around two polarities, an "Ambrosian" or corporeal understanding, and an "Augustinian" or more spiritual interpretation requiring Neoplatonic participation—had ended.[269] These debates were resolved, at least in theory, at the Fourth Lateran Council in 1215 by the doctrinal mandate that the body and

---

[268] Brian Stock, *Listening for the Text: On the Uses of the Past* (1990; Philadelphia: University of Pennsylvania Press, 1996), 150.

[269] Gary Macy, "Introduction" to *The Theologies of the Eucharist in the Early Scholastic Period: A Study of the Salvific Function of the Sacrament According to the Theologians, c. 1080–c.1220* (Oxford: Clarendon Press, 1984), 5; Brian Stock, "Interpreting the Eucharist," in his *Implications of Literacy*.

blood of Jesus Christ were transubstantiated into the bread and wine respectively.[270] However, as Macy clearly states: "elaboration of the doctrine was not achieved till the acceptance of Aristotelian metaphysics later in the thirteenth century, when it found classic formulation in the teaching of St. Thomas Aquinas."[271] Therefore, it is easy to surmise that *Animarum cibus* does not have an entirely consistent theological interpretation of the Eucharist, a topic taken up in great detail in the discussion and analysis of the liturgical manuscripts. The texts were drawn together from eucharistic doctrines of the preceding century that relied extensively on the eucharistic theologies of Hugh of Saint-Victor and Alger of Liège. Most likely, these are limited by what was available to Juliana though the Liège libraries. The first antiphon, *Animarum cibus dei sapientia nobis carnem assumptam proposuit in edulium ut per cibum humanitatis invitaret ad gustum divinitatis* [Food for souls, the wisdom of God has offered to us for food the flesh that he has assumed, so that through the food for our humanity he might invite us to taste of his divinity], invokes the authority of *Sapientia*, a feminine source of authority and among the most popular of medieval goddesses. Newman notes that *Sapientia*, "located on the boundary between the divine and human," was the "most protean of goddesses."[272] Nonetheless, she isolates a relevant stream in the later fourteenth-century tradition of devotion to Christ as Eternal Wisdom and the foundation for the later Dominican promulgation of Henry Suso's devotion *Horologium Sapientiae*, alongside the *Hours of Eternal Wisdom*, which formed the standard prayer book of the Modern Devout.[273]

Sapiencia [a]edificavit, the second version, invokes its authority through textual references to the Eucharist taken directly from the Bible, while confirming the reliance on *sapientia*, or wisdom, so popular among women prophetesses.[274] This version thus demonstrates requisite careful study, diligence, and memory of a complete compilation of biblical texts used to interpret the Eucharist in the late twelfth and early thirteenth centuries, and invokes the power of the Holy Spirit. If it was not authored by Hugh of Saint-Cher, it nonetheless bears his imprimatur through extensive use of texts drawn from his biblical compilations and commentaries. It also shares themes from the "original office," and especially in its opening antiphon for first vespers, which again refers directly to wisdom: "*Sapiencia edificavit sibi domum, excidit columpnas septem; immolavit victimas suas, miscuit vinum et posuit mensam suam*" [Wisdom has built herself a house, she has erected her seven pillars, she has slaughtered her beasts, prepared her wine; she has laid her table].[275] Wisdom here might represent the seven liberal arts, the seven principle virtues,[276] or the seven gifts of the Holy Spirit.[277]

[270] Gary Macy, "'The Dogma of Transubstantiation' in the Middle Ages," *Journal of Ecclesiastic History* 81 (1994), 11–41.

[271] Ibid., 11.

[272] Newman, *God and the Goddesses*, 193.

[273] Ibid., 193. See also John Van Engen, ed. and trans. *Devotio Moderna: Basic Writings* (New York: Paulist Press, 1988).

[274] Cf. Mulder-Bakker, *Lives of the Anchoresses*; see also Corrigan's critical edition of SAS in Strahov.

[275] See antiphon #1 in first vespers in Corrigan's critical edition of SAS; see also *Prov* 9: 1–2.

[276] Newman, *God and the Goddesses*, 193.

[277] See Barbara R. Walters, "*O verge de droiture ki de Jessé eissis.*"

The third version of the liturgy, *Sacerdos in [a]eternum*, can be found in BNF 1143, and most certainly represents the work of Saint Thomas Aquinas. The eternal priesthood here replaces Lady Wisdom. The concordances of *Sacerdos* with other versions, which precede and follow it in time, including *Sapiencia*, are treated extensively in the introduction to the liturgical manuscripts. These, as well as the other analyses in the accompanying tables, show its structure and its depth, as well as outline the path of its travels. The lectionary contains the famous Aquinas homily with its logically consistent explanation of transubstantiation. Antiphons and responsories in the office are paraphrased rather than directly quoted from biblical texts, all musical items are arranged in ascending modal order, and the prose employs Latin tense structures to highlight basic themes. Each musical item is set to the melody of an existing chant to create both a text and subtext so as to amplify its message regarding the special place of those invited to the supper—the "eternal priesthood."

Mulder-Bakker has noted similarities between the liturgical versions of the office by Saints Juliana and Aquinas. Both conceived of offices for city churches, cathedrals, or collegiate churches rather than monasteries. Both envisioned a feast day in which the entire community of the faithful might participate. Both rejected the allegorical versions and highly individual meditation so popular during their historical time period. And, both resist a purely spiritual communion.[278] This public liturgy functioned well for the urban working women of the thirteenth century—certainly more clearly than a "mystique courtoise"—in defining orientation, and dovetailed with the religious imagery, biblical message, and religious purpose of the Mosan psalters, which shape the foundation of Part III in this book.

POEMS OF THE MOSAN PSALTERS

Poems in the Mosan Psalters, or thirteenth-century psalters from the diocese of Liège, form a different strand or thread perhaps for a different textual audience than the literature emanating from the Cistercian Gerard. The poems are biblical and show the influence of the Dominicans. The psalters in which they appear were made for and by the béguines, highlighting the Dominican emphasis on book production and work. Their greatest contribution is spiritual, and Oliver claims that they are "the immediate precursors of the vernacular psalters and books of hours written by the Brethern of the Common Life."[279] She summarizes:

> Major themes of the Devotio Moderna are already found in the thirteenth-century Mosan psalters. Geert Grote (d. 1284) insisted on daily attendance at mass and prayer several times a day. The Beguine psalters, as we have seen, contain mass prayers and offices of the Virgin for these purposes. The illustrations of the psalter divisions for an early version of Grote's septenary of devotions, which focused each day on a single subject for meditation. Grote stressed the translation of scripture and prayers into the vernacular. The first steps toward this goal can be seen in the interspersing of Latin mass prayers and translations of them in French in the Mosan psalters. Latin poems and vernacular ones also appear at either end of Mosan psalters, and vernacular rubrics guide

the reader through the Latin hours of the Virgin. The Mosan psalters are books of private devotion, "lay breviaries" adapting monastic offices to individual use, just as the Beguines adopted a monastic life while remaining in the world and living by their own labor. . . . Most importantly, the Devotio Moderna stressed book production by its members, an activity that the Beguines had also practiced over a century earlier.[280]

The two types of texts presented in Parts II and III of this volume document profound intellectual interaction between men and women and the significant power and influence of lay religious women on interpreting and communicating the central theological doctrine of the thirteenth-century Church. The texts inform us of a genuine textual community that included both men and women and through which people interacted and experienced growth and change. The critical editions of the liturgical manuscripts and of the poems in Old French therefore provide a rich portrait of the complex spiritual world of thirteenth-century Europe. They offer an invaluable research resource to scholars in a wide range of discipline fields, one to be savored, treasured, and analyzed within its own textual community: a community that remembers with gratitude the work of Vincent Corrigan and Peter T. Ricketts and their respective contributions to Medieval Studies.

---

[280] Ibid., 207.

PART II

MATERIALS FOR THE STUDY OF CORPUS CHRISTI:
SOURCES

INTRODUCTION TO THE LITURGICAL MANUSCRIPTS

Barbara R. Walters

Twentieth-century critical scholarship on the liturgy for the feast of Corpus Christi was initiated by Browe[1] and significantly expanded in conjunction with the seventh centenary celebration of the feast in 1946. Lambot and his critic Delaissé provided the foundational research, with intellectual expertise reinforced by intimate familiarity with Latin liturgy, gleaned by daily repetition of the prayer cycle.[2] Identification and analysis of primary source materials, manuscripts to which components and versions of the liturgy were added in the late thirteenth and early fourteenth centuries, were central to their investigations. These and subsequent research endeavors focused principally on questions of authorship of the new office and Mass, the multiple versions of the liturgy added to existing manuscripts, and concordances among the chant materials across office versions that emerged in tandem with the inception of the new feast. More recently, Gy[3] and Zawilla[4] have challenged, corroborated, and expanded the research initiated by Browe, Lambot, and Delaissé. Their work included extensive analyses of the source documents transcribed by Lambot and new source documents not included in this earlier research. Taken together, these five scholars provide an indispensable cornerstone for the new critical editions by Vincent Corrigan. Corrigan's critical edi-

[1] Peter Browe, "Die Ausbreitung des Fronleichnamsfestes," *Jahrbuch für Liturgiewissenschaft* 8 (1928), 107–43, and *Textus antiqui de festo Corporis Christi*, Opuscula et textus, series liturgica IV (Münster: Aschendorff, 1934).

[2] Cyrille Lambot, "L'Office de la Fête-Dieu: Aperçu nouveaux sur ses origines," *Revue bénédictine* 54 (1942), 61–123, and "La bulle d'Urbaine IV à Eve of Saint-Martin sur l'institution de la Fête-Dieu," *Scriptorium* 2 (1948), 69–77, repr. in *Revue bénédictine* 79 (1969), 215–22; Cyrille Lambot and Irenée Fransen, *L'Office de la Fête-Dieu primitive: Textes et mélodies retrouvés* (Maredsous: Editions de Maredsous, 1946); see also L. M. J. Delaissé, "A la recherche des origines de l'office du Corpus Christi dans les manuscrits liturgiques," *Scriptorium* 4 (1950), 220–39.

[3] Pierre-Marie Gy, "L'Office du Corpus Christi et s. Thomas d'Aquin: état d'une recherché," *Revue des sciences philosophiques et théologiques* 64 (1980), 491–507, "L'office du Corpus Christi et la théologie des accidents eucharistique," *Revue des sciences philosophiques et théologiques* 66 (1982), 81–86, and "Office liégeois et office romain de la Fête-Dieu," in *Fête-Dieu (1246–1996)*, vol. 1, *Actes du Colloque de Liège*, ed. André Haquin (Louvain-la-Neuve: Institut d'Études Médiévales de l'Université Catholique de Louvain, 1999), 117–26.

[4] Ronald Zawilla, *The Biblical Sources of the Historia Corporis Christi Attributed to Thomas Aquinas: A Theological Study to Determine Their Authenticity* (Ph.D. diss. University of Toronto, 1985); see also Thomas J. Mathiesen, "'The Office of the New Feast of Corpus Christi' in the Regimen Animarum at Brigham Young University," *The Journal of Musicology* 2 (1983), 13–44.

tions represent the first new transcriptions of manuscripts central to the study of the feast of Corpus Christi since the 1940s, the first English translations, and the most comprehensive editions to date because they include transcriptions of melodies in modern musical notation. His analyses also include a set of analytic tables that can assist future researchers to navigate with ease through the manuscript editions.

BNF 755 AND OFFICES A, B, AND C

Lambot and Delaissé[5] identified ten late thirteenth- and early fourteenth-century manuscripts to which the feast of Corpus Christi was added. Their analyses of the chants for newly composed versions of the liturgy resulted in the clustering of material into three versions of the office: Forms I, II, and III,[6] or A, B, and C.[7] Lambot and Delaissé proposed different hypothetical patterns of sequential creation and adoption of the three versions to account for differences and similarities between them, a topic central to this discussion of the research literature and introduction to the Corrigan editions.

In 1983, musicologist Mathiesen[8] reviewed the manuscripts and research by Lambot and Delaissé in an article analyzing a previously unknown fourteenth-century manuscript at Brigham Young University, which contains an early version of the office. He identified the known manuscripts to which the new feast was added in a heuristic chart modified here to include Edinburgh University Library, MS 211.iv, the Inchcolm Antiphonary (EU), which was identified and described by Isobel Woods in 1987[9] (see Table 1). Mathiesen in 1983 also identified three versions, labeling them Forms A, B, and C, basing his classification for the most part on the work of the earlier scholars.

Table 1[10]

Manuscripts to which the Feast of Corpus Christi was Added

1. Brussels, Bibliothèque royale, 139
      Dominican cantatory of Marienthal (1269; fols. added ca. 1300)
      fols. 107–109: 10 responsories and versicles for Matins
      fols. 109–110: responsories and versicles based on office for S. Dominic
      fols. 162–63: gradual and alleluia for the Mass *Cibavit eos*
2. Paris, Bibliothèque nationale de France, lat. 755
      Roman lectionary
      fols. 367–69: Mathiesen's Office A

                                                        Mathiesen's Office C
      fols. 370–82: Mathiesen's Office B
3. Prague, Abbey of Strahov MS D.E.I.7
      Premonstratensian breviary (14th c.)
      fols. 213–21: Office B, lections grouped in four nocturnes

---

[5] Lambot, "L'Office de la Fête-Dieu"; Delaissé, "A la recherche."

[6] Delaissé, "A la recherche."

[7] See Mathiesen, "'The Office of the New Feast of Corpus Christi.'"

[8] Ibid.

[9] Isobel Woods, "'Our Awin Scottis Use': Chant Usage in Medieval Scotland," *Journal of the Royal Musical Association* 112 (1987), 21–37. This article contains an inventory and history of the manuscript. Warwick Edwards is preparing a study of this manuscript for publication in the near future.

[10] Table adapted from Mathiesen, "'The Office of the New Feast of Corpus Christi,'" 15.

4. Troyes, Bibliothèque municipale, MS 1974
    Benedictine breviary of the abbey of Montier-la-Celle (late 13th c.)
    fols. 434–38: Troy Office 1: Office B
    fols. 438v–444v: Troy Office 2: Office A
5. Graz, Universitätsbibliothek, MS 134
    Benedictine breviary (later 13th c.)
    fols. 241–46: Office A
6. Paris, Bibliothèque nationale de France, lat. 1143
    Musical manuscript (late 13th c. or early 14th c.)
7. Troyes, Bibliothèque municipale, MS 1980
    Cistercian breviary (13th c.)
8. Hague, National Library of the Netherlands, MS 70.E.4
    Composite manuscript (need paleographic dating)
    Part I: fols. 52–63: Lections from Office C
    Part II: fols. 86–96: Possible copy of "original" Liege office
9. Paris, Bibliothèque nationale de France, lat. 1023
    Breviary of Philippe le Bel (late 13th c.)
    fols. 551–64: Office C
10. Paris, Bibliothèque nationale de France, lat. 1266
    Breviary for the church at Meaux
11. Brigham Young University, Harold B. Lee Library, Special Collections, Vault 091 R263 1343:
    Office C
12. Edinburgh University Library, MS 211.iv. (Inchcolm Antiphonary)
    Parts of Office

The theory of Offices A, B, and C originated with Lambot's transcription and publication in 1942 of the lectionary material found in Paris, Bibliothèque nationale de France, lat. 755 (BNF 755).[11] Lambot reports that BNF 755 was first identified by Victor Leroquais, who believed it to have been in use in the papal chapel.[12] This manuscript most likely was completed in 1253, with *legenda* on folios 367–82 added perhaps as early as 1264 or 1279, and most likely not after 1296.[13] The additions, each marked with a rubric, testify to several profound reorganizations of the lections for the feast of Corpus Christi office. Lambot's 1942 article with his transcription and analysis of BNF 755 highlights intertextual relationships among component parts of the legendarium, the lections of Strahov (Item 3 on Table 1), and the lections of BNF 1143 (Item 6), a topic taken up below.

Mathiesen developed a second heuristic table[14] to summarize and explain Lambot's analysis of BNF 755. Presented here as Table 2, it facilitates an understanding of the folios and texts added to the manuscript and the concordances among lections in hypo-

---

[11] Lambot, "L'Office de la Fête-Dieu"; Delaissé, "A la recherche," 74–94, 97–118; see also S. J. P. Van Dijk, "Three Manuscripts of a Liturgical Reform by John Cajetan Orsini (Nicholas III)," *Scriptorium* 6 (1952), 213–42.

[12] Lambot, "L'Office de la Fête-Dieu," 69–70. Cf. Victor Leroquais, *Les bréviaires manuscrits des bibliothèques publiques de France*, vol. 4 (Paris: Macon, Protat frères, imprimeurs, 1934). Van Dijk, "Three Manuscripts of a Liturgical Reform," believed that BNF 755 was from a different Roman church. The debate between Lambot ("L'Office de la Fête-Dieu") and Delaissé ("A la recherche") on dating and other issues pertaining to BNF 755 is taken up at length by Gy, "L'Office du Corpus Christi et s. Thomas d'Aquin," 496 n 21, and by Zawilla, *Biblical Sources of the Historia Corporis Christi*, 57–74.

[13] Delaissé, "A la recherche," 224–25; Van Dijk, "Three Manuscripts of a Liturgical Reform," 222–23; see Zawilla, *Biblical Sources of the Historia Corporis Christi*, 57–63, for a summary of the contradictory evidence regarding dating of the added legendarium.

[14] Mathiesen, "'The Office of the New Feast of Corpus Christi,'" 22.

thetical Offices A, B, and C. The first addition was placed on folios 370r–382v, where the lections for an office, *Dominus Jesus ad invisibilia* (DJI), were added. This office consists of four nocturns with three lessons each: (I) *Dominus Jesus ad invisibilia*; (II) *Panis est in altari usitatus*; (III) *Secundum Ioannem*; and (IV) *Omnia quaecumque*. DJI was referred to by Delaissé as Form II and then by Mathiesen as Office B; it consists largely of readings taken or adapted, for the most part, from Gratian's *Decretum* and from an Augustine homily. Delaissé, in response to Lambot's initial article, concluded that the lections inserted on folios 367r–368r of BNF 755 were the second and third nocturns of a later edition of the lectionary for the office and that the first nocturn had been "excised":

> Les fol. 367 à 369 comportent les 2e et 3e nocturnes de l'office du Saint Sacrement. Le premier nocturne, dont le texte nous est inconnu, se trouvait sur un premier feuillet, avant le fol. 367. . . . Le second nocturne commençait par les mots 'Immensa divine largitatis.'[15]

> [Folios 367 to 369 contain the second and third nocturns of the office of the Blessed Sacrament. The first nocturn, for which the text is unknown to us, is found on the first page, before folio 367. . . . The second nocturn begins with the words "Immesa divine largitatis."]

The rubric at the top of BNF 755, folio 367r, marks the lections as for the feast of Corpus Christi: *In solempnitate Corporis Domini Jesu Christi . . . Ad matutinum.* The rubric *lectio prima* clearly notates the beginning of the first lesson as *Immensa divine largitatis.* Delaissé, nonetheless, and then Mathiesen, referred to this set of lections as a theoretical Form I, or Office A, with a missing nocturn. Theoretical Office A as described does not exist as such in any known manuscript.

Table 2
Mathiesen's Outline of the Lections for Offices A, B, and C: BNF 755

	Office A	Office B	Office C
I.	Excised[16]	*Dominus Jesus ad invisibilia*	*Immensa divine largitatis*
II.	Excised	*Considera utrum*	*Manducatur utique*
III.	Excised	*Marath fluvius*	*Convenit itaque devotioni*
IV.	*Immensa divine*	*Panis est in altari*	*Huius sacramenti figura*
V.	*Manducatur utique*	*Christus panis est de quo*	*Forte dicis: aliud*
VI.	*Convenit itaque devotioni*	*Iteratur cotidie haec oblatio*	*Marath fluvius*
VII.	*Secundum Ioannem*	*Secundum Ioannem*	*Secundum Ioannem*
VIII.	*Denique iam*	*Sicut me misit*	*Denique iam*
IX.	*Sicut misit me*	*Spiritus est qui*	*Sicut misit me*
X.		*Utrum sub figura*	
XI.		*Omnia quecumque*	
XII.		*Qui scelerate vivunt*	

Mathiesen's table shows the first three lessons of Office A as "excised" to illustrate Delaissé's hypothesis of a missing nocturn. The second nocturn, according to Delaissé, began with *Immensa divine*, now widely recognized as the homily of Aquinas, which is divided on folios 367r–368r into three lessons: (I) *Immensa divine*; (II) *Manducatur utique*;

[15] Delaissé, "A la recherche," 225.

[16] Mathiesen derived most of this information from Lambot, "L'Office de la Fête-Dieu," and Delaissé, "A la recherche."

and (III) *Convenit itaque*. A marking on the manuscript at the end of the third lesson, at the bottom of folio 268r, directs the reader to a fourth lection, which begins on folio 370v with *Huius sacramenti*. A third nocturn was inserted on folios 368v–369r, between the first nocturn and the fourth. The inserted nocturn contains the homily of Saint Augustine on *Secundum Ioannem*, divided into three lections, clearly marked on the manuscript as lessons seven, eight, and nine: (VII) *Secundum Ioannem: in illo tempore . . .*; *Quomodo quidem* (VIII); *Denique iam*; and (IX) *Sicut misit me*. Folio 369r is blank. On folio 370v, the first lesson of DJI is crossed out and a marginal note indicates that *Huis sacramenti* is lection IV. Both Lambot and Delaissé used BNF 755 to show that Form III (Mathiesen's Office C) is a rearrangement and amalgamation of hypothetical Office A and Office B. Office C begins with *Immensa divine largitatis* and thus is referred to as IDL.

Contemporary scholars continue to recognize three major offices for the feast of Corpus Christi. This more contemporary understanding is in continuity with the research executed on BNF 755, research that was expanded considerably by Lambot and other scholars in the late 1940s and early 1950s to include musical items and other manuscripts. The more extensive analyses of other manuscripts identified three versions of the office through clustering musical items from separate manuscripts into three groups.

The first version, *Animarum cibus*, the incipit of its first antiphon, represents the "original office" composed by Juliana of Mont Cornillon, aided by the young monk John. Lambot discovered this office in 1946 in a composite manuscript from Notre Dame at Tongres, The Hague, National Library of the Netherlands, MS 70.E.4 (KB 70.E.4), through the incipit of the first antiphon that matched a description of the office composed by Juliana and John in a note added to Juliana's *vita* in 1475.[17] A *glossateur* inserted a note in the *vita* at the end of Part I, indicating that the office was preserved at the church at Tongres and elsewhere, and that the first antiphon began with the incipit *Animarum cibus*: "Hoc officium incipit, *Animarum cibus*; et reperitur plenum in Ecclesia Tungrensi et alliis locis. Deinde Urbanus IV, officium quod ubique cantatur, instituit"[18] [This is the office incipit, *Animarum cibus*; it can be found in its entirety in the church at Tongres and other places. Afterwards Urban IV, instituted an office that is celebrated everywhere].[19]

Animarum cibus, is a secular office intended for celebration in a church setting. It stands apart, having virtually no overlapping texts with the other two versions. The Latin text has a *rusticitas* quality, betraying the provincial origins and scholarly limitations of its authoress, Juliana of Mont Cornillon.[20] The texts are doctrinal, drawn from "multorum sanctorum libros"[21] pertaining to the Eucharist by twelfth-century scholars, which were rearranged and set to music. Text sources include Alger of Liège (1055–1131), Hugh of Saint-Victor (1096–1141), Gratian (d. 1179), Anselm of Canterbury (1033–1109), Guibert of Nogent (ca. 1055–1124), and Jacques de Vitry (1180–1240).

17 Lambot and Fransen, *L'Office de la Fête-Dieu primitive*, 21.

18 Jean-Pierre Delville, *Vie de Sainte Julienne de Cornillon*, Critical Edition, vol. 2 of *Fête-Dieu (1246–1996)* (Louvain-la-Neuve: Institut d'Études Médiévales de l'Université Catholique de Louvain, 1999), 138 n 665.

19 Lambot and Fransen, *L'Office de la Fête-Dieu primitive*.

20 See Anneke B. Mulder-Bakker, *Lives of the Anchoresses: The Rise of the Urban Recluse in Medieval Europe*, trans. Myra Heerspink Scholz (Philadelphia: University of Pennsylvania Press, 2005); J. Cottiaux, "L'Office liégeois de la Fête-Dieu, sa valeur et son destin," *Revue d'histoire ecclésiastique* 58 (1963), 5–81, 405–59.

21 Delville, *Vie de Sainte Julienne de Cornillon*, 138.

Mulder-Bakker notes a central theme developed around a theological point empha-sized by Guibert, as well as Anselm of Canterbury and Alger of Liège: "Jesus was not daily 'crucified' on the altar, as some theologians had maintained, but had died on the cross once and for all, *semel*, and this was daily represented in the Mass."[22]

Folios 52–63v contain the lections described above for BNF 755 as Form III or Office C, IDL. These are written in the same or a similar hand as folios 86–96v. Lectio III refers to Urban IV and his decree instituting the feast for the universal Church within the text.

> Unde ut integro celebritatis officio institutionem tanti sacramenti sollempniter recoleret plebs fidelis: romanus pontifex Urbanus quartus huius sacramenti devotione affectus, pie statuit prefate institutionis memoriam, prima ferio quinta post octavas pentecostes, a cunctis fidelibus celebrari: ut qui per totum anni circulum hoc sacramentuo utimur ad salutem, eius institutionem illo specialiter tempore recolamus: quo spiritus sanctus dis-cipulorum corda edocuit, ad plene cognoscenda huius misteria sacramenti.

> [Hence, so that the faithful may solemnly honor again the institution of such a great sac-rament by a complete office of celebration, the Roman Pope Urban IV, influenced by the devotion of this sacrament, piously decreed commemoration of the aforementioned in-stitution on feria five after the octave of Pentecost, to be celebrated by all the faithful, so that we, who use this sacrament throughout the year for salvation, may honor again, at that time especially, its institution, by which the Holy Spirit taught the hearts of the dis-ciples to understand fully the mysteries of this sacrament.][23]

Since the institution by Urban IV occurred in 1264, long after the original celebration in Liège, it is a virtual certainty that Form III, or IDL, is not the correct *legendum* for the *Animarum cibus* office. Lambot and Fransen, in their reconstruction,[24] inserted Form II, DJI, in the *legendum*. The actual lections for the original office remain unknown, a topic open to future research. Gy and later Zawilla[25] have suggested another *legendum*, *In mysterio corporis*, which can be found in Oxford, Bodleian Library A 263, folios 49r–62r, but theirs is an admittedly speculative hypothesis.

The second version, Office B, *Sapiencia [a]edificavit sibi* (SAS), the incipit of its first antiphon, can be found in its entirety in another manuscript identified by Lambot:[26] Prague, Abbey of Strahov, MS D.E.I.7 (Strahov), a Premonstratensian breviary dating from the mid-fourteenth century, with an office for the feast Corpus Christi on folios 213v–221r. Its texts are entirely biblical, and fourteen of its items are concordant with the version found in BNF 1143. An overview of the Strahov office—its sources and con-cordances with BNF 1143—can be found below in Table 3.[27] SAS is for monastic use and is associated with the DJI lectionary readings.[28] It also was added to another early manuscript, MS Troyes, Bibliothèque Municipale 1974. Gy later observed that the Mass

---

[22] Mulder-Bakker, *Lives of the Anchoresses*, 33.

[23] See KB 70.E.4 transcription and translation.

[24] Lambot and Fransen, *L'Office de la Fête-Dieu primitive*.

[25] Gy, "L'Office du Corpus Christi," 497 n 23; Zawilla, *Biblical Sources of the Historia Corporis Christi*, 18.

[26] Lambot, "L'Office de la Fête-Dieu," 87–94, 118–23.

[27] Corrigan provides a far more extensive analysis in his indices.

[28] SAS is derived from *Sapiencia [a]edificavit sibi*, as used by Zawilla, *Biblical Sources of the Historia Corporis Christi*.

for SAS, *Ego sum panis*, is preserved in a number of manuscripts from Troyes, which was the birthplace of Urban IV. [29]

The third version, Office C, referred to as *Sacerdos in [a]eternum* (SIA), the incipit of its first antiphon, is the official Roman office traditionally attributed to Aquinas. The lections for Office C from BNF 755 and all of its musical items can be found in a manuscript exclusively devoted to the feast of Corpus Christi, Paris, Bibliothèque nationale de France, lat. 1143.[30] BNF 1143 is an elegant and remarkable manuscript, in part because of its formal and official appearance but also because of notations in the margin that identify the source chant from which the music was taken for each musical item in the office and Mass. Like *Animarum cibus*, it is a secular office, with a fourth nocturn for monastic use added at the end of the manuscript. It shares a significant number of items with SAS. It is also biblical, but in this instance the texts are paraphrases rather than quotations. An overview of the BNF 1143 office—its sources and concordances with Strahov—can be found below in Table 4.

CHRONOLOGICAL ORDERING OF THE THREE OFFICES AND THE PAPAL BULL *TRANSITURUS*

Delaissé[31] initially concluded from the transcription and analyses of the manuscripts presented in Table 1 that the new feast celebrating the sacrament first developed in the entourage around Juliana of Mont Cornillon in Liège, ca. 1246. He suggested that the new feast was fostered by the Cistercians at Villers, who, not satisfied with the original office by Juliana and John, developed their own based on biblical inspiration. When celebration of the office spread to Germany in 1252, several rhymed offices were available. Finally, at the prompting of Urban IV, Aquinas developed a version that brought together the earlier versions and was stabilized as the accepted practice after 1323.

Mathiesen summarized Delaissé's interpretation of the development in his article on the Brigham Young manuscript:

> There was certainly an original Liège office written around 1246. The Cistercians, who along with the Romans were among the first to celebrate the Feast, were dissatisfied with the naïve Office of John and developed their own with Biblical text. In Germany after 1252, a number of rhymed offices appeared. The support of Pope Urban IV led to the development of a Roman Office, Office A, sometime in the mid-13th century. The Premonstratensians and Benedictines developed another Office, Office B, with the lections in four nocturns. Then, around 1300, or a little before, these two were modified and combined to form a new Office, Office C, which also appears in France [Item 6 on Table 1]. At the beginning of the 14th century, Office C prevailed . . . but it was not known as the Aquinas office and it was not used exclusively . . . [until the Dominican] Chapter in Barcelona announced in favor of Office C because it was composed, *ut asseritur*, by their brother Thomas Aquinas.[32]

[29] Gy, "L'Office du Corpus Christi," 498, 498 n 15.

[30] A facsimile of the manuscript can be found in Vincent Corrigan, ed., *Paris, Bibliothèque Nationale Fonds Latin 1143* (Ottawa: The Institute of Medieval Music, 2001).

[31] Delaissé, "A la recherche," 237–38.

[32] Mathiesen, "'The Office of the New Feast of Corpus Christi,'" 24–25; see also Delaissé, "A la recherche," 237–38.

Codicologist Van Dijk in 1952 argued against a slow process in the development of multiple versions and suggested a different explanation, one which followed more closely the initial work of Lambot.[33] Lambot concluded from the codicological evidence that both SAS and SIA were composed by Aquinas, but at two different times. He hypothesized that Urban IV commissioned Aquinas to compose an office for the new feast while he was serving as Conventual Lector in Orvieto between 1261 and 1265.[34] According to Lambot, Saint Thomas must have completed only the hymns when the pope, perhaps influenced by knowledge of his imminent death, decided to hold a special celebration of the new feast in the curia in August 1264. Thomas adapted what he had already completed for the occasion, hastily assembled texts for the antiphons, responsories, and versicles from the Bible, and developed a set of readings from Gratian's *Decretum*.[35] This provisional version, SAS, was attached to the *Transiturus* sent to the Patriarch of Jerusalem by Urban IV in August 1264, and perhaps also to his letter to the bishops in September. Lambot concluded that later, after the death of Urban IV, Aquinas completed the more fully developed Roman office, IDL and SIA, as found in BNF 1143.[36]

Gy and then Zawilla corroborated Lambot's thesis of an Aquinas authorship, amplifying the explanation with manuscript evidence not available to Lambot in 1946. Gy referred to three redactions of the *Transiturus*, later labeled by Zawilla as T-1, T-2, and T-3,[37] which were discovered by Bertamini and Franceschini in the 1960s.[38] T-1 is dated 11 August 1264 and addressed to the Patriarch of Jerusalem. It makes specific mention of a liturgical office included in the correspondence: "cum novem lectionibus, cum responsoriis, versiculis, antifonis, psalmis, [h]ymnis et orationisbus ipsi festo specialiter congruentibus, que cum proprio misse officio vobis sub bulla nostra mittimus interclusa"[39] [with nine lections, with responsories, versicles, antiphons, psalms, hymns, and orations especially in conformity with the nature of this feast, which with the proper office for the Mass are included under the bull we are sending to you]. This statement also is found in T-2, but not in T-3.[40] T-2 was addressed to the Church hierarchy and was undated; it was edited by Bertamini from a libellus with the bull and the office SIA. It also specifically mentions the above-noted inclusion of a liturgical office and states: "Intelleximus autem olim, dum in minori essemus officio constitute, quod fuerat quibusdam catholicis divinitus revelatum festum huiusmodi generaliter in ecclesia

---

[33] Van Dijk, "Three Manuscripts of a Liturgical Reform"; see also Lambot, "L'Office de la Fête-Dieu," 92–94.

[34] Lambot, "L'Office de la Fête-Dieu," 93–94; see also Jean-Pierre Torrell, *Saint Thomas Aquinas*, vol. 1, trans. Robert Royal (Washington, D.C.: Catholic University of America Press, 1996), 129–41.

[35] Lambot later hypothesized that the lections were drawn from the lections of the earlier *Animarum cibus* office. See Lambot and Fransen, *L'Office de la Fête-Dieu primitive*.

[36] Lambot, "L'Office de la Fête-Dieu," 94.

[37] Gy, "L'Office du Corpus Christi," 495 n 17; Zawilla, *Biblical Sources of the Historia Corporis Christi*, 29–34.

[38] Tulllio Bertamini, "La bolla 'Transiturus' di papa Urbano IV e l'uffizio del 'Corpus Christi' secondo il codice di S. Lorenzo di bognanco," *Aevum* 42 (1968), 29–58; Ezio Franceschini, "Origine e stile della bolla 'Transiturus,'" *Aevum* 39 (1965), 218–43.

[39] Gy, "L'Office du Corpus Christi," 494.

[40] Ibid., 494; see also Zawilla, *Biblical Sources of the Historia Corporis Christi*, 31.

celebrandum"[41] [Once when we held a lesser office we came to know that it had been divinely revealed to certain catholics that a feast of this kind should be generally observed in the Church].[42] T-3 also contains this statement, which is not found in T-1. T-3 was incorporated into the bull issued by Clement V following the Council of Vienne in 1312, later promulgated by John XXII in the Clementines of 1317.[43]

Franceschini examined the codicological evidence, including the dates of the letters sent by Urban IV to Henry of Gueldre on 7 September 1264 and Eve of Saint-Martin on 8 September 1264. He concluded that Urban IV must have celebrated the feast using SAS in the curia on 19 June, the Thursday after Pentecost, a slightly different chronology and date than that suggested by Lambot.[44] Gy agreed with Lambot regarding the provisional office SAS; he also noted the wide diffusion of *Transiturus* addressed to the bishops (T-2) during the late thirteenth century and concluded that Urban IV, when he instituted the new feast among the bishops, promulgated and distributed the office with which he wished it to be celebrated.[45] Gy saw evidence "du lien primitive entre l'Office [SIA] et la bull" [of a primitive relationship between the office and the bull],[46] and from this concluded that BNF 1143 was a curial prototype from which all libelli were copied and that it represented the most authentic form of SIA. He further concluded that SAS may well have been the earlier version performed in the curia and sent to the Patriarch of Jerusalem with T-1 in August 1264. "Nous pouvons, je pense, inférer avec certitude que l'Office *Sacerdos* a été diffusé en 1264, *interclusum* dans la bull *Transiturus*"[47] [We can, I think, infer with certainty, that the Office *Sacerdos* was distributed in 1264, and included in the bull *Transiturus*]. Zawilla and Bertamini indicate with less certainty that the bull may have been sent after the death of Urban IV. These questions remain open to further investigation.

GY AND ZAWILLA'S ANALYSES

Gy's conclusive attribution of the Roman office SIA to Aquinas is based in part on the omission from SIA of Matthew 28: 20: "Behold I am with you until the end of time," an omission also characteristic of SAS. The gospel passage has been linked through biblical glosses to an early scholastic and doctrinal interpretation of the Eucharist as a "corporeal presence." The biblical passage appears in the *vita* of Juliana of Mont Cornillon, in the bull *Transiturus*, in the actual *Animarum cibus* office, in Bonaventure, and in other early thirteenth-century sources. Gy argues that the absence of the Matthew passage from SAS and SIA suggests the authorship of Saint Thomas, who did not use this reading in his other theological work written in Orvieto or later, including *Summa theologiae*.

---

[41] Franceschini, "Origine e stile della bolla 'Transiturus,'" 238–39; Bertamini, "La bolla 'Transiturus,'" 47.

[42] See Zawilla, *Biblical Sources of the Historia Corporis Christi*, 32.

[43] Gy, "L'Office du Corpus Christi," 494; see also Zawilla, *Biblical Sources of the Historia Corporis Christi*, 31–32.

[44] Franceschini, "Origine e stile della bolla 'Transiturus,'" 224–25; see also Zawilla, *Biblical Sources of the Historia Corporis Christi*, 54.

[45] Gy, "L'Office du Corpus Christi," 495.

[46] Ibid., 496, 501; see also Zawilla, *Biblical Sources of the Historia Corporis Christi*, 66.

[47] Gy, "L'Office du Corpus Christi," 501.

He noted in particular that Aquinas thought about the real presence in an entirely different way than earlier theologians and never used the idea of a corporeal presence. Based primarily on Gy's observations regarding the Aristotelian language in the SIA lections, Aquinas biographer Torrell highlights this thesis:

> ["Accidentia enim sine subiecto in eodem existent, ut fides locum habeat dum visibile invisibiliter sumitur, aliena specie occultatum, et *sensus a deceptione immunes redantur, qui de accidentibus iudicant sibi notis."*][48] The entire passage certainly appears a little bit incongruous in a liturgical celebration, but it is in fact the equivalent of a signature. The italicized words, which show to best advantage a judgment on the meaning of the Eucharistic accidents, express a position that occurs five times in the context of this *Legenda*. Although this is not a point of view that is exclusively Thomas's own, his rigorous Aristotelian perspective makes him probably the only one of his contemporaries who would think to use it in such a context. . . .[49]

Bataillon noted a parallel phenomenon with Luke 14: 16, which was rarely used in reference to the Eucharist prior to Saint Thomas' sermon *Homo quidam fecit cenam magnam.*[50] The appearance of the Luke reading in SIA is thus another argument for the Aquinas authorship of this version of the office.

Taking Gy and Batillon as his starting point, Zawilla executed a far more extensive and systematic analysis and comparison of the antiphons, responsories, and versicles in SAS and SIA.[51] First, noting that medieval theologians typically relied on commentaries rather than original biblical sources, he created four dossiers presented as tables and discussion: (1) a table comparing the biblical texts used in SAS and SIA with writings and commentaries before 1264; (2) a table comparing SAS and SIA with the writings of Saint Thomas after 1264; (3) a table comparing SAS and SIA with the writings of Saint Bonaventure; and (4) illustrative material from sermons and sermon literature.[52] He then observed that the first two tables formed a diptych, with a striking contrast between the two offices in terms of the texts proper to each.[53] For the texts proper to SAS, only two are cited in the later works of Aquinas: Exodus 25: 23–24, 30 and 1 Corinthians 10: 3–4. By contrast, for the texts proper to SIA, only seven of twenty-three texts are not cited at least once in these later works.[54] Zawilla thus notes both a continuity and discontinuity between the two offices.

Zawilla executed further analyses of both SAS and SIA. He observes that nineteen of the biblical texts employed in SAS were part of a common theological tradition. Another twenty-five were rarely, if ever, employed in discussions of the Eucharist prior to

---

[48] [The accidents, however, remain here without any subject. And this, that faith may be exercised when what is visible is invisibly received, hidden under another appearance; furthermore, that the senses, which judge of the accidents according to appearances, may be preserved from the same error.]

[49] Torrell, *Saint Thomas Aquinas,* 131–32.

[50] L.-J. Bataillon, "Le sermon inédit de saint Thomas 'Homo quidam fecit cenam magnam': introduction et édition," *Revue des sciences philosophiques et théologiques* 67 (1983), 353–69.

[51] Zawilla, *Biblical Sources of the Historia Corporis Christi.*

[52] Ibid., 88–117.

[53] Ibid., 120.

[54] Ibid.

their use in SAS. Of these twenty-five, eighteen had as their source the *Postilla* by Hugh of Saint-Cher.[55] Hugh also had cited most of the text sources new to the tradition in his exposition of the texts in the common tradition. On the basis of this painstaking analysis of SAS, Zawilla concluded that Hugh was a likely candidate for authorship, but that his analysis should not be taken as evidence that Thomas did not write it.

> This information, however, indicates that Hugh could be considered as likely a candidate for the composer of the *historia*, that is, of the biblical parts of the office, as Thomas. It must be acknowledged that nothing links SAS to Thomas in a way that excludes others.[56]

On the basis of his close analysis of SIA, Zawilla notes that over half of the biblical texts are common to both SAS and SIA. In a summary and concluding section of his dissertation, Zawilla presents a table with four partitions: (1) biblical texts proper to SAS; (2) texts common to SAS and SIA; (3) texts proper to SIA; and (4) texts used in pairs in SIA. For each biblical text in each partition Zawilla notes the source in terms of items in the biblical commentary dossiers described above, and where (if at all) the text was used by Thomas.

Tables 3 and 4 below summarize and expand the analysis by Zawilla by organizing the information so as to provide the biblical source of each item and integrate it with the analytic work of musicologist Corrigan. These tables contain only those musical items from SAS and SIA that have biblical texts (hymns, for example, are excluded). Focusing on Table 4, for each SIA item there are five types of possible intertextuality with SAS: (1) exact quotation of music and text; (2) exact quotation of text only; (3) text source in identical biblical passage but paraphrased; (4) exact musical quotation; and (5) musical paraphrasing.

Zawilla's original analysis, Corrigan's indices, and the adapted tables corroborate a close relationship between the two offices in exact quotes, common sources in biblical texts, and the extensive reliance on biblical sources found in the Postilla. However, there is also evidence for some independence; several important variations distinguish the two offices, as initially reported by Zawilla. Table 3 reveals the low likelihood of items proper to SAS appearing in the late works of Aquinas and their more frequent source in earlier medieval sources. Table 4, by contrast, reveals the higher likelihood of items proper to SIA also being utilized by Aquinas in his later writings. While the SAS antiphons come from the Psalms and other biblical books, the SIA antiphons rely exclusively on the Psalms. An exception to this is in the fourth nocturn for monastic use. Here the SIA antiphons and responsories are exact concordances of both the text and music of SAS. (While the fourth nocturn is presented in the Table 4 immediately after nocturn three, it is in fact the last entry in the actual BNF 1143 manuscript).

---

[55] The *Postilla* were encyclopedic commentary compiled by a group of Dominicans between 1230 and 1235 under the direction of Hugh of Saint-Cher, which supplemented the *Glossa ordinaria*. They incorporated the biblical commentary of Parisian Masters from the preceding century. See Zawilla's description, *Biblical Sources of the Historia Corporis Christi*, 92.

[56] Ibid., 206.

Table 3
Strahov (SAS) Ccx Office: Proper and Common Texts, Music, and Sources
(in Relation to SIA Only)*
Adapted from Zawilla (1985) and Corrigan (2001)

	Title	Biblical Source	Text Source Proper to SAS	T/S Common to SAS & SIA	Music Proper to SAS	Source of Text*	Used by Aquinas
Legend:	* See Dossier of Biblical Sources at the end of Table 4						
	/ = no known use by Thomas or no known commentary source						
	X′ = same biblical source text with different phrasing						
1st V							
A1	Sapiencia edificavit	Prv 9:1–2		X′	X	POST	HQF
A2	Melchisedech rex	Gn 14:18–19		X′	X	Decr/4SNT	In4SNT ST3
A3	Immolabit edum	Ex 12:6–7		X′	X	4SNT	In4SNT ST3
A4	Et edent carnes	Ex 12:8–9		X′	X	4SNT	In4SNT ST3
A5	Pluit illis	Ps 77:24–25		X′	X	4SNT	In4SNT InMt In Jo6 HQF
R	Cumque operuisset/ Iste est panis/ Gloria patri	Ex 16:14–15		X′	X	/	/
A/M	Angelorum esca/ Magnificat	Sap 16:20–21		X′	X	DSAM	In4SNT InJo6 HQF ST3
M/Inv/N1							
Inv	Venite comedite	Prv 9:5		X	X	POST	InMt26 In1Cor11 InJo6 HQF ST#
A1	Numquid poterit	Ps 77:19–20	X		X	POST	/
A2	Parasti in conspectu	Ps 22:5		X′	X	4SNT	HQF
A3	De fructu operum	Ps 103: 13–15		X′	X	P Comester	InJo6 HQF ST3
R1	Cenantibus discipulis/V Hic est sanguis	Matt 26:26–28		X′	X	Lanfranc	In4SNT InJo6 HQF ST3
R2	Accepto pane/ V Similiter et calicem	Lk 22:19–20		X′	X	Lanfranc	ST3
R3	Manducantibus discipulis/	Mk 14: 22–24	X		X	Lanfranc	/
N2							
A1	Faciens mensam	Ex 25:23–24,30	X		X	POST>Ps22	In Ps22
A2	Sacerdotes sancti	Lev 21:6		X′	X	/	InHbr
A3	Faciet Dominus	Is 25:6	X		X	POST>Prv24 Jo6	
R1	Dominus Ihesus/ V Similiter et calicem	1Cor 11:23–25	X		X	4SNT	/
R2	Quicumque mandu-caverit/V Qui enim manducat	1Cor 11: 27–29	X		X	Decr	/

	Title	Biblical Source	Text Source Proper to SAS	T/S Common to SAS & SIA	Music Proper to SAS	Source of Text*	Used by Aquinas
R3	*Calix benedictionis/ V Quoniam unus panis/Gloria*	1Cor 10:16–17		X		4SNT	HQF
N3							
A1	*Tulit Manue*	Jud 13:19–20	X		X	W Militona	/
A2	*Erit quasi oliva*	Hos 14:7–8	X		X	POST>Prv9 Sir24 Jo6	/
A3	*Quid enim bonum*	Zach 9:17	X		X	POST>Ps80 Prv 9	/
R1	*Ego sum/ Ego sum/Gloria*	Jo 6:48–51		X		GO	InMt26 In1Cor11 HQF ST3
R2	*Amen, amen/ Caro enim/Gloria*	Jo 6:53–56		X'	X	POST	InJo6
R3	*Sicut vivens/Non sicut patres/Gloria*	Jo 6: 57–59		X'	X	Decr/4SNT	In4SNT HQF ST3
N4							
A1	*Extendit Jonathas*	1 Sam 14:27	X		no music in MS	/	/
A2	*Comede fili mi*	Prv 24:13, 25,16	X		no music in MS	POST>Prv24 Jo6	/
A3	*Venite emite*	Is 55:1–2	X		no music in MS	POST>Ct5 Prv9 Jo6	/
R1	*Melchisedech viro/ Benedictus*	Gen 14:18–19		X		Decr/4SNT	In4SNT ST3
R2	*Immolabit hedum/ Et edent*	Ex 12:6–8		X'	X	4SNT	In4SNT ST3
R3	*Cumque operuisset/ Iste est panis/Gloria*	Ex 16:14–15	X		X	/	/
Lauds							
A1	*Memoriam fecit*	Ps 110:4–5		X		POST	In1Cor11
A2	*Memoria mea*	Sir 24:28–29		X		POST>Jo6	
A3	*Omnes eandem*	1 Cor 10:3–4	X		X	Decr	InJo6 ST3
A4	*Nolo vos socios*	1 Cor 10:20–21	X		X	?	/
A5	*Qui habet aures*	Apc 2:17 (Rev)		X		G Orchelles	HQF
A/B	*Dixit Ihesus/Benedictus*	Jo 6:35	X		X	GO	
Day Hours: Prime: Terce, Sext, None							
A/P	*Memoria fecit*	see Lauds					
A/T	*Memoria mea*	see Lauds					
R/T	*Parasti in conspectu/ Adversos eos/Gloria*	Ps 22:5		X'	X	4SNT	HQF
A/S	*Omnes eandem*	see Lauds					
R/S	*Panem angelorum/ Cibaria misit/Gloria*	Ps 77:25		X'	X	4SNT	HQF
A/N	*Qui habet aures*	see Lauds					
R/N	*Calicem salutaris/*	Ps 115:13		X'	X	POST	InMt

Second Vespers is written in the margin in a different hand and is not clearly legible.

Table 4
BNF 1143 (SIA) Ccx Office: Proper and Common Texts, Music, and Sources
(in Relation to SAS Only)
Adapted from Zawilla (1985) and Corrigan (2001)

	Title	Biblical Source	Text Source Proper to SIA	Text Source Common to SAS & SIA	Music Proper to SIA	Source of Text	Used by Aquinas	Office Source of Music
1st V								
A1	Sacerdos in eternum	Cf aPs 109:4; bGn14:18	aX	bX'	X	Innocent III	/	Trinitate
A2	Miserator dominus	Cf Ps 110:4		X'	X	POST	In1Cor11	Thoma Canterbury
A3	Calicem salutaris	Cf Ps 115: 13,17		X'	X	POST	InMt	Nicholao
A4	Sicut novelle	Cf Ps 127:3	X		X	POST	/	Nicholao
A5	Qui pacem ponit	Cf Ps 147:14	X		X	POST	/	Nicholao
R	Homo quidam fecit/	Lk 14: 16–17	X		X	POST	HQF	Katharina
	Venite comedite	V Prv 9:5		X	X	POST	InMt26 In1Cor11 In Jo6 HQF ST3	
A/M	O quam suavis/ Magnificat	Sap a12:1; b16:20 Lk 1:53	AX X	bX'	X	/ /	HQF /	Nicholao
M N1								
Inv	Christum regem/Venite	Cf Ps 21:29	X		X	/	InPs21	Andrea (Andrew)
A1	Fructum salutiferem	Cf Ps 1:3	X		X	POST	/	Thoma
A2	A fructu frumenti	Cf Ps 4:8–9	X		X	POST	InPs4	Thoma
A3	Communione calicis	Cf Ps 15:4–5	X		X	POST	/	Bernardo
R1	Immolabit hedum/	Ex 12:6–8		X'	X	4SNT	In4SNT ST 3	All Saints
	Pascha nostrum	1Cor 5:7–8	X		X	POST>1Cor	ST1–2 ST3	
R2	Comedetis carnes/ Non Moyses	Cf Ex 16: 12,15 V Jo 6:32	X	X'	X X	/ GO	/ InJo6	Stirps Iesse de S. Maria
R3	Respexit Helyas/	1Reg 19: 6–8	X		X	G Or- chelles	HQF ST3	Vespers for Purification of Mary
	Si quis mandu- caverit	V Jo 6:53–58		X'	X	Decr/4SNT POST	In4SNT HQF InJo6 ST3	
N2								
A1	Memor sit dominus	Cf Ps 19:4	X		X	POST	InPs4	Common of Virgins
A2	Paratur nobis	Cf Ps 22:5		X'	X	4SNT	HQF	Common of Martyrs
A3	In voce exultationis	Cf Ps 41:5	X		X	POST	InPs21 InPs41	Omnibus Sanctis

	Title	Biblical Source	Text Source Proper to SIA	Text Source Common to SAS & SIA	Music Proper to SIA	Source of Text	Used by Aquinas	Office Source of Music
R1	Panis quem ego dabo/	Jo a6:51–52; b6:53	BX	aX′	X	GO POST	InJo6 InMt26 In1Cor11 HQF ST3	Deus qui sedes super thronos (Quadam Domin)
	Locutus est populus	V Cf Nm 21:5	X		X	POST> Lk14	InJo6	
R2	Cenantibus illis/	Mt 26:26		X′	X	Lanfranc	In4SNT ST3	Nicholao
	Dixerunt viri	V Cf Job 31:31	X		X	John Chrysostom	InJo6 HQF	
R3	Accepit Ihesus/ memoria memor/Gloria	Lk 22:20,19 V Lament 3:20	X	X′	X X	Lanfranc Bonaventure	ST3 HQF	Bernardo
N3								
A1	Introibo ad altare Dei	Cf Ps 42:4	X		X	POST	InPs42	Ascencione
A2	Cibavit nos Dominus	Cf Ps 80:17		X′	X	POST	/	Nicholao
A3	Ex altari tuo	Cf. Ps 83:3–4	X		X	POST	/	Nicholao
R1	Qui manducat/	Jo 6:57		X′	X	Decr/4SNT	In4SNT HQF ST3	Dominico
	Non est alia	V Dt 4:7	X		X	/	HQF	
R2	Misit me pater/	Jo 6:58		X′	X	Decr/4SNT	/	Circumcisione
	Cibavit eum	V Cf Sir 15:3 (Ecc)	X		X	POST	InJo6	
R3	Unus panis/	Cf 1Cor 10:16–17		X′	X	4SNT	HQF	Nicholao
	Parasti in dulcedine/Gloria	V Cf Ps 67:7,11	X		X	Augustine	InJo6	
N4 (monastic): follows Mass in BNF 1143 (See Corrigan Transcriptions in Part II)								
A1	Memoriam fecit mirabilium	Ps 110:4–5		X		POST	In1Cor11	Maria
A2	Memoria mea in generac	Sir 24:28–29		X		POST> Jo6		Stephano
A3	Qui habet aures	Apc 2:17 (Rev)		X		G Orchelles	HQF	Katharina
R1	Melchisedech vero/ Benedictus	Gn 14:18–20		X		Decr 4SNT G Orchelles	In4SNT ST3 InJo6	Common of Virgins
R2	Calix benedictionis/ Quoniam unus panis	1Cor 10:16–17		X		4SNT	HQF	Beata Maria
R3	Ego sum panis/ Ego sum panis	Jo 6:48–51		X		GO	InMt26 In1Cor11 HQF ST3	Augustino
Lauds								
A1	Sapiencia edificavit	Prov 9:1–2		X′	X	POST	HQF	Dominico
A2	Angelorum esca	Cf Sap 16:20		X′	X	DSAM	In4SNT InJo6 HQF ST3	Dominico
A3	Pinguis est panis	Cf Gn 49:20		X′	X	G Orchelles	InJo6	Dominico

	Title	Biblical Source	Text Source Proper to SIA	Text Source Common to SAS & SIA	Music Proper to SIA	Source of Text	Used by Aquinas	Office Source of Music
A4	*Sacerdotes sancti*	Cf Lev 21:6		X'	X	/	InHbr	Annunciacione sca Marie
A5	*Vincenti dabo*	Cf Apc 2:17		X'	X	G Orchelles	HQF	Trinitate
A/M	*Ego sum panis/ Benedictus*	Jo 6:51–52		X	X	GO	InMt26 In1Cor11 HQF ST3	Dedicacione
Prime								
A	*Sapiencia edificavit*							
Terce								
A	*Angelorum esca*	see Lauds						
R	*Panem celi/ Panem angelorum/Gloria*	Ps 77:24–25		X'	X	4SNT	In4SNT InMt InJo6 HQF	
Sext								
A	*Pinguis est panis*	see Lauds						
R	*Cibavit illos*	Ps 80:17		X'	X	POST	/	
None								
A	*Vincenti dabo*	see Lauds						
R	*Educas panem/ Et vinam*	Ps 103:14–15		X'	X	P Comester	InJo6 HQF ST3	

"SOURCE OF TEXT": DOSSIER OF PRE-1264 BIBLICAL TEXTS/COMMENTARIES Adapted from Zawilla (1985)		
GO	*Glossa ordinaria*	summary of twelfth-century biblical scholarship by Anselm of Laon
POST	*Postilla*	encyclopedic commentaries by Hugh of Saint-Cher compiled by Dominicans (1230–33)
4SNT	*Sententiae in IV libris distinctae*	composed by Peter Lombard in 1158
DeCons.2 (Decr)	*Corpus iuris cononici, De cons. 2*	Gratian's selection of text on the Eucharist
SA	*Summa aurea*	William of Auxerre's commentary (1215–29)
Innocent III	*De sacramento altaris mysterio*	contemporary of Aquinas
G Orchelles	*Tract de sacramentis et summa de sacramentis*	written 1215–20
John Chrysostom		Aquinas used John Chrysostom (347–407) in his commentary on Matthew in the *Cantena aurea*
Lanfranc	*De corpore et sanguine Domine*	written 1063–1168: debate against Berengar of Tours
Hugh of St.-Victor	*De sacramentis fidei christianae*	early twelfth century
Peter Comester	*De sacramentis fidei christianae*	written 1165–70
Bonaventure	*In quartum librum sententiarum*	commentary on 4SNT written between 1245 and 1249
W Militona	*Questiones de sacramentis*	lector at Paris from 1245–53

"USED BY THOMAS": DOSSIER OF BIBLICAL TEXTS BY THOMAS Adapted from Zawilla (1985) and Torrell (1996)	
In4SNT	commentary on 4STN dating 1252–54
InJob	commentary on Job written 1261–65
Cantena aurea	commentary on the four evangelists written ca. 1262–64
SIA	Ccx office centonated in ca. 1264
InMt	commentary on Matthew written 1269–70 (second Paris regency)
In1Cor11	*reportatio* on 1 Cor 11 written 1269–72
InHbr	*reportatio* on Hebrews written 1269–72
InJo6	*reportatio* on John 6 written 1270–72
ST 1–2	*Summa theologiae* written 1265–66; 1271–72
HQF	sermon *Homo quidam fecit cenam* written between 1269 and 1272
ST3	last part of *Summa theologiae* written 1273
InPss	commentary on Psalms interrupted by death in 1263

In SAS, each responsory is a quotation from one biblical text whereas in SIA each responsory is composed of two texts, one from the Old Testament and one from the New Testament. Exceptions to this are the SIA responsories of terce, sext, and none. As is the case for the antiphons of lauds, here the composer used biblical texts common to SAS with different music. And, finally, in SAS the biblical texts are used word for word whereas in SIA they are often paraphrased, again with the noted exceptions in the fourth nocturn.[57]

While others examining his tables and data[58] might form a different conclusion, Zawilla, based on the close relationship between the two offices, corroborates Gy[59] and attributes authorship of both SAS and SIA to Aquinas. Both Gy and Zawilla explain the differences between the two offices by contrasting the theological work of Aquinas before and after Orvieto. Thus, the continuity is attributed "to a tradition to which Thomas was heir and in particular the influence of the biblical exegesis of Hugh of St. Cher."[60] The discontinuity is attributed to the influence of the *Cantena aurea*, estimated to have been written at about the same time as at least SAS, and functioning as a turning point in Thomas's theological formation. Gy, Zawilla, and Torell concur that SIA contains language about the Eucharist that is unique to Aquinas, with specific reference to his signature Aristotelian language in the SIA lections and the absence of reference to a corporeal presence.

In his analysis of the material unique to SIA, Zawilla views the relationship between SIA and the Aquinas sermon *Homo quidam fecit cenam magnam* (HQF) to be compelling evidence for the Aquinas authorship of SIA. If perhaps initially inspired by Hugh of Saint-Cher's commentary, the Aquinas sermon on Luke 14: 16 interprets the Eucharist as a three-fold supper: of sacrament, of intellect (scripture), and of will (grace). Zawilla

---

[57] Ibid., 214.

[58] Ibid., Table 7, 324–25.

[59] Gy, "Office liégeois et office romain de la Fête-Dieu," 117–26.

[60] Zawilla, *Biblical Sources of the Historia Corporis Christi*, 120.

claims: "Besides being virtually the only know medieval sermon to interpret the supper in this manner, *HFQ* cites many of the same biblical texts used in *SIA*."[61]

Five themes corroborate the thesis of a common author for SIA and HFQ. First, biblical texts used in SIA intersect with those used in HQF. Second, biblical texts are paraphrased for artistic effect in SIA. Biblical texts likewise are paraphrased in HQF. Third, the matins responsories are organized systematically in an alternation of reflections on the Old and New Testaments. This is a central theme in HQF: "In ista refeccione et est prandium et est cena. Prandium est refeccio sacramentalis in ueteri testamento, cena in nouo testamento"[62] [In this refreshment there is both a dinner and a supper. Dinner is the sacramental refreshment in the Old Testament; supper is in the New Testament]. Fourth, SIA "is highly stylized with prayers which move from past (*Deus qui*), to the present (*Ecclesie tue*), to the future tense (*Fac nos*)."[63] In HQF, this describes the source of delight in the supper: "Delectacio causatur ex tribus, ex momoria preteritorum, ex spe futurorum et ex sensu presencium"[64] [This delight is caused by three sources: from the memory of past things, from the hope of the future, and from the experience of the present]. And, finally, thematic content, such as musical borrowings in SIA, creates a textual/musical imagery for theological ideas in HQF.

THE NEW CRITICAL EDITIONS

Contemporary scholars have corroborated the initial identification of three versions of the office for the feast of Corpus Christi: *Animarum cibus, Sapiencia (a)edificavit sibi* (SAS), and *Sacerdos in (a)eternum* (SIA). In his most recent article,[65] Gy views the office composed at Mont Cornillon as most certainly dating before the two later versions and as most appropriate to the context of early scholasticism. Relying to a certain extent on the work of Cottiaux,[66] he notes that the early office is replete with quotations from Alger of Liège and other early scholastics, who argued against Berengar and his initially heretical interpretation of the Eucharist as a spiritual presence. Gy concludes that the later two offices, but especially SIA, represent the summit of high scholasticism and a new set of theological principles eventually articulated in the discursive writings of Aquinas in the Second Part of *Summa Theologica*. Thus Gy interprets the three offices as evidence of a linear progression from the early scholastic theologians, a progression culminating in the work of Saint Thomas.

The new critical editions by Corrigan reveal that the early Liège office as found in KB 70.E.4 may be less systematic in its theological content than suggested by Gy. Rather, its texts constitute a pastiche drawn from a number of authors across a period of more than two hundred years: Alger of Liège, Hugh of Saint-Victor, Gratian, and Jacques de Vitry. While each of these authors wrote against heretical interpretations of the Eucharist, they do not present a unified interpretation of the Real Presence as nec-

---

[61] Ibid., 231.

[62] Saint Thomas Aquinas, "Sermo Homo quidam fecit cenam magnam," ed. L.-J. Bataillon, *Revue des Sciences Philosopohiques et Théologiques* 63 (1983); see note 50. Also available online at http://www.corpusthomisticum.org/hhf.html

[63] Miri Rubin, *Corpus Christi: The Eucharist in Late Medieval Culture* (Cambridge: Cambridge University Press, 1991), 188.

[64] Saint Thomas Aquinas, "Sermo Homo quidam fecit cenam magnam."

[65] Gy, "Office liégeois et office romain de la Fête-Dieu."

[66] Cottiaux, "L'Office liégeois de la Fête-Dieu."

essarily corporeal. Highlighting this lack of consistency, each document introducing the feast of Corpus Christi to a new audience specifically mentions a rationale that includes combating the error of heretics: Bishop Robert Thourette's letter, Hugh of Saint-Cher's letter, and the three redactions of the papal bull *Transiturus*. Only Urban IV's *Transiturus* refers specifically to a corporeal presence.[67] Another specific reference to the idea of a corporeal presence in the original office from Liège was noted by Zawilla.[68] The reference appears in the prayer at lauds in the critical edition by Lambot and Fransen.[69] However, this prayer does not appear in the actual KB 70.E.4 manuscript. Rather, it was taken from an 1846 publication by Lavalleye[70] and inserted as a hypothesis into the lauds office as part of Lambot and Fransen's goal of producing a critical edition of the entire office.[71] The methodological issue is similar to the one discussed by Wright in relationship to the Jesus seminar.[72] The authors decided on an interpretation of the office and then selected material that fit the interpretation. They cannot, therefore, argue that the added material supports their initial interpretation.

Moreover, there is far more continuity between the early Liège office and the later versions than prior scholars have noted. First, the Victorine sequence in KB 70.E.4, *Laureata plebs fidelis*, refers to, without directly quoting, many of the biblical passages that shape the *historia* of later versions of the office: Melchisedech (Gen 14: 18–19), Aser (Gen 49: 20), the pascal lamb (Ex 12: 6–7 and 8–9); and the manna in the desert (Ex 16: 15). None of these is proper to SAS. Second, the sequence has its musical source in an *Alleluia* and *prosula*, which was also used in the famous sequence *Lauda Syon* in BNF 1143 (SIA): *Alleluia dulce lignum*. A tenth-century *Alleluia* provided musical motifs shared by both offices, and this apparent melodic borrowing may have resulted in similarities between the early Liège sequence and the popular Parisian sequence, *Laudes cruces*, composed in the twelfth century to celebrate the finding of the true cross. *Lauda Syon* from SIA was a text contrafactum to its music. Third, a number of source chants in SIA point to the Liège source, especially the items in the fourth nocturn: three musical items, including the initial antiphon *Sacerdos in [a]eternum*, are contrafacta to chants from the Liège office of the Trinity; seven musical items use source chants from the office of Saint Nicholas, the dedication name for the church of Marie D'Oignie and the *béguines* in the diocese of Liège; two musical items relate to themes prominent in the *Ave* prayers found in the Mosan psalters, *Paradisi porta de sca Maria* and *Solem iusticie regem paritura suppremum Stella Maria maris;* a

---

[67] See Gary Macy, *Treasures from the Storehouse: Medieval Religion and the Eucharist* (Collegeville, MN: The Liturgical Press, 1999); see also Brian Stock, *The Implications of Literacy: Written Language and Models of Interpretation in the Eleventh and Twelfth Centuries* (Princeton: Princeton University Press, 1983).

[68] Zawilla, *Biblical Sources of the Historia Corporis Christi*, 19.

[69] Lambot and Fransen, *L'Office de la Fête-Dieu primitive*, 65: "Deus qui gloriosum corporis et sanguinis Domini nostri Iesu Christi mysterium nobiscum manere voluisti, da nobis quaesumus eius praesentiam corporalem ita venerari in terris, ut de eius visione gaudere mereamur in caelis."

[70] See Lambot and Fransen, *L'Office de la Fête-Dieu primitive*, 95.

[71] On this complex topic, see Joseph Dyer, "The 'Rite Way' of Studying the Old Roman and Gregorian Tradition" (Paper delivered at the International Congress of Medieval Studies, Kalamazoo, MI, 2004); see also *The Divine Office in the Latin Middle Ages: Methodology and Source Studies, Regional Developments, Hagiography*, ed. Margot E. Fassler and Rebecca A. Baltzer (New York: Oxford University Press, 2000).

[72] N. T. Wright, *Jesus and the Victory of God* (Minneapolis, MN: Fortress Press, 1996).

number of other musical items use source chants that relate to themes prominent in the community of women, the Tree of Jesse, the Purification of Mary, the Ascension, the Annunciation. And, finally, Corrigan has identified manuscripts with evidence of the inevitable meeting of *Animarum cibus* and *Sacerdos in [a]eternum*.[73] Taken together, these factors suggest a shared religious culture, interdependent communities, and supportive coexistence during the thirteenth century, rather than dominance and succession, which most likely occurred only after the Council of Trent.

Certainly there are different versions of the Eucharist and different levels of literacy manifest in the three versions. *Animarum cibus* is simpler; the texts do not distinguish between phenomenon and appearance as presence in the Eucharist, a view characteristic of the earlier period from which the texts were drawn. Christ and the Holy Spirit simply are really present, and this understanding supported the community liturgical celebration, as well as the spiritual autonomy of women. In contrast, Corrigan's work on BNF 1143, which identifies the source of each chant and provides the complete musical-text setting for both the chant and its source, demonstrates a far higher level of expression than previously described matter-of-factly as late scholastic. This version goes well beyond a doctrinal statement of transubstantiation, although this, too, is included in the famous homily by Saint Thomas. His version of the liturgy transcends the discursive reasoning characteristic of High Medieval scholasticism and even his late works, including the sermon *Homo quidem fecit cenam.*

Both Juliana and Saint Thomas would have contemned the irony of history and uses to which their works were put both contemporaneously in different geographic locations and later more broadly throughout Europe. Both were religious thinkers who chose contemplation rather than collaboration with an institutional epicenter of Crown and Church. A generation of scholars will find ample resources within the details of their work for continued research on problems of dating and interpretations of meaning.

---

[73] Vincent Corrigan, "Travel and Transformation: The Corpus Christi Office in Germany" (Paper delivered at the 23rd Annual Medieval Forum, Plymouth, NH: Plymouth State College, 19–29 April 2002).

CRITICAL EDITIONS OF THE LITURGICAL MANUSCRIPTS

Vincent Corrigan

THE MANUSCRIPTS

Included in this chapter are editions of seven late-thirteenth- and fourteenth-century manuscripts that are generally regarded as the central musical sources for the Corpus Christi office.[1] Although the dates of these sources are still a matter of conjecture, they seem to come from the period 1269–1320. Together these seven manuscripts transmit a record of the three major offices. The Hague, National Library of the Netherlands, MS 70.E.4 (KB 70.E.4) contains the "original office," *Animarum cibus*. *Sapiencia [a]edificavit* is preserved in Prague, Abbey of Strahov, MS D.E.I.7 (Strahov). The Roman office attributed to Saint Thomas Aquinas is preserved in Paris, Bibliothèque nationale de France, lat. 1143 (BNF 1143). Graz, Universitätsbibliothek, MS 134 (Graz 134) contains the entire BNF 1143 service in monastic format, but in staffless unheighted notation. The solo portions of the BNF 1143 responsories are transmitted in Brussels, Bibliothèque royale, 139 (BR 139). BR 139 also records an alternative set of responsories based on the office for Saint Dominic. The service derived from the Dominic office in BR 139 is of the same type as *Animarum cibus*, that is, an independent liturgy with no relation to BNF 1143. Strahov, *Sapiencia [a]edificavit*, likewise may have been an independent service, but some of its texts and music were incorporated into the standard service, embodied first in BNF 1143. Both Brigham Young University, Special Collections, Harold B. Lee Library, *Regimen animarum* (BYU) and Edinburgh University Library, MS 211.iv, the Inchcolm Antiphonary (EU) contain variations on the prototype in BNF 1143.

BYU and EU contain versions of *Sacerdos in eternum* that differ from each other and from the central sources in many ways. Four of the central sources, KB 70.E.4, Strahov, BNF 1143, and Graz 134, contain music for all or nearly all of the service. BR 139 contains only the solo portions of the responsories and an invitatory. This chapter first discusses the musical contents of each manuscript, beginning with the "original" office

---

[1] See L. M. J. Delaissé, "A la recherche des origines de l'office du Corpus Christi dans les manuscrits liturgiques," *Scriptorium* 4 (1950), 220–39; Cyrille Lambot, "L'office de la Fête-Dieu: Aperçus nouveaux sur ses origines," *Revue bénédictine* 54 (1942), 61–123.

and ending with the various versions of *Sacerdos in eternum*. It then presents a transcription of the text and music from each manuscript.

THE HAGUE, NATIONAL LIBRARY OF THE NETHERLANDS, KB 70.E.4

128 fols. in 5 gatherings of different eras and formats; 29 x 19 cm (1st gathering only)

KB 70.E.4 is a composite manuscript from the thirteenth century and contains parts originally distinct but grouped together in 1537 at Tongres.[2] The manuscript contains material for the Corpus Christi service in two different places. The lections occupy folios 52 to 63v, while the music for the office is found on folios 86–96v. According to Lambot, this service, beginning with the antiphon *Animarum cibus*, may be the original Corpus Christi service composed by Juliana of Mont Cornillon for the first celebration of the feast in Liège in 1246.[3]

The office is a secular one in the standard format of three nocturns at Matins, each composed of three antiphons and three responsories. There is some evidence of modal organization, suggesting a deliberate compositional strategy, but it is not of the standard sort that ascends through all the modes, returning to the first mode at the end. Here the antiphons at Vespers and Lauds, and the antiphons and responsories at Matins, begin in the normal way but deviate from the pattern shortly thereafter. These deviations often arise from what appears to be an avoidance of mode 4. The only mode 4 piece is the 2 Vespers antiphon *Ore quidem*. Elsewhere, wherever that mode should occur (1 Vespers, antiphon 4; Matins nocturn 2, antiphon 1) it is replaced by another mode.[4]

At the conclusion of the office services are two independent pieces, the Victorine Mass sequence *Laureata plebs fidelis*,[5] and the single hymn *Ad cenam agni providi*, which presumably was to be sung at Vespers, Matins, and Lauds where the hymn should fall. No other hymns are mentioned in the manuscript.

[2] Cyrille Lambot and Irenée Fransen, *L'Office de la Fête-Dieu primitive. Textes et mélodies retrouvés* (Maredsous: Editions de Maredsous, 1946). This contains an edition of the music and text, and a detailed descrtiption of the entire manuscipt (99–101).

[3] See Lambot and Fransen, *L'Office de la Fête-Dieu primitive*, 9–37. See also Peter Browe, *Textus antiqui de festo Corporis Christi*, Opuscula et textus, series liturgica IV (Münster: Aschendorff, 1934), 12–13. This contains those portions of Juliana's *vita* which relate to the feast of Corpus Christi. See *The Life of Juliana of Mont Cornillon*, trans. Barbara Newman (Toronto: Peregrina, 1988); and, more recently, *Vie de Sainte Julienne de Cornillon*, Critical Edition, vol. 2 of *Fête-Dieu (1246–1996)*, ed. Jean-Pierre Delville (Louvain-la-Neuve: Institut d'Études Médiévales de l'Université Catholique de Louvain, 1999).

[4] See Andrew Hughes, "Modal Order and Disorder in the Rhymed Office," *Musica disciplina* 37 (1983), 29–43.

[5] On the Victorine sequence in general, see Margot Fassler, *Gothic Song: Victorine Sequences and Augustinian Reform in Twelfth-Century Paris* (Cambridge: Cambridge University Press, 1993).

Table 5
Office for Corpus Christi in KB 70.E.4

FIRST VESPERS

A. Animarum cibus
A. Discipulis competentem
A. Totum Cristus
A. Et sic
A. Panem angelorum
R. Sacerdos summus/Leta laudum
V. Notum fecit
Mag. A. Dominus Ihesus Cristus

MATINS

Inv. Cristum regum regem

FIRST NOCTURN

A. Suo Cristus
A. Visibilis creature
A. Sanguis eius
R. Invisibilis sacerdos/Ipse conviva
R. Dixit Ihesus/Nisi meam
R. Vere mira/Hoc celesti/Gloria patri

SECOND NOCTURN

A. Hostia Cristus
A. Hic et ibi
A. Verus Deus
R. Ad ipsius/Suam carnem
R. Alieni/Viva vivo
R. [Sacerdos summus/Leta laudum/Gloria patri]

THIRD NOCTURN

A. Dominus Ihesus
A. Sacri ministerio
A. Hec igitur
R. Cristus corpus/Ut perhennis
R. O vere miraculum/Vere bonus
R. Panis vive/Ideoque tu/Gloria patri
[Te Deum]

LAUDS

A. Celestis artificio
A. Cristus enim
A. Illa nobis
A. Nulla nobis
A. Ecce vobiscum
Bene. A. Panis vite

SECOND VESPERS

A. Sacramentum pietatis
A. Misterii veritatem
A. Qui semel
A. Ore quidem
A. Ore vero
R. Ad nutum/Ubi virtus
Mag. A. Ihesu bone

[VARIAE]

Seq. Laureata plebs fidelis
H. Ad cenam agni providi

PRAGUE, ABBEY OF STRAHOV, MS D.E.I.7 (HUGHES LMLO XCXO)[6]

Parchment; 328 numbered folios and 1 unnumbered folio after fol. 155; 23 x 36 cm (writing area only)

Strahov is a Premonstratensian breviary for the *Temporale*, dating, perhaps from the mid-fourteenth century, although the date remains uncertain.[7] There is no indication of contemporaneous foliation in the manuscript, but the pages have been cropped and so an original foliation, if there was one, has been lost. There is a foliation in modern hand, containing some errors,[8] that runs from folio 1 to folio 328v. The library seal *Strahoviensis Bibliothecae* appears on folio 1 and here and there throughout the manuscript. The shelf number also is written in modern hand at the top of folio 1.[9]

Szendrei gives a comprehensive description of the manuscript, so only that portion of the manuscript containing the Corpus Christi service is described here.[10] This material is part of an addition to the main body of the manuscript comprising folios 206–222v and was inserted at very nearly the same time the manuscript was copied. The addition contains material for both Trinity Sunday and Corpus Christi. The Corpus Christi office begins on folio 213v and extends through much of folio 221; it is immediately followed on folio 221 by the First Sunday after Pentecost.[11] Originally the manuscript had a heading for the beginning of Corpus Christi, but much of it has been lost because of cropping.

The liturgy is monastic, but its structure is unusual. Instead of three nocturns of 6+6+1 antiphons and 4+4+4 responsories, this service has four nocturns with three antiphons and three responsories each, as well as the necessary lections. Someone later provided marginal annotations to these lections, assigning them to the various ferias.

---

[6] See Andrew Hughes, *Late Medieval Liturgical Offices* (Toronto: Pontifical Institute of Mediaeval Studies, 1994), [126–27].

[7] The Order of Premonstratensians (Norbertines) was founded in 1120 following the Rule of St. Augustine. Henry Zdik, bishop of Olmütz (d. 1150), established the Abbey of Mt. Syon at Strahov, Prague, in 1140, and it became a center for Premonstratensians. It was burned in 1258 and destroyed by the Hussites in 1420.

[8] For example, an erroneous entry 93 has been crossed over and replaced by 94, and some sheets were bound upside down before the folio numbers were added (e.g., fols. 10, 15).

[9] A facsimile is available: Janka Szendrei, *Breviarium notatum Strigoniense: saeculi XIII*, Musicalia Danubiana 17 (Budapest: Magyar Tudományos Akadémia Zenetudomáhyi Intézet, 1998).

[10] See Szendrei, *Breviarum*, 40–42.

[11] Lambot ("L'Office de la Fête-Dieu," 88), Delaissé ("A la recherche," 226), and Thomas J. Mathiesen ("'The Office of the New Feast of Corpus Christi' in the Regimen Animarum at Brigham Young University," *The Journal of Musicology* 2 [1983], 15, 23) all say that the service extends from fol. 427v to fol. 443, and on that basis Delaissé concludes that the service is a late addition to the manuscript. The erroneous foliation stems from Lambot. However, he never stated that he saw the manuscript, only that the abbot G. Beyssac communicated the contents to him with permission to publish. I think that Beyssac mistook page numbers for folio numbers. Fol. 213v would equal p. 427, and the service begins on the verso side. To translate the Beyssac/Lambot numbers into the manuscript folios, divide the even numbers by two; odd numbers are the verso sides of the preceding even numbers. Thus Beyssac/Lambot 432 equals MS fol. 216r, and 433 equals 216v.

Table 6
Musical Portions of the Corpus Christi Service in Strahov

FIRST VESPERS

A. Sapiencia edificavit
A. Melchisedech rex Salem
A. Immolabit edum
A. Et edent carnes
A. Pluit illis
R. [Cumque operuisset][12]
H. Pange lingua
Mag. A. Angelorum esca

MATINS

Inv. Venite comedite
H. Sacris sollempniis

FIRST NOCTURN

A. Numquid poterit
A. Parasti in conspectu
A. De fructu operum
R. Cenantibus discipulis/Hic est sanguis
R. Accepto pane/Similiter et calicem
R. Manducantibus discipulis/Et ait illis

SECOND NOCTURN

A. Faciens mensam
A. Sacerdotes sancti
A. Faciet Dominus
R. Dominus Ihesus/Similiter et calicem
R. Quicumque manducaverit/Qui enim manducat
R. Calix benedictionis/Quoniam unus panis/Gloria patri

THIRD NOCTURN

A. Tulit Manue
A. Erit quasi oliva
A. Quid enim bonum
R. Ego sum/Ego sum/Gloria patri
R. Amen, amen/Caro enim/Gloria patri
R. Sicut vivens/Non sicut patres/Gloria patri

FOURTH NOCTURN[13]

A. Extendit Jonathas
A. Comede fili mi
A. Venite emite
R. Melchisedech viro [sic]/Benedictus Abraham
R. Immolabit hedum/Et edent
R. Cumque operuisset/Iste est panis/Gloria patri

LAUDS

A. Memoriam fecit
A. Memoria mea
A. Omnes eandem
A. Nolo vos socios
A. Qui habet aures
H. Verbum supernum prodiens
Bene. A. Dixit Ihesus

---

[12] Items in brackets show portions that are indicated by incipit only.

[13] There are staves for the three antiphons, but no music was ever entered on them.

PRIME

A. [Memoriam fecit]

TERCE

A. [Memoria mea]
R. Parasti in conspectu

SEXT

A. [Omnes eandem]
R. Panem angelorum

NONES

A. [Qui habet aures]
R. Calicem salutaris

SECOND VESPERS[14]

R. [Ego sum panis v(ite)]
Mag. A. Amen, amen dico vobis

Three of Strahov's antiphons (*Memoriam fecit, Memoria mea,* and *Qui habet aures*) and three of its responsories (*Calix benedictionis, Ego sum,* and *Melchisedech viro* (*sic* for *vero*) are common to BNF 1143, where they are included in the fourth nocturn. The hymn *Pange lingua* is also common to BNF 1143. All of the pieces in BNF 1143 are contrafacta of existing chants, and the presence of these seven concordances in Strahov shows that the process of adapting these particular chants to the new texts must have been in place when the Strahov liturgy was constructed. It turns out that seven other items in Strahov are melodically identical to existing chants; these are listed in Table 7.

Table 7
Additional Contrafacta in the Strahov Manuscript

FIRST VESPERS

A3	Immolabit edum	Beata Dei genetrix, Office of BVM, WA 361, Wales 249v
A4	Et edent carnes	Tu decus virgineum, antiphons of the BVM throughout the year, Pm 271
A6	Angelorum esca/Magnificat\	O Christi pietas, Office of St. Nicholas; C.f. O quam suavis, BNF 1143 fol. 2v (#10)

MATINS

SECOND NOCTURN

A11	Sacerdotes sancti	Pater manifestavi, Ascension, Strahov fol. 190v; LA 244 (NOT Wales and WA)
R4	Dominus Ihesus/ Similiter et calicem	Ecce iam coram, St. Stephen, Pm 31

THIRD NOCTURN

A15	Quid enim bonum	O quam gloriosum est regnum, Utrecht 31v

---

[14] The Second Vespers material was written by a later hand in the margin and is very difficult to read. The responsory *Amen, amen* is likewise a later addition, written across the bottom of the page and nearly illegible.

SECOND VESPERS

A22	Amen, amen/Magnificat	Benedictus Dominus, Office of St. Bernard; C.f. O sacrum convivium, BNF 1143 fol. 16v (#74)

Only one of these sources, *Pater manifestavi*, is part of the Strahov manuscript. This may imply that the other chants, or at least their texts, were imported from elsewhere and were not part of the standard liturgy at the abbey. At the same time, the Strahov manuscript contains only feasts of the *Temporale*, and the source melodies may have been part of the *Sanctorale*, as is the case for BNF 1143. Most interesting are the two Magnificat antiphons *Angelorum esca* and *Amen, amen*, which have the same the melodies and liturgical placement as the Magnificat antiphons in BNF 1143, but different texts. If we add the seven other pieces that Strahov shares with BNF 1143, we arrive at a total of 14 pieces, about one-third of the musical items in Strahov, which are contrafacta. This encourages the speculation that the entirety of Strahov is composed of contrafacta, just like the service in BNF 1143. Perhaps construction by contrafacta was characteristic of the Roman curia, and these two services show different manifestations of the same procedure.

Two other responsories, *Immolabit edum* and *Cenantibus discipulis*, have responsory texts similar to those in BNF 1143, but the verses are completely different, as are the melodies. The Matins hymn *Sacris sollempniis* agrees with the version in Graz 134, but not with the other versions. The notation is sometimes difficult to read, and the relationship of the notes to the syllables unclear. The melodic lines are often remarkably disjunct (see #33 over *corporis*), giving a passion in expression not found in the standard service.

PARIS, BIBLIOTHÈQUE NATIONALE DE FRANCE, LAT. 1143 (HUGHES LMLO XCX)

Parchment; 33 fols. in 2 cols.; 24 x 16.5 cm

BNF 1143 is a small manuscript devoted exclusively to Corpus Christi, dating anywhere from the second half of the thirteenth century to the early fourteenth century. Its importance is two-fold: it is the first extant version of much of Office C, and it contains marginal annotations to the melodies indicating their sources.

These annotations, which extend through the manuscript, are present whenever a new text has been added to a pre-existing tune. When the text has not been changed, as, for instance, in the Gradual, no annotation appears. However, all melodies in the service are taken from other feasts. These sources are given in Table 8.

Table 8
Office for Corpus Christi in BNF 1143 and Sources for its Chants

FIRST VESPERS

A. Sacerdos in eternum	Contra Gloria tibi Trinitas de Trinitate
A. Miserator Dominus	Contra Totus orbis de sco Thoma
A. Calicem salutaris	Contra Pudore bono de sco Nicholao
A. Sicut novelle	Contra Iuste et sancte vivendo de sco Nicholao

A. Qui pacem ponit   Contra Innocenter puerilia iura de sco Nicholao
R. Homo quidam   Contra Virgo flagellatur de sca Katharina
H. Pange lingua   Contra Pange lingua gloriosi prelium
                              certaminis in passione Domini
Mag. A. O quam suavis   Contra O Christi pietas de sco Nicholao

MATINS

Inv. Christum regem   Contra Christum regem regum adoremus
                              Dominum de sco Andrea
H. Sacris sollempniis   Contra Sanctorum meritis

FIRST NOCTURN

A. Fructum salutiferum   Contra Granum cadens [*sic* for *cadit*] de sco Thoma
A. A fructu frumenti   Contra Novus homo [actually Monachus sub
                              clerico] de sco Thoma
A. Communione calicis   Contra Crescente etate de sco Bernardo
R. Immolabit hedum   Contra Te sanctum Dominum de Angelis
R. Comedetis carnes   Contra Stirps Iesse de sca Maria
R. Respexit Helyas   Contra Videte miraculum matris Domini

SECOND NOCTURN

A. Memor sit Dominus   Contra In celis gaudent virgines et cantant
                              canticum [Common of Virgins]
A. Paratur nobis   Contra Sanguis sanctorum martyrum pro Christo
                              effusus est in terra [Common of Martyrs]
A. In voce exultationis   Contra O quam gloriosum est regnum de
                              Omnibus Sanctis
R. Panis quem   Contra Deus qui sedes super thronos [*sic* for
                              thronum] et iudicas de Quadam Dominica
R. Cenantibus illis   Contra Qui cum audissent de sco Nicholao
R. Accepit Ihesus   Contra Virtute multa de sco Bernardo

THIRD NOCTURN

A. Introibo ad altare Dei   Contra Ascendo ad Patrem meum de Ascencione
A. Cibavit nos Dominus   Contra O per omnia laudabilem virum de
                              sco Nicholao
A. Ex altari tuo   Contra Gloriam mundi sprevit de sco Nicholao
R. Qui manducat   Contra Felix vitis de sco Dominico
R. Misit me pater   Contra Verbum caro factum est de Circumcisione
R. Unus panis   Contra Ex eius tumba de sco Nicholao

LAUDS

A. Sapiencia edificavit   Contra Adest dies de sco Dominico
A. Angelorum esca   Contra Pauper esca [*sic* for *Pauper in peculio*]
                              de sco Dominico
A. Pinguis est panis   Contra Scala celo de sco Dominico
A. Sacerdotes sancti   Contra Ingressus angelus de Annunciacione
                              sce Marie
A. Vincenti dabo   Contra Ex quo omnia de Trinitate
H. Verbum supernum   Contra Eterne rex altissime de Ascensione
Bene. A. Ego sum panis   Contra Pax eterna de Dedicacione

SECOND VESPERS

Mag. A. O sacrum convivium   Contra Benedictus Dominus Deus patris nostri
                              de sco Bernardo

MASS

Introit: Cibavit eos   [Feria II post Pentecost "ad sanctum Petrum"]
Kyrie   Fons bonitatis   [Mass II]
Gloria   [Mass IV]

Gradual:	Oculi omnium	[Feria V post Domin. III. Quadragesime]
Alleluia:	Caro mea	Contra Nativitas gloriose de sca Maria
Prosa:	Lauda Syon	Contra Laudes crucis attollamus de sca cruce
Offert.:	Sacerdotes incensum	Contra Confirma hoc D[eus] de sco Spiritu
Sanctus		[Mass IV]
Agnus Dei		[Mass IV]
Comm.:	Quocienscumque	Contra Factus est repente de sco Spiritu

FOURTH NOCTURN "PRO MONACHIS"

A. Memoriam fecit	Contra Paradisi porta de sca Maria
A. Memoria mea	Contra Patefacte sunt ianue celi de sco Stephano
A. Qui habet aures	Contra Post plurima supplicia martyr alma de sca Katharina
R. Melchisedech vero	Contra Regnum mundi de Virginibus
R. Calix benedictionis	Contra Solem iusticie regem de Beata Maria
R. Ego sum	Contra Vulneraverat caritas Christi cor eius de sco Augustino

It often is said that BNF 1143 contains the earliest version of the standard service, but a comparison with EU and BYU show that this is only partially true. The texts in BNF 1143 are those of the standard service, but some of the melodies are not. This indicates that the text stabilized earlier than the melodies, which continued to vary well into the fourteenth century. In some cases (*Memor sit Dominus*, *Paratur nobis*, *Accepit Ihesus*), new melodies replaced the ones in BNF 1143. Even when the melodies are clearly related (*In voce exultationis*), there are differences in how the source melody is arranged for the new text.

GRAZ, UNIVERSITÄTSBIBLIOTHEK, MS 134

Parchment; 548 folios; 36 x 24 cm

This is a breviary from the Benedictine abbey of Saint Lambert dating from ca. 1280, in which the Corpus Christi office extends from folio 241 to 246, with lections for the octave following. The music is written in unheighted neumes, surprising for such a late date.[15]

The version in Graz is the standard office, but in a monastic format, and includes an antiphon for Compline, the only early source to do so.[16]

---

[15] A complete description of the manuscript (size, contents, bibliography, etc.) by Hans Zotter is available online at http://www-ub.kfunigraz.ac.at/SOSA/katalog/katalog-frame.html. Many other Graz manuscripts have material of relevance to Corpus Christi studies. To cite a few:
  Graz 56, a Benedictine breviary from St. Lambert (ca. late 12th c.) contains, as an addition from about 1300, lections for Corpus Christi (*In festo corporis et sanguinis dni.*) between fols. 338 and 347v.
  Graz 65, fols. 186–93, contains a copy of Urban's bull establishing the feast.
  The first part of Graz 83 contains lections for Corpus Christi added in the14th c.
  Copies of Hugh of St.-Victor's *De sacramentis* are found in Graz 101 and 149.
  Graz 171 contains five sections on Corpus Christi between fols. 44 and 120v, including ones by Augustine and Paschasius Radbertus.
  Graz 114, 129, 1226, and 1254 transmit the first four antiphons of the Liège office. See Kern, "Das Offizium *De Corpore Christi*," esp. 56–57.

[16] The Edinburgh MS also contains a Compline antiphon, but it is not the same as this one.

Table 9
Office for Corpus Christi in Graz 134

FIRST VESPERS

A. Sacerdos in eternum
A. Miserator Dominus
A. Calicem salutaris
A. Sicut novelle
A. Qui pacem ponit
R. Homo quidam
[H. Pange lingua][17]
Mag. A. O quam suavis

MATINS

Inv. Christum regem
[H. Sacris sollempniis]

FIRST NOCTURN

A. Fructum salutiferum
A. A fructu frumenti
A. Communione calicis
A. Memor sit Dominus
A. Paratur nobis
A. In voce exultationis
V. [Panem celi dedit eis][18]
R. Immolabit hedum/Pascha nostrum
R. Panis quem/Locutus est
R. Comedetis carnes/Non Moyses
R. Respexit Helyas/Si quis manducaverit/Gloria patri

SECOND NOCTURN

A. Introibo ad altare Dei
A. Cibavit nos Dominus
A. Ex altari tuo Domine
A. Memoriam fecit
A. Memoria mea
A. Qui habet aures
V. Pecierunt et . . .
R. Misit me pater/Cibavit eum
R. Cenantibus illis/Dixerunt viri
R. Qui manducat/Non est alia
R. Accepit Ihesus/Memoria memor/Gloria patri

THIRD NOCTURN

Ad Cant. A. Comedi favum
V. [Educas panem]
R. Unus panis/Parasti in dulcedine
R. Melchisedech vero/Benedictus Abraham
R. Calix benedictionis/Quoniam unus panis
R. Ego sum/Ego sum/Gloria patri

---

[17] Graz 134 contains the complete text for the hymns (*Pange lingua, Sacris sollempniis*), but only *Sacris sollempniis* carries music.

[18] Space was left for neumes for this versicle, but none were entered.

LAUDS

A. Sapientia edificavit
A. Angelorum esca
A. Pinguis est panis
A. Sacerdotes sancti
A. Vincenti dabo
V. Panem de celo/Omne delectamentum
[H. Verbum supernum]
[V. Posuit fines]
Bene. A. Ego sum panis

PRIME

A. Sapientia

TERCE[19]

SEXT

NONES

SECOND VESPERS

Mag. A. O sacrum convivium

COMPLINE

Nunc dimittis A. O gustu mirabilis

Because of the notation used in the manuscript, it is not possible to transcribe this source in the same way that other sources can be transcribed. However it is possible to recognize when the sequence of notational symbols matches other sources, where pitch is notated precisely, and, more importantly, where it does not match. The method is to compare each piece in Graz 134 with versions preserved in the other sources. Kern believed that such a comparison would show that the Graz 134 melodies corresponded exactly to the version in BNF 1143.[20] However, this is not entirely the case. The Matins hymn *Sacris sollempniis* follows the Strahov melody and no other, and the Matins Nocturn 1 antiphons *Memor sit* and *Paratur nobis* agree only with the Inchcolm Antiphonary.

Again because of the notation, it is not possible to read the melodies to the Nocturn 3 antiphon *Comedi favum*, the Lauds short responsory *Panem de celo*, or the Compline antiphon *O gustu mirabilis*. Further work may unearth concordances for the last two of these, but a melodic source for *Comedi favum* has appeared. The Worcester Antiphonary uses this text and melody for Matins on the Feast of the Assumption, Nocturn II, the second of the six antiphons (WA 355). The placement of single notes, two-note figures, and melismas, is nearly identical to the pattern in Graz 134.

---

[19] Items for Terce, Sext, and Nones are indicated by incipit and contain no music. Texts for some of the prayers and chapters are given complete.

[20] Kern, "Das Offizium *De Corpore Christi*," 48–49.

BRUSSELS, BIBLIOTHÈQUE ROYALE, 139
(ALTERNATIVE SERVICE: HUGHES LMLO XCX4)

Parchment; 219 ff.; 35 x 23 cm

This is a Dominican cantatory from Marienthal, dated from 1269 on the basis of the following inscription on folio 218: "Hunc librum fecit priorissa soror Yoles viennensis scribi sororibus in valle sancte Marie anno domini mcc lxix ut habetur ibi in memoriam sui" [Prioress sister Yoles of Vienne had this book made for the sisters in Marienthal in the year 1269 to be held there in her memory]. 'Yoles' may be Yolanda von Vianden, the daughter of Heinrich von Vianden and Margareta, who was born in 1231. She became a Dominican nun and entered the recently founded cloister of Marienthal on 6 January 1248, assuming the position of prioress in 1258. She died on 17 December 1283.[21]

There is an overall division in the manuscript between the office and the Mass, and each section is subdivided into the *Temporale* and the *Sanctorale*. The manuscript begins with recitation formulas for the Gloria in all modes. There follow invitatories with the psalm *Venite* in seven modes; separate invitatories are given for the period from Christmas through Epiphany and for Easter. The *Temporale* begins with Lauds antiphons for the Christmas vigil and concludes with Trinity Sunday and the office for the dedication of a church.

The *Sanctorale* portion of the office begins on folio 47 with the feast of Saint Andrew and extends through the feast of Katherine on folio 98. It contains entries for the Translation of Dominic (fol. 63v) and Dominic's feast (fol. 73). This is followed by the Common of One or Several Apostles. It closes with the Common of Confessors (fol. 99v), which concludes in the middle of folio 100. This is the end of the original office portion of the manuscript.

The Corpus Christi section is part of a series of leaves (fols. 100v and 114v) that contain a potpourri of Mass and office items that Delaissé thought were added between 1269 and 1323.[22] The manuscript actually contains two Corpus Christi offices, one corresponding to the standard office and a second based on the office for Saint Dominic.[23] The first, with no heading, extends from folio 107 through 108v and contains the solo portions of the Matins responsories and the 2 Vespers responsory for the standard office. The second, with the heading "De sacramento" covers folios 109–10 and contains the invitatory and nine Matins responsories to the service patterned on the office for Saint Dominic. This is followed by more office and Mass pieces, concluding with the Mass for Aquinas on folios 111–113v[24] and the Commemoration of Saint Paul on folio 114.

---

[21] This description is drawn from Hieronymus Wilms O.P., *Geschichte der deutschen Dominikanerinnen: 1206–1916.* (Dülman i. W.: A. Laumann, 1920), 59–61.

[22] See Delaissé "A la recherche," 220–39; Lambot, "L'Office de la Fête-Dieu," 61–123; Mathiesen, "The New Feast of Corpus Christi," 21.

[23] The Corpus Christi office text was edited by Guido M. Dreves and Clemens Blume, *Analecta Hymnica medii aevi*, 55 vols. (Leipzig, 1886–1922; repr. New York: Johnson Reprint Corporation, 1961) 5: 30–32. The Dominic office is in AH 25: 239–43.

[24] Thomas Aquinas was canonized on 18 July 1323 by John XXII at Avignon. This gives an earliest possible date for the insertion of the Mass for Thomas into this manuscript.

The Mass portion of the manuscript begins on folio 115 with the First Sunday of Advent. There follow Graduals and Alleluias for the *Temporale*. The Gradual and Alleluia for the Corpus Christi Mass, bearing the heading "In festo sacramenti," is found on folios 162–163v. It is preceded by music for Trinity Sunday and followed by the First Sunday after Trinity Sunday. Thus, it occurs in its proper liturgical position, and because it is part of the original portion of the manuscript, this Mass must have been associated with Corpus Christi from 1269, that is, from its earliest days. Because the manuscript contains only the solo portions of the responsories, it does not tell us all we would like to know about either service. However, it gives enough to show the nature of the service (secular) and melodic relationships with other sources. The texts and melodies of the first service are all common with those in BNF 1143, although the order is very different, and three of them are common with Strahov D.E.I7.[25]

Table 10

Responsories for Standard Service in BR 139

Immolabit/Pascha nostrum (=BNF 1143 #20)
Comede[tis]/Non Moyses (=BNF 1143 #21)
Melchisedech/Benedictus/Gloria (=BNF 1143 #96; Strahov #49)
Cenantibus/Dixerunt (=BNF 1143 #31)
Qui manducat/Non est alia (=BNF 1143 #39)
Accepit/Memoria/Gloria (=BNF 1143 #33)
Calix/Quoniam (=BNF 1143 #98 but more ornate and closer to source chant
        Solem iusticie; Strahov #33)
Ego sum/Ego sum (=BNF 1143 #100; Strahov #39)
Unus/Parasti/Gloria (=BNF 1143 #43)
Homo/Venite/Gloria (=BNF 1143 #7)

The second service, which follows immediately in the manuscript, is derived from the corresponding sections of the office for Saint Dominic.

Table 11

Responsories for Alternative Service in BR 139

Carnis/Venite[26] (=Assunt Dominici)
Mundum/Ad hoc continuum (=Mundum/Ad hoc)
Mundo/Pater namque (=Datum/Stella micans)
Verbum/Sole panis/Gloria (=Verbum/Ter inflammas/Gloria)
Pauperibus/Apostolo (=Paupertatis/Nocte celi)
Panis/Confortantem (=Panis signo crucis)
Granum/Nisi locus/Gloria (=Granum/Flos in florum/Gloria)
Felix vitis/Omnes in fide (=Felix/Ex ubertate)
Discedentem/Quicumque digne (=Ascendenti/Per quem multos)
Terminatis/Presens in mentis/Gloria (=O [spem]/Qui tot signis/Gloria)

---

[25] Two other chants are often cited as common with Strahov, *Immolabit* and *Cenantibus*, but they are not.

[26] BR 139 does not contain an invitatory in its version of the service for Dominic, but *Carnis* is melodically identical to the Dominic invitatory *Assunt Dominici* found in Vat. Lat. 10770, fol. 168v.

BRIGHAM YOUNG UNIVERSITY, HAROLD B. LEE LIBRARY, SPECIAL COLLECTIONS, VAULT 091 R263 1343

Vellum; 222 fols. (unfoliated); 2.75 x 19.5 cm

This manuscript was written for Canterbury in 1343 and opens with thirty-seven items from Office C, twenty-nine of which have music. Most are identical to the version in BNF 1143, but eight of them, while using the standard texts, have different music. These are: *Sacris solemniis*; *Communione calicis*; *Memor sit dominus*; *Paratur nobis*; *In voce exultationis*; *Accepit Ihesus*; *Qui manducat*; and *Sapientia edificavit*.

Table 12
Office for Corpus Christi in BYU

FIRST VESPERS

A. Sacerdos in eternum
A. Miserator Dominus
A. Calicem salutaris
A. Sicut novelle
A. Qui pacem ponit
R. Homo quidam/Venite comedite
H. Sacris solemniis
Mag. A. O quam suavis

MATINS

Inv. Christum regem
H. Pange lingua

FIRST NOCTURN

A. Fructum salutiferum
A. A fructu frumenti
A. Communione calicis
R. Immolabit hedum
R. Comedetis carnes
R. Respexit Helyas

SECOND NOCTURN

A. Memor sit Dominus
A. Paratur nobis
A. In voce exultationis
R. Panis quem ego dabo
R. Cenantibus illis
R. Accepit Ihesus

THIRD NOCTURN

A. Introibo ad altare Dei
A. Cibavit nos Dominus
A. Ex altari tuo
R. Qui manducat
R. Misit me pater
R. Unus panis

LAUDS

A. Sapientia edificavit

EDINBURGH UNIVERSITY LIBRARY, MS 211.IV (INCHCOLM ANTIPHONARY)

2 bifolia; 28 x 19.5 cm

Although not one of the five central sources, the Inchcolm Antiphonary contains some concordances with the five main manuscripts, as well as some significant differences. It is a fragmentary manuscript containing thirty-one items for the Corpus Christi office, twenty-one of which carry music.[27]

Most of these pieces are also found in BNF 1143, but two of them, the second nocturn antiphons *Memor sit Dominus* and *Paratur nobis*, are common only with Graz 134 and BYU. Moreover, three items, the hymn *Sacris sollempniis* and the responsories *Accepit Ihesus* and *Qui manducat*, have the same texts as the other sources but different melodies. Finally, the manuscript contains two items for Compline, the antiphon *Salvator miserere* and the *Nunc dimittis* antiphon *O admirabile misterium*, both of which are unique.

Table 13
Office for Corpus Christi in EU

FIRST VESPERS

Mag. A. O quam suavis

COMPLINE

A. Salvator miserere
Nunc dimittis A. O admirabile misterium

MATINS

Inv. Christum regem
H. Sacris solempniis

FIRST NOCTURN

A. Fructum salutiferum
A. A fructu frumenti
A. Communione calicis
R. Immolabit hedum
R. Comedetis carnes
R. Respexit Helyas

SECOND NOCTURN

A. Memor sit Dominus
A. Paratur nobis
A. In voce exultationis
R. Panis quem ego dabo
R. Cenantibus illis (end only)
R. Accepit Ihesus

THIRD NOCTURN

A. Introibo ad altare Dei
A. Cibavit nos Dominus
A. Ex altari tuo
R. Qui manducat (beginning only)

---

[27] Isobel Woods, "'Our Awin Scottis Use': Chant Usage in Medieval Scotland," *Journal of the Royal Musical Association* 112 (1987), 21–37.

SUMMARY

A comparison of the seven manuscripts gives an idea of how rich the early history of this feast is. The earliest service, according to Lambot, is the one preserved in KB 70.E.4. A glance at Manuscript Index 1, below, shows that this service is completely independent of later sources in both melodies and texts. Apparently it was a local service, intended for use only in Liège, with little influence elsewhere.[28] The service derived from the Dominic office in BR 139 is of the same type: an independent liturgy with no relation to the international service being developed at the same time. For that matter, Strahov may have been an independent service as well, but some of its texts and music were incorporated into the standard service, embodied first in BNF 1143. Both BYU and EU contain variations on the prototype in BNF 1143.

The final version of the standard office came into being through waves of stabilization. The texts were established first. Some of the texts in Strahov, and all of those in BNF 1143, became standard for later versions. Often, but not always, the melodies associated with them became standard as well. The next step was the modal organization of the antiphons and responsories. BNF 1143 has it, but KB 70.E.4 and Strahov do not. Nor does the first service in BR 139, although the second one does. The insular manuscripts, BYU and EU, are, like BNF 1143, modally organized, but in some cases with different melodies.

The final wave was the stabilization of the melodies. I refer here to the antiphon and responsory melodies, not the hymns, whose melodies appear to vary more widely. Much of melodic material in BNF 1143 returns in BYU and EU, but some of the melodies from BNF 1143 were discarded in favor of others in the same mode.

INDICES

The following indices record the individual musical items from all seven manuscripts. Indices 1 through 7 are organized by manuscript. The first column gives the title of the piece. The second and third columns specify the manuscript and folio number, and the fourth shows the piece's place in the overall structure of the service. This number refers to a scheme in which each item in the office, textual as well as musical, is given a separate number. The fifth and sixth columns give the office hour and the category of composition (antiphon, responsory, etc.).

The next twelve columns contain the incipits of the individual melodies using the code invented by David Hughes and John Bryden, in which the numbers represent distance above (positive numbers) or below (negative numbers) the starting pitch.[29] The next column gives the mode of the individual melody, and the last provides information on concordances among the seven manuscripts.

The eighth index contains the same information but is organized by title. The purpose of this Title Index is to compare items with the same text to see if they use the same melodies. Frequently, it will be noted, the melodies differ.

---

[28] Some of it forms part of the service in Graz 1254, a Cistercian manuscript from 1396.

[29] John R. Bryden and David Hughes, *An Index of Gregorian Chant*, 2 vols. (Cambridge MA: Harvard University Press, 1969).

Manuscript Index 1
KB 70.E.4

Title	MS	Folio	MS #	Service													Mode	Concordances
Animarum cibus	70.E.4	86r	1	1 Vesp	A1	2	10	9	7	9	7	5	7	9	7	5	Mode 1	
Discipulis competentem	70.E.4	86r	2	1 Vesp	A2	-2	-2	0	-5	-2	2	0	2	3	2	0	Mode 2	
Totum Cristus	70.E.4	86v	3	1 Vesp	A3	2	2	5	2	4	0	2	0	-2	-3	-5	Mode 3	
Et sic	70.E.4	86v	4	1 Vesp	A4	-5	-2	-3	0	2	4	0	2	0	5	4	Mode 8	
Panem angelorum	70.E.4	86v	5	1 Vesp	A5	1	0	-2	-4	0	1	0	1	3	5	7	Mode 5	
Sacerdos summus/Leta laudum/Gloria	70.E.4	87r	6	1 Vesp	R1	5	5	7	5	7	7	5	9	12	14	12	Mode 5	70.E.4 #23
Notum fecit	70.E.4	87v	7	1 Vesp	Vers1	-1	-5	-3	-3	-1	-3					5	Mode 1	
Dominus Ihesus Cristus/Magnificat	70.E.4	87v	8	1 Vesp	A6	2	2	5	0	7	5	9	11	9	7	5	Mode 1	
Cristum regem regem/Venite	70.E.4	88r	9	Matins	Inv	-2	3	2	3	0	-2	2	3	5	3	0	Mode 1	
Suo Cristus	70.E.4	88r	10	Matins Noct. 1	A7	3	3	0	-2	3	5	3	5	3	2	3	Mode 1	
Visibilis creature	70.E.4	88r	11	Matins Noct. 1	A8	-2	-5	-2	-2	0	5	3	2	0	3	7	Mode 2	
Sanguis eius	70.E.4	88r	12	Matins Noct. 1	A9	-2	-3	-2	-2	0	-3	-5	0	2	4	2	Mode 3	
Invisibilis sacerdos/Ipse conviva	70.E.4	88v	14	Matins Noct. 1	R2	-2	0	3	3	2	-2	2	0	0	3	5	Mode 1	
Dixit Ihesus/Nisi meam	70.E.4	88v	15	Matins Noct. 1	R3	-2	0	-5	0	-2	0	2	0	0	3	2	Mode 2	
Vere mira/Hoc celesti/Gloria	70.E.4	89r	16	Matins Noct. 1	R4	4	5	7	5	4	2	4	5	2	0	2	Mode 5	
Hostia Cristus	70.E.4	89r	17	Matins Noct. 2	A10	2	4	2	5	2	5	9	7	7	5	7	Mode 1	
Hic et ibi	70.E.4	89v	18	Matins Noct. 2	A11	-2	-1	-5	-3	-3	0	-2	-3	-7	-7	-7	Mode 5	
Verus Deus	70.E.4	89v	19	Matins Noct. 2	A12	-1	2	-1	-3	0	2	0	0	4	2	4	Mode 6	
Ad ipsius/Suam carnem	70.E.4	89v	21	Matins Noct. 2	R5	-2	0	2	3	2	0	-2	0	3	7	5	Mode 1	
Alieni/Viva vivo	70.E.4	90r	22	Matins Noct. 2	R6	4	5	7	9	10	7	5	5	4	2	5	Mode 7	
Sacerdos sum[mus/Leta laudem/Gloria]	70.E.4	90v	23	Matins Noct. 2	R7	5	7	5	7	9	9	9					Mode 5	70.E.4 #6
Dominus Ihesus	70.E.4	90v	24	Matins Noct. 3	A13	7	7	5	4	5	7	10	9	7	5	4	Mode 7	
Sacri ministerio	70.E.4	90v	25	Matins Noct. 3	A14	2	0	-2	-3	-3	-5	-2	-3	-2	-3	-2	Mode 8	
Hec igitur	70.E.4	90v	26	Matins Noct. 3	A15	2	4	5	4	2	0	2	0	5	9	7	Mode 1	

Title	MS	Folio	MS #	Service															Mode	Concordances
Cristus corpus/Ut perhennis	70.E.4	91r	28	Matins Noct. 3	R8	2	4	2	0	-1	0	2	0	4	7	6	4	Mode 7	
O vere miraculum/Vere bonus	70.E.4	91r	29	Matins Noct. 3	R9	-2	0	2	3	0	2	-2	0	2	3	2	0	Mode 2	
Panis vive/Ideoque tu/Gloria	70.E.4	91v	30	Matins Noct. 3	R10	-2	0	2	3	2	3	0	-2	0	3	5	7	Mode 1	
Te Deum	70.E.4	92r	31	Matins	Te D.	3	5											Mode 3	
Celestis artificio	70.E.4	92r	32	Lauds	A16	2	5	7	5	4	2	5	4	2	0	5	7	Mode 1	
Cristus enim	70.E.4	92r	33	Lauds	A17	-2	-5	-2	0	2	3	2	0	-2	0	3	2	Mode 2	
Illa nobis	70.E.4	92r	34	Lauds	A18	2	5	4	2	5	4	0	2	0	-2	0	2	Mode 3	
Nulla nobis	70.E.4	92v	35	Lauds	A19	2	3	2	0	-2	0	-2	3	2	0	2	3	Mode 6	
Ecce vobiscum	70.E.4	92v	36	Lauds	A20	-2	2	5	4	0	4	4	5	2	0	2	0	Mode 8	
Panis vite/Benedictus	70.E.4	92v	38	Lauds	A21	-2	-3	-2	0	-2	-5	0	0	2	5	4	2	Mode 6	
Sacramentum pietatis	70.E.4	93r	39	2 Vesp	A22	-4	-2	-4	-5	-7	-5	-4	-5	-7	-9	-4	-2	Mode 1	
Misterii veritatem	70.E.4	93r	40	2 Vesp	A23	2	-2	3	2	0	5	3	3	2	0	-2	3	Mode 2	
Qui semel	70.E.4	93r	41	2 Vesp	A24	1	3	1	0	-2	3	3	5	8	7	5	7	Mode 3	
Ore quidem	70.E.4	93v	42	2 Vesp	A25	-2	0	1	0	-2	-4	-4	-2	-4	0	3	5	Mode 4	
Ore vero	70.E.4	93v	43	2 Vesp	A26	2	0	2	4	5	4	2	2	0	5	4	2	Mode 6	
Ad nutum/Ubi virtus/Gloria	70.E.4	93v	44	2 Vesp	R11	2	4	5	4	2	2	4	2	0	-1	2	0	Mode 5	
Ihesu bone/Magnificat	70.E.4	94r	45	2 Vesp	A27	3	2	0	-2	0	0	3	5	7	5	3	5	Mode 1	
Laureata plebs fidelis	70.E.4	94v	46	Sequence	Seq	2	-2	0	2	5	2	3	2	0	7	8	7	Mode 1	
Ad cenam agni providi	70.E.4	96r	47	Hymn	H1	4	7	9	5	7	9	9	11	7	12	9	11	Mode 5	

Manuscript Index 2
Strahov

Title	MS	Folio	MS #	Service														Mode	Concordances
Sapiencia edificavit	Strahov	213v	1	1 Vesp	A1	-1	-3	-5	-3	0	2	4	2	4	5	4	2	Mode 6	Not concord w/ others of same text
Melchisedech rex	Strahov	213v	2	1 Vesp	A2	-5	-2	0	-5	0	2	0	-2	2	5	7	5	Mode 8	
Immolabit edum	Strahov	213v	3	1 Vesp	A3	-2	-3	-5	-3	-2	2	0	-2	0	5	2	5	Mode 8	Beata Dei genetrix WA 361; Wales 249v
Et edent carnes	Strahov	213v	4	1 Vesp	A4	2	5	4	5	7	5	4	2	4	5	7	5	Mode 4	Tu decus virgineum PM 271
Pluit illis	Strahov	213v	5	1 Vesp	A5	3	0	-2	0	3	5	7	5	3	2	0	3	Mode 1	
Pange lingua	Strahov	213v	8	1 Vesp	H1	1	0	-2	3	5	8	10	8	7	5	8	7	Mode 3	1143 #8; BYU #10
Angelorum esca/Magnificat	Strahov	214r	10	1 Vesp	A6	2	4	0	2	0	-1	-3	-5	0	2	4	5	Mode 6	134 #10; 1143 #10; BYU #10; EU #3, all w/ diff. text
Venite comedite/Venite	Strahov	214r	12	Matins	Inv	-1	-3	-1	0	2	0	-1	2	2	2	0	-1	Mode 4	
Sacris sollempniis	Strahov	214r	13	Matins	H2	-3	-2	-5	-3	0	-5	0	2	0	-2	-3	-5	Mode 8	134 #13
Numquid poterit	Strahov	214r	14	Matins Noct. 1	A7	3	0	-2	3	5	7	8	5	3	5	7	10	Mode 1	
Parasti in conspectu	Strahov	214r	15	Matins Noct. 1	A8	2	4	2	0	2	4	0	2	4	2	4	2	Mode 1	
De fructu operum	Strahov	214r	16	Matins Noct. 1	A9	3	0	-2	3	5	7	5	3	5	3	0	3	Mode 1	
Cenantibus discipulis/Hic est sanguis	Strahov	214v	19	Matins Noct. 1	R1	-2	0	-2	0	3	0	-2	0	3	0	3	0	Mode 7	
Accepto pane/Similiter et calicem	Strahov	215r	21	Matins Noct. 1	R2	5	7	5	7	5	7	9	7	9	7	5	4	Mode 6	
Manducantibus discipulis/Et ait illis	Strahov	215v	23	Matins Noct. 1	R3	2	0	2	0	-2	2	5	7	5	7	9	7	Mode 7	
Faciens mensam	Strahov	215v	24	Matins Noct. 2	A10	-2	0	-7	-5	-2	0	2	0	2	0	-2	0	Mode 8	
Sacerdotes sancti	Strahov	215v	25	Matins Noct. 2	A11	-3	-1	0	-3	0	2	5	4	5	2	0	2	Mode 6	Pater manifestavi Strahov D.E.I.7 190v
Faciet Dominus	Strahov	215v	26	Matins Noct. 2	A12	-2	3	5	8	5	3	5	3	1	0	1	3	Mode 3	
Dominus Ihesus/Similiter et calicem	Strahov	216r	29	Matins Noct. 2	R4	2	5	7	4	2	5	4	5	2	4	2	0	Mode 1	
Quicumque manducaverit/Qui enim manducat	Strahov	216v	31	Matins Noct. 2	R5	2	0	2	0	-2	2	5	4	5	7	5	7	Mode 7	

Title	MS	Folio	MS #	Service														Mode	Concordances
Calix benedictionis/Quoniam unus panis/Gloria	Strahov	217r	33	Matins Noct. 2 R6	3	0	-2	3	2	0	3	0	-2	0	-2	3	Mode 1	134 #53; 139 #7; 1143 #98
Melchisedech rex Salem	Strahov	217r	34	Matins Noct. 3 A13	2	4	5	2	5	4	5	7	2	7	9	7	Mode 1	
Erit quasi oliva	Strahov	217r	35	Matins Noct. 3 A14	2	3	0	-2	0	3	5	7	8	7	5	3	Mode 1	
Quid enim bonum	Strahov	217r	36	Matins Noct. 3 A15	-3	-5	0	2	2	2	4	0	2	0	2	4	Mode 6	O quam gloriosum est regnum 1412, 11
Ego sum/Ego sum/Gloria	Strahov	217v	39	Matins Noct. 3 R7	4	5	7	9	7	5	7	9	10	12	10	9	Mode 7	134 #55; 139 #8; 1143 #100
Amen, amen/Caro enim/Gloria	Strahov	218v	41	Matins Noct. 3 R8	2	0	2	0	2	-2	5	7	10	7	10	7	Mode 7	
Sicut vivens/Non sicut patres/Gloria	Strahov	219r	43	Matins Noct. 3 R9	2	0	2	4	2	4	2	0	-3	-1	0	-1	Mode 6	
Melchisedech viro/Benedictus Abraham	Strahov	219v	49	Matins Noct. 4 R10	4	7	4	2	7	9	7	9	11	12	11	9	Mode 5	134 #51; 139 #3; 1143 #96
Immolabit hedum/Et edent	Strahov	220r	51	Matins Noct. 4 R11	2	0	2	0	-2	2	5	4	5	7	5	7	Mode 7	
Cumque operuisset/Iste est panis/Gloria	Strahov	220v	53	Matins Noct. 4 R12	2	0	2	4	2	4	4	0	5	4	2	7	Mode 6	
Memoriam fecit	Strahov	220v	54	Lauds A16	-2	3	5	7	5	3	5	3	5	7	5	3	Mode 1	134 #33; 1143 #91
Memoria mea	Strahov	220v	55	Lauds A17	-2	-5	-2	0	7	0	2	0	-2	2	2	7	Mode 8	134 #34; 1143#92
Omnes eandem	Strahov	220v	56	Lauds A18	-1	-3	-5	0	0	-1	0	2	4	5	4	2	0	Mode 6	
Nolo vos socios	Strahov	220v	57	Lauds A19	-1	-3	2	4	2	7	6	6	9	7	9	7	Mode 3	
Qui habet aures	Strahov	220v	58	Lauds A20	-1	-3	2	4	4	7	6	6	9	7	6	4	Mode 3	134 #35; 1143 #93
Verbum supernum	Strahov	221r	60	Lauds H3	4	5	7	9	7	4	5	7	4	7	5	4	Mode 5	Not concord w/ others of same text
Dixit Ihesus/Benedictus	Strahov	221r	62	Lauds A21	-2	-4	-2	0	3	-1	-2	3	-2	-4	-7	-5	Mode 1	
Parasti in conspectu/Adversos eos/Gloria	Strahov	221r	65	Terce Rb1	2	0	2	0	-1	-3	-5	0	2	5	7	5	Mode 6	
Panem angelorum/Cibaria misit/Gloria	Strahov	221r	69	Sext Rb2	2	0	2	0	2	-1	-3	-5	2	5	7	5	Mode 6	
Calicem salutaris/Et nomen Domini/Gloria	Strahov	221r	73	Nones Rb3	7	8	7	5	7	3	3	3	5	7	10	8	Mode 1	
Amen, amen/Magnificat	Strahov	221r	78	2 Vesp A22	-2	-4	0	3	5	3	5	3	8	7	5	3	Mode 5	134 #83; 1143 #74, both w/ diff. text

Manuscript Index 3
BNF 1143

Title	MS	Folio	MS #	Service													Mode	Concordances
Sacerdos in eternum	1143	1r	1	A1	3	0	-2	3	3	5	5	7	10	7	5	3	Mode 1	134 #1; BYU #1
Miserator dominus	1143	1r	2	A2	3	5	3	5	8	7	8	3	5	12	10	8	Mode 2	134 #2; BYU #2
Calicem salutaris	1143	1r	3	A3	-2	3	5	8	8	7	8	8	7	5	8	7	Mode 3	134 #3; BYU #3
Sicut novelle	1143	1v	4	A4	-1	-3	0	2	4	4	2	2	4	2	0	-1	Mode 4	134 #4; BYU #4
Qui pacem ponit	1143	1v	5	A5	4	7	4	7	9	9	7	12	11	9	7	5	Mode 5	134 #5; BYU #5
Homo quidam/Venite comedite/Gloria	1143	1v	7	R1	2	0	2	4	0	0	2	5	4	2	5	7	Mode 6	134 #7; 139 #10; BYU #6
Pange lingua	1143	2r	8	H1	1	0	-2	3	5	8	8	8	7	5	8	7	Mode 3	BYU #10; Strahov #8;
O quam suavis/Magnificat	1143	2v	10	A6	2	4	0	2	0	-1	-3	-5	0	2	4	7	Mode 6	134 #10; BYU #10; EU #3; Strahov #10 w/ diff. text
Christum regem/Venite	1143	3r	12	Inv	2	4	2	5	4	2	0	2	4	2	9	7	Mode 4	134 #12; BYU #9; EU #11
Sacris sollempniis	1143	3v	13	H2	7	8	7	5	7	8	10	8	7	5	7	5	Mode 1	Not concord w/ others of same text
Fructum salutiferum	1143	4r	14	A7	2	0	5	4	2	0	5	7	9	10	7	9	Mode 1	134 #14; BYU #11; EU #13
A fructu frumenti	1143	4r	15	A8	3	2	0	-2	3	5	3	2	0	3	5	7	Mode 2	134 #15; BYU #12; EU #14
Communione calicis	1143	4v	16	A9	-2	3	5	8	7	5	3	5	8	7	8	10	Mode 3	134 #16; EU #15
Immolabit hedum/Pascha nostrum	1143	5r	19	R2	-2	0	-2	0	2	3	0	-2	0	-2	0	3	Mode 1	134 #23; 139 #1; BYU #14; EU #17
Comedetis carnes/Non Moyses	1143	6r	21	R3	-2	0	2	3	2	3	2	0	0	-2	0	3	Mode 2	134 #27; 139 #2; BYU #15; EU #18
Respexit Helyas/Si quis manducaverit/Gloria	1143	7r	23	R4	2	-3	-2	0	0	2	5	2	2	4	5	4	Mode 3	134 #29; BYU #16; EU #19
Memor sit Dominus	1143	8r	24	A10	-1	-3	-1	0	-3	-5	0	-1	0	2	0	-1	Mode 4	Not concord w/ others of same text
Paratur nobis	1143	8r	25	A11	-2	-4	0	3	2	0	-2	3	5	8	7	5	Mode 5	Not concord w/ others of same text
In voce exultationis	1143	8r	26	A12	1	-2	-4	1	3	1	1	3	3	1	3	6	Mode 6	134 #19; EU #22
Panis quem/Locutus est	1143	9r	29	R5	2	0	-3	0	-1	2	4	0	-1	0	-1	0	Mode 4	134 #25; BYU #20; EU #24

Title	MS	Folio	MS #	Service													Mode	Concordances
Cenantibus illis/Dixerunt viri	1143	10r	31	Matins Noct. 2 R6	4	2	7	9	7	6	4	2	7	11	12	11	Mode 5	134 #40; 139 #4; BYU #21; EU #25
Accepit Ihesus/Memoria memor/Gloria	1143	10v	33	Matins Noct. 2 R7	2	0	2	4	0	-3	-2	0	-3	-5	0	2	Mode 6	134 #44; 139 #6
Introibo ad altare Dei	1143	11r	34	Matins Noct. 3 A13	4	5	7	9	12	7	9	7	4	5	7	5	Mode 7	134 #30; BYU #23; EU #27
Cibavit nos Dominus	1143	11r	35	Matins Noct. 3 A14	-2	-5	-3	-2	2	0	-2	0	2	5	4	2	Mode 8	134 #31; BYU #24; EU #28
Ex altari tuo	1143	11v	36	Matins Noct. 3 A15	2	4	0	-3	-5	-3	0	2	5	4	5	7	Mode 6	134 #32; BYU #25; EU #29
Qui manducat/Non est alia	1143	12r	39	Matins Noct. 3 R8	7	5	4	5	7	9	7	5	4	5	2	0	Mode 7	134 #42; 139 #5
Misit me pater/Cibavit eum	1143	12v	41	Matins Noct. 3 R9	5	3	5	7	5	7	9	7	5	7	10	5	Mode 8	134 #38; BYU #27
Unus panis/Parasti in dulcedine/Gloria	1143	13v	43	Matins Noct. 3 R10	-2	0	3	0	2	0	-2	0	-2	3	2	5	Mode 1	134 #49; 139 #9; BYU #28
Sapiencia edificavit	1143	14r	46	Lauds A16	7	8	7	5	7	5	3	2	0	2	3	2	Mode 1	134 #56
Angelorum esca	1143	14r	47	Lauds A17	-2	-5	-2	0	2	3	0	2	0	-2	0	3	Mode 2	134 #57
Pinguis est panis	1143	14v	48	Lauds A18	2	4	5	4	5	7	5	4	2	4	2	0	Mode 3	134 #58
Sacerdotes sancti	1143	14v	49	Lauds A19	-1	-3	-1	-3	0	-1	0	2	0	-1	-3	-5	Mode 4	134 #59
Vincenti dabo	1143	14v	50	Lauds A20	-2	-4	0	3	5	3	5	8	7	5	7	5	Mode 5	134 #60
Verbum supernum	1143	15r	52	Lauds H3	2	5	4	2	0	-2	2	0	2	4	2	0	Mode 8	Not concord w/ others of same text
Ego sum panis/Benedictus	1143	15v	54	Lauds A21	7	5	3	5	7	8	7	5	3	5	3	0	Mode 1	134 #66
Panem celi/Panem angelorum/Gloria	1143	15v	59	Terce Rb1	2	0	-1	-3	-5	0	2	5	7	5	4	2	Mode 6?	
Cibavit illos/Et de petra/Gloria	1143	16r	64	Sext Rb2	2	0	2	0	0	-3	-5	0	2	5	7	5	Mode 6?	
Educas panem/Et vinum/Gloria	1143	16v	68	None Rb3	2	0	0	-3	-5	0	2	5	7	5	4	2	Mode 6?	
O sacrum convivium/Magnificat	1143	16v	74	2 Vesp A22	-2	-4	0	3	5	3	5	8	7	5	5	3	Mode 5	134 #83; Strahov #78 w/ diff. text
Cibavit eos	1143	17r	75	Mass Intr	3	5	3	5	7	5	3	5	3	5	8	5	Mode 2	
Kyrie Fons bonitatis	1143	17v	76	Mass K	2	4	2	4	5	4	4	2	4	0			Mode 3	From Mass II (K. Fons bonitatis)
Gloria	1143	17v	77	Mass Gl	2	5	4	5	7	5	5	4	4	5	4	2	Mode 4	From Mass IV (K. Cunctipotens)

Title	MS	Folio	MS #	Service														Mode	Concordances
Oculi omnium/Aperis	1143	18r	80	Mass	Grad	2	5	7	5	4	2	0	2	4	2	4	0	Mode 7	139 #21
Alleluia/Caro mea	1143	18v	81	Mass	All	2	4	0	2	4	2	0	4	7	6	4	7	Mode 7	139 #22
Lauda Syon	1143	19r	82	Mass	Seq	3	5	3	8	7	5	3	5	7	3	0	1	Mode 7	
Sacerdotes incensum	1143	22v	84	Mass	Off	3	2	3	2	3	5	7	3	8	7	8	5	Mode 4	
Sanctus	1143	23r	87	Mass	San	5	2	0	-3	-2	0	2	0					Mode 4	From Mass IV (K. Cunctipotens)
Agnus Dei	1143	23r	88	Mass	Ag	2	0	2	4	2	0	-1	0					Mode 6	From Mass IV (K. Cunctipotens)
Quocienscumque	1143	23r	89	Mass	Com	7	0	7	5	10	9	10	7	9	7	5	7	Mode 7	
Memoriam fecit	1143	23v	91	Matins Noct. 4	A23	-2	3	5	3	5	7	5	3	5	7	5	3	Mode 1	134 #33; Strahov #54
Memoria mea	1143	23v	92	Matins Noct. 4	A24	-2	-5	-2	0	2	0	2	0	-2	2	5	7	Mode 8	134 #34; Strahov #55;
Qui habet aures	1143	24r	93	Matins Noct. 4	A25	1	0	-2	3	5	8	7	8	10	8	7	5	Mode 3	134 #35; Strahov #58
Melchisedech vero/Benedictus Abraham	1143	24v	96	Matins Noct. 4	R11	4	7	4	2	7	9	7	9	11	12	11	9	Mode 5	134 #51; 139 #3; Strahov #49;
Calix benedictionis/ Quoniam unus panis	1143	25r	98	Matins Noct. 4	R12	2	0	2	0	-2	0	-2	3	5	7	5	3	Mode 1	134 #53; 139 #7; Strahov #33
Ego sum/Ego sum/Gloria	1143	26r	100	Matins Noct. 4	R13	4	5	7	9	7	5	7	9	10	12	10	9	Mode 7	134 #55; 139 #8; Strahov #39;

Manuscript Index 4
Graz 134

Title	MS	Folio	MS #	Service	Mode	Concordances
Sacerdos in eternum	134	241r	1	1 Vesp	A1	Mode 1	1143 #1; BYU #1
Miserator Dominus	134	241r	2	1 Vesp	A2	Mode 2	1143 #2; BYU #2
Calicem salutaris	134	241r	3	1 Vesp	A3	Mode 3	1143 #3; BYU #3
Sicut novelle	134	241r	4	1 Vesp	A4	Mode 4	1143 #4; BYU #4
Qui pacem ponit	134	241r	5	1 Vesp	A5	Mode 5	1143 #5; BYU #5
Homo quidam/Venite comedite	134	241r	7	1 Vesp	R1	Mode 6	139 #10; 1143 #7; BYU #6
O quam suavis/Magnificat	134	241v	10	1 Vesp	A6	Mode 6	1143 #10; BYU #10; EU #3; Strahov #10 w/ diff. text
Christum regem/Venite	134	241v	12	Matins	Inv	Mode 4	1143 #12; BYU #9; EU #11
Sacris sollempniis	134	241v	13	Matins	H1	Mode 8	Strahov #13
Fructum salutiferum	134	242r	14	Matins Noct. 1	A7	Mode 1	1143 #14; BYU #11; EU #13
A fructu frumenti	134	242r	15	Matins Noct. 1	A8	Mode 2	1143 #15; BYU #12; EU #14
Communione calicis	134	242r	16	Matins Noct. 1	A9	Mode 3	1143 #16; EU #15
Memor sit Dominus	134	242r	17	Matins Noct. 1	A10	Mode 4	EU #20
Paratur nobis	134	242r	18	Matins Noct. 1	A11	Mode 5	EU #21
In voce exultationis	134	242r	19	Matins Noct. 1	A12	Mode 6	1143 #26; EU #22
Immolabit hedum/Pascha nostrum	134	242r	23	Matins Noct. 1	R2	Mode 1	139 #1; 1143 #19; BYU #14; EU #17
Panis quem/Locutus est	134	242v	25	Matins Noct. 1	R3	Mode 4	1143 #29; BYU #20; EU #24
Comedetis carnes/Non Moyses	134	242v	27	Matins Noct. 1	R4	Mode 2	139 #2; 1143 #21; BYU #15; EU #18
Respexit Helyas/Si quis mandu-caverit/Gloria	134	243r	29	Matins Noct. 1	R5	Mode 3	1143 #23; BYU #16; EU #19
Introibo ad altare Dei	134	243r	30	Matins Noct. 2	A13	Mode 7	1143 #34; BYU #23; EU #27
Cibavit nos Dominus	134	243r	31	Matins Noct. 2	A14	Mode 8	1143 #35; BYU #24; EU #28
Ex altari tuo	134	243r	32	Matins Noct. 2	A15	Mode 6	1143 #36; BYU #25; EU #29
Memoriam fecit	134	243r	33	Matins Noct. 2	A16	Mode 1	1143 #91; Strahov #45
Memoria mea	134	243r	34	Matins Noct. 2	A17	Mode 8	1143 #92; Strahov #55

Title	MS	Folio	MS #	Service													Mode	Concordances
Qui habet aures	134	243r	35	Matins Noct. 2	A18												Mode 3	1143 #93; Strahov #58
Misit me pater/Cibavit eum	134	243v	38	Matins Noct. 2	R6												Mode 8	1143 #41; BYU #27
Cenantibus illis/Dixerunt viri	134	243v	40	Matins Noct. 2	R7												Mode 5	139 #4; 1143 #31; BYU 21; EU #25
Qui manducat/Non est alia	134	244r	42	Matins Noct. 2	R8												Mode 7	139 #5; 1143 #39
Accepit Iesus/Memoria memor/Gloria	134	244r	44	Matins Noct. 2	R9												Mode 6	139 #6; 1143 #33
Comedi favum	134	244r	45	Matins Noct. 3	A19													
Unus panis/Parasti in dulcedine	134	244v	49	Matins Noct. 3	R10												Mode 1	139 #9; 1143 #43; BYU #28
Melchisedech vero/Benedictus Abraham	134	244v	51	Matins Noct. 3	R11												Mode 5	139 #3; 1143 #96; Strahov #49
Calix benedictionis/Quoniam unus panis	134	245r	53	Matins Noct. 3	R12												Mode 1	139 #7; 1143 #98; Strahov #33
Ego sum/Ego sum/Gloria	134	245r	55	Matins Noct. 3	R13												Mode 7	139 #8; 1143 #100; Strahov #39
Sapientia edificavit	134	245r	56	Lauds	A20												Mode 1	1143 #46
Angelorum esca	134	245v	57	Lauds	A21												Mode 2	1143 #47
Pinguis est panis	134	245v	58	Lauds	A22												Mode 3	1143 #48
Sacerdotes sancti	134	245v	59	Lauds	A23												Mode 4	1143 #49
Vincenti dabo	134	245v	60	Lauds	A24												Mode 5	1143 #50
Panem de celo	134	245v	62	Lauds	Rb1													
Ego sum panis/Benedictus	134	245v	66	Lauds	A25												Mode 1	1143 #54
O sacrum convivium[/Magnificat]	134	246r	83	2 Vesp	A26												Mode 5	1143 #74; Strahov #78 w/ diff. text
O gustu mirabilis	134	246r	84	Compline	A27													

Manuscript Index 5
BR 139

Title	MS	Folio	MS #	Service													Mode	Concordances
Immolabit[hedum]/Pascha nostrum	139	107r	1	Matins Noct. 1	R1	-2											Mode 1	134 #23; 1143 #19; BYU #14; EU #17
Comede[tis]/Non moyses	139	107r	2	Matins Noct. 1	R2	-2	0	2	3	0	2	3	2	0	-2	0	Mode 2	134 #27; 1143 #21; BYU #15; EU #18
Melchisedech vero/Benedictus/Gloria	139	107v	3	Matins Noct. 1	R3	4	7	4	2	7	9	7					Mode 5	134 #51; 1143 #96; Strahov #49
Cenantibus illis/Dixerunt viri	139	107v	4	Matins Noct. 2	R4	4	2	7									Mode 5	134 #40; 1143 #31; BYU #21; EU #25;
Qui manducat/Non est alia	139	107v	5	Matins Noct. 2	R5	7	5	4	5	7	9	7					Mode 7	134 #42; 1143 #39
Accepit [Ihesus]/Memoria memor/Gloria	139	107v	6	Matins Noct. 2	R6	2	0	2	4	0							Mode 6	134 #44; 1143 #33
Calix [benedictionis]/Quoniam unus panis	139	108r	7	Matins Noct. 3	R7	2	0	-2	3	2	0	2	0	-2	0	-2	Mode 1	134 #53; 1143 #98; Strahov #33
Ego sum/Ego sum	139	108r	8	Matins Noct. 3	R8	4	5	7									Mode 7	134 #55; 1143 #100; Strahov #39
Unus [panis]/Parasti in dulcedine/Gloria	139	108r	9	Matins Noct. 3	R9	-2	0	2	0								Mode 1	134 #49; 1143 #43; BYU #28
Homo[quidam]/Venite comedite/Gloria	139	108v	10	2 Vesp	R10	2	0										Mode 6	134 #7; 1143 #7; BYU #6
Carnis/Venite	139	109r	11	Matins	Inv	-2	0	2	3	2	0	-2	0				Mode 4	
Mundum/Ad hoc convivium	139	109r	12	Matins Noct. 1	R11	2	0	-2	3	2	0						Mode 1	
Mundo/Pater namque	139	109r	13	Matins Noct. 1	R12	-2	-5	-2	0								Mode 2	
Verbum/Sole panis/Gloria	139	109r	14	Matins Noct. 1	R13	1	0	-2	3	1	0						Mode 3	
Pauperibus/Apostolus	139	109r	15	Matins Noct. 2	R14	2	4	2	5	4							Mode 4	
Panis/Confortantem	139	109v	16	Matins Noct. 2	R15	-2	1	0	-2	0	-4						Mode 5	
Granum/Nisi lotus/Gloria	139	109v	17	Matins Noct. 2	R16	2	0	-3	-1	0							Mode 6	
Felix vitis/Omnes in fide	139	109v	18	Matins Noct. 3	R17	7	5	4	5	7							Mode 7	
Discedentem/Quicumque	139	109v	19	Matins Noct. 3	R18	-2	0	-2	-3	-5	-3	-2	0	2	0		Mode 8	
Terminatis/Presens in mente/Gloria	139	110r	20	Matins Noct. 3	R19	-2	0	3	2	2	3	0	3	5	7	5	Mode 1	
Oculi omnium/Aperis	139	162r	21	Mass	Grad	2	5	7	5	4	2	0	4	7	6	4	Mode 7	1143 #80
Alleluia/Caro mea	139	162v	22	Mass	All	2	4	0	2	4	2	0	4	7	6	4	Mode 7	1143 #81

Manuscript Index 6
BYU

Title	MS	Folio	MS #	Service															Mode	Concordances
Sacerdos in eternum	BYU	1v	1	1 Vesp	A1	3	0	-2	3	5	3	3	5	7	10	7	5	3	Mode 1	134 #1; 1143 #1
Miserator Dominus	BYU	1v	2	1 Vesp	A2	3	5	3	5	7	8	8	5	12	10	8	7	5	Mode 2	134 #2; 1143 #2
Calicem salutaris	BYU	1v	3	1 Vesp	A3	-2	3	5	8	7	8	8	10	8	7	5	8	7	Mode 3	134 #3; 1143 #3
Sicut novelle	BYU	1v	4	1 Vesp	A4	-1	-3	0	2	4	2	2	0	2	4	2	2	-1	Mode 4	134 #4; 1143 #4
Qui pacem ponit	BYU	1v	5	1 Vesp	A5	4	7	4	2	9	7	7	9	12	11	9	7	5	Mode 5	134 #5; 1143 #5
Homo quidam/Venite comedite/Gloria	BYU	1v	7	1 Vesp	R1	2	0	2	4	2	4	4	0	5	4	2	5	7	Mode 6	134 #7; 139 #10; 1143 #7
Sacris sollempniis	BYU	1v	8	1 Vesp	H1	4	5	7	9	5	7	7	0	2	4	5	4	2	Mode 7	Not concord w/ others of same text
O quam suavis/Magnificat	BYU	2r	10	1 Vesp	A6	2	4	0	2	0	-1	0	-3	-5	0	2	4	7	Mode 6	134 #10; 1143 #10; EU #3; Strahov #10 w/ diff. text
Christum regem/Venite	BYU	2v	12	Matins	Inv	2	4	2	5	4	2	2	0	2	4	2	2	9	Mode 4	134 #12; 1143 #12; EU #11
Pange lingua	BYU	2v	13	Matins	H2	-2	3	5	8	10	8	5	5	8	7	5	3	5	Mode 3	1143 #8; Strahov #8 but simpler
Fructum salutiferum	BYU	2v	14	Matins Noct. 1	A7	2	0	5	4	2	0	2	2	5	7	9	12	7	Mode 1	134 #14; 1143 #14; EU #13
A fructu frumenti	BYU	2v	15	Matins Noct. 1	A8	3	2	0	-2	3	5	3	3	2	0	3	5	7	Mode 2	134 #15; EU #14; 1143 #15
Communione calicis	BYU	3r	16	Matins Noct. 1	A9	-2	3	5	8	7	8	8	7	5	3	5	0	1	Mode 3	Not concord w/ others of same text
Immolabit hedum/Pascha nostrum	BYU	3r	19	Matins Noct. 1	R2	-2	0	2	3	0	-2	0	0	-2	0	3	5	2	Mode 1	134 #23; 139 #1; 1143 #19; EU #17
Comedetis carnes/Non Moyses	BYU	3r	20	Matins Noct. 1	R3	-2	0	3	2	2	0	0	2	3	0	-2	0	3	Mode 2	134 #27; 139 #2; 1143 #21; EU #18
Respexit Helyas/Si quis manducaverit	BYU	3r	21	Matins Noct. 1	R4	2	-3	0	2	2	2	0	2	4	2	4	5	4	Mode 3	134 #29; 1143 #23; EU #19
Memor sit Dominus	BYU	3v	22	Matins Noct. 2	A10	-1	-3	-1	0	2	0	0	-1	0	2	2	2	4	Mode 4	Not concord w/ others of same text
Paratur nobis	BYU	3v	23	Matins Noct. 2	A11	-3	-5	0	2	0	-3	-1	-1	-3	-7	-5	-7	0	Mode 5	Not concord w/ others of same text
In voce exultationis	BYU	3v	24	Matins Noct. 2	A12	1	-2	-4	1	3	1	3	3	1	1	3	5	7	Mode 6	Not concordant in 2nd half
Panis quem/Locutus est	BYU	3v	26	Matins Noct. 2	R5	2	0	-3	-1	2	4	0	4	-1	0	-1	0	2	Mode 4	134 #25; 1143 #29; EU #24
Cenantibus illis/Dixerunt viri	BYU	3v	27	Matins Noct. 2	R6	4	2	7	4	2	7	9	9	11	9	7	9	7	Mode 5	134 #40; 139 #4; 1143 #31; EU #25;

Title	MS	Folio	MS #	Service														Mode	Concordances
Accepit Jesus/Memoria memor	BYU	4r	28	Matins Noct. 2	R7	2	0	-2	-3	-5	-3	-2	0	2	4	0	2	Mode 6	Not concord w/ others of same text
Introibo ad altare Dei	BYU	4r	29	Matins Noct. 3	A13	4	5	7	9	12	7	9	7	4	5	7	5	Mode 7	134 #30; 1143 #34; EU #27
Cibavit nos dominus	BYU	4r	30	Matins Noct. 3	A14	-2	-5	-2	0	2	0	-2	0	2	5	4	2	Mode 8	134 #31; 1143 #35; EU #28
Ex altari tuo	BYU	4r	31	Matins Noct. 3	A15	2	4	0	-1	-3	-1	0	2	5	4	5	7	Mode 6	134 #32; 1143 #36; EU #29
Qui manducat/Non est alia	BYU	4r	33	Matins Noct. 3	R8	-2	-3	-2	0	3	2	-2	2	0	3	2	0	Mode 7	Not concord w/ others of same text
Misit me pater/Cibavit eum	BYU	4v	34	Matins Noct. 3	R9	5	2	5	7	9	7	5	7	10	5	7	5	Mode 8	134 #38; 1143 #41
Unus panis/Parasti in dulcedine/Gloria	BYU	4v	35	Matins Noct. 3	R10	-2	0	3	0	2	0	-2	0	-2	3	2	5	Mode 1	134 #49; 139 #9; 1143 #43
Sapiencia edificavit	BYU	4v	37	Lauds	A16	7	8	7	10	7	5	7	8	7	5	3	5	Mode 1	Not concord w/ others of same text

Manuscript Index 7
EU

Title	MS	Folio	MS #	Service														Mode	Concordances
O quam suavis/Magnificat	EU	1r	3	1 Vesp	A1	2	4	0	2	0	-1	-3	-5	0	2	4	2	Mode 6	134 #10; 1143 #10; BYU #10; Strahov #10 w/ diff. text
Salvator miserere	EU	1r	5	Compline	A2	3	0	2	3	-2	3	5	7	5	3	5	7	Mode 1	
O admirabile misterium/Nunc dimittis	EU	1r	9	Compline	A3	1	-2	-4	1	3	1	3	5	3	1	3	1	Mode 6	
Christum regem[/Venite]	EU	1r	11	Matins	Inv	2	4	2	5	4	2	0	2	4	2	9	7	Mode 4	134 #12; 1143 #12; BYU #9
Sacris sollempniis	EU	1v	12	Matins	H1	2	5	4	0	2	5	0	2	0	2	-3	-2	Mode 2	Not concord w/ others of same text
Fructum salutiferum	EU	1v	13	Matins Noct. 1	A4	2	0	5	4	2	0	5	7	9	10	7	9	Mode 1	134 #14; 1143 #14; BYU #11
A fructu frumenti	EU	1v	14	Matins Noct. 1	A5	3	2	0	-2	3	5	3	2	0	3	5	7	Mode 2	134 #15; 1143 #15; BYU #12
Communione calicis	EU	1v	15	Matins Noct. 1	A6	-2	3	5	8	7	5	3	5	8	7	8	10	Mode 3	134 #16; 1143 #16
Immolabit hedum/Pascha nostrum	EU	1v	17	Matins Noct. 1	R1	-2	0	2	3	0	-2	0	-2	0	3	5	2	Mode 1	134 #23; 139 #1; 1143 #19; BYU #14
Comedetis carnes/Non Moyses	EU	1v	18	Matins Noct. 1	R2	-2	0	2	3	0	2	3	2	0	-2	0	3	Mode 2	134 #27; 139 #2; 1143 #21; BYU #15
Respexit Helyas/Si quis manducaverit/Gloria	EU	4r	19	Matins Noct. 1	R3	2	-3	-2	0	2	0	2	5	2	4	5	4	Mode 3	134 #29; 1143 #23; BYU #16
Memor sit Dominus	EU	4r	20	Matins Noct. 2	A7	-1	-3	0	2	4	2	0	-1	2	4	2	0	Mode 4	134 #17
Paratur nobis	EU	4r	21	Matins Noct. 2	A8	3	0	3	5	3	5	8	7	5	3	1	3	Mode 5	134 #18
In voce exultationis	EU	4r	22	Matins Noct. 2	A9	1	-2	-4	-2	1	3	1	3	5	3	1	3	Mode 6	134 #19; 1143 #26
Panis quem/Locutus est	EU	4r	24	Matins Noct. 2	R4	2	0	-3	0	-1	2	4	0	-1	0	-1	0	Mode 4	134 #25; 1143 #29; BYU #20
Cenantibus illis/Dixerunt viri	EU	4v	25	Matins Noct. 2	R5													Mode 5	134 #40; 139 #4; 1143 #31; BYU #21
Accepit Ihesus/Memoria memor	EU	4v	26	Matins Noct. 2	R6	-5	-2	0	2	0	-2	2	5	7	7	0	-2	Mode 8	Not concord w/ others of same text
Introibo ad altare Dei	EU	4v	27	Matins Noct. 3	A10	4	5	7	9	12	7	9	7	4	5	7	5	Mode 7	134 #30; 1143 #34; BYU #23
Cibavit nos Dominus	EU	4v	28	Matins Noct. 3	A11	-2	-5	-3	-2	0	0	-2	0	2	2	4	2	Mode 8	134 #31; 1143 #35; BYU #24
Ex altari tuo	EU	4v	29	Matins Noct. 3	A12	2	4	0	4	-3	-3	0	2	4	5	7	5	Mode 6	134 #32; 1143 #36; BYU #25
Qui manducat/Non est alia	EU	4v	31	Matins Noct. 3	R7	3	5	7	5	7	5	7	10	5	3	7	5	Mode 8	Not concord w/ others of same text

Title Index

Title	MS	Folio	MS #	Service														Mode	Concordances
A fructu frumenti	EU	1v	14	Matins Noct. 1	A5	3	2	0	-2	3	5	3	2	0	3	5	7	Mode 2	134 #15; 1143 #15; BYU #12
A fructu frumenti	134	242r	15	Matins Noct. 1	A8													Mode 2	1143 #15; BYU #12; EU #14
A fructu frumenti	1143	4r	15	Matins Noct. 1	A8	3	2	0	-2	3	5	3	2	0	3	5	7	Mode 2	134 #15; BYU #12; EU #14
A fructu frumenti	BYU	2v	15	Matins Noct. 1	A8	3	2	0	-2	3	5	3	2	0	3	5	7	Mode 2	134 #15; EU #14; 1143 #15
Accepit Iesus/Memoria memor/Gloria	134	244r	44	Matins Noct. 2	R9													Mode 6	139 #6; 1143 #33
Accepit Ihesus/Memoria memor	EU	4v	26	Matins Noct. 2	R6	-5	-2	0	2	0	2	2	5	7	2	0	-2	Mode 8	Not concord w/ others of same text
Accepit Ihesus/Memoria memor/Gloria	1143	10v	33	Matins Noct. 2	R7	2	0	2	4	0	-3	-2	0	-3	-5	0	2	Mode 6	134 #44; 139 #6
Accepit Jesus/Memoria memor	BYU	4r	28	Matins Noct. 2	R7	2	0	-2	-3	-5	-3	-2	0	2	4	0	2	Mode 6	Not concord w/ others of same text
Accepit [Ihesus]/Memoria memor/Gloria	139	107v	6	Matins Noct. 2	R6	2	0	2	0	4	0							Mode 6	134 #44; 1143 #33
Accepto pane/Similiter et calicem	Strahov	215r	21	Matins Noct. 1	R2	5	7	5	7	5	9	9	9	7	5	4		Mode 6	
Ad cenam agni providi	70.E.4	96r	47	Hymn	H1	4	7	9	7	5	9	11	7	12	9	11	7	Mode 5	
Ad ipsius/Suam carnem	70.E.4	89v	21	Matins Noct. 2	R5	-2	0	2	0	3	2	-2	3	5	7	5		Mode 1	
Ad nutum/Ubi virtus/Gloria	70.E.4	93v	44	2 Vesp	R11	2	4	5	4	2	4	2	0	-1	2	0	4	Mode 5	
Agnus Dei	1143	23r	88	Mass	Ag	2	0	2	4	2	0	-1	0					Mode 6	From Mass IV (K. Cunctipotens)
Alieni/Viva vivo	70.E.4	90r	22	Matins Noct. 2	R6	4	5	7	9	9	7	5	4	2	4	5		Mode 7	
Alleluia/Caro mea	139	162v	22	Mass	All	2	4	0	2	4	2	0	4	6	4	7		Mode 7	1143 #81
Alleluia/Caro mea	1143	18v	81	Mass	All	2	4	0	2	4	2	0	4	6	4	7		Mode 7	139 #22
Amen, amen/Caro enim/Gloria	Strahov	218v	41	Matins Noct. 3	R8	2	0	-2	0	-2	2	5	7	10	7	10	7	Mode 7	
Amen, amen/Magnificat	Strahov	221r	78	2 Vesp	A22	-2	-4	0	3	5	5	3	7	8	7	5	3	Mode 5	134 #83; 1143 #74, both w/ diff. text
Angelorum esca	134	245v	57	Lauds	A21													Mode 2	1143 #47
Angelorum esca	1143	14r	47	Lauds	A17	-2	-5	-2	0	2	3	0	2	0	-2	0	3	Mode 2	134 #57
Angelorum esca/Magnificat	Strahov	214r	10	1 Vesp	A6	2	4	0	2	0	-1	-3	-5	-3	0	2	4	5	Mode 6	134 #10; 1143 #10; BYU #10; EU #3, all w/ diff. text
Animarum cibus	70.E.4	86r	1	1 Vesp	A1	2	9	10	9	7	9	9	7	5	7			Mode 1	
Calicem salutaris	134	241r	3	1 Vesp	A3													Mode 3	1143 #3; BYU #3

Title	MS	Folio	MS #	Service															Mode	Concordances
Calicem salutaris	1143	1r	3	1 Vesp	A3	-2	3	5	8	7	8	10	8	7	5	8	7	Mode 3	134 #3; BYU #3
Calicem salutaris	BYU	1v	3	1 Vesp	A3	-2	3	5	8	7	8	10	8	7	5	8	7	Mode 3	134 #3; 1143 #3
Calicem salutaris/Et nomen Domini/Gloria	Strahov	221r	73	Nones	Rb3	7	8	7	5	7	3	5	5	7	7	10	8	Mode 1	
Calix benedictionis/Quoniam unus panis	134	245r	53	Matins Noct. 3	R12	2	0	2	0	-2	2	0	3	5	7	5	3	Mode 1	139 #7; 1143 #98; Strahov #33
Calix benedictionis/Quoniam unus panis	1143	25r	98	Matins Noct. 4	R12	2	0	2	0	-2	2	0	3	5	7	5	3	Mode 1	134 #53; 139 #7; Strahov #33
Calix benedictionis/Quoniam unus panis/Gloria	Strahov	217r	33	Matins Noct. 2	R6	3	0	-2	3	2	2	0	3	-2	0	-2	3	Mode 1	134 #53; 139 #7; 1143 #98;
Calix [benedictionis/Quoniam unus panis]	139	108r	7	Matins Noct. 3	R7	2	0	-2	3	2	2	0	2	0	-2	0	-2	Mode 1	134 #53; 1143 #98; Strahov #33
Carnis/Venite	139	109r	11	Matins	Inv	-2	0	2	0	2	0	-2	0					Mode 4	
Celestis artificio	70.E.4	92r	32	Lauds	A16	2	5	7	5	4	2	5	5	0	5	3	7	Mode 1	
Cenantibus discipulis/Hic est sanguis	Strahov	214v	19	Matins Noct. 1	R1	-2	0	-2	0	3	0	-2	0	-2	0	3	0	Mode 7	134 #40; 139 #4; 1143 #31; BYU #21
Cenantibus illis/Dixerunt viri	EU	4v	25	Matins Noct. 2	R5	4	2	7										Mode 5	134 #40; 1143 #31; BYU #21; EU #25;
Cenantibus illis/Dixerunt viri	139	107v	4	Matins Noct. 2	R4	4	2	7										Mode 5	134 #40; 143 #31; BYU #21; EU #25;
Cenantibus illis/Dixerunt viri	BYU	3v	27	Matins Noct. 2	R6	4	2	7	4	2	7	11	9	11	7	9	7	Mode 5	134 #40; 139 #4; 1143 #31; EU #25;
Cenantibus illis/Dixerunt viri	1143	10r	31	Matins Noct. 2	R6	4	2	7	9	7	6	9	4	2	7	11	12	Mode 5	134 #40; 139 #4; BYU #21; EU #25
Cenantibus illis/Dixerunt viri	134	243v	40	Matins Noct. 2	R7	4	2	7										Mode 5	139 #4; 1143 #31; BYU 21; EU #25
Christum regem/Venite	134	241v	12	Matins	Inv													Mode 4	1143 #12; BYU #9; EU #11
Christum regem/Venite	1143	3r	12	Matins	Inv	2	4	2	5	4	2	4	2	9	2	2	9	Mode 4	134 #12; BYU #9; EU #11
Christum regem/Venite	BYU	2v	12	Matins	Inv	2	4	2	5	4	2	4	2	9	2	2	9	Mode 4	134 #12; 1143 #12; EU #11
Christum regem/[Venite]	EU	1r	11	Matins	Inv	2	4	2	5	4	2	4	2	9	2	2	9	Mode 4	134 #12; 1143 #12; BYU #9
Cibavit eos	1143	17r	75	Mass	Intr	3	5	3	5	7	5	3	5	3	5	8	5	Mode 2	
Cibavit illos/Et de petra/Gloria	1143	16r	64	Sext	Rb2	2	0	2	0	-1	-3	0	-5	-2	0	7	5	Mode 6?	
Cibavit nos Dominus	EU	4v	28	Matins Noct. 3	A11	-2	-5	2	2	0	2	0	-2	0	2	2	4	Mode 8	134 #31; 1143 #35; BYU #24
Cibavit nos Dominus	134	243r	31	Matins Noct. 2	A14													Mode 8	1143 #35; BYU #24; EU #28
Cibavit nos Dominus	1143	11r	35	Matins Noct. 3	A14	-2	-5	2	2	0	2	0	-2	0	2	5	4	Mode 8	134 #31; BYU #24; EU #28
Cibavit nos Dominus	BYU	4r	30	Matins Noct. 3	A14	-2	-5	2	2	0	2	0	-2	0	2	5	4	Mode 8	134 #31; 1143 #35; EU #28

Title	MS	Folio	MS #	Service															Mode	Concordances
Comedetis carnes/Non Moyses	EU	1v	18	Matins Noct. 1	R2	-2	0	2	0	3	0	2	2	0	-2	0	0	3	Mode 2	134 #27; 139 #2; 1143 #21; BYU #15
Comedetis carnes/Non Moyses	134	242v	27	Matins Noct. 1	R4				0	3	2	0			-2	0		3	Mode 2	139 #2; 1143 #21; BYU #15; EU #18
Comedetis carnes/Non Moyses	BYU	3r	20	Matins Noct. 1	R3	-2	0	2	0	3	2	3	3	0	-2	0	0	3	Mode 2	134 #27; 139 #2; 1143 #21; EU #18
Comedetis carnes/Non Moyses	1143	6r	21	Matins Noct. 1	R3	-2	0	2	0	3	3	2	2	0	-2	0	0	3	Mode 2	134 #27; 139 #2; BYU #15; EU #18
Comede[tis]/Non moyses	139	107r	2	Matins Noct. 1	R2	-2	0	2	0	3	3	2	2	0	-2	0			Mode 2	134 #27; 1143 #21; BYU #15; EU #18
Comedi favum	134	244r	45	Matins Noct. 3	A19															
Communione calicis	EU	1v	15	Matins Noct. 1	A6	-2	3	5	8	7	5	3	5	8	7	8	10		Mode 3	134 #16; 1143 #16
Communione calicis	134	242r	16	Matins Noct. 1	A9		3	5	8	7	5	3	5	8	7	8	10		Mode 3	1143 #16; EU #15
Communione calicis	1143	4v	16	Matins Noct. 1	A9	-2	3	5	8	7	5	3	5	8	7	8	10		Mode 3	134 #16; EU #15
Communione calicis	BYU	3r	16	Matins Noct. 1	A9	-2	3	5	8	7	8	7	5	3	5	3	0	1	Mode 3	Not concord w/ others of same text
Cristum regum regem/Venite	70.E.4	88r	9	Matins	Inv	-2	2	3	0	-2	0	2	3	5	3	5	2	0	Mode 1	
Cristus corpus/Ut perhennis	70.E.4	91r	28	Matins Noct. 3	R8	2	4	2	0	-1	0	2	0	4	7	6	4		Mode 7	
Cristus enim	70.E.4	92r	33	Lauds	A17	-2	-5	-2	0	2	3	2	0	-2	0	3	2		Mode 2	
Cumque operuisset/Iste est panis/Gloria	Strahov	220v	53	Matins Noct. 4	R12	2	0	2	4	2	4	0	5	4	2	5	7		Mode 6	
De fructu operum	Strahov	214r	16	Matins Noct. 1	A9	3	0	-2	3	5	7	5	3	5	3	0	3		Mode 1	
Discedentem/Quicumque	139	109v	19	Matins Noct. 3	R18	-2	0	-2	-3	-3	-5	-3	-2	0	0				Mode 8	
Discipulis competentem	70.E.4	86r	2	1 Vesp	A2	-2	0	-2	-5	-2	0	2	3	5	3	2	0		Mode 2	
Dixit Ihesus/Benedictus	Strahov	221r	62	Lauds	A21	-2	-4	-2	-4	0	3	0	-2	-4	-4	-7	-5		Mode 1	
Dixit Ihesus/Nisi meam	70.E.4	88v	15	Matins Noct. 1	R3	-2	0	-5	-2	0	3	3	0	-2	0	3	2		Mode 2	
Dominus Ihesus	70.E.4	90v	24	Matins Noct. 3	A13	7	5	4	5	7	5	7	10	9	7	5	4		Mode 7	
Dominus Ihesus Cristus/Magnificat	70.E.4	87v	8	1 Vesp	A6	2	5	2	0	5	10	9	11	9	9	5			Mode 1	
Dominus Ihesus/Similiter et calicem	Strahov	216r	29	Matins Noct. 2	R4	2	7	4	2	5	4	5	2	4	2	0			Mode 1	Ecce iam coram PM 31
Ecce vobiscum	70.E.4	92v	36	Lauds	A20	-2	5	4	0	4	5	2	0	2	0	-2			Mode 8	
Educas panem/Et vinum/Gloria	1143	16v	68	None	Rb3	2	0	-1	-3	-5	-5	0	2	5	7	5	4	2	Mode 6?	
Ego sum panis/Benedictus	134	245v	66	Lauds	A25														Mode 1	1143 #54
Ego sum panis/Benedictus	1143	15v	54	Lauds	A21	7	3	3	5	7	8	5	3	5	3	0			Mode 1	134 #66
Ego sum/Ego sum	139	108r	8	Matins Noct. 3	R8	4	5	7	9	9	7	5	5	3	5	3			Mode 7	134 #55; 1143 #100; Strahov #39
Ego sum/Ego sum/Gloria	Strahov	217v	39	Matins Noct. 3	R7	4	5	7	9	9	7	5	5	9	7	12	10	9	Mode 7	134 #55; 139 #8; 1143 #100;

Title	MS	Folio	MS #	Service													Mode	Concordances
Ego sum/Ego sum/Gloria	134	245r	55	Matins Noct. 3	R13	4	5	7	9	7	7	5	9	10	12	10	9	Mode 7	139 #8; 1143 #100; Strahov #39
Ego sum/Ego sum/Gloria	1143	26r	100	Matins Noct. 4	R13	2	3	0	-2	0	5	3	7	8	7	5	3	Mode 7	134 #55; 139 #8; Strahov #39
Erit quasi oliva	Strahov	217r	35	Matins Noct. 3	A14	2	5	4	5	7	4	5	2	4	5	7	5	Mode 1	
Et edent carnes	Strahov	213v	4	1 Vesp	A4	2	5	4	5	7	5	5	0	2	0	5	5	Mode 4	Tu decus virgineum PM 271
Et sic	70.E.4	86v	4	1 Vesp	A4	-5	-3	-2	0	2	-2	4	2	0	5	5	4	Mode 8	
Ex altari tuo	EU	4v	29	Matins Noct. 3	A12	2	4	0	-3	-5	0	2	4	5	7	5		Mode 6	134 #32; 1143 #36; BYU #25
Ex altari tuo	134	243r	32	Matins Noct. 2	A15													Mode 6	1143 #36; BYU #25; EU #29
Ex altari tuo	BYU	4r	31	Matins Noct. 3	A15	2	4	0	-1	-3	0	2	5	4	5	7		Mode 6	134 #32; 1143 #36; EU #29
Ex altari tuo	1143	11v	36	Matins Noct. 3	A15	2	4	0	-3	-5	0	2	5	4	5	7		Mode 6	134 #32; BYU #25; EU #29
Faciens mensam	Strahov	215v	24	Matins Noct. 2	A10	-2	0	-7	-5	-2	0	2	0	2	0	-2	0	Mode 8	
Faciet Dominus	Strahov	215v	26	Matins Noct. 2	A12	-2	3	5	8	5	3	5	3	1	0	1	3	Mode 3	
Felix vitis/Omnes in fide	139	109v	18	Matins Noct. 3	R17	7	5	4	5	7								Mode 7	
Fructum salutiferum	EU	1v	13	Matins Noct. 1	A4	2	0	5	4	2	0	5	7	9	10	7	9	Mode 1	134 #14; 1143 #14; BYU #11
Fructum salutiferum	134	242r	14	Matins Noct. 1	A7	2												Mode 1	1143 #14; BYU #11; EU #13
Fructum salutiferum	1143	4r	14	Matins Noct. 1	A7	2	0	5	4	2	0	5	7	9	10	7	9	Mode 1	134 #14; BYU #11; EU #13
Fructum salutiferum	BYU	2v	14	Matins Noct. 1	A7	2	0	5	4	2	0	5	7	9	12	7		Mode 1	134 #14; EU #13
Gloria	1143	17v	77	Mass	G1	2	5	4	5	7	5	4	2	4	5	4	2	Mode 4	From Mass IV (K. Cunctipotens)
Granum/Nisi lotus/Gloria	139	109v	17	Matins Noct. 2	R16	2	0	-3	-1	0								Mode 6	
Hec igitur	70.E.4	90v	26	Matins Noct. 3	A15	2	4	5	4	2	0	2	0	5	7	9	7	Mode 1	
Hic et ibi	70.E.4	89v	18	Matins Noct. 2	A11	-2	-3	-5	0	2	-2	-3	-5	-5	-7	-3	-7	Mode 5	
Homo quidam/Venite comedite	134	241r	7	1 Vesp	R1													Mode 6	139 #10; 1143 #7; BYU #6
Homo quidam/Venite comedite/Gloria	1143	1v	7	1 Vesp	R1	2	0	2	4	0	2	2	4	2	5		7	Mode 6	134 #7; 139 #10; BYU #6
Homo quidam/Venite comedite/Gloria	BYU	1v	7	1 Vesp	R1	2	0	2	4	2	0	4	0	5	4	2	5	7	Mode 6	134 #7; 139 #10; 1143 #7
Homo[quidam]/Venite comedite/Gloria	139	108v	10	2 Vesp	R10	2	0											Mode 6	134 #7; 1143 #7; BYU #6
Hostia Cristus	70.E.4	89r	17	Matins Noct. 2	A10	2	5	4	2	5	7	9	7	5	7	5	7	Mode 1	
Ihesu bone/Magnificat	70.E.4	94r	45	2 Vesp	A27	3	2	0	-2	0	3	5	7	5	3	5	7	Mode 1	

Title	MS	Folio	MS #	Service																Mode	Concordances
Illa nobis	70.E.4	92r	34	Lauds	A18	2	5	4	2	5	0	2	4	0	2	0	-2	0	2	Mode 3	
Immolabit edum	Strahov	213v	3	1 Vesp	A3	-2	-3	0	-5	-3	0	-2	2	0	-2	0	5	2	5	Mode 8	Beata Dei genetrix WA 361; Wales 249v
Immolabit hedum/Et edent	Strahov	220r	51	Matins Noct. 4	R11	2	0	2	0	5	5	4	5	0	5	7	5	0	7	Mode 7	
Immolabit hedum/Pascha nostrum	EU	1v	17	Matins Noct. 1	R1	-2	0	2	3	0	-2	2	-2	0	-2	0	3	5	2	Mode 1	134 #23; 139 #1; 1143 #19; BYU #14
Immolabit hedum/Pascha nostrum	134	242r	23	Matins Noct. 1	R2															Mode 1	139 #1; 1143 #19; BYU #14; EU #17
Immolabit hedum/Pascha nostrum	1143	5r	19	Matins Noct. 1	R2	-2	0	-2	0	2	3	0	-2	0	-2	0	3	5	3	Mode 1	134 #23; 139 #1; BYU #14; EU #17
Immolabit hedum/Pascha nostrum	BYU	3r	19	Matins Noct. 1	R2	-2	0	2	3	0	-2	0	-2	0	3	5	2			Mode 1	134 #23; 139 #1; 1143 #19; EU #17
Immolabit[hedum]/Pascha nostrum	139	107r	1	Matins Noct. 1	R1	-2														Mode 1	134 #23; 1143 #19; BYU #14; EU #17
In voce exultationis	134	242r	19	Matins Noct. 1	A12															Mode 6	1143 #26; EU #22
In voce exultationis	EU	4r	22	Matins Noct. 2	A9	1	-2	-4	-2	1	3	1	5	1	3	3	1	3		Mode 6	134 #19; 1143 #26
In voce exultationis	BYU	3v	24	Matins Noct. 2	A12	1	-2	-4	1	3	1	3	5	1	3	5	3	5	7	Mode 6	Not concordant in 2nd half
In voce exultationis	1143	8r	26	Matins Noct. 2	A12	1	-2	-4	1	3	1	3	5	3	1	3	1	3	6	Mode 6	134 #19; EU #22
Introibo ad altare Dei	EU	4v	27	Matins Noct. 3	A10	4	5	7	9	12	7	9	7	4	5	7	5			Mode 7	134 #30; 1143 #34; BYU #23
Introibo ad altare Dei	134	243r	30	Matins Noct. 2	A13															Mode 7	1143 #34; BYU #23; EU #27
Introibo ad altare Dei	BYU	4r	29	Matins Noct. 3	A13	4	5	7	9	12	7	9	7	4	5	7	5			Mode 7	134 #30; 1143 #34; EU #27
Introibo ad altare Dei	1143	11r	34	Matins Noct. 3	A13	4	5	7	9	12	7	9	7	4	5	7	5			Mode 7	134 #30; BYU #23; EU #27
Invisibilis sacerdos/Ipse conviva	70.E.4	88v	14	Matins Noct. 1	R2	-2	0	3	2	-2	3	2	0	-2	0	3	5			Mode 1	
Kyrie	1143	17v	76	Mass	K	2	4	2	4	5	2	0								Mode 3	From Mass II (K. Fons bonitatis)
Lauda Syon	1143	19r	82	Mass	Seq	3	5	8	7	5	3	5	7	3	0	1				Mode 7	
Laureata plebs fidelis	70.E.4	94v	46	Sequence	Seq	2	-2	0	2	5	-2	0	7	8	7	5				Mode 1	
Manducantibus discipulis/Et ait illis	Strahov	215v	23	Matins Noct. 1	R3	2	0	2	0	-2	2	5	7	5	7	9	7	9		Mode 7	
Melchisedech rex Salem	Strahov	213v	2	1 Vesp	A2	-5	-2	0	2	0	-2	0	2	0	-2	2	5	7	5	Mode 8	
Melchisedech vero/Benedictus Abraham	134	244v	51	Matins Noct. 3	R11															Mode 5	139 #3; 1143 #96; Strahov #49
Melchisedech vero/Benedictus Abraham	1143	24v	96	Matins Noct. 4	R11	4	7	4	2	7	7	9	9	7	9	11	12	11	9	Mode 5	134 #51; 139 #3; Strahov #49
Melchisedech vero/Benedictus/Gloria	139	107v	3	Matins Noct. 1	R3	4	7	4	2	7	7	9	9	7	9					Mode 5	134 #51; 1143 #96; Strahov #49

Title	MS	Folio	MS #	Service															Mode	Concordances
Melchisedech viro/Benedictus Abraham	Strahov	219v	49	Matins Noct. 4	R10	4	7	4	2	7	9	7	9	11	12	11	9		Mode 5	134 #51; 139 #3; 1143 #96
Memor sit Dominus	134	242r	17	Matins Noct. 1	A10														Mode 4	EU #20
Memor sit Dominus	EU	4r	20	Matins Noct. 2	A7	-1	-3	0	-1	-3	2	0	-1	2	2	4	0		Mode 4	134 #17
Memor sit Dominus	BYU	3v	22	Matins Noct. 2	A10	-1	-3	-1	0	-3	0	2	0	0	0	2	0		Mode 4	Not concord w/ others of same text
Memor sit Dominus	1143	8r	24	Matins Noct. 2	A10	-1	-3	-1	0	-3	-5	-3	-1	-1	0	0	-1		Mode 4	Not concord w/ others of same text
Memoria mea	134	243r	34	Matins Noct. 2	A17														Mode 8	1143 #92; Strahov #55
Memoria mea	Strahov	220v	55	Lauds	A17	-2	-5	-2	0	2	0	2	0	0	-2	-2	5	7	Mode 8	134 #34; 1143#92
Memoria mea	1143	23v	92	Matins Noct. 4	A24	-2	-5	-2	0	2	0	2	0	0	-2	-2	5	7	Mode 8	134 #34; Strahov #55;
Memoriam fecit	134	243r	33	Matins Noct. 2	A16														Mode 1	1143 #91; Strahov #45
Memoriam fecit	Strahov	220v	54	Lauds	A16	-2	3	5	3	5	7	5	3	3	5	5	3		Mode 1	134 #33; 1143 #91
Memoriam fecit	1143	23v	91	Matins Noct. 4	A23	-2	3	5	3	5	7	5	3	3	5	5	3		Mode 1	134 #33; Strahov #54
Miserator Dominus	134	241r	2	1 Vesp	A2														Mode 2	1143 #2; BYU #2
Miserator Dominus	BYU	1v	2	1 Vesp	A2	3	5	3	5	7	8	5	12	10	8	7	5		Mode 2	134 #2; 1143 #2
Miserator Dominus	1143	1r	2	1 Vesp	A2	3	5	3	5	7	8	5	3	5	12	10	8		Mode 2	134 #2; BYU #2
Misit me pater/Cibavit eum	BYU	4v	34	Matins Noct. 3	R9	5	2	5	7	9	7	5	7	10	5	7	5		Mode 8	134 #38; 1143 #41
Misit me pater/Cibavit eum	134	243v	38	Matins Noct. 2	R6														Mode 8	1143 #41; BYU #27
Misit me pater/Cibavit eum	1143	12v	41	Matins Noct. 3	R9	5	3	5	7	5	7	9	7	5	10	5	5		Mode 8	134 #38; BYU #27
Misterii veritatem	70.E.4	93r	40	2 Vesp	A23	2	-2	3	2	0	5	3	2	0	-2	3	5		Mode 2	
Mundo/Pater namque	139	109r	13	Matins Noct. 1	R12	-2	-5	-2	0										Mode 2	
Mundum/Ad hoc convivium	139	109r	12	Matins Noct. 1	R11	2	0	-2	3	2	0								Mode 1	
Nolo vos socios	Strahov	220v	57	Lauds	A19	-1	-3	2	4	7	6	7	9	9	7	9	6		Mode 3	
Notum fecit	70.E.4	87v	7	1 Vesp	Vers1	-1	-3	-3	-5	-3	-1	-3								
Nulla nobis	70.E.4	92v	35	Lauds	A19	2	3	2	0	2	3	3	5	3	2	2	3		Mode 6	
Numquid poterit	Strahov	214r	14	Matins Noct. 1	A7	3	0	-2	3	5	7	8	5	3	7	5	10		Mode 1	
O admirabile misterium/Nunc dimittis	EU	1r	9	Compline	A3	1	-2	-4	1	3	1	3	3	5	3	1	3		Mode 6	
O gustu mirabilis	134	246r	84	Compline	A27															

Title	MS	Folio	MS #	Service														Mode	Concordances
O quam suavis/Magnificat	EU	1r	3	1 Vesp	A1	2	4	0	2	0	-1	-3	-5	0	2	4	2	Mode 6	134 #10; 1143 #10; BYU #10; Strahov #10 w/ diff. text
O quam suavis/Magnificat	134	241v	10	1 Vesp	A6													Mode 6	1143 #10; BYU #10; EU #3; Strahov #10 w/ diff. text
O quam suavis/Magnificat	1143	2v	10	1 Vesp	A6	2	4	0	2	0	-1	-3	-5	0	2	4	7	Mode 6	134 #10; BYU #10; EU #3; Strahov #10 w/ diff. text
O quam suavis/Magnificat	BYU	2r	10	1 Vesp	A6	2	4	0	2	0	-1	-3	-5	0	2	4	7	Mode 6	134 #10; 1143 #10; EU #3 Strahov #10 w/ diff/ text
O sacrum convivium/Magnificat	1143	16v	74	2 Vesp	A22	-2	-4	0	3	5	3	5	7	8	7	5	3	Mode 5	134 #83; Strahov #78 w/ diff. text
O sacrum convivium[/Magnificat]	134	246r	83	2 Vesp	A26													Mode 5	1143 #74; Strahov #78 w/ diff. text
O vere miraculum/Vere bonus	70.E.4	91r	29	Matins Noct. 3	R9	-2	0	2	3	0	2	-2	0	2	3	2	0	Mode 2	
Oculi omnium/Aperis	139	162r	21	Mass	Grad	2	5	7	5	4	2	0						Mode 7	1143 #80
Oculi omnium/Aperis	1143	18r	80	Mass	Grad	2	5	7	5	4	2	0	2	4	2	0	0	Mode 7	139 #21
Omnes eandem	Strahov	220v	56	Lauds	A18	-1	-3	-5	0	2	0	2	4	5	4	2	0	Mode 6	
Ore quidem	70.E.4	93v	42	2 Vesp	A25	-2	0	1	0	-2	-4	-2	-4	0	3	5	3	Mode 4	
Ore vero	70.E.4	93v	43	2 Vesp	A26	2	0	2	4	5	4	2	0	5	4	2	4	Mode 6	
Panem angelorum	70.E.4	86v	5	1 Vesp	A5	1	0	-2	0	-2	0	3	1	0	1	3	5	Mode 5	
Panem angelorum/Cibaria misit/Gloria	Strahov	221r	69	Sext	Rb2	2	0	2	0	-1	-3	-5	0	2	5	7	5	Mode 6	
Panem celi/Panem angelorum/Gloria	1143	15v	59	Terce	Rb1	2	0	-3	-3	-5	0	2	5	7	5	4	2	Mode 6?	
Panem de celo	134	245v	62	Lauds	Rb1	2	0	-3	-3	-5	0	2	5	7	5	4	2		
Pange lingua	1143	2r	8	1 Vesp	H1	1	0	-2	3	5	5	8	10	8	7	5	8	Mode 3	BYU #10; Strahov #8;
Pange lingua	Strahov	213v	8	1 Vesp	H1	1	0	-2	3	5	5	8	10	8	7	5	8	Mode 3	1143 #8; BYU #10
Pange lingua	BYU	2v	13	Matins	H2	-2	3	5	8	10	8	5	5	7	5	3	5	Mode 3	1143 #8; Strahov #8 but simpler
Panis quem/Locutus est	EU	4r	24	Matins Noct. 2	R4	2	0	-3	0	-1	2	4	0	-1	0	0	-1	Mode 4	134 #25; 1143 #29; BYU #20
Panis quem/Locutus est	134	242v	25	Matins Noct. 1	R3													Mode 4	1143 #29; BYU #20; EU #24
Panis quem/Locutus est	BYU	3v	26	Matins Noct. 2	R5	2	0	-3	-1	2	4	0	-1	-1	-1	0	2	Mode 4	134 #25; 1143 #29; EU #24
Panis quem/Locutus est	1143	9r	29	Matins Noct. 2	R5	2	0	-3	0	-1	2	4	0	-1	0	0	-1	Mode 4	134 #25; BYU #20; EU #24
Panis vite/Benedictus	70.E.4	92v	38	Lauds	A21	-2	-3	-2	0	-2	-5	0	2	5	4	3	0	Mode 6	
Panis vive/Ideoque tu/Gloria	70.E.4	91v	30	Matins Noct. 3	R10	-2	0	2	3	2	3	0	-2	0	3	5	7	Mode 1	

Title	MS	Folio	MS #	Service														Mode	Concordances
Panis/Confortantem	139	109v	16	R15	-2	1	0	-2	0	0	-4		0	2	4	2	2	Mode 5	
Parasti in conspectu	Strahov	214r	15	A8	2	4	2	2	2	4	4		2	5	2	4	7	5	Mode 1	
Parasti in conspectu/Adversos eos/Gloria	Strahov	221r	65	Rb1	2	0	2	0	-1	0	-3	-5	0	2	5	0	5	Mode 6	
Paratur nobis	134	242r	18	A11														Mode 5	EU #21
Paratur nobis	EU	4r	21	A8	3	0	3	5	5	3	8	7	5	3	3	1	3	Mode 5	134 #18
Paratur nobis	BYU	3v	23	A11	-3	-5	0	2	0	0	-3	-1	-3	-7	-5	-7	0	Mode 5	Not concord w/ others of same text
Paratur nobis	1143	8r	25	A11	-2	-4	0	3	2	2	0	-2	3	5	8	7	5	Mode 5	Not concord w/ others of same text
Pauperibus/Apostolus	139	109r	15	R14	2	4	2	5	4									Mode 4	
Pinguis est panis	1143	14v	48	A18	2	4	5	4	5	5	7	5	4	2	4	2	0	Mode 3	134 #58
Pinguis est panis	134	245v	58	A22														Mode 3	1143 #48
Pluit illis	Strahov	213v	5	A5	3	0	-2	0	3	3	5	7	5	3	2	0	3	Mode 1	
Qui habet aures	134	243r	35	A18														Mode 3	1143 #93; Strahov #58
Qui habet aures	Strahov	220v	58	A20	-1	-3	2	4	7	7	6	7	9	7	6	4	6	Mode 3	134 #35; 1143 #93
Qui habet aures	1143	24r	93	A25	1	0	-2	3	5	5	8	7	8	10	8	7	5	Mode 3	134 #35; Strahov #58
Qui manducat/Non est alia	139	107v	5	R5	7	5	4	5	7	7	9	7						Mode 7	134 #42; 1143 #39
Qui manducat/Non est alia	EU	4v	31	R7	3	5	7	5	7	7	5	7	10	5	3	7	5	Mode 8	Not concord w/ others of same text
Qui manducat/Non est alia	134	244r	42	R8														Mode 7	139 #5; 1143 #39
Qui manducat/Non est alia	BYU	4r	33	R8	-2	-3	0	0	3	3	2	2	0	3	2	2	0	Mode 7	Not concord w/ others of same text
Qui manducat/Non est alia	1143	12r	39	R8	7	5	4	5	7	7	9	7	5	4	5	2	0	Mode 7	134 #42; 139 #5
Qui pacem ponit	134	241r	5	A5														Mode 5	1143 #5; BYU #5
Qui pacem ponit	BYU	1v	5	A5	4	7	4	7	9	9	7	9	12	11	9	7	5	Mode 5	134 #5; 1143 #5
Qui pacem ponit	1143	1v	5	A5	4	7	4	7	9	9	7	9	12	11	9	7	5	Mode 5	134 #5; BYU #5
Qui semel	70.E.4	93r	41	A24	1	3	1	0	-2	0	3	5	8	7	5	7	8	Mode 3	
Quicumque manducaverit/Qui enim manducat	Strahov	216v	31	R5	2	0	2	0	-2	0	2	5	4	5	7	5	7	Mode 7	
Quid enim bonum	Strahov	217r	36	A15	-3	-5	0	2	0	2	4	0	2	0	2	2	4	Mode 6	O quam gloriosum est regnum Utrecht 31v
Quocienscumque	1143	23r	89	Com	7	0	7	5	10	9	10	7	9	7	5	5	7	Mode 7	

Title	MS	Folio	MS #	Service																	Mode	Concordances
Respexit Helyas/Si quis manducaverit	BYU	3r	21	Matins Noct. 1	R4	2	-3	-2	0	2	0	2	2	0	2	4	2	4	5	4	Mode 3	134 #29; 1143 #23; EU #19
Respexit Helyas/Si quis manducaverit/Gloria	EU	4r	19	Matins Noct. 1	R3	2	-3	-2	0	2	0	2	2	0	2	5	2	4	5	4	Mode 3	134 #29; 1143 #23; BYU #16
Respexit Helyas/Si quis manducaverit/Gloria	134	243r	29	Matins Noct. 1	R5																Mode 3	1143 #23; BYU #16; EU #19
Respexit Helyas/Si quis manducaverit/Gloria	1143	7r	23	Matins Noct. 1	R4	2	-3	-2	0	2	0	2	2	0	2	5	2	4	5	4	Mode 3	134 #29; BYU #16; EU #19
Sacerdos in eternum	134	241r	1	1 Vesp	A1																Mode 1	1143 #1; BYU #1
Sacerdos in eternum	1143	1r	1	1 Vesp	A1	3	0	-2	3	5	3	5	7	10	7	5	3				Mode 1	134 #1; BYU #1
Sacerdos in eternum	BYU	1v	1	1 Vesp	A1	3	0	-2	3	5	3	5	7	10	7	5	3				Mode 1	134 #1; 1143 #1
Sacerdos summus/Leta laudum/Gloria	70.E.4	87r	6	1 Vesp	R1	5	5	7	5	7	9	5	7	5	12	14	12				Mode 5	70.E.4 #23
Sacerdos sum[mus/Leta laudem/Gloria]	70.E.4	90v	23	Matins Noct. 2	R7	5	7	5	7	9	7	9									Mode 5	70.E.4 #6
Sacerdotes incensum	1143	22v	84	Mass	Off	3	2	3	2	3	5	7	3	8	7	8	5				Mode 4	
Sacerdotes sancti	Strahov	215v	25	Matins Noct. 2	A11	-3	-1	0	-3	0	-1	2	5	4	2	0	-3				Mode 6	Pater manifestavi Strahov 190v
Sacerdotes sancti	1143	14v	49	Lauds	A19	-1	-3	-1	-3	0	0	2	0	-1	2	-3	-5				Mode 4	134 #59
Sacerdotes sancti	134	245v	59	Lauds	A23																Mode 4	1143 #49
Sacramentum pietatis	70.E.4	93r	39	2 Vesp	A22	-4	-2	-4	-5	-7	-5	-4	-5	-7	-9	-4	-2				Mode 1	
Sacri ministerio	70.E.4	90v	25	Matins Noct. 3	A14	2	0	-2	-3	-5	-3	-2	-5	-2	-2	-3	-2				Mode 8	
Sacris solempniis	BYU	1v	8	1 Vesp	H1	4	5	7	9	5	7	0	4	2	5	4	2				Mode 7	Not concord w/ others of same text
Sacris sollempniis	EU	1v	12	Matins	H1	2	5	4	0	2	5	5	0	2	2	-3	-2				Mode 2	Not concord w/ others of same text
Sacris sollempniis	134	241v	13	Matins	H1																Mode 8	Strahov #13
Sacris sollempniis	Strahov	214r	13	Matins	H2	-3	-2	-5	-3	0	-3	0	0	2	-2	-3	-5				Mode 8	134 #13
Sacris sollempniis	1143	3v	13	Matins	H2	7	8	7	5	7	8	10	8	7	5	7	5				Mode 1	Not concord w/ others of same text
Salvator miserere	EU	1r	5	Compline	A2	3	0	2	0	-2	0	3	5	7	5	3	7				Mode 1	
Sanctus	1143	23r	87	Mass	San	5	2	0	-3	-2	-2	2	0	5							Mode 4	From Mass IV (K. Cunctipotens)
Sanguis eius	70.E.4	88r	12	Matins Noct. 1	A9	-2	-3	-2	0	-2	-3	-5	0	2	5	4	2				Mode 3	
Sapiencia edificavit	Strahov	213v	1	1 Vesp	A1	-1	-3	-3	0	2	0	2	2	4	5	4	2				Mode 6	Not concord w/ others of same text

Title	MS	Folio	MS #	Service															Mode	Concordances
Sapiencia edificavit	BYU	4v	37	Lauds	A16	7	8	7	10	7	5	7	8	7	5	3	5		Mode 1	Not concord w/ others of same text
Sapiencia edificavit	1143	14r	46	Lauds	A16	7	8	7	5	7	5	3	2	0	2	3	2		Mode 1	134 #56
Sapientia edificavit	134	245r	56	Lauds	A20														Mode 1	1143 #46
Sicut novelle	134	241r	4	1 Vesp	A4														Mode 4	1143 #4; BYU #4
Sicut novelle	BYU	1v	4	1 Vesp	A4	-1	-3	0	2	4	2	0	2	4	2	0	-1		Mode 4	134 #4; 1143 #4
Sicut novelle	1143	1v	4	1 Vesp	A4	-1	-3	0	2	4	2	0	2	4	2	0	-1		Mode 4	134 #4; BYU #4
Sicut vivens/Non sicut patres/Gloria	Strahov	219r	43	Matins Noct. 3	R9	2	0	2	4	2	2	0	-3	-1	0	0	-1		Mode 6	
Suo Cristus	70.E.4	88r	10	Matins Noct. 1	A7	3	0	-2	3	5	7	5	3	2	0	2	3		Mode 1	
Te Deum	70.E.4	92r	31	Matins	Te D.	3	5												Mode 3	
Terminatis/Presens in mente/Gloria	139	110r	20	Matins Noct. 3	R19	-2	0	3	2	-2	2	3	0	3	-2	7	5		Mode 1	
Totum Cristus	70.E.4	86v	3	1 Vesp	A3	2	5	2	5	4	2	0	2	0	-2	-3	-5		Mode 3	
Tulit Manue	Strahov	217r	34	Matins Noct. 3	A13	2	4	5	2	5	4	5	7	2	7	9	7		Mode 1	
Unus panis/Parasti in dulcedine	134	244v	49	Matins Noct. 3	R10														Mode 1	139 #9; 1143 #43; BYU #28
Unus panis/Parasti in dul-cedine/Gloria	BYU	4v	35	Matins Noct. 3	R10	-2	0	3	0	2	0	-2	0	-2	3	2	5		Mode 1	134 #49; 139 #9; 1143 #43
Unus panis/Parasti in dul-cedine/Gloria	1143	13v	43	Matins Noct. 3	R10	-2	0	3	0	2	0	-2	0	-2	3	2	5		Mode 1	134 #49; 139 #9; BYU #28
Unus [panis]/Parasti in dul-cedine/Gloria	139	108r	9	Matins Noct. 3	R9	-2	0												Mode 1	134 #49; 1143 #43; BYU #28
Venite comedite/Venite	Strahov	214r	12	Matins	Inv	-1	-3	-1	0	2	0	-1	2	4	4	2	0	-1	Mode 4	Not concord w/ others of same text
Verbum supernum	1143	15r	52	Lauds	H3	2	5	4	2	2	-2	2	0	2	4	2	0		Mode 8	Not concord w/ others of same text
Verbum supernum	Strahov	221r	60	Lauds	H3	4	5	7	9	7	4	5	7	4	7	5	4		Mode 5	
Verbum/Sole panis/Gloria	139	109r	14	Matins Noct. 1	R13	1	0	-2	3	1	0								Mode 3	
Vere miraHoc celesti/Gloria	70.E.4	89r	16	Matins Noct. 1	R4	4	5	7	5	4	2	4	5	4	2	0	2		Mode 5	
Verus Deus	70.E.4	89v	19	Matins Noct. 2	A12	-1	-3	-1	-3	0	-5	0	2	0	5	4	2	4	Mode 6	
Vincenti dabo	1143	14v	50	Lauds	A20	-2	-4	0	3	3	0	3	5	8	7	5	7	5	Mode 5	134 #60
Vincenti dabo	134	245v	60	Lauds	A24	-2	-5												Mode 5	1143 #50
Visibilis creature	70.E.4	88r	11	Matins Noct. 1	A8	-2	-5	7	0	3	3	5	3	2	0	3	5	7	Mode 2	

EDITIONS

INTRODUCTION TO THE EDITIONS

The following are transcriptions of the Corpus Christi material in each of the manuscripts containing readable musical notation. There are no transcriptions for Graz 134 because the notation cannot be read with certainty, although it can be compared to concordant manuscripts.

The transcriptions try to give as clear a picture as possible of the manuscript situation. Each liturgical item bears a number. In the transcriptions, stemless note heads indicate individual pitches. Note groups in the manuscripts are shown by slurs. Liquiescent neumes are treated as note groups (slurred) in which the main note is represented by a standard note head, and the liquiescent pitch itself by a note head of reduced size. Small note heads are also used to show material that has been added to what is in the manuscript (e.g., versicle responses).

IN FESTO EUCHARISTIE
THE HAGUE, NATIONAL LIBRARY OF THE NETHERLANDS, MS 70.E.4

In festo nove sollempnitate corporis domini nostri Ihesu Christi (fols. 52–63v)

Lco i

Immensa divine largitatis beneficia, exhibita populo christiano: inestimabilem ei conferunt dignitatem. Neque enim est, aut fuit aliquando tam grandis nacio, que habeat deos appropinquantes sibi: sicut adest nobis deus noster. Unigenitus siquidem dei filius, sue divinitatis volens nos esse participes: naturam nostram assumpsit, ut homines deos faceret factus homo. Et hoc insuper quod de nostro assumpsit: totum nobis contulit ad salutem. Corpus namque suum pro nostra reconciliatione in ara crucis hostiam obtulit deo patri, sanguinem suum fudit in precium simul et lavachrum: ut redempti a miserabili servitute, a peccatis omnibus mundaremur. Et ut tanti beneficii iugis in nobis maneret memoria: corpus suum in cibum, et sanguinem suum in potum, sub specie panis et vini sumendum: fidelibus dereliquit. O preciosum et ammirandum convivium, salutiferum et omni suavitate repletum. Quid enim hoc convivio preciosius esse potest, in quo non carnes vitulorum et hyrcorum ut olim in lege, sed nobis Christus sumendus proponitur verus deus? Quid hoc sacramento mirabilius? In ipso namque panis et vinum, in corpus Christi et sanguinem substancialiter convertuntur. Ideoque Christus deus et homo perfectus sub modici panis specie continetur.

[The boundless favors of divine generosity, shown to the Christian people, bestow an inestimable dignity on them. There neither is nor ever was so great a nation having gods so near to itself as our God is to us. The only-begotten Son of God, desiring that we be participants in his divinity, took on our nature, so that, having become man, he might make men gods. Whatever he assumed of our nature he made instrumental in the work of our salvation. He offered to God the Father his own body as sacrifice for our reconciliation on the altar of the cross, shed his own blood for our ransom and rebirth, so that, having been redeemed from wretched servitude, we might be washed clean of all sins. And, so that a memory of such great kindnesses might remain always in us, he left behind his body as food and his blood as drink, to be consumed by the faithful in the form of bread and wine. O most precious and wondrous banquet, full of health and filled with every delicacy! What can be more precious than this banquet, in which not the flesh of goats and calves, as once was the rule, but Christ the true God, is given to us as nourishment? What is more wondrous than this sacrament? For in it, bread and wine are changed substantially into the body and blood of Christ. Indeed Christ, the perfect God and man, is contained under the appearance of a little bread.]

Lco ii

Manducatur utique a fidelibus, sed minime laceratur: quinimmo diviso sacramento integer sub qualibet divisionis particula perseverat. Accidencia eciam sine subiecto in eodem existunt, ut fides locum habeat, dum visibile invisibiliter sumitur, aliena specie occultatum: et sensus a deceptione immunes reddantur, qui de accidentibus iudicant sibi notis. Nullum enim sacramentum est isto salubrius, quo purgantur peccata, virtutes augentur, et mens omnium spritualium carismatum habundancia impinguatur.

Offertur in ecclesia pro vivis et pro mortuis: ut omnibus prosit, quod est pro salute omnium institutum. Suavitatem namque huius sacramenti nullus exprimere sufficit, per quod spiritualis dulcedo in suo fonte gustatur: et recolitur memoria illius quam in sua passione Christus monstravit excellentissime caritatis. Unde ut arcius huius caritatis inmensitas cordibus infigeretur fidelium, in ultima cena quando pascha cum discipulis celebrato, transiturus erat ex hoc mundo ad patrem, hoc sacramentum instituit, tamquam passionis sue memoriale perhenne: figurarum veterum impletivum, miraculorum ab ipso factorum maximum, et de sua contristatis absencia solacium singulare. Tu [autem . . .]

[He is consumed entirely by the faithful, but he is in no way broken up, but rather, even though the sacramental sign is divided, he remains entire in each particle of division. For the accidents exist in it without material form in order that faith may have its place, when the visible is invisibly consumed, hidden in the form of another thing, and our senses, which judge events that happen to them, are restored safely from deception. For no sacrament is more salubrious than this, through which sins are purged, virtues are increased, and the soul is filled with an abundance of every spiritual gift. It is offered in the Church for the living and the dead, so that what was instituted for the salvation of all may benefit all. No one suffices to express the delicacy of this sacrament, through which spiritual sweetness is tasted in its source, and the memory of the most excellent charity, which Christ showed in his passion, is recalled. Whereby, so that the immensity of this charity might be impressed more profoundly on the hearts of the faithful, at the last supper, when, having celebrated the passover with his disciples, he was about to leave this world and return to the father, he instituted this sacrament as an eternal remembrance of his passion, the fulfillment of ancient precursors, the greatest of the miracles performed by him, and sole solace to those saddened by his absence.]

L. iii

Convenit itaque devotioni fidelium sollempniter recolere institutionem tam salutiferi, tamquam mirabilis sacramenti: ut ineffabilem modum divine presencie in sacramento visibili veneremur: et laudetur dei potencia que in sacramento eodem tot mirabilia operatur, nec non et de tam salubri, tamquam suavi beneficio exsolvantur deo graciarum debite actiones. Verum etsi in die cene quando sacramentum predictum noscitur institutum, inter missarum sollempnia de institutione ipsius specialis mencio habeatur: totum tamen residuum eiusdem officium diei ad Christi passionem pertinet, circa cuius venerationem ecclesia illo tempore occupatur. Unde ut integro celebritatis officio institutionem tanti sacramenti sollempniter recoleret plebs fidelis: romanus pontifex Urbanus quartus huius sacramenti devotione[30] affectus, pie statuit prefate institutionis memoriam, prima feria quinta post octavas pentecostes, a cunctis fidelibus celebrari: ut qui per totum anni circulum hoc sacramentuo utimur ad salutem, eius institutionem illo specialiter tempore recolamus: quo spiritus sanctus discipulorum corda edocuit, ad plene cognoscenda huius misteria sacramenti. Nam et in eodem tempore cepit hoc sacramentum a fidelibus frequentari. Legitur enim in actibus apostolo-

---

[30] This word is written in the margin.

rum: quod erant perseverantes in doctrina apostolorum et communicatione fractionis panis, et orationibus: statim post sancti spiritus missionem. Ut autem predicta quinta feria, et per octavas sequentes eiusdem institutionis salutaris, honorificencius agatur memoria, et sollempnitas de hoc celebrior habeatur, loco distributionum materialium, que in ecclesiis cathedralibus largiuntur: existentibus canonicis horis, nocturnis pariterque diurnis, prefatus romanus pontifex, eis qui huiusmodi horis in hac sollemnitate personaliter in ecclesiis interessent, stipendia spiritualia apostolica largitione concessit: quatinus per hec fideles ad tanti festi celibritatem, avidius et copiosius convenirent. Unde omnibus vere penitentibus et confessis, qui matutinali officio huius festi, presencialiter in ecclesia ubi celebraretur adessent centum. Qui vero misse totidem. Illis autem qui interessent in primis ipsius festi vesperis similiter centum. Qui vero in secundis totidem. Eis quoque qui prime, tercie, sexte, none, ac completorii, adessent officiis, pro qualibet horarum ipsarum quadraginta. Illis vero qui per ipsius festi octavas in matutinalibus, vespertinis, misse, ac predictarum horarum officiis presentes existerent: singulis diebus octavarum ipsarum centum dierum indulgenciam misericorditer tribuit, perpetuis temporibus duraturam.

[It is fitting therefore for the devotion of the faithful, solemnly to honor again the institution of such a salubrious and miraculous sacrament, so that we may venerate the ineffable mode of the divine presence in a visible sacrament, and so that the power of God may be praised, which, in the same sacrament, works so many miracles, and indeed so that the thanks owed to God for such a salubrious and sweet kindness may be discharged. But, although on the day of the last supper, when the aforesaid sacrament is known to have been instituted, special mention is made of its institution within the solemnities of the mass, nevertheless all the remaining worship of this same day is concerned with Christ's suffering, around whose veneration the church at that time is occupied. Hence, so that the faithful may solemnly honor again the institution of such a great sacrament by a complete office of celebration, the Roman Pope Urban IV, influenced by the devotion of this sacrament, piously decreed commemoration of the aforementioned institution on feria five after the octave of Pentecost, to be celebrated by all the faithful, so that we, who use this sacrament throughout the year for salvation, may honor again, at that time especially, its institution, by which the Holy Spirit taught the hearts of the disciples to understand fully the mysteries of this sacrament. For at the same time this sacrament began to be frequented by the faithful. It is indeed read in the Acts of the Apostles that they were persevering in the apostolic doctrine by sharing in the breaking of bread, and by prayers, immediately after the departure of the Holy Spirit. So that, on the the aforesaid feria five and the following octave, remembrance of this same saving institution may be performed more honorably and its ceremony have greater participation, in place of the distributions of material goods that are bestowed in cathedral churches, during current established times, night as well as day, the aforesaid Roman pope grants to those who, during its times, personally take part in this ceremony at church spiritual stipends through apostolic generosity, so that by them the faithful more eagerly and more numerously may come together for the celebration of so great a feast. Hence, to all the truly penitent and to those having confessed, who are present at the office of matins of this feast in person in the church where it is celebrated, one hundred [days' indulgence]. To those who attend mass, the same number. To those who take part in first vespers of the feast, similarly one hundred. The same number to those in second vespers. To those who attend the offices of prime, terce, sext, none, and compline, forty for any of those hours. To those who personally appear through the octave of this feast at matins, vespers, mass, and the aforesaid office hours, for each of the days of the octave he mercifully allots one hundred days in perpetuity.]

L. iiii

[Gratian, De consecratione, *Dist. II, can. 69 beginning]*[31]

Huius sacramenti figura precessit, quando manna pluit deus patribus in deserto: qui cotidiano celi pascebantur alimento. Unde dictum est. Panem angelorum manducavit homo. Sed[32] tamen panem illum qui manducaverunt: omnes in deserto mortui sunt. Ista autem esca quam accipitis, iste panis vivus qui de celo descendit: vite eterne substanciam ministrat. Et quicumque hunc panem manducaverit, non morietur in eternum: quia corpus Christi est. Considera utrum nunc prestancior sit panis angelorum, aut caro Christi: que utique est corpus vite. Manna illud de celo: hoc super celum. Illud celi: hoc domini celorum. Illud corrupcioni obnoxium, si in diem alterum servaretur: hoc alienum ab omni corruptione. Quicumque religiose gustaverit: corruptionem sentire non poterit. Illis aqua de petra fluxit: tibi sanguis ex Christo. Illos ad horam saciavit aqua: te sanguis aluit in eternum. Iudeus bibit et sitit: tu cum biberis sitire non poteris. Et illud in umbra: hoc in veritate. Si illud quod miraris umbra est: quantum istud est cuius umbram miraris? Audi quia umbra est: que aput patres facta est. Bibebant inquit de spirituali: consequenti eos petra. Petra autem erat Christus. Sed non in pluribus eorum complacitum est deo. Nam prostrati sunt in deserto. Hec autem facta sunt in figura nostri. Cognovisti pociora. Pocior est enim lux: quam umbra, veritas quam figura: corpus auctoris quam manna de celo.

[A precursor of this sacrament occurred earlier, when God rained manna on the fathers in the desert, who daily ate the food of heaven. Wherefore it is said: Man ate the bread of the angels. But yet those who ate that bread all died in the desert. However, this bread which you take, this living bread which descended from heaven, provides the substance of eternal life. And whoever shall eat this bread, will not die forever, because it is the body of Christ. Consider which now is more precious, the bread of angels, or Christ's flesh, which is wholly the body of life. That manna is from heaven, this above heaven. That is of heaven, this, of the Lord of heavens. That, subject to corruption, if kept for another day, this free from all corruption. Whoever religiously eats, will not experience corruption. To them water flowed from the rock, to you the blood [flows] from Christ. The water satisfied them for a time, the blood cleanses you for

---

[31] Based on Ambrosius, *De mysteriis,* Ch. VIII, n. 47 et seq. (*Patrologia cursus completus: series latina,* ed. J.-P. Migne, 221 vols. [Paris, 1841–64], 16, cols. 404 ff.; hereafter PL).

[32] In KB 70.E.4, the word is *sed,* but in BNF 1143 it is *set.* This distinction is maintained whenever the word is written out fully, i.e., not abbreviated. It may indicate a difference in pronunciation: voiced consonances in KB 70.E.4, unvoiced consonances in BNF 1143. Other word differences, e.g., *obtulit* (KB 70.E.4) vs. *optulit* (BNF 1143), support this, although the difference is not consistently observed.

eternity. The Jews drank and thirsted, you, when you drink, cannot thirst. That [happened] in a shadow, this in truth. If that at which you marvel is a shadow, how much more is this whose shadow you admire. Hear why this is a shadow, which was done in the time of the forefathers. They drank, he said, from the spiritual rock which followed them. The rock, however, was Christ. But God was not well pleased with many of them. Thus they were cast down in the desert. This was done as a symbol to us. You know which is better. Light is better that shadow, truth better than a symbol, the body of the creator better than manna from heaven.]

L. v

[Gratian, De consecratione, *Dist. II, can. 69 continued]*

Forte dicis: aliud video. Quomodo tu michi asseris quod corpus Christi accipiam? Et hoc nobis super est ut probemus. Quantis igitur utimur exemplis ut probemus hoc non esse quod natura formavit, sed quod benedictio consecravit: maioremque vim esse benedictionis quam nature, quia benedictione eciam ipsa natura mutatur. Unde virgam tenebat Moyses, proiecit eam: et facta est serpens. Rursus apprehendit caudam serpentis: et in virge naturam revertitur. Vides ergo prophetica gratia bis mutatam naturam esse: et serpentis et virge. Currebant Egypti flumina, puro meatu aquarum, subito de foncium venis sanguis cepit erumpere: non erat potus in fluviis. Rursus ad prophete preces cruor fluminum cessavit, aquarum natura remeavit, circumclusus undique erat populus Hebreorum: hinc Egyptiis vallatus inde mari conclusus. Virgam levavit Moyses, separavit se aqua, et in murorum speciem se congelavit: atque inter undas via pedestris apparuit. Iordanis retrorsum conversus: contra naturam in sui fontis revertitur exordium. Nonne claret naturam vel maritimorum fluctuum, vel cursus fluvialis esse mutatam. Siciebat populus patrum, tetigit Moyses petram: et aqua de petra fluxit. Numquid non preter naturam operata est gratia: ut aquam vomeret petra, quam non habebat natura?

[Perhaps you say: I see something different. How can you claim to me that I am receiving the body of Christ? And this is what we must show. How many examples, therefore, do we use, to show that this is not what nature has formed, but what blessing has consecrated, and that there is greater power in blessing than in nature, because by blessing even nature itself can be changed. Hence, Moses held a rod, threw it, and it became a serpent. Again, he grasped the serpent's tail, and it reverted into its nature as a rod. You see therefore, by prophetic will, its nature is twice changed, both of a serpent and a rod. The rivers of Egypt flowed with a pure course of waters, suddenly from the source of the waters blood began to burst forth, there was no drinkable water in the rivers. Conversely, at the prayers of the prophet, the blood of the rivers ceased, the nature of waters returned. The Hebrew nation was surrounded on all sides, on one side blocked by the Egyptians, on the other side cut off by the sea. Moses raised a rod, the water parted and solidified itself into a kind of wall, and between the waves a foot path appeared. The Jordan reversed course, and it returned, against nature, to the beginning of its source. Is it not clear that the nature of the ocean's waves or of the river's course was changed? The people of the forefathers thirsted, Moses touched the rock, and water flowed from the rock. Has not grace acted contrary to nature, so that a rock might spew forth water, which it did not have by nature?]

L. vi

[Gratian, De consecratione, Dist. II, can. 69 continued]

Marath fluvius amarissimus erat, ut siciens populus bibere non posset. Moyses misit lignum in aquam, et amaritudinem suam aquarum natura deposuit: quam infusa subito gracia temperavit. Sub Helyseo propheta uni ex filiis prophetarum excussum est ferrum de securi, et statim immersum est. Rogavit Helyseum: qui amiserat ferrum. Misit eciam Helyseus lignum in aquam, et ferrum natavit. Utique eciam hoc preter naturam factum cognovimus. Gravior est enim ferri species: quam aquarum liquor. Advertimus igitur maiorem esse gratiam quam naturam: et adhuc tamen prophetice benedictionis numeramus[33] gratiam. Quod si tantum valuit humana benedictio, ut naturam converteret, o[34] quid dicimus de ipsa consecratione divina: ubi ipsa verba domini salvatoris operantur? Nam sacramentum istud quod accipis: Christi sermone conficitur. Quod si tantum valuit sermo Helye, ut ignem de celo deponeret: non valebit Christi sermo ut species mutet elementorum.

[The Marath River was very bitter, so that the thirsting people were not able to drink. Moses threw a branch into the water, and nature eliminated the bitterness of its waters, which grace, suddenly intermixed, tempered. During the time of Elias the prophet, the blade fell off the battle ax of one of the sons of the prophets and immediately sank. He who had let the iron slip sought out Elias. Elias put a stick into the water, and the blade floated. Certainly we know that this is an act beyond nature. The species of iron is heavier than the liquid of water. We perceive therefore that grace is greater than nature, but yet we still reckon grace to be of prophetic blessing. But if a human blessing has such great strength that it can change nature, O what can we say of that divine consecration, in which the words themselves of the Savior act? For this sacrament you receive is accomplished by the words of Christ. If the word of Elias had such great strength that it could bring down fire from heaven, will not the word of Christ have the power to change the species of the elements?]

[Versus]
Educas panem de terra alleluia. R. Et vinum letificet cor hominis, alleluia.
[May you produce bread from the earth, alleluia. R. And may wine gladden the heart of man, alleluia.]

[Gospel] secundum Iohanne [Jo 6: 55]
In illo tempore: Dixit Ihesus d[iscipulis] s[uis] et turbis Iudeorum. Caro mea vere est cibus: et sanguis meus vere est potus. Et. rel:
[At that time. Jesus said to his disciples and to the multitude of the Jews: My flesh truly is food, and my blood is truly drink. And so forth.]

---

[33] *Miramur* in Lambot and Fransen, but *numeramus* in all sources.

[34] This word is only in KB 70.E.4.

[Lectio vii] Omel[ia] beati Augustini epi[scopi] de eadem lectione

[Alcuin, Commentaria in S. Joannis evangelium, *Lib. 3: Ch. XV, Vers. 56]*[35]

Cum enim cibo et potu id appetant homines, ut non esuriant necque siciant: hoc vere non prestat nisi iste cibus et potus, qui eos a quibus sumitur, immortales, et incorruptibiles facit, id est societas ipsorum sanctorum: ubi pax erit, et unitas plena atque perfecta. Propterea quippe sicut eciam ante nos intellexerunt hoc homines dei, dominus noster Ihesus Christus corpus et sanguinem suum in eis rebus commendavit: que ad unum aliquid rediguntur. Ex multis namque granis unus panis conficitur, et ex multis racemis vinum confluit.

[Although men desire from food and drink, that they neither hunger nor thirst, this is not assured, unless it is that food and drink which makes those, by whom it is consumed, immortal and incorruptible, that is, a community of the saints themselves, where there will be peace and full and perfect unity. Therefore, indeed, as men of God understood before us, our Lord Jesus Christ put his body and blood into these things things, which are made into some one thing. Now, one bread is made from many grains, and wine flows together from many clusters of grapes.]

Lco viii

[Alcuin, Commentaria in S. Joannis evangelium, *Lib. 3: Ch. XV, Vers. 56–57]*[36]

Denique iam exponit quomodo id fiat quod loquitur, et quid sit manducare corpus eius et sanguinem bibere. Et qui manducat meam carnem, et bibit meum sanguinem: in me manet et ego in eo. Hoc est ergo manducare illam escam, et illum bibere potum: in Christo manere, et illum manentem in se habere, ac per hoc qui non manet in Christo, et in quo non manet Christus, proculdubio non manducat spiritualiter eius carnem, licet carnaliter, et visibiliter premat dentibus sacramenta corporis et sanguinis Christi: sed magis tante rei sacramentum ad iudicium sibi manducat et bibit, qui immundus presumit ad Christi accedere sacramenta: que alius non digne sumit nisi qui mundus est. De quibus dicitur. Beati mundo corde: quoniam ipsi deum videbunt.

[Finally he now explains how what he has spoken happens, and what it is to eat his body and drink his blood. "He who eats my body and drinks my blood abides in me and I in him." To eat that food and to drink that drink is, therefore, to abide in Christ, and to have him abiding in oneself, and thus the person who does not abide in Christ, and in whom Christ does not abide, without doubt does not eat spiritually his flesh, although physically and visibly he chews with his teeth the sacraments of the body and blood of Christ, but rather he eats and drinks the sacrament of such great importance to his own condemnation, who, impure, presumes to approach the sacraments of Christ, which no one rightly takes except the one who is pure. About whom it is said: Blessed are the pure of heart, because they shall see God.]

---

[35] PL 100, col. 835. The verse numbers in PL do not agree with current ones. From verse 52 on, the PL numbers are one too high. This is because PL divides verse 52 into two parts, each with its own number.

[36] PL 100, cols. 835–36.

L. ix

[Alcuin, Commentaria in S. Joannis evangelium, *Lib. 3: Ch. XV, Vers. 58[37]]*

Sicut misit me inquit vivens pater: et ego vivo propter patrem. Et qui manducat me: et ipse vivet propter me. Non enim filius participatione patris fit melior, qui est natus equalis sicut participatione filii, per unitatem corporis et sanguinis quam illa manducatio potacioque significat: efficit nos meliores. Vivimus ergo nos propter ipsum, manducantes eum, id est ipsum accipientes vitam eternam: quam non habemus ex nobis. Vivit autem ipse propter patrem, missus ab eo: quia semetipsum exinanivit factus obediens usque ad signum crucis. Sicut misit me vivens pater, et ego vivo propter patrem. Et qui manducat me, et ipse vivet propter me. Ac si diceret. Et ego vivo propter patrem, id est ut ad illum tanquam ad maiorem referam vitam meam: exinanicio mea fecit in qua me misit. Ut autem quisque vivat propter me, participatio facit qui manducat me. Ego itaque humiliatus vivo propter patrem, ille rectus vivit propter me. Non de ea natura dixit, qua[38] semper est equalis patri, sed ea in qua minor factus est patre: de qua eciam superius dixit. Sicut pater habet vitam in semetipso, sic dedit et filio vitam habere in semetipso, id est genuit filium habentem vitam in semetipso. Tu [autem . . .]

[As the living father, he said, sent me, I live because of the father. And he who eats me, will live because of me. Certainly the son, who was born equal, is not made better through the participation of the father, as he makes us better through the participation of the son through the unity of the body and blood which that food and drink signifies. We live on behalf of him, by eating him, that is, receiving him as eternal life, which we do not have by ourselves. He himself lives on behalf of the father, sent by him, because he emptied himself, made obedient up to the sign of the cross. As the living father sent me, I live on behalf of the father. And he who eats me, he himself will live on behalf of me. This is as if to say: I live on behalf of the father, that is, I direct my life to him as to one greater, he brought about my emptying, in which form he sent me. Participation brings about for the one who eats me, that each one lives on behalf of me. Thus, I, humbled, live on behalf of the father, this man, uplifted, lives on behalf of me. He said this not about his nature, in which he is always equal to the father, but about that in which he was made lesser in relation to the father, about which earlier he said: Just as the father has life in and of himself, he gave his son life to have in and of himself, that is, he begot a son having life in and of himself.]

Per ebdomadam Lco prima

[Gratian, De consecratione, *Dist. II, can. 57][39]*

Christus panis est, de quo qui manducat, vivit in eternum. De quo ipsemet dixit, et panis quem ego dabo ei caro mea est: pro mundi vita. Determinat quomodo sit panis, non solum secundum verbum quo vivunt omnia: sed secundum carnem assumptam,

---

[37] PL 100, col. 836.

[38] *Quia* in BNF 1143

[39] From Augustinus, *In Iohannis Evangelium tractatus CXXIV*, ed. Radbotus Willems, Corpus Christianorum, Series latina, 36 (Turnholt: Brepols, 1954), tr. XXVI, n. 13.

pro mundi vita. Humana enim caro, que erat peccato mortua, carni munde unita, incorporata, unum cum illa effecta: vivit de spiritu eius, sicut vivit corpus de suo spiritu. Qui vero non est de corpore Christi: non vivit de spiritu Christi.

[Gratian, De consecratione, *Dist. II, can. 60]*

Corpus et sanguinem Christi dicimus illud, quod ex fructibus terre acceptum, et prece mistica consecratum, recte sumimus ad salutem spiritualem: in memoriam dominice passionis. Quod cum per manus hominis ad illam visibilem speciem perducatur, non sanctificatur ut sit tam magnum sacramentum, nisi operante invisibiliter spiritu sancto, cum hec omnia que per corporales motus in illo opere fiunt: deus operetur.

[Christ is the bread, of which whoever eats, lives forever. About this he himself said: "And the bread which I will give him is my flesh, for the life of the world." He prescribes in what way it is bread for the life of the world, not only in accordance with the word, by which all things live, but in accordance with the assumed flesh. His human flesh, which was dead to sin, united to the flesh of the world, incorporated, made one with it, lives by his spirit, just as the body lives by its spirit. Whoever is not truly of the body of Christ, does not live by the spirit of Christ.

We call the body and blood of Christ that which, taken from the fruits of the earth, and blessed by sacred prayer, we properly consume for spiritual salvation, in memory of the passion of the Lord. Since it is brought into its visible form by the hand of man, it is not sanctified to be such a great sacrament, except by the Holy Spirit working invisibly, since God makes all these things which come about from the body's movements in that work.]

L. ii

[Gratian, De consecratione, *Dist. II, can. 63]*

Hoc est sacramentum pietatis, et est signum unitatis: et vinculum caritatis. Qui vult vivere, accedat et credat, incorporet hunc cibum et potum: societatem vult intelligi corporis et membrorum suorum: quod est ecclesie in predestinatis.

[Gratian, De consecratione, *Dist. II, can. 48]*

Hoc est quod dicimus, quod omnibus modis approbare contendimus, sacrificium ecclesie duobus confici, duobus constare: visibili elementorum specie, et invisibili domini nostri Ihesu Christi carne et sanguine: et sacramento, et re sacramenti, id est corpore Christi, sicut Christi persona constat, et conficitur ex deo et homine, cum ipse Christus verus sit deus, et verus homo: quia omnis res illarum rerum naturam et veritatem in se continet ex quibus conficitur. Conficitur autem sacrificium ecclesie duobus, sacramento et re sacramenti: id est corpore Christi. Est igitur sacramentum, et res sacramenti: id est corpus Christi. Caro eius est quam forma panis opertam in sacramento accipimus, et sanguis eius quem sub vini specie ac sapore potamus. Caro videlicet est carnis: et sanguis est sacramentum sanguinis. Carne et sanguine utroque invisibili, intelligibili, spirituali, significatur visibile corpus domini nostri Ihesu Christi, et palpabile plenum gracia omnium virtutum: et divina maiestate.

[This is the sacrament of piety, it is both a sign of unity and a bond of love. Whoever wishes to live, let him approach and believe, let him consume this food and drink. He wishes the society of the body and its members to be understood, because it is among the things predestined in/for the church.[40]

This is what we say, what we work to prove in every way, that the sacrifice of the church is composed of two things, consists of two things, of the visible species of the elements, and of the invisible body and blood of our Lord Jesus Christ, both of the sacrament and of the object of the sacrament, that is, of the body of Christ, just as the person of Christ comprises and is composed of God and man, since Christ himself is truly God and truly man, because each thing contains in itself the nature and truth of those things of which it is composed. Thus the sacrifice of the church is composed of two things, the sacrament and the object of the sacrament, that is the body of Christ. There is therefore the sacrament and the object of the sacrament, that is the body of Christ. His flesh is what, hidden in the form of bread, we receive in the sacrament, and his blood what we drink under the appearance and taste of wine. His flesh is the sacrament of his flesh, and his blood the sacrament of his blood. By his flesh and blood both invisible, understandable, spiritual, is symbolized the visible body of our Lord Jesus Christ, and it is touchable, full of the grace of all virtues and of divine majesty.]

Lco iii

[Gratian, De consecratione, Dist. II, can. 48 cont'd]

Sicut ergo celestis panis qui vere Christi caro est, suo modo vocatur corpus Christi, cum re vera sit sacramentum corporis Christi illius videlicet quod visibile, quod palpabile, mortale in cruce est positum: vocaturque ipsa carnis immolacio, que sacerdotis manibus fit Christi passio, mors, crucifixio, non rei veritate, sed significanti misterio: sic sacramentum fidei, quod baptismus intelligitur: fides est.

[Gratian, De consecratione, Dist. II, can. 71]

Iteratur cotidie hec oblatio, licet Christus semel passus in carne, per unam eandemque mortis passionem, semel salvavit mundum: ex qua morte idem resurgens ad vitam, mors illi ultra non dominabitur. Quod profecto sapiencia dei patris necessarium: pro multis causis providit. Primo quidem quia cotidie peccamus, saltem in peccatis sine quibus mortalis infirmitas vivere non potest, quia licet omnia peccata condonata sint in baptismo: infirmitas tamen peccati adhuc manet in carne. Unde psalmista. Benedic anima mea dominum, qui propiciatur omnibus iniquitatibus tuis: qui sanat omnes infirmitates tuas. Et ideo quia cotidie labimur, cotidie Christus pro nobis mistice immolatur, et passio Christi in misterio traditur, ut qui semel moriendo mortem vicerat: cotidie recidiva delictorum per hec sacramenta corporis et sanguinis peccata relaxet. Unde oramus: dimitte nobis debita nostra. Quia si dixerimus quia peccatum non habemus, ipsi nos seducimus: et veritas in nobis non est.

---

[40] All sources have: "Qui vult vivere, accedat et credat, incorporet hunc cibum et potum, societatem vult intelligi corporis et membrorum suorum, quod est ecclesie in predestinatis." But Friedberg has: "Qui vult vivere, accedat et credat, incorporetur. Hunc cibum et potum, societatem vult intelligi corporis et membrorum suorum, quod est ecclesie in predestinatis"; see *Corpus juris canonici*, ed. E. Friedberg (1879–81; repr. Graz: Akademische Druck- u. Verlagsanstalt, 1959.

[Therefore, just as the celestial bread, which is truly the flesh of Christ, is called in its own way the body of Christ, although actually it is the sacrament of the body of Christ, which visibly, which palpably, subject to death, was placed on the cross, and just as it is called that sacrifice of the flesh, which is the suffering, death, and crucifixion of Christ at the priest's hands, not because of the truth of the matter, but because of a symbolic mystery, so the sacrament of faith, which is called baptism, is faith.

This offering is repeated daily, although Christ having died once in the flesh through one and the same suffering of death, saved the world a single time, from which death rising again to life, death will have no more dominion over him. Indeed the wisdom of God[41] foresaw this necessity for many reasons. First of all because we sin daily, at least in sins without which mortal infirmity it is not possible to live,[42] because although all sins are pardoned in baptism, nevertheless the infirmity of sin still remains in the flesh. Hence the psalmist: Bless the Lord, my soul, who forgives all your sins, who heals all your infirmities. And because daily we fall, daily Christ is mystically sacrificed for us, and the passion of Christ is handed down in mystery, so that he who, by dying a single time, conquered death, might forgive daily the faults of recurring transgressions through the sacraments of the body and blood. Hence we pray: Forgive us our sins. Because if we would say that we do not have sin, we delude ourselves, and truth is not within us.]

[L. i]

[Gratian, De consecratione, *Dist. II, can. 71]*

Iteratur eciam hoc misterium, et ob commemorationem passionis Christi: sicut ipse ait. Hoc quocienscumque agitis, in meam commemoracionem facite. Quocienscumque ergo hunc panem sumitis, et bibitis hunc calicem: mortem domini annunciabitis donec veniat. Non itaque sic accipiendum est, donec Christi mors veniat, quia iam ultra non morietur: sed donec ipse dominus ad iudicium veniat. Interdum autem semper mors est Christi per seculi vitam posteris nuncianda: ut discant qua caritate dilexit suos, qui pro eis mori dignatus est, cui omnes vicem debemus rependere caritatis, quia ad hoc nos prior dilexit, cum essemus gehenne filii: ut diligeremus eum a morte iam liberati.

[Gratian, De consecratione, *Dist. II, can. 50]*

Quia morte domini liberati sumus, huius rei memoriam[43] in edendo carnem, et potando sanguinem eius, que pro nobis oblata sunt significamus.

[This mystery is repeated, indeed for the purpose of a commemoration of the passion of Christ, just as he himself said: So often as you do this, do it in memory of me. Therefore, as often as you eat this bread, and drink this cup, you proclaim the death of the Lord until he comes. This is not to be understood as: "until the death of Christ comes," because he will not die any more, but "until the Lord himself comes for judg-

---

[41] "Sapientia Dei" [Wisdom of God] is the name given to Christ as the second person of the Trinity.

[42] That is, each day we commit at least venial sins.

[43] *memores* in BNF 1143.

ment." In the meanwhile the death of Christ for the life of time must always be proclaimed to posterity, so that they may learn with what love he loved his own, who
deigned to die for them, to whom we all should return an equivalence of love, because
he loved us first, although we were the sons of Gehenna, so that we, now liberated
from death, might love him.

Because by the death of the Lord we have been freed, we signify the memory of this
event in eating his flesh and drinking his blood, which were offered up for us.]

L. ii

[Gratian, De consecratione, *Dist. II, can.72]*

Utrum sub figura, an sub veritate hoc misticum calicis sacramentum fiat, veritas ait,
caro mea vere est cibus: et sanguis meus vere est potus. Alioquin quomodo magnum
erit, panis quem ego dabo caro mea est pro mundi vita: nisi vera sit caro? Sed quia
Christum fas vorari dentibus non est, voluit hunc panem et vinum, in ministerio vere
carnem suam, et sanguinem suum consecratione spiritus sancti potencialiter creari, et
cotidie pro mundi vita mistice immolari, ut sicut de virgine per spiritum sanctum vera
caro sine cohitu creatur: ita per eundem ex substancia panis et vini mistice idem corpus
Christi consecretur. Corpus Christi et veritas et figura est. Veritas dum corpus Christi et
sanguis in virtute spiritus sancti et in virtute ipsius, ex panis vinique substancia efficitur. Figura vero est: id quod exterius sentitur.

[Whether by symbolism or by truth the mystery of the chalice becomes a sacrament,
truth tells: My flesh truly is food, and my blood truly is drink. Otherwise how will it be
a great thing—"the bread which I will give is my flesh for the life of the world"—unless
it be true flesh? But because it is not right that Christ be devoured with the teeth, he
wanted this bread and wine truly in the ministry to become powerfully his flesh and
blood by the consecration of the Holy Spirit, and daily to be sacrificed mystically for
the life of the world, so that, just as his true flesh is created from a virgin through the
Holy Spirit without intercourse, through the same Holy Spirit the same body of Christ
may be mystically consecrated from the substance of bread and wine. The body of
Christ is both truth and a symbol. Truth when the body and blood of Christ is produced by the power of the Holy Spirit and by his own power, from the substance of
bread and wine. The symbol is that which is perceived externally.]

Lco iii

[Gratian, De consecratione, *Dist. II, can.72 continued]*

Intra catholicam ecclesiam, in misterio[44] corporis Christi, nichil a bono maius, nichil
a malo minus perficitur sacerdote, quia non in merito consecrantis, sed in verbo efficitur creatoris: et in virtute spiritus sancti. Si enim in merito esset sacerdotis: nequaquam
ad Christum pertineret. Nunc autem sicut ipse est qui baptizat, ita ipse est qui per spiritum sanctum hanc suam efficit carnem: et transit vinum in sanguinem. Unde et sacerdos. Iube inquit hec offerri per manus angeli tui sancti in sublime altare tuum: in cons-

---

[44] Originally *ministerio*. The word has been changed to *misterio* by crossing out the third and fourth letters.
BNF 1143 has *misterio*, Strahov has *ministerio*.

pectu divine maiestatis tue. Ut quid deferenda in lucem deposcit, nisi ut intelligatur: quod ista fiant in eo sacerdocio. Hanc ergo oblationem benedictam per quam benedicimur, asscriptam, per quam homines in celo asscribuntur, ratam, per quam visceribus Christi esse censeamur, rationabilem, per quam a bestiali sensu exuamur, acceptabilem, ut qui nobis ipsis displicemus: per hanc acceptabiles eius unico filio simus. Nichil rationabilius ut quia nos iam similitudinem mortis eius in baptismo accepimus, similitudinem quoque carnis et sanguinis sumamus, ita ut veritas non desit in sacramento, et ridiculum nullum fiat a paganis: quod cruorem occisi hominis bibamus.

[Within the catholic church, in the mystery of the body of Christ, nothing greater by a good priest, nor inferior by a bad priest is accomplished, because it is accomplished, not by the merit of the one consecrating, but by the word of the creator, and by the power of the Holy Spirit. If it were by the merit of the priest, it would in no way pertain to Christ. Now however, just as it is he himself who baptizes, so it is he himself who, through the Holy Spirit, makes it his flesh, and changes wine into his blood. Hence the priest: Command, he says, these offerings to be carried up by the hands of your holy angels to your sublime altar, in the sight of your divine majesty. How is it that he demands these offerings be brought into the light, if not that it be understood that these things are done in his priesthood? Therefore this offering is blessed, through which we are blessed, it is enrolled, through which men are enrolled in heaven, it is certified, through which we are deemed to be of the flesh of Christ, it is intelligent, through which we are freed from bestial understanding, it is accepting, so that we who are displeasing to ourselves may become by it acceptable to his only son. Nothing is more sensible than that, because we receive the likeness of his death in baptism, we also consume the likeness of his body and blood, so that truth may not be lacking in the sacrament, and that there be no mockery by pagans, that we drink the blood of a dead man.]

Lco prima

[Gratian, De consecratione, *Dist. II, can.72 conclusion]*

Credendum est quod in verbis Christi, sacramenta conficiantur. Cuius enim potencia creantur prius: eius utique verbo ad melius procreantur. Reliqua omnia que sacerdos dicit, aut clerus chori canit: nichil aliud quam laudes, et gratiarum actiones sunt: aut certe obsecrationes: aut fidelium petitiones.

[Gratian, De consecratione, *Dist. II, can.74]*

Omnia quecumque voluit dominus, fecit in celo et in terra. Et quia voluit: sic factum est. Ita licet figura panis et vini videatur: nichil tamen aliud quam caro Christi, et sanguis post consecrationem credenda sunt. Unde veritas ad discipulos. Hec inquit caro mea est: pro mundi vita. Et ut mirabilius loquar, non alia plane quam que nata est de Maria, et passa in cruce: et resurrexit de sepulchro. Hec inquam ipsa est, et ideo Christi est caro, que pro mundi vita adhuc hodie offertur: et cum digne percipitur, vita utique eterna in nobis reparatur. Panem quidem istum quem sumimus in misterio, illum utique intelligo panem, qui manu sancti spiritus formatus est in utero virginis: et igne passionis decoctus in ara crucis. Panis enim angelorum factus est hominum cibus. Unde ipse ait. Ego sum panis vivus: qui de celo descendi. Et iterum, panis quem ego dabo caro mea est: pro mundi vita.

[It must be believed that the sacraments are produced by the words of Christ, by whose power they are created beforehand, by his word especially they are produced for the better. All the remaining things which the priest says, or which the group of the chorus sings, are nothing other than praises and thanksgivings, or even supplications, or prayers of the faithful.

All things that the Lord wished, he did in heaven and on earth. And because he wished it, it was done. Thus, although it seems to be the form of bread and wine, these things, after consecration, must be believed to be nothing other than the flesh of Christ and his blood. Whence he spoke the truth to his disciples: This, he said, is my flesh, for the life of the world. And that I may speak more remarkably, it is clearly nothing other than what was born of Mary, and suffered on the cross, and rose again from the tomb. This, I say, it is, and therefore it is the flesh of Christ, which is offered for the life of the world even today, and when it is taken worthily, eternal life certainly is restored in us. This bread which we consume in mystery, I certainly understand to be that bread which was formed by the hand of the Holy Spirit in the womb of the virgin, and destroyed by the fire of his passion on the altar of the cross. The bread of the angels has become the food of men. Whence he himself said: I am the living bread, who descended from heaven. And again: The bread which I will give is my flesh, for the life of the world.]

Lco ii

[Gratian, De consecratione, *Dist II, can. 13]*

Cotidie eucharistie communionem accipere: nec laudo nec vitupero. Omnibus tamen dominicis diebus communicandum hortor. Si tamen mens in affectu peccandi est: gravari magis dico eucharistie perceptione quam purificari. Et ideo quamvis quis peccato mordeatur, peccandi tamen de cetero non habeat voluntatem, et communicaturus satisfaciat lacrimis et orationibus, et confidens de domini miseratione: accedat ad eucharistiam intrepidus et securus. Sed hoc dico de illo, quem mortalia peccata non gravant. Item[45] dixerit quispiam non cotidie accipiendam eucharistiam, alius affirmat cotidie: faciat unusquisque quod secundum fidem suam pie credit esse faciendum. Necque enim litigaverunt inter se, aut quisquam eorum se alteri preposuit, Zacheus, et ille centurio, cum alter eorum gaudenter in domo sua susceperit dominum, alter dixerit domino, domine non sum dignus ut intres sub tectum meum: ambo salvatorem honorificantes, quamvis non uno modo, ambo peccatis miseri, ambo misericordiam consecuti. Ad hoc valet quod manna secundum propriam volu[n]tatem in ore cuiusque sapiebat.

[To receive communion of the eucharist daily I neither praise nor censure. I urge communion on all Sundays. If however the soul is in a state of sin, I say that he is more to be burdened by receiving communion, than to be purfied. And therefore someone is consumed by sin, but yet does not have a wish to sin further, let him receive communion in tears and prayers, and, confident in the mercy of the Lord, let him approach the eucharist undaunted and secure. But I say this to the one whom mortal sins do not burden. Thus one person says that the Eucharist must not be received daily, another

---

[45] *idem* in BNF 1143.

asserts that it be done daily, let each one do what he conscientiously believes must be done according to his own faith. Nor did either of them put himself before the other, Zacheus and that centurion, when one of them gladly received the Lord into his house, the other said to the Lord: "Lord I am not worthy that you should enter my house," both honoring the Saviour, although not in one way, both having been pitied for their sins, both having attained mercy. To this it applies that manna tastes in the mouth of each according to his own desire.]

Lco iii

[Gratian, De consecratione, *Dist. II, can. 14]*

Si quocienscumque effunditur sanguis Christi, in remissionem peccatorum funditur: debeo illum semper accipere: ut semper michi peccata dimittantur.

[Gratian, De consecratione, *Dist. II, can. 24]*

Qui semper pecco: debeo semper habere medicinam. Qui scelerate vivunt in ecclesia, et communicare non desinunt, putantes se tali communione mundari: discant nichil ad emundationem proficere sibi dicente propheta. Quid est quod dilectus meus fecit in domo mea scelera multa? Numquid carnes sancte auferunt a te malicias tuas? Et apostolus. Probet inquit se homo, et sic de pane illo edat: et de calice bibat.

[Gratian De consecratione, *Dist. II, can. 56]*

Non iste panis est qui vadit in corpus, sed panis vite eterne: que anime nostre substanciam fulcit. Iste panis cotidianus est: accipe cotidie: quod cotidie tibi prosit. Sic vive: ut cotidie merearis accipere.

[If, however often the blood of Christ is poured out, it is shed for the remission of sins, I ought always to receive it, so that always my sins may be forgiven.

I who always sin, ought always to have a remedy. Those who live wickedly in the church, and do not cease to receive communion, considering themselves to be purified by such communion, let them learn that they acquire nothing for their purification, as the prophet says: How is it that my beloved commits crimes in my house? Do the consecrated pieces of flesh take away from you your maliciousness? As the apostle [says]: Let a man examine himself, he said, and thus eat of that bread and drink from that chalice.

This bread is not that which goes into the body, but the bread of eternal life, which supports the substance of our soul. This is a daily bread, receive it daily, so that daily it may be of benefit to you. Live in such a way that you may be worthy to receive it.]

L. I

[Gratian, De consecratione, *Dist. II, can. 66]*

Sancta malis possunt obesse. Bonis sunt ad salutem: malis ad iudicium. Unde apostolus. Qui manducat et bibit indigne: iudicium sibi manducat et bibit. Non quia illa res mala est, sed quia malus male accipit quod bonum est. Non enim mala erat buccella:

que Iude data est a domino. Salutem medicus dedit. Sed quia ille qui indignus [erat][46] accepit: ad perniciem suam accepit.

[Gratian, De consecratione, Dist. II, can. 67]

Non prohibeat dispensator pingues terre mensam domini manducare: sed exactorem moneat timere.

[Gratian, De consecratione, Dist. II, can. 68]

Sicut Iudas cum buccellam tradidit Christus non malum accipiendo, sed bonum male accipiendo, locum prebuit dyabolo: sic indigne quisquis sumens corpus Christi, non efficit ut quia malus est malum sit: aut quia non ad salutem accipit: nichil accipit. Corpus enim et sanguis domini, nichilominus erat in illis: quibus dicebat apostolus. Qui manducat et bibit indigne: iudicium sibi manducat et bibit.

[Gratian, De consecratione, Dist. II, can. 46]

Multi indigne corpus Christi accipiunt: de quibus ait apostolus. Qui manducat et bibit calicem domini indigne: iudicium sibi manducat et bibit. Sed quomodo manducandus est Christus? Quomodo ipse dicit. Qui enim manducat carnem meam et bibit meum sanguinem digne, in me manet et ego in eo, et si indigne accipit sacramentum: acquirit magnum tormentum.

[Sacred things can be harmful to the wicked. They work to the salvation of the good, to the judgment of the wicked. Hence the apostle: He who eats and drinks unworthily, eats and drinks judgment on himself. Not because that thing is evil, but because the evil one receives evilly what is good. It was not an evil morsel which was given by the Lord to Judas. The doctor gives health. But because he who was unworthy received it, he received it to his destruction.

Let the steward not forbid the rich of the land from eating at the Lord's table, but let him advise them to fear the bringer of judgment.

Just as Judas, when Christ handed a morsel to him, did not receive evil but badly received good, gave room to the devil, so when someone unworthily consumes the body of Christ, it is not the case that because he is wicked, it is wicked, or because he does not receive it to his benefit he receives nothing. The body and blood of the Lord nonetheless was in them, to whom the apostle said: Whoever eats and drinks unworthily, eats and drinks judgment on himself.

Many receive the body unworthily, about whom the apostle said: He who eats and drinks from the chalice of the Lord unworthily, eats and drinks judgment on himself. But how must Christ be eaten? He himself described the way: He who eats my flesh and drinks my blood worthily, remains in me and I in him, and if he receives the sacrament unworthily, he obtains great torment.]

---

[46] This word is missing in KB 70.E.4 but is present in BNF 1143 and Strahov.

Lco ii

[Gratian, De consecratione, *Dist. II, can. 35 beginning]*

Quia corpus assumptum ablaturus erat dominus ab oculis, et illaturus syderibus, necessarium erat ut die cene sacramentum nobis corporis et sanguinis consecraret, ut coleretur iugiter per misterium, quod semel offerebatur in precium, ut quia cotidiana et indefessa currebat pro hominum salute redemptio, perpetua esset redemptionis oblatio, et perhennis victima illa viveret in memoria, et semper presens esset in gracia vere unica et perfecta hostia, fide existimanda non specie, neque exteriori censanda visu, sed interiori affectu. Unde merito celestis confirmat auctoritas, quia caro mea vere est cibus: et sanguis meus vere est potus. Recedat ergo omne infidelitatis ambiguum, quoniam quidem qui auctor est muneris: ipse est et testis veritatis. Nam et invisibilis sacerdos visibiles creaturas, in substanciam corporis sui et sanguinis verbo suo secreta potestate convertit: ita dicens. Accipite et comedite: hoc est corpus meum. Et sanctificatione repetita, accipite et bibite: hic est sanguis meus. Ergo sicut ad nutum precipientis domini repente ex nichilo substiterunt, excelsa celorum, profunda fluctuum, vasta terrarum: ita pari potestate in spiritualibus sacramentis, ubi precipit virtus servit effectus.

[Because the Lord was going to take away from our eyes his assumed body and place it in the heavens, it was necessary that, on the day of the last supper, he consecrate a sacrament of his body and blood for us, so that what once was offered as ransom might be worshiped continuously through the mystery, so that because daily and indefatigably redemption flowed for the well-being of men, it might be a perpetual offering of redemption, and so that everlasting sacrifice might live in memory, and so the truly unique and perfect sacrifice might always be present in grace, appraised by faith, not by money, and valued not by external appearance but by internal influence. Whence heavenly authority justly confirms, because ". . . my flesh truly is food, and my blood truly is drink." Therefore, let every doubt of disbelief depart, because certainly he who is the giver of the gift, is himself witness of its truth. For the invisible priest converts visible creations into the substance of his body and blood by his word and secret power, saying: "Take and eat, this is my body." And, when the blessing is repeated, "Take and drink, this is my blood." Therefore just as at the command of the directing Lord suddenly from nothing there existed the heights of the heavens, the depths of the waters, the vastness of the earth, so by equal power in the spiritual sacraments, when goodness commands, the results obey.]

Lco iii

[Gratian, De consecratione, *Dist. II, can. 35 conclusion]*

Quanta itaque et quam celebranda beneficia vis divine benedictionis operetur, et quomodo tibi novum et inpossibile esse non debeat, quod in Christi substanciam terrena, et mortalia convertuntur te ipsum qui in Christo es regeneratus interroga. Dudum alienus a vita, peregrinus a misericordia, et a salutis via intrinsecus mortuus exulabas: subito iniciatus Christi legibus, et salutaribus ministeriis innovatus, in corpus ecclesie non videndo sed credendo transtulisti: et de filio perditionis, adoptivus dei fieri occulta puritate meruisti, in mensura visibili permanens, maior factus es, te ipso invisibiliter: sine quantitatis augmento. Cum idem atque ipse esses multo alter fidei processibus extitisti. In exteriori nichil additum est: et totum in interiori mutatum est, ac sic homo

Christi filius effectus: et Christus hominis in mente formatus est. Sicut ergo sine corporali sensu, vilitate preterita deposita, subito novam indutus es dignitatem, et sicut hoc quod deus in te lesa curavit, infecta diluit, maculata detersit, non oculis sed sensibus tuis sunt credita, et cum reverendum ad altare cibis spiritualibus saciandus ascendis sacrum dei tui corpus, et sanguinem fide respice, honora, et mirare, mente continge, cordis manu suscipe, et maxime mente totum haustu interioris hominis assume.

[Therefore ask yourself, you who were reborn in Christ, how much and in what way the beneficent power of divine blessing works, and how it ought not to be new and impossible for you, that earthly and mortal things are converted into the substance of Christ. Formerly you were estranged from life, banished from mercy, and from the path of salvation, dead inside, you were exiled. Suddenly, admitted to the laws of Christ and restored by his healthful ministries, you crossed over into the body of the church, not by seeing but by believing, and from a son of perdition you merited to become adopted of God by hidden goodness, though remaining the same in outward form, you were made imperceptively greater, without the addition of anything. Although you were one and the same you stood out as much different by your advances in the faith. On the outside nothing was added, and all was changed on the inside, and thus man was made the son of Christ, and Christ was formed in the mind of men. Just as, therefore, without actual feeling, with past worthlessness put aside, you have suddenly assumed a new worth, and just as, because God cured in you the wound, washed away the stains, wiped away the blemish, these things are believed not by your eyes but by your feelings, and so when you come to worship at the altar, to be satisfied with spiritual food, look with faith upon the holy body of your Lord and his blood, honor and marvel at them, hold them in your soul, take them in heart's hand, and especially with heart partake fully of the nourishment of man's soul.]

L. I

[Gratian, De consecratione, *Dist. II, can. 53]*

In Christo semel oblata est hostia: ad salutem sempiternam potens. Quid ergo nos dicimus? Nonne per singulos dies offerimus. Sed ad recordationem mortis eius: et una est hostia non multe. Quomodo una et non multe? Quia semel oblatus est Christus. Hoc autem sacrificium est exemplum illius: idipsum, et semper idipsum.[47] Proinde hoc idem est sacrificium: unum solum. Alioquin diceretur, quoniam in multis locis offertur: multi sunt Christi. Nequaquam. Sed unus ubique Christus, et hic[48] plenus existens: et illic plenus. Sicut enim quod ubique offertur, unum est corpus, et non multam corpora: ita et unum sacrificium. Pontifex autem est ille qui hostiam obtulit[49] nos mundantem, ipsam offerimus eciam nunc, que tunc oblata consumi non potest. Quod nos facimus, in commemoratione fit eius quod factum est. Hoc enim facite ait: in meam commemorationem.

---

[47] Originally *inidipsum* but the first two letters were crossed out.

[48] Originally *hinc* but the *n* has been crossed out.

[49] Cf. *optulit* in BNF 1143.

[In Christ the sacrifice was offered once, potent for eternal salvation. What therefore can we say? Do we not offer every day? Yes, but for the commemoration of his death, for the sacrifice is one and not several. Why is it one and not several? Because Christ was sacrificed once. This sacrifice is an imitation of that one, itself and always itself. Hence this is one and the same sacrifice. Some may say that because he is offered in many places, there are many Christs. In no way! Christ is but one everywhere, both here and there, existing in full. Just as, because wherever he is offered, there is one body and not many bodies, so there is one sacrifice. The priest however is the one who offered the sacrifice which cleanses us, [and] we offer the same now, that when offered then was not to be consumed. What we do is done in commemoration of that which was done. Do this, he said, in my memory.]

L. ii

[Gratian, De consecratione, *Dist. II, can. 1]*

In sacramentorum oblationibus que inter missarum sollempnia offeruntur, panis tantum et vinum aqua permixtum: in sacrificium offerantur. Non enim debet in calice domini, aut vinum solum, aut aqua sola offerri, sed utrumque permixtum, quia utrumque ex latere eius in passione sua profluxisse legitur.

[Gratian, De consecratione, *Dist. II, can. 7]*

Calix eciam dominicus vino et aqua permixtus debet offerri, quia videmus in aqua populum intelligi, in vino vero ostendi sanguinem Christi. Ergo cum in calice vinum aqua misceatur,[50] Christo populus adunatur, et credencium plebs ei in quem credit copulatur et iungitur: que copulatio et coniunctio aque et vini, sic miscetur in calice domini: ut mixtio illa non possit separari. Nam si vinum tantum quis offerat: sanguis Christi incipit esse sine nobis. Si vero aqua sit sola: plebs incipit esse sine Christo. Ergo quando botrus solus offertur, in quo vini efficiencia tantum designatur: salutis nostre sacramentum necligitur, quod aqua significatur.

[Among the offerings of the sacraments which are presented during the solemnities of the masses, let bread alone as well as wine mixed with water be offered in sacrifice. There must not be, in the chalice of the Lord, either wine alone, or water alone, but both mixed, because it is read that both flowed from his side in his passion.

The chalice of the Lord ought to be offered with wine and water mixed, because we see the people represented by the water, the blood of Christ shown by the wine. Therefore, when wine and water are mixed in the chalice, the people are joined with Christ, and the crowd of believers are combined and united with him in whom they believe, and this combination and union of water and wine is mixed in the chalice of the Lord in such a way that the mixture cannot be separated. For if one offers wine alone, the blood of Christ comes into being without us. If the water is alone, the people come into being without Christ. Therefore, when the cluster of grapes is offered alone, in which the power of wine alone is represented, the sacrament of our health is neglected, which is signified by water.]

---

[50] *Miscetur* in Lambot.

L. iii

[Gratian, De consecratione, *Dist. II, can. 83]*

Huius sacramenti ritum Melchisedech ostendit, ubi panem et vinum Abrahe obtulit. Sed tu michi dicis. Quomodo ergo Melchisedech vinum et panem tantum obtulit? Quid sibi vult ammixtio aque? Rationem accipe. Primo omnium figura fuit, que ante precessit tempore Moysi. Quia cum sitiret populus iudeorum, et murmuraret quod aquam invenire non posset, iussit dominus Moysi, ut tangeret petram cum virga tetigit petram, et petra undam maximam fudit, sicut apostolus dicit. Bibebant autem de consequenti petra. Petra autem erat Christus. Non immobilis petra: que populum sequebatur. Et tu bibe: ut te Christus sequatur. Vide misterium. Moyses hoc est propheta. Virga: hoc est verbum dei. Sacerdos verbo dei tangit petram, et fluit aqua: et bibit populus dei. Tangit ergo sacerdos calicem, redundat aquam in calice, et salit in vitam eternam: et bibit populus dei, qui dei graciam consecutus est.

[Melchisedech showed the rite of this sacrament, when he offered Abraham bread and wine. But you say to me: How therefore did Melchisedech offer bread and wine alone? Why is an admixture of water preferred? Learn this reason. First of all it was a symbol, which preceded before at the time of Moses. Because, when the Jewish people thirsted, and they complained that it was not possible to find water, the Lord ordered Moses to touch the rock with a rod, he touched the rock and the rock poured out a great wave, just as the apostle says: They drank from the rock which followed them. The rock was Christ. It was not an immobile rock that followed the people. And you, drink, so that Christ may follow you. Behold the mystery. Moses is the prophet. The rod is the word of God. The priest touches the rock with the word of God, and water flows, and the people of God drink. Therefore the priest touches the chalice, he pours water into the chalice, and it springs into eternal life, and the people of God drink, who followed the grace of God.]

Lco prima

[Gratian, De consecratione, *Dist. II, can. 83]*

Didicisti hoc: ergo accipe et aliud. In tempore dominice passionis cum sabbatum magnum instaret, quia diu in cruce vivebat dominus noster Ihesus Christus et latrones: missi sunt qui percuterent eos. Qui venientes: invenerunt defunctum dominum nostrum Ihesum Christum. Tunc unus de militibus lancea latus tetigit: et de latere eius aqua fluxit et sanguis. Aqua autem ut mundaret: sanguis ut redimeret. Quare de latere? Quia unde culpa: inde gracia. Culpa per feminam: gracia per dominum nostrum Ihesum Christum.

[Gratian, De consecratione, *Dist. II, can. 2]*

Sic vero calix domini non est aqua sola et vinum solum, nisi utrumque misceatur: quomodo nec corpus domini potest esse farina sola, nisi utrumque adunatum fuerit et copulatum, et unius conpage solidatum.

[Gratian, De consecratione, *Dist. II, can. 5]*

In sacramento corporis et sanguinis nichil amplius offeratur, quam quod ipse dominus tradidit, hoc est panis et vinum aqua mixtum, nec amplius in sacrificiis offeratur: quam de uvis et frumento.

[Gratian, De consecratione, *Dist. II, can. 4]*

Hec tria unum sunt in Christo Ihesu. Hec hostia et oblatio dei in odorem suavitatis.

[You have learned this; therefore learn something else. At the time of the passion of the Lord, when the great Sabbath was at hand, because our Lord Jesus Christ was still alive on the cross, along with the thieves, soldiers were sent to kill them. On approaching, they found our Lord Jesus Christ dead. Then one of the soldiers pierced his side with a spear, and from his side water and blood flowed. Water to purify, blood to redeem. Why from his side? Because where there is guilt, there is grace. Guilt through woman, grace through our Lord Jesus Christ.

Thus the chalice of the Lord is not water alone and wine alone, unless both are combined, just as the body of the Lord cannot be flour alone, unless it is united and joined, and made firm into the structure of one thing.

In the sacrament of the body and blood, nothing more is offered, than that which our Lord himself passed on to us, that is, bread and wine mixed with water, nor is anything more offered in sacrifices, than what comes from grapes and grain.

These three are one in Christ Jesus. This sacrifice is an offering to God in the aroma of sweetness.]

Lco I

[Gratian, De consecratione, *Dist. II, can. 82 beginning]*

In Christo pater, et Christus in nobis: unum in hiis esse nos[51] faciunt. Si vere carnem corporis nostri Christus assumpsit, et vere homo ille Christus est: nos quoque vere sub misterio carnem corporis sui sumimus, et per hoc unum erimus: quia pater in eo est: et ille in nobis. Quomodo enim voluntatis unitas asseritur, cum naturalis per sacramentum proprietas, perfectum sacramentum sit unitatis? Non est humano aut seculari[52] sensu de hiis rebus loquendum, neque per violenciam, atque imprudentem predicationem dictorum celestium: sanitati aliene, atque impie intelligencie perversitas extorquenda est. De naturali enim in nobis Christi veritate, vel unitate que dicimus: nisi que dixerimus, ab eo didicimus, stulte atque impie dicemus. Ipse enim ait. Caro mea vere est esca: et sanguis meus vere est potus. Qui edit carnem meam, et bibit sanguinem meum: in me manet et ego in eo.

[The Father in Christ, and Christ in us, make us as one in them. If truly Christ took on the flesh of our body, and that man is truly Christ, we also truly consume the flesh of his body in a mystery, and through it we will be one, because the father is in him,

---

[51] Appears to be an abbreviated *Non* in both KB 70.E.4 and BNF 1143.

[52] *Saeculi* in Lambot.

and he is in us. For how is the unity of will claimed, when in the sacrament the substance is of nature, and the sacrament of unity is perfect? It is not in the human or worldly sense that we must speak about these things, and not by violence must the foolish utterance of divine words, hostile to salvation, as well as the perversity of intelligence be eliminated. Concerning the natural truth or unity of Christ in us, what we say, we will say foolishly and impiously, unless what we say we have learned from him. He himself said: My flesh truly is food, and my blood truly is drink. He who eats my flesh and drinks my blood, remains in me and I in him.]

Lco. Ii

[Gratian, De consecratione, *Dist. II, can. 82 continued]*

De veritate carnis et sanguinis: non relictus est ambigendi locus. Nunc enim et ipsius domini professione et fide nostra vere caro est: et vere sanguis est, et hec accepta atque hausta efficiunt: ut et nos in Christo et Christus in nobis sit. Est ergo ipse in nobis per carnem. Quod autem in eo per sacramentum communicate carnis et sanguinis simus: ipse testatur dicens. Vos autem me videbitis, quia ergo vivo et vos vivetis, quia ego in patre meo, et vos in me, et ego in vobis.[53] Si voluntatis tantum intelligi unitatem vellet ut heretici asserunt, cur gradum quendam atque ordinem consumande unitatis exposuit, nisi ut ille in patre per naturam divinitatis, nos contra in eo per corporalem eius nativitatem, et ille rursus in nobis per sacramentorum inesse misterium crederetur? Ac sic perfecta mediatorem unitas doceret, cum nobis in se permanentibus ipse maneret in patre, manensque in patre, maneret in nobis, et ita ad unitatem proficisceremur: cum qui in eo naturaliter secundum nativitatem inest, nos quoque in eo naturaliter essemus: ipso in nobis naturaliter permanente.

[Concerning the truth of the flesh and blood, no room for ambiguity remained. Now indeed, according to both the profession of the Lord himself and our faith, it is truly flesh, and it is truly blood, and they, eaten and drunk, cause both us to be in Christ and Christ in us. Therefore he himself is in us through the flesh. That, moreover, we are in him through the sacrament of the union of flesh and blood, he himself testifies, saying: "You indeed will see me, because I live, you too will live, because I am in my father, and you are in me, and I am in you." If he wished only the unity of will to be understood, as the heretics claim, why did he detail a specific degree and series of unity to be gone through, except that he might be believed to be present in the father through the nature of his divinity, and we, consequently to be in him through his physical birth, and he in us through the mystery of the sacraments. And so perfect unity might instruct the mediator that, with us still in him, he remained in the Father, and, still in the Father, he remained in us, and in this way we advanced to unity, since we would also naturally exist in the one who is naturally in him on account of birth, and he naturally would remain in us.]

---

[53] John 14: 19–20.

L. iii

[Gratian, De consecratione, *Dist. II, can. 82 conclusion]*

Quod autem hec in nobis, naturaliter unitas sit: ipse testatus est. Qui edit carnem meam, et bibit sanguinem meum: in me manet et ego in eo. Non enim in eo erit nisi in quo ipse fuerit, eius tamen in se assumptam habens[54]carnem, qui suam sumpserat, sicut misit me inquit pater vivens, et ego vivo per patrem, qui manducaverit carnem meam: ipse vivit per me. Quomodo per patrem vivit: eodem modo nos per carnem eius vivimus. Hec ergo vite nostre causa est, quod in nobis manere per carnem Christi habemus, victuri per eum: ea conditione qua vivit ille per patrem. Si ergo nos naturaliter secundum carnem per eum vivimus, id est naturam carnis sue adepti, quomodo non naturaliter secundum spiritum in se patrem habeat: cum vivat ipse per patrem? Corpus Christi quod sumitur de altari figura est: cum panis et vinum extra videtur. Veritas autem dum corpus Christi et sanguis et in veritate interius creditur.

[That this unity is naturally in us he himself has testified: "Whoever eats my flesh and drinks my blood abides in me and I in him." For he will not be in anyone except in the one in whom he already was, having taken upon himself the flesh of him who had eaten his flesh. "Just as," he said "the living father sent me, and I live through the father, whoever shall eat my flesh will live through me." Just as he lives through the father, we likewise live through his flesh. This therefore is the cause of our life, that what abides in us we have on account of Christ's flesh, living through him, by virtue of him living through the father. If therefore we naturally live through him according to his flesh, that is having acquired the nature of his flesh, how does he not have naturally, through the spirit, the father in himself, since he lives through the father? The body of Christ, which is consumed at the altar, is a symbol, since bread and wine is seen outwardly. It is truth when the body and blood of Christ is in truth believed within.]

L. I

[Gratian, De consecratione, *Dist. II, can. 73 beginning]*

Hec salutaris victima illam nobis mortem unigeniti per misterium reparat, qui licet surgens a mortuis iam non moritur, mors illi ultra non dominabitur, tamen in se ipso inmoraliter, et incorruptibiliter vivens: iterum in hoc ministerio moritur, eius quoque ubique corpus sumitur, eius caro in populi salutem patitur, eius sanguis non iam in manus infidelium, sed in ora fidelium funditur. Hinc ergo pensemus quale sit hoc sacrificium, quod pro nostra absolutione passionem unigeniti filii semper imitatur. Quis enim fidelium habere dubium possit, ut in ipsa immolationis hora, ad sacerdotis vocem celos aperiri, et in illo Ihesu Christi misterio choros angelorum adesse, summa, et yma sociari, unum quid ex invisibilibus atque visibilibus fieri? Idem uno eodemque inquit tempore, ac momento, et in celo rapitur, ministerio angelorum consociandum corpori Christi: et ante oculos sacertotis in altari videtur.

---

[54] Abbreviated *hns* in KB 70.E.4, so it is unclear whether *habens* or *hominis* was intended. The word is clearly *habens* in BNF 1143, although Lambot uses *hominis*.

[This salutary sacrifice renews for us that death of the only begotten son through mystery, who, rising from the dead, dies no more—death will have no more dominion over him—nevertheless, living immortally and incorruptibly in himself, he dies again in this ministry, and his body is consumed everywhere, his flesh suffers for the salvation of the people, his blood now is poured out, not into the hands of the unfaithful, but into the mouths of the faithful. Consequently let us think of what nature is this sacrifice, which always imitates the passion of the only begotten son for our absolution. For who of the faithful can have doubt that, in that hour of sacrifice, at the voice of the priest the heavens are opened, and in that mystery of Jesus Christ the choruses of angels are present, the highest and lowest are joined together, made one out of invisible and visible things? At one and the same time and moment, he said, the same is both carried off into heaven, by the ministry of the angels to be joined to the body of Christ, and is seen before the eyes of the priest on the altar.]

Lco ii

[Gratian, De consecratione, *Dist. II, can. 73 continued*]

Tanta est unitas ecclesie in Christo ut unus ubique sit panis corporis Christi: et unus sit calix sanguinis eius. Calix enim quem sacerdos catholicus sacrificat, non est alius nisi ipse quem dominus apostolis tradidit, quia sicut divinitas verbi dei una est: sive totum implet mundum: ita licet multis locis, et innumerabilibus diebus illud consecretur: non sunt tamen multa corpora Christi, neque multi calices, sed unum corpus Christi, et unus sanguis cum illo, quod sumpsit in utero virginis: et quod dedit apostolis. Divinitas enim verbi replet illud quod ubique est, et coniungit ac facit, ut sicut ipsa una est, ita et unum corpus eius sit in veritate. Unde animadvertendum est, quia sive plus, sive minus inde percipiat: omnes equaliter corpus Christi integerrime sumunt, et generaliter omnes: et specialiter unusquisque.

[So great is the unity of the church in Christ, that everywhere the bread of the body of Christ is one, and the chalice of his blood is one. For the chalice which the catholic priest offers, is none other than that which the Lord entrusted to the apostles, because just as the divinity of the word of God is one, although it fills up the whole world, so, notwithstanding the fact that it is consecrated in many places and on innumerable days, there are not many bodies of Christ, nor many chalices, but one body of Christ, and one blood with it, which he obtained in the womb of the virgin, and which he gave to the apostles. For the divinity of the word fills that which is everywhere, and unites it and is the reason why, just as it is one, so also his body is one in truth. Hence it must be observed, that, whether several or fewer partake of it, all consume equally the body of Christ completely whole, both generally all, and specifically each one.]

Lco iii

[Gratian, De consecratione, *Dist. II, can. 73 conclusion*]

Misterium fidei dicitur quod credere debes: quod ibi salus nostra consistat. Providens enim nobis dominus, dedit hoc sacramentum salutis, ut quia nos cotidie peccamus: et ille iam mori non potest, per istud sacramentum remissionem consequamur. Cotidie enim ipse comeditur, et bibitur in veritate: sed integer et vivus atque immaculatus permanet. Et ideo magnum et pavendum misterium est: quia et aliud videtur: et aliud intelligitur. Sed cum misterium sit unum: corpus et sanguis dicitur, figuram panis et vini habet faciente domino, quia non habemus in usum carnem crudam comedere: et bibere sanguinem.

[Gratian, De consecratione, *Dist. II, can. 84]*

Sicut verus filius dei dominus noster Ihesus Christus non quemadmodum homines per graciam, sed quasi filius et substancia patris: ita vera est Christi caro, sicut ipse dixit quam accipimus, et verus sanguis est potus. Ego sum inquit panis vivus: qui de celo descendi. Sed caro non descendit de celo. Quomodo ergo descendit de celo panis vivus? Quia idem dominus Ihesus consors est divinitatis et corporis, et tu qui accipis carnem divine eius substancie: in illo participas alimento.

[What you must believe is called the mystery of faith, because our salvation rests on it. Looking out for us, our Lord gave us this sacrament of salvation, so that, because we sin daily, and he cannot die any more, through this sacrament we might obtain remission. Daily he himself is truly eaten and drunk, but he remains whole and living and immaculate. And so it is a great and fearful mystery, because one thing is seen and another understood. But although the mystery is one, it is called the body and blood, it has the appearance of bread and wine, through the Lord's doing, because we are not used to eating crude flesh and drinking blood.

Just as our Lord Jesus Christ is the true son of God, not in the manner that men are, through grace, but just as a son is the substance of the father, so it is the true flesh of Christ, as he himself said, which we receive, and true blood is drink. I am, he said, the living bread, who descended from heaven. But his flesh did not descend from heaven. How, therefore, did the living bread descend from heaven? Because the same Lord Jesus is a sharer of divinity and flesh, and you who receive the flesh of his divine substance, participate in that food.]

L. i (In 8va sacramenti in another hand)

[Gratian, De consecratione, *Dist. II, can. 36 beginning]*

Quia passus est pro nobis dominus, commendavit nobis in isto sacramento sanguinem suum et corpus: quod eciam fecit nos metipsos. Nam et nos corpus ipsius facti sumus: et per misericordiam ipsius quod accepimus nos sumus. Recordamini et vos non fuistis, et creati estis, et ad aream dominicam comportati estis: laboribus boum id est annunciancium evangelium triturati estis. Quando cathecumini deferebamini, in horreo servabamini: nomina vestra dedistis, moli cepistis ieuiniis exorcismis. Postea ad aquam venistis, et conspersi estis: et panis dominicus facti estis. Ecce quod accepistis. Quomodo ergo unum videtis esse quod factum est, sic unum estote vos, diligentes vos, scilicet tenendo unam fidem, unam spem, individuam caritatem. Heretici quando hoc accipiunt sacramentum, testimonium contra se accipiunt, quia illi querunt divisionem: cum panis iste indicet unitatem. Sic et vinum in multis[55] racemis fuit: et modo unum est. Vinum est in sua nativitate, calix est post pressuram torcularis, et vos post illa ieiu-

---

[55] *In multis* erroneously recopied.

nia, post labores, post humilitatem, et contritionem, iam in nomine domini tanquam ad calicem Christi venistis, et ibi vos estis in mensa, et in calice nobiscum vos estis. Simul enim hoc sumimus, simul bibimus: quia simul vivimus.

[Because he died for us, the Lord gave his blood and body to us in this sacrament, which also makes us his own. For we have become his body, and through his mercy we are what we receive. Remember that you did not exist, that you were born and you were brought together to the Lord's altar, and you were formed by the labor of cows, that is, of proclaiming angels. When you were catechumens you were brought down, you served in the barn, you gave your names, you received grain to drive out your hunger. After you came to the water, you were sprinkled, and you became the Lord's bread. Behold what you have received. Just as you see that which was made is one, so you will be one, and you shall be faithful, namely by holding one faith, one hope, individual charity. Heretics, when they receive this sacrament, receive testimony against themselves, because they seek division, while this bread proclaims unity. Thus wine was in many grapes, and now it is one. This is wine in its origin, it is that chalice after the pressure of the grape press, and, after those fasts, after labors, after humility and contrition, now in the name of the Lord, in the same way, you come to the chalice of Christ, and you are at the table, and you are at the chalice with us. Together we consume this, together we drink, because together we live.]

L. ii

[Gratian, De consecratione, *Dist. II, can. 36 conclusion]*

Ita dominus noster Ihesus Christus nos significavit, nos ad se pertinere voluit: misterium pacis et unitatis nostre in mensa consecravit. Qui accipit misterium unitatis, et non tenet vinculum pacis, non misterium accipit pro se, sed testimonium contra se. Nulli est aliquatenus ambigendum, unumquemque fidelium corporis et sanguinis dominici, tunc esse participem: quando in baptismate efficitur membrum Christi, nec alienari ab illius panis calicisque consorcio, eciam si antequam panem illum comedat calicemque bibat, de hoc seculo migraverit, in unitate corporis constitutus. Sacramenti quippe illius participacione ac beneficio non privatur: quando in se hoc quod illud sacramentum significat invenitur.

[Gratian, De consecratione, *Dist. II, can. 58 beginning]*

Qui manducant et bibunt Christum: vitam manducant et bibunt. Illud manducare est refici: illud bibere est vivere. Quod in sacramento visibiliter sumitur: in ipsa veritate spiritualiter manducatur et bibitur.

[In this way our Lord Jesus Christ showed us that he wished us to belong to him, he consecrated the sacrament of peace and of our unity at the table. Whoever receives the sacrament of unity, and does not keep the bond of peace, does not receive the sacrament for himself, but testimony against himself. It is in no way to be doubted by anyone that each of the faithful is a participant in the body and blood of the Lord from the time when he is made by baptism a member of Christ, and is not kept from the fellowship of that bread and cup even if he left this world before he could eat that bread and drink the cup, since he was already a part of the unity of the body. Certainly he is not deprived of participation in, and the benefit of, that sacrament, since found in him is the very thing which that sacrament testifies.

Those who eat and drink Christ eat and drink life. To consume it is to be refreshed, to drink it is to live. What is consumed visibly in the sacrament, in truth itself is consumed and drunk spiritually.]

L. iii

[Gratian, De consecratione, *Dist. II, can. 58 continued, overlapping with can. 75]*

Manducatur Christus, vivit manducatus: quia surrexit occisus. Nec quando manducamus: partes de illo facimus. Et quidem in sacramento sic fit. Et norunt fideles, quando manducent carnem Christi: unusquisque accipit partem suam. Per partes manducatur in sacramento: et manet integer totus in celo. Per partes manducatur in sacramento: et manet integer totus in corde tuo. Totus enim erat apud patrem, quando venit in virginem, implevit illam: nec recessit ab illo. Veniebat in carnem, ut homines eum manducarent: et manebat integer aput patrem: et[56] angelos pasceret.

[Gratian, De consecratione, *Dist. II, can. 70]*

Invitat dominus servos, et preparat eis cibum seipsum. Quis audeat dominum suum manducare: et tamen ait. Qui manducat me: vivit propter me. Quando manducatur, vita manducatur: nec occiditur ut manducetur, sed mortuos vivificat. Quando manducatur, reficit: sed non deficit.

[Gratian, De consecratione, *Dist. II, can. 75]*

Non ergo timeamus, fratres manducare istum panem, ne forte finiamus illum: et postea quod manducemus non inveniamus.

[Gratian, De consecratione, *Dist. II, can. 58 continued]*

Quod videtur panis est et calix, quod eciam oculi renunciant. Quod autem fides postulat instruenda, panis est corpus Christi: et calix est sanguis. Ista ideo dicuntur sacramenta, quia in eis aliud videtur: et aliud intelligitur. Quod videtur, speciem habet corporalem: quod intelligitur, fructum habet spiritualem.

[Christ is eaten, eaten he lives, because he arose, though slain. Nor, when we eat, do we make parts of him. For in the sacrament the situation is the following. The faithful know, when they eat the flesh of Christ, that everyone receives his share. He is eaten in the sacrament in parts, yet he remains entirely whole in heaven. He is eaten in the sacrament in parts, yet he remains entirely whole in your heart. He was one with the father, when he came into the virgin, he filled her, but he did not withdraw from him. He became flesh, so that men might consume him, yet he remained one with the father, so that he might nourish the angels.

The Lord invites his servants, and serves to them himself as food. Who dares to consume his Lord? Nevertheless he said: Whoever eats me, lives according to me.

---

[56] *Ut* in BNF 1143.

When he is eaten, life is eaten, and he does not die that he might be eaten, but to make the dead live. When he is eaten, he refreshes, but he does not perish.

Therefore let us not fear, brothers, to eat this bread, lest by chance we finish it, and afterwards we do not discover what we eat.

What appears to be bread and cup is indeed what the eyes report. Because faith demands to be taught, the bread is the body of Christ, and the chalice is the blood. These things are called sacraments, because in them one thing is seen, and something else understood. What is seen has a corporeal substance, what is understood has spiritual benefit.]

L. iiii (originally L. i)

[Gratian, De consecratione, *Dist. II, can. 8]*

Nichil in sacrificiis maius potest esse quam corpus et sanguis Christi, nec ulla oblacio hac pocior est, sed hec omnes precellit: que pura consciencia domino offerenda est: et pura mente sumenda, atque ab omnibus veneranda. Et sicuti pocior est ceteris: ita pocius excoli et venerari debet.

[Gratian, De consecratione, *Dist. II, can. 22]*

Triforme est corpus domini. Pars oblate in calicem missa, corpus Christi quod iam resurrexit monstrat, pars comesta, ambulans adhuc super terram, pars in altari, usque ad finem misse remanens, corpus in sepulchro: quia usque in finem seculi corpora sanctorum in sepulchris erunt.

[Gratian, De consecratione, *Dist. II, can. 37]*

Dum frangitur hostia, dum sanguis de calice in ora funditur fidelium, quid aliud quam dominici corporis in cruce immolatio eiusque sanguinis de latere effuso designatur.

[Gratian, De consecratione, *Dist. II, [can. 39]]*

Panis et calix non qualibet, sed certa consecratione misticus nobis fit. Non nascitur proinde quod ita fit nobis. Quamvis sit panis et calix: alimentum est resurrectionis.

[Gratian, De consecratione, *Dist. II, can. 40]*

Ante benedictionem alia species nominatur: post benedictionem Christi corpus significatur. In illo sacramento Christus est. Qui manducaverit hoc corpus: fiat ei remissio peccatorum.

[Nothing in sacrifices can be greater than the body and blood of Christ, nor is any oblation more powerful than this, but it surpasses all, which, with a pure conscience, must be offered to the Lord, and consumed with a pure heart, and must be venerated by all. And just as it is better than others, so it ought to be better worshipped and venerated.

The body of the Lord is of three forms: The part of the offering put in the chalice at mass shows the body of Christ which has now risen; the part consumed, still walking on the earth; and the part on the altar, remaining at the end of mass, the body in the sepulchre, because the bodies of the saints will be in the sepulchres until the end of time.

When the host is broken, when the blood from the chalice is poured out into the mouths of the faithful, what else is designated than the sacrifice of the body of the Lord on the cross, and of his blood gushing from his side? The bread and chalice become mystical for us not by an uncertain, but a definite, consecration. What consequently happens for us is not born. Although it be bread and chalice, it is the food of resurrection.

Before the blessing it is called one species, after the blessing it is designated the body of Christ. Christ is in that sacrament. Whoever shall have eaten this body, let there be for him the remission of sins.]

L. v (originally L. ii)

[Gratian, De consecratione, *Dist. II, can. 40]*

In illa mistica distributione spiritualis alimonie, hoc impertitur, hoc sumitur: ut accipientes virtutem celestis cibi, in carnem ipsius qui caro nostra factus est: transeamus. Est cibus refectionis: est cibus sanguinis. Sicut enim caro Christi vere est cibus, ita sanguis eius vere est potus. Idem est corpus de quo dictum est. Caro mea vere est cibus: et sanguis meus vere est potus. Circa hoc corpus aquile sunt: que alis circumvolant spiritualibus. Unde et idem corpus Christi edimus: ut vite eterne possimus esse participes.

[Gratian, De consecratione, *Dist. II, can. 41]*

Nos autem in specie panis et vini quam[57] videmus: res invisibiles id est carnem et sanguinem honoramus. Nec similiter comprehendimus has duas species, quemadmodum ante consecrationem comprehendebamus: cum fideliter fateamur ante consecrationem panem esse, et vinum, quod natura formavit, post consecrationem, vere esse carnem, et sanguinem Christi: quod benedictio consecravit.

[In that symbolic distribution of his spiritual inheritance, this is shared, this is consumed, so that, receiving the strength of heavenly food, we may be transformed into the flesh of the very one who became our flesh. This is the food of refreshment, this is the food of blood. Just as the flesh of Christ truly is food, so his blood truly is drink. It is the same body of which it is said: My flesh is truly food, and my blood is truly drink. Around this body there are eagles, which fly around on spiritual wings. Wherefore we eat the body of Christ, so that we may be participants in eternal life.

In the appearance of bread and wine that we see, we honor the invisible things, that is, his flesh and blood. Nor do we similarly perceive these two species in the way we perceived them before consecration, since we honestly say that they are bread and wine before consecration, which nature fashioned, but after consecration they are truly the flesh and blood of Christ, which the blessing has consecrated.]

L. vi (originally L. iii)

[Gratian, De consecratione, *Dist. II, can. 43]*

Forte dicas. Quomodo vera caro, quomodo verus sanguis, quia sumilitudinem non video carnis, non video sanguinis veritatem? Primo omnium dixi tibi de sermone Christi qui operatur, ut possit mutare et convertere genera: et instituta nature. Deinde ubi non tulerunt sermonem Christi discipuli eius, sed audientes quod carnem suam daret manducare, et sanguinem suum ad bibendum: recedebant. Solus tamen Petrus

---

[57] The scribe began to write *ed*, then crossed it out.

dixit. Verba vite eterne habes: et ego a te quomodo recedam? Ne igitur plures hoc dicerent, et ne veluti quidam esset horror cruoris, sed maneret gracia redemptoris: ideo in similitudine quidem accipis sacramentum, sed vere naturam gloriam virtutemque consequeris. Ego sum inquit panis vivus: qui de celo descendi.

[Peter Lombard, Sententiae, *Bk. IV, Dist. XI, ch. 62 (3)]*

Sub alia autem specie tribus de causis carnem et sanguinem tradidit Christus, et deinceps sumendum instituit, ut scilicet fides haberet meritum, que est de hiis que non videntur, quia fides non habet meritum: cui humana ratio prebet experimentum. Et ideo ne abhorreret animus quod cerneret oculus: quia non habemus usum carnem crudam et sanguinem comedere. Quia ergo Christum vorari dentibus fas non est, in misterio carnem et sanguinem nobis commendavit. Et ideo ne ab incredulis religioni christiane insultaretur.

[Perhaps you may say: In what way is this true flesh, in what way true blood, because I do not see the similarity to flesh, I do not see the reality of blood? First of all I told you about the word of Christ, which works so that it can change and convert the divisions and designs of nature. Afterwards his apostles did not endure the word of Christ, but hearing that he would give his flesh to eat, and his blood to drink, they backed away. Only Peter said: You have words of eternal life, and how can I withdraw from you? So that, therefore, more might not say this, and so that there might not be any such bristling at blood, but that the grace of the redeemer might remain, for those reasons you receive the sacrament under a certain likeness, but really you obtain nature, glory, and strength. I am, he said, the living bread, who descended from heaven.

There are three reasons why Christ transmitted his flesh and blood under a different appearance, and instituted their consumption successively, namely: so that faith, which concerns those things that are not seen, might have value, because faith does not have value, for that which human reason gives proof. And so the soul might not shrink from what the eye perceives, because we are not accustomed to eat raw flesh and blood. Because it is not right for Christ to be eaten with the teeth, he commended his body and blood to us in the mystery. And so that nothing of the Christian religion might be reviled by unbelievers.]

L. vii (originally L. prima)

[Peter Lombard, Sententiae, *Bk. IV, Dist. XI, ch. 62 (3) continued]*

Nichil rationabilius: quam ut sanguinis similitudinem sumamus. Ut ita et veritas non desit, et ridiculum nullum fiat a paganis: quod cruorem occisi bibamus.

[Peter Lombard Sententiae, *Bk. IV, Dist. XI, ch. 63 (4)]*

Sed quare sub duplici specie sumitur, cum substantialiter unum totus sit Christus? Ut ostenderetur totam humanam naturam assumpsisse: ut totam redimeret. Panis enim ad carnem refertur, vinum ad animam, quia vinum operatur sanguinem: in quo sedes anime a fisicis esse dicitur. Ideo ergo in duabus speciebus celebratur, ut anime et carnis susceptio in Christo, et utriusque liberatio: in nobis significetur. Valet enim ad tuitionem corporis et anime quod percipimus: quia caro Christi pro salute corporis. Sanguis vero pro anima nostra offertur: sicut prefiguravit Moyses. Caro inquit pro corpore vestro[58] offertur, sanguis vero pro anima, sed tamen sub utraque specie sumitur, quod ad utrumque valet: quia sub utraque specie sumitur totus Christus.

[There is nothing more sensible than that we should consume the likeness of blood. So that in this way both truth may not be lacking, and no mockery may be made by the pagans, that we drink the blood of the dead.

But why is it consumed under two species, since Christ is substantially one whole? So that he might be shown to have assumed all of human nature, in order that he might redeem all of it. Bread refers to the flesh, wine to the soul, because wine affects the blood, in which the seat of the soul is said to be by physicians. For that reason, therefore, it is celebrated under two species, so that the taking on of soul and body may be shown in Christ, and the liberation of both, may be shown in us. What we take in is good for the preservation of the body and the soul, because the flesh of Christ is offered for the health of the body. His blood is offered for our soul, just as Moses prefigured. Flesh, he said, is offered for your body, blood for the soul, but yet what is good for both is consumed in each food, because the complete Christ is consumed under each species.]

L. viii (originally L. ii)

[Peter Lombard, Sententiae, *Bk. IV, Dist. VIII, ch. 54 (7)]*

Porro illa species visibilis sacramentum est gemine rei, quia utramque rem significat: et utriusque rei similitudinem gerit expressam. Nam sicut panis pre ceteris cibis corpus reficit et sustentat, et vinum hominem letificat atque inebriat: sic caro Christi interiorem hominem plus ceteris graciis spiritualiter reficit et saginat.

[Peter Lombard, Sententiae, *Bk. IV, Dist. VIII, ch. 48 (1)]*

Unde excellenter eucharistia dicitur, id est bona gratia, quia in hoc sacramento non modo est augmentum virtutis et gracie, sed ille totus sumitur: qui est fons et origo tocius gracie.

[Peter Lombard, Sententiae, *Bk. IV, Dist. VIII, ch. 54 (7)]*

Habet eciam similitudinem cum re mistica, quod est unitas fidelium: quia sicut ex multis granis conficitur unus panis, et ex plurimis acinis vinum in unum confluit, sic ex multis fidelium personis unitas ecclesiastica constat. Unde apostolus. Unus panis et unum corpus multi sumus. Unus panis, et unum corpus ecclesia dicitur, pro eo quod sicut unus panis ex multis granis, et unum corpus ex multis membris componitur: sic ecclesia ex multis fidelibus caritate copulante connectitur.

[Furthermore that visible species is a sacrament of two natures, because it represents each one, and it bears each one's stamped out likeness. For just as bread above all other foods refreshes and sustains the body, and wine elates and inebriates man, so the flesh of Christ more than other gifts spiritually refreshes and satiates the inner man.

---

[58] *Nostro* in BNF 1143.

Hence it is excellently called "Eucharist," that is "good grace," because in this sacrament there is not only an increase of virtue and grace, but he, who is the font and origin of all grace, is wholly consumed.

That which is the unity of the faithful has a similarity with the sacred event, because just as one bread is made from many grains, and wine flows from many grapes into one, so the ecclesiastical unity exists from many faithful people. Hence the Apostle: We many are one bread and one body. One bread and one body is called the church, for the reason that, just as bread is composed of many grains, and one body is composed of many members, so the church is composed of many faithful people, love uniting it.]

L. ix (originally L. iii)

[Gratian, De consecratione, *Dist. II, can. 59]*

Credere in Iesum Christum: hoc est manducare panem et vinum. Qui credit, manducat invisibiliter, saginatur: quia invisibiliter renascitur. Et qui manducat carnem Christi, et bibit sanguinem illius: vitam habet eternam. Participatione enim filii, quod est per unitatem corporis et sanguinis eius homo manducans vivit, non sumens tantum in sacramento, quod et mali faciunt: sed usque ad spiritus participationem, ut in corpore domini tamquam membrum maneat, et eius spiritu vegetetur: quod est dum eius mandata servat. Ad altare dei invisibile quo non accedit iniustus ille pervenit, qui ad hoc presens iustificatus accedit. Invenit illic vitam: qui hic discernit causam suam.

[Gratian, De consecratione, *Dist. II, can. 77]*

Singuli autem accipiunt Christum dominum, et in singulis portionibus totus est: nec per singulos minuitur: sed integrum se prebet in singulis.

[Gratian, De consecratione, *Dist. II, can. 78]*

Ubi pars est corporis: est et totum. Eadem ratio est in corpore domini, que in manna, quod in eius figura precessit: de quo dicitur. Qui plus collegerat, non habuit amplius: neque qui minus paraverat, habuit minus.

[Peter Lombard, Sententiae, *Bk. IV, Dist. VIII, ch. 49 (2)]*

Illud datum fuit antiquitus post transitum Maris Rubri: ubi submersis Egyptiis liberati sunt Hebrei. Ita hoc celeste manna, non nisi regeneratis prestari debet. Corporalis panis ille: populum antiquum ad terram promissionis per desertum eduxit. Hic celestis, fideles huius seculi desertum transeuntes: in celum subvehit. Unde recte viaticum appellatur: quia in via nos reficiens: usque in patriam deducit. Tu autem domine.

[To believe in Jesus Christ is to eat the bread and wine. He who believes, consumes invisibly, is satiated, because he is reborn invisibly. And whoever eats the flesh of Christ, and drinks his blood, has eternal life. Man eating lives through participation with the Son, that is through the unity of his body and blood, not just consuming the sacrament, just as evil ones do, but to the extent of participation with the spirit, so that he may abide as a member in the body of the Lord, and he may be invigorated by His spirit, that is as long as he follows His mandates. He, who at this time comes justified, arrives invisibly at the altar of God, whither the unjust does not come. He finds there life, who here understands its source.

Individuals receive Christ the Lord, and the whole is in the single portions, nor is he diminished in the single parts, but he offers himself whole in the individual pieces.

Where there is a part of the body, there the whole is. The same circumstance exists in the body of the Lord as in manna, which preceded it as a symbol, about which it is said: He who gathered more, did not have a greater amount, nor did the one who had acquired less, have less.

That had been given long ago after the crossing of the Red Sea, where the Hebrews were freed from the drowned Egyptians. Thus, this heavenly manna ought to be furnished to none except the reborn (baptized). That actual bread led the ancient people through the desert to the promised land. This celestial bread conducts the faithful crossing the desert of this era into heaven. Hence it is rightly called "viaticum," because, refreshing us on the way, it leads into the homeland.]

[The remainder in at least three later hands]

Capitulum

Dominus Ihesus in qua nocte tradebatur accepit panem: et gratias agens fregit et dixit Accipite et manducate. Hoc est corpus meum quod pro vobis tradetur. Deo gratias.

[The Lord Jesus, on the night he was betrayed, took bread, and giving thanks broke it and said: Take and eat, this is my body which will be given up for you. Thanks be to God.]

Collecta

[Ad terciam] Deus qui nobis sub sacramento mirabili passionis tue memoriam reliquisti: tribue quesumus, ita nos corporis et sanguinis tui sacra misteria venerari: ut redemptionis tue fructum in nobis iugiter sentiamus. Qui vivis et [regnas cum deo patre in unitate spiritu sancti deus per omnia secula seculorum. Amen.]

[God, you who have left us a memorial of your passion under this wondrous sacrament, grant, we ask, that we venerate the sacred mystery of your body and blood in such a way that we feel always in us the fruit of your redemption. Who lives and reigns with God the Father in the unity of the Holy Spirit, God, for ever and ever. Amen.]

[Ad sextam] Quociens enim manducabitis panem hunc, et calicem bibetis, mortem domini annunciabitis donec veniat. Deo gratias.

[As often as you shall eat this bread, and drink this cup, you will proclaim the death of the Lord until he comes. Thanks be to God.]

[Ad nonam] Quicumque manducaverit panem vel biberit calicem domini indigne reus erit corporis et sanguinis Domini.

[Whoever eats this bread or drinks the cup of the Lord unworthily, will be a criminal of the body and blood of the Lord.]

[Versicle] Educas panem de terra, alleluia. R. Et vinum letificet cor hominis, alleluia.

[May you produce bread from the earth, alleluia. R. And may wine gladden the heart of man, alleluia.]

CORPUS CHRISTI
THE HAGUE, NATIONAL LIBRARY OF THE NETHERLANDS, MS 70.E.4

Ad primas vesperas
[Antiphona]
1. Animarum cibus [Ps Dixit Dominus][59]

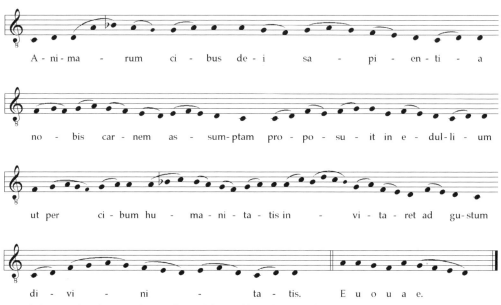

A - ni - ma - rum ci - bus de - i sa - pi - en - ti - a

no - bis car - nem as - sum-ptam pro - po - su - it in e - dul-li - um

ut per ci - bum hu - ma - ni - ta - tis in - vi - ta - ret ad gu-stum

di - vi - ni - ta - tis. E u o u a e.

[Food for souls, the wisdom of God has offered to us for food the flesh that he has assumed, so that through the food for our humanity he might invite us to taste of his
divinity.]

---

[59] Hugh of Saint-Victor, *De sacramentis corporis et sanguinis Dominici*, Book II, pt. 8, Ch. 8 (PL 176, col. 467):
"Voluit enim sapientia Dei, quae se per visibilia manifestat ostendere quod ipsa animarum refectio est et
cibus, et propterea carnem assumptam in edulium proposuit, ut per cibum carnis ad gustum invitaret divinitatis." "Sapientia Dei" here refers to Christ. See the Catholic Encyclopedia, s.v. The Blessed Trinity: "The
Greek Fathers regarded the Son as the Wisdom and power of the Father (I Cor, 1: 24) in a formal sense, and in
like manner, the Spirit as His Sanctity. Apart from the Son the Father would be without His Wisdom; apart
from the Spirit He would be without His Sanctity. . . . [T]he Son is the Wisdom and Power of the Father in the
full and formal sense. This teaching constantly recurs from the time of Origen to that of St. John Damascene
(Origen apud Athan., "De decr. Nic.," 27; Athanasius, "Con. Arianos," I, 19; Cyril of Alexandria, "Thesau-
rus"; John Damascene, "Fid.orth.," I, xii). It is based on the Platonic philosophy accepted by the Alexandrine
School. . . . Not a few writers of great weight hold that there is sufficient consensus among the Fathers and
Scholastic theologians as to the meaning of the names Word and Wisdom (Proverbs 8), applied to the Son."
    "Sapientia Dei" was sometimes applied to the Holy Spirit. See Theophilus of Antioch (ca. A.D. 180), who
refers to "the Trinity of God [the Father], His Word and His Wisdom ("Ad Autolychum," II, 15).

2.   Discipulis competentem [Ps Confitebor tibi Domine]

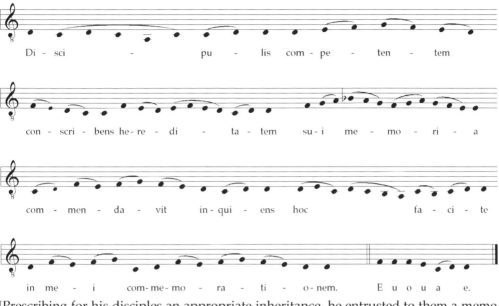

[Prescribing for his disciples an appropriate inheritance, he entrusted to them a memorial, saying: Do this in memory of me.]

3.   Totum Cristus [Ps Credidi propter]

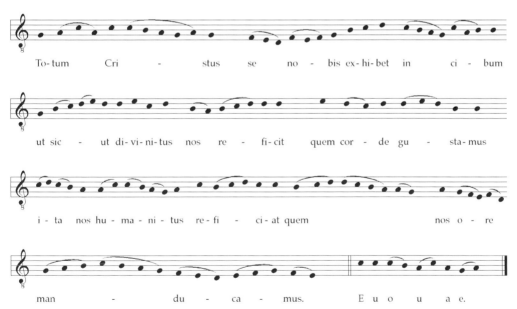

[Christ presents himself entirely to us for food so that, just as his divinity restores us when we partake him with our hearts, so his humanity might restore us when we partake him with our mouths.]

4.   Et sic[60] [Ps Beati omnes]

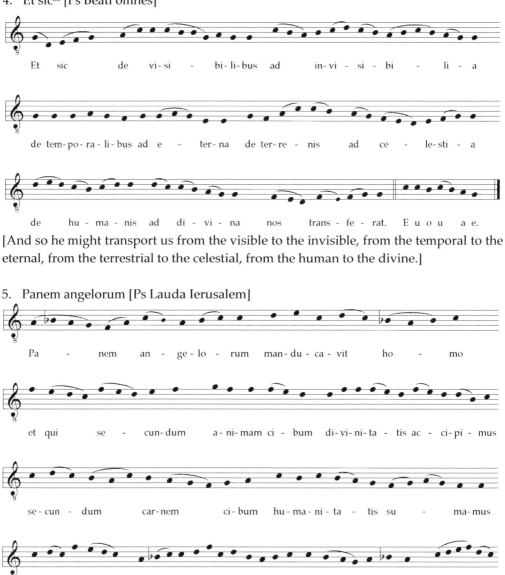

Et   sic   de   vi- si - bi- li- bus   ad   in- vi - si - bi   -   li - a

de tem- po- ra - li- bus ad e - ter - na   de ter- re - nis   ad   ce   - le- sti - a

de   hu - ma - nis   ad   di - vi - na   nos   trans - fe - rat.   E u o u   a e.

[And so he might transport us from the visible to the invisible, from the temporal to the
eternal, from the terrestrial to the celestial, from the human to the divine.]

5.   Panem angelorum [Ps Lauda Ierusalem]

Pa   -   nem   an - ge- lo - rum   man- du - ca - vit   ho   -   mo

et qui   se   -   cun- dum   a - ni- mam ci - bum   di- vi- ni- ta - tis ac - ci- pi - mus

se - cun - dum   car- nem   ci- bum   hu- ma - ni- ta - tis su   -   ma- mus

qui- a   sic- ut   a - ni ma ra- ti- o- na- lis et ca- ro u- nus   est ho- mo   i - ta

De- us   et ho - mo   u - num   est   Cri   -   stus.   E u o u a e.

[Man has eaten the bread of angels, so that we, who partake in his divinity through his
food for souls, may partake in his humanity through his food for flesh, because just as
the rational soul and flesh are one man, so the one Christ is God and man.]

---

[60] Fourth word is *visibibus* in MS.

6.   Responsory: Sacerdos summus/Leta laudum

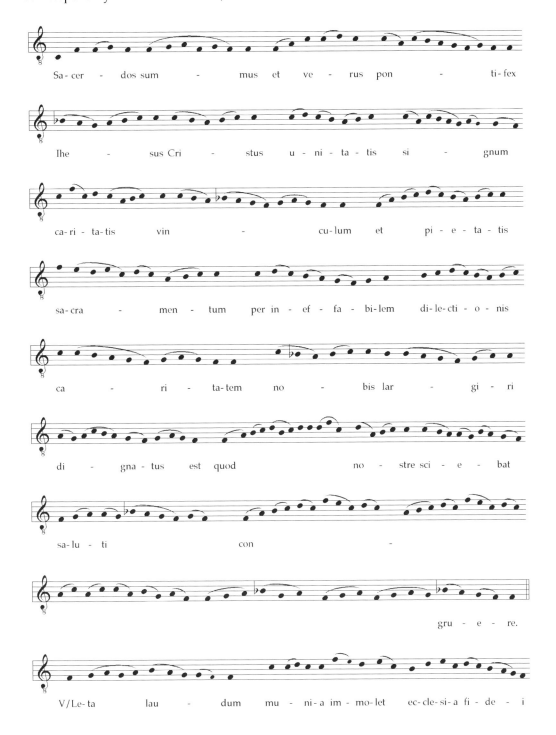

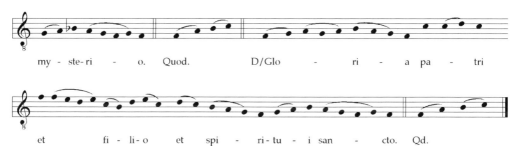

my - ste-ri - o.   Quod.   D/Glo - ri - a pa - tri

et   fi - li- o   et   spi - ri - tu - i san - cto.   Qd.

[By the ineffable charity of his love the high priest and true pontiff, Jesus Christ, has deigned to lavish upon us what he knew to be fitting for our salvation: a sign of unity, a bond of charity and a sacrament of piety.[61] V. Let the church offer the joyful gifts of its praises to the mystery of faith.]

7. [Versiculus]: Notum fecit

No- tum fe - cit Do- mi- nus.   Sa- lu- ta- re su- um.

[V. The Lord has made known. R. His salvation.]

---

[61] See Alger of Liège, *De sacramentis*, Book I, Ch. 3 (PL 180, col. 748). See also Gratian, *De consecratione*, Dist. II, can. 63.

8. Ad Magnificat antiphona: Dominus Ihesus Cristus[62]

Do – mi – nus Ihe – sus Cri – stus mun – di de – cus, ho – nor

sa – lus spes et glo – ri – a, ca – ri – ta – tis

ar – te pro – vi – da pig – men – ta com – po – su – it, qui – bus le – tar – gi – cam

men – tem re – no – va – tam co – ti – di – e su – e

sa – lu – tis me – mo – ri – a pro – pel – le – ret

qui e – den – tu – lam ple – bem que ver – bum an – ti – quum

et e – ter – num prin – ci – pi – um qua – si so – li – dum ci – bum

---

[62] MS has *edentulam*, not *edulentam* as in Fransen. This does not seem to be a garbling.

ru - mi - na - re non po - te - rat hoc pre-dul - cis - si - mo con - fe - cto li - qua-mi - ne in pa - nis et vi - ni sa - cra - men - to con - su - e - fe - cit sor - bi - la - re. E u o u a e. Ps/Ma- gni - fi- cat.

[Lord Jesus Christ, dignity, honor, and salvation of the world, hope and glory, with the provident art of his love, composed the ingredients by which he might drive forward the lethargic mind, renewed daily by the memory of his salvation; when the toothless people were unable to chew the solid food of the ancient word and eternal principle, he accustomed them to sip from the most sweet liquid in the sacrament of bread and wine.]

[Ad matutinas]

9. Invitatory: Cristum regum regem

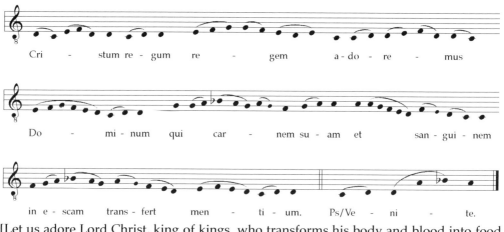

Cri - stum re - gum re - gem a - do - re - mus Do - mi - num qui car - nem su - am et san - gui - nem in e - scam trans - fert men - ti - um. Ps/Ve - ni - te.

[Let us adore Lord Christ, king of kings, who transforms his body and blood into food for our hearts.]

In primo noctorno
Antiphona[63]
10. Suo Cristus /Ps Beatus vir

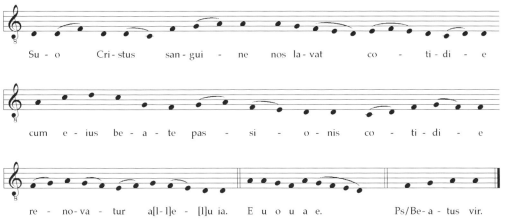

Su - o   Cri - stus   san - gui - ne   nos la - vat   co - ti - di - e

cum e - ius be - a - te pas - si - o - nis co - ti - di - e

re - no - va - tur a[l- l]e - [l]u ia.   E u o u a e.   Ps/Be- a - tus vir.

[Each day Christ washes us with his blood when each day the memory of his blessed passion is renewed, alleluia.]

11. Visibilis creature/Ps Cum invocarem

Vi- si - bi - lis cre-a - tu-re   in car- nis et   san-gui- nis e - ius   in- ef- fa- bi- li spi- ri - tus

san - cti- fi- ca- ti- o - ne   trans - fer - tur sa - cra - men - tum.   E u o u a   e.

Ps/Cum in- vo- ca- rem.

[A visible creation is transformed into the sacrament of his flesh and blood by the ineffable work of the Spirit.]

---

[63] For antiphon texts, see Alger of Liège, *De sacramentis*, Book I, Ch. 16 (PL 180, col. 788).

12. Sanguis eius/Ps Exaudiat te.

San - guis e - ius   non in - fi - de - li - um   ma — ni - bus   ad i - pso - rum

per - ni - ci - em   fun - di - tur   sed co - ti - di - e   fi - de — li - um

su - am   o - re su - mi - tur   in sa - lu - tem.   E u o u   a   e.   Ps/Ex - au - di - at te.

[His blood is not shed by the hands of unbelievers unto their destruction, but each day it is received by the mouths of believers unto their salvation.[64]]

13. Versiculus

V. Viderunt omnes termini terre. R. Salutare Dei nostri.

[V. All the ends of the earth have seen. R. The salvation of our God.]

V. Notum fecit Dominus. R. Saluta[re suum.]

[V. The Lord has made known. R. His salvation.]

---

[64] Alger of Liege, *De sacramentis . . .* , Bk. 1, Ch. 16, quoting Bede (PL 180, col. 788): ". . . corpus et sanguis illius non infidelium manibus ad perniciem ipsorum funditur et occiditur, sed fidelium ore suam sumitur in sa- lutem."

[Lectio i]

14. Responsory: Invisibilis sacerdos/Ipse conviva[65]

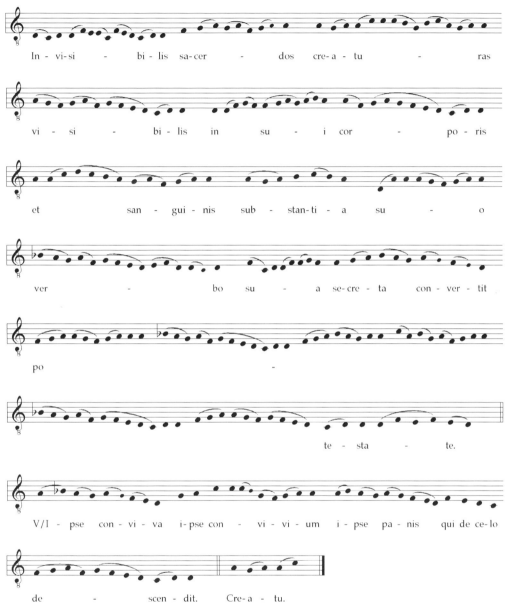

[The invisible priest by his word and by his secret power converts visible creatures into the substance of his body and blood. V. He himself the guest, himself the banquet, himself the bread which comes down from heaven.]

---

[65] Gratian, *De consecratione*, Dist. II, can. 35. See Alger of Liège, *De sacramentis*, Book I, Ch. 10 (PL 180, col. 771).

[Lectio ii]

15. Responsory: Dixit Ihesus/Nisi meam[66]

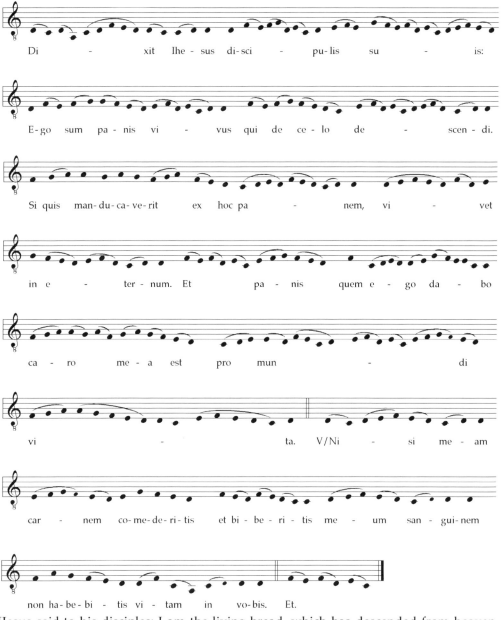

Di - xit Ihe - sus di-sci - pu-lis su - is:

E-go sum pa - nis vi - vus qui de ce - lo de - scen - di.

Si quis man-du-ca-ve-rit ex hoc pa - nem, vi - vet

in e - ter - num. Et pa - nis quem e - go da - bo

ca - ro me - a est pro mun - di

vi - ta. V/Ni - si me - am

car - nem co-me-de-ri-tis et bi - be - ri-tis me - um san - gui-nem

non ha-be-bi - tis vi - tam in vo-bis. Et.

[Jesus said to his disciples: I am the living bread, which has descended from heaven. Whoever eats of this bread shall have eternal life. And the bread that I give is my flesh for the life of the world. V. Unless you shall eat my flesh and drink my blood you shall not have life within you.]

---

[66] John 6: 51–53.

[Lectio iii]

16. Responsory: Vere mira/Hoc celesti/Gloria patri

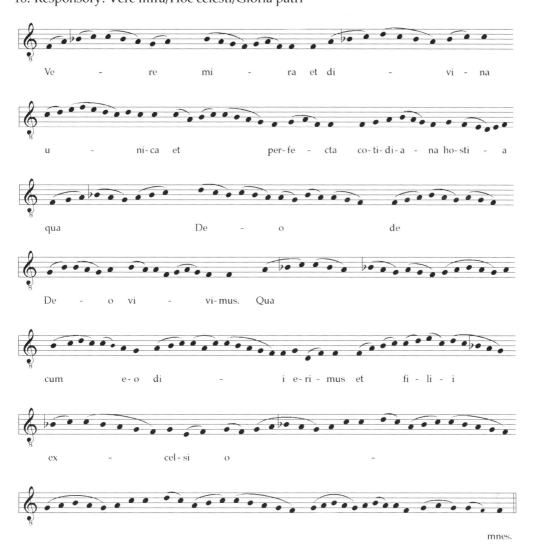

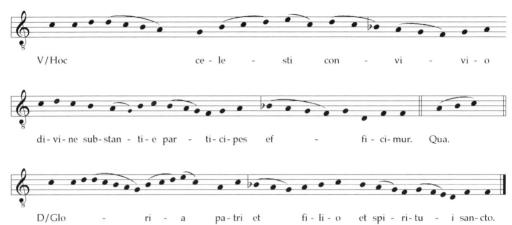

V/Hoc   ce - le - sti   con - vi - vi - o

di - vi - ne sub - stan - ti - e par - ti - ci - pes ef - fi - ci - mur.   Qua.

D/Glo - ri - a   pa - tri et   fi - li - o   et spi - ri - tu - i san - cto.

[Truly wonderful and divine, unique and perfect daily sacrifice,[67] by which we live with God and of God, by which we will be gods with him and all sons of the Most High. V. By this celestial banquet we are made participants of the divine substance.]

In secundo noctorno
Antiphona[68]
17. Hostia Cristus/Ps Dominus reg[navit]

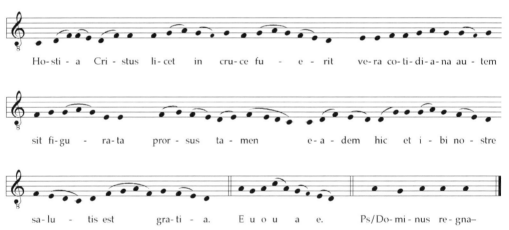

Ho - sti - a   Cri - stus li - cet   in   cru- ce fu - e - rit   ve - ra co- ti- di- a- na au - tem

sit fi- gu - ra- ta   pror - sus   ta - men   e- a - dem hic   et i - bi no - stre

sa - lu - tis est   gra- ti - a.   E u o u   a   e.   Ps/Do- mi - nus re- gna–

[Although Christ was once truly a victim on the cross, but now is daily such as a figure, still there and here he is the grace of our salvation.]

---

[67] Alger of Liège, *De sacramentis*, Book I, Ch. 15 (PL 180, col. 785).

[68] For antiphon texts, see Alger of Liège, *De sacramentis*, Book I, Ch. 16 (PL 180, col. 787).

18. Hic et ibi/Ps Benedicam

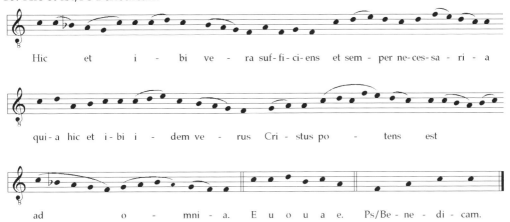

Hic   et   i - bi ve - ra suf-fi-ci-ens et sem - per ne-ces-sa - ri - a

qui-a hic et i-bi i - dem ve - rus Cri - stus po   tens   est

ad   o - mni - a.   E u o u a e.   Ps/Be - ne - di - cam.

[Here and there [On the cross and on the altar he is] a necessary and sufficient sacrifice, because here and there Christ is mighty in all things.]

19. Verus Deus/Ps Quam dilecta

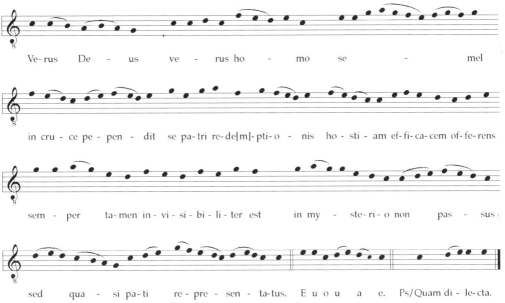

Ve - rus   De - us   ve - rus ho - mo   se   mel

in cru - ce pe - pen - dit se pa-tri re-de[m]-pti-o - nis ho - sti - am ef-fi-ca-cem of-fe-rens

sem - per ta-men in - vi - si - bi - li - ter est in my - ste-ri-o non   pas - sus

sed qua - si pa-ti re - pre - sen - ta-tus. E u o u a e.   Ps/Quam di - le-cta.

[True God, true man, Christ, who once hung on the cross, offering himself to the Father as an efficacious and redeeming sacrifice, now ever offers himself invisibly in the mystery where he does not suffer, but is represented as if suffering.]

20. Pater noster.
   [Versiculus]

   V. Ipse est vite. R. Credere [in Jesum Christum]
   [V. It is life itself. R. To believe in Jesus Christ]

   V. Viderunt omnes termini [terre. R. Salutare Dei nostri.]
   [V. All the ends of the earth have seen. R. The salvation of our God.]

[Lectio iv]

21. Responsory: Ad ipsius/Suam carnem[69]

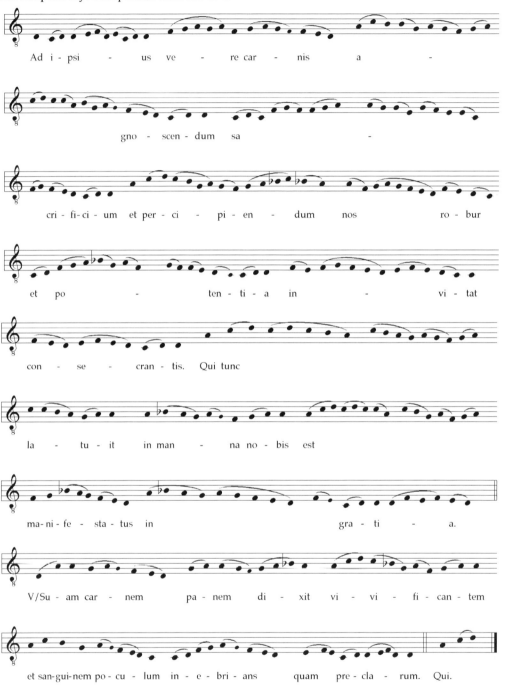

Ad i - psi - us ve - re car - nis a -

gno - scen - dum sa -

cri - fi - ci - um et per - ci - pi - en - dum nos ro - bur

et po - ten - ti - a in - vi - tat

con - se - cran - tis. Qui tunc

la - tu - it in man - na no - bis est

ma - ni - fe - sta - tus in gra - ti - a.

V/Su - am car - nem pa - nem di - xit vi - vi - fi - can - tem

et san-gui-nem po - cu - lum in - e - bri - ans quam pre - cla - rum. Qui.

---

[69] For responsory text, see Alger of Liège, *De sacramentis*, Book I, Ch. 11 (PL 180, col. 771).

[The strength and power of one who consecrates invites us to acknowledge and receive his true flesh. The one who lay hidden in the manna was manifest to us in grace. V. He said that his body is life-giving bread and his blood a drink more spendid than inebriating.]

[Lectio v]
22. Responsory: Alieni/Viva vivo

A - li - e - ni et ex - te - ri

in-trin - se - cus mor - tu - i a vi - ta

a mi - se - ri - cor - di - a et a sa - lu - tis

vi - a du-dum ex-u - la - vi - mus.

Nunc re-fe - cti sa - lu - ta - ri my - ste - ri - o.

V/Vi - va vi - vo men-bra su - o cor - po - ri

non vi - den - do sed cre - den - do in se - ri - mur. Nunc.

[Formerly alien and foreign, dead inside, for a long time we were in exile from life, from compassion, and from the path of salvation. Now we are restored by the mystery of salvation. V. Now we are planted as living members in his living body, not by seeing but by believing.]

[Lectio vi]

23. Responsory: Sacerdos sum[/Leta laudum/Gloria patri (See #6)

Sa- cer   -   dos sum   -

In tertio nocturno
Antiphona

24. Dominus Ihesus/Ps Cantate ii[70]

Do   -   mi - nus Ihe - sus   Cri - stus   si- ne   vul   -   ne- re

co   -   ti- di - e   sa   -   cri - fi- ca - tus   mor- ta- les   in   ter   -   ra

pre- sti- tit   ce   -   le - sti   su - o   fun   -   gi   mi- ni - ste- ri - o.

E   u   o   u   a   e.   Ps/Can- ta - te.

[The Lord Jesus Christ, sacrificed each day without wound, has appointed earthly mortals to perform his heavenly ministry.]

---

[70] In the manuscript, the seventh word was initially *sacrificantes*. An editor scratched out the final *e* and replaced it with the *u*, yielding *sacrificantus*, which Fransen and others have changed to *sacrificatus*.

25. Sacri ministerio/Ps Dominus reg. Iras.[71]

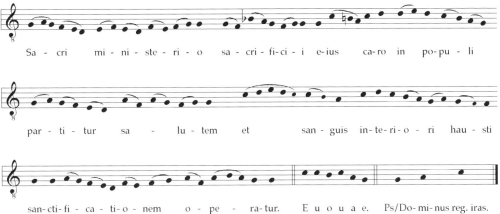

[In the administration of his sacred sacrifice his flesh bestows salvation upon his people and his blood, drunk by their hearts, effects their sanctification.]

26. Hec igitur/Ps Benedic anima ii

[This unique sacrifice recalls the death of Christ, cleanses us from our sins, fulfills the devoted service of the faithful, and enables them to attain eternal life.]

27. Versiculi

V. Ipse est vita. R. Credere [in Jesum Christum.]
[V. It is life itself. R. To believe in Jesus Christ]

V. Benedictus qui venit. [R. In nomine Domini.]
[V. Blessed is he who comes. R. In the name of the Lord.]

---

[71] Alger of Liège, *De sacramentis*, Book I, Ch. 11 (PL 180, col. 771).

[Lectio vii]

28. Responsory: Cristus corpus/Ut perhennis[72]

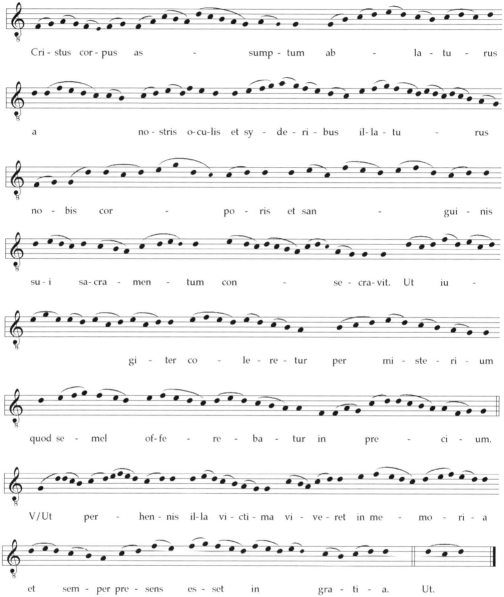

Cri - stus cor - pus as - sump - tum ab - la - tu - rus

a no - stris o - cu - lis et sy - de - ri - bus il - la - tu - rus

no - bis cor - po - ris et san - gui - nis

su - i sa - cra - men - tum con - se - cra - vit. Ut iu -

gi - ter co - le - re - tur per mi - ste - ri - um

quod se - mel of - fe - re - ba - tur in pre - ci - um.

V/Ut per - hen - nis il - la vi - cti - ma vi - ve - ret in me - mo - ri - a

et sem - per pre - sens es - set in gra - ti - a. Ut.

[Christ, when he was ready to remove from our eyes the body he had taken on and bring it into heaven, consecrated for us the sacrament of his body and blood, so that what he once offered as the price of our redemption might continually be revered through this mystery. V. So that this eternal victim might live in memory and ever be present in grace.]

---

[72] Gratian, *De consecratione*, Dist. II, can. 35 beginning (quoting Eusebius Emisenus).

[Lectio viii]

29. Responsory: O vere miraculum/Vere bonus[73]

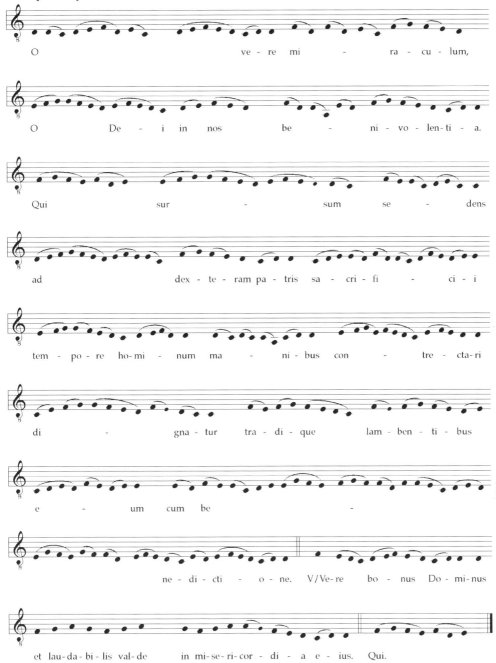

[O true miracle! O God's kindness to us! He who is seated at the right hand of his father deigns in time to be touched by human hands and to be handed over to those sipping him with blessing. V. Truly a good God and very praiseworthy in his mercy.]

---

[73] For responsory text, see Alger of Liège, *De sacramentis*, Book I, Ch. 12 (PL 180, cols. 777–78).

[Lectio ix]

30. Responsory: Panis vive/Ideoque tu/Gloria patri

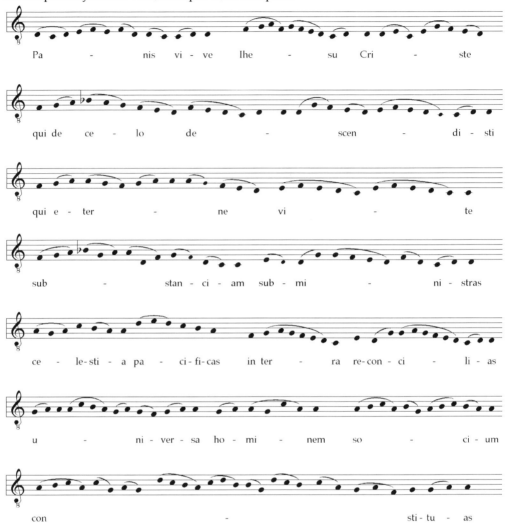

Pa - nis vi - ve Ihe - su Cri - ste

qui de ce - lo de - scen - di - sti

qui e - ter - ne vi - te

sub - stan - ci - am sub - mi - ni - stras

ce - le - sti - a pa - ci - fi - cas in ter - ra re - con - ci - li - as

u - ni - ver - sa ho - mi - nem so - ci - um

con - sti - tu - as

an - ge - lo - rum. Te no - stris men - ti - bus

con - fe - ras e - dul - li - um

sa - ci - e - ta - tis per -

pe - tu - e.

V/I - de - o - que tu fi - li - us De - i vi - si - bi - li sub spe - ci - e

no - bis - cum es - se vo - lu - i - sti ut tu - i par -

ti - ci - pi - bus. Te no - stris. D/Glo - ri - a pa - tri

et fi - li - o et spi - ri - tu - i san - cto. Te.

[Jesus Christ, living bread, who has descended from heaven, who provides the substance of eternal life, who brings the peace of heaven, and who reconciles all things on earth, you make humanity the companion of angels, you give yourself to our hearts as the food that satisfies eternally. V. Therefore you, the son of God, has chosen to be with us under a visible species so that we might share in your life.]

31. Te Deum (cued after last verse of previous responsory)

Te   Deu - um.

Laudes

32. Celestis[74] artificio [Ps Dominus regnavit]

Ce - le - stis   ar - ti - fi - ci - o   mi - se - ri - cor - di - e

in- du- tam car - ne di- vi- ni - ta- tem at- que dul- cis- si- mam Cri - sti pre - sen - ti - am

de - vo - tis - si - me   ho - no - ri - fi - ce- mus.   E u o u a e.

[Let us with utmost devotion honor the most sweet presence of Christ, the God that by the merciful art of heaven assumed flesh.]

33. Cristus enim [Ps Iubilate][75]

Cri - stus   e - nim   est   sa - lu- bris a - ni - ma - rum   re - fe- cti - o.

Re- so - net   vox lau - dis o- mni - um iu - bi - lo.   E u o u a   e.

[Christ is the healthy restoration of souls; let the voice of praise resound with the joy of all people.]

---

[74] The first word is clearly *Cristus* in the manuscript. Lambot/Fransen edited it to *celestis*. Perhaps the scribe of KB 70.E.4 mistakenly copied the first word of Antiphon 2.

[75] See Hugh of Saint-Victor, *De sacramentis corporis et sanguinis Dominici*, Book II, pt. 8, Ch. 8.

34. Illa nobis [Ps Deus deus]

Il - la   no - bis ex - pec - ta-mus in qui - bus   est ve - ri - tas, in   qui-bus est

per - fe - cti - o, ut vi-de-re va - le - a - mus

Chri - sti   vir - tu-tem et glo-ri-am in ce - le-sti - bus. E u o   u   a   e.

[Let us await those things in which there is truth, in which there is perfection, so that we might be worthy of seeing the power and glory of Christ in the heavens.]

35. Nulla nobis [Ps Benedicite]

Nul - la no-bis me - mo - ri - a   e - rit ne-ces-sa - ri-a   cum in e-ius vi - si - o - ne

o - bli - vi - o nul - la   po - te - rit   in - ter - ci - de - re. E u o u   a   e.

[Memory will no longer be necessary for us since the vision will preclude forgetting.]

36. Ecce vobiscum [Ps Laudate]

Ec- ce vo-bis-cum sum o - mni-bus di-e-bus us - que ad con-su-ma - ti-o-nem mun - di,

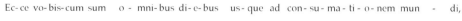

a[l- l]e-[l]u- ia. E u o   u   a   e.

[Behold I am with you always until the end of the world.[76]]

[76] Matt 28: 20.

37. Versiculus

V. Constituite diem sollemp[nem. R. Usque ad cornu altare.]

[V. Celebrate the solemn day . R. Up to the corner of the altar.

38. Ad Benedictus antiphona: Panis vite/Benedictus

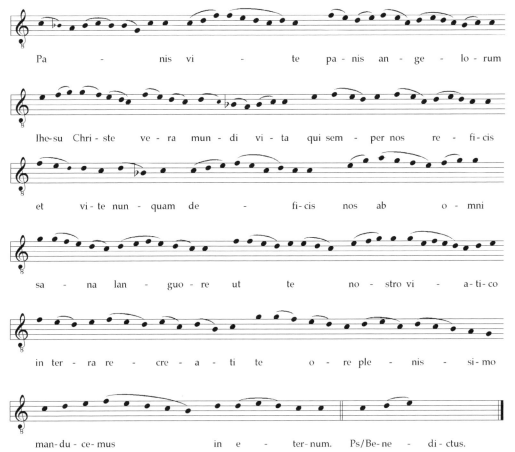

Pa — nis vi — te pa- nis an - ge - lo - rum

Ihe-su Chri - ste ve - ra mun - di vi - ta qui sem - per nos re - fi- cis

et vi- te nun - quam de - fi- cis nos ab o - mni

sa - na lan - guo- re ut te no - stro vi - a- ti- co

in ter - ra re - cre - a - ti te o - re ple - nis - si- mo

man- du - ce- mus in e - ter- num. Ps/Be- ne - di- ctus.

[Bread of life, bread of angels, Jesus Christ, true life of the world, you who perpetually restores us and never fails us; guard us from all languor so that recreated by you through the food for our journey on earth we might partake of you most fully in heaven.]

Ad ii vesperas
[Antiphona]
39. Sacramentum pietatis/Ps Dixit Do[minus]

Sa- cra- men- tum pi- e- ta - tis hu- ic mun - do cre- di- tum a - li - e- na spe - ci - e

li - cet   oc - cul - ta- tum   ve- rump- ta - men   ve - ri - ta - te

est   am - mi - ni- stra- tum.   E u o u a e.   Ps/Di- xit Do - mi - nus.

[The sacrament of piety, entrusted to this world, although hidden under a foreign species, truly was administered in truth.]

40. Misterii veritatem/Ps Confitebor tibi[77]

Mi - ste- ri - i ve- ri - ta- tem fi - li- us   a- stri- xit   quem au- di - re De- us pa - ter

no - bis   in - dul- sit   in   quo si - bi com- pla- ce - re   ma- ni - fe - sta - vit

e- um es- se quem ge - nu - it dum   de- cla - ra- vit.   E u o u a e.   Ps/Confi- te-bor ti-bi.

[The Son has demonstrated the truth of the mystery. God the Father enjoined us to hear
the one in whom he was well pleased when he declared him to be his only-begotten
son.]

---

[77] See Alger of Liège, *De sacramentis*, Book I, Ch. 12 (PL 180, col. 776).

41. Qui semel/Ps Beati o[mnes] qui [timent][78]

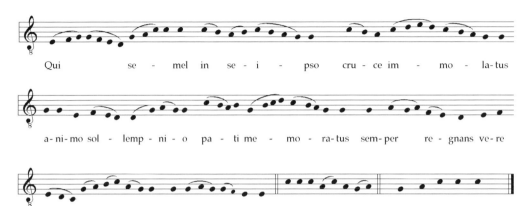

Qui se - mel in se - i - pso cru - ce im - mo - la-tus

a - ni-mo sol - lemp - ni - o pa - ti me - mo - ra-tus sem-per re - gnans ve-re

co - ti - di - e est li - ta-tus. E u o u a e. Ps/Be-a - ti o. qui.

[He who sacrificed himself a single time on the cross, his passion commemorated daily with solemn mind, always truly reigning, was made an acceptable offering.]

42. Ore quidem/Ps Confitemini Do[mino] q[uonia]m bo[nus][79]

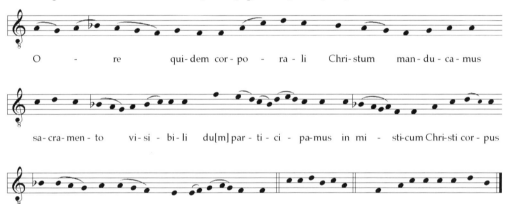

O - re qui- dem cor- po - ra - li Chri- stum man - du - ca - mus

sa- cra-men - to vi- si - bi- li du[m] par - ti - ci - pa-mus in mi - sti-cum Chri-sti cor - pus

per quod trans - mi - gra-mus. E u o u a e. Ps/Con-fi-te-mi-ni do. qm bo.

[Indeed with our bodily mouth we eat Christ as we participate in the visible sacrament through which we become the mystical body of Christ.]

---

[78] See Alger of Liège, *De sacramentis*, Book I, Ch. 16 (PL 180, col.. 790).

[79] For the texts to this and the following antiphon, see Alger of Liège, *De sacramentis*, Book I, Ch. 20 (PL 180, cols. 797–98).

43. Ore vero/Ps Lauda Iher[ulsa]lem[80]

O- re ve- ro   spi - ri- ta- li   Chri - stum man - du - ca- mus   si pro no- bis   i- psum pas- sum

men- te   re - cor - da- mus   fi - de- li- ter et   vi - ti - is   si

nos   cru - ci - a- mus.   E   u   o   u   a   e.   Ps/ Lau- da   Ihr - lm.

[Indeed with our spiritual mouth we eat Christ if we faithfully recall that he suffered for us and if we grieve over our sins.]

[80] The last word is *conciamus* in Fransen, but clearly *cruciamus* in the manuscript.

44. Ad nutum/Ubi virtus/Gloria patri[81]

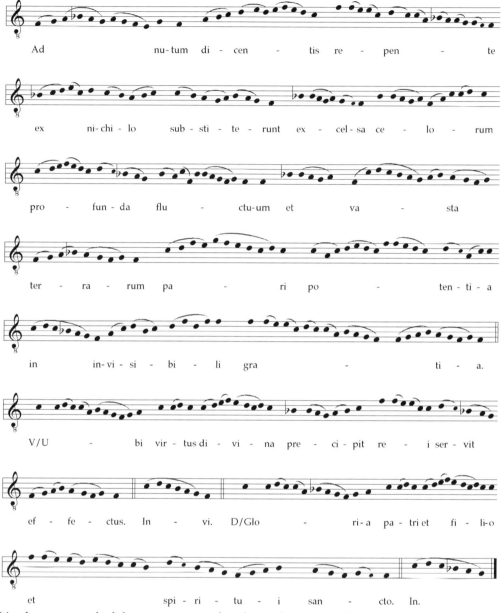

Ad   nu-tum di - cen - tis re - pen - te

ex   ni-chi - lo   sub - sti - te - runt ex - cel - sa ce - lo - rum

pro - fun - da flu - ctu-um et   va - sta

ter - ra - rum pa - ri po - ten - ti - a

in   in-vi - si - bi - li gra - ti - a.

V/U - bi vir - tus di - vi - na pre - ci - pit re - i ser - vit

ef - fe - ctus. In - vi. D/Glo - ri-a pa - tri et fi - li-o

et   spi - ri - tu - i san - cto. In.

[At the command of the creator, out of nothing, there arose the heights of the heavens, depths of the waves, and expanses of the earth, by an invisible force equal in power and grace. V. Where divine power rules, it produces its effects.]

---

[81] Gratian, *De consecratione*, Dist. II, can. 35. See Alger of Liège, *De sacramentis*, Book I, Ch. 10 (PL 180, col. 771).

45. Ad Magnificat: Ihesu bone/Magnificat

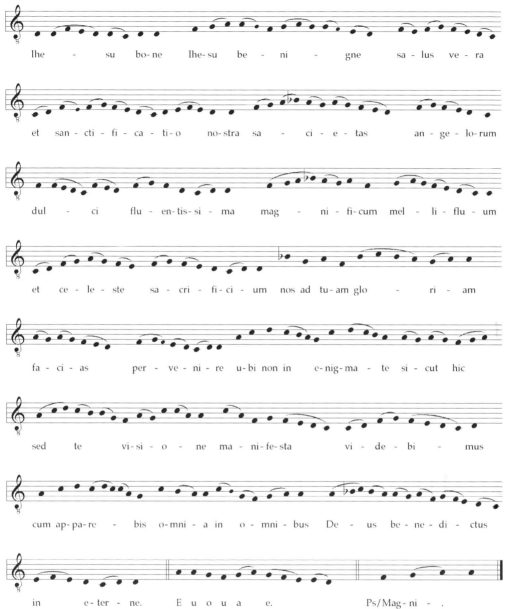

Ihe - su bo-ne Ihe-su be - ni - gne sa - lus ve - ra

et san-cti-fi-ca-ti-o no-stra sa - ci-e-tas an-ge-lo-rum

dul - ci flu-en-tis-si-ma mag - ni-fi-cum mel - li-flu - um

et ce-le-ste sa-cri-fi-ci-um nos ad tu-am glo - ri - am

fa-ci-as per-ve-ni-re u-bi non in e-nig-ma - te si-cut hic

sed te vi-si-o - ne ma-ni-fe-sta vi-de-bi - mus

cum ap-pa-re - bis o-mni-a in o-mni-bus De - us be-ne-di - ctus

in e-ter - ne. E u o u a e. Ps/Mag-ni - .

[Jesus full of good, Jesus full of kindness, true salvation and our sanctification, most sweet satiety of the angels, most sweetly flowing celestial sacrifice, you make us come to your glory, whereby we shall see you no longer obscurely, as here, but in open vision, where you will appear everything in all things, God blessed for all ages.]

[Ad missam]

46. Sequencia: Laureata plebs fidelis

Lau-re-a-ta plebs fi-de lis sa-cra-men-to Christi car-nis lau-da re-gem glo-ri-e.
Nam cum re-gnans sit in ce-lis cum ef-fe-ctu su-e mor-tis se pre-bet co-ti-di-e.

Ut pre-ci-um pro pec-ca-tis fi-at vir-tus pas-si o-nis et aug-men-tum gra-ti-e.
Mis-sa con fert i-sta no-bis er-go di-gne sit sol-lemp-nis mis-se cul-tus ho-di-e.

Hoc si-gna-vit vi-te li-gnum Mel-chi-se-dech pa-nem vi-vum ut pla-ce-ret tri-num u-num

of-fe-rens al-tis-si-mo. A-ser quo-que pin-guis ci-bus de-li-ci-as dans re-gi-bus

nam re-ga-lis hic est ci-bus pa-ne sa-cra-tis-si-mo. Et hoc qui-dem de-si-gna-vit

a-gnus si-ne ma-cu-la quem e-den-dum im-mo-la-vit quon-dam lex Mo-sa-y-ca.

A-gnus le-gis iam ces-sa-vit su-per ve-nit gra-ti-a Chri-sti san-guis dum ma-na-vit

mun-di tol-lens cri-mi-na. Ca-ro cu-ius tam se-re-na no-bis e-sca fit a-me-na

fi-de-i mi-ste-ri-o. Quam pro-vi-de man-na ce-li fi-gu-ra-vit Is-ra-he-li

no-bi-li pre-sa-gi-o. E-sca fu-it tem-po-ra-lis in de-ser-to da-tum man-na
Hic est pa-nis sa-lu-ta-ris per quem da-tur no-bis vi-ta

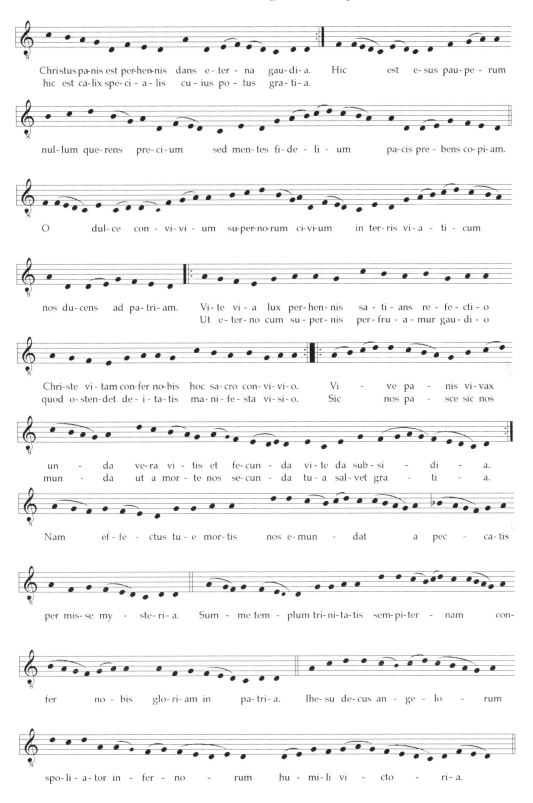

Christus pa-nis est per-hen-nis dans e - ter - na gau-di- a.   Hic   est e-sus pau-pe - rum
hic est ca-lix spe-ci - a - lis   cu - ius po - tus   gra - ti - a.

nul-lum que-rens   pre-ci- um   sed men-tes fi- de - li - um   pa-cis pre - bens co-pi-am.

O   dul-ce   con - vi-vi - um   su-per-no-rum ci-vi-um   in ter-ris vi-a - ti - cum

nos du-cens   ad pa-tri- am.   Vi-te vi - a lux per-hen - nis   sa - ti-ans re-fe-cti- o
Ut e-ter-no cum su-per-nis   per-fru - a - mur gau-di- o

Chri-ste vi - tam con-fer no-bis   hoc sa-cro con-vi-vi- o.   Vi   ve pa   nis vi-vax
quod o-sten-det de - i-ta-tis   ma-ni-fe-sta vi-si- o.   Sic   nos pa   sce sic nos

un   da   ve-ra vi - tis et fe-cun - da vi-te da sub-si   di   a.
mun   da   ut a mor - te nos se-cun - da tu-a sal-vet gra   ti   a.

Nam   ef - fe - ctus tu - e mor-tis   nos e-mun   dat   a pec   ca-tis

per mis-se my - ste-ri- a.   Sum - me tem - plum tri-ni-ta-tis sem-pi-ter - nam   con-

fer   no - bis   glo-ri-am in   pa-tri- a.   Ihe-su de-cus an - ge - lo - rum

spo-li - a-tor in - fer - no - rum   hu - mi-li vi - cto - ri- a.

Ho-nor ce-li lux san - cto - rum sa-lus mun- di fons ho - no - rum ti - bi laus et   glo - ri-a.

A   -   men.

[1. Faithful people, crowned with the sacrament of the body of Christ, praise the king of glory. Although reigning in heaven, by the effect of his death, he gives himself each day.

2. In order that the virtue of his passion may be the price for our sins and an increase of grace, this mass confers these things upon us. Therefore, let the celebration of mass be worthily solemn today.

3. The tree of life signified this [mystery]: Melchisedech offering bread and wine to the Most High to please the triune God, and like Aser, giving delights to kings in the form of rich foods. This is also royal food, by means of the most sacred bread.

4. And the lamb without blemish also signified this, the one which the law of Moses once sacrificed and had to be eaten. The lamb of the old law has now ceased, for grace has come instead, when the blood of Christ flowed, expiating the sins of the world,

5. May his flesh so serene be pleasant food for us in the mystery of faith. The manna from heaven given to Israel symbolized a noble exemplar.

6. Temporal food it was, that manna given in the desert; Christ is perennial bread, giving eternal joys. Here is the bread of salvation, through which life is given to us; here is the special chalice, whose beverage is grace.

7. Here is the food of the poor, requiring no price, but granting the minds of the faithful an abundance of peace. O sweet banquet of celestial citizens, viaticum on earth, leading us to our homeland.

8. Way of life, continual light, satisfying refreshment, Christ, confer life to us by this sacred banquet, that, with those above, we may eternally enjoy the joy, which the manifest vision of the deity will bestow.

9. Living bread, lively flow of water, true and fruitful vine, give us succor for life. Thus nourish us, thus cleanse us, so that your favorable grace may preserve us from death.

10. For the effect of your death cleanses us from our sins through the mysteries of the mass. O temple of the most high Trinity, confer upon us everlasting glory in heaven.

11. Jesus, glory of angels, despoiler of hell by your humble victory, the honor of heaven, the light of the saints, the salvation of the world, the font of good things, to you be praise and glory. Amen.

47. Hymnus: Ad cenam agni providi

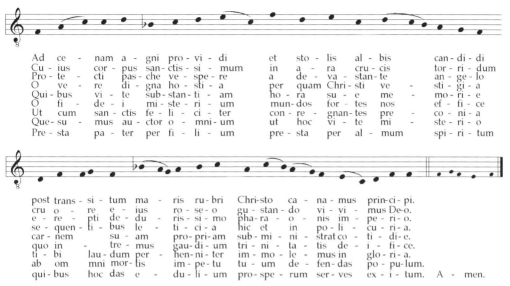

Ad ce - nam a - gni pro - vi - di   et sto - lis al - bis   can - di - di
Cu - ius cor - pus san - ctis - si - mum   in a - ra cru - cis   tor - ri - dum
Pro - te - cti pas - che ve - spe - re   a de - va - stan - te   an - ge - lo
O ve - re di - gna ho - sti - a   per quam Chri - sti ve -   sti - gi - a
Qui - bus vi - te sub - stan - ti - am   ho - ra su - e me -   mo - ri - e
O fi - de - i mi - ste - ri - um   mun - dos for - tes nos   ef - fi - ce
Ut cum san - ctis fe - li - ci - ter   con - re - gnan - tes pre - co - ni - a
Que - su - mus au - ctor o - mni - um   ut hoc vi - te mi -   ste - ri - o
Pre - sta pa - ter per fi - li - um   pre - sta per al - mum   spi - ri - tum

post trans - si - tum ma - ris ru - bri   Chri - sto ca - na - mus   prin - ci - pi.
cru o - re e - ius   ro - se - o gu - stan - do vi - vi - mus De - o.
e - re - pti de - du - ris - si - mo   pha - ra - o - nis im -   pe - ri - o.
se - quen - ti - bus le - ti - ci - a   hic et in po - li -   cu - ri - a.
car - nem su - am pro - pri - am   sub - mi - ni - strat co - ti - di - e.
quo in tre - mus gau - di - um   tri - ni - ta - tis de -   i - fi - ce.
ti - bi lau - dum per - hen - ni - ter   im - mo - le - mus in   glo - ri - a.
ab om - mni mor - tis im - pe - tu   tu - um de - fen - das   po - pu - lum.
qui - bus hoc das e - du - li - um   pro - spe - rum ser - ves   ex - i - tum. A - men.

[1. At the feast of the sacrificial lamb, and attired in white robes, after the crossing of the Red Sea, let us sing praises to Christ the King.

2. We subsist by partaking of God, whose most sacred body, with his rose colored blood, was parched on the altar of the cross.

3. Protected on the eve of Passover from the angel of destruction, we were snatched away from the most oppressive rule of the Pharaoh.

4. O true worthy sacrifice, through which there is joy for those who follow in the footsteps of Christ, here and in the hall of heaven.

5. For whom, in the hour of his remembrance, he daily offers the substance of life through his own flesh.

6. O mystery of faith make us clean, strong, so that we may enter into the joy of the deified Trinity.

7. So that, happily reigning with the saints, we may perpetually offer the announcements of praises to you in glory.

8. We pray, author of all, that by means of this mystery of life, you defend your people from every attack of death.

9. Be present, Father, through the Son. Be present through the nourishing spirit. To those to whom you give this food, grant a favorable end. Amen.]

[IN FESTO CORPORIS[82] CHRISTI
PRAGUE, ABBEY OF STRAHOV, MS D.E.I.7

In Primis vesperis
Antiphona
1. Sapiencia edificavit/Ps Dixit dominus domino
    [Text Source: Prov 9: 1–2]

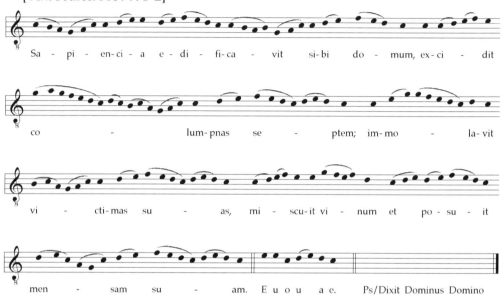

[Wisdom has built herself a house, she has erected her seven pillars, she has slaughtered her beasts, prepared her wine, she has laid her table.]

---

[82] Only *xpi* is clearly visible. The rest has been cut off.

2. Melchisedech rex Salem/Ps Confitebor
    [Text Source: Gen 14: 18–19]

Mel - chi - se-dech rex Sa - lem pro-fe - rens pa - nem et vi - num–

e- rat e - nim sa - cer - dos De-i sum - mus– be-ne-di - xit

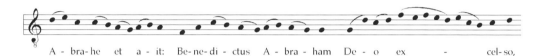

A - bra-he et a - it: Be-ne-di - ctus A - bra - ham De - o ex - cel- so,

qui cre - a- vit ce - lum et ter- ram.   E u o u a e.   Ps/Confitebor.

[Melchisedech king of Salem offered bread and wine; he was the priest of the highest God. He blessed Abraham and said. Blessed be Abraham by the most high God, who created heaven and earth.]

3. Immolabit edum/Ps Credidi propter
    [Text Source: Ex 12: 6–7]

Im-mo-la - bit e-dum u - ni - ver-sa mul-ti - tu - do fi-li-o - rum Is - ra- el.

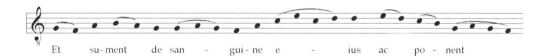

Et su-ment de san - gui-ne e - ius ac po - nent

su - per u - trum-que po - stem et in su - per - li-mi - na-ri - bus

do - mo- rum, in qui- bus co - me-dent il- lum.   E u o u a e.   Ps/Credidi propter

[The multitude of the sons of Israel shall kill the lamb. And they shall take its blood, and place it on doorposts and lintels of the houses in which it is eaten.]

4. Et edent carnes/Ps Beati omnes
    [Text Source: Ex 12: 8–9]

Et e - dent car - nes no-cte il - la as - sas i - gni

et a - zi-mos pa - nes cum la-ctu - cis a - gre - sti - bus;

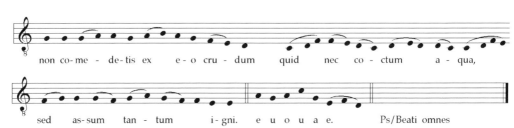

non co-me - de-tis ex e - o cru - dum quid nec co - ctum a - qua,

sed as-sum tan - tum i - gni. e u o u a e.   Ps/Beati omnes

[And they shall eat flesh on that night roasted over fire and unleavened bread with bitter herbs; do not eat any of it raw or boiled in water, but over fire.]

5. Pluit illis/Ps Lauda Iherusalem
    [Text Source: Ps 77a (Latin), 78 (Hebrew): 24–25]

Plu - it il - lis man - na ad man-du - can - dum

et pa-nem ce - li de - dit e - is; pa-nem an-ge - lo - rum

man-du-ca-vit ho - mo, ci - ba - ri - a mi - sit e - is

in ha - bun - dan-ci - a. E u o u a e.   Ps/Lauda Iherusalem Dominum

[He rained down manna to feed them, and he gave them the bread of heaven. Mankind ate the bread of the angels; he sent them food in abundance.]

6. Capitulum

Dominus ihesus christus in qua nocte tradebatur, accepit panem, et gratias agens fregit et dixit, accipite et manducate, hoc est corpus meum quod pro vobis tradetur, hoc facite in meam commemoracionem.

[The Lord Jesus Christ, on the night he was betrayed, took bread and, giving thanks, broke it and said: Take and eat; This is my body, which will be given up for you. Do this in my memory.]

7. Responsory: Cumque operuisset (See #53)

Cumque operuisset [ros superficiem terre apparuit in solutidine minutum et quasi pilo tunsum in similitudinem pruine super terram. V/ Iste est panis quem dominus dedit vobis ad vescendum.]

[When the dew had gone up there appeared on the ground a fine and flake-like thing, similar to hoarfrost on the ground. V. It is the bread that the Lord has given you to eat.]

8.   Hymn: Pange lingua

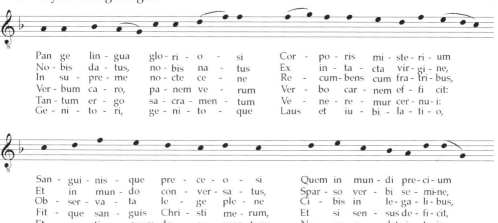

[1. Praise, my tongue, the mystery of the glorious body and of the precious blood, which the king of nations, fruit of a noble womb, poured out in ransom of the world.

2. Given to us, born to us from a pure virgin, and having lived in the world, the seed of his word having been scattered, he closed in a wondrous way his span of life.

3. At the night of the last supper, reclining with his brothers, the law of permitted foods having been fully observed, he gives himself as food with his own hands to the group of twelve.

4. The Word made flesh changes true bread into flesh by a word. And pure wine becomes Christ's blood becomes pure wine. And if the sense fails, only faith suffices to convince the sincere heart.

5. Therefore let us eagerly venerate such a great sacrament. Let the old example cede to the new rite. Let faith render assistance to the limitations of the senses.

6. To the Father, and to the Son be praise and jubilation, salvation, honor, strength, and blessing. To the One who proceeds from them both be equal praise. Amen.]

9. Versiculus
    [Text Source: Gen 49: 20]
    Aser pinguis panis eis alleluia. R. Et prebebit delicias regibus alleluia.

    [Asher, his bread is rich, alleluia. R. And he provides food for kings, alleluia.]

10. [Ad Magnificat antiphona] Angelorum esca [/Magnificat]
    [Text Source: Sap 16: 20–21]

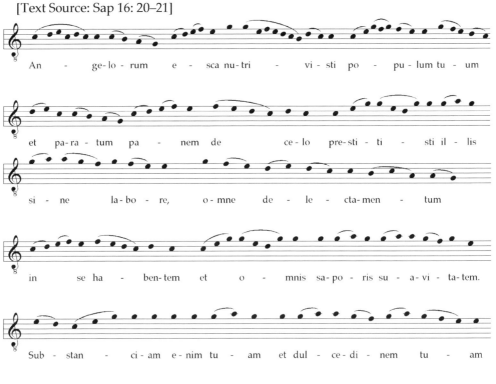

An - ge-lo-rum e - sca nu-tri - vi-sti po - pu-lum tu - um

et pa-ra-tum pa - nem de ce-lo pre-sti-ti - sti il-lis

si - ne la-bo - re, o-mne de - le - cta-men - tum

in se ha - ben-tem et o - mnis sa-po-ris su - a-vi-ta-tem.

Sub - stan - ci-am e-nim tu - am et dul - ce-di-nem tu - am

quam in fi-li-os ha - bes o - sten - de-bas. E u o u a e.

[You have nourished your people with the food of the angels, and you have furnished them with the prepared bread of heaven without labor, containing in it every delight, and satisfying every taste. You have shown your substance and your sweetness which you give to your children.]

11. Collect

Deus qui nobis sub sacramento mirabili passionis tue memoriam reliquisti, tribue quesumus: ita nos corporis et sanguinis tui sacra misteria venerari, ut redemptionis tue fructum in nobis iugiter senciamus. Qui vivis et regnas deus [per omnia secula seculorum. Amen.]

[Lord, who has left us, in a wonderful sacrament, a memorial of your passion, grant, we pray, that we may venerate the mystery of your body and blood, so that we may always feel within ourselves the fruit of your redemption. Who lives and reigns, God, world without end. Amen.]

[Ad matutinas]

12. Invitatory: Venite comedite

[Text Source: Prov 9: 5]

Ve - ni - te   co - me - di-te   pa - nem   me - um   et   bi-bi-te   vi - num

quod   mi - scu - i   vo - bis. Ps/Ve-ni - te

[Come eat my bread and drink the wine which I have mixed for you.]

13. Hymn: Sacris sollempniis

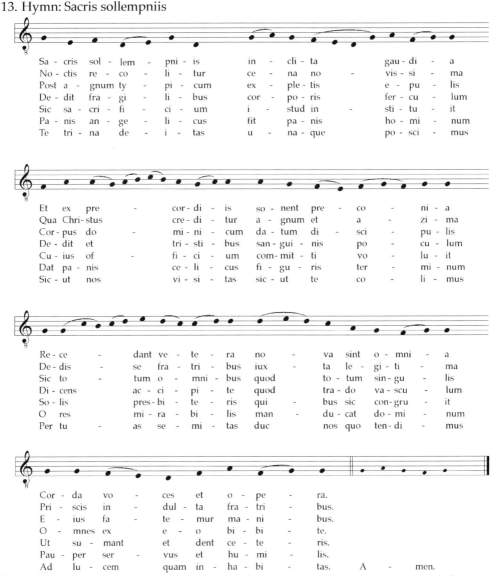

Sa - cris sol - lem - pni - is in - cli - ta gau - di - a
No - ctis re - co - li - tur ce - na no - vis - si - ma
Post a - gnum ty - pi - cum ex - ple - tis e - pu - lis
De - dit fra - gi - li - bus cor - po - ris fer - cu - lum
Sic sa - cri - fi - ci - um i - stud in - sti - tu - it
Pa - nis an - ge - li - cus fit pa - nis ho - mi - num
Te tri - na de - i - tas u - na - que po - sci - mus

Et ex pre - cor - di - is so - nent pre - co - ni - a
Qua Chri- stus cre - di - tur a - gnum et a - zi - ma
Cor - pus do - mi - ni - cum da - tum di - sci pu - lis
De - dit et tri - sti - bus san - gui - nis po - cu - lum
Cu - ius of - fi - ci - um com- mit - ti vo - lu - it
Dat pa - nis ce - li - cus fi - gu - ris ter - mi - num
Sic - ut nos vi - si - tas sic - ut te co - li - mus

Re - ce - dant ve - te - ra no - va sint o - mni - a
De - dis - se fra - tri - bus iux - ta le - gi - ti - ma
Sic to - tum o - mni - bus quod to - tum sin - gu - lis
Di - cens ac - ci - pi - te quod tra - do va - scu - lum
So - lis pres- bi - te - ris qui - bus sic con- gru - it
O res mi - ra - bi - lis man - du - cat do - mi - num
Per tu - as se - mi - tas duc nos quo ten- di - mus

Cor - da vo - ces et o - pe - ra.
Pri - scis in - dul - ta fra - tri - bus.
E - ius fa - te - mur ma - ni - bus.
O - mnes ex e - o bi - bi - te.
Ut su - mant et dent ce - te - ris.
Pau - per ser - vus et hu - mi - lis.
Ad lu - cem quam in - ha - bi - tas. A - men.

[1. Let joys be joined with the sacred solemnities, and let prayers sound from our hearts. Let the old depart, let all things be new, hearts, voices, and works.

2. The night of last supper is recalled, in which Christ is believed to have given to his brethren lamb and unleavened bread, according to the rights granted to the forefathers.

3. The meal completed, after the symbolic lamb, the divine body was given to his disciples, entirely to all, entirely to each, by his own hands, this we proclaim.

4. He gave to the weak the meal of his body, and he gave to the sorrowful the drink of his blood, saying: Take the vessel which I give; all of you drink from it.

5. Thus he established this sacrifice, whose ceremony he wished to be entrusted only to those elders who were fit to consume it and give to others.

6. The bread of the angels becomes the bread of mankind, the celestial bread gives an end to symbols. O wondrous thing! the poor, the slave, the humble consumes the Lord.

7. We implore you, God three and one, just as you visit us, so do we honor you. Lead us on your pathway, by which we strive to the light which you inhabit. Amen.

[First Nocturn]

Antiphona

14. Numquid poterit/Ps.Conserva me

[Text Source: Ps 77 (Latin), 78 (Hebrew): 19–20]

Num - quid po - te-rit De- us pa-ra-re men - sam in de-ser - to?

Num - quid et pa-nem po - te - rit da - re aut pa-ra - re

men-sam po - pu - lo su - o? E u o u a e. Ps/Conserva me

[Is it likely that God can prepare a table in the desert? Can he give bread or prepare a table for his people?]

15. Parasti in conspectu/Ps Exaudiat te Dominus

[Text Source: Ps 22 (Latin), 23 (Hebrew): 5]

Pa-ra - sti in con-spe - ctu me - o men-sam ad - ver - sus e - os,

qui tri - bu-lant me; in-pin-gua-sti in o - le-o ca-put me - um,

et ca - lix me-us in - e-bri-ans quam pre-cla-rus est.

E u o u a e. Ps/Exaudiat te Dominus

[You have prepared a table for me in the face of those who torment me; you have annointed my head with oil and my cup brims over.]

16. De fructu operum/Ps Deus Deus meus respice
   [Text Source: Ps 103 (Latin), 104 (Hebrew): 13–15]

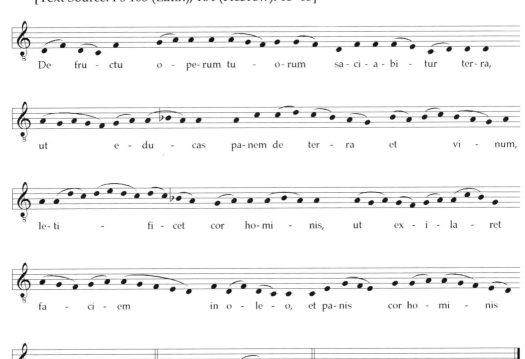

De fru - ctu   o - pe-rum tu - o-rum   sa - ci - a - bi - tur   ter- ra,

ut   e - du - cas   pa-nem de   ter - ra   et   vi - num,

le- ti -   fi - cet   cor   ho- mi - nis,   ut   ex - i - la - ret

fa - ci - em   in o - le - o,   et pa-nis   cor ho - mi - nis

con - fir- met.   E   u   o   u   a   e.   Ps/Deus   Deus   meus   respice

[The earth is satiated with the fruit of your works, you bring forth bread from the earth, and wine to gladden the heart of mankind, oil to make the face shine, and bread to strengthen the heart of mankind.]

17. Versiculus
   [Text Source: Ps 104a (Latin), 105 (Hebrew): 40]
   Petierunt et venit coturnix alleluia. R. Et pane celi saturavit eos alleluia.

   [They asked, and quail came, alleluia. R And he filled them with bread from heaven.]

18. Lectio Prima
[Peter Lombard, Sententiae, *Bk. IV, Dist. VIII, ch. 5 (52)]*

   Dominus ihesus ad invisibilia paterne maiestatis migraturus, celebrato cum discipulistypico pasca, quoddam memoriale eis commendare volens sub specie panis et vini, corpus et sanguinem suum eis tradidit, ut ostenderet legis veteris sacramenta, inter que precipuum erat agni pascalis, sacrificium in morte sua terminari, ac legis nove sacramenta substitui: in quibus excellit misterium eucharistie.

[Gratian, De consecratione, *Dist. II, can. 54]*

   Liquido eciam apparet, quando primo acceperunt discipuli corpus et sanguinem domini, non eos accepisse ieiunos. Numquam tamen propterea calumpniandum est universe ecclesie, quod a ieiunis semper accipitur. Hoc enim placuit spiritu sancto, ut in honore tanti sacramenti, prius in os christiani dominicum corpus intraret quam exteri cibi. Nam ideo per universum mos iste servatur. Neque enim, quia post cibos dominus dedit, propterea pransi aut cenati ad illud sacramentum accipiendum convenire debent, aut sicut faciebant quos apostolus arguit, et emendat mensis suis ista miscere. Namque salvator quo vehemencius commendaret misterii illius altitudinem, ultimum hoc voluit infigere cordibus et memorie discipulorum, a quibus ad passionem digressurus erat. Et ideo non precepit quo deinceps ordine summetur, ut per quos ecclesiam dispositurus erat, servarent hunc locum.

[Gratian, De consecratione, *Dist. II, can. 69 beginning]*

Huius sacramenti figura precessit, quando manna pluit deus patribus in deserto, qui cotidiano celi pascebantur alimento. Unde dictum est, panem angelorum manducavit homo. Sed tamen panem illum qui manducaverunt, omnes in deserto mortui sunt. Ista autem esca quam accipitis, iste panis vivus qui de celo descendit, vite eterne substanciam ministrat, et quicumque hunc panem manducaverit, non morietur in eternum quia corpus Christi est.

[The Lord Jesus, about to pass over into the invisible realms of paternal majesty, after having celebrated the symbolic paschal feast with his disciples, and wishing to entrust to them a certain remembrance, bequeathed to them his body and blood in the form of bread and wine, so that he might show that the sacraments of the old law, within which the sacrifice of the paschal lamb was principal, were terminated in his death, and that the sacraments of the new law took their place.

Clearly it is certainly apparent, when the disciples first received the body and blood of the Lord, that they did not receive it when fasting. Therefore it must never be falsely charged to the universal Church, that it is always received by those who are fasting. However it was pleasing to the Holy Spirit, that, in honor of such a great sacrament, the divine body enter the mouth of the Christian before other foods. For thus this custom is observed universally. But because the Lord gave it after dining, it does not follow that they ought to come to receive the sacrament after having eaten, or that they ought to combine it with their own meals as those were doing whom the apostle faulted and corrected. For the Savior, so that he might convey more strongly the height of this mystery, wished to implant it last on the hearts and memory of his disciples, from whom he was departing for his passion. And therefore he did not prescribe that they to whom he was about to entrust the church preserve the sequence by which it was taken.

A precursor of this sacrament occurred earlier, when God rained manna on the fathers in the desert, who daily ate the food of heaven. Wherefore it is said: Man ate the bread of the angels. But yet those who ate that bread all died in the desert. However, this bread which you take, this living bread which descended from heaven, provides the substance of eternal life. And whoever shall eat this bread, will not die forever, because it is the body of Christ.]

19. Responsory: Cenantibus discipulis/Hic est sanguis
[Text Source: Matt 26: 26–28]

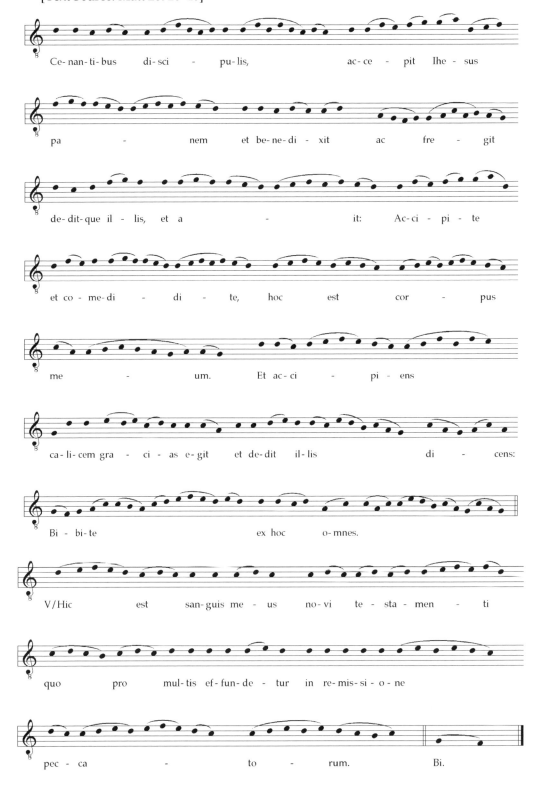

Ce- nan- ti- bus   di- sci - pu- lis,   ac- ce - pit   Ihe - sus

pa - nem   et be-ne-di - xit   ac   fre - git

de- dit- que il - lis,   et a - it: Ac- ci - pi - te

et co - me- di - di - te,   hoc   est   cor - pus

me - um.   Et ac- ci - pi - ens

ca- li- cem gra - ci - as e- git   et de- dit   il- lis   di - cens:

Bi - bi- te   ex hoc   o- mnes.

V/Hic   est   san- guis me - us   no- vi   te - sta - men - ti

quo   pro   mul- tis ef- fun- de - tur   in re- mis- si - o - ne

pec - ca - to - rum.   Bi.

[As the disciples were eating, Jesus took bread and blessed it and broke it and gave it to them, and he said: Take and eat, this is my body. And taking the cup he gave thanks and gave it to them, saying: Drink from this all of you. V. This is my blood of the new testament, which will be shed for many for the forgiveness of sin. R. Drink.]

20. Lectio ii

[Gratian, De consecratione, *Dist. II, can. 69 continued]*

Considera utrum prestancior sit panis angelorum, an caro christi, que utique est corpus vite. Manna illud de celo, hoc super celum: illud celi, hoc domini celorum. Illud corrupcioni obnoxium: si in diem alterum servaretur. hoc alienum ab omni corrupcione. Quicumque religiose gustaverit: corruptionem sentire non poterit. Illis aqua de petra fluxit: tibi sanguis ex christo. Illos ad horam saciavit aqua: te sanguis diluit in eternum. Iudeus bibit et sitit: tu cum biberis sitire non poteris. Et illud in umbra: hoc in veritate. Si illud quod miraris umbra est: quantum istud est cuius umbram miraris? Audi quia umbra est, que apud patres facta est. Bibebant autem de spirituali, consequenti eos petra. Petra autem erat christus. Sed non in pluribus eorum complacitum est deo. Nam prostrati sunt in deserto. Hec autem facta sunt in figura nostri. Cognovisti pociora. Pocior enim est lux quam umbra, veritas, quam figura, corpus auctoris, quam manna de celo, forte dicis aliud video. Quantis igitur utimur exemplis, ut probemus. Hoc non esse, quod natura formavit, sed quod benediccio consecravit, maioremque vim esse benediccionis quam nature, quia benediccione etiam natura ipsa mutatur. Unde virgam tenebat moises, proiecit eciam et facta est serpens. Rursus apprehendit caudam serpentis, et in virge naturam revertitur. Videns ergo prophetica gratia bis mutata naturam esse, et serpentis et virge. Currebant egypti flumina puro meatu aquarum, subito de foncium venis, sanguis cepit erumpere, non erat potus in fluviis. Rursus ad prophete preces, cruor fluminum cessavit, aquarum natura remeavit, circumclusus undique erat populus ebreorum: Hinc egyptiis vallatus, inde mari conclusus. Virgam levavit moyses, separavit se aqua, et in murorum speciem se congellavit, atque inter undas, via pedestris apparuit. Iordanis retrosum conversus contra naturam in sui fontis revertitur exordium. Nonne claret naturam vel maritimorum fluctuum, vel cursus fluvialis esse mutatam? Siciebat populus petram, tecigit moyses petram, et aqua de petra fluxit. Numquid non preter naturam operata est gratia, ut aquam moveret petra, quam non habebat natura?

[Consider which now is more precious, the bread of angels, or Christ's flesh, which is wholly the body of life. That manna is from heaven, this above heaven. That is of heaven, this, of the Lord of heavens. That, subject to corruption, if kept for another day, this free from all corruption. Whoever religiously eats, will not experience corruption. To them water flowed from the rock, to you the blood [flows] from Christ. The water satisfied them for a time, the blood cleanses you for eternity. The Jews drank and thirsted, you, when you drink, cannot thirst. That [happened] in a shadow, this in truth. If that at which you marvel is a shadow, how much more is this whose shadow you admire? Hear why this is a shadow, which was done in the time of the forefathers. They drank indeed from the spiritual rock which followed them. The rock, however, was Christ. But God was not well pleased with many of them. Thus they were cast down in the desert. This was done as a symbol to us. You know which is better. Light is better that shadow, truth better than a symbol, the body of the creator better than manna from heaven. Perhaps you say: I see something different. How many examples, therefore, do we use, to show that this is not what nature has formed, but what blessing has consecrated, and that there is greater power in blessing than in nature, because by blessing even nature itself can be changed. Hence, Moses held a rod, threw it, and it became a serpent. Again, he grasped the serpent's tail, and it reverted into its nature as a rod. You see therefore, by prophetic will, its nature is twice changed, both of a serpent and a rod. The rivers of Egypt flowed with a pure course of waters, suddenly from the source of the waters blood began to burst forth, there was no drinkable water in the rivers. Conversely, at the prayers of the prophet, the blood of the rivers ceased, the nature of waters returned. The Hebrew nation was surrounded on all sides, on one side blocked by the Egyptians, on the other side cut off by the sea. Moses raised a rod, the water parted and solidified itself into a kind of wall, and between the waves a foot path appeared. The Jordan reversed course, and it returned, against nature, to the beginning of its source. Is it not clear that the nature of the ocean's waves or of the river's course was changed? The people of the forefathers thirsted, Moses touched the rock, and water flowed from the rock. Has not grace acted contrary to nature, so that a rock might spew forth water, which it did not have by nature?]

21. Responsory: Accepto pane/Similiter et calicem
   [Text Source: Luke 22: 19–20]

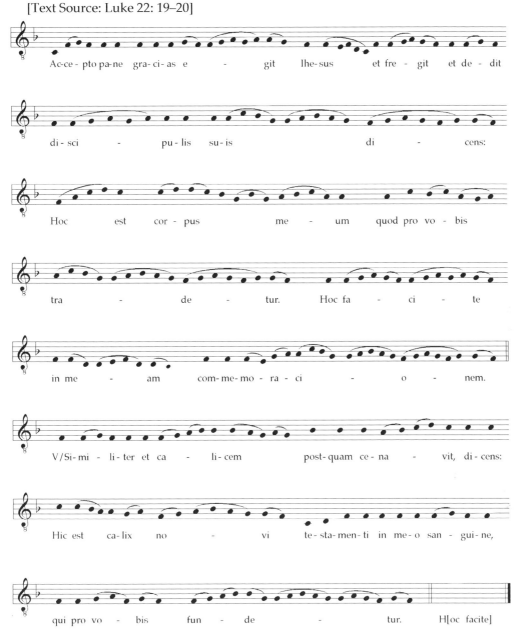

[Having taken the bread Jesus gave thanks and broke it and gave it to his disciples, saying: This is my body which will be given up for you. Do this in my memory. V. Similarly, he took a cup, after he had eaten, saying: This is the chalice of the new testament in my blood, which will be shed for you. R. Do this.]

22. Lectio iii

[Gratian, De consecratione, *Dist. II, can. 69 concluded]*

Marath fluvius amarissimus erat, ut siciens populus bibere non posset. Moises misit lignum in aquam et amaritudinem suam aquarum natura deposuit, quam infusa subito gratia temperavit. Sub elyseo propheta uni ex filiis prophetarum excussum est ferrum de securi et statim inmersum est. Rogavit heliseum qui amiserat ferrum. Misit eciam heliseus lignum in aquam, et ferrum natavit. Utique eciam hoc preter naturam factum cognovimus. Gravior est enim ferri species, quam aquarum liquor. Advertimus igitur maiorem esse gratiam quam naturam, et adhuc tamen prophetice benediccionis numeramus gratiam. Quod si tantum valuit humana benediccio, ut naturam converteret, quid dicimus de ipsa consecracione divina, ubi ipsa verba domini salvatoris operantur? Nam sacramentum istud quod accipis: sermone conficitur, quod si tantum valuit sermo helye, ut ignem de celo deponeret, non valebit Christi sermo, ut species mutet elementorum? De tocius mundi operibus legisti, quia ipse dixit et facta sunt, ipse mandavit et creata sunt. Sermo igitur qui potuit ex nichilo facere quod non erat, non potuit in id mutare quod non erat? Non enim minus dare quam mutare novas naturas rebus. Sed quid? Cuius argumentis utimur, suis utamur exemplis, incarnationisque astruamus misterii veritatem. Numquid nature usus persensit, cum dominus ihesus christus ex maria nasceretur? Si ordinem querimus viro mixta femina generare consueverat. Liquet igitur quod preter nature ordinem virgo generavit. Et hoc quod conficimus corpus, ex virgine est. Quid hic queris nature ordinem in christi corpore, cum preter naturam sit ipse dominus ihesus partus ex virgine? Vera namque caro christi que crucifixa, que sepulta est. Vere ergo illius carnis sacramentum est. Ipse clamat dominus noster ihesus, hoc est corpus meum. Ante benediccionem verborum celestium, alia species nominatur, post consecrationem, corpus significatur. Ipse dicit sanguinem suum, ante consecrationem aliud dicitur. Post consecrationem sanguis Christi nuncupatur. Tu dicis amen: hoc est verum est. Quod sermo sonat, affectus senciat.

[The Marath River was very bitter, so that the thirsting people were not able to drink. Moses threw a branch into the water, and nature eliminated the bitterness of its waters, which grace, suddenly intermixed, tempered. During the time of Elias the prophet, the blade fell off the battle ax of one of the sons of the prophets and immediately sank. He who had let the iron slip sought out Elias. Elias put a stick into the water, and the blade floated. Certainly we know that this is an act beyond nature. The species of iron is heavier than the liquid of water. We perceive therefore that grace is greater than nature, but yet we still reckon grace to be of prophetic blessing. But if a human blessing has such great strength that it can change nature, What can we say of that divine consecration, in which the words themselves of the Savior act? For this sacrament you receive is accomplished by the words of Christ. If the word of Elias had such great strength that it could bring down fire from heaven, will not the word of Christ have the power to change the species of the elements? You have read about the creation of the entire world, that he spoke, and it was made, that he commanded, and it was created. Thus speech, which was able from nothing to create what did not exist, now was able to change existing things into that which they were not. For it is not less to give, than to change new natures in things. Why is this so? Let us use the example of the one whose argument we use, and let us add the truth of the mystery of his incarnation. Do you doubt that he perceived clearly the custom of nature, since the Lord Jesus was born of Mary. If we seek order, it had been the custom to procreate by man combined with woman. It is clear, therefore that, against the order of nature, a virgin gave birth. And that which we celebrate is the body of Christ from a virgin. What order of nature do you find here in the body of Christ, since against nature the Lord Jesus himself was born of a virgin? Certainly real was the flesh of Christ which was crucified, which was buried. Truly his flesh is the sacrament. Our Lord Jesus himself proclaims: This is my body. Before the blessing of the celestial words, it is called another species; after the consecration his body is signified. He himself calls it his blood. Before the consecration it is called another thing; after the consecration it is called the blood of Christ. You say: Amen, this is so, this is true. May that which speech proclaims perceive the condition.]

23. Responsory: Manducantibus discipulis/Et ait illis
[Text Source: Mark 14: 22–24]

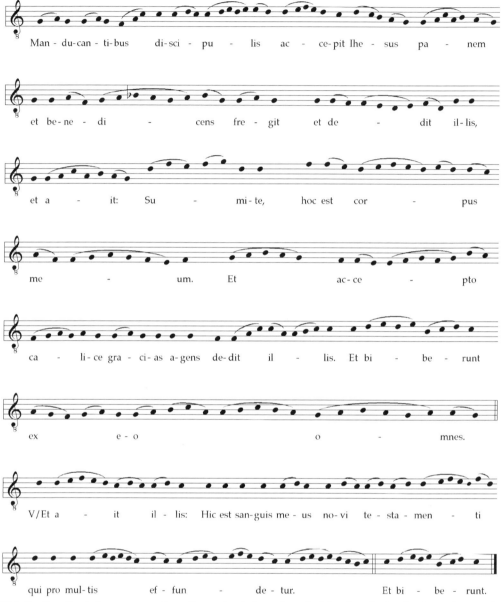

[While the disciples were eating, Jesus took bread and, blessing it, broke it and gave it to them, and he said: Take this, this is my body, and having taken a cup, giving thanks, he gave it to them. And they all drank from it. V. And he said to them: This is my blood of the new testament which will be poured out for many.]

In ii nocturno
Antiphona

24. Faciens mensam/Ps Dominus regit
    [Text Source: Ex 25: 23–24, 30]

Fa- ci- ens   men- sam de   li - gnis Se- thim   et in- au- ra - bis   e- am

au - ro pu - ris - si- mo, et po- nes su- per e   -   am   pa- nes pro- po- si- ci- o- nis

in   con- spe- ctu   me - o sem- per.   E u o u a e.   Ps/Dominus regit

[Making a table of acacia wood, plate it with purest gold, and you will place on it the
bread of the presence always before me.]

25. Sacerdotes sancti/Ps Benedicam
    [Text Source: Lev 21: 6]

Sa- cer   -   do - tes   san - cti e - runt de - o   su- o   et   non pol- lu - ent

no- men   e - ius in   -   cen- sum e- nim do- mi - ni   et pa- nes de - o of- fe- runt

et i - de   o   san - cti e- runt. E u o u   a e.   Ps/Benedicam

[The priests shall be consecrated to their God, and shall not profane his name; they
shall offer burnt offerings of the Lord and breads to God, and they shall be holy.]

26. Faciet Dominus/Ps Iudica me Deus

[Text Source: Is 25: 6]

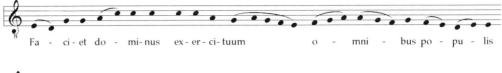

Fa - ci - et do - mi - nus ex - er - ci - tuum   o - mni - bus po - pu - lis

in mon - te   Sy - on   con - vi - vi - um pin - gui - um

con - vi - vi - um vin - de - mi - e   pin - gui - um   me - du - la - to - rum vin - de - mi - e

de - fe - ca - te. E u o u a e.   Ps/Iudica me Deus

[The Lord will prepare for all peoples on Mount Zyon a rich banquet, a banquet of rich vintage, of rich marrows, of strained wine.]

27. Versiculus

[Text Source: Ps 80 (Latin), 81 (Hebrew): 17]

Cibavit illos ex adipe frumenti alleluia. R. Et de petra melle saturavit eos alleluia.

[He fed them from the finest grain, alleluia. R. And he filled them with honey from a rock, alleluia.]

28. Lectio iiii

[Gratian, De consecratione, *Dist. II, can. 55]*

Panis est in altari usitatus ante verba sacramentorum. Ubi accessit consecratio, de pane fit caro christi. Quomodo autem potest: qui panis est esse corpus christi? Consecracio igitur quibus verbis, et cuius sermonibus est domini ihesu. Nam per reliqua que dicuntur, laus deo offertur, oracione petitur, pro populo, pro regibus, pro ceteris. Ubi autem sacramentum conficitur, iam non suis sermonibus sacerdos, sed utitur sermonibus christi. Ergo sermo christi hoc conficit sacramentum. Quis sermo christi? Hic nempe quo facta sunt omnia celum, terra, maria. Vides ergo quam operatorius sit sermo christi. Si ergo tanta vis est in sermone domini nostri ihesu christi, ut inciperet esse quod non erat, quanto magis operatorius est, ut sint que erant, et in aliud convertantur. Et sic quod erat panis ante consecrationem: iam corpus christi post consecrationem est, quia sermo christi creaturam mutat, et sic ex pane fit corpus christi. Et vinum cum aqua in calice mixtum, fit sanguis consecratione verbi celestis. Set forte dicis speciem sanguinis non video, sed habet similitudinem. Sicut enim mortis similitudinem assumpsisti, ita etiam christi similitudinem sanguinis bibis, ut nullus horror cruoris sit, et precium tamen operetur redemptionis. Didicisti quia corpus accipis christi, vis scire quia verbis celestibus consecratur: accipe que sunt verba. Dicit sacerdos, fac nobis inquit hanc oblacionem ascriptam, racionabilem, et cetera. Inde omnia illa evangeliste sunt usque ad accipite, sive corpus, sive sanguinem, inde verba christi sunt. Accipite et bibite ex hoc omnes, hic est enim sanguis meus, vide. Qui pridie quam pateretur, accepit inquit in sanctis manibus panem. Antequam consecretur panis est. Ubi autem verba christi accesserint, corpus christi est. Deinde audi dicentem. Accipite, et edite ex hoc omnes, hoc est enim corpus meum. Et ante verba Christi. Calix est vino et aqua plenus. Ubi autem verba Christi operata fuerint, ibi sanguis efficitur, qui plebem redemit. Ergo vide quam potens est sermo christi, universa convertere. Deinde ipse Christus testificatur quod corpus suum et sanguinem suum accipiamus, de cuius fide et testificatione dubitare non debemus. Tu autem.

[There is the bread used on the altar before the words of the sacraments. When the consecration comes, from bread it becomes the body of Christ. How can what is bread be the body of Christ? Consecration by whose words, by whose speech? The Lord Jesus.[83] Because through all the rest that is said, praise is offered to God, through prayer he is petitioned for the people, for kings, and for other things. However when the sacrament is made ready, now the priest uses not his own words, but the words of Christ. Therefore Christ's word makes this a sacrament. What word of Christ? That, of course, by which all things were created: heaven, earth, seas. You see therefore how efficacious is the word of Christ. If therefore so much power is in the word of our Lord Jesus, so that what was not might begin to be, how much more efficacious is it, so that they may be which were, and that they may be converted into something else? And thus what was bread before the consecration now is the body of Christ after the consecration, because the word of Christ changes the object, and thus from bread it becomes the body of Christ. And the wine mixed with water in the chalice, becomes blood by the consecration of the heavenly word. But perhaps you say: I do not see the species of blood, but it is similar. Indeed, just as you took on the likeness of death, so also you drink the likeness of the blood of Christ, so that there be no horror of blood, and so that it still serve as the price of redemption. You have learned that you receive the body of Christ. Do you wish to know how, by the celestial words, it is consecrated? Learn what the words are. The priest says: Make this offering for us approved, worthy, and so forth. After that, there are all the things of the evangelist up to: Take either the body or the blood. Then there are the words of Christ: Take and drink from this all of you. This is my blood. Look at them one at a time. Who the day before he suffered took, he said, bread into his holy hands. Before it is consecrated, it is bread. When however the words of Christ draw near, it is the body of Christ. Then hear him saying: Take and eat of this all of you: This is my body. And before the words of Christ the chalice is filled with wine and water. When however the words of Christ were spoken, then it became blood, which redeems the people. Therefore see how powerful is the word of Christ to change all things. Then Jesus himself bears witness, that we receive his body and his blood, whose faith and testimony we ought not doubt.]

---

[83] Philip Peek suggested the following translation: "How can what is bread be the body of Christ? Consecration. By whose words, by whose speech? The Lord Jesus."

29. Responsory: Dominus Ihesus/Similiter et calicem
[Text Source: 1 Cor 11: 23–25]

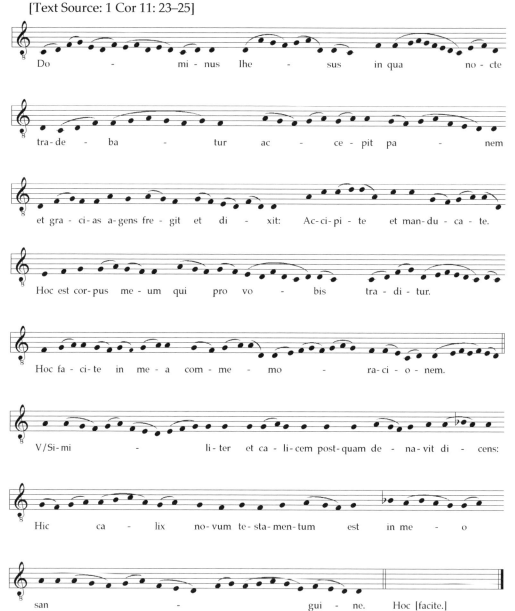

[The Lord Jesus, on the night he was betrayed, took bread and, giving thanks, broke it and said: Take and eat. This is my body which will be given up for you. Do this in my memory. V. Similarly he took the cup after he had eaten, saying: This chalice is a new testament in my blood. R. Do this.]

30. Lectio v

[Gratian, De consecratione *Dist. II, can. 57]*[84]

Christus panis est de quo qui manducat, vivit in eternum. De quo ipsemet dixit, et panis quem ego dabo caro mea est pro mundi vita. Determinat quomodo sit panis, non solum secundum verbum quo vivunt omnia, sed secundum carnem assumptam pro mundi vita. Humana enim caro que erat peccato mortua, carni munde unita incorporata, unum cum illa effecta, vivit de spiritu eius, sicut vivit corpus de suo spiritu.

[Gratian, De consecratione *Dist. II, can. 60]*

Corpus et sanguinem christi dicimus illud, quod ex fructibus terre acceptum: et prece mistica consecratum recte sumimus ad salutem spiritualem, in memoriam dominice passionis. Quod cum per manus hominis ad illam visibilem speciem per-ducatur, non sanctificatur, ut sit tam magnum sacramentum, nisi operante invisibi-liter spiritu sancto cum hec omnia que per corporales motus in illo opere fiunt, deus operetur.

[Gratian, De consecratione *Dist. II, can. 63]*

Hoc est sacramentum pietatis, et signum unitatis, et vinculum caritatis. Qui vult vi-vere, accedat et credat, incorporet hunc cibum et potum, societatem vult intelligi corporis, et membrorum suorum quod est ecclesie in predestinatis.

[Gratian, De consecratione *Dist. II, can. 48]*

Hoc est quod dicimus, quod omnibus modis approbare concedimus sacrificium ec-clesie duobus confici, duobus constare, visibili elementorum specie, et invisibili domini nostri ihesu christi carne et sanguine, et sacramento, et re sacramenti, id est corpore christi, sicut christi persona constat et conficitur ex deo et homine, cum ipse christus, verus sit deus et verus homo. Quia omnis res illarum rerum naturam et ve-ritatem in se continet ex quibus conficitur. Conficitur autem sacrificium ecclesie duobus, sacramento, et re sacramenti: id est corpore christi. Est igitur sacramentum et res sacramenti, id est corpus christi. Caro eius est, quam forma panis opertam in sacramento accipimus, et sanguis eius quem sub vini specie ac sapore potamus. Ca-ro videlicet est carnis et sanguis est sacramentum sanguinis. Carne et sanguine utroque invisibili, intelligibili, spirituali, significatur corpus domini nostri ihesu christi, et palpabile plenum gracia omnium virtutum et divina maiestate. Sicut ergo celestis panis qui vere christi caro est, suo modo vocatur corpus christi cum re vera sit sacramentum corporis christi, illud videlicet quod visibile quod palpabile, mor-tale in cruce est positum, vocaturque ipsa carnis immolatio, que sacerdotis manibus, fit christi passio, mors crucifixio, non rei veritate, sed significanti misterio sic sa-cramentum fidei, quo baptismus, intelligitur fides est.

[Christ is the bread, of which whoever eats, lives forever. About this he himself said: "And the bread which I will give him is my flesh, for the life of the world." He prescribes in what way it is bread for the life of the world, not only in accordance

---

[84] From Augustinus, *In Iohannis* tr. XXVI, n. 13.

with the word, by which all things live, but in accordance with the assumed flesh. His human flesh, which was dead to sin, united to the flesh of the world, incorporated, made one with it, lives by his spirit, just as the body lives by its spirit. Whoever is not truly of the body of Christ, does not live by his spirit.

We call the body and blood of Christ that which, taken from the fruits of the earth, and blessed by sacred prayer, we properly consume for spiritual salvation, in memory of the passion of the Lord. Since it is brought into its visible form by the hand of man, it is not sanctified to be so a great sacrament, except by the Holy Spirit working invisibly, since God makes all these things which come about from the body's movements in that work.

This is the sacrament of piety, and a sign of unity, and a bond of love. Whoever wishes to live, let him approach and believe, let him consume this food and drink. He wishes the society of the body and its members to be understood, because it is among the things predestined in/for the church.

This is what we say, what we work to prove in every way, that the sacrifice of the church is composed of two things, consists of two things, of the visible species of the elements, and of the invisible body and blood of our Lord Jesus Christ, both of the sacrament and of the object of the sacrament, that is, of the body of Christ, just as the person of Christ comprises and is composed of God and man, since Christ himself is truly God and truly man, because each thing contains in itself the nature and truth of those things of which it is composed. Thus the sacrifice of the church is composed of two things, the sacrament and the object of the sacrament, that is the body of Christ. There is therefore the sacrament and the object of the sacrament, that is the body of Christ. His flesh is what, hidden in the form of bread, we receive in the sacrament, and his blood what we drink under the appearance and taste of wine. His flesh is the sacrament of his flesh, and his blood the sacrament of his blood. By his flesh and blood both invisible, understandable, spiritual, is symbolized the visible body of our Lord Jesus Christ, and it is touchable, full of the grace of all virtues and of divine majesty.

Therefore, just as the celestial bread, which is truly the flesh of Christ, is called in its own way the body of Christ, although actually it is the sacrament of the body of Christ, that which visibly, which palpably, subject to death, was placed on the cross, and just as it is called that sacrifice of the flesh, which is the suffering, death, and crucifixion of Christ at the priest's hands, not because of the truth of the matter, but because of a symbolic mystery, so the sacrament of faith, which is called baptism, is faith.]

31. Responsory: Quicumque manducaverit/Qui enim manducat
[Text Source: 1 Cor 11: 27–29]

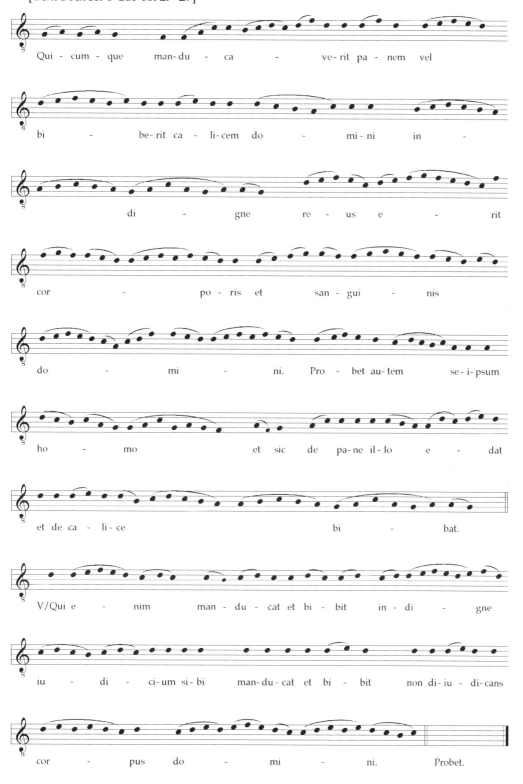

Qui - cum - que   man - du - ca   -   ve - rit pa - nem vel

bi   -   be - rit ca - li - cem do   -   mi - ni   in   -

di   -   gne   re - us   e   -   rit

cor   -   po - ris et   san - gui   -   nis

do   -   mi   -   ni.   Pro - bet au - tem   se - i - psum

ho   -   mo   et sic de pa - ne il - lo   e   -   dat

et de ca - li - ce   bi   -   bat.

V/Qui e   -   nim   man - du - cat et bi - bit   in - di   -   gne

iu   -   di   -   ci - um si - bi   man - du - cat et bi - bit   non di - iu - di - cans

cor   -   pus   do   -   mi   -   ni.   Probet.

[Anyone who eats the bread or drinks the cup unworthily will be guilty of profaning the body and blood of the Lord. Let each man examine himself and so eat the bread and drink the cup. V. Who eats and drinks unworthily, eats and drinks judgment on himself, not recognizing the body of the Lord.]

32. Lectio vi

[Gratian, De consecratione Dist. II, can. 71]

Iteratur cotidie hec oblatio, licet christus semel passus carne, per unam eandemque mortis passionem semel salvavit mundum, ex qua morte idem resurgens ad vitam mors ei ultra non dominabitur. Quod profecto sapientia dei patris necessarium pro multis causis providit. Primo quidem, quia cotidie peccamus, saltem in peccatis, sine quibus mortalis infirmitas vivere non potest, quia licet omnia peccata condonata sint in baptismo, infirmitas tamen peccati adhuc manet in carne. Unde psalmista. Benedic anima dominum, qui propiciatur omnibus iniquitatibus tuis qui sanat omnes infirmitates tuas. Et ideo quia cotidie labimur, cotidie Christus pro nobis mistice immolatur, et passio christi in misterio traditur, ut qui semel moriendo mortem vicerat, cotidie recidiva delictorum per hec corporis sacramenta et sanguinis, peccata relaxet. Unde oramus, dimitte nobis debita nostra. Quia si dixerimus quia peccatum non habemus: ipsi nos seducimus, et veritas in nobis non est. Iteratur eciam hoc misterium et ob commemorationem passionis christi, sicut ipse ait. Hoc quocienscumque agitis in meam commemoracionem facite. Quocienscumque hunc panem sumitis, et bibitis hunc calicem: mortem domini anunciabitis donec veniat. Non itaque sic accipiendum est: donec christi mors veniat, quia iam ultra non morietur sed donec ipse dominus ad iudicium veniat. Interdum autem semper mors est christi per seculi vitam posteris nuncianda, ut discant qua caritate dilexit suos, qui pro eis mori dignatus est. Cui omnes vicem debemus rependere caritatis, quia ad hoc nos prior dilexit, cum essemus gehenne filii. Ut diligeremus eum a morte iam liberati.

[Gratian, De consecratione Dist. II, can. 50]

Quia morte domini liberati sumus, huius rei memores in edendo carnem, et potando sanguinem eius, que pro nobis oblata sunt significamus.

[This offering is repeated daily, although Christ having died once in the flesh through one and the same suffering of death, saved the world a single time, from which death rising again to life, death will have no more dominion over him. Indeed the wisdom of God foresaw this necessity for many reasons. First of all because we sin daily, at least in sins without which mortal infirmity it is not possible to live,[85] because although all sins are pardoned in baptism, nevertheless the infirmity of sin still remains in the flesh. Hence the psalmist: Bless the Lord, my soul, who forgives all your sins, who heals all your infirmities. And because daily we fall, daily Christ is mystically sacrificed for us, and the passion of Christ is handed down in mystery, so that he who, by dying a single time, conquered death, might forgive daily the faults of recurring transgressions through the sacraments of the body and blood. Hence we pray: Forgive us our sins. Because if we would say that we do not have sin, we delude outselves, and truth is not within us. This mystery is repeated, indeed for the purpose of a commemoration of the passion of Christ, just as he himself said: So often as you do this, do it in memory of me. Therefore, as often as you eat this bread, and drink this cup, you proclaim the death of the Lord until he comes. This is not to be understood as: "until the death of Christ comes," because he will not die any more, but "until the Lord himself comes for judgment." In the meanwhile the death of Christ for the life of time must always be proclaimed to posterity, so that they may learn with what love he loved his own, who deigned to die for them, to whom we all should return an equivalence of love, because he loved us first, although we were the sons of Gehenna, so that we, now liberated from death, might love him.

Because by the death of the Lord we have been freed, we signify the memory of this event in eating his flesh and drinking his blood, which were offered up for us.]

---

[85] That is, each day we commit at least venial sins.

33. Responsory: Calix benedictionis/Quoniam unus panis/Gloria patri
[Text Source: 1 Cor 10: 16–17]

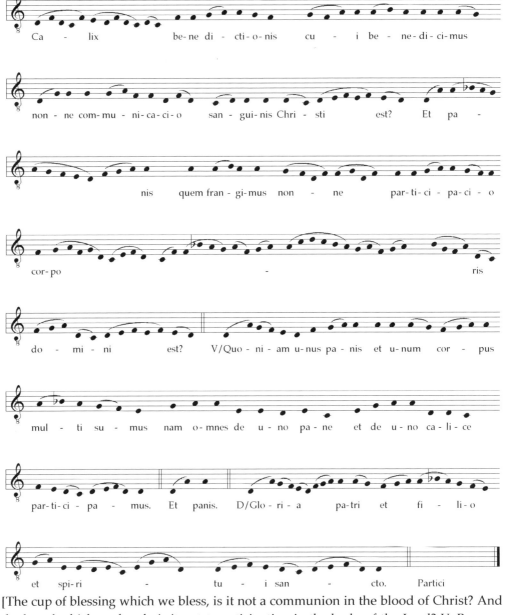

Ca - lix be- ne di - cti- o- nis cu - i be - ne- di- ci- mus

non - ne com- mu - ni- ca- ci- o san - gui- nis Chri - sti est? Et pa -

nis quem fran - gi- mus non - ne par- ti- ci - pa- ci - o

cor- po - ris

do - mi - ni est? V/Quo - ni - am u- nus pa - nis et u- num cor - pus

mul - ti su - mus nam o- mnes de u - no pa - ne et de u - no ca - li - ce

par- ti- ci - pa - mus. Et panis. D/Glo - ri - a pa- tri et fi - li- o

et spi- ri - tu - i san - cto. Partici

[The cup of blessing which we bless, is it not a communion in the blood of Christ? And the bread which we break, is it not a participation in the body of the Lord? V. Because there is one bread, we who are many are one body, for we all participate in one bread and one cup. R. And the bread.]

In tercio nocturno
Antiphona
34. Tulit Manue/Ps Te decet
     [Text Source: Iud 13: 19–20]

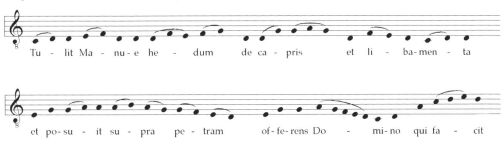

Tu – lit Ma – nu-e he – dum   de ca – pris   et li – ba-men – ta

et po-su – it su – pra   pe – tram   of-fe-rens Do – mi-no qui fa – cit

mi-ra – bi – li-a. Cum a-scen – de-ret   flam – ma   al-ta-ris in ce-lum

an – ge-lus   do-mi-ni   pa-ri-ter in   flam – ma   a – scen – dit.

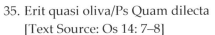

E u o u a   e.   Ps/Te   decet

[Manoah took the kid and the libation and placed it on the rock, offering it to the Lord who works miracles. When the flame ascended into heaven from the altar, the angel of the Lord ascended in the flame as well.]

35. Erit quasi oliva/Ps Quam dilecta
     [Text Source: Os 14: 7–8]

E – rit   qua – si o-li – va   glo – ri – a   e – ius et o – dor   e – ius

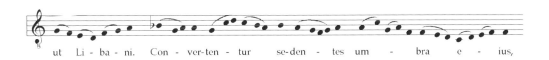

ut Li – ba – ni. Con – ver-ten – tur   se-den – tes um – bra   e – ius,

vi – vent   tri – ti-co. E u o u a   e.   Ps/Quam dilecta

[His glory will be like the olive, and his odor like Lebanon. They will return to sit in his shade, they will live on wheat.]

36. Quid enim bonum/Ps Inclina
    [Text Source: Zach 9: 17]

Quid   e - nim   bo - num   e - ius   est   et   quid   pul- chrum e - ius

ni- si   fru - men - tum   e - le - cto   -   rum   et   vi - num   ger- mi - nans

vir - gi - nes.   [E   u   o   u   a   e.]   Ps/Inclina   D[omine]

[How good it is and how beautiful; grain will make the young men thrive, and new wine the young women.]

37. Versiculus
    [Text Source: Is 30: 23]
    Panis frugum terre alleluia. R. Erit uberrimus et pinguis alleluia.

    [The bread, the fruit of the earth, alleluia. R. Will be most abundant and rich, alleluia.]

38. [Gospel] secundum Iohanne [Jo 6: 53].
    In illo tempore. Dixit ihesus discipulis suis, et turbis iudeorum. Amen amen dico vobis, nisi manducaveritis carnem filii, hominis et biberitis eius sanguinem, non habebitis vitam in vobis. Et reliqua.

    [At that time. Jesus said to his disciples, and to the crowd of the Jews: Amen, amen, I say to you, unless you shall eat the flesh of the son of man and drink his blood, you will not have life in you.]

[Lectio vii]
Omelia beati Augustini episcopi
    [Alcuin, *Commentaria in S. Joannis evangelium*, Lib. 3: Ch. XV, Vers. 54–57][86]

    [Vers. 54] Quomodo quidem detur et quisnam modus sit manducandi istum panem: ignoratis. Verumptamen nisi manducaveritis carnem filii hominis et bibitis eius sanguinem, non habebitis vitam in vobis. Hec utique non cadaveribus, sed viventibus loquebatur. Unde ne vitam istam intelligentes, et de hac re litigarent, secutus adiunxit. [Vers. 55] Qui manducat meam carnem, et bibit meum sanguinem, habet vitam eternam. Hanc ergo non habet qui istum panem non manducat, nec istum

---

[86] PL 100, cols. 835–36.

sanguinem bibit. Nam temporalem vitam sine illo utcumque homines in hoc seculo qui non sunt in corpore eius per fidem habere possunt, eternam autem numquam, que sanctis promittitur. Ne autem putarent sic in isto cibo et potu eius qui carnaliter sumunt, et spiritualiter non intelligunt in fide promitti in vitam eternam ut qui eam sumerent: iam nec corpore morerentur, huic cogitacioni est dignatus occurrere. Nam cum dixisset qui manducat meam carnem et bibit meum sanguinem: habet vitam eternam. Continuo subiecit et dixit. Et ego resuscitabo eum in novissimo die, ut habeat interim vitam[87] secundum spiritum eternam in requie, que sanctorum spiritus suscipit. Quod autem ad corpus attinet, nec eos vita eterna fraudabitur in resurrectione mortuorum in novissimo die. Caro inquit mea vere est cibus, et sanguis meus vere est potus.

[Vers. 56] Cum enim cibo et potu id appetant homines, ut non esuriant necque sitiant, hoc vere non prestat nisi iste cibus et potus qui eos a quibus sumitur immortales et incorruptibiles facit, id est societas ipsorum sanctorum, ubi pax erit et unitas plena atque perfecta. Propterea quippe sicut eciam ante nos hoc intellexerunt homines dei dominus noster ihesus christus corpus et sanguinem suum in eis rebus commendavit, que ad unum aliquid rediguntur. Ex multis namque granis panis conficitur, et ex multis racemis confluit. Denique iam exponit, quomodo id fiat quod loquitur, et quid sit manducare corpus eius et sanguinem bibere.

[Vers. 57] Et qui manducat carnem meam et bibit meum sanguinem, in me manet, et ego in eo dicit dominus. Hoc est ergo manducare illam escam, et illum bibere potum in christo manere, et illum manentem in se habere, ac per hoc qui non manet in christo, et in quo non manet christus, proculdubio non manducat spiritualiter eius carnem, licet carnaliter et visibiliter, premat dentibus sacramenta corporis et sanguinis christi, sed magis tante rei sacramentum, ad iudicium sibi manducat et bibit, qui immundus presumpsit ad christi accedere sacramenta, que alius non digne sumit, nisi qui mundus est. De quibus dicitur. Beati mundo corde quoniam ipsi deum videbunt.

---

[87] This word is added in the margin.

[You do not know how, in fact, it is given and what the method is for eating this bread. However, unless you shall eat the flesh of the son of man and drink his blood, you will not have life in you. He said this, of course, not to the dead but to the living. Whereby, so that those understanding this life would not argue about this matter, he added next: He who eats my flesh and drinks my blood, has eternal life. Therefore he does not have it, who does not eat this bread or drink this blood. For without it, men in this age who are not in his body through faith are able to have temporal life, but never eternal life, which is promised to the faithful. So that they, who partake in this food and drink of his carnally, and spiritually do not understand that in faith they are sent into eternal life, do not think that those who take it now also do not die in the flesh, he deemed it worthy to oppose this thought. For when he said: "Whoever eats my flesh and drinks my blood has eternal life," immediately he added and said: "And I will raise him up on the last day," so that meanwhile he may have eternal life according to the spirit in the repose which overtakes the spirits of the faithful. What pertains to the body, however, and not to them will be deprived of eternal life in the resurrection of the dead on the last day. "My flesh" he said "truly is food, and my blood truly is drink."

Although men desire from food and drink, that they neither hunger nor thirst, this is not assured, unless it is that food and drink which makes those, by whom it is consumed, immortal and incorruptible, that is, a community of the saints themselves, where there will be peace and full and perfect unity. Therefore, indeed, as men of God understood before us, our Lord Jesus Christ put his body and blood into these things things, which are made into some one thing. Now, one bread is made from many grains, and wine flows together from many clusters of grapes. Finally he now explains how what he has spoken happens, and what it is to eat his body and drink his blood.

"He who eats my body and drinks my blood abides in me and I in him," says the Lord. To eat that food and to drink that drink is, therefore, to abide in Christ, and to have him abiding in oneself. And thus the person who does not abide in Christ, and in whom Christ does not abide, without doubt does not eat spiritually his flesh, although physically and visibly he chews with his teeth the sacraments of the body and blood of Christ, but rather he eats and drinks the sacrament of such great importance to his own condemnation, who, impure, presumes to approach the sacraments of Christ, which no one rightly takes except the one who is pure. About whom it is said: Blessed are the pure of heart, because they shall see God.]

39. Responsory: Ego sum/Ego sum/Gloria patri
[Text Source: Jo 6: 48–51]

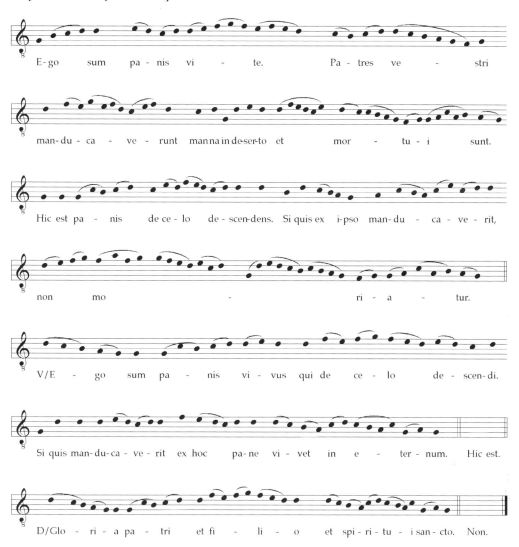

E-go   sum   pa - nis   vi - te.   Pa - tres ve - stri

man-du-ca - ve - runt man na in de-ser-to et   mor - tu - i   sunt.

Hic est pa - nis   de ce - lo   de - scen-dens. Si quis ex i-pso man-du - ca - ve - rit,

non   mo -   ri - a - tur.

V/E - go   sum pa - nis   vi - vus qui de   ce - lo   de - scen- di.

Si quis man-du-ca - ve - rit ex hoc   pa - ne vi - vet   in e - ter - num.   Hic est.

D/Glo - ri - a pa - tri   et fi - li - o   et spi - ri - tu - i san - cto.   Non.

[I am the bread of life. Your fathers ate manna in the desert and they died. This is the bread which descends from heaven. If anyone eats of it, he will not die. V. I am the living bread which descended from heaven. If anyone shall eat from this bread, he will live forever.]

40. [Lectio viii]

[Alcuin, Commentaria in S. Joannis evangelium, *Lib. 3: Ch. XV, Vers. 58–61]*[88]

[Vers. 58] Sicut me misit inquit vivens pater, et ego vivo propter patrem. Et qui manducat me, et ipse vivet propter me. Non enim filius participatione patris fit melior, qui est natus equalis. Sicut participatione filii per unitatem corporis et sanguinis, quam illa manducatio potacioque significat, efficit nos meliores. Vivimus ergo nos propter ipsum manducantes eum, id est ipsum accipientes vitam eternum quam non habemus ex nobis. Vivit autem ipse propter patrem missus ab eo, quia semetipsum exinanivit, factus obediens usque ad signum crucis. Sicut misit me vivens pater, et ego vivo propter patrem. Et qui manducat me, et ipse vivet propter me. Ac si diceret. Et ego vivo propter patrem, id est ut ad illum tamquam ad maiorem referam vitam meam. Exinanicio mea fecit in qua me misit. Ut autem quisque vivat propter me, participatio facit qui manducat me. Ego itaque humiliatatus vivo propter patrem, ille rectus, vivit propter me. Non de ea natura dixit, quia semper est equalis patri, sed ea in qua minor est patre factus. De qua eciam superius dixit. Sicut pater habet vitam in semetipso, sic dedit filio vitam habere in semetipso.

[Vers. 59] Hic est panis qui de celo descendit, ut illum manducando vivamus, quia eternam vitam ex illo[89] habere possumus. Non sicut manducaverunt inquit patres vestri manna et mortui sunt? Qui manducat hunc panem, vivet in eternum. Quod ergo illi mortui sunt, ita vult intelligi, ut non vivant in eternum. Nam temporaliter profecto et hic morientur qui christum manducant, sed vivunt in eternum, quia christus est vite eterne signum. Qui manducat et bibit hoc est si manet et manetur, si habitat, et inhabitatur, si heret et non deseritur. Hoc ergo nos docuit ut ammonuit misticis verbis ut simus in eius corpore, sub ipso capite, in membris eius edentes carnem eius, non relinquentes unitatem eius, sed quia aderant plures non intelligendo scandalizati sunt. Non enim cogitabant hec audiendo nisi carnem quod ipsi erant. Apostolus autem dicit et verum dicit. Sapere secundum carnem mors est. Carnem suam dicit nobis dominus manducare et sapere. Sapere secundum carnem mors est, cum de carne sua dicat, quia cibus est vita eterna. Ergo nec carnem debemus sapere secundum carnem, sicut in hiis verbis.

[Vers. 61] Multique audientes non ex inimicis sed ex discipulis eius dixerunt. Durus est hic sermo. Quis potest eum audire? Si discipuli durum habuerunt istum sermonem, quid inimici? Et tamen sic oportebat ut diceretur, quod non ab hominibus intelligeretur. Secretum intentos debet facere non aversos.

---

[88] PL 100, cols. 836–37.

[89] *Nihilo* scratched out in MS and replaced with *illo.*

[As the living father, he said, sent me, I live because of the father. And he who eats me, will live because of me. Certainly the son, who was born equal, is not made better through the participation of the father, as he makes us better through the participation of the son through the unity of the body and blood which that food and drink signifies. We live on behalf of him, by eating him, that is, receiving him as eternal life, which we do not have by ourselves. He himself lives on behalf of the father, sent by him, because he emptied himself, made obedient up to the sign of the cross. As the living father sent me, I live on behalf of the father. And he who eats me, he himself will live on behalf of me. This is as if to say: I live on behalf of the father, that is, I direct my life to him as to one greater, he brought about my emptying, in which form he sent me. Participation brings about for the one who eats me, that each one lives on behalf of me. Thus, I, humbled, live on behalf of the father, this man, uplifted, lives on behalf of me. He said this not about his nature, in which he is always equal to the father, but about that in which he was made lesser in relation to the father, about which earlier he said: Just as the father has life in and of himself, he gave his son life to have in and of himself, that is, he begot a son having life in and of himself.

This is the bread which descended from heaven, that by eating it we may live, because we can have eternal life from it. Not like the manna, he said, your fathers ate, and died. Whoever eats this bread, will live forever. Because they died, it is to be understood that they do not live in eternity. For certainly here on earth they will die who eat Christ, but they live in eternity, because Christ is the sign of eternal life. The one who eats and drinks, it is as if he abides and is abided, dwells and is dwelt in, holds fast and is not abandoned. Therefore he taught us this when he admonished us with mystical words, that we are in his body, under his head, in his limbs by eating his flesh, not abandoning his unity, but because there were several participating who did not understand, they were scandalized. They did not imagine anything except the flesh that they were. The Apostle himself said, and said truly: To be wise in the flesh is death. The Lord tells us to eat his flesh and be wise. To be wise in the flesh is death, although he may speak of his own flesh, because his food is eternal life. Therefore we must not be wise in the flesh according to flesh, just as in these words.

And many hearing this who were not his enemies but his disciples, said: This is a hard saying. Who can listen to it? If his disciples found this saying hard, what of his enemies? And in spite of this it was thus necessary for him to say it, although it might not be understood by men. The mystery ought to create proponents, not opponents.]

41. Responsory: Amen, Amen/Caro enim/Gloria patri
[Text Source: Jo 6: 53–56]

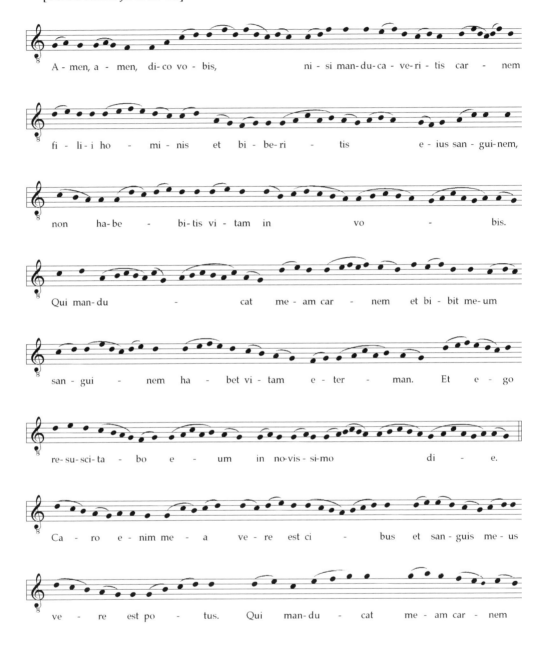

A - men, a - men, di - co vo - bis, ni - si man-du-ca - ve-ri - tis car - nem

fi - li - i ho - mi - nis et bi - be-ri - tis e - ius san - gui-nem,

non ha-be - bi-tis vi - tam in vo - bis.

Qui man-du - cat me - am car - nem et bi - bit me-um

san - gui - nem ha - bet vi - tam e - ter - man. Et e - go

re-su-sci-ta - bo e - um in no-vis - si-mo di - e.

Ca - ro e - nim me - a ve - re est ci - bus et san - guis me - us

ve - re est po - tus. Qui man-du - cat me - am car - nem

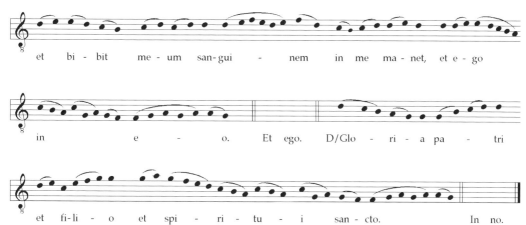

et bi - bit me - um san - gui - nem in me ma - net, et e - go

in e - o. Et ego. D/Glo - ri - a pa - tri

et fi - li - o et spi - ri - tu - i san - cto. In no.

[Amen, amen I say to you, unless you eat the flesh of the son of man and drink his blood, you will not have life in you. Whoever eats my flesh and drinks my blood will have eternal life. And I will raise him up on the last day. V. My flesh indeed is truly food and my blood truly drink. He who eats my flesh and drinks my blood abides in me, and I in him.]

42. Lectio ix

[*Alcuin,* Commentaria in S. Joannis evangelium, *Lib. 3: Ch. XVI, Vers. 64–69]*[90]

[Vers 64, Ch. XVI] Spiritus est qui vivificat, caro autem non prodest quicquam. Diximus enim hoc dominum commendasse in manducatione carnis sue, et potacione sanguinis sui, ut in illo commaneamus et ipse in nobis. Manet autem ipse in nobis, cum simus templum eius. Ut autem simus membra eius: unitas nos compaginat. Unitas autem ex caritate eius, caritas ex spiritu. Ergo est spiritus qui vivificat, spiritus enim facit viva membra. Nec viva membra spiritus facit, nisi que in corpore quod vegetat, ipse spiritus invenit. Nam spiritus qui est in te o homo, quo constas ut homo sis: quomodo vivificat membrum quod separatum invenerit a carne tua? Spiritum tuum dico animam tuam, anima tua non vivificat nisi membra qui sunt in carne tua. Unum si tollas iam ex anima tua non vivificatur, quia unitate corporis tui non copulatur. Hec dicuntur, ut amemus unitatem, et timeamus separacionem. Nichil enim sic debet formidare christianus: quam separari a corpore christi. Si enim separatur a corpore christi: non est membrum eius. Si non est membrum eius: non vegetatur spiritu eius. Quisquis inquit apostolus spiritum christi non habet: hic non est eius. Spiritus est ergo qui vivificat, caro non prodest quicquam. Verba que ego locutus sum vobis spiritus et vita sunt, spiritualiter intelligenda sunt. Intellexistis spiritualiter. Spiritus et vita sunt. Sed tibi non sunt o homo qui spiritualiter ea non intelligis, nec fide ea venerari nosti.

---

[90] PL 100, cols. 838–40.

[Vers 65] Sunt enim quidam in vobis qui non credunt, et ideo non intelligunt, quia non credunt. Propheta enim dixit. Nisi credideritis: non intelligetis. Per fidem copulamur, per intellectum vivificamur, prius habeamus fidem: ut sic post vivificemur, per intellectum.

[Vers 67] Ex hoc multi discipulorum eius abierunt retro,[91] quomodo precisi a corpore christi, nec ultra redeuntes ad eum, quia fideliter in corpore eius non fuerunt, et hii non pauci sed multi. Audiamus ergo quid ad paucos dixerit qui remanserunt.

[Vers. 68] Dixit ergo ihesus ad duodecim. Numquid et vos vultis abire? Non discessit nec iudas. Sed quare manebat cum Domino iam apparebat. Postea manifestus est. Respondit pro omnibus, unus pro multis, unitas pro universis. Respondit ergo ei Symon Petrus. Domine ad quem ibimus? Repellis nos a te, da nobis alium similem tui ad quem ibimus. Si a te recedemus ad quiem ibimus?

[Vers. 69] Verba vite eterne habes. Videte quemadmodum petrus dante domino, recreante spiritu sancto intellixit. Unde nisi quia credidit verba vite eterne? Vitam enim eternam habes, in ministracione corporis tui et sanguinis. Et nos credimus et cognovimus. Credimus enim ut cognosceremus. Nam si prius cognoscere et deinde credere vellemus:[92] Quid credidimus et quid cognovimus? quia tu es christus filius dei vivi, id est quia in ipsa vita eterna tu es, et non das in carne et sanguine tuo, nisi quod es.

[It is the spirit that gives life, the flesh on the other hand does not benefit anyone. We have said that the Lord instructed us in eating his flesh and drinking his blood, so that we may abide in him and he in us. Moreover, he himself abides in us, since we are his temple. So that we too may be members of him, union joins us into a whole. Unity then through love of him, love through the spirit. Therefore it is the spirit that gives life, for the spirit makes living members. But the spirit does not make the members live, except those things the spirit itself finds which are in the body which invigorates them. For how can the spirit which is in you, O man, by which you are held together so that you are man, vivify a member which it finds separate from your flesh? If you take one thing away from your soul it does not live, because it is not joined to the unity of your body. These things are said, so that we may love unity and fear separation. Nothing indeed ought a Christian fear as much as being separated from the body of Christ. If indeed he is separated from the body of Christ, he is not a member of him. If he is not a member of him, he is not animated by his spirit. Whoever, the Apostle says, does not have the spirit of Christ, he is not of his body. It is the spirit, therefore, that gives life, the flesh does not benefit anyone. The words that I have spoken to you are spirit and life, they must be understood spiritually. You have understood spiritually, they are spirit and life. But

---

[91] Perhaps the passage "et iam non cum illo ambulant. Abierunt retro non post Christum sed post Satanum. Isti autem sic abierunt retro" is missing here. See PL 100, col. 839; Lambot, "L'Office de la Fête-Dieu," 105.

[92] Perhaps the phrase "nec cognoscere nec credere valeremus [we will be able neither to come to know nor to believe]" is missing here. See PL 100, col. 840; Lambot, "L'Office de la Fête-Dieu," 105.

they are not yours, O man, you who do not understand them spiritually, nor know to venerate them with faith.

There are, however, some among you who do not believe, and therefore do not understand because they do not believe. The prophet said: "Unless you shall believe, you shall not understand." We are united by faith, we are given life by understanding; first let us have faith, so that afterwards we may be given life by understanding.

From this time many of his disciples turned away, in such a way as to be cut off from the body of Christ, and did not follow him any longer, because they were not faithfully in his body, and these were not a few but many. Let us hear therefore what he said to the few who remained.

Jesus therefore said to the twelve: "Do you also wish to go away?" The twelve did not go away, not even Judas, but why the group remained with the Lord now appeared. Later it was made manifest. One responded for all, one for many, a single one for the whole group. Simon Peter therefore answered him: "Lord, to whom shall we go?" If you drive us from you, give us another similar to you to whom we shall go. If we withdraw from you, to whom shall we go?

"You have words of eternal life." Behold how Peter understood because the Lord gives the Holy Spirit renews. How else unless it was because he believed the words of eternal life? You have eternal life in the ministration of your body and blood. And we believe and have come to know. We believe indeed that we might come to know. For if first we wish to come to know and then believe, what have we believed and what have we come to know? That you are Christ the son of the living God, that is, that you are in eternal life itself, and you do not give in your flesh and blood, anything except what you are.]

43. Responsory: Sicut vivens/Non sicut patres/Gloria patri
[Text Source: Jo 6: 57–59]

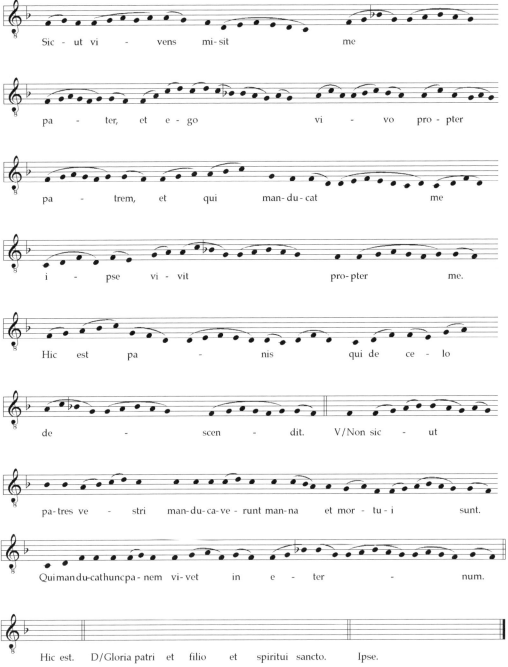

[As the living father sent me, and I live because of the father, so he who eats me lives because of me. This is the bread which descended from heaven. V. Not like the manna your fathers ate and died. He who eats this bread will live forever.]

In quarto nocturno
Antiphona[93]

44. Extendit Jonathas/Ps Domine exaudi
[Text Source: 1 Sam 14: 27]
Extendit Ionatas sumitatem virgule quam habebat in manu et intinxit in favum mellis et convertit manum suam ad os suum et illuminati sunt oculi eius. Euouae. Ps Domine exaudi.

[Jonathan extended the tip of the staff he had in his hand and dipped it in the honeycomb and put his hand to his mouth and his eyes became bright.]

45. Comede fili mi/Ps Benedic ii
[Text Source: Prov 24: 13, 25: 16]
Comede fili mi mel quia bonum est et favum dulcissimum gutturi tuo mel invenisti comede quod sufficit tibi. Euouae. Ps Benedic ii

[Eat honey, my son, because it is good, and the drippings of the honeycomb are sweet to your taste. You have found honey. Eat enough to satisfy yourself.]

46. Venite emite/Ps Confitemini domino et invocate
[Text Source: Is 55: 1–2]
Venite emite absque argento et absque ulla commutacione vinum et lac audite audientes me et comedite bonum et d[el]ectabitur in crassitudine anima vestra. Euouae. Ps Confitemini domino et invocate.

[Come, buy wine and milk without money and without any exchange. Listen, you hearing me, and eat well, and let your soul delight in richness.]

47. Versiculus
[Text Source: Cant 5: 1]
Comedi favum cum melle meo alleluia. R. Bibi vinum meum cum lacte meo alleluia.

[I eat honeycomb with my honey, alleluia. R. I drink my wine with my milk, alleluia.]

---

[93] There are staves for these three antiphons and the versiculus, but no music was entered on them.

48. Lectio x[94]

[Gratian, De consecratione, *Dist. II, can. 72]*

Utrum sub figura an sub veritate hoc misticum calicis sacramentum fiat, veritas ait. Caro mea est cibus, et sanguis meus vere est potus. Alioquin quomodo magnum erit, panis quem ego dabo caro mea est pro mundi vita nisi vera sit caro? Sed quia christum fas vorari dentibus non est, voluit hunc panem et vinum in ministerio vere carnem suam et sanguinem suum consecratione spiritus sancti potencialiter creari, et cotidie pro mundi vita mistice immolari, ut sicut de virgine per spiritum sanctum vera caro sine coitu creatur, ita per eundem ex substancia panis et vini: mistice idem corpus christi consecretur. Corpus christi et veritas et figura est. Veritas: dum corpus christi et sanguis in virtute spiritus sancti et in virtute ipsius, ex panis vinique substancia efficitur. Figura vero est, id quod exterius sentitur. Intra catholicam ecclesiam in ministerio corporis christi nichil a bono maius, nichil a malo minus perficitur sacerdote, quia non in merito consecrantis, sed in verbo efficitur creatoris et in virtute spiritus sancti.[95] Si enim in merito esset sacerdotis, nequaquam ad christum pertineret. Nunc autem sicut ipse est qui baptizat, ita ipse est qui per spiritum sanctum hanc suam efficit carnem, et transit vinum in sanguinem. Unde et sacerdos. Iube hec inquit offeri per manus angeli tui sancti in sublime altare tuum in conspectu divine maiestatis tue. Ut quid deferenda in lucem deposcit, nisi ut intelligatur: quod ista fiant in eo sacerdocio. Hanc ergo oblacionem benedictam per quam benedicimur, ascriptam, per quam homines in celo ascribuntur. Ratam, per quam visceribus christi esse censeamur. Rationabilem, per quam a bestiali sensu exuamur. Acceptabilem, ut qui nobis ipsis displicemus, per hanc acceptabiles eius unico filio simus. Nichil rationabilius, ut quia nos iam similitudinem mortis eius in baptismo accepimus, similitudinem quoque carnis et sanguinis sumamus, ita ut veritas non desit in sacramento, et ridiculum nullum fiat a paganis quod cruorem occisi hominis bibamus. Credendum est quod in verbis christi sacramenta conficiantur. Cuius enim potencia creantur prius, eius utique verbo ad melius procreantur. Reliqua omnia que sacerdos dicit aut chori clerus canit, nichil aliud quam laudes et gratiarum actiones sunt, aut certe obsecraciones, et fidelium peticiones.

---

[94] The *x* has been crossed out and replaced with what looks like a *iii*. This is the last of the readings to be given the inscription *lectio.*

[95] In margin, *lecto.*

[Whether by symbolism or by truth the mystery of the chalice becomes a sacrament, truth tells: My flesh truly is food, and my blood truly is drink. Otherwise how will it be a great thing—"the bread which I will give is my flesh for the life of the world"—unless it be true flesh? But because it is not right that Christ be devoured with the teeth, he wanted this bread and wine truly in the ministry to become powerfully his flesh and blood by the consecration of the Holy Spirit, and daily to be sacrificed mystically for the life of the world, so that, just as his true flesh is created from a virgin through the Holy Spirit without intercourse, through the same Holy Spirit the same body of Christ may be mystically consecrated from the substance of bread and wine. The body of Christ is both truth and a symbol. Truth when the body and blood of Christ is produced by the power of the Holy Spirit and by his own power, from the substance of bread and wine. The symbol is that which is perceived externally. Within the catholic church, in the ministry of the body of Christ, nothing greater by a good priest, nor inferior by a bad priest is accomplished, because it is accomplished, not by the merit of the one consecrating, but by the word of the creator, and by the power of the Holy Spirit. If it were by the merit of the priest, it would in no way pertain to Christ. Now however, just as it is he himself who baptizes, so it is he himself who, through the Holy Spirit, makes it his flesh, and changes wine into his blood. Hence the priest: Command, he says, these offerings to be carried up by the hands of your holy angels to your sublime altar, in the sight of your divine majesty. How is it that he demands these offerings be brought into the light, if not that it be understood that these things are done in his priesthood? Therefore this offering is blessed, through which we are blessed, it is enrolled, through which men are enrolled in heaven, it is certified, through which we are deemed to be of the flesh of Christ, it is intelligent, through which we are freed from bestial understanding, it is accepting, so that we who are displeasing to ourselves may become by it acceptable to his only son. Nothing is more sensible than that, because we receive the likeness of his death in baptism, we also consume the likeness of his body and blood, so that truth may not be lacking in the sacrament, and that there be no mockery by pagans, that we drink the blood of a dead man. It must be believed that the sacraments are produced by the words of Christ, by whose power they are created beforehand, by his word especially they are produced for the better. All the remaining things which the priest says, or which the group of the chorus sings, are nothing other than praises and thanksgivings, or even supplications, or prayers of the faithful.]

49. Responsory: Melchisedech viro/Benedictus Abraham
[Text Source: Gen 14: 18–19]

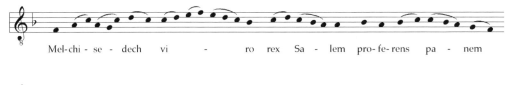

Mel-chi - se - dech vi - ro rex Sa - lem pro-fe- rens pa - nem

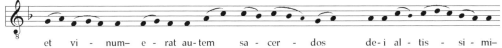

et vi - num— e - rat au- tem sa - cer - dos de- i al - tis - si - mi—

be - ne- di - xit A - bra - he et a it.

V/Be- ne - di - ctus A - bra - ham de- o ex - cel- so qui cre - a - vit

ce - lum et ter - ram. Be - ne- di - xit.

[Melchisedech king of Salem offered bread and wine; he was the priest of the highest God. He blessed Abraham and said. V. Blessed be Abraham by the most high God, who created heaven and earth.]

50. [Lectio xi][96]

[Gratian, De consecratione, *Dist. II, can. 74]*

Omnia quecumque voluit dominus, fecit in celo et in terra. Et quia voluit sic factum est. Ita licet figura panis et vini videatur, nichil tamen aliud quam caro christi et sanguis post consecracionem credenda sunt. Unde ipsa veritas ad discipulos. Hec inquit caro mea est pro mundi vita, et ut mirabilius loquar, non alia plane quam que nata est de maria et passa in cruce, et resurrexit de sepulchro. Hec inquam ipsa est, et ideo christi est caro, que pro mundi vita adhuc hodie offertur, et cum digne percipitur: vita utique eternam nobis reparatur. Panem quidem istum quem sumimus in misterio illum utique intelligo panem qui manu sancti spiritus formatus est in utero virginis, et igne passionis decoctus in ara crucis. Panis angelorum enim factus est hominum cibus. Unde ipse ait. Ego sum panis vivus qui de celo descendi. Et iterum. Panis quem ego dabo caro mea est pro mundi vita.[97]

---

[96] In margin, *iiia lecto.* Note that there is no indication of *lectio xi.*

[97] In upper margin, *lecto iiii.*

[Gratian, De consecratione, *Dist II, can. 13]*

Cotidie eucharistie communionem accipere, non laudo nec vitupero. Omnibus tamen dominicis diebus communicandum ortor. Si tamen mens in affectu peccandi
est, gravari magis dico eucharistie perceptione quam purificari. Et ideo quamvis
quis peccato mordeatur, peccandi tamen de cetero non habeat voluntatem, et communicaturus satisfaciat lacrimis et orationibus, et confidens de domini miseratione,
accedat ad eucharistiam intrepidus et securus. Sed hoc de illo dico quem mortalia
peccata non gravant. Idem, dixerit quispiam non cotidie accipiendam eucharistiam,
alius affirmat cotidie, faciat unusquisque quod secundum fidem suam pie credit
esse faciendum. Necque enim litigarunt inter se, aut quisquam eorum se alteri proposuit Zacheus et ille centurio, cum alter eorum gaudenter in domo sua susceperit
dominum, alter dixerit domino: Domine non sum dignus ut intres sub tectum
meum. Ambo salvatorem honorificantes quamvis non uno modo, ambo peccatis
miseri, ambo misericordiam consecuti. Ad hoc valet, quod manna secundum propriam voluntatem in ore cuiusque sapiebat.

[Gratian, De consecratione, *Dist. II, can. 14]*

Si quocienscumque effunditur sanguis christi, in remissionem peccatorum funditur,
debeo illum semper accipere, ut semper michi peccata dimittantur.

[Gratian, De consecratione, *Dist. II, can. 24 beginning]*

Qui semper pecco, debeo semper habere medicinam.

[All things that the Lord wished, he did in heaven and on earth. And because he
wished it, it was done. Thus, although it seems to be the form of bread and wine,
these things, after consecration, must be believed to be nothing other than the flesh
of Christ and his blood. Whence he spoke the truth to his disciples: This, he said, is
my flesh, for the life of the world, and that I may speak more remarkably, it is
clearly nothing other than what was born of Mary, and suffered on the cross, and
rose again from the tomb. This, I say, it is, and therefore it is the flesh of Christ,
which is offered for the life of the world even today, and when it is taken worthily,
eternal life certainly is restored in us. This bread which we consume in mystery, I
certainly understand to be that bread which was formed by the hand of the Holy
Spirit in the womb of the virgin, and destroyed by the fire of his passion on the altar
of the cross. The bread of the angels has become the food of men. Whence he himself said: I am the living bread, who descended from heaven. And again: The bread
which I will give is my flesh, for the life of the world.

   To receive communion of the eucharist daily I do not either praise or censure. I
urge communion on all Sundays. If however the soul is in a state of sin, I say that he
is more to be burdened by receiving communion, than to be purfied. And therefore
someone is consumed by sin, but yet does not have a wish to sin further, let him receive communion in tears and prayers, and, confident in the mercy of the Lord, let
him approach the eucharist undaunted and secure. But I say this to the one whom
mortal sins do not burden. Thus one person says that the Eucharist must not be received daily, another asserts that it be done daily, let each one do what he conscien-

tiously believes must be done according to his own faith. Nor did either of them put himself before the other, Zacheus and that centurion, when one of them gladly received the Lord into his house, the other said to the Lord: "Lord I am not worthy that you should enter my house," both honoring the Saviour, although not in one way, both having been pitied for their sins, both having attained mercy. To this it applies that manna tastes in the mouth of each according to his own desire.

If, however often the blood of Christ is poured out, it is shed for the remission of sins, I ought always to receive it, so that always my sins may be forgiven. I who always sin, ought always to have a remedy.]

51. Responsory: Immolabit hedum/Et edent
   [Text Source: Ex 12: 6–8]

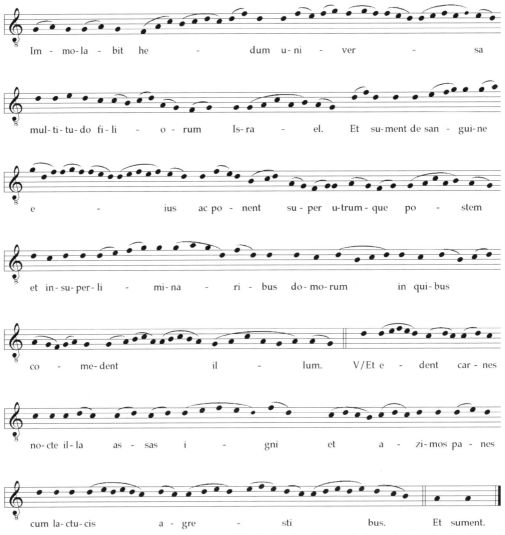

[The multitude of the sons of Israel shall kill the lamb. And they shall take its blood, and place it on doorposts and lintels of the houses in which they eat it. V. And they shall eat flesh on that night roasted over fire and unleavened bread with bitter herbs.]

52. [Lectio xi][98]

[Gratian, De consecratione, *Dist. II, can. 24 concluded]*

Qui scelerate vivunt in ecclesia, et communicare non desinunt, putantes se tali communione mundari, discant nichil ad emundationem proficere sibi, dicente propheta. Quid est quod dilectus meus fecit in domo mea scelera multa? Numquid carnes sancte auferunt a te malicias tuas? Et apostolus. Probet inquit se homo, et sic de pane illo edat, et de calice bibat.

[Gratian, De consecratione, *Dist. II, can. 56]*

Non iste panis est qui vadit in corpus sed panis vite eterne qui anime nostre substanciam fulcit. Iste panis cotidianus est. Accipe cotidie, quod cotidie tibi prosit. Sic vive, ut cotidie merearis accipere.

[Gratian, De consecratione, *Dist. II, can. 66]*

Sancta malis possunt obesse, bonis sunt ad salutem, malis ad iudicium. Unde apostolus. Qui manducat et bibit indigne: iudicium sibi manducat, et bibit. Non quia illa res mala est, sed quia malus male accipit quod bonum est. Non enim mala erat buccella que iude data est a domino. Salutem medicus dedit. Sed quia ille qui indignus erat accepit: ad perniciem suam accepit.

[Gratian, De consecratione, *Dist. II, can. 67]*

Non prohibeat dispensator pingues terre mensam domini manducare, sed exactorum moneat timere.

[Gratian, De consecratione, *Dist. II, can. 68]*

Sicut iudas cum buccellam tradidit christus, non malum accipiendo, sed bonum male accipiendo locum prebuit dyabolo, sic indigne quisquis sumens corpus christi non efficit, ut quia malus est malum sit, aut quia malus est malum sit,[99] aut quia non ad salutem accipit, nichil accipit. Corpus enim et sanguis domini nichilominus erat in illis, quibus dicebat apostolus. Qui manducat et bibit indigne, iudicium sibi manducat et bibit.

[Gratian, De consecratione, *Dist. II, can. 46]*

Multi indigne corpus christi accipiunt, de quibus apostolus. Qui manducat et bibit calicem domini indigne, iudicium sibi manducat et bibit. Sed quomodo manducandus est christus? Quomodo ipse dicit. Qui enim manducat carnem meam et bibit sanguinem meum digne, in me manet et ego in eo, et si indigne accipit sacramentum, acquirit magnum tormentum.

---

[98] In margin, *l va.*

[99] The previous five words seem to have been recopied erroneously.

[If, however often the blood of Christ is poured out, it is shed for the remission of sins, I ought always to receive it, so that always my sins may be forgiven.

I who always sin, ought always to have a remedy. Those who live wickedly in the church, and do not cease to receive communion, considering themselves to be purified by such communion, let them learn that they acquire nothing for their purification, as the prophet says: How is it that my beloved commits crimes in my house? Do the consecrated pieces of flesh take away from you your maliciousness? As the apostle [says]: Let a man examine himself, he said, and thus eat of that bread and drink from that chalice.

This bread is not that which goes into the body, but the bread of eternal life, which supports the substance of our soul. This is a daily bread, receive it daily, so that daily it may be of benefit to you. Live in such a way that you may be worthy to receive it.

Sacred things can be harmful to the wicked. They work to the salvation of the good, to the judgment of the wicked. Hence the apostle: He who eats and drinks unworthily, eats and drinks judgment on himself. Not because that thing is evil, but because the evil one receives evilly what is good. It was not an evil morsel which was given by the Lord to Judas. The doctor gives health. But because he who was unworthy received it, he received it to his destruction.

Let the steward not forbid the rich of the land from eating at the Lord's table, but let him advise them to fear the bringer of judgment.

Just as Judas, when Christ handed a morsel to him, did not receive evil but badly received good, gave room to the devil, so when someone unworthily consumes the body of Christ, it is not the case that because he is wicked, it is wicked, or because he does not receive it to his benefit he receives nothing. The body and blood of the Lord nonetheless was in them, to whom the apostle said: Whoever eats and drinks unworthily, eats and drinks judgment on himself.

Many receive the body unworthily, about whom the apostle said: He who eats and drinks from the chalice of the Lord unworthily, eats and drinks judgment on himself. But how must Christ be eaten? He himself described the way: He who eats my flesh and drinks my blood worthily, remains in me and I in him, and if he receives the sacrament unworthily, he obtains great torment.]

53. Responsory: Cumque operuisset/Iste est panis/Gloria patri
    [Text Source: Ex 16: 14–15]

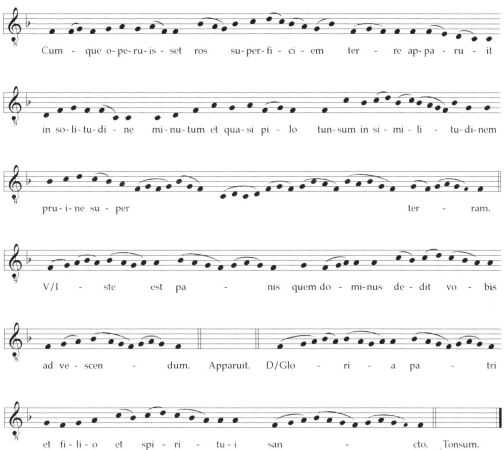

Cum - que o-pe-ru-is - set   ros   su-per-fi - ci - em   ter - re ap-pa - ru - it

in so-li-tu-di - ne   mi-nu-tum et qua-si pi - lo   tun-sum in si - mi - li - tu-di-nem

pru-i-ne su - per   ter - ram.

V/I - ste   est pa - nis   quem do - mi-nus de - dit vo - bis

ad ve - scen - dum.   Apparuit.   D/Glo - ri - a pa - tri

et fi - li - o   et spi - ri - tu - i   san - cto.   Tonsum.

[When the dew had gone up there appeared on the ground a fine and flake-like thing,
similar to hoarfrost on the ground. V. It is the bread that the Lord has given you to eat.]

In laudibus
Antiphona

54. Memoriam fecit/Ps Dominus regnavit

[Text Source: Ps 110 (Latin), 111 (Hebrew): 4–5]

Me- mo – ri- am fe – cit   mi - ra - bi - li – um su – o – rum,

mi- se – ri- cors et mi- se – ra- tor   do- mi – nus. E- scam   se   de- dit

ti- men- ti- bus se,   al – le – lu- ia.   E u o u a   e.   Ps/Dominus regnavit.

[He has made a memorial of his wonderful works, the gracious and merciful Lord. He himself has given food to those who fear him, alleluia.]

55. Memoria mea/Ps Iubilate

[Text Source: Sir (Ecclesiasticus) 24: 28–29]

Me - mo – ri- a me - a   in   ge- ne- ra – ci- o- nes   se – cu- lo- rum.

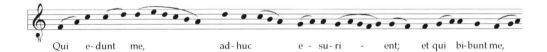

Qui   e- dunt   me,   ad- huc   e - su- ri – ent;   et qui bi- bunt me,

ad – huc   si – ci- ent, al – le- lu- ia.   E u o u a e.   Ps/Iubilate.

[My memory will be in the generations of ages. Those who eat me will hunger for more; and those who drink me will thirst for more, alleluia.]

56. Omnes eandem/Ps Deus Deus meus

[Text Source: 1 Cor 10: 3–4]

O - mnes e-an- dem e-scam spi-ri - ta - lem man-du - ca-ve - runt

et o-mnes e-un - dem po-tum spi-ri-ta-lem bi-be - runt; bi-be - bant

au-tem de spi-ri-ta - li con - se - quen - te e-os pe-tra: pe - tra au - tem

e - rat Chri-stus, al - le-lu-ia. E u o u a e. Ps/Deus Deus meus.

[They all ate the same spiritual food, and they all drank the same spiritual drink. They drank from the spiritual rock which followed them: the rock was Christ, alleluia.]

57. Nolo vos socios/Ps Benedicite

[Text Source: 1 Cor 10: 20–21]

No-lo vos so - ci-os fi - e-ri de - mo - ni - o-rum, qui-a non po-te - stis

ca - li-cem do - mi - ni bi-be - re et ca - li-cem de-mo-ni-o - rum;

non po-te - stis men-se do-mi - ni par-ti-ci - pes es-se et men-se

de - mo-ni-o-rum, al - le - lu - ia. E u o u a e. Ps/Benedicite.

[I do not want you to be associates of demons, because you cannot drink the chalice of the Lord and the chalice of demons; you cannot be participants in the table of the Lord and the table of demons, alleluia.]

58. Qui habet aures/Ps Laudate Dominum

[Text Source: Apoc 2: 17]

Qui ha - bet au - res au - di - en - di, au - di - at quid spi - ri - tus

di - cat ec - cle - siis. Vin - cen - ti da - bo man - na

ab - scon - di - tum, al - le - lu - ia. E u o u a e. Ps/Laudate Dominum.

[Let the one who has ears for hearing, let him hear what the Spirit says to the churches. To him who conquers I will give hidden manna, alleluia.]

59. Capitulum

[Text Source: Heb 5: 1]

Omnis pontifex ex hominibus assumptus pro hominibus constituitur in hiis que sunt ad deum ut offerat dona et sacrificia pro peccatis.

[Every priest chosen from among men is appointed to act for men in their relations with God, to offer gifts and sacrifices for sins.]

60. Hymn: Verbum supernum prodiens[100]

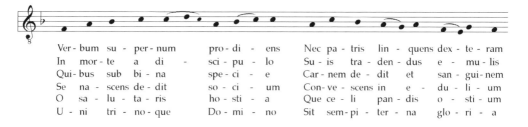

Ver - bum su - per - num pro - di - ens Nec pa - tris lin - quens dex - te - ram
In mor - te a di - sci - pu - lo Su - is tra - den - dus e - mu - lis
Qui- bus sub bi - na spe - ci - e Car - nem de - dit et san - gui - nem
Se na - scens de - dit so - ci - um Con - ve - scens in e - du - li - um
O sa - lu - ta - ris ho - sti - a Que ce - li pan - dis o - sti - um
U - ni tri - no - que Do - mi - no Sit sem - pi - ter - na glo - ri - a

Ad o - pus su - um ex - i - ens Ve - nit - ad vi - te ve - spe - ram.
Pri- us in vi - te fer - cu - lo Se tra - di - dit di - sci - pu - lis.
Ut du- pli- cis sub-stan- ci - e To- tum ci - ba - ret ho - mi - nem.
Se mo- ri- ens in pre - ti - um Se re - gnans dans in pre - mi - um.
Bel- la pre- munt ho- sti - li - a Da ro - bur fer au - xi - li - um.
Qui vi- tam si - ne ter - mi - no No-bis do - net in pa - tri - a. A - men.

---

[100] The music is in a different hand.

[1. The celestial word coming forth, but not leaving the right hand of the father, going out to his work, comes to the evening of life.

2. Handed over by a disciple to his enemies for his death, he first gave himself to his disciples in the food of life.

3. He gave them his flesh and blood under two species, so that he might feed the whole man of twofold substance.

4. Being born he gave himself as a companion, dining he gave himself as nourishment, dying he gave himself as a ransom, reigning he gives himself as a reward.

5. O saving victim who opens the door of heaven, wars and enemies press us, give us strength, bring us help.

6. To the Lord, one and three, be eternal praise, may he give us eternal life in the homeland. Amen.]

61. Versiculus
    [Text Source: Ps 103 (Latin), 104 (Hebrew): 27]
    Omnia a te expectant alleluia. R. Ut des illis escam in tempore oportuno alleluia.

    [All creatures depend on you, alleluia. R. To give them food at the proper time, alleluia.]

62. Ad benedictus antiphona: Dixit Ihesus/Benedictus
    [Text Source: Jo 6: 35]

[Jesus said: I am the bread of life; he who comes to me will not hunger, and he who believes in me will never thirst, alleluia.]

    [Day Hours]
    Ad primam
63. Antiphona: Memoriam fecit (See #54)/Ps Deus in [nomine]

Ad terciam

64. Memoria mea (See #55)

Capitulum

Dominus Ihesus Christus (See #6)

65. Responsory: Parasti in conspectu

[Text Source: Ps 22 (Latin), 23 (Hebrew): 5]

Pa-ra-sti in con-spe-ctu me - o   men - sam,   al - le   -   lu - ia,   al - le   -   lu - ia.

V/Ad- ver-sos e- os qui tri - bu - lant   me,   alleluia, alleluia.   D/Glo- ri- a pa   -   tri

et   fi - li - o   et   spi - ri - tu   -   i   san - cto.   Paras[ti.]

[You have prepared a table for me, alleluia, alleluia. V. In the face of those who torment me, alleluia, alleluia.]

66. Versiculus

[Text Source: Ps 144 (Latin), 145 (Hebrew): 15]

Oculi omnium in te sperant domine alleluia. R. Et tu das escam illorum in tempore oportuno alleluia.

[The eyes of all hope in you Lord, alleluia. R. And you give their food at the proper time, alleluia.]

Ad sextam

67. Antiphona: Omnes eandem (See #56)

68. Capitulum

Quocienscumque manducabitis panem hunc et calicem bibetis: mortem Domini an-nunciabitis donec veniat.

[As often as you shall eat this bread and drink this chalice, you will proclaim the death of the Lord until he comes.]

69. Responsory: Panem angelorum
[Text Source: Ps 77 (Latin), 78 (Hebrew): 25]

Pa- nem an - ge - lo- rum man- du - ca - vit   ho - mo,   al - le   -   lu - ia,

al - le   -   lu- ia.   V/Ci- ba - ri- a mi- sit e- is   in ha - bun - dan- ci - a,

alleluia, alleluia.   D/Gloria patri et filio   et spiritui sancto.   Panem.

[Mankind ate the bread of the angels, alleluia, alleluia. V. He sent them food in abundance, alleluia, alleluia.]

70. Versiculus
[Text Source: Ps 15 (Latin), 16 (Hebrew): 5]
Dominus pars hereditatis mee et calicis mei alleluia. R. Tu es qui restitues hereditatem meam mea alleluia.

[The Lord is my inheritance and my cup, alleluia. R. You are the one who restores my interitance to me, alleluia.]

Ad nonam
71. Antiphona: Qui habet aures audiendi (See #58)

72. Capitulum
[Text Source: 1 Cor 11: 27]
Quicumque manducaverit panem vel biberit calicem Domini indigne, reus erit corporis et sanguinis Domini.

[Anyone who eats the bread or drinks the cup unworthily will be guilty of profaning the body and blood of the Lord.]

73. Responsory: Calicem salutaris[101]
   [Text Source: Ps 115 (Latin): 4, 116 (Hebrew): 13]

Ca - li-cem sa - lu-ta - ris ac-ci - pi - am,

al - le-lu-ia,   al- le - lu- ia.   V/Et no - men

Do - mi-ni in-vo-ca - bo, alleluia.

D/Glo-ri - a pa - tri et fi - li-o

et spi- ri - tu- i san - cto. Calicem

[I will take up the cup of salvation, alleluia, alleluia. V. And I will invoke the name of the Lord, alleluia.]

74. Versiculus
   [Text Source: Ps 22 (Latin), 23 (Hebrew): 5]
   Inpinguasti in oleo caput meum alleluia. R. Et calix meus inebrians quam preclarus est alleluia.

   [You have annointed my head with oil, alleluia. R. And my cup brims over.]

In secundis vesperis de primis vesperis[102]
75. Capitulum
   Probet autem seipsum homo et sic de pane illo edat et de calice bibat; qui enim manducat et bibit indigne iudicium sibi manducat et bibit non diiudicans corpus domini.

   [Let each man examine himself and so eat the bread and drink the cup. V. Who eats and drinks unworthily, eats and drinks judgment on himself, not recognizing the body of the Lord.]

---

[101] A different hand again for the music.

[102] All that follows is written by a later hand in the margin and is very difficult to read. Thus, much is conjectural. The responsory *Amen Amen* is written across the bottom of the page and is also nearly illegible.

76. Responsory: Ego sum panis v[ite] (See #39?)

77. Versiculus
[Text Source: Ps 110 (Latin), 111 (Hebrew): 4]
Memoriam fecit mirabilium suorum. R. Misericors et miserator dominus alleluia.

[He has made a memorial of his wonderful works. R. The gracious and merciful Lord, alleluia.]

78. [Ad Magnificat antiphona: Amen, amen dico vobis/Magnificat]
[Text Source: Jo 6: 32]

A - men, a - men di - co vo - bis: Non de - dit Mo - y - ses vo - bis

pa - nem de ce - lo sed pa - ter me - us dat vo - bis

pa - nem ve - rum de ce - lo. Pa - nis e - nim ve - rus est

qui de ce - lo de - scen - dit et dat vi - tam mun - do, al - le -

lu - ia. Ps/Mag[nificat.]

[Amen, Amen I say to you: Moses did not give you the bread from heaven, but my father gives you the true bread from heaven. For the true bread is that which comes down from heaven and gives life to the world, alleluia, alleluia.]

CORPUS CHRISTI
BNF 1143

Officium nove sollempnitatis corporis
Domini Jesu Christi celebrande singulis annis.fr.
Quinta post Octavas penthecostes.

In Primis vesperis
Antiphona

1. Sacerdos in eternum/Ps Dixit Dominus
    [Text Source: Ps 109 (Latin), 110 (Hebrew): 4b; Heb. 5: 6; Gen 14: 18]
    [Christ the Lord, a priest forever after the order of Melchisedech, offered bread and wine.]

    Contra Gloria tibi Trinitas de Trinitate, CAO 2948
    [Glory to you, Trinity of equals, one God, before all ages, now, and forever.]

    [Musical Source: AS 286, Vespers Ant. 1]

2. Miserator Dominus/Ps Confitebor tibi Domine
    [Text Source: Cf. Ps 110 (Latin), 111 (Hebrew): 4]
    [The merciful Lord gave food to those who fear him in memory of his wonderful works.]

    Contra Totus orbis de sco Thoma [Canterbury], AH XIII, 240
    [The whole of the world strives in love of the martyr, whose singular signs excite astonishment.]

    [Musical Source: Wales 23v, Lauds Ant. 2]

3. Calicem salutaris/Ps Credidi propter
   [Text Source: Cf. Ps 115: 4, 7 (Latin); 116 (Hebrew): 13, 17]
   [I will take up the chalice of salvation and I will offer up a sacrifice of praise.]

   Contra Pudore bono. de sco Nicholao, CAO 4408, Jones 19[103]
   [For Nicholas: Filled with perfect modesty, the follower of God, through money given, prevented the evil of defilement.]
   [For James: Preserving the palm of purity, the minister of God gave himself completely to the divine voice.]

   [Musical Sources: AS 355, Matins Noct. 1, Ant. 3; 1051 195v, ODO 51 (Pudoris palmam), Matins Noct. 1, Ant. 3]

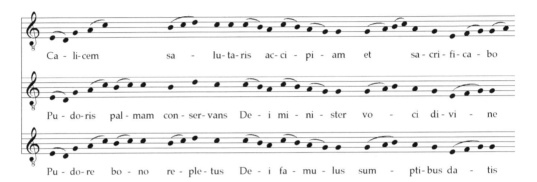

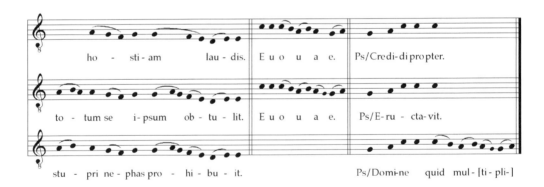

---

[103] The entirety of the Nicholas Office was transformed into an Office for St. James the Greater, used in Paris from the 14th through the 16th centuries and published by the Parisian church of St. Jacques de la Boucherie as *Ordo divini officii beati Jacobi Apostoli Maioris, patroni ecclesie parrochialis eiusdem sancti Jacobe de Carnificeria* (Paris: Jean LeBlanc, 1581) (ODO). For information on ODO, see Alejandro Enrique Planchart, "Guillaume Dufay's Masses: A View of the Manuscript Tradition," *Dufay Quincentenary Conference: Papers Read at the Dufay Quincentenary Conference, Brooklyn College, Dec. 6–7, 1974* (Dept. of Music, Brooklyn College, 1976): 26–53. In this and the other pieces derived from the Nicholas office, I have given the corresponding piece from the James office on the middle staff.

4. Sicut novelle/Ps Beati omnes

    [Text Source: Cf. Ps 127 (Latin), 128 (Hebrew): 3]

    [Let the sons of the church be like olive shoots around the table of the Lord.]

    Contra Iuste et sancte vivendo de sco Nicholao, CAO 3532, Jones 37

    [For Nicholas: Living justly and piously, he merited to be advanced to the honor of the priesthood.]

    [For James: Rightly and piously let us sing, celebrating the glorious solemnity of the most kind apostle.]

    [Musical Sources: AS 361, Lauds Ant. 3; ODO 80 (Iuste et pie), Lauds Ant. 3]

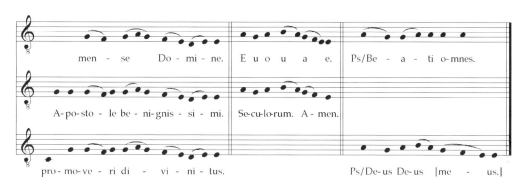

5. Qui pacem ponit/Ps Lauda Ierusalem
   [Text Source: Cf. Ps 147 (Latin): 3; 147 (Hebrew): 14]
   [He imposes peace in the territory of the church; the Lord fills us with the finest grain.]

   Contra Innocenter puerilia iura de sco Nicholao, CAO 3348, Jones 20
   [For Nicholas: Innocently transcending youthful duties, he was made a disciple of the teaching of the gospel.]
   [For James: Innocently studying to surpass secular things, he was made a disciple by the preaching of St. James.]

   [Musical Sources: AS 357, Matins Noct. 2 Ant. 5; 1051 198v, ODO 59 (Innocenter secularia), Matins Noct. 2, Ant. 5]

6. Capitulum

Dominus Ihesus Christus in qua nocte tradebatur; accepit panem; et gratias agens fregit et dixit. accepite et manducate; hoc est corpus meum; quod pro vobis tradetur.

[The Lord Jesus Christ, on the night he was betrayed, took bread and, giving thanks, broke it and said: Take and eat; This is my body, which will be given up for you.]

7. Responsory: Homo quidam/Venite comedite/Gloria patri
[Text Source: R. Cf. Luke 14: 16–17; V. Prov 9: 5]
[R. A man once gave a great feast and sent his servant at the hour of the feast to tell those invited to come, because all was prepared. V. Come eat my bread and drink the wine which I have mixed for you.]

Contra Virgo flagellatur de Sca Katharina, AH XVIII, 106
[R. The virgin is scourged, about to be tortured for ill fame, she is bound fast, she remains shut up in jail; a copious heavenly light shines, a sweet smell arises, sweetly the heavenly hosts sing praises. V. The bridegroom esteems the bride, the savior visits her.]

[Musical Source: AS pl. Y, Matins Noct. 2, Resp. 6]

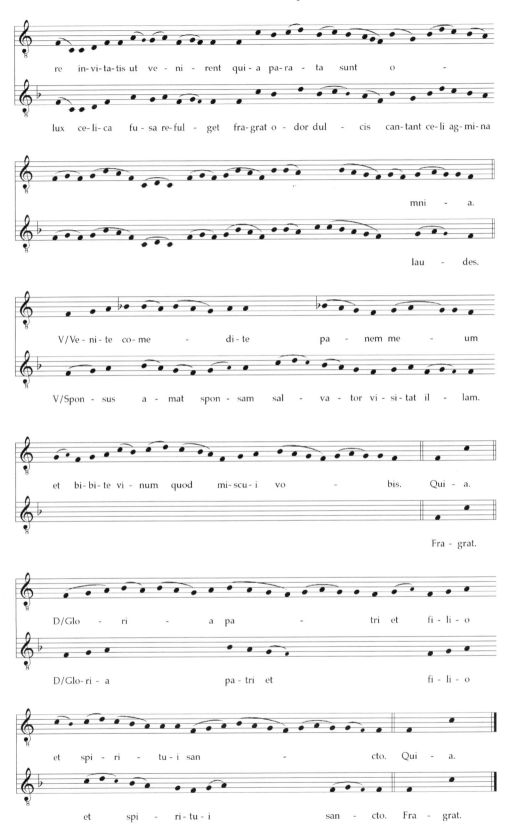

8. Hymn: Pange lingua

[1. Praise, my tongue, the mystery of the glorious body and of the precious blood, which the king of nations, fruit of a noble womb, poured out in ransom of the world.

2. Given to us, born to us from a pure virgin, and having lived in the world, the seed of his word having been scattered, he closed in a wondrous way his span of life.

3. At the night of the last supper, reclining with his brothers, the law of permitted foods having been fully observed, he gives himself as food with his own hands to the group of twelve.

4. The Word made flesh changes true bread into flesh by a word. And pure wine becomes Christ's blood. And if the sense fails, only faith suffices to convince the sincere heart.

5. Therefore let us eagerly venerate such a great sacrament. Let the old example cede to the new rite. Let faith render assistance to the limitations of the senses.

6. To the Father, and to the Son be praise and jubilation, salvation, honor, strength, and blessing. To the One who proceeds from them both be equal praise. Amen.]

Contra Pange lingua gloriosi prelium certaminis. In passione domini, AH L, 71, RH 14481, CAO 8367

[1. Sing my tongue the battle of the glorious struggle and tell of the noble triumph over the memorial of the cross, how the Redeemer of the world, sacrificed, has conquered.

2. The creator, pitying the deception of the primal parent, when, through a bite of the noxious fruit, he fell into death, he then marked the tree to make good the damages of the tree.

3. His order demanded this work of our salvation, so that His art might deceive the art of the multiform betrayer, and so that He might carry the remedy from that place where the enemy struck.

4. Glory and honor to God in the highest, to the Father and to the Son, along with with the Holy Spirit, to whom there is praise and power forever. Amen.]

[Musical Sources: Ut 83v; BNF 1235, 159v–160v, "In passione Domini," Matins Hymn (ST 90)][104]

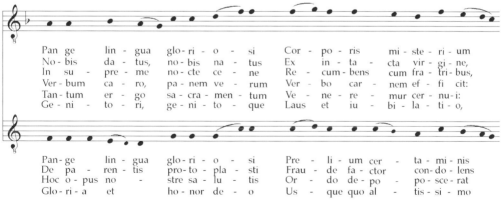

---

[104] Wales 131v has *Pange lingua/corporis* for the feast of Corpus Christi; the text *Pange lingua/prelium* is in WA 216, but with a different melody.

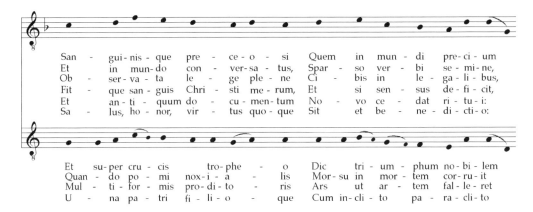

San	gui-nis-que	pre	ce-o-si	Quem	in	mun -	di	pre-ci-um
Et	in mun-do	con	ver-sa-tus,	Spar	so	ver -	bi	se - mi-ne,
Ob	ser-va-ta	le	ge ple-ne	Ci	bis	in	le -	ga-li-bus,
Fit	que san-guis Chri	sti me-rum,	Et	si	sen	sus	de-fi-cit,
Et	an-ti-quum do	cu-men-tum	No	vo	ce -	dat	ri-tu-i:
Sa	lus, ho-nor, vir	tus quo-que	Sit	et	be	ne - di-cti-o:

Et	su-per cru-cis	tro-phe	o	Dic	tri - um -	phum no-bi-lem
Quan	do po-mi	nox-i-a	lis	Mor-su in	mor - tem	cor-ru-it
Mul	ti-for-mis pro-di-to	ris	Ars	ut	ar - tem	fal-le-ret
U	na pa-tri	fi-li-o	que	Cum in-cli-to	pa - ra-cli-to

Fructus ven-tris	ge-ne-ro-si	Rex ef-fu - dit gen-ci-um.	Nobisdatusno
Su-i mo-ras	in-co-la-tus	Mi-ro clau-sit	or-di-ne.
Ci-bun-tur-be	du-o-de-ne	Se dat su-is	ma-ni-bus.
Ad fir-man-dum	cor sin-ce-rum	So-la fi - des suf-fi-cit.
Pre-stet fi-des	sup ple-mentum	Sen-su-um	de-fe-ctui.
Proce-den-tis	ab u-tro-que	Comparsit	lau-da-ti-o.		A - men.

Qua-li-ter	re-demptoror-bis	Im-mo-la-tus	vi-ce-rit.
I - pse li-gnumtuncno-ta-vit	Da-mnali-gniut	sol-ve-ret.
Et me-de-lam fer-ret in-de	Ho-stis un - de	le-se-rat.
Cu-i laus est et po-te-stas	Per e-ter-ne	se-cu-la.		A - men.

9. **Versiculus**

[Text Source: Sap 16: 20–21]

Panem de celo prestitisti eis, alleluia. R. Omne delectamentum in se habentem, alleluia.

[You have furnished them with the bread of heaven, alleluia. R. Having in it every delight, alleluia.]

10. **Ad Magnificat antiphona: O quam suavis/Magnificat**

[Text Source: Cf. Wisdom 12: 1; 16: 21; Luke 1: 53]

[O how kind is your spirit Lord, who, to show your sweetness towards your children, provides the sweetest bread from heaven, filling the hungry with good things, sending the haughty rich away empty.]

Contra O Christi pietas de sco Nicholao, CAO 4008, Jones 38

[For Nicholas: O piety of Christ, deserving of every praise, which declares far and wide the merits of his follower Nicholas. For from his marble tomb oil emanates, and cures all illnesses.]

[For James: O Christ our savior, grant to us the reward of life, singing worthily for the glory of your follower James, who reigns with the palm, his blood shed for you.]

[Musical Sources: AS 361, 2 Vesp. Mag. Ant.; ODO 113 (O Christe), 2 Vesp. Mag. Ant.]

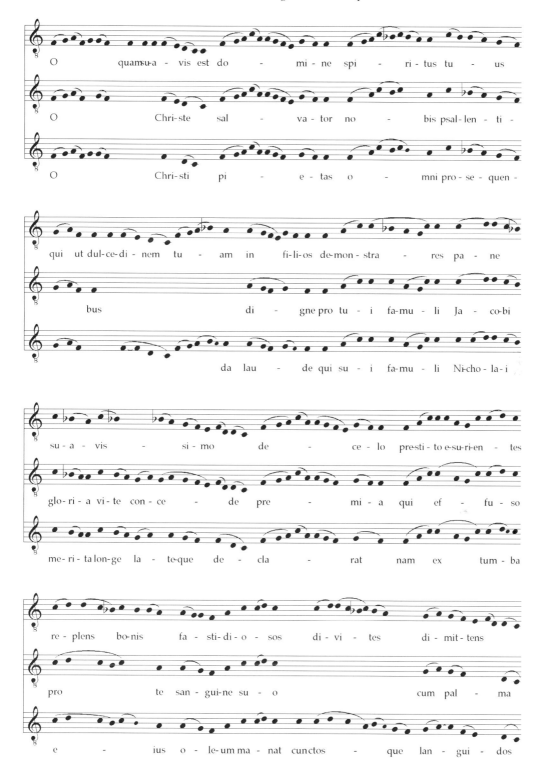

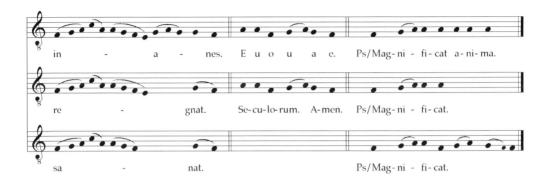

in - a - nes. E u o u a e. Ps/Mag-ni - fi-cat a-ni-ma.

re - gnat. Se-cu-lo-rum. A-men. Ps/Mag-ni - fi-cat.

sa - nat. Ps/Mag-ni - fi-cat.

11. Oratio

Deus qui nobis sub sacramento mirabili passionis tue memoriam reliquisti; tribue quesumus ita nos corporis et sanguinis tui sacra misteria venerari; ut redemptionis tue fructum in nobis iugiter senciamus. Qui vivis et regnas cum deo patre in unitate spiritu sancti deus per omnia secula seculorum. Amen.

[God, who has left us, in a wonderful sacrament, a memorial of your passion, grant, we pray, that we may venerate the mystery of your body and blood, so that we may always feel within ourselves the fruit of your redemption. Who lives and reigns with God the father in unity with the holy spirit, God, world without end. Amen.]

Ad matutinas

12. Invitatory: Christum regem

[Text Source: Cf. Ps 21 (Latin), 22 (Hebrew): 29 (LU 750, line 32)]

[Let us adore Christ the king, the Lord of all peoples, who gives nourishment of the spirit to those who eat.]

Contra Christum regem regum adoremus de sco Andrea, CAO 1051[105]

[Let us adore Christ the Lord, the King of kings, who glorified the blessed apostle Peter/Andrew with martyrdom of the cross.]

---

[105] This invitatory appears for St. Andrew in three early sources, among them the Ivrea Antiphoner, Ivrée, Chapitre 106. Also in Rome: Bibl. Ap. Vat. Burges 5, fol. 1v, and Rome: Bibl. Ap. Vat. Vat. lat. 4749, fol. 18. Elsewhere it is used for St. Peter. See CAO, vol. 1, #120: same tune as LR 441 *Christum Dei filium* for Precious Blood.

[Musical Sources: 4749, 18r, Invitatory for St. Andrew; Ut 130r, Invitatory for Passion of St. Peter]

13. Hymn: Sacris sollempniis

1. Let joys be joined with the sacred solemnities, and let prayers sound from our hearts. Let the old depart, let all things be new, hearts, voices, and works.

2. The night of last supper is recalled, in which Christ is believed to have given to his brethren lamb and unleavened bread, according to the rights granted to the forefathers.

3. The meal completed, after the symbolic lamb, the divine body was given to his disciples, entirely to all, entirely to each, by his own hands, this we proclaim.

4. He gave to the weak the meal of his body, and he gave to the sorrowful the drink of his blood, saying: Take the vessel which I give; all of you drink from it.

5. Thus he established this sacrifice, whose ceremony he wished to be entrusted only to those elders who were fit to consume it and give to others.

6. The bread of the angels becomes the bread of mankind, the celestial bread gives an end to symbols. O wondrous thing! the poor, the slave, the humble consumes the Lord.

7. We implore you, God three and one, just as you visit us, so do we honor you. Lead us on your pathway, by which we strive to the light which you inhabit. Amen.

Contra Sanctorum meritis, AH L, 204, RH 18607, CAO 8390, Text in Utrecht 34 but different melody

1. Let us celebrate, friends, the glorious joys of those hallowed by their services and their brave deeds, for the soul blazes up to tell through songs the noble line of victors.

2. These are the ones against whom the restraining world inveighed; because they inwardly disdained it, withered with sterile blossom, and followed you, Christ, good heavenly king.

3. These men for your sake trampled the furies and ferocities of men, and their fierce words: The claw fiercely lacerating yielded to them, and did not rend their innards.

4. They are cut down by swords in the manner of sacrificial animals; no murmur resounds, nor complaint; but with a quiet heart, their mind well aware maintains patience.

5. What voice, what tongue will be able to reveal what rewards you are preparing for the martyrs? For, red with flowing blood, they are enriched by laurels well shining.

6. We beg you, highest and one God, to absolve our sins, to take away harmful things, grant peace to your followers; we in turn give you glory forever. Amen.

[Musical Source: Cistercian Hymnal Heiligenkreuz 20, 12, 240v (ST 70)][106]

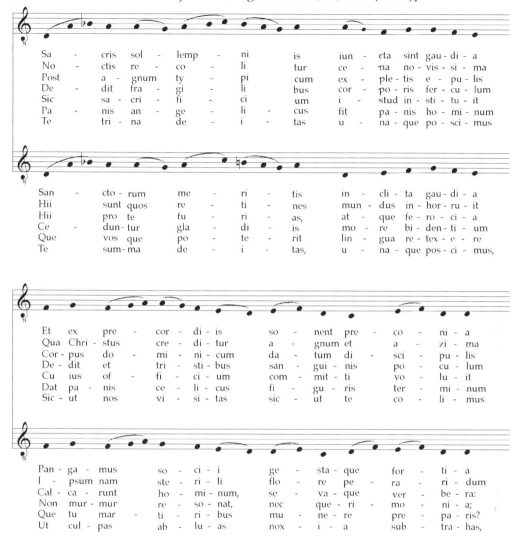

[106] The melody is taken from Stäblein; the text is taken from Vatican Library, San Pietro B 87, fol. 75v.

In primo nocturno
Antiphona
14. Fructrum salutiferum/Ps Beatus vir
    [Text Source: Cf. Ps 1: 3]
    [The Lord gave a saving fruit to taste at the time of his death.]

    Contra Granum cadens (sic for cadit) de sco Thoma
    [The seed drops, it yields an abundance of grain, the jar is shattered, the strength of
    ointment emits a sweet smell.]

    [Musical Source: Wales 23v, Lauds Ant. 1]

Fru - ctum sa-lu - ti - fe - rum gu - stan-dum de - dit do - mi-nus mor - tis

Gra - num ca-dit co-pi-am ger - mi - nat fru - men-ti a-la-ba-strum fran - gi - tur

su - e tem - po - re. E u o u a e. Ps/Be-a - tus vir.

fra - grat vis un - guen-ti. Ps/Do- ns. re- gn.

15. A fructu frumenti/Ps Cum invocarem

[Text Source: Cf. Ps 4: 8–9]

[Having increased by the fruit of grain and wine, the faithful rest in the peace of Christ.]

Contra Novus homo [*sic*] de sco Thoma (Monachus sub clerico)

[The monk, secretly hair-shirted under clerical garb, flesh stronger than flesh, overcomes its impluses.]

[Musical Source: Wales 21, Matins Noct. 1, Ant. 2]

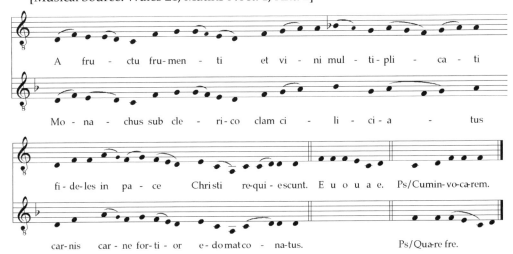

16. Communione calicis/Ps Conserva me

[Text Source: Cf. Ps 15 (Latin), 16 (Hebrew): 5, 4]

[The Lord has assembled us by the communion of the chalice in which God himself is consumed, not by the blood of calves.]

Contra Crescente etate de sco Bernardo

[With increasing age, he was growing both in wisdom and grace, gleaming in all miracles.]

[Musical Source: Chigi 351r, Sext Ant.; Pat 119r, Lauds Ant. 3 for St. Rubberto (Vat. Lib. RG Lit. VI–133, fol. 444 Lauds Ant. 2—text only)]

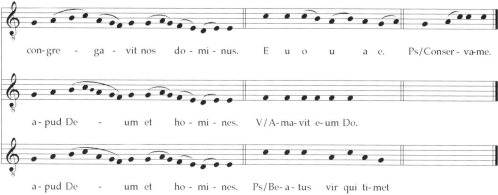

17. Versiculus

[Text Source: Ps 77 (Latin), 78 (Hebrew): 24–25]

Panem celi dedit eis, alleluia. R. Panem angelorum manducavit homo, alleluia.

[He gave them the bread of heaven, alleluia. R. Mankind ate the bread of the angels, alleluia.]

18. Lectio Prima

Immensa divine largitatis beneficia, exhibita populo christiano inextimabilem ei conferunt dignitatem. Neque enim est aut fuit aliquando tam grandis nacio que habeat deos appropinquantes sibi, sicut adest nobis deus noster. Unigenitus siquidem dei filius sue divinitatis volens nos esse participes, naturam nostram assumpsit, ut homines deos faceret factus homo. Et hoc insuper quod de nostro assumpsit totum nobis contulit ad salutem. Corpus namque suum pro nostra reconciliacione in ara crucis hostiam optulit deo patri, sanguinem suum fudit in precium simul et lavachrum, ut redempti a miserabili servitute a peccatis omnibus mundaremur. Et ut tanti beneficii iugis in nobis maneret memoria, corpus suum in cibum et sanguinem suum in potum sub specie panis et vini sumendum fidelibus dereliquit. O preciosum et admirandum convivium salutiferum et omni suavitate repletum. Quid enim hoc convivio preciosius esse potest, in quo non carnes vitulorum et hyrcorum ut olim in lege, sed nobis Christus sumendus proponitur verus deus? Quid hoc sacramento mirabilius? In ipso namque panis et vinum in corpus Christi et sanguinem substancialiter convertuntur. Ideoque Christus deus et homo perfectus sub modici panis specie continetur.

[The boundless favors of divine generosity, shown to the Christian people, bestow an inestimable dignity on them. There neither is nor ever was so great a nation having gods so near to itself as our God is to us. The only-begotten Son of God, desiring that we be participants in his divinity, took on our nature, so that, having become man, he might make men gods. Whatever he assumed of our nature he made instrumental in the work of our salvation. He offered to God the Father his own body as sacrifice for our reconciliation on the altar of the cross, shed his own blood for our ransom and rebirth, so that, having been redeemed from wretched servitude, we might be washed clean of all sins. And, so that a memory of such great kindnesses might remain always in us, he left behind his body as food and his blood as drink, to be consumed by the faithful in the form of bread and wine. O most precious and wondrous banquet, full of health and filled with every delicacy! What can be more precious than this banquet, in which not the flesh of goats and calves, as once was the rule, but Christ the true God, is given to us as nourishment? What is more wondrous than this sacrament? For in it, bread and wine are changed substantially into the body and blood of Christ. Indeed Christ, the perfect God and man, is contained under the appearance of a little bread.]

19. Responsory: Immolabit hedum/Pascha nostrum
[Text Sources: R. Ex 12: 6, 8; V. 1 Cor 5: 7–8]
[R. The multitude of the sons of Israel shall kill the lamb on the Passover evening, and they shall eat meat and unleavened bread. V. Christ our Paschal lamb has been sacrificed. Therefore let us feast on the unleavened bread of sincerity and truth.]

Contra Te sanctum Dominum de Angelis, CAO 7757[107]

[R. All the angels praise you holy Lord in the highest, saying: To you be praise and honor Lord. V. The Cherubim and the holy Seraphim and all of the heavenly host proclaim, saying.]

[Musical Source: WA 382, Matins Noct. 2, Resp. 8; see also Wales, 275v (All Saints) Matins Noct. 1, Resp. 1; Wales, 269 (St. Michael) Matins Noct. 3, Resp. 9; Ut 179 (St. Michael) 1 Vesp. Resp.]

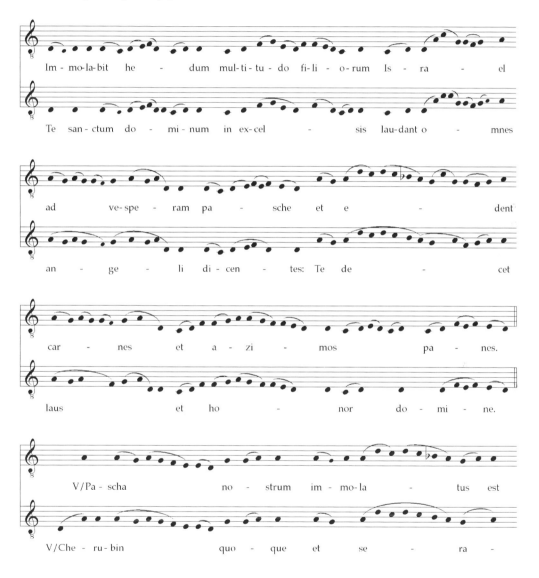

---

[107] In Hesbert, this responsory is used for St. Michael and All Saints.

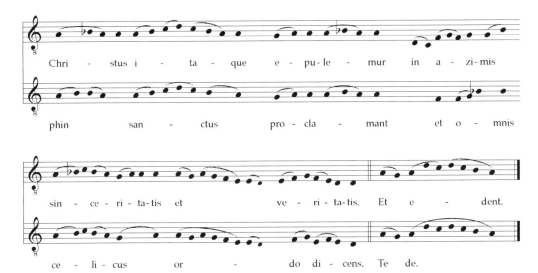

Chri - stus i - ta - que e - pu - le - mur in a - zi- mis

phin san - ctus pro - cla - mant et o - mnis

sin - ce - ri - ta-tis et ve - ri - ta- tis. Et e - dent.

ce - li - cus or - do di - cens. Te de.

20. Lectio ii

Manducatur utique a fidelibus, sed minime laceratur, quinimmo diviso sacramento integer sub qualibet divisionis particula perseverat. Accidencia eciam sine subiecto in eodem existunt, ut fides locum hebeat dum visibile invisibiliter sumitur, aliena specie occultatum, et sensus a deceptione immunes reddantur qui de accidentibus iudicant sibi notis. Nullum eciam sacramentum est isto salubrius quo purgantur peccata, virtutes augentur, et mens omnium spritualium carismatum habundancia impinguatur. Offertur in ecclesia pro vivis et mortuis, ut omnibus prosit quod est pro salute omnium institutum. Suavitatem denique huiusmodi sacramenti nullus exprimere sufficit, per quod spiritualis dulcedo in suo fonte gustatur, et recolitur memoria illius quam in sua passione Christus monstravit excellentissime caritatis. Unde ut arcius huiusmodi caritatis immensitas cordibus infigeretur fidelium in ultima cena quando pascha cum discipulis celebrato, transiturus erat ex hoc mundo ad patrem, hoc sacramentum instituit tanquam passionis sue memoriale perhenne, figurarum veterum impletivum, miraculorum ab ipso factorum maximum. Et de sua contristatis absentia solacium singulare.

[He is consumed entirely by the faithful, but he is in no way broken up, but rather, even though the sacramental sign is divided, he remains entire in each particle of division. For the accidents exist in it without material form in order that faith may have its place, when the visible is invisibly consumed, hidden in the form of another thing, and our senses, which judge events that happen to them, are restored safely from deception. For no sacrament is more salubrious than this, through which sins are purged, virtues are increased, and the soul is filled with an abundance of every spiritual gift. It is offered in the Church for the living and the dead, so that what was instituted for the salvation of all may benefit all. No one suffices to express the delicacy of this kind of sacrament, through which spiritual sweetness is tasted in its source, and the memory of the most excellent charity, which Christ showed in his passion, is recalled. Whereby, so that the immensity of this kind of charity might be impressed more profoundly on the hearts of the faithful, at the last supper, when, having celebrated the passover with his disciples, he was about to leave this world and return to the father, he instituted this sacrament as an eternal remembrance of his passion, the fulfillment of ancient precursors, the greatest of the miracles performed by him, and sole solace to those saddened by his absence.]

21. Responsory: Comedetis carnes/Non moÿses
[Text Source: R. Cf. Ex 16: 12, 15; V. Jo 6: 32]
[R. You will eat meats, and you will be satiated with breads. This is the bread the Lord has given to you to be eaten. V. Moses did not give you bread from heaven but my father gives you true bread from heaven.]

Contra Stirps Iesse de sca Maria, CAO 7709
[The root of Jesse put forth a shoot and the shoot a flower. And over this flower rested a nourishing spirit. V. The virgin mother of God is the shoot, the flower her son.]

[Musical Source: WA 303r, Noct. 3 Resp. 10; see also Wales 250r, 1 Vesp. Resp. (also Matins Noct. 1, Resp. 3)]

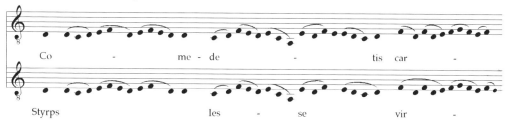

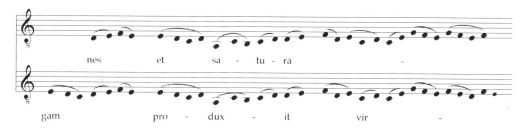

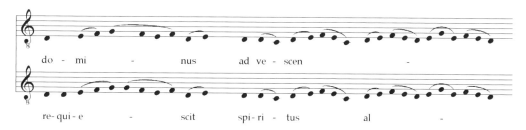

dum.

mus.

V/Non Mo — y‑ses de ‑ dit vo ‑ bis pa ‑ nem de ce ‑ lo

V/Vir ‑ go De ‑ i ge‑ni ‑ trix vir ‑ ga est

sed pa ‑ ter me‑us dat vo ‑ bis pa ‑ nem de ce ‑ lo

flos fi ‑ li ‑ us e ‑

ve ‑ rum. I ‑ ste.

ius. Et su‑per.

22. Lectio iii

Convenit itaque devotioni fidelium sollempniter recolere institutionem tam salu‑
tiferi tamquam mirabilis sacramenti, ut ineffabilem modum divine presencie in sac‑
ramento visibili veneremur, et laudetur dei potencia que in sacramento eodem tot
mirabilia operatur, nec non et de tam salubri tamquam suavi beneficio exsolvantur
deo gratiarum debite actiones. Verum et si in die cene quando sacramentum predic‑
tum noscitur institutum inter missarum sollempnia de institutione ipsius specialis
mentio habeatur, totum tamen residuum eiusdem diei officium ad Christi pas‑
sionem pertinet, circa cuius venerationem ecclesia illo tempore occupatur. Unde ut
integro celebritatis officio institutionem tanti sacramenti sollempniter recoleret
plebs fidelis, romanus pontifex Urbanus quartus huius sacramenti devotione affec‑
tus, pie statuit prefate institutionis memoriam prima feria quinta post octabas pen‑
thecostes a cunctis fidelibus celebrari, ut qui per totum anni circulum hoc sacramen‑
tuo utimur ad salutem, eius institutionem illo specialiter tempore recolamus, quo

spiritus sanctus discipulorum corda edocuit ad plene cognoscenda huius misteria sacramenti. Nam et in eodem tempore cepit hoc sacramentum a fidelibus frequentari. Legitur enim in actibus apostolorum quod erant perseverantes in doctrina apostolorum et communicatione fractionis panis et orationibus, statim post sancti spiritus missionem. Ut autem predicta quinta feria et per octavas sequentes eiusdem salutaris institutionis honorificencius agatur memoria et sollempnitas de hoc celebrior habeatur loco distributionem materialium que in ecclesiis cathedralibus largiuntur existentibus canonicis horis nocturnis pariterque diurnis prefatus romanus pontifex eis qui huiusmodi horis in hac sollemnitate personaliter in ecclesiis interessent stipendia spiritualia apostolica largitione concessit quatinus per hec fideles ad tanti festi celibritatem avidius et copiosius convenirent. Unde omnibus vere penitentibus et confessis qui matutinali officio huius festi presencialiter in ecclesia ubi celebraretur adessent centum. Qui vero misse totidem. Illis autem qui interessent in primis ipsius festi vesperis similiter centum. Qui vero in secundis totidem. Eis quoque qui prime tercie sexte none ac completorii adessent officiis pro qualibet horarum ipsarum quadraginta. Illis vero qui per ipsius festi octavas in matutinalibus vespertinis misse ac predictarum horarum officiis presentes existerent singulis diebus octavarum ipsarum, centum dierum indulgenciam misericorditer tribuit perpetuis temporibus duraturam.

[It is fitting therefore for the devotion of the faithful, solemnly to honor again the institution of such a salubrious and miraculous sacrament, so that we may venerate the ineffable mode of the divine presence in a visible sacrament, and so that the power of God may be praised, which, in the same sacrament, works so many miracles, and indeed so that the thanks owed to God for such a salubrious and sweet kindness may be discharged. But, although on the day of the last supper, when the aforesaid sacrament is known to have been instituted, special mention is made of its institution within the solemnities of the mass, nevertheless all the remaining worship of this same day is concerned with Christ's suffering, around whose veneration the church at that time is occupied. Hence, so that the faithful may solemnly honor again the institution of such a great sacrament by a complete office of celebration, the Roman Pope Urban IV, influenced by the devotion of this sacrament, piously decreed commemoration of the aforementioned institution on feria five after the octave of Pentecost, to be celebrated by all the faithful, so that we, who use this sacrament throughout the year for salvation, may honor again, at that time especially, its institution, by which the Holy Spirit taught the hearts of the disciples to understand fully the mysteries of this sacrament. For at the same time this sacrament began to be frequented by the faithful. It is indeed read in the Acts of the Apostles that they were persevering in the apostolic doctrine by sharing in the breaking of bread, and by prayers, immediately after the departure of the Holy Spirit. So that, on the the aforesaid feria five and the following octave, remembrance of this same saving institution may be performed more honorably and its ceremony have greater participation, in place of the distributions of material goods that are bestowed in cathedral churches, during current established times, night as well as day, the aforesaid Roman pope grants to those who, during its times, personally take part in this ceremony at church spiritual stipends through apostolic generosity, so that by them the faithful more eagerly and more numerously may come together for the celebration of so great a feast. Hence, to all the truly penitent and to those having confessed, who are present at the office of matins of this feast in person in the church where it is celebrated, one hundred [days' indulgence]. To those who attend mass, the same number. To those who take part in first vespers of the feast, similarly one hundred. The same number to those in second vespers. To those who attend the offices of prime, terce, sext, none, and compline, forty for any of those hours. To those who personally appear through the octave of this feast at matins, vespers, mass, and the aforesaid office hours, for each of the days of the octave he mercifully allots one hundred days in perpetuity.]

23. Responsory: Respexit Helyas/Si quis manducaverit/Gloria patri
[Text Source: R. 1 Reg 19: 6–8; V. Jo 6: 53–58]
[R. Elias saw a hearth bread by his head and arising he ate and drank. And he walked in the strength of this food up to the mountain of God. V. If anyone eats this bread, he will live forever.]

Contra Videte miraculum matris Domini/Hec speciosum, CAO 7869[108]
Videte miraculum matris Domini: concepit virgo, virilis ignara consorcii. Stans honerata nobili onere Maria, et matrem se letam cognoscet que se nescit uxorem. V. Hec speciosum forma pre filiis hominum castis concepit visceribus et benedicta in eternum Deum nobis protulit et hominem.
[Behold the miracle of the mother of the Lord: a virgin conceived without a male consort. Mary, remaining honored for her noble burden, will realize that she is blessed, a blessed mother who has no knowledge of being a wife. V. She conceived in her chaste womb one outstanding in form above all the sons of men, and, blessed forever, gave us God and man.]

[Musical Sources: Wales 197v, 1 Vesp. Resp. for Purification of Mary; WA 268, 1 Vesp. Resp. for Purification of Mary]

---

[108] Hesbert lists two verses for this responsory: *Casta parentis* and *Virgo concepit.*

Re- spe- xit   He- ly   -   as   ad ca   -   pud   su   -   um

Vi- de   -   te   mi- ra   -   cu- lum   ma - tris   do- mi   -   ni

sub- ci   -   ne- ri- ci   -   um   pa- nem   qui   sur- gens   co   -   me   -   dit

con   -   ce- pit   vir   -   go   vi - ri   -   lis   i - gna   -   ra

et   bi   -   bit.   Et   am- bu- la   -   vit

con   -   sor- ci   -   i.   Stans   ho- ne- ra   -   ta

in   for   -   ti   -   tu - di- ne   ci   -   bi   il - li   -   us

no - bi   -   li   o - ne- re   Ma- ri   -   a   et   ma   -   trem

us - que ad mon - tem

se le - tam co - gno - scet que se-ne - scit ux -

- de - i.   V/Si   quis

o - rem.   V/Hec   spe- ci - o- sum

man - du - ca - ve - rit ex hoc pa- ne

for - ma pre-fi - li- is   ho - mi - num ca-stis con - ce- pit vi - sce-ri - bus

vi -

et be - ne - di - cta in e - ter- num de - um no- bis pro- tu - lit et

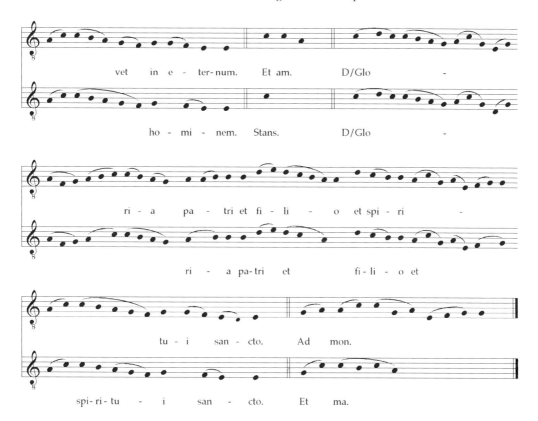

In secundo nocturno

Antiphona

24. Memor sit Dominus/Ps Exaudiat te Dominus

[Text Source: Cf. Ps 19: 4 (Latin), 20: 4 (Hebrew)]

[May the Lord remember our sacrifices and may he make our burnt offering rich.]

Contra In celis gaudent virgines et cantant canticum

[In the heavens virgins praise and they sing a new song before the throne of God, because the Lord has made known his salvation.]

[Musical Source: WA 432, Common of virgins, Noct. 2, Resp. 11]

25. Paratur nobis/Ps Dominus regit me
    [Text Source: Cf. Ps 22: 5 (Latin), 23: 5 (Hebrew)]
    [The table of the Lord is prepared for us against those who oppress us.]

    Contra Sanguis sanctorum martyrum pro Christo effusus est in terra, CAO 4809
    [The blood of the holy martyrs has been poured out on the earth for Christ; there-
    fore they have obtained eternal rewards.]

    [Musical Sources: WA 421r, Common of Martyrs, Noct. 2, Ant. 11; see also Ut 178v,
    Common of Martyrs]

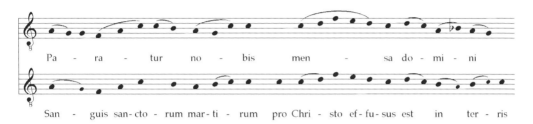

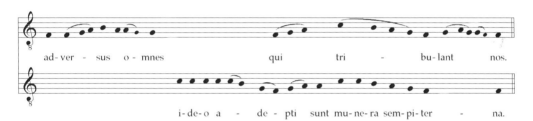

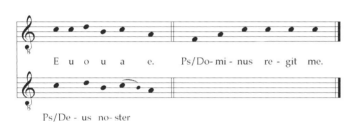

26. In voce exultationis/Ps Quemadmodum
   [Text Source: Cf. Ps 41 (Latin), 42 (Hebrew): 5]
   [May the banqueters resound in a voice of exultation at the table of the Lord.]

   Contra O quam gloriosum est regnum de Omnibus Sanctis, CAO 4063
   [O how glorious is the kingdom in which, with Christ, all the faithful rejoice; dressed in white garments they follow the lamb wherever he goes.]

   [Musical Source: Wales 274, All Saints, 1 Vesp., Ant. 2 transp. up a fifth; WA 45, Holy Innocents, Ant. at Canticles]

27. Versiculus
   [Text Source: Ps 80 (Latin), 81 (Hebrew): 17]
   Cibavit illos ex adype frumenti, alleluia. R. Et de petra melle saturavit eos, alleluia.

   [He fed them from the finest grain, alleluia. R. And he filled them with honey from a rock, alleluia.]

28. Lectio iv

[Gratian, De consecratione, *Dist. II, can. 69 beginning]*[109]

Huius sacramenti figura precessit, quando manna pluit Deus patribus in deserto, qui cotidiano celi pascebantur alimento. Unde dictum est: Panem angelorum manducavit homo. Set tamen panem illum qui manducaverunt, omnes in deserto mortui sunt. Ista autem esca quam accipitis, iste panis vivus qui de celo descendit, vite eterne substanciam ministrat. Et quicumque hunc panem manducaverit non morietur in eternum, quia corpus Christi est. Considera utrum nunc prestancior sit panis angelorum an caro Christi, que utique est corpus vite. Manna illud de celo, hoc super celum. Illud celi, hoc domini celorum. Illud corrupcioni obnoxium si in diem alterum servaretur, hoc alienum ab omni corrupcione. Quicumque religiose gustaverit, corruptionem sentire non poterit. Illis aqua de petra fluxit, tibi sanguis ex Christo. Illos ad horam satiavit aqua, te sanguis diluit in eternum. Iudeus bibit et sitit, tu cum biberis sitire non poteris. Et illud in umbra, hoc in veritate. Si illud quod miraris umbra est, quantum istud est cuius umbram miraris? Audi quia umbra est, que apud patres facta est. Bibebant inquit de spirituali consequenti eos petra. Petra autem erat Christus. Set non in pluribus eorum complacitum est deo. Nam prostrati sunt in deserto. Hec autem facta sunt in figura nostri. Cognovisti pociora. Pocior est enim lux quam umbra, veritas quam figura, corpus auctoris quam manna de celo.

[A precursor of this sacrament occurred earlier, when God rained manna on the fathers in the desert, who daily ate the food of heaven. Wherefore it is said: Man ate the bread of the angels. But yet those who ate that bread all died in the desert. However, this bread which you take, this living bread which descended from heaven, provides the substance of eternal life. And whoever shall eat this bread, will not die forever, because it is the body of Christ. Consider which now is more precious, the bread of angels, or Christ's flesh, which is wholly the body of life. That manna is from heaven, this above heaven. That is of heaven, this, of the Lord of heavens. That, subject to corruption, if kept for another day, this free from all corruption. Whoever religiously eats, will not experience corruption. To them water flowed from the rock, to you the blood [flows] from Christ. The water satisfied them for a time, the blood cleanses you for eternity. The Jews drank and thirsted, you, when you drink, cannot thirst. That [happened] in a shadow, this in truth. If that at which you marvel is a shadow, how much more is this whose shadow you admire. Hear why this is a shadow, which was done in the time of the forefathers. They drank, he said, from the spiritual rock which followed them. The rock, however, was Christ. But God was not well pleased with many of them. Thus they were cast down in the desert. This was done as a symbol to us. You know which is better. Light is better that shadow, truth better than a symbol, the body of the creator better than manna from heaven.]

---

[109] Based on Ambrosius, *De mysteriis*, Ch. VIII, n. 47 et seq. (PL 16, cols. 404 ff.)

29. Responsory: Panis quem ego dabo/Locutus est populus
[Text Source: Jo 6: 51–53; V. Cf. Nm 21: 5]
[R. The bread which I give is my flesh for the life of the world. The Jews disputed saying: How can this man give us his own flesh as food? V. The people spoke against the Lord: Our spirit is sickened by this most trifling food.]

Contra Deus qui sedes super thronos [*sic* for *thronum*] et iudicas de Quadam Dominica, CAO 6433
[R. O God, you who sits on the throne and judges equity, be the refuge of the poor in their tribulation, because you alone consider their toil and sorrow. V. The abandoned pauper is yours; you will be the aid to the orphan.]

[Musical Source: Wales 41v, Sundays throughout the year, Matins, Noct. 1, Resp. 2; see also WA 60, 1st Sun. after Epiphany, Matins, Noct. 1, Resp. 2]

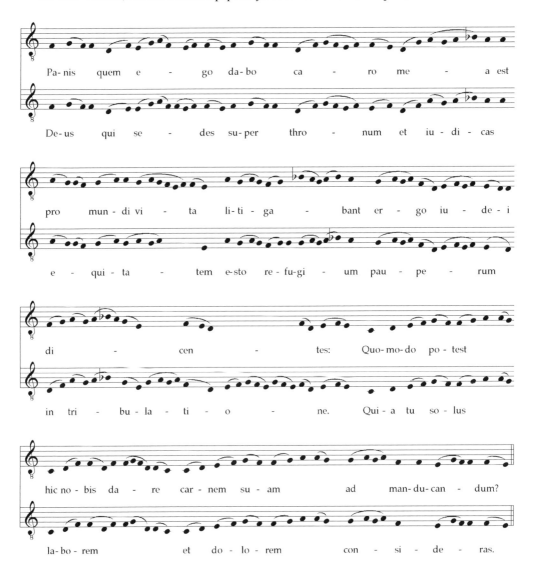

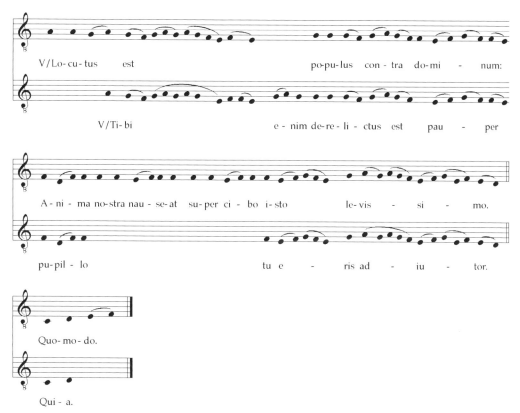

V/Lo-cu-tus   est   po-pu-lus con - tra do-mi - num:

V/Ti- bi   e - nim de-re - li - ctus est   pau - per

A - ni - ma no-stra nau - se- at su-per ci - bo i-sto   le-vis - si - mo.

pu-pil - lo   tu e - ris ad - iu - tor.

Quo- mo- do.

Qui - a.

30. Lectio v

[Gratian, De consecratione, *Dist. II, can. 69 continued]*

Forte dicis. Aliud video. Quomodo tu mihi asseris quod corpus Christi accipiam? Et hoc nobis super est ut probemus. Quantis igitur utimur exemplis, ut probemus hoc non esse, quod natura formavit, sed quod benedictio consecravit, maioremque vim esse benedictionis quam nature, quia benedictione etiam natura ipsa mutatur? Unde virgam tenebat Moyses, proiecit eam et facta est serpens. Rursus apprehendit caudam serpentis et in virge naturam revertitur. Vides ergo prophetica gratia bis mutatam naturam esse, et serpentis et virge. Currebant Egypti flumina puro meatu aquarum, subito de fontium venis sanguis cepit erumpere, non erat potus in fluviis. Rursus ad prophete preces cruor fluminum cessavit, aquarum natura remeavit. Circumclusus undique erat populus Hebreorum, hinc Egyptiis vallatus, inde mari conclusus. Virgam levavit Moyses, separavit se aqua et in murorum speciem se congelavit, atque inter undas via pedestris apparuit. Iordanis retrorsum conversus contra naturam in sui fontis revertitur exordium. Nonne claret naturam, vel maritimorum fluctuum, vel cursus fluvialis esse mutatam? Siciebat populus patrum, tetigit Moyses petram, et aqua de petra fluxit. Numquid non preter naturam operata est gratia ut aquam vomeret petra quam non habebat natura?

[Perhaps you say: I see something different. How can you claim to me that I am receiving the body of Christ? And this is what we must show. How many examples, therefore, do we use, to show that this is not what nature has formed, but what blessing has consecrated, and that there is greater power in blessing than in nature, because by blessing even nature itself can be changed. Hence, Moses held a rod, threw it, and it became a serpent. Again, he grasped the serpent's tail, and it reverted into its nature as a rod. You see therefore, by prophetic will, its nature is twice changed, both of a serpent and a rod. The rivers of Egypt flowed with a pure course of waters, suddenly from the source of the waters blood began to burst forth, there was no drinkable water in the rivers. Conversely, at the prayers of the prophet, the blood of the rivers ceased, the nature of waters returned. The Hebrew nation was surrounded on all sides, on one side blocked by the Egyptians, on the other side cut off by the sea. Moses raised a rod, the water parted and solidified itself into a kind of wall, and between the waves a foot path appeared. The Jordan reversed course, and it returned, against nature, to the beginning of its source. Is it not clear that the nature of the ocean's waves or of the river's course was changed? The people of the forefathers thirsted, Moses touched the rock, and water flowed from the rock. Has not grace acted contrary to nature, so that a rock might spew forth water, which it did not have by nature?]

31. Responsory: Cenantibus illis/Dixerunt viri

[Text Source: Mt 26: 26; V. Cf. Job 31: 31]

[While they were eating, Jesus took bread and blessed and broke it, and gave it to his disciples and said: Take and eat. This is my body. V. The men of my tent said: Who will give of his flesh that we may be satisfied?]

Contra Qui cum audissent de sco. Nicholao, CAO 7474, Jones 29

[For Nicholas: R. When they heard the name of St. Nicholas, they immediately stretched their hands to heaven, praising the mercy of the Saviour. V. In a clear voice in the presence of the men, they were calling him the worthy follower of God.]

[For James: R. When they heard him invoking God, they immediately laid evil hands on him, not believing in the mercy of Christ born. V. In a clear voice in the presence of the soldiers, he was declaring Christ to be the Son of God.]

[Musical Sources: AS 357 Matins, Noct. 2, Resp. 5; ODO 63 Matins, Noct. 2, Resp. 5 (Qui cum audissent illum)]

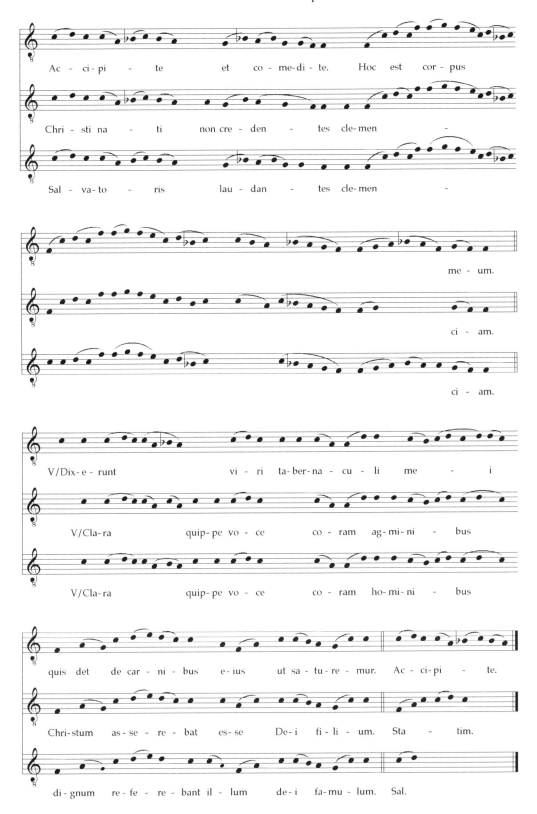

32. Lectio vi

[Gratian, De consecratione, *Dist. II, can. 69 continued]*

Marath fluvius amarissimus erat, ut siciens populus bibere non posset. Moyses misit lignum in aquam, et amaritudinem suam aquarum natura deposuit, quam infusa subito gratia temperavit. Sub Helyseo propheta uni ex filiis prophetarum excussum est ferrum de securi, et statim immersum est. Rogavit Helyseum, qui amiserat ferrum. Misit etiam Heliseus lignum in aquam, et ferrum natavit. Utique etiam hoc preter naturam factum cognovimus. Gravior est enim ferri species, quam aquarum liquor. Advertimus enim maiorem esse gratiam quam naturam, et adhuc tamen prophetice benedictionis numeramus gratiam. Quod si tantum valuit humana benedictio ut naturam converteret, quid dicimus de ipsa consecratione divina, ubi ipsa verba domini salvatoris operantur? Nam sacramentum istud quod accipis Christi sermone conficitur. Quod si tantum valuit sermo Helye, ut ignem de celo deponeret, non valebit Christi sermo, ut species mutet elementorum?

[The Marath River was very bitter, so that the thirsting people were not able to drink. Moses threw a branch into the water, and nature eliminated the bitterness of its waters, which grace, suddenly intermixed, tempered. During the time of Elias the prophet, the blade fell off the battle ax of one of the sons of the prophets and immediately sank. He who had let the iron slip sought out Elias. Elias put a stick into the water, and the blade floated. Certainly we know that this is an act beyond nature. The species of iron is heavier than the liquid of water. We perceive therefore that grace is greater than nature, but yet we still reckon grace to be of prophetic blessing. But if a human blessing has such great strength that it can change nature, what can we say of that divine consecration, in which the words themselves of the Savior act? For this sacrament you receive is accomplished by the words of Christ. If the word of Elias had such great strength that it could bring down fire from heaven, will not the word of Christ have the power to change the species of the elements?]

33. Responsory: Accepit Ihesus/Memoria memor/Gloria patri
[Text Source: Luke 22: 20, 19; V. Lamentations 3: 20]
[After he had eaten, Jesus took the cup, saying: This cup is a new testament in my blood. Do this in my memory. V. I shall recall this memory, and my soul will be sorrowful within me.]

Contra Virtute multa de sco Bernardo
[Gifted with great virtue and knowledge, the holy man of God approached the dignity of the saints with the fruit of his works, bringing forth words of heavenly wisdom. V. From boyhood he sought the author of life, and gave his spirit to eloquent speeches of God.]

[Musical Source: Chigi 348v]

Ac - ce - pit Ihe - sus ca - li - cem post - quam ce - na - vit

Vir - tu - te mul - ta et sci - en - ti - a pre -

di - cens: Hic ca - lix no - vum te - sta - men - tum est

di - tus san - ctus De - i pro - xi - ma - bat di-gni-ta - ti

in me - o san - gui - ne. Hoc fa - ci - te

san - cto - rum cum fru - ctu o - pe - rum

in me - am com-mem - mo - ra - ci - o -

pro-fe - rens ce - le - stis sa-pi - en - ti - e ver -

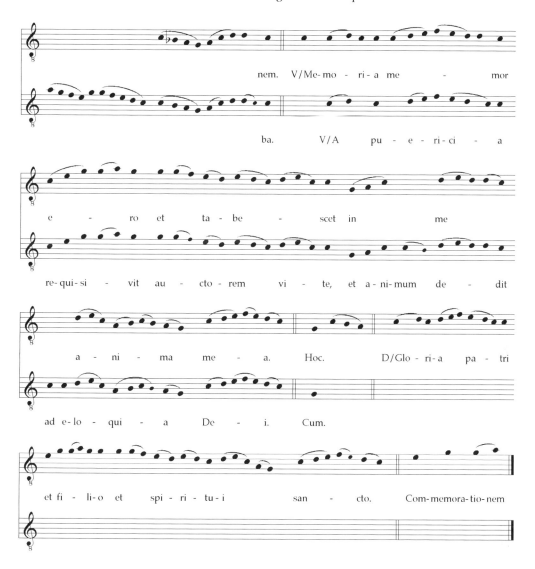

In tertio Nocturno

Antiphona

34. Introibo ad altare Dei/Ps Iudica me Deus

[I go will into the altar of God, I will take on Christ who renews my youth.]

[Text Source: Cf. Ps 42 (Latin), 43 (Hebrew): 4]

Contra Ascendo ad Patrem meum de Ascencione, CAO 1493

[I ascend to my father and your father, to my God and your God.]

[Musical Source: Wales 117; see also WA 150]

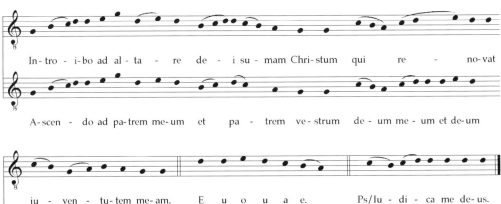

In-tro-i-bo ad al-ta - re de - i su - mam Chri-stum qui re - no-vat

A-scen - do ad pa-trem me-um et pa - trem ve-strum de - um me - um et de-um

iu - ven - tu-tem me-am.   E   u   o   u   a   e.   Ps/Iu - di - ca me de-us.

ve - strum   al - le - lu - ya.   Ps/Be ne - di-ctus.

35. Cibavit nos Dominus/Ps Exultate Deo adiutori

[The Lord has fed us from the finest grain, and he has filled us with honey from a rock.]

[Text Source: Cf. Ps 80 (Latin), 81 (Hebrew): 17 (15 in LU 936)]

Contra O per omnia laudabilem virum de sco Nicholao, CAO 4052, Jones 38

[For Nicholas: O man praiseworthy for everything, through whose merits they are freed from every disaster who seek him with all their heart.]

For James: [O father, merciful through all things, aid us your servants when you, dutiful aide, come to judge the world.]

[Musical Sources: AS 361, Lauds Ant. 5; ODO 83v (O per omnia misericors), Lauds Ant. 5]

36. Ex altari tuo Domine/Ps Quam dilecta

  [From your altar, Lord, we receive Christ, in whom our soul and body rejoice.]
  [Text Source: Cf. Ps 83 (Latin), 84 (Hebrew): 3–4]

  Contra Gloriam mundi sprevit de sco Nicholao, CAO 2949, Jones 20
  [For Nicholas: He rejected the glory of the world with its delights, and he merited to
  be raised to the highest level of priesthood.]
  [For James: James, the blessed man of God, was preaching the glory of God by word
  and deed, affirming the true God to be in heaven.]

  [Musical Sources: AS 357 Matins Noct. 2 Ant. 5; ODO 60 (Gloriam Dei)]

37. Versiculus

[Text Source: Ps 103 (Latin), 104 (Hebrew): 14–15]

Educas panem de terra, alleluia. R. Et vinum letificet cor hominis, alleluia.

[May you produce bread from the earth, alleluia. R. And let wine gladden the heart of man, alleluia.]

38. [Gospel] secundum Iohanne [Jo 6: 55].

In illo tempore. Dixit Ihesus discipulis suis, et turbis Iudeorum: Caro mea vere est cibus et sanguis meus vere est potus. Et. rel.

[At that time. Jesus said to his disciples and to the multitude of the Jews: My flesh truly is food, and my blood is truly drink. And so forth.]

Omelia beati Augustini episcopi de eadem lectione. Lectio vii

[*Alcuin,* Commentaria in S. Joannis evangelium, *Lib. 3: Ch. XV, Vers. 56]*[110]

[Vers. 56] Cum enim cibo et potu id appetant homines ut non esuriant necque siciant, hoc vere non prestat nisi iste cibus et potus, qui eos a quibus sumitur immortales et incorruptibiles facit, id est societas ipsorum sanctorum ubi pax erit et unitas plena atque perfecta. Propterea quippe sicut etiam ante nos hoc intellexerunt homines dei, dominus noster Ihesus Christus corpus et sanguinem suum in eis rebus comendavit, que ad unum aliquid rediguntur. Ex multis namque granis unus panis conficitur, et ex multis racemis vinum confluit.

[Although men desire from food and drink, that they neither hunger nor thirst, this is not assured, unless it is that food and drink which makes those, by whom it is consumed, immortal and incorruptible, that is, a community of the saints themselves, where there will be peace and full and perfect unity. Therefore, indeed, as men of God understood before us, our Lord Jesus Christ put his body and blood into these things, which are made into some one thing. Now, one bread is made from many grains, and wine flows together from many clusters of grapes.]

---

[110] PL 100, col. 835. The verse numbers in PL do not agree with current ones. From verse 52 on, the PL numbers are one too high. This is because PL divides verse 52 into two parts, each with its own number.

39. Responsory: Qui manducat/Non est alia

[He who eats my flesh and drinks my blood remains in me and I in him. V. There is not another nation so great who has gods so near to itself as our God is to us.]
[Text Source: R. Jo 6: 57; V. Dt 4: 7]

Contra Felix vitis de sco Dominico AH XXV, 240

[Fruitful vine, from whose branch such a shoot overflows for our age, passing on to the people the wine of heaven in the cup of life. V. From the abundance of the vines he has now encircled the circumference of the world.]

[Musical Source: 10770 172v, Matins Noct. 3, Resp. 7]

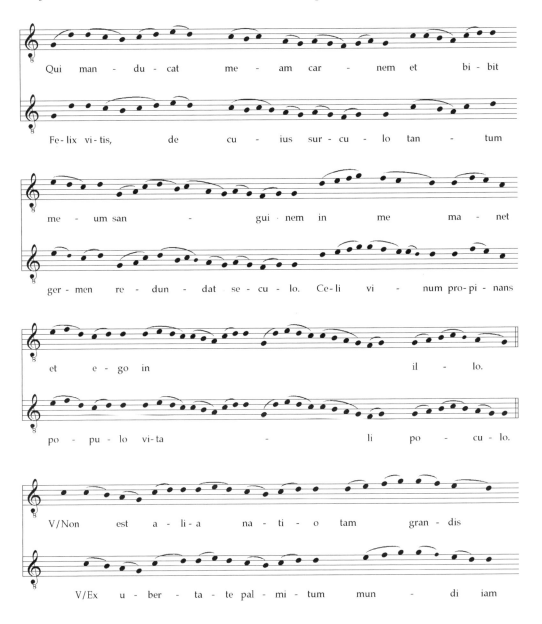

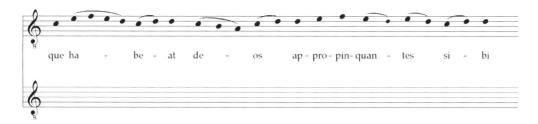

que ha - be - at de - os ap - pro - pin- quan - tes si - bi

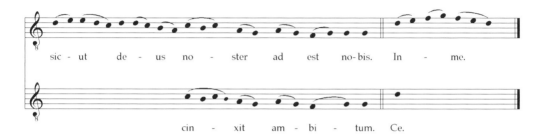

sic - ut de - us no - ster ad est no- bis. In - me.

cin - xit am - bi - tum. Ce.

40. Lectio viii

[*Alcuin,* Commentaria in S. Joannis evangelium, *Lib. 3: Ch. XV, Vers. 56–57*][111]

Denique iam exponit quomodo id fiat quod loquitur et quid sit manducare corpus eius et sanguinem bibere.

[Vers. 57] Et qui manducat meam carnem et bibit meum sanguinem in me manet et ego in eo. Hoc est ergo manducare illam escam et illum bibere potum, in Christo manere, et illum manentem in se habere, ac per hoc qui non manet in Christo, et in quo non manet Christus, proculdubio non manducat spiritualiter eius carnem licet carnaliter et visibiliter premat dentibus sacramenta corporis et sanguinis Christi, sed magis tante rei sacramentum ad iudicium sibi manducat et bibit, qui immundus presumpsit ad Christi accedere sacramenta, que alius non digne sumit nisi qui mundus est. De quibus dicitur: Beati mundo corde quoniam ipsi Deum videbunt.

[Finally he now explains how what he has spoken happens, and what it is to eat his body and drink his blood. "He who eats my body and drinks my blood abides in me and I in him." To eat that food and to drink that drink is, therefore, to abide in Christ, and to have him abiding in oneself, and thus the person who does not abide in Christ, and in whom Christ does not abide, without doubt does not eat spiritually his flesh, although physically and visibly he chews with his teeth the sacraments of the body and blood of Christ, but rather he eats and drinks the sacrament of such great importance to his own condemnation, who, impure, presumes to approach the sacraments of Christ, which no one rightly takes except the one who is pure. About whom it is said: Blessed are the pure of heart, because they shall see God.]

---

[111] PL 100, cols. 835–36.

41. Responsory: Misit me pater/Cibavit eum
   [Text Source: R. Jo 6: 58; V. Cf. Sir 15: 3]
   [The living Father sent me and I live because of the Father. And he who eats me lives because of me. V. The Lord fed him with the bread of life and understanding.]

   Contra Verbum caro factum est de Circumcisione, CAO 7840
   [The Word was made flesh and dwelt among us, whose glory we saw as the Only-Begotten of the Father, full of grace and truth. V. In the beginning was the Word and the Word was with God and the Word was God.]

   [Musical Source: Wales 3, Nativity, Noct. 2, Resp. 6; see also WA 30, Nativity, Noct. 3, Resp. 11 (and indicated on 50 for Circumcision)]

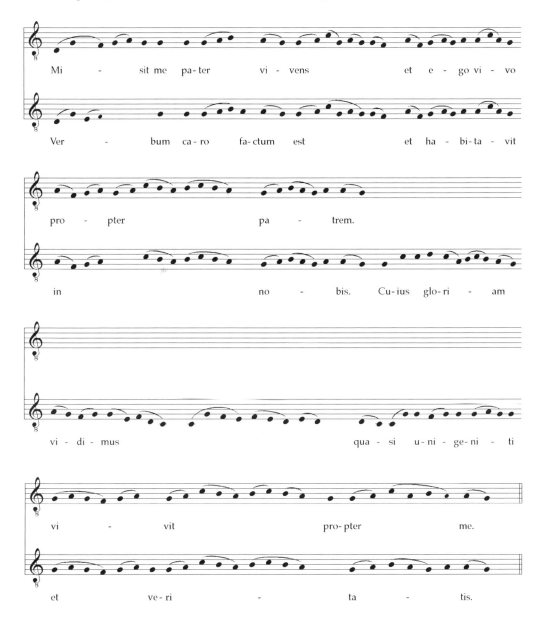

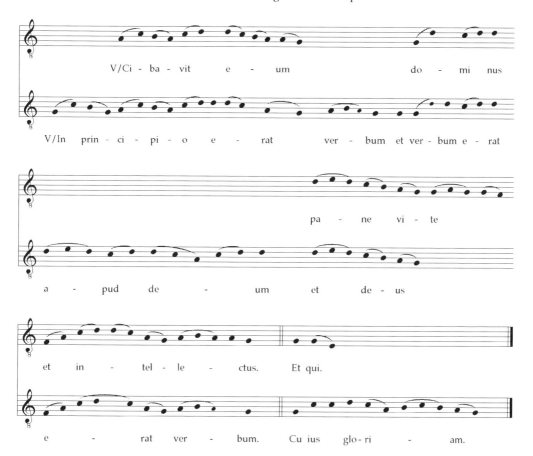

42. Lectio nona

[*Alcuin,* Commentaria in S. Joannis evangelium, *Lib. 3: Ch. XV, Vers. 58*][112]

[Vers. 58] Sicut me misit inquit vivens pater, et ego vivo propter patrem. Et qui manducat me, et ipse vivet propter me. Non enim filius participatione patris fit melior qui est natus equalis sicut participatione filii per unitatem corporis et sanguinis quam illa manducatio potacioque significat, efficit nos meliores. Vivimus ergo nos propter ipsum manducantes eum, id est ipsum accipientes vitam eternam, quam non habemus ex nobis. Vivit autem ipse propter patrem missus ab eo, quia semetipsum exinanivit, factus obediens usque ad signum crucis. Sicut misit me vivens pater, et ego vivo propter patrem. Et qui manducat me, et ipse vivet propter me. Ac si diceret: Et ego vivo propter patrem, id est ut ad illum tanquam ad maiorem referam vitam meam, exinanicio mea fecit in qua me misit. Ut autem quisque vivat propter me participatio facit qui manducat me. Ego itaque humiliatus vivo propter patrem, ille rectus vivit propter me. Non de ea natura dixit, quia semper est equalis patri, sed ea in qua minor factus est patre de qua eciam superius dixit: Sicut pater habet vitam in semetipso, sic dedit filio vitam habere in semetipso, id est genuit filium habentem vitam in semetipso.

[As the living father, he said, sent me, I live because of the father. And he who eats me, will live because of me. Certainly the son, who was born equal, is not made better through the participation of the father, as he makes us better through the participation of the son through the unity of the body and blood which that food and drink signifies. We live on behalf of him, by eating him, that is, receiving him as eternal life, which we do not have by ourselves. He himself lives on behalf of the father, sent by him, because he emptied himself, made obedient up to the sign of the cross. As the living father sent me, I live on behalf of the father. And he who eats me, he himself will live on behalf of me. This is as if to say: I live on behalf of the father, that is, I direct my life to him as to one greater, he brought about my emptying, in which form he sent me. Participation brings about for the one who eats me, that each one lives on behalf of me. Thus, I, humbled, live on behalf of the father, this man, uplifted, lives on behalf of me. He said this not about his nature, because he is always equal to the father, but about that in which he was made lesser in relation to the father, about which earlier he said: Just as the father has life in and of himself, he gave his son life to have in and of himself, that is, he begot a son having life in and of himself.]

---

[112] PL 100, col. 836.

43. Responsory: Unus panis/Parasti in dulcedine/Gloria patri[113]

[Text Source: R. Cf. 1 Cor 10: 16–17; V. Cf. Ps 67 (Latin), 68 (Hebrew): 11, 7]

[We many are one bread and one body, we all who are made participants in one bread and one cup. V. You have prepared in your goodness for the needy, O God, You who cause us to live of one mind in your house.]

Contra Ex eius tumba de sco Nicholao, CAO 6679, Jones 30

[For Nicholas: From his marble tomb there exudes a holy oil, smeared with which the blind man is cured, the deaf is given back hearing, every lame person is returned to health. V. In throngs the people rush in, desiring to see what miracles are done through him.]

[For James: O Christ, grant us grace through the intercession of him, at whose reception the saints rejoice, to whom the crown is given, and who is made a faithful companion with you. V. In throngs let the people sing hymns to James, who frees those justly asking on land and sea.]

[Musical Sources: AS 359, Matins Noct. 3, Resp. 9; ODO 75 (Ex eius Christe); see also 1051 205v]

---

[113] The nine pitches over the last word of the first sentence (*sumus*) are a third too high in BNF 1143—perhaps a change of clef occurred in the source at this point.

44. Te Deum (cued after last verse of previous responsory)

45. Versiculus

[Text Source: Sap 16: 20–21]

Panem de celo prestitisti eis, alleluia. R. Omne delectamentum in se habentem, alleluia.

[You have furnished them with the bread of heaven, alleluia. R. Having in it every delight, alleluia.]

In laudibus

Antiphona

46. Sapiencia edificavit/Ps Dominus regnavit

[Wisdom has built herself a house, she has prepared her wine, she has laid her table, alleluia.]

[Text Source: Prov 9: 1–2]

Contra Adest dies de sco Dominico, AH XXV, 241

[The day of rejoicing is at hand, on which blessed Dominic enters the hall of the celestial court as a distinguished citizen.]

[Musical Sources: 10770 173v, Lauds Ant. 1]

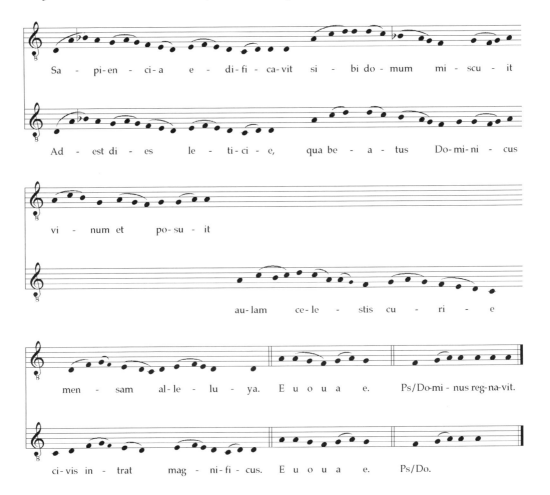

47. Angelorum esca/Ps Iubilate

[You have nourished your people with the food of the angels, and you have provided them bread from heaven, alleluia.]

[Text Source: Cf. Sap 16: 20]

Contra Pauper esca. de sco Dominico (Pauper in peculio), AH XXV, 241

[Poor in belongings, rich in a pure life, He swears a vow of poverty for the reward of heaven.]

[Musical Source: 10772 177, Lauds Ant. 2]

An-ge - lo - rum e - sca nu - tri - vi-sti po - pu-lum tu - um

Pau - per in pe-cu - li - o, di - ves vi - ta pu - ra,

et pa - nem de ce - lo pre-sti-ti - sti il - lis al-le - lu-ya. E u o u a e. Ps/Iu-bi-la - te.

pau-per - ta - tis pre - ci - o ce - li te - net iu - ra. E u o u a e.

48. Pinguis est panis/Ps Deus deus

[Rich is the bread of Christ and he will offer delicacies to kings, alleluia.]
[Text Source: Cf. Gen 49: 20]

Contra Scala celo de sco Dominico, AH XXV 241
[A ladder extending from heaven is revealed to the brother, by which the father, coming from below, was being taken up.]

[Musical Source: 10772 177, Lauds Ant. 3]

49. Sacerdotes sancti/Ps Benedicite

[Text Source: Dn 3: 57–58? (Cf. Lev 21: 6)]
[The holy priests offer incense and breads to God, alleluia.]

Contra Ingressus angelus de Annunciacione sce Marie, CAO 3339
[An angel having approached Mary said: Hail, Mary, full of grace, the Lord is with you.]

[Musical Sources: WA 301, 1 Vesp, Mag. Ant.]

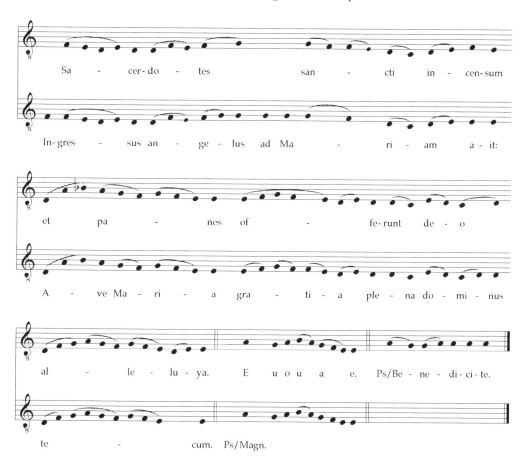

50. Vincenti dabo/Ps Laudate

[To the one who conquers I will give hidden manna and a new name, alleluia.]
[Text Source: Cf. Apoc 2: 17]

Contra Ex quo omnia de Trinitate CAO 2751
[From whom all things, through whom all things, in whom all things, to him be glory forever.]

[Musical Sources: WA 159, Matins Noct. 2, Ant. 11; see also AS 287, Vesp. 1, Ant. 5; Wales 127]

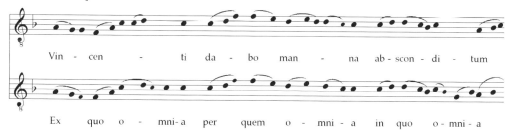

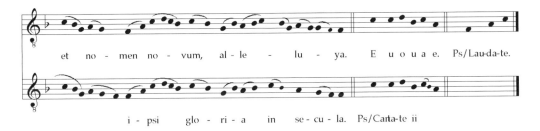

et no - men no - vum, al - le - lu - ya. E u o u a e. Ps/Lau-da-te.

i - psi glo - ri - a in se - cu - la. Ps/Carta-te ii

51. Capitulum

Dominus Ihesus Christus in qua nocte tradebatur; accepit panem et gratias agens fregit et dixit. accipite et manducate hoc est corpus meum; quod pro vobis tradetur. hoc facite in meam commemorationem.

[The Lord Jesus Christ, on the night he was betrayed, took bread and, giving thanks, broke it and said: Take and eat. This is my body, which will be given up for you. Do this in my memory.]

52. Hymn: Verbum supernum

[1. The celestial word coming forth, not leaving the right hand of the father, going out to its work, comes to the evening of life.

2. Handed over by a disciple to his enemies for his death, he first gave himself to his disciples on a plate of life.

3. He gave them his flesh and blood under two species, so that he might feed all men of twofold substance.

4. Being born he gave himself as a companion, dining he gave himself as a nourishment, dying he gave himself as a ransom, reigning he gives himself as a reward.

5. O saving victim, you who opens the door of heaven, wars and enemies press us, give us strength, bring us help.

6. To the Lord, one and three, be eternal praise, may he give us eternal life in the homeland. Amen.]

Contra Eterne rex altissime de Ascensione, AH XXVII 96, LI 94; RH 654; CAO 8255
[1. Eternal most high king, and redeemer of the faithful, by whom death, removed, perished, and to whom is given the triumph of grace.

2. Ascending the judgment seat on the right hand of the father, power over all was bestowed on Jesus from heaven, which was not of a human sort.

3. So that the three-fold system of things, celestial, terrestrial, and the hidden realms of the underworld, may bend their knees now subdued.

4. The angels tremble seeing the changes caused by mortals, flesh sins, flesh cleanses, God reigns as God's flesh.

5. May you be our joy, you who are our future reward, may the glory of life be ours always through all ages.

6. Glory to you Lord who ascends over the stars, wih the father and holy spirit in everlasting age. Amen.]

[Musical Source: Wales 115v; see also LR 95 with LU 940 and 952n; ST 37, 93)]

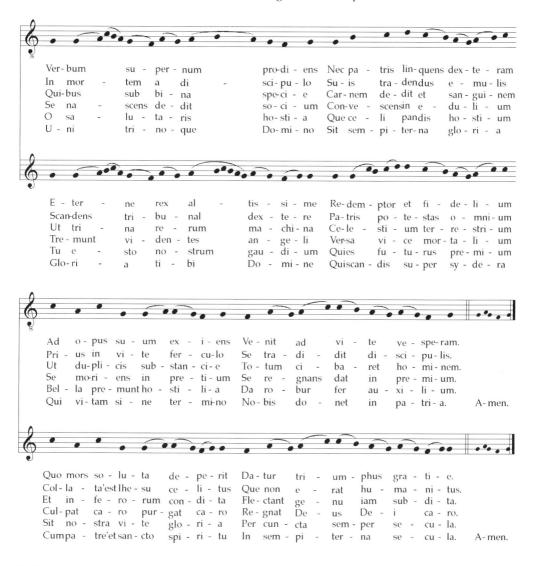

Ver-bum   su - per-num   pro-di - ens Nec pa - tris lin-quens dex-te - ram
In   mor -   tem   a   di -   sci-pu - lo   Su - is   tra-dendus   e - mu - lis
Qui-bus   sub   bi - na   spe-ci - e   Car-nem   de-dit et   san-gui - nem
Se   na -   scens de-dit   so-ci - um Con-ve - scensin e -   du - li - um
O   sa -   lu - ta - ris   ho-sti - a   Que ce - li   pandis   ho-sti - um
U - ni   tri - no - que   Do-mi - no   Sit sem-pi - ter-na   glo - ri - a

E - ter - ne   rex   al -   tis - si - me Re-dem - ptor et fi - de - li - um
Scan-dens   tri - bu - nal   dex - te - re   Pa-tris   po - te-stas o - mni-um
Ut tri - na   re - rum   ma - chi - na   Ce-le - sti - um ter - re - stri - um
Tre - munt   vi - den - tes   an - ge - li   Ver-sa   vi - ce mor - ta - li - um
Tu e - sto   no - strum   gau - di - um   Quies   fu - tu - rus   pre - mi - um
Glo-ri - a   ti - bi   Do - mi - ne   Quiscan - dis   su - per   sy - de - ra

Ad o - pus su - um   ex - i - ens Ve - nit   ad   vi - te   ve - spe-ram.
Pri - us in   vi - te   fer - cu-lo Se   tra - di - dit   di - sci - pu-lis.
Ut   du-pli - cis sub - stan - ci-e To - tum ci - ba - ret   ho - mi-nem.
Se   mo-ri - ens in   pre - ti - um Se   re - gnans dat in   pre - mi-um.
Bel - la pre - munt ho - sti - li - a Da ro - bur   fer   au - xi - li - um.
Qui vi-tam si - ne   ter - mi-no No-bis   do - net   in   pa - tri - a.   A-men.

Quo mors so - lu - ta   de - pe - rit Da-tur   tri - um - phus gra - ti - e.
Col - la - ta'est Ihe - su   ce - li - tus Que non e - rat   hu - ma - ni - tus.
Et in - fe - ro - rum con - di - ta   Fle-ctant ge - nu   iam   sub - di - ta.
Cul-pat ca - ro   pur - gat ca - ro   Re - gnat De - us De - i   ca - ro.
Sit no - stra vi - te   glo - ri - a   Per cun - cta   sem - per   se - cu - la.
Cumpa - tre'et san - cto   spi - ri - tu   In sem - pi - ter - na   se - cu - la.   A-men.

53. Versiculus

[Text Source: Cf. Ps 147 (Latin): 3; 147 (Hebrew): 14]

Posuit fines tuos pacem, alleluia. R. Et adipe frumenti saciat te alleluia.

[He has established peace in your borders, alleluia. R. And with the finest grain he has filled you, alleluia.]

54. Ad Benedictus antiphona: Ego sum panis/Benedictus

[Text Source: Jo 6: 51–52]

[I am the living bread who descended from heaven. If anyone eats of this bread, he will live forever.]

Contra Pax eterna de Dedicacione, CAO 4252

[Eternal peace from the eternal Father to this house. Let the everlasting peace, the Word of the Father, be the peace to this house. Let the Holy Consoler ensure the peace for this house.]

[Musical Source: Pm 240]

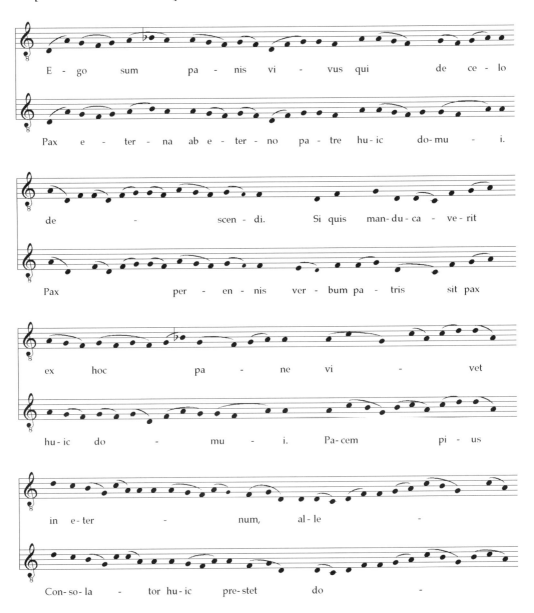

lu - ya.

mu - i.

[E u o u a   e.]   Ps/Be- ne - di- ctus.

55. Oratio

Deus qui nobis sub sacramento mirabili passionis tue memoriam reliquisti: tribue quesumus ita nos corporis et sanguinis tui sacra mysteria venerari; ut redemptionis tue fructum in nobis iugiter senciamus. Qui vivis [et regnas cum Deo Patre in unitate Spiritu sancti Deus per omnia secula seculorum. Amen.]

[God, who left us in a wonderful sacrament a memorial of your passion, grant, we ask, that we so venerate the sacred mystery of your body and blood, that we always feel in ourselves the fruit of your redemption. Who lives and reigns with God the Father in unity with the Holy Spirit, God, world without end. Amen.]

[Day Hours]

Ad primam

56. Antiphona: Sapiencia. Ps Deus in nomine

Ad terciam

57. Antiphona: Angelorum esca

58. Capitulum

Dominus Ihesus Christus in qua nocte tradebatur; accepit panem et gratias agens fregit et dixit. accipite et manducate hoc est corpus meum; quod pro vobis tradetur.

[The Lord Jesus Christ, on the night he was betrayed, took bread and, giving thanks, broke it and said: Take and eat; This is my body, which will be given up for you.]

59. Responsory: Panem celi

[Text Source: Ps 77 (Latin), 78 (Hebrew): 24–25]

[He gave them the bread of heaven, alleluia. V. Mankind ate the bread of the angels, alleluia.]

Pa-nem ce-li de - dit   e - is,   al - le - lu - ya,   al - le -

lu - ya.   V/Pa-nem an - ge - lo - rum man - du - ca - vit   ho - mo

al - le - lu - ya,   al - le - lu - ya.

D/Glo-ri - a pa - tri   et fi - li - o   et spi-ri-tu - i   san - cto. Pa - nem.

60. Versiculus

[Text Source: Ps 80 (Latin), 81 (Hebrew): 17]

Cibavit illos ex adype frumenti, alleluia. R. Et de petra melle saturavit eos, alleluia.

[He fed them from the finest grain, alleluia. R. And he filled them with honey from a rock, alleluia.]

61. Oratio: Deus qui nobis.

Ad sextam

62. Antiphona: Pinguis est panis

63. Capitulum

Quociens manducabitis panem hunc et calicem bibetis; mortem domini annunciabitis donec veniat.

[As often as you shall eat this bread and drink this chalice, you will proclaim the death of the Lord until he comes.]

64. Responsory: Cibavit illos

[Text Source: Ps 80 (Latin), 81 (Hebrew): 17]

[He fed them from the finest grain, alleluia. R. And he filled them with honey from a rock, alleluia.]

Ci-ba-vit il-los ex a-dy - pe fru-men - ti al - le   -   lu - ya,   al - le -

lu   -   ya.   V/Et de pe- tra mel - le   sa-tu- ra - vit   e - os,

al - le   -   lu - ya,   al - le   -   lu   -   ya.

D/Glo-ri - a pa - tri   et fi - li - o et spi- ri - tu - i   san - cto. Ci - ba- vit.

65. Versiculus

[Text Source: Ps 103 (Latin), 104 (Hebrew): 14–15]

Educas panem de terra, alleluia. R. Et vinum letificet cor hominis, alleluia.

[May you produce bread from the earth, alleluia. R. And may wine gladden the heart of man, alleluia.]

Ad nonam

66. Antiphona: Vincenti dabo

67. Capitulum

Quicumque manducaverit panem et biberit calicem domini indigne; reus erit corporis et sanguinis domini.

[Whoever shall eat this bread and drink the chalice of the Lord unworthily, will be answerable for the body and blood of the Lord.]

68. Responsory: Educas panem

Text Source: Ps 103 (Latin), 104 (Hebrew): 14–15

[May you produce bread from the earth, alleluia. V. And may wine gladden the heart of man.]

E- du- cas pa - nem   de ter - ra   al - le - lu - ya,   al - le -

lu - ya.   V/Et vi- num le- ti- fi- cet   cor   ho - mi - nis.   E- du- cas.

D/Glo- ri- a pa - tri   et fi - li- o   et spi- ri- tu - i   san - cto.   E - du- cas.

69. Versiculus

[Text Source: Cf. Ps 147 (Latin): 3; 147 (Hebrew): 14]

Posuit fines tuos pacem, alleluia. R. Et adype frumenti saciat te, alleluia.

[He has established peace in your borders, alleluia. R. And with the finest grain he has filled you, alleluia.]

In secundis vesperis antiphona et psalmii de primis vesperis

70. Capitulum

Dominus Ihesus [Christus in qua nocte tradebatur; accepit panem et gratias agens fregit et dixit. accipite et manducate hoc est corpus meum; quod pro vobis tradetur.]

[The Lord Jesus Christ, on the night he was betrayed, took bread and, giving thanks, broke it and said: Take and eat; This is my body, which will be given up for you.]

71. Responsory: Respexit Helyas [/Si quis manducaverit/Gloria patri]

72. Hymn: Pange lingua

73. Versiculus

[Text Source: Ps 77 (Latin), 78 (Hebrew): 24–25]

Panem de celo prestitisti eis, alleluia. R. Panem angelorum manducavit homo, alleluia.

[You have furnished them with the bread of heaven, alleluia. R Mankind ate the bread of the angels, alleluia.]

74. Ad Magnificat: O sacrum convivium/Magnificat
[Text Source: No biblical source, the only such text besides the hymns]
[O sacred banquet in which Christ is received, the memory of his passion renewed, the soul is filled with grace, and a pledge of future glory is given to us, alleluia.]

Contra Benedictus Dominus Deus patris nostri de sco Bernardo
[Blessed Lord God of our father, who, through his teaching and example, has built his church, through his felicitous assumption has made joyful his celestial community, through his solemn commemoration consoles his followers present today.]

[Musical Source: Chigi 351r, Lauds Ant. 2]

al - le   lu - ya.

pre-sen - tem ho - di - e conso-la-tur fa - mi   -   li - am   su   -   am.

E u o u a e.   Ps/Ma-gni-fi-cat.

E u o u a e.

Ad missam

75. Officium (Introit): Cibavit eos/Ps Exultate Deo/Gloria patri[114]

[Text Source: Ps 80 (Latin), 81 (Hebrew): 17]

[He fed them from the finest grain, alleluia. R. And he filled them with honey from a rock, alleluia.]

[Musical Sources: GS 138 Feria II post Pentecost "ad sanctum Petrum"; see also Syg 184 (92v)]

---

[114] There is no notation in the margin to indicate that the Introit has been borrowed from elsewhere, but in fact it has. It uses the same text as the introit to feria II after Pentecost, but since neither the text nor the music has been altered, no marginal remark is necessary. The same holds true for the Gradual.

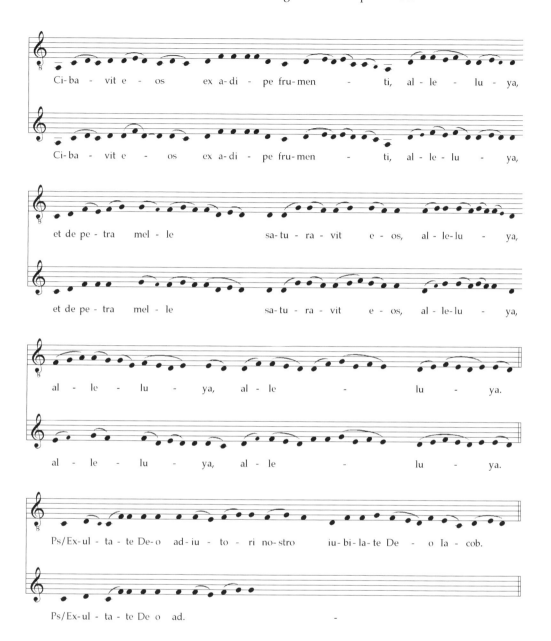

Ci-ba - vit e - os   ex a-di - pe fru-men - ti, al - le - lu - ya,

Ci-ba - vit e - os   ex a-di - pe fru-men - ti, al - le-lu - ya,

et de pe-tra   mel - le   sa-tu - ra - vit   e - os,   al - le-lu - ya,

et de pe-tra   mel - le   sa-tu - ra - vit   e - os,   al - le-lu - ya,

al - le - lu - ya,   al - le - lu - ya.

al - le - lu - ya,   al - le - lu - ya.

Ps/Ex-ul - ta - te De-o   ad-iu - to - ri no-stro   iu-bi-la-te De - o Ia - cob.

Ps/Ex-ul - ta - te De o   ad.   -

D/Glo-ri-a   pa-tri et fi-li-o   et spi-ri - tu - i san - cto   sic-ut e-rat in prin-ci-pi-o

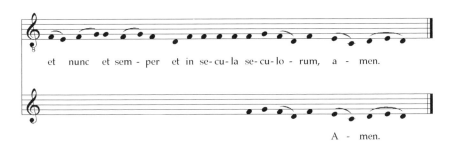

et   nunc   et sem - per   et in se-cu-la se-cu-lo - rum,   a - men.

A - men.

76. Kyrie: Fons bonitatis (Mass II)

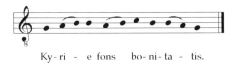

Ky-ri - e fons   bo-ni-ta - tis.

77. Gloria in excelsis Deo. Et in terra pax . . . (Mass IV)

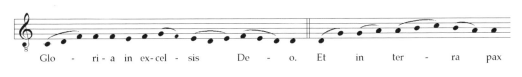

Glo - ri-a in ex-cel - sis   De - o.   Et   in   ter - ra   pax

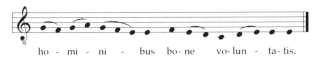

ho - mi - ni - bus bo-ne   vo-lun - ta-tis.

78. Oratio

Deus qui nobis sub sacramento mirabili passionis tue memoriam reliquisti: tribue quesumus ita nos corporis et sanguinis tui sacra mysteria venerari; ut redemptionis tue fructum in nobis iugiter senciamus. Qui vivis et regnas cum Doe Patre in unitate Spiritu sancti Deus per omnia secula seculorum. Amen.

[Lord, who has left us, in a wonderful sacrament, a memorial of your passion, grant, we pray, that we may venerate the mystery of your body and blood, so that we may always feel within ourselves the fruit of your redemption. Who lives and reigns with God the father in unity with the holy spirit, God, world without end. Amen.]

79. [Epistle] ad Corinthios [I,11,23–29][115]

Fratres: Ego accepi a Domino quod et tradidi vobis; quoniam Dominus noster Ihe-sus in qua nocte tradebatur accepit panem et gratias agens **fre**git et dixit Accipite: et **man**ducate. hoc est corpus meum; quod pro **vo**bis tradetur. Hoc facite; in meam commemo**ra**tionem. Similiter et calicem: postquam ce**na**vit dicens. Hic calix novum testamentum est in meo sanguine; hoc facite quocienscumque sumetis. in meam commemo**ra**tionem. Quocienscumque enim manducaveritis panem hunc. et calicem bibetis; mortem Domini annunciabitis **do**nec veniat. Itaque quicumque manducaverit hunc panem vel biberit calicem Domini indigne. reus erit corporis et **san**guinis Domini. Probet autem seipsum homo; et sic de pane illo edat. et de **ca**lice bibat. Qui enim manducat et bibit indigne iudicium sibi manducat et bibit non di**iu**dicans corpus Domini.

[Brothers: I received from the Lord what I also delivered to you, that our Lord Je-sus, on the night he was betrayed, took bread and, giving thanks, broke it and said: Take and eat. This is my body, which will be given up for you. Do this in my memory. Similarly [he took] also the cup, after he ate, saying: This chalice is the new covenant in my blood. Do this, as often as you drink it, in my memory. For whenever you shall eat this bread and drink this chalice, you proclaim the death of the Lord until he comes. Therefore, whoever shall eat this bread or drink this chalice unworthily, will be answerable for the body and blood of the Lord. Let a man examine himself, and so eat of the bread and drink from the chalice. For whoever eats and drinks unworthily, not discerning the body of the Lord, eats and drinks judgment on himself.]

---

[115] Syllables in boldface have two-note ligatures over them to indicate structural points in the recitation for-mula.

80. Gradual: Oculi omnium/Aperis tu manum tuam[116]

    Text Source: Ps 144 (Latin), 145 (Hebrew): 15–16

    [The eyes of all hope in you Lord, and you give them food in the suitable time. V. You open your hand and fill every creature with blessing.]

    [Musical Sources Syg 97 [fol. 49] Feria V post Domin. III. Quadragesimae; see also GS 59]

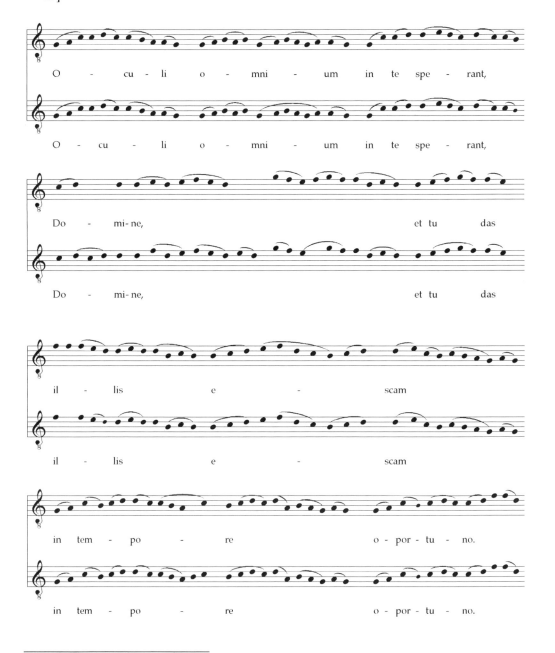

---

[116] See note 114 above.

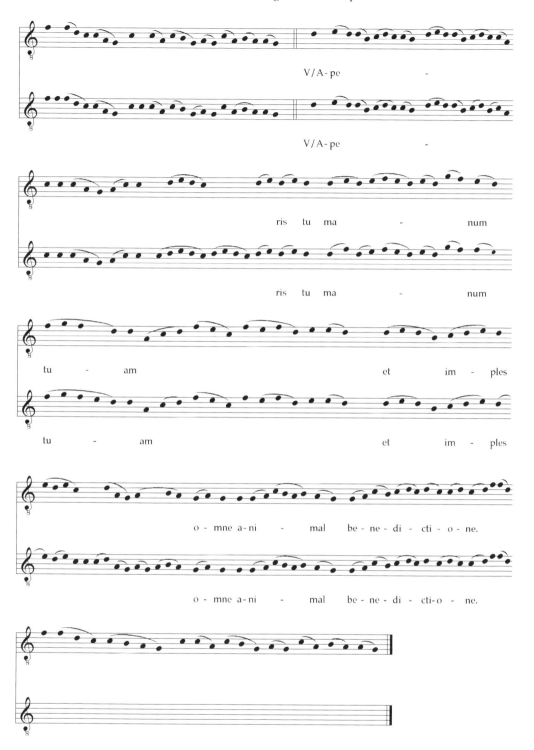

81. Alleluia: Caro mea

[Text Source: John 6: 55–56]

[Alleluia. My flesh is true food et my blood is true drink: whoever eats my flesh and drinks my blood will remains in me and I in him.]

Contra Nativitas gloriose de sca Maria

[Alleluia. The nativity of the glorious virgin Mary from the seed of Abraham, sprung from the tribe of Judah, from the renowned lineage of David.]

[Musical Source: GS u][117]

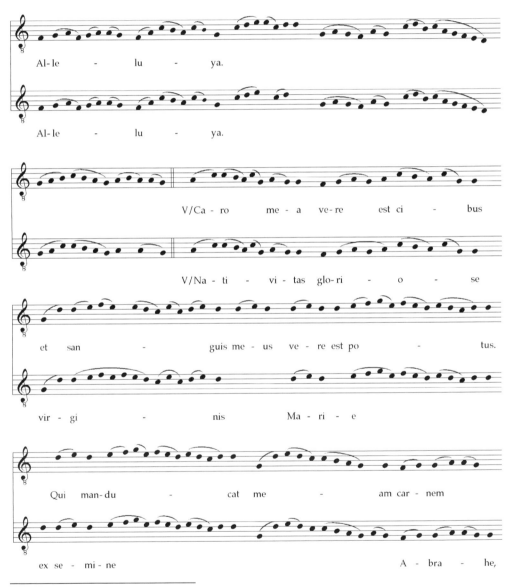

---

[117] Member of large family of Alleluias, incl. *All. Sanctissime apostole Iacobe* in Codex Calixtinus, *All. Concussum est mare* in GS 198, *All. Letabitur iustus* in SYG 209 [fol. 105] and GS 207. See Schlager #274, 196 which gives 19 verse texts, not including *Caro mea*.

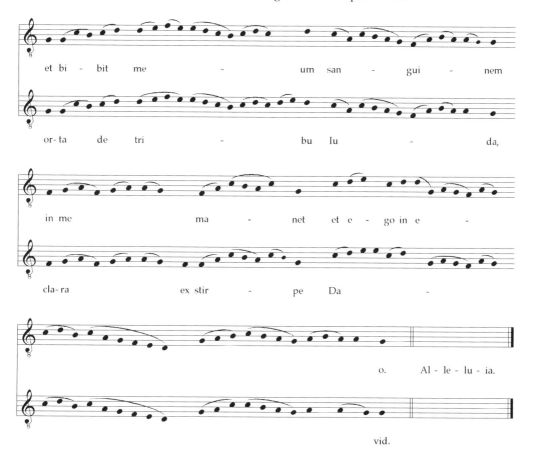

et bi - bit me - um san - gui - nem

or- ta de tri - bu Iu - da,

in me ma - net et e - go in e -

cla- ra ex stir - pe Da -

o.   Al - le - lu - ia.

vid.

82. Prosa: Lauda Syon

[1. Zion, praise the saviour, praise the leader and shepherd in hymns and songs.

2. As much as you can, dare that much, because he is greater than all praise, nor can you praise him adequately.

3. The theme of special praise , the living and vital bread, today is offered.

4. Which without doubt was given in the meal at the sacred table to the group of twelve brethren.

5. Let praise be full, let it be sonorous, let the jubilation of the spirit be joyful, let it be decorous.

6. The solemn day be solemnly observed when first is renewed the custom of this table.

7. At this table of the new king, the new paschal offering of the new law ends the old phase.

8. The new truth drives away the old, truth drives out the dark, light eliminates the night.

9. What Christ brought forth at the meal he said must be done in memory of him.

10. Taught by sacred practices, we consecrate the host, bread and wine, for our salvation.

11. The teaching is given to Christians that bread transforms into flesh and wine into blood.

12. Undaunted faith confirms what you do not touch, what you do not see, against the order of things.

13. Under diverse species, symbols only, not objects, lie hidden extraordinary things.

14. His flesh as food, his blood as drink; yet Christ remains whole under each species.

15. Not cut, not broken, not divided by the consumer, He is received whole.

16. One consumes, thousands consume, he is as much as they consume, and, consumed, he is undiminished.

17. The good people consume, the wicked consume, yet with an unequal outcome, of life or of death.

18. Death is for the wicked, life for the good; behold, of equal consumption, how unequal is the result.

19. When the sacrament has just been broken, do not doubt but remember that there is as much contained in each fragment as in the whole.

20. There is no rending of the substance, only a breaking of the symbol, by which neither the state nor the stature of the signified is diminished.

21. This is the bread of the angels, made into the food of travellers, truly the bread of the sons, not to be given to dogs.

22. It was prefigured in symbols, when Isaac was sacrificed, when the lamb of the passover was delegated, when manna was given to the fathers.

23. Good shepherd, truly bread, Jesus, have mercy on us. You feed us, you watch over us, you make us see good things in the land of the living.

24. You who knows all things and prevails, who nourishes us mortals here, make us there your table companions, joint heirs, and members of the community of saints. Amen.]

Contra Laudes crucis attollamus de sca cruce

[1. Let us raise praises of the cross, we who exult in the special glory of the cross.

2. Let sweet song strike the heavens; we believe the sweet wood worthy of sweet melody.

3. Let life not contradict the voice; when the voice does not disturb life, the symphony is sweet.

4. Let the servants of the cross praise the cross, who, through the cross, rejoice that the rewards of life are given to them.

5. Let all say and let each say: Hail, deliverance of the people, health-bringing tree.

6. O how happy, how esteemed was this altar of salvation, made red by the blood of the lamb.

7. Without the fault of the lamb, which cleansed the world from ancient sin.

8. This is the ladder of sinners through which Christ, the king of the heavens, brings all things over to himself.

9. Its form shows this, and includes the four ends of the earth.

10. These are not new rituals, nor was this reverence of the cross recently invented.

11. It made the waters sweet, through it the rock sent forth water, by the order of Moses.

12. There is no health in a house unless a man protects his lintel with a cross.

13. Whoever has done such things neither feels the sword nor loses a son.

14. The poor little woman gathering wood in Sarepta gained the hope of salvation.

15. Without the wood of faith, neither the flask of oil nor grain is effective.

16. The benefits of the cross lie hidden in scriptures under a symbol, but now they are revealed.

17. Kings believe, enemies yield, by the cross alone, with Christ as leader, he puts to flight thousands of the enemy.

18. This always makes its followers stronger and victorious, it cures illnesses and languors, it drives back demons.

19. It gives freedom to captives, it confers newness to life, the cross has returned all things to their former dignity.

20. O cross, triumphal sign, true salvation of the world, hail. Among woods there is none like you with leaf, flower, seed.

21. Christian medicine, save the healthy, cure the sick, what human power cannot do, is done in your name.

22. Hear, Consecrator of the cross, the followers in praise of the cross, and protect the servants of your cross; after this life, transport them to the palaces of true light.

23. Those whom you wish to submit to torture, make them feel no pains, but when the day of wrath comes, grant and bestow on us eternal joys.]

[Musical Source: Ox 111v]

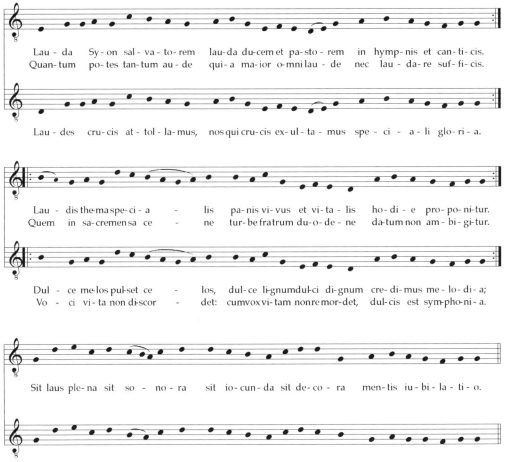

Lau - da   Sy - on sal - va - to- rem   lau- da du-cem et pa-sto - rem   in hymp- nis et can- ti- cis.
Quan- tum   po- tes tan-tum au- de   qui- a ma-ior o-mni lau- de   nec lau - da- re suf- fi- cis.

Lau- des   cru- cis at - tol - la- mus,   nos qui cru-cis ex- ul - ta - mus spe - ci - a - li glo- ri - a.

Lau - dis the-ma spe- ci - a   -   lis   pa- nis vi- vus et vi- ta - lis   ho- di - e   pro- po- ni- tur.
Quem   in sa-cre men sa ce   -   ne   tur- be fratrum du-o-de - ne   da- tum non am - bi- gi- tur.

Dul - ce me-los pul- set ce   -   los,   dul- ce li-gnum dul-ci di-gnum cre- di- mus me - lo- di - a;
Vo - ci vi- ta non di-scor   -   det: cum vox vi- tam non re mor- det,   dul- cis est sym-pho-ni - a.

Sit laus ple- na sit so - no- ra   sit io- cun- da sit de-co - ra   men- tis iu- bi- la - ti- o.

Ser- vi cru- cis cru- cem   lau- dent   qui per cru- cem si- bi gau- dent   vi - te da- ri mu- ni - a.

Di - es e - nim sol-lem-pnis a - gi-tur in qua men - se pri-ma re-co - li-tur hu - ius in-sti-tu-ci - o.

Di-cant o - mnes et di - cant sin-gu-li: A - ve, sa - lus to - ti-us po-pu-li,   ar-bor sa-lu - ti-fe-ra.

In hac men-sa   no - vi   re-gis no-vum pa-scha no - ve le-gis pha - se ve-tus ter - mi-nat.

O quam fe - lix, quam pre - cla-ra   fu - it hec sa - lu - tis a - ra,   ru-bens a - gni san-gui - ne,

Ve - tu-sta - tem no - vi - tas   um-bram fu - gat ve - ri-tas   no-ctem lux e - li - mi-nat.

A - gni si - ne ma - cu - la   qui pur-ga - vit se - cu - la   ab an - ti-quo cri-mi - ne.

Quod in ce-na Chri-stus ges - sit   fa - ci - en-dum hoc ex-pres-sit   in su - i me-mo-ri-am.
Do - cti sa-cris in - sti-tu - tis   pa - nem vi - num in sa - lu - tis   con-se - cra-mus ho-sti-am.

Hec est sca - la   pec - ca - to - rum per quam Chri-stus rex ce - lo-rum ad se tra - xit o - mni - a;
For-ma cu-ius hoc o-sten-dit que ter - ra - rum com-pre-hen-dit qua-tu - or con - fi - ni - a.

Dog-ma da-tur chri-sti - a - nis quod in car-nem tran-sit pa-nis   et vi-num in   san-gui-nem.
Quod non ca-pis quod non vi-des   a - ni-mo-sa fir-mat fi-des pre-ter re - rum   or - di-nem.

Non sunt no-va   sa-cra-men-ta,   nec re-cen-ter est in-ven-ta   cru-cis hec   re - li - gi - o:
I - sta dul-ces a-quas fe-cit,   per hanc si - lex a-quas ie-cit Mo-y - si   of - fi - ci - o.

Sub di - ver - sis   spe-ci-e-bus   si - gnis tan-tum et non re - bus
Ca - ro ci - bus san-guis po-tus   ma - net ta - men Chri-stus to - tus

Nul-la   sa - lus   est in do-mo   ni - si cru-ce mu - nit ho - mo
Ne - que sen - sit gla-di - um, nec a - mi-sit fi - li - um

la - tent res ex - i - mi-e.   A su - men - te non con - ci-sus non con-fra ctus non di - vi sus
sub u - tra-que spe- ci - e.   Su-mit   u - nus su-munt mil-le quantum i - sti tan-tum il - le

su - per - li - mi - na - ri - a; Li-gna   le-gens in Sa - re-pta spem sa-lu-tis est a-depta
quis-quis e - git ta - li - a. Si - ne   li - gnis fi - de - i   nec le-chi-tus o - le - i

in - te - ger ac - ci - pi-tur.   Su - munt bo - ni   su-munt ma - li
nec sum-ptus ab - su - mi-tur.   Mors est ma - lis vi - ta bo - nis

pau - per mu - li - er - cu - la;   In scri - ptu - ris sub fi - gu - ra
va - let, nec fa - ri - nu - la. Re - ges cre - dunt, ho - stes ce - dunt

sor - te   ta - men   in - e - qua - li   vi - te   vel   in - ter - ri - tus.
vi - de   pa - ris   sum - pti - o - nis   quam sit   dis - par   ex - i - tus.

i - sta   la - tent, sed   iam   pa - tent   cru - cis   be - ne - fi - ci - a;
so - la   cru - ce, Chri - sto   du - ce,   ho - stis   fu - gat   mi - li - a.

Fra - cto de-mum sa - cra-men-to   ne va - cil - les set me-men-to   tan-tum es - se sub frag-men - to
Nul - la re - i   fit scis - su - ra   si - gni tan-tum fit fra - ctu - ra   qua nec sta - tus nec sta - tu - ra

I - sta su - os for - ti - o - res   sem-per fa - cit et vi - cto-res,   mor-bos sa - nat et lan - go - res,
Dat ca-pti - vis li - ber - ta-tem,   vi - te con-fert no - vi - ta-tem,   ad an - ti-quam di - gni - ta - tem

quan - tum to - to   te   gi - tur.   Ec - ce pa - nis   an - ge - lo - rum   fa-ctus ci-bus vi - a - to-rum
si - gna - ti   mi - nu   i - tur.   In   fi - gu - ris   pre - si - gna-tur   cum Y - sa - ac im-mo-la - tur

re - pri - mit de - mo - ni - a;   O crux, si-gnum tri - um - pha - le,   mun-di ve - ra sa-lus, va - le,
crux   re - du - xit   o - mni - a.   Me - di - ci - na chri - sti - a - na,   sal - va sa-nos, e-gros sa - na,

ve - re   pa - nis   fi - li - o - rum   non   mit - ten - dus   ca - ni - bus.
a - gnus pa - sche   de - pu - ta - tur   da - tur man - na   pa - tri - bus.

in - ter   li - gna   nul - lum   ta - le,   fron - de,   flo - re,   ger - mi - ne;
quod non   va - let   vis   hu - ma - na   fit   in   tu - o   no - mi - ne.

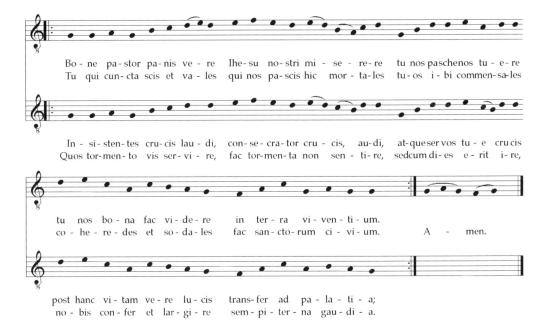

Bo - ne pa-stor pa-nis ve - re   Ihe-su no-stri mi - se - re-re   tu nos paschenos tu - e - re
Tu qui cun-cta scis et va - les   qui nos pa-scis hic mor - ta-les   tu-os i - bi commen-sa-les

In - si-sten-tes cru-cis lau - di,   con-se-cra-tor cru-cis, au-di,   at-queser vos tu - e cru cis
Quos tor-men-to vis ser-vi - re,   fac tor-men-ta non sen - ti- re, sedcum di- es e - rit i-re,

tu   nos bo - na fac vi - de - re   in ter - ra   vi - ven - ti- um.
co - he - re - des et so - da - les   fac san - cto-rum ci - vi - um.   A - men.

post hanc vi - tam ve - re lu - cis   trans-fer ad pa - la - ti - a;
no - bis con - fer et lar - gi - re   sem - pi - ter - na gau - di - a.

83. Gospel secundum Iohan. [Jo 6: 55–58]

In illo tempore. Dixit Ihesus [discipulis suis et[118]] turbis Iudeorum. Caro mea vere est cibus: et sanguis meus vere est potus. Qui manducat meam carnem et bibit meum sanguinem: in me manet et ego in illo. Sicut misit me vivens pater: et ego vivo propter patrem. Et qui manducat me: et ipse vivet propter me. Hic est panis: qui de celo descendit. Non sicut manducaverunt patres vestri manna: et mortui sunt. Qui manducat hunc panem vivet in eternum.

[At that time Jesus said [to his disciples and] to the multitude of the Jews My flesh is truly food, and my blood truly is drink. He who eats my flesh and drinks my blood abides in me, and I in him. As the living father sent me, and I live because of the father, so he who eats me, will himself live because of me. This is the bread which came down from heaven, not such as the manna your fathers ate and died. He who eats this bread will live forever.]

---

[118] These three words are written in the margin, with a sign indicating that they be inserted into the text.

84. Offertory: Sacerdotes incensum

[Text Source: Lv 21: 6]

[The priests of the Lord offer incense and bread to God and they will be holy to their God and they will not profane his name, alleluia.]

Contra Confirma hoc d[eus]s de sco Spiritu

[Confirm, O God, what you have wrought in us; from your temple which is in Jerusalem, kings shall offer gifts to you, alleluia.]

[Musical Source: GS 137; see also Syg 183 [Offertory w/ 3 verses for Pentecost]]

no - men e - ius, al - le -

re - ges mu - ne - ra, al - le -

lu - ya.

lu - ya.

85. Secret: Ecclesie tue quesumus Domine unitatis et pacis

Ecclesie tue quesumus Domine unitatis et pacis propicius dona concede que sub oblatis muneribus mistice designantur. Per Dominum nostrum [Jesum Christum Filium tuum, qui tecum vivit et regnat in unitate Spiritus Sancti Deus, per omnia saecula saeculorum. R. Amen.]

[We ask, Lord that you mercifully grant to your church the gifts of unity and peace, which are mystically signified beneath the gifts we offer. Through our Lord Jesus Christ your Son, who lives and reigns with you in the unity of the Holy Spirit, world without end. Amen.]

86. Preface

[Vere dignum et justum est, aequm et salutare, nos tibi semper, et ubique gratias agere: Domine, sancte Pater,] omnipotens eterne deus. Quia per incarnati verbi misterium. nova mentis nostre oculis lux tue claritatis infulsit. Ut dum visibiliter deum cognoscimus per hunc in invisibilium amorem rapiamur. Et ideo cum angelis et archangelis cum thronis et dominationibus. Cumque omni milicia celestis exercitus ympnum glorie tue canimus sine fine dicentes.

[It is truly right and just, proper and salutary, always and everywhere to give you thanks. Holy Lord, omnipotent Father, eternal God. Because of the mystery of the word incarnate, the light of your glory has shone anew on the eyes of our mind. That, while we acknowledge him to be God visible, we may be drawn by him to the love of invisible things. And therefore with the angels and archangels, thrones and dominations, and with all the heavenly hosts, we sing a hymn to your glory, saying without end.]

87. Sanctus (Mass IV, incipit only)

San - ctus.

88. Agnus Dei (Mass IV, incipit only)

A - gnus De - i.

89. Communion: Quocienscumque
[Text Source: 1 Cor 11: 26–27]

[For as often as you eat this bread and drink this cup, you proclaim the Lord's death until he comes. Whoever, therefore, eats the bread or drinks the cup of the Lord unworthily will be guilty of profaning the body and blood of the Lord, alleluia.]

Contra Factus est repente de sco Spiritu
[Suddenly there came a sound from heaven, as of a mighty wind where they were sitting, alleluia. And they were all filled with the Holy Spirit speaking the wonders of God, alleluia, alleluia.]

[Musical Source: GS 137; see also Syg 184 Pentecost]

Quo - ci - ens-cum-que   man- du - ca - bi - tis   pa - nem hunc

Fa- ctus   est re - pen - te   de ce - lo so - nus ad - ve - ni - en - tis

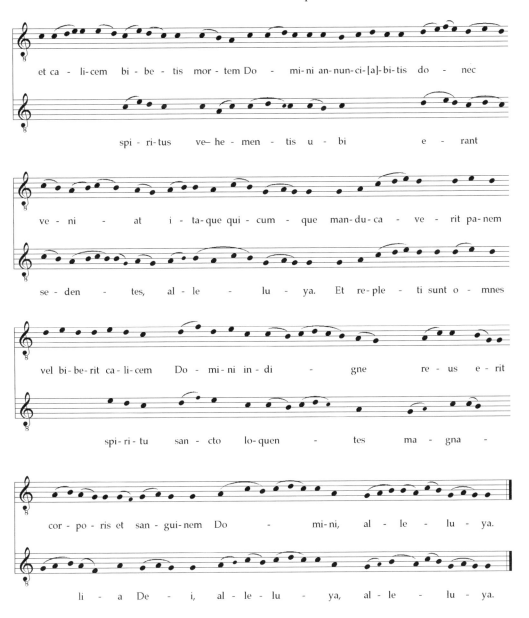

et ca - li-cem bi - be - tis mor - tem Do - mi - ni an - nun-ci-[a]-bi-tis do - nec

spi - ri-tus ve- men - tis u - bi e - rant

ve - ni - at i - ta-que qui - cum - que man-du-ca - ve - rit pa-nem

se - den - tes, al - le - lu - ya. Et re-ple - ti sunt o - mnes

vel bi-be-rit ca - li-cem Do - mi-ni in - di - gne re - us e - rit

spi-ri-tu san - cto lo-quen - tes ma - gna -

cor - po - ris et san-gui-nem Do - mi-ni, al - le - lu - ya.

li - a De - i, al - le - lu - ya, al - le - lu - ya.

90. Postcommunion

Fac nos quesumus domine divinitatis tue sempiterna fruitione repleri quam preciosi corporis et sanguinis tui temporalis perceptio prefigurat. Qui vivis [et regnas cum deo patre in unitate spiritu sancti deus per omnia secula seculorum. Amen.

[Grant, we ask, O Lord, that we be filled with the everlasting enjoyment of your divinity, which the temporal perception of your precious body and blood prefigures. Who lives and reigns with God the father in unity with the holy spirit, God, world without end. Amen.]

In quarto nocturno pro monachis
Antiphona
91. Memoriam fecit/Ps Domine exaudi
[Text Source: Ps 110 (Latin), 111 (Hebrew): 4–5]
[He has made a memorial of his wonderful works, the gracious and merciful Lord.
He himself has given food to those who fear him, alleluia.]

Contra Paradisi porta de sca Maria, CAO 4214
[Through Eve the gate of Paradise has been closed, and through the Virgin Mary it
has been opened again.]

[Musical Sources: WA 135 (Vigil of Assumption), Vesp. 1, Mag. Ant.; see also Wales
108—Commemoration of Mary, Feria 2 after Easter; Lucca 442—Vesp. 1 Mag. Ant.]

92. Memoria mea/Ps Benedic ii.

[Text Source: Sir (Ecclesiasticus) 24: 28–29]

[My memory will be in the generations of ages. Those who eat me will hunger for more; and those who drink me will thirst for more, alleluia.]

Contra Patefacte sunt ianue celi de sco Stephano, CAO 4228

[The gates of heaven have opened to blessed Stephen, martyr of Christ, who is found first in the number of saints, and therefore he triumphs, crowned in heaven.]

[Musical Sources: Wales 12v—2 Vesp. Mag. Ant.; LA 47—Lauds, Ant. 4 (different melody)]

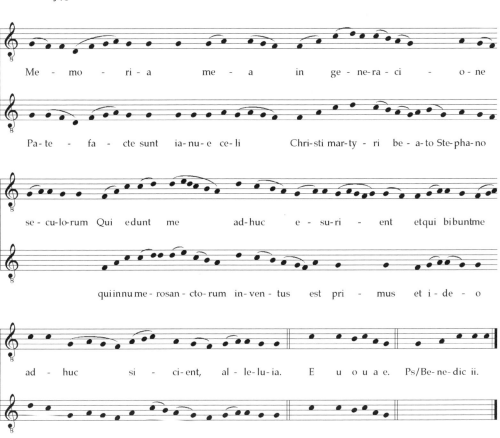

93. Qui habet aures/Ps Confitemini Domino et invocate
    [Text Source: Apoc 2: 17]
    [Let the one who has ears for hearing, hear what the Spirit says to the churches. To him who conquers I will give hidden manna, alleluia.]

    Contra Post plurima supplicia martyr alma de sca Katharina
    [After many torments, the benevolent martyr was led to the beheading. Fixing her eyes on heaven, she submitted her neck to the sword, praying she gave glory to God.]

    [Musical Sources: 10770 253v Lauds Ant. 2; 10772 250v; AS pl. Z, Lauds Ant. 2 (different melody), AH XXVI, 199 (but with variations in the text)]

94. Versiculus

[Text Source: Cant. 5: 1]

Comedi favum cum melle meo, alleluia. R. Bibi vinum cum lacte meo, alleluia.

[Eat the honeycomb with my honey, alleluia. R. Drink wine with my milk, alleluia.]

95. Lectio Decima[119]

[Gratian, De consecratione, Dist. II, can. 69 conclusion]

De tocius mundi operibus legisti quia ipse dixit et facta sunt, ipse mandavit et creata sunt. Sermo igitur qui potuit ex nichilo facere quod non erat, nun potuit eaque sunt in id mutare quod non erant? Non est enim minus dare, quam mutare novas naturas rebus. Set quid? Cuius argumentis utimur, suis utamur exemplis, incarnationisque astruamus misterii veritatem. Nunquid nature usus persensit, cum dominus Ihesus ex Maria nasceretur? Si ordinem querimus, viro mixta femina generare consueverat. Liquet igitur quod preter nature ordinem virgo generavit. Et hoc quod conficimus, corpus Christi ex virgine est. Quid hic queris nature ordinem in Christi corpore, cum preter naturam sit ipse dominus Ihesus partus ex virgine? Vera utique caro Christi que crucifixa, que sepulta est. Vere ergo illius carnis sacramentum est. Ipse clamat dominus noster Ihesus: Hoc est corpus meum. Ante benedictionem verborum celestium, alia species nominatur; post consecrationem, corpus significatur. Ipse dicit sanguinem suum. Ante consecrationem aliud dicitur; post consecrationem sanguis Christi nuncupatur. Tu dicis: Amen, hoc est verum est. Quod sermo sonat, affectus senciat.

[You have read about the creation of the entire world, that he spoke, and it was made, that he commanded, and it was created. Thus speech, which was able from nothing to create what did not exist, now was able to change existing things into that which they were not. For it is not less to give, than to change new natures in things.[120] Why is this so? Let us use the example of the one whose argument we use, and let us add the truth of the mystery of his incarnation. Do you doubt that he perceived clearly the custom of nature, since the Lord Jesus was born of Mary. If we seek order, it had been the custom to procreate by man combined with woman. It is clear, therefore that, against the order of nature, a virgin gave birth. And that which we celebrate is the body of Christ from a virgin. What order of nature do you find here in the body of Christ, since against nature the Lord Jesus himself was born of a virgin? Certainly real was the flesh of Christ which was crucified, which was buried. Truly his flesh is the sacrament. Our Lord Jesus himself proclaims: This is my body. Before the blessing of the celestial words, it is called another species; after the consecration his body is signified. He himself calls it his blood. Before the consecration it is called another thing; after the consecration it is called the blood of Christ. You say: Amen, this is so, this is true. May that which speech proclaims perceive the condition.]

---

[119] Lambot, "L'Office de la Fête-Dieu," 99, line 78.

[120] Perhaps the meaning is: "For surely giving is less than changing new natures in things." If so, then "Non est enim" should read "Nonne est enim." I thank my colleague Philip Peek for this suggestion.

96. Responsory: Melchisedech vero/Benedictus Abraham

[Text Source: Gen 14: 18–20]

[Melchisedech king of Salem offered bread and wine; he was the priest of the highest God. He blessed Abraham and said. V. Blessed be Abraham by the most high God, who created heaven and earth.]

Contra Regnum mundi de Virginibus

[I have disdained the power of the world and all the finery of the age, because of my love for my Lord Jesus Christ, whom I saw, whom I loved, in whom I believed, whom I cherish. V. My heart has poured forth the good word, I tell the king of my works.]

[Musical Sources: WA 432 Noct. 2, R. 4; see also Ut 219]

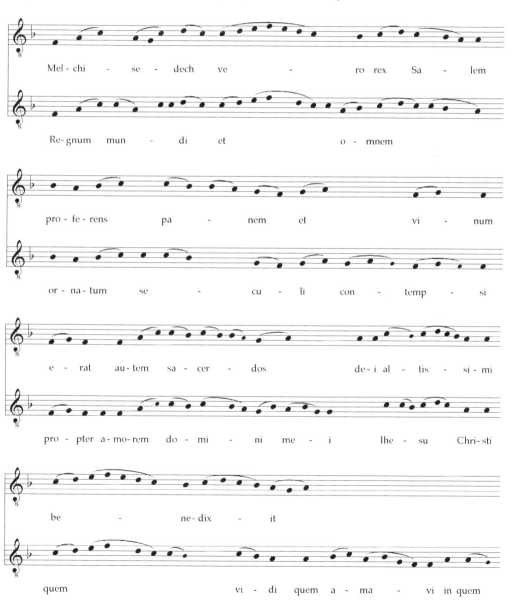

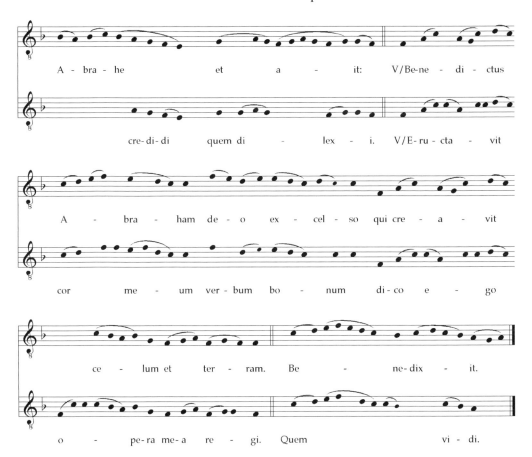

A - bra - he   et   a - it: V/Be-ne - di - ctus

cre-di- di   quem di - lex - i. V/E - ru - cta - vit

A - bra - ham de - o   ex - cel - so   qui cre - a - vit

cor   me - um ver - bum bo - num   di - co   e - go

ce - lum et   ter - ram. Be - ne - dix - it.

o - pe-ra me-a   re - gi. Quem   vi - di.

97. Lectio Undecima[121]

[Gratian, De consecratione, *Dist. II, can. 55 = Ambrosius.* De sacramentis, *L. IV, Ch 4–5]*

Panis est in altari usitatus ante verba sacramentorum. Ubi accessit consecratio, de pane fit caro Christi. Quomodo autem potest qui panis est esse corpus Christi? Consecratio igitur quibus verbis et cuius sermonibus est? Domini Ihesu. Nam per reliqua omnia que dicuntur, laus deo offertur, oratione petitur pro populo, pro regibus, pro ceteris. Ubi autem sacramentum conficitur, iam non suis sermonibus sacerdos, sed utitur sermonibus Christi. Ergo sermo Christi hoc conficit sacramentum. Quis sermo christi? Hic nempe quo facta sunt omnia: celum, terra, maria. Vides ergo quam operatorius sit sermo Christi. Si ergo tanta vis est in sermone domini nostri Ihesu, ut inciperet esse quod non erat, quanto magis operatorius est ut sint que erant et in aliud convertantur? Et sic quod erat panis ante consecrationem iam corpus Christi post consecrationem est, quia sermo Christi creaturam mutat, et sic ex pane fit corpus Christi. Et vinum cum aqua in calice mixtum, fit sanguis consecratione verbi celestis.

---

[121] Lambot, "L'Office de la Fête-Dieu," 100, [4].

[There is the bread used on the altar before the words of the sacraments. When the consecration comes, from bread it becomes the body of Christ. How can what is bread be the body of Christ? Consecration by whose words, by whose speech? The Lord Jesus.[122] Because through all the rest that is said, praise is offered to God, through prayer he is petitioned for the people, for kings, and for other things. However when the sacrament is made ready, now the priest uses not his own words, but the words of Christ. Therefore Christ's word makes this a sacrament. What word of Christ? That, of course, by which all things were created: heaven, earth, seas. You see therefore how efficacious is the word of Christ. If therefore so much power is in the word of our Lord Jesus, so that what was not might begin to be, how much more efficacious is it, so that they may be which were, and that they may be converted into something else? And thus what was bread before the consecration now is the body of Christ after the consecration, because the word of Christ changes the object, and thus from bread it becomes the body of Christ. And the wine mixed with water in the chalice, becomes blood by the consecration of the heavenly word.]

98. Responsory: Calix benedictionis/Quoniam unus panis
[Text Source: 1 Cor 10: 16–17]
[The cup of blessing which we bless, is it not a participation in the blood of Christ? And the bread which we break, is it not a participation in the body of the Lord? V. Because there is one bread, we who are many are one body, for we all partake of the one bread.]

Contra Solem iusticie regem de Beata Maria, CAO 7677
[About to give birth to the highest sun, the King of justice, Mary, the Star of the Sea today proceded to the east. V. Faithful ones, rejoice in seeing the divine light.]

Musical Sources: WA 366; see also Wales 252v, Ut 150

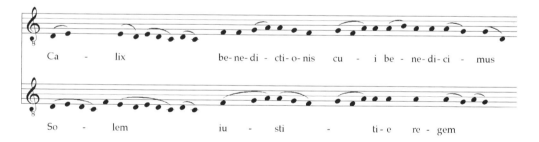

---

[122] Philip Peek suggested the following translation: How can what is bread be the body of Christ? Consecration. By whose words, by whose speech? The Lord Jesus."

u-nus pa - nis et u-num   cor - pus mul - ti su - mus   nam o-mnes de u-no pa-ne   et de u-no ca-li-ce

di - vi - num   lu - men   gau - de -

par-ti - ci - pa - mus.   Et   pa - nis.

te fi - de - les.   Stel - la.

99. Lectio duodecima[123]

[Gratian, De consecratione, *Dist. II, can. 55 concluded]*

Set forte dicis: Speciem sanguinis non video, sed habet similitudinem. Sicut enim mortissimilitudinem assumpsisti, ita etiam Christi similitudinem sanguinis bibis, ut nullus horror cruoris sit, et precium tamen operetur redemptionis. Didicisti quia corpus accipis Christi. Vis scire quia verbis celestibus consecratur? Accipe que sunt verba. Dicit sacerdos: Fac nobis hanc oblationem ascriptam, rationabi-lem, et cetera.[124] Inde, omnia evangeliste sunt usque ad: Accipite, sive corpus, sive sanguinem. Inde verba Christi sunt: Accipite et bibite ex hoc omnes. Hic est enim sanguis meus. Vide singula. Qui pridie quam pateretur accepit, inquit, in sanctis manibus panem. Antequam consecretur panis est. Ubi autem verba Christi acces-serint, corpus Christi est. Deinde audi dicentem: Accipite et edite ex hoc omnes: hoc est enim corpus meum. Et ante verba Christi, calix est vino et aqua plenus. Ubi autem verba Christi operata fuerint, ibi sanguis efficitur, qui plebem redemit. Ergo vide quam potens est sermo Christi universa convertere. Deinde ipse Ihesus testificatur, quod corpus suum et sanguinem suum accipiamus, de cuius fide et testificatione dubitare non debemus.

---

[123] Lambot, "L'Office de la Fête-Dieu," 100, line 111.

[124] Much of the remainder of this reading quotes from the prayer in the canon of the Mass preceding the consecration of the host.

[But perhaps you say: I do not see the species of blood, but it is similar. Indeed, just as you took on the likeness of death, so also you drink the likeness of the blood of Christ, so that there be no horror of blood, and so that it still serve as the price of redemption. You have learned that you receive the body of Christ. Do you wish to know how, by the celestial words, it is consecrated? Learn what the words are. The priest says: Make this offering for us approved, worthy, and so forth. After that, there are all the things of the evangelist up to: Take either the body or the blood. Then there are the words of Christ: Take and drink from this all of you. This is my blood. Look at them one at a time. "Who the day before he suffered took, he said, bread into his holy hands. Before it is consecrated, it is bread. When however the words of Christ draw near, it is the body of Christ. Then hear him saying: Take and eat of this all of you: This is my body. And before the words of Christ the chalice is filled with wine and water. When however the words of Christ were spoken, then it became blood, which redeems the people. Therefore see how powerful is the word of Christ to change all things. Then Jesus himself bears witness, that we receive his body and his blood, whose faith and testimony we ought not doubt.]

100.   Responsory: Ego panis/Ego panis/Gloria patri
[Text Source: Jo 6: 48–51]
[I am the bread of life. Your fathers ate manna in the desert and they died. This is the bread which comes down from heaven. If anyone shall eat of it, he will not die. V. I am the living bread who came down from heaven. If anyone shall eat of this bread he will live forever.]

Contra Vulneraverat caritas Christi cor eius de sco Augustino[125]
[The love of Christ pierced his heart and he carried his word in his entrails like a sharp arrow. And, like burning devastators, the examples of the servants of God, whom he raised from the dead to the living. V. To him [Augustine] coming up from the vale of tears and singing the gradual canticle, He gave sharp arrows.]

[Musical Source: AS 508 Noct. 3 Resp. 7]

---

[125] See Jacobus de Voragine, *The Golden Legend: Readings on the Saints*, trans. William Granger (Princeton, Princeton University Press, 1993), 2: 121.

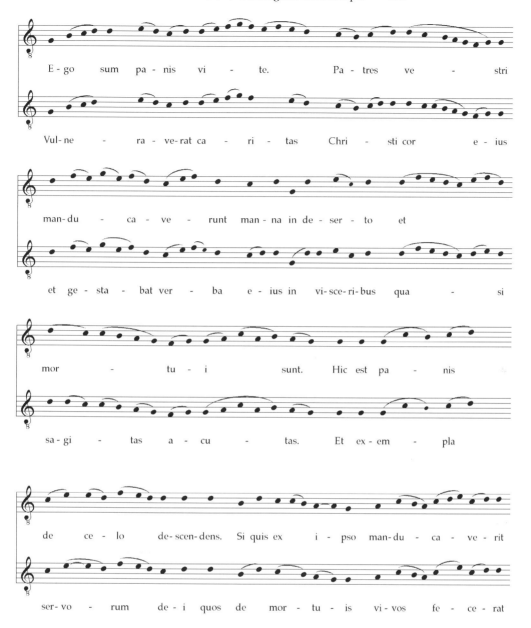

E - go   sum   pa - nis   vi - te.   Pa - tres   ve - stri

Vul - ne - ra - ve - rat ca - ri - tas   Chri - sti cor   e - ius

man - du - ca - ve - runt man - na in de - ser - to   et

et   ge - sta - bat ver - ba   e - ius in   vi - sce - ri - bus   qua - si

mor - tu - i   sunt.   Hic est pa - nis

sa - gi - tas   a - cu - tas.   Et   ex - em - pla

de   ce - lo   de - scen - dens.   Si quis ex   i - pso   man - du - ca - ve - rit

ser - vo - rum   de - i   quos de   mor - tu - is   vi - vos   fe - ce - rat

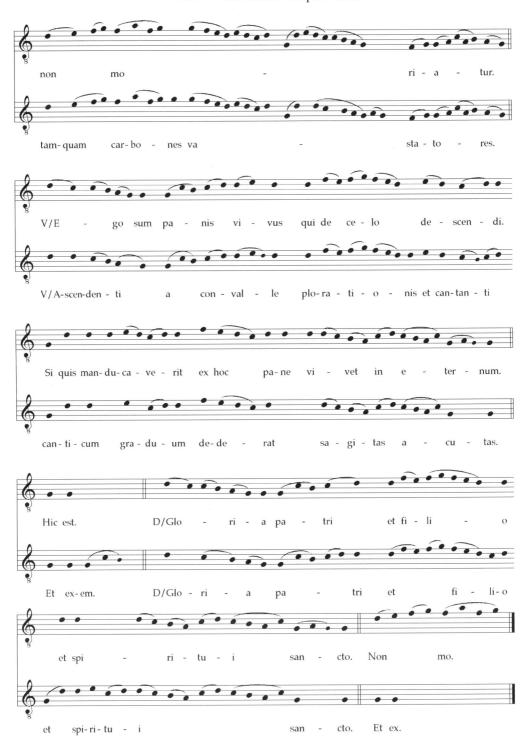

non   mo   -   ri - a - tur.

tam- quam   car-bo - nes va   -   sta - to - res.

V/E - go sum pa - nis vi - vus qui de ce - lo   de - scen - di.

V/A-scen-den - ti   a   con - val - le   plo-ra - ti - o - nis et can-tan - ti

Si quis man-du-ca - ve - rit ex hoc   pa-ne vi - vet in e - ter - num.

can - ti - cum   gra - du - um de-de - rat   sa - gi - tas a - cu - tas.

Hic est.   D/Glo - ri - a pa - tri   et fi - li   -   o

Et ex-em.   D/Glo - ri - a pa - tri et   fi - li-o

et spi - ri - tu - i   san - cto. Non   mo.

et spi-ri-tu - i   san - cto. Et ex.

Infra Octavas

101.   Lectio prima[126]

[Gratian, De consecratione,*] Dist. II, can 57 [Augustinus,* In Iohannis *tr. XXVI, n. 13]*

Christus panis est de quo qui manducat, vivit in eternum.[127] De quo ipsemet dixit: Et panis quem ego dabo caro mea est pro mundi vita. Determinat quomodo sit panis, non solum secundum verbum quo vivunt omnia, sed secundum carnem assumptam pro mundi vita. Humana enim caro que erat peccato mortua, carni munde unita, incorporata, unum cum illa effecta, vivit de spiritu eius, sicut vivit corpus de suo spiritu. Qui vero non est de corpore Christi, non vivit de spiritu Christi.

Augustinus in lib. De trinitate. *[Gratian]* De con[secratione,] *Dist. II, [can 60]*

Corpus et sanguinem Christi dicimus illud quod ex fructibus terre acceptum, et prece mistica consecratum recte sumimus ad salutem spiritualem, in memoriam dominice passionis. Quod, cum per manus hominis ad illam visibilem speciem perducatur, non sanctificatur ut sit tam magnum sacramentum, nisi operante invisibiliter spiritu sancto, cum hec omnia que per corporales motus in illo opere fiunt, deus operetur.

[Christ is the bread, of which whoever eats, lives forever. About this he himself said: "And the bread which I will give him is my flesh, for the life of the world." He prescribes in what way it is bread for the life of the world, not only in accordance with the word, by which all things live, but in accordance with the assumed flesh. His human flesh, which was dead to sin, united to the flesh of the world, incorporated, made one with it, lives by his spirit, just as the body lives by its spirit. Whoever is not truly of the body of Christ, does not live by the spirit of Christ.

We call the body and blood of Christ that which, taken from the fruits of the earth, and blessed by sacred prayer, we properly consume for spiritual salvation, in memory of the passion of the Lord. Since it is brought into its visible form by the hand of man, it is not sanctified to be such a great sacrament, except by the Holy Spirit working invisibly, since God makes all these things which come about from the body's movements in that work.]

102.   Lectio[128]

[Gratian, De consecratione, *Dist. II, can. 63]*

Hoc est sacramentum pietatis et est signum unitatis, et vinculum caritatis. Qui vult vivere, accedat et credat, incorporet hunc cibum et potum. Societatem vult intelligi corporis et membrorum suorum quod est ecclesie in predestinatis.

---

[126] Lambot, "L'Office de la Fête-Dieu," 100, [5].

[127] Last seven words of this sentence not in Lambot.

[128] Lambot, "L'Office de la Fête-Dieu," 101, [7].

Augustinus in libro sentenciarum Prosperi.[129] *[Gratian,]* De con[secratione,] *can. 48*

Hoc est quod dicimus, quod omnibus modis approbare contendimus, sacrificium ecclesie duobus confici, duobus constare: visibili elementorum specie, et invisibili domini nostri Ihesu Christi carne et sanguine et sacramento, et re sacramenti, id est corpore Christi, sicut Christi persona constat et conficitur ex deo et homine, cum ipse Christus verus sit deus et verus homo, quia omnis res illarum rerum naturam et veritatem in se continet ex quibus conficitur. Conficitur autem sacrificium ecclesie duobus, sacramento et re sacramenti, id est corpore Christi. Est igitur sacramentum et res sacramenti, id est corpus Christi. Caro eius est quam forma panis opertam in sacramento accipimus, et sanguis eius quem sub vini specie ac sapore potamus. Caro videlicet est carnis et sanguis est sacramentum sanguinis. Carne et sanguine utroque invisibili intelligibili spirituali, significatur visibile corpus domini nostri Ihesu Christi et palpabile plenum gracia omnium virtutum et divina maiestate.

[This is the sacrament of piety, it is both a sign of unity and a bond of love. Whoever wishes to live, let him approach and believe, let him consume this food and drink. He wishes the society of the body and its members to be understood, because it is among the things predestined in/for the church.[130]

This is what we say, what we work to prove in every way, that the sacrifice of the church is composed of two things, consists of two things, of the visible species of the elements, and of the invisible body and blood of our Lord Jesus Christ, both of the sacrament and of the object of the sacrament, that is, of the body of Christ, just as the person of Christ comprises and is composed of God and man, since Christ himself is truly God and truly man, because each thing contains in itself the nature and truth of those things of which it is composed. Thus the sacrifice of the church is composed of two things, the sacrament and the object of the sacrament, that is the body of Christ. There is therefore the sacrament and the object of the sacrament, that is the body of Christ. His flesh is what, hidden in the form of bread, we receive in the sacrament, and his blood what we drink under the appearance and taste of wine. His flesh is the sacrament of his flesh, and his blood the sacrament of his blood. By his flesh and blood both invisible, understandable, spiritual, is symbolized the visible body of our Lord Jesus Christ, and it is touchable, full of the grace of all virtues and of divine majesty.]

---

[129] In reality from Lanfranc, *De corpore et sanguine domini*, ch. 10.

[130] All sources have: "Qui vult vivere, accedat et credat, incorporet hunc cibum et potum, societatem vult intelligi corporis et membrorum suorum, quod est ecclesie in predestinatis." But Gratian (*Corpus juris canonici*, ed. Friedberg) has: "Qui vult vivere, accedat et credat, incorporetur. Hunc cibum et potum, societatem vult intelligi corporis et membrorum suorum, quod est ecclesie in predestinatis."

103.   Lectio[131]

[*Gratian,* De consecratione, *Dist. II, can. 48 cont'd*]

Sicut ergo celestis panis qui vere Christi caro est, suo modo vocatur corpus Christi, cum revera sit sacramentum corporis Christi, illius videlicet quod visibile, quod palpabile mortale in cruce est positum, vocaturque ipsa carnis immolatio, que sacerdotis manibus fit, Christi passio mors crucifixio, non rei veritate, set significanti misterio, sic sacramentum fidei, quo baptismus intelligitur fides est.

Paschasius[132] [*Radbertus*], De corpore et sanguine domini; [*Gratian,*] De con[secratione,] *Dist. II, [can, 71]*

Iteratur cotidie hec oblatio, licet Christus semel passus in carne per unam eandemque mortis passionem semel salvavit mundum, ex qua morte idem resurgens ad vitam, mors ei ultra non dominabitur. Quod profecto sapientia dei patris necessarium pro multis causis providit. Primo quidem quia cotidie peccamus, saltem in peccatis sine quibus mortalis infirmitas vivere non potest, quia licet omnia peccata condonata sint in baptismo, infirmitas tamen peccati adhuc manet in carne. Unde psalmista: Benedic anima dominum qui propiciatur omnibus iniquitatibus tuis, qui sanat omnes infirmitates tuas. Et ideo, quia cotidie labimur, cotidie Christus pro nobis mistyce immolatur, et passio Christi in misterio traditur, ut qui semel moriendo mortem vicerat, cotidie recidiva delictorum per hec sacramenta corporis et sanguinis peccata relaxet. Unde oramus: Dimitte nobis debita nostra. Quia si dixerimus quia peccatum non habemus, ipsi nos seducimus, et veritas in nobis non est.

[Therefore, just as the celestial bread, which is truly the flesh of Christ, is called in its own way the body of Christ, although actually it is the sacrament of the body of Christ, which visibly, which palpably, subject to death, was placed on the cross, and just as it is called that sacrifice of the flesh, which is the suffering, death, and crucifixion of Christ at the priest's hands, not because of the truth of the matter, but because of a symbolic mystery, so the sacrament of faith, which is called baptism, is faith.

This offering is repeated daily, although Christ having died once in the flesh through one and the same suffering of death, saved the world a single time, from which death rising again to life, death will have no more dominion over him. Indeed the wisdom of God[133] foresaw this necessity for many reasons. First of all because we sin daily, at least in sins without which mortal infirmity it is not possible to live,[134] because although all sins are pardoned in baptism, nevertheless the infirmity of sin still remains in the flesh. Hence the psalmist: Bless the Lord, my soul, who forgives all your sins, who heals all your infirmities. And because daily we fall, daily Christ is mystically sacrificed for us, and the passion of Christ is handed down in mystery, so that he who, by dying a single time, conquered death, might forgive

---

[131] Lambot, "L'Office de la Fête-Dieu," 101, line 161.

[132] See Paschasius Radbertus, *De corpore et sanguine domini,* ch. 9, lines 4–19.

[133] "Sapientia Dei" [Wisdom of God] is the name given to Christ as the second person of the Trinity.

[134] That is, each day we commit at least venial sins.

daily the faults of recurring transgressions through the sacraments of the body and blood. Hence we pray: Forgive us our sins. Because if we would say that we do not have sin, we delude ourselves, and truth is not within us.]

104.   Lectio[135]

[Gratian, De consecratione, *Dist. II, can. 71]*

Iteratur eciam hoc misterium et ob commemoracionem passionis Christi, sicut ipse ait: Hoc quocienscumque agitis, in meam commemoracionem facite. Quocienscumque ergo hunc panem sumitis et bibitis hunc calicem, mortem domini anunciabitis donec veniat. Non itaque sic accipiendum est: donec Christi mor[s] veniat, quia iam ultra non morietur, sed: donec ipse dominus ad iudicium veniat. Interdum autem semper mors est Christi per seculi vitam posteris nuncianda, ut discant qua caritate dilexit suos, qui pro eis mori dignatus est, cui omnes vicem debemus rependere caritatis, quia ad hoc nos prior dilexit cum essemus gehenne filii, ut diligeremus eum a morte iam liberati.

Augustinus, De trinitate; *[Gratian,]* De con[secratione,] *Dist. II, can. 50]*

Quia morte domini liberati sumus, huius rei memores[136] in edendo carnem et potando de sanguinem eius, que pro nobis oblata sunt significamus.

[This mystery is repeated, indeed for the purpose of a commemoration of the passion of Christ, just as he himself said: So often as you do this, do it in memory of me. Therefore, as often as you eat this bread, and drink this cup, you proclaim the death of the Lord until he comes. This is not to be understood as: "until the death of Christ comes," because he will not die any more, but "until the Lord himself comes for judgment." In the meanwhile the death of Christ for the life of time must always be proclaimed to posterity, so that they may learn with what love he loved his own, who deigned to die for them, to whom we all should return an equivalence of love, because he loved us first, although we were the sons of Gehenna, so that we, now liberated from death, might love him.

Because by the death of the Lord we have been freed, we signify the memories of this event in eating his flesh and drinking his blood, which were offered up for us.]

105.   Lectio[137] Augustinus[138]

[Gratian,] De con[secratione, *can.72]*

Utrum sub figura an sub veritate hoc misticum calicis sacramentum fiat, veritas ait: Caro mea vere est cibus, et sanguis meus vere est potus. Alioquin quomodo magnum erit: Panis quem ego dabo caro mea est pro mundi vita nisi vera sit caro? Set quia Christum fas vorari dentibus non est, voluit hunc panem et vinum in ministerio vere carnem suam et sanguinem suum consecratione spiritus sancti potencialiter creari, et cotidie pro mundi vita mistice immolari, ut sicut de virgine per spiritum

---

[135] Lambot, "L'Office de la Fête-Dieu," 102, line 183.

[136] *memoriam* in KB 70.E.4.

[137] Lambot, "L'Office de la Fête-Dieu," 106, [11].

[138] In reality, Paschasius Radbertus, *De corpore et sanguine domini,* ch. 4, lines 1–20.

sanctum vera caro sine coitu creatur, ita per eundem ex substancia panis et vini mistice idem corpus Christi consecretur. Corpus Christi et veritas et figura est. Veritas dum corpus Christi et sanguis in virtute spiritus sancti et in virtute ipsius ex panis vinique substancia efficitur. Figura vero est id quod exterius sencitur.

[Whether by symbolism or by truth the mystery of the chalice becomes a sacrament, truth tells: My flesh truly is food, and my blood truly is drink. Otherwise how will it be a great thing—"the bread which I will give is my flesh for the life of the world"—unless it be true flesh? But because it is not right that Christ be devoured with the teeth, he wanted this bread and wine truly in the ministry to become powerfully his flesh and blood by the consecration of the Holy Spirit, and daily to be sacrificed mystically for the life of the world, so that, just as his true flesh is created from a virgin through the Holy Spirit without intercourse, through the same Holy Spirit the same body of Christ may be mystically consecrated from the substance of bread and wine. The body of Christ is both truth and a symbol. Truth when the body and blood of Christ is produced by the power of the Holy Spirit and by his own power, from the substance of bread and wine. The symbol is that which is perceived externally.]

106.   Lectio[139]

[Gratian, De consecratione, can.72 cont'd]

Intra catholicam ecclesiam in misterio[140] corporis Christi nichil a bono maius, nichil a malo minus perficitur sacerdote, quia non in merito consecrantis, set in verbo efficitur creatoris, et in virtute spiritus sancti. Si enim in merito esset sacerdotis, nequaquam ad Christum pertineret. Nunc autem sicut ipse est qui baptizat, ita ipse est qui per spiritum sanctum hanc suam efficit carnem, et transit vinum in sanguinem. Unde et sacerdos: Iube hec, inquit, offeri per manus angeli tui sancti in sublime altare tuum, in conspectu divine maiestatis tue. Ut quid deferenda in lucem deposcit, nisi ut intelligatur, quod ista fiant in eo sacerdocio? Hanc ergo oblationem, benedictam, per quam benedicimur, ascriptam, per quam homines in celo ascribuntur, ratam, per quam visceribus Christi esse censeamur, rationabilem, per quam a bestiali sensu exuamur, acceptabilem, ut qui nobis ipsis displicemus, per hanc acceptabiles eius unico filio simus. Nichil rationabilius ut quia nos iam similitudinem mortis eius in baptismo accepimus, similitudinem quoque carnis et sanguinis sumamus, ita ut veritas non desit in sacramento, et ridiculum nullum fiat a paganis, quod cruorem occisi hominis bibamus.

[Within the catholic church, in the mystery of the body of Christ, nothing greater by a good priest, nor inferior by a bad priest is accomplished, because it is accomplished, not by the merit of the one consecrating, but by the word of the creator, and by the power of the Holy Spirit. If it were by the merit of the priest, it would in no way pertain to Christ. Now however, just as it is he himself who baptizes, so it is he

---

[139] Lambot, "L'Office de la Fête-Dieu," 106, line 209.

[140] Lambot has *ministerio.*

himself who, through the Holy Spirit, makes it his flesh, and changes wine into his blood. Hence the priest: Command, he says, these offerings to be carried up by the hands of your holy angels to your sublime altar, in the sight of your divine majesty. How is it that he demands these offerings be brought into the light, if not that it be understood that these things are done in his priesthood? Therefore this offering is blessed, through which we are blessed, it is enrolled, through which men are enrolled in heaven, it is certified, through which we are deemed to be of the flesh of Christ, it is intelligent, through which we are freed from bestial understanding, it is accepting, so that we who are displeasing to ourselves may become by it acceptable to his only son. Nothing is more sensible than that, because we receive the likeness of his death in baptism, we also consume the likeness of his body and blood, so that truth may not be lacking in the sacrament, and that there be no mockery by pagans, that we drink the blood of a dead man.]

107.   Lectio[141]

[Gratian, De consecratione, *can.72 conclusion]*

Credendum est quod in verbis Christi sacramenta conficiantur. Cuius enim potencia creantur prius, eius utique verbo ad melius procreantur. Reliqua omnia que sacerdos dicit aut clerus chori canit, nichil aliud quam laudes et gratiarum actiones sunt aut certe obsecrationes, et fidelium peticiones.

[Ambrosius;[142] *[Gratian,]* De con[secratione, *can.74]*

Omnia quecumque voluit dominus fecit in celo et in terra. Et quia voluit, sic factum est. Ita licet figura panis et vini videatur, nichil tamen aliud quam caro Christi et sanguis post consecrationem credenda sunt. Unde ipsa veritas ad discipulos: Hec, inquit, caro mea est, pro mundi vita, et ut mirabilius loquar, non alia plane quam que nata est de Maria, et passa in cruce, et resurrexit de sepulchro. Hec, inquam, ipsa est, et ideo Christi est caro, que pro mundi vita adhuc hodie offertur, et cum digne percipitur, vita utique eterna in nobis reparatur. Panem quidem istum quem sumimus in misterio illum utique intelligo panem qui manu sancti spiritus formatus est in utero virginis, et igne passionis decoctus in ara crucis. Panis enim angelorum factus est hominum cibus. Unde ipse ait: Ego sum panis vivus qui de celo descendi. Et iterum: Panis quem ego dabo, caro mea est pro mundi vita.

[It must be believed that the sacraments are produced by the words of Christ, by whose power they are created beforehand, by his word especially they are produced for the better. All the remaining things which the priest says, or which the group of the chorus sings, are nothing other than praises and thanksgivings, or even supplications, or prayers of the faithful.

All things that the Lord wished, he did in heaven and on earth. And because he wished it, it was done. Thus, although it seems to be the form of bread and wine,

---

[141] Lambot, "L'Office de la Fête-Dieu," 106, line 226.

[142] See Paschasius Radbertus, *De corpore et sanguine domini,* ch. 1, lines 46–55.

these things, after consecration, must be believed to be nothing other than the flesh of Christ and his blood. Whence he himself spoke the truth to his disciples: This, he said, is my flesh, for the life of the world. And that I may speak more remarkably, it is clearly nothing other than what was born of Mary, and suffered on the cross, and rose again from the tomb. This, I say, it is, and therefore it is the flesh of Christ, which is offered for the life of the world even today, and when it is taken worthily, eternal life certainly is restored in us. This bread which we consume in mystery, I certainly understand to be that bread which was formed by the hand of the Holy Spirit in the womb of the virgin, and destroyed by the fire of his passion on the altar of the cross. The bread of the angels has become the food of men. Whence he himself said: I am the living bread, who descended from heaven. And again: The bread which I will give is my flesh, for the life of the world.]

108.   Lectio[143]

Augustinus; [Gratian] De con[secratione,] *Dist II, [can. 13]*

Cotidie eucharistie communionem accipere, nec laudo nec vitupero. Omnibus tamen dominicis diebus communicandum ortor. Si tamen mens in affectu peccandi est, gravari magis dico eucharistie perceptione quam purificari. Et ideo quamvis quis peccato mordeatur, peccandi tamen de cetero non habeat voluntatem, et communicaturus satisfaciat lacrimis et orationibus, et confidens de domini miseratione, accedat ad eucharistiam intrepidus et securus. Set hoc de illo dico quem mortalia peccata non gravant. Idem,[144] dixerit quispiam non cotidie accipiendam eucharistiam, alius affirmat cotidie, faciat unusquisque quod secundum fidem suam pie credit esse faciendum. Necque enim litigarunt inter se, aut quisquam eorum se alteri proposuit Zacheus et ille centurio, cum alter eorum gaudenter in domo sua susceperit dominum, alter dixerit domino: Domine non sum dignus ut intres sub tectum meum, ambo salvatorem honorificantes quamvis non uno modo, ambo peccatis miseri, ambo misericordiam consecuti. Ad hoc valet, quod manna secundum propriam voluntatem in ore cuiusque sapiebat.

[To receive communion of the eucharist daily I neither praise nor censure. I urge communion on all Sundays. If however the soul is in a state of sin, I say that he is more to be burdened by receiving communion, than to be purfied. And therefore someone is consumed by sin, but yet does not have a wish to sin further, let him receive communion in tears and prayers, and, confident in the mercy of the Lord, let him approach the eucharist undaunted and secure. But I say this to the one whom mortal sins do not burden. Thus one person says that the Eucharist must not be received daily, another asserts that it be done daily, let each one do what he conscientiously believes must be done according to his own faith. Nor did either of them put himself before the other, Zacheus and that centurion, when one of them gladly received the Lord into his house, the other said to the Lord: "Lord I am not worthy

---

[143] Lambot, "L'Office de la Fête-Dieu," 107, [13].

[144] *item* in KB 70.E.4.

that you should enter my house," both honoring the Saviour, although not in one way, both having been pitied for their sins, both having attained mercy. To this it applies that manna tastes in the mouth of each according to his own desire.]

109.   Lectio[145]

Ambrosius, De sacramentis; *[Gratian,]* De con[secratione,] *Dist. II, [can. 14]*

Si quocienscumque effunditur sanguis Christi, in remissionem peccatorum funditur, debeo illum semper accipere, ut semper michi peccata dimittantur.

Sergius [?]; [Gratian,] De con[secratione,] *Dist. II, [can. 24]*

Qui semper pecco, debeo semper habere medicinam. Qui scelerate vivunt in ecclesia et communicare non desinunt, putantes se tali communione mundari, discant nichil ad emundationem proficere sibi dicente propheta: Quid est quod dilectus meus fecit in domo mea scelera multa? Numquid carnes sancte auferunt a te malicias tuas? Et apostolus: Probet, inquit, se homo, et sic de pane illo edat, et de calice bibat.

Ambrosius, de sacramentis; *[Gratian,]* De con[secratione,] *Dist. II, [can. 56]*

Non iste panis est qui vadit in corpus, sed panis vite eterne, qui anime nostre substanciam fulcit. Iste panis cotidianus est. Accipe cotidie, quod cotidie tibi prosit. Sic vive, ut cotidie merearis accipere.

[If, however often the blood of Christ is poured out, it is shed for the remission of sins, I ought always to receive it, so that always my sins may be forgiven.

I who always sin, ought always to have a remedy. Those who live wickedly in the church, and do not cease to receive communion, considering themselves to be purified by such communion, let them learn that they acquire nothing for their purification, as the prophet says: How is it that my beloved commits crimes in my house? Do the consecrated pieces of flesh take away from you your maliciousness? As the apostle [says]: Let a man examine himself, he said, and thus eat of that bread and drink from that chalice.

This bread is not that which goes into the body, but the bread of eternal life, which supports the substance of our soul. This is a daily bread, receive it daily, so that daily it may be of benefit to you. Live in such a way that you may be worthy to receive it.]

110.   Lectio[146]

Augustinus, De trinitate; *[Gratian,]* De con[secratione,] *Dist. II, [can. 66]*

Sancta malis possunt obesse. Bonis sunt ad salutem, malis ad iudicium. Unde apostolus: Qui manducat et bibit indigne, iudicium sibi manducat et bibit. Non quia illa res mala est, set quia malus male accipit, quod bonum est. Non enim mala erat buccella que Iude data est a domino. Salutem medicus dedit. Set quia ille qui indignus erat accepit, ad perniciem suam accepit.

---

[145] Lambot, "L'Office de la Fête-Dieu," 107, [14].

[146] Ibid., 108, [17].

[Gratian, De consecratione, *Dist. II, can. 67]*

Non prohibeat dispensator pingues terre mensam domini manducare, set exactorem moneat timere.

[Gratian, De consecratione, *Dist. II, can. 68]*

Sicut Iudas cum buccellam tradidit Christus non malum accipiendo, set bonum male accipiendo, locum prebuit dyabolo. Sic indigne quisquis sumens corpus Christi, non efficit ut quia malus est malum sit, aut quia non ad salutem accipit, nichil accipit. Corpus enim et sanguis domini nichilominus erat in illis quibus dicebat apostolus: Qui manducat et bibit indigne, iudicium sibi manducat et bibit.

[Augustinus; Gratian, De consecratione, *Dist. II, can. 46]*

Multi indigne corpus Christi accipiunt, de quibus ait apostolus: Qui manducat et bibit calicem domini indigne, iudicium sibi manducat et bibit. Set quomodo manducandus est Christus? Quomodo ipse dicit: Qui enim manducat carnem meam et bibit sanguinem meum digne, in me manet et ego in eo. Et si indigne accipit sacramentum, adquirit magnum tormentum.

[Sacred things can be harmful to the wicked. They work to the salvation of the good, to the judgment of the wicked. Hence the apostle: He who eats and drinks unworthily, eats and drinks judgment on himself. Not because that thing is evil, but because the evil one receives evilly what is good. It was not an evil morsel which was given by the Lord to Judas. The doctor gives health. But because he who was unworthy received it, he received it to his destruction.

Let the steward not forbid the rich of the land from eating at the Lord's table, but let him advise them to fear the bringer of judgment.

Just as Judas, when Christ handed a morsel to him, did not receive evil but badly received good, gave room to the devil, so when someone unworthily consumes the body of Christ, it is not the case that because he is wicked, it is wicked, or because he does not receive it to his benefit he receives nothing. The body and blood of the Lord nonetheless was in them, to whom the apostle said: Whoever eats and drinks unworthily, eats and drinks judgment on himself.

Many receive the body unworthily, about whom the apostle said: He who eats and drinks from the chalice of the Lord unworthily, eats and drinks judgment on himself. But how must Christ be eaten? He himself described the way: He who eats my flesh and drinks my blood worthily, remains in me and I in him, and if he receives the sacrament unworthily, he obtains great torment.]

111.   Lectio[147]

Eusebius Emisenus [?]; [Gratian,] De con[secratione,] Dist. II, [can. 35 beginning]

Quia corpus assumptum ablaturus erat dominus ab oculis, et illaturus syderibus, necessarium erat ut die cene sacramentum nobis corporis et sanguinis consecraret, ut coleretur iugiter per misterium, quod semel offerebatur in precium, ut quia cotidiana et indefessa currebat pro hominum salute redemptio, perpetua esset redemptionis oblacio et perhennis victima illa viveret in memoria, et semper presens esset in gracia vere unica et perfecta hostia, fide existimanda non specie, neque exteriori censanda visu, set interiori affectu. Unde merito celestis confirmat auctoritas quia: Caro mea vere est cibus, et sanguis meus vere est potus. Recedat ergo omne infidelitatis ambiguum, quoniam quidem qui auctor est muneris, ipse est et testis veritatis. Nam et invisibilis sacerdos visibiles creaturas in substanciam corporis sui et sanguinis verbo suo secreta potestate convertit, ita dicens: Accipite et commedite: Hoc est corpus meum. Et sanctificatione repetita: Accipite et bibite: Hic est sanguis meus. Ergo sicut ad nutum precipientis domini repente ex nichilo substiterunt excelsa celorum profunda fluctuum, vasta terrarum, ita pari potestate in spiritualibus sacramentis ubi precipit virtus servit effectus.

[Because the Lord was going to take away from our eyes his assumed body and place it in the heavens, it was necessary that, on the day of the last supper, he consecrate a sacrament of his body and blood for us, so that what once was offered as ransom might be worshiped continuously through the mystery, so that because daily and indefatigably redemption flowed for the well-being of men, it might be a perpetual offering of redemption, and so that everlasting sacrifice might live in memory, and so the truly unique and perfect sacrifice might always be present in grace, appraised by faith, not by money, and valued not by external appearance but by internal influence. Whence heavenly authority justly confirms, because ". . . my flesh truly is food, and my blood truly is drink." Therefore, let every doubt of disbelief depart, because certainly he who is the giver of the gift, is himself witness of its truth. For the invisible priest converts visible creations into the substance of his body and blood by his word and secret power, saying: "Take and eat, this is my body." And, when the blessing is repeated, "Take and drink, this is my blood." Therefore just as at the command of the directing Lord suddenly from nothing there existed the heights of the heavens, the depths of the waters, the vastness of the earth, so by equal power in the spiritual sacraments, when goodness commands, the results obey.]

112.   Lectio[148]

[Gratian, De consecratione, Dist. II, can. 35 conclusion]

Quanta itaque et quam celebranda beneficia vis divine benedictionis operetur, et quomodo tibi novum et impossibile esse non debeat quod in Christi substanciam terrena et mortalia convertuntur, te ipsum qui in Christo es regeneratus interroga.

---

[147] Ibid., 108, [21].

[148] Ibid., 109, line 314.

Dudum alienus a vita, peregrinus a misericordia, et a salutis via intrinsecus mortuus exulabas, subito iniciatus Christi legibus et salutaribus ministeriis innovatus in corpus ecclesie non videndo set credendo transilisti, et de filio perdicionis adoptivus dei fieri occulta puritate meruisti, in mensura visibili permanens maior factus es te ipso invisibiliter sine quantitatis augmento. Cum idem atque ipse esses multo alter fidei processibus extitisti. In exteriori nichil additum est, et totum in interiori mutatum est. Ac sic homo Christi filius effectus, et Christus hominis in mente formatus est. Sicut ergo sine corporali sensu vilitate preterita deposita. Subito novam indutus es dignitatem, et sicut hoc quod deus in te lesa curavit, infecta diluit, maculata detersit non oculis sed sensibus tuis sunt credita. Et cum reverendum ad altare cibis spiritualibus saciendus ascendis sacrum dei tui corpus et sanguinem fide respice honora et mirare, mente continge, cordis manu suscipe, et maxime mente totum haustu interioris hominis assume.

[Therefore ask yourself, you who were reborn in Christ, how much and in what way the beneficent power of divine blessing works, and how it ought not to be new and impossible for you, that earthly and mortal things are converted into the substance of Christ. Formerly you were estranged from life, banished from mercy, and from the path of salvation, dead inside, you were exiled. Suddenly, admitted to the laws of Christ and restored by his healthful ministries, you hastened over into the body of the church, not by seeing but by believing, and from a son of perdition you merited to become adopted of God by hidden goodness, though remaining the same in outward form, you were made imperceptively greater, without the addition of anything. Although you were one and the same you stood out as much different by your advances in the faith. On the outside nothing was added, and all was changed on the inside, and thus man was made the son of Christ, and Christ was formed in the mind of men. Just as, therefore, without actual feeling, with past worthlessness put aside, you have suddenly assumed a new worth, and just as, because God cured in you the wound, washed away the stains, wiped away the blemish, these things are believed not by your eyes but by your feelings, and so when you come to worship at the altar, to be satisfied with spiritual food, look with faith upon the holy body of your Lord and his blood, honor and marvel at them, hold them in your soul, take them in heart's hand, and especially with heart partake fully of the nourishment of man's soul.]

113.   Lectio[149]

Ambrosius (?); [Gratian, De consecratione, Dist. II, can. 53]

In Christo semel oblata est hostia ad salutem sempiternam potens. Quid ergo nos dicimus? Nonne per singulos dies offerrimus? Set ad recordacionem mortis eius, et una est hostia et non multe. Quomodo una et non multe? Quia semel oblatus est Christus. Hoc autem sacrificium exemplum est illius, idipsum et semper idipsum. Proinde hoc idem est sacrificium unum solum. Alioquin diceretur quoniam in mul-

---

[149] Ibid., 109, [22].

tis locis offertur, multi sunt Christi. Nequaquam, sed unus ubique Christus, et hic plenus existens et illic plenus. Sicut enim quod ubique offertur unum est corpus et non multam corpora, ita et unum sacrificium. Pontifex autem est ille qui hostiam optulit nos mundantem, ipsam offerimus eciam nunc que tunc oblata consumi non potest. Quod nos facimus in commemoratione fit eius quod factum est. Hoc enim facite ait in meam commemorationem.

[In Christ the sacrifice was offered once, potent for eternal salvation. What therefore can we say? Do we not offer every day? Yes, but for the commemoration of his death, for the sacrifice is one and not several. Why is it one and not several? Because Christ was sacrificed once. This sacrifice is an imitation of that one, itself and always itself. Hence this is one and the same sacrifice. Some may say that because he is offered in many places, there are many Christs. In no way! Christ is but one everywhere, both here and there, existing in full. Just as, because wherever he is offered, there is one body and not many bodies, so there is one sacrifice. The priest however is the one who offered the sacrifice which cleanses us, [and] we offer the same now, that when offered then was not to be consumed. What we do is done in commemoration of that which was done. Do this, he said, in my memory.]

114.   Lectio[150]

[Gratian, De consecratione, *Dist. II, can. 1]*

In sacramentorum oblationibus que inter missarum sollempnia domino[151] offeruntur, panis tantum, et vinum aqua permixtum in sacrificium offerantur. Non enim debet in calice domini aut vinum solum, aut aqua sola offerri, set utrumque permixtum, quia utrumque ex latere eius in passione sua profluxisse legitur.

[Gratian, De consecratione,] *Dist. II, [can. 7]*[152]

Calix etiam dominicus vino, et aqua permixtus debet offeri, quia videmus in aqua populum intelligi, in vino vero ostendi sanguinem Christi. Ergo cum in calice vinum aqua misceatur,[153] Christo populus adunatur, et credentium plebs ei in quem credit copulatur, et iungitur, que copulatio et coniunctio aque et vini sic miscetur in calice domini, ut mixtio illa non possit seperari. Nam si vinum tantum quis offerat, sanguis Christi incipit esse sine nobis. Si vero aqua sit sola, plebs incipit esse sine Christo. Ergo quando botrus solus offertur in quo vini efficiencia tantum designatur, salutis nostre sacramentum negligitur quod aqua significatur.

[Among the offerings of the sacraments which are presented during the solemnities of the masses, let bread alone as well as wine mixed with water be offered in sacrifice. There must not be, in the chalice of the Lord, either wine alone, or water alone, but both mixed, because it is read that both flowed from his side in his passion.

---

[150] Ibid., 110, [23].

[151] *Domino* missing in KB 70.E.4.

[152] There is more to this marginal note, but it cannot be read.

[153] *Miscetur* in Lambot.

The chalice of the Lord ought to be offered with wine and water mixed, because we see the people represented by the water, the blood of Christ shown by the wine. Therefore, when wine and water are mixed in the chalice, the people are joined with Christ, and the crowd of believers are combined and united with him in whom they believe, and this combination and union of water and wine is mixed in the chalice of the Lord in such a way that the mixture cannot be separated. For if one offers wine alone, the blood of Christ comes into being without us. If the water is alone, the people come into being without Christ. Therefore, when the cluster of grapes is offered alone, in which the power of wine alone is represented, the sacrament of our health is neglected, which is signified by water.]

115.   Lectio[154]

Ambrosius, De sacramentis; *[Gratian,]* De con[secratione,] *Dist. II, [can. 83]*[155]

Huius sacramenti ritum Melchisedech ostendit ubi panem et vinum Abrahe obtulit, sed tu michi dicis: Quomodo ergo Melchisedech vinum et panem tantum obtulit? Quid sibi vult amixtio aque? Rationem accipe. Primo omnium figura fuit que ante precessit tempore Moysi. Quia cum sitiret populus iudeorum et murmuraret quod aqua inveniri non posset, iussit dominus Moysi ut tangeret petram cum virga, tetigit petram et petra undam maximam fudit, sicut apostolus dicit: Bibebant autem de consequenti petra. Petra autem erat Christus. Non immobilis petra, que populum sequebatur. Et tu bibe, ut te Christus sequatur. Vide misterium: Moyses, hoc est propheta. Virga, hoc est verbum dei. Sacerdos verbo dei tangit petram et fluit aqua et bibit populus dei. Tangit ergo sacerdos calicem, redundat aquam in calice et salit in vitam eternam, et bibit populus dei, qui dei graciam consecutus est.

[Melchisedech showed the rite of this sacrament, when he offered Abraham bread and wine. But you say to me: How therefore did Melchisedech offer bread and wine alone? Why is an admixture of water preferred? Learn this reason. First of all it was a symbol, which preceded before at the time of Moses. Because, when the Jewish people thirsted, and they complained that it was not possible for water to be found, the Lord ordered Moses to touch the rock with a rod, he touched the rock and the rock poured out a great wave, just as the apostle says: They drank from the rock which followed them. The rock was Christ. It was not an immobile rock that followed the people. And you, drink, so that Christ may follow you. Behold the mystery. Moses is the prophet. The rod is the word of God. The priest touches the rock with the word of God, and water flows, and the people of God drink. Therefore the priest touches the chalice, he pours water into the chalice, and it springs into eternal life, and the people of God drink, who followed the grace of God.]

---

[154] Lambot, "L'Office de la Fête-Dieu," 110, [25].

[155] Much of this reading is not in Gratian, *De consecratione*, Dist. II, can. 83.

116.   Lectio[156]

[Gratian, De consecratione, *Dist. II, can 83]*

> Didicisti hoc ergo accipe et aliud. In tempore dominice passionis cum sabbatum magnum instaret, quia diu in cruce vivebat dominus noster Ihesus Christus et latrones, missi sunt qui percuterent eos. Qui venientes, invenerunt defunctum dominum nostrum Ihesum Christum. Tunc unus de militibus lancea tetigit latus, et de latere eius aqua fluxit et sanguis. Aqua autem ut mundaret, sanguis ut redimeret. Quare de latere? Quia unde culpa, inde gracia. Culpa per feminam, gracia per dominum nostrum Ihesum Christum.

Cyprianus; [Gratian, De consecratione, *Dist. II, can 2]*

> Sic vero calix domini non est aqua sola et vinum solum, nisi utrumque misceatur, quomodo nec corpus domini potest esse farina sola, nisi utrumque adunatum fuerit, et copulatum, et panis[157] unius compage solidatum.

[Gratian, De consecratione, *Dist. II, can 5]*

> In sacramento corporis et sanguinis domini[158] nichil amplius offeratur, quam quod ipse dominis tradidit, hoc est panis et vinum aqua mixtum, nec amplius in sacrificiis offeratur, quam de uvis et frumento.

Concilio Martini Papae; [Gratian, De consecratione, *Dist. II, can 4]*

> Hec tria unum sunt in Christo Ihesu. Hec hostia, et oblatio dei in odorem suavitatis.

[You have learned this; therefore learn something else. At the time of the passion of the Lord, when the great Sabbath was at hand, because our Lord Jesus Christ was still alive on the cross, along with the thieves, soldiers were sent to kill them. On approaching, they found our Lord Jesus Christ dead. Then one of the soldiers pierced his side with a spear, and from his side water and blood flowed. Water to purify, blood to redeem. Why from his side? Because where there is guilt, there is grace. Guilt through woman, grace through our Lord Jesus Christ.

Thus the chalice of the Lord is not water alone and wine alone, unless both are combined, just as the body of the Lord cannot be flour alone, unless it is united and joined, and made firm into the structure of one thing.

In the sacrament of the body and blood, nothing more is offered, than that which our Lord himself passed on to us, that is, bread and wine mixed with water, nor is anything more offered in sacrifices, than what comes from grapes and grain.

These three are one in Christ Jesus. This sacrifice is an offering to God in the aroma of sweetness.]

---

[156] Lambot, "L'Office de la Fête-Dieu," 110, line 381.

[157] 'Panis' missing in KB 70.E.4.

[158] *Domini* missing in KB 70.E.4.

117.   Lectio[159]

Hilarius, De trinitate; *[Gratian,* De consecratione,] *Dist. II, [can. 82 beginning]*

In Christo pater et Christus in nobis unum in hiis esse nos[160] faciunt. Si vere carnem corporis nostri Christus assumpsit, et vere homo ille Christus est, nos quoque vere sub misterio carnem corporis sui sumimus, et per hoc unum erimus, quia pater in eo est et ille in nobis. Quomodo enim voluntatis unitas asseritur, cum naturalis per sacramentum propriatas perfectum sacramentum sit unitatis? Non est humano aut seculari[161] sensu de hiis rebus loquendum, neque per violenciam atque impruden-tem predicationem dictorum celestium, sanitati aliene atque impie intelligencie per-versitas extorquenda est. De naturali enim in nobis Christi veritate vel unitate que dicimus, nisi que dixerimus ab eo didicimus stulte atque impie dicemus. Ipse enim ait: Caro mea vere est esca, et sanguis meus vere est potus. Qui edit carnem meam et bibit sanguinem meum, in me manet et ego in eo.

[The Father in Christ, and Christ in us, make us as one in them. If truly Christ took on the flesh of our body, and that man is truly Christ, we also truly consume the flesh of his body in a mystery, and through it we will be one, because the father is in him, and he is in us. For how is the unity of will claimed, when in the sacrament the substance is of nature, and the sacrament of unity is perfect? It is not in the human or worldly sense that we must speak about these things, and not by violence must the foolish utterance of divine words, hostile to salvation, as well as the perversity of intelligence be eliminated. Concerning the natural truth or unity of Christ in us, what we say, we will say foolishly and impiously, unless what we say we have learned from him. He himself said: My flesh truly is food, and my blood truly is drink. He who eats my flesh and drinks my blood, remains in me and I in him.]

118.   Lectio[162]

[Gratian, De consecratione, *Dist. II, can. 82 continued]*

De veritate carnis et sanguinis non relictus est ambigendi locus. Nunc enim et ipsius domini professione et fide nostra vere caro est, et vere sanguis est, et hec accepta at-que hausta efficiunt, ut et nos in Christo et Christus in nobis sit, est ergo ipse in nobis per carnem. Quod autem in eo per sacramentum communicate carnis et sanguinis si-mus, ipse testatur dicens: Vos autem me videbitis, quia ergo vivo et vos vivetis. Quo-niam[163] ego in patre meo et vos in me, et ego in vobis. Si voluntatis tantum intelligi unitatem vellet, ut heretici asserunt, cur gradum quendam atque ordinem consu-mande unitatis exposuit, nisi ut ille in patre per naturam divinitatis, nos contra in eo per corporalem eius nativitatem, et ille rursus in nobis per sacramentorum inesse mis-

---

[159] Lambot, "L'Office de la Fête-Dieu," 111, [29].

[160] Appears to be an abbreviated *non* in BNF 1143 and KB 70.E.4.

[161] *Saeculi* in Lambot.

[162] Lambot, "L'Office de la Fête-Dieu," 111, line 413.

[163] *Quia* in Lambot.

terium crederetur. Ac si perfecta mediatorem unitas doceret, cum nobis in se permanentibus ipse maneret in patre, et in patre manens maneret in nobis, et ita ad unitatem
proficisceremur, cum qui in eo naturaliter secundum nativitatem inest, nos quoque in
eo naturaliter inessemus, ipso in nobis naturaliter permanente.

[Concerning the truth of the flesh and blood, no room for ambiguity remained.
Now indeed, according to both the profession of the Lord himself and our faith, it is
truly flesh, and it is truly blood, and they, eaten and drunk, cause both us to be in
Christ and Christ in us. Therefore he himself is in us through the flesh. That, moreover, we are in him through the sacrament of the union of flesh and blood, he himself testifies, saying: "You indeed will see me, because I live, you too will live, because I am in my father, and you are in me, and I am in you." If he wished only the
unity of will to be understood, as the heretics claim, why did he detail a specific degree and series of unity to be gone through, except that he might be believed to be
present in the father through the nature of his divinity, and we, consequently to be
in him through his physical birth, and he in us through the mystery of the sacraments. And so perfect unity might instruct the mediator that, with us still in him, he
remained in the Father, and, still in the Father, he remained in us, and in this way
we advanced to unity, since we would also naturally exist in the one who is naturally in him on account of birth, and he naturally would remain in us.]

119.   Lectio[164]

[Gratian, De consecratione, Dist. II, can. 82 conclusion]

Quod autem hec in nobis naturaliter unitas sit, ipse testatus est: Qui edit carnem
meam, et bibit sanguinem meum, in me manet et ego in eo. Non enim in eo erit nisi
in quo ipse fuerit, eius tamen in se assumptam habens[165] carnem, qui suam sumpserat. Sicut misit me inquit pater vivens, et ego vivo per patrem, qui manducaverit
carnem meam ipse vivit per me. Quomodo per patrem vivit, eodem modo nos per
carnem eius vivimus. Hec ergo vite nostre causa est, quod in nobis manere per
carnem Christi habemus victuri per eum, ea conditione qua vivit ille per patrem. Si
ergo nos naturaliter secundum carnem per eum vivimus, id est naturam carnis sue
adepti, quomodo non naturaliter secundum spiritum in se patrem habeat, cum
vivat ipse per patrem? Corpus Christi quod sumitur de altari figura est, dum panis
et vinum extra videtur, veritas autem dum corpus Christi et sanguis in veritate interius creditur.

[That this unity is naturally in us he himself has testified: "Whoever eats my flesh
and drinks my blood abides in me and I in him." For he will not be in anyone except in the one in whom he already was, having taken upon himself the flesh of him
who had eaten his flesh. "Just as," he said "the living father sent me, and I live
through the father, whoever shall eat my flesh will live through me." Just as he lives

---

164 Lambot, "L'Office de la Fête-Dieu," 112, line 430.

165 Clearly *habens* in BNF 1143, but abbreviated *hns* in KB 70.E.4. *Hominis* in Lambot.

through the father, we likewise live through his flesh. This therefore is the cause of our life, that what abides in us we have on account of Christ's flesh, living through him, by virtue of him living through the father. If therefore we naturally live through him according to his flesh, that is having acquired the nature of his flesh, how does he not have naturally, through the spirit, the father in himself, since he lives through the father? The body of Christ, which is consumed at the altar, is a symbol, since bread and wine is seen outwardly. It is truth when the body and blood of Christ is in truth believed within.]

120.   Lectio[166]

Gregorius; [Gratian,] De con[secratione,] Dist. II, [can. 73 beginning]

Hec salutaris victima illam nobis mortem unigeniti per misterium reparat, qui licet surgens a mortuis iam non moritur mors illi ultra non dominabitur, tamen in seipso immoraliter et incorruptibiliter vivens, iterum in hoc ministerio moritur, eius quoque ubique corpus sumitur, eius caro in populi salutem patitur, eius sanguis non iam in manus infidelium, sed in ora fidelium funditur. Hinc ergo pensemus quale sit hoc sacrificium, quod pro nostra absolutione passionem unigeniti filii semper imitatur. Quis enim fidelium habere dubium possit, ut in ipsa immolacionis hora ad sacerdotis vocem celos aperiri, et in illo Ihesu Christi misterio choros angelorum adesse summa et yma sociari, unum quid ex invisibilibus atque visibilibus fieri? Idem uno inquit eodemque tempore ac momento, et in celo rapitur, ministerio angelorum consociandum corpori Christi, et ante oculos sacertotis in altari videtur.

[This salutary sacrifice renews for us that death of the only begotten son through mystery, who, rising from the dead, dies no more—death will have no more dominion over him—nevertheless, living immortally and incorruptibly in himself, he dies again in this ministry, and his body is consumed everywhere, his flesh suffers for the salvation of the people, his blood now is poured out, not into the hands of the unfaithful, but into the mouths of the faithful. Consequently let us think of what nature is this sacrifice, which always imitates the passion of the only begotten son for our absolution. For who of the faithful can have doubt that, in that hour of sacrifice, at the voice of the priest the heavens are opened, and in that mystery of Jesus Christ the choruses of angels are present, the highest and lowest are joined together, made one out of invisible and visible things? At one and the same time and moment, he said, the same is both carried off into heaven, by the ministry of the angels to be joined to the body of Christ, and is seen before the eyes of the priest on the altar.]

---

[166] Lambot, "L'Office de la Fête-Dieu," 112, [30].

121.   Lectio:[167]

[Gratian, De consecratione, *Dist. II, can. 73 continued]*

Tanta est unitas ecclesie in Christo, ut unus ubique sit panis corporis Christi, et unus sit calix sanguinis eius. Calix enim quem sacerdos catholicus sacrificat, non est aliud nisi ipse quem dominus apostolis tradidit, quia sicut divinitas verbi dei una est, que totum implet mundum, ita licet multis locis, et innumerabilibus diebus illud corpus consecretur, non sunt tamen multa corpora Christi, neque multi calices, sed unum corpus Christi, et unus sanguis cum illo, quod sumpsit in utero virginis et quod dedit apostolis. Divinitas enim verbi replet illud quod ubique est, et coniungit ac facit, ut sicut ipsa una est, ita et unum corpus eius sit in veritate. Unde animadvertendum est quia sive plus sive minus quis inde percipiat, omnes equaliter corpus Christi integerrime sumunt, et generaliter omnes, et specialiter unusquisque.

[So great is the unity of the church in Christ, that everywhere the bread of the body of Christ is one, and the chalice of his blood is one. For the chalice which the catholic priest offers, is none other than that which the Lord entrusted to the apostles, because just as the divinity of the word of God is one, which it fills up the whole world, so, notwithstanding the fact that it is consecrated in many places and on innumerable days, there are not many bodies of Christ, nor many chalices, but one body of Christ, and one blood with it, which he obtained in the womb of the virgin, and which he gave to the apostles. For the divinity of the word fills that which is everywhere, and unites it and is the reason why, just as it is one, so also his body is one in truth. Hence it must be observed, that, whether several or fewer, whoever partakes of it, all consume equally the body of Christ completely whole, both generally all, and specifically each one.]

122.   Lectio[168]

[Gratian, De consecratione, *Dist. II, can. 73 conclusion]*

Misterium fidei dicitur quod credere debes, quod ibi salus nostra consistat. Providens enim nobis dominus dedit hoc sacramentum salutis, ut quia nos cotidie peccamus, et ille iam mori non potest per istud sacramentum remissionem consequamur. Cotidie enim ipse comeditur et bibitur in veritate, sed integer, et vivus et immaculatus permanet. Et ideo magnum et pavendum misterium est, quia aliud videtur, et aliud intelligitur. Sed cum misterium sit unum, corpus et sanguis dicitur, figuram panis et vini habet faciente domino, quia non habemus in usum carnem crudam commedere et bibere sanguinem.

Ambrosius, De sacramentis; *[Gratian,]* De con[secratione,] *Dist. II, [can. 84]*

Sicut verus est filius dei dominus noster Ihesus Christus non quemadmodum homines per graciam, sed quasi filius et substancia patris, ita vera est Christi caro, sicut ipse dixit quam accipimus, et verus sanguis est potus. Ego sum inquit panis vi-

---

[167] Ibid., 113, line 461.

[168] Ibid., 113, line 474.

vus, qui de celo descendi. Sed caro non descendit de celo. Quomodo ergo descendit de celo panis vivus? Quia idem dominus Ihesus consors est divinitatis et corporis, et tu qui accipis carnem, divine eius substancie, in illo participas alimento.

[What you must believe is called the mystery of faith, because our salvation rests on it. Looking out for us, our Lord gave us this sacrament of salvation, so that, because we sin daily, and he cannot die any more, through this sacrament we might obtain remission. Daily he himself is truly eaten and drunk, but he remains whole and living and immaculate. And so it is a great and fearful mystery, because one thing is seen and another understood. But although the mystery is one, it is called the body and blood, it has the appearance of bread and wine, through the Lord's doing, because we are not used to eating crude flesh and drinking blood.

Just as our Lord Jesus Christ is the true son of God, not in the manner that men are, through grace, but just as a son is the substance of the father, so it is the true flesh of Christ, as he himself said, which we receive, and true blood is drink. I am, he said, the living bread, who descended from heaven. But his flesh did not descend from heaven. How, therefore, did the living bread descend from heaven? Because the same Lord Jesus is a sharer of divinity and flesh, and you who receive the flesh of his divine substance, participate in that food.]

123.   Lectio[169]

Augustinus; [Gratian,] De con[secratione,] Dist. II, [can. 36 beginning]

Quia passus est pro nobis dominus commendavit nobis in isto sacramento sanguinem suum et corpus, quod eciam fecit nosmetipsos. Nam et nos corpus ipsius facti sumus, et per misericordiam ipsius quod accepimus nos sumus. Recordamini et vos non fuistis, et creati estis, et ad aream dominicam comportati estis, laboribus boum id est annunciancium evangelium triturati estis. Quando cathecumini deferebamini, in orreo servabamini, nomina vestra dedistis, moli cepistis ieuiniis, exorcismis. Postea ad aquam venistis, et conspersi estis, et panis dominicus facti estis. Ecce quod accepistis. Quomodo ergo unum videtis esse quod factum est, sic unum estote vos, diligentes vos, scilicet tenendo unam fidem, unam spem, individuam caritatem. Heretici quando hoc accipiunt sacramentum, testimonium contra se accipiunt, quia illi querunt divisionem, cum panis iste indicet unitatem. Sic et vinum in multis racemis fuit, et modo unum est. Vinum est in sua nativitate, calix est post pressuram torcularis et vos post illa ieiunia, post labores, post humilitatem et contricionem iam in nomine domini tanquam ad calicem Christi venistis, et ibi vos estis in mensa et in calice nobiscum vos estis. Simul enim hoc sumimus, simul bibimus, quia simul vivimus.

[Because he died for us, the Lord gave his blood and body to us in this sacrament, which also makes us his own. For we have become his body, and through his mercy we are what we receive. Remember that you did not exist, that you were born and

---

[169] Ibid., 114, [32].

you were brought together to the Lord's altar, and you were formed by the labor of cows, that is, of proclaiming angels. When you were catechumens you were brought down, you served in the barn, you gave your names, you received grain to drive out your hunger. After you came to the water, you were sprinkled, and you became the Lord's bread. Behold what you have received. Just as you see that which was made is one, so you will be one, and you shall be faithful, namely by holding one faith, one hope, individual charity. Heretics, when they receive this sacrament, receive testimony against themselves, because they seek division, while this bread proclaims unity. Thus wine was in many grapes, and now it is one. This is wine in its origin, it is that chalice after the pressure of the grape press, and, after those fasts, after labors, after humility and contrition, now in the name of the Lord, in the same way, you come to the chalice of Christ, and you are at the table, and you are at the chalice with us. Together we consume this, together we drink, because together we live.]

124.   Lectio[170]

Augustinus De sermone de infantibus *et continuatur littere precedenti in decretis; [Gratian,* De consecratione, *Dist. II, can. 36 conclusion]*

Ita dominus noster Ihesus Christus nos significavit, nos ad se pertinere voluit, misterium pacis et unitatis nostre in mensa consecravit. Qui accipit misterium unitatis, et non tenet vinculum pacis, non misterium accipit pro se, sed testimonium contra se. Nulli est aliquatenus ambigendum unumquemque fidelium corporis et sanguinis dominici tunc esse participem quando in baptismate efficitur membrum Christi, nec alienari ab illius panis calicisque consorcio eciam si antequam panem illum comedat calicemque bibat de hoc seculo migraverit, in unitate corporis constitutus. Sacramenti quippe illius participacione ac beneficio non privatur, quando in se hoc quod illud sacramentum significat invenitur.

[Gratian, De consecratione, *Dist. II, can. 58 beginning]*

Qui manducant et bibunt Christum, vitam manducant et bibunt. Illud manducare est refici, illud bibere est vivere. Quod in sacramento visibiliter sumitur, in ipsa veritate spiritualiter manducatur et bibitur.

[In this way our Lord Jesus Christ showed us that he wished us to belong to him, he consecrated the sacrament of peace and of our unity at the table. Whoever receives the sacrament of unity, and does not keep the bond of peace, does not receive the sacrament for himself, but testimony against himself. It is in no way to be doubted by anyone that each of the faithful is a participant in the body and blood of the Lord from the time when he is made by baptism a member of Christ, and is not kept from the fellowship of that bread and cup even if he left this world before he could eat that bread and drink the cup, since he was already a part of the unity of the body. Certainly he is not deprived of participation in, and the benefit of, that sacrament, since found in him is the very thing which that sacrament testifies.

---

[170] Ibid., 114, line 513.

Those who eat and drink Christ eat and drink life. To consume it is to be refreshed, to drink it is to live. What is consumed visibly in the sacrament, in truth itself is consumed and drunk spiritually.]

125.   Lectio[171]

[Gratian, De consecratione, Dist. II, can. 58 continued, overlapping with can. 75]

Manducatur Christus, vivit manducatus, quia surrexit occisus. Nec quando manducamus, partes de illo facimus. Et quidem in sacramento sic fit. Et norunt fideles quando manducent carnem Christi, unusquisque accipit partem suam. Per partes manducatur in sacramento, et manet integer totus in celo. Per partes manducatur in sacramento, et manet integer totus in corde tuo. Totus enim erat apud patrem quando venit in virginem, implevit illam nec recessit ab illo. Veniebat in carnem ut homines eum manducarent, et manebat integer apud patrem ut angelos pasceret.

[Gratian, De consecratione, Dist. II, can. 70]

Invitat dominus servos, et preparat eis cibum seipsum. Quis audeat dominum suum manducare? Et tamen ait: Qui manducat me, vivit propter me. Quando manducatur vita manducatur, nec occiditur ut manducetur sed mortuos vivificat. Quando manducatur, reficit, sed non deficit.

[Gratian, De consecratione, Dist. II, can. 75]

Non ergo timeamus fratres manducare istum panem, ne forte finiamus illum, et postea quid[172] manducemus non inveniamus.

[Gratian, De consecratione, Dist. II, can. 58 continued]

Quod videtur panis est et calix, quod eciam oculi renunciant. Quod autem fides postulat instruenda, panis est corpus Christi, et calix est sanguis. Ista ideo dicuntur sacramenta, quia in eis aliud videtur et aliud intelligitur. Quod videtur speciem habet corporalem, quod intelligitur fructum habet spiritualem.

[Christ is eaten, eaten he lives, because he arose, though slain. Nor, when we eat, do we make parts of him. For in the sacrament the situation is the following. The faithful know, when they eat the flesh of Christ, that everyone receives his share. He is eaten in the sacrament in parts, yet he remains entirely whole in heaven. He is eaten in the sacrament in parts, yet he remains entirely whole in your heart. He was one with the father, when he came into the virgin, he filled her, but he did not withdraw from him. He became flesh, so that men might consume him, yet he remained one with the father, so that he might nourish the angels.

The Lord invites his servants, and serves to them himself as food. Who dares to consume his Lord? Nevertheless he said: Whoever eats me, lives according to me. When he is eaten, life is eaten, and he does not die that he might be eaten, but to make the dead live. When he is eaten, he refreshes, but he does not perish.

---

[171] Ibid., 115, [34].

[172] *Quod* in Lambot.

Therefore let us not fear, brothers, to eat this bread, lest by chance we finish it, and afterwards we do not discover what we eat.

What appears to be bread and cup is indeed what the eyes report. Because faith demands to be taught, the bread is the body of Christ, and the chalice is the blood. These things are called sacraments, because in them one thing is seen, and something else understood. What is seen has a corporeal substance, what is understood has spiritual benefit.]

126.   Lectio[173]

Alexander papa, Quintus a Petro;[174] *[Gratian,]* De con[secratione,] *Dist. II, [can. 8]*

> Nichil in sacrificiis maius potest esse quam corpus et sanguis Christi, nec ulla oblacio hac pocior est, sed hec omnes precellit, que pura consciencia domino offerenda est et pura mente sumenda, atque ab omnibus veneranda. Et sicuti pocior est ceteris, ita pocius excoli et venerari debet.

Sergius papa; [Gratian,] De con[secratione,] *Dist. II, [can. 22] et ponitur quarto sententiarum.*

> Triforme est corpus domini. Pars oblate in calicem missa, corpus Christi quod iam resurrexit monstrat, pars commesta, ambulans adhuc super terram, pars in altari usque ad finem misse remanens, corpus in sepulchro, quia usque in finem seculi corpora sanctorum in sepulchris erunt.

Augustinus in libro sententiarum Prosperi *et ponitur decretis; [Gratian,]* De con[secratione,] *Dist. II, [can. 37]*

> Dum frangitur hostia, dum sanguis de calice in ora fidelium funditur, quid aliud quam dominici corporis in cruce immolatio eiusque sanguinis de latere effuso designatur?

Ambrosius in libro de catecizandis rudibus et ponitur decretis; [Gratian,] De con[secratione,] *Dist. II, [can. 39]*

> Panis et calix non qualibet sed certa consecratione misticus nobis fit. Non nascitur proinde quod ita fit nobis, quamvis sit panis et calix, alimentum est resurrectionis.

Augustinus (Ambrosius?) in libro officiis; [Gratian,] De con[secratione,] *Dist. II, [can. 40]*

> Ante benedictionem alia species nominatur, post benedictionem Christi corpus significatur. In illo sacramento Christi est. Qui manducaverit[175] hoc corpus, fiat ei remissio peccatorum.

> [Nothing in sacrifices can be greater than the body and blood of Christ, nor is any oblation more powerful than this, but it surpasses all, which, with a pure conscience, must be offered to the Lord, and consumed with a pure heart, and must be venerated by all. And just as it is better than others, so it ought to be better worshipped and venerated.

---

[173] Lambot, "L'Office de la Fête-Dieu," 115, [38].

[174] This remark seems to refer to the earliest papal tradition, in which Alexander is listed as the fifth pope after Peter.

[175] *Manducat* in Lambot.

The body of the Lord is of three forms: The part of the offering put in the chalice at mass shows the body of Christ which has now risen; the part consumed, still walking on the earth; and the part on the altar, remaining at the end of mass, the body in the sepulchre, because the bodies of the saints will be in the sepulchres until the end of time.

When the host is broken, when the blood from the chalice is poured out into the mouths of the faithful, what else is designated than the sacrifice of the body of the Lord on the cross, and of his blood gushing from his side?

The bread and chalice become mystical for us not by an uncertain, but a definite, consecration. What consequently happens for us is not born. Although it be bread and chalice, it is the food of resurrection.

Before the blessing it is called one species, after the blessing it is designated the body of Christ. Christ is in that sacrament. Whoever shall have eaten this body, let there be for him the remission of sins.]

[Lectio][176]

Leo papa; [Gratian, De consecratione, *Dist. II, can. 40]*

In illa mistica distributione spiritualis alimonie hoc impertitur, hoc sumitur, ut accipientes virtutem celestis cibi, in carnem ipsius qui caro nostra factus est transeamus. Est[177] cibus refeccionis, est cibus sanguinis. Sicut enim caro Christi vere est cibus, ita sanguis eius vere est potus. Idem est corpus de quo dictum est: Caro mea vere est cibus, et sanguis meus vere est potus.[178] Circa hoc corpus aquile sunt, que alis circumvolant spiritualibus. Unde et idem corpus Christi edimus, ut vite eterne possimus esse participes.

Augustinus [in libro] sententiarum; [Gratian,] De con[secratione,] *Dist. II, [can. 41]*

Nos autem in specie panis et vini quam videmus, res invisibiles, id est carnem et sanguinem honoramus. Nec similiter comprehendimus has duas species, quemadmodum ante consecrationem comprehendebamus, cum fideliter fateamur ante consecrationem[179] panem esse et vinum, quod natura formavit, post consecracionem vere esse carnem et sanguinem Christi, quod benedictio consecravit.

[In that symbolic distribution of his spiritual inheritance, this is shared, this is consumed, so that, receiving the strength of heavenly food, we may be transformed into the flesh of the very one who became our flesh. This is the food of refreshment, this is the food of blood. Just as the flesh of Christ truly is food, so his blood truly is drink. It is the same body of which it is said: My flesh is truly food, and my blood is truly drink. Around this body there are eagles, which fly around on spiritual wings. Wherefore we eat the body of Christ, so that we may be participants in eternal life.

---

[176] There is no indication in BNF 1143 that a separate reading begins here, but there is such an indication in KB 70.E.4.

[177] *Et* in Lambot.

[178] This sentence erroneously recopied in BNF 1143, then crossed out.

[179] "Comprehendebamus, cum fideliter fateamur" erroneously recopied, then crossed out.

In the appearance of bread and wine that we see, we honor the invisible things, that is, his flesh and blood. Nor do we similarly perceive these two species in the way we perceived them before consecration, since we honestly say that they are bread and wine before consecration, which nature fashioned, but after consecration they are truly the flesh and blood of Christ, which the blessing has consecrated.]

127.   Lectio[180]

[Ambrosius, De officiis; *Gratian,* De consecratione, *Dist. II, can. 43]*

Forte dicas: Quomodo vera caro quomodo verus sanguis, quia sumilitudinem non video carnis, non video sanguinis veritatem? Primo omnium dixi tibi de sermone Christi, qui operatur ut possit mutare et convertere genera et instituta nature. Deinde ubi non tulerunt sermonem Christi discipuli eius sed audientes quod carnem suam daret manducare et sanguinem suum ad bibendum, recedebant, solus tamen Petrus dixit: Verba vite eterne habes, et ego a te quomodo recedam? Ne igitur plures hoc dicerent et ne veluti quidam esset horror cruoris, sed maneret gratia redemptoris, ideo in similitudine quidem accipis sacramentum, sed vere nature gloriam virtutemque consequeris. Ego sum inquit panis vivus qui de celo descendi.

Quarto Sententiarum de sacramento altaris [Peter Lombard, Sententiae, Bk. IV, Dist. XI, ch. 62 (3)]

Sub alia autem specie tribus de causis carnem et sanguinem tradidit Christus, et deinceps sumendum instituit. Ut scilicet fides haberet meritum que est de hiis que non videntur, quia fides non habet meritum cui humana ratio prebet experimentum. Et ideo ne abhorreret animus quod cerneret oculus, quia non habemus usum carnem crudam et sanguinem comedere. Quia ergo Christum vorari dentibus fas non est, in misterio carnem et sanguinem nobis comendavit. Et etiam ideo ne ab incredulis religioni christiane insultaretur.

[Perhaps you may say: In what way is this true flesh, in what way true blood, because I do not see the similarity to flesh, I do not see the reality of blood? First of all I told you about the word of Christ, which works so that it can change and convert the divisions and designs of nature. Afterwards his apostles did not endure the word of Christ, but hearing that he would give his flesh to eat, and his blood to drink, they backed away. Only Peter said: You have words of eternal life, and how can I withdraw from you? So that, therefore, more might not say this, and so that there might not be any such bristling at blood, but that the grace of the redeemer might remain, for those reasons you receive the sacrament under a certain likeness, but really you obtain nature, glory, and strength. I am, he said, the living bread, who descended from heaven.

There are three reasons why Christ transmitted his flesh and blood under a different appearance, and instituted their consumption successively, namely: so that faith, which concerns those things that are not seen, might have value, because faith does not have value, for that which human reason gives proof. And so the soul

---

[180] Lambot, "L'Office de la Fête-Dieu," 116, [45]. Seems to be a new hand in BNF 1143.

might not shrink from what the eye perceives, because we are not accustomed to eat raw flesh and blood. Because it is not right for Christ to be eaten with the teeth, he commended his body and blood to us in the mystery. And so that nothing of the Christian religion might be reviled by unbelievers.]

128.   Lectio[181]

Augustinus et ponitur quarto sententiarum; [Peter Lombard, Sententiae, *Bk. IV, Dist. XI, ch. 62 (3) continued]*

Nichil racionabilius quam ut sanguinis similitudinem sumamus, ut ita et veritas non desit et ridiculum nullum fiat a paganis, quod cruorum occisi bibamus.[182]

[Peter Lombard, Sententiae, *Bk. IV, Dist. XI, ch. 63 (4)]*

Sed quare sub duplici specie sumitur, cum substantialiter unum totus sit Christus? Ut ostenderetur totam humanam naturam assumpsisse,[183] ut totam redimeret. Panis enim ad carnem refertur vinum ad animam quia vinum operatur sanguinem, in quo sedes anime a phisicis esse dicitur. Ideo ergo in duabus speciebus celebratur ut anime et carnis susceptio in Christo et utriusque liberatio in nobis significetur.

Ambrosius et ponitur quarto sententiarum

Valet enim ad tuicionem corporis et anime quod percipimus quia caro Christi pro salute corporis, sanguis vero pro anima nostra offertur, sicut prefiguravit[184] Moyses. Caro inquit pro corpore nostro[185] offertur sanguis vero pro anima. Sed tamen sub utraque specie sumitur quod ad utrumque valet quia sub utraque specie sumitur totus Christus.

[There is nothing more sensible than that we should consume the likeness of blood. So that in this way both truth may not be lacking, and no mockery may be made by the pagans, that we drink the blood of the dead.

But why is it consumed under two species, since Christ is substantially one whole? So that he might be shown to have assumed all of human nature, in order that he might redeem all of it. Bread refers to the flesh, wine to the soul, because wine affects the blood, in which the seat of the soul is said to be by physicians. For that reason, therefore, it is celebrated under two species, so that the taking on of soul and body may be shown in Christ, and the liberation of both, may be shown in us.

What we take in is good for the preservation of the body and the soul, because the flesh of Christ is offered for the health of the body, his blood for our soul, just as Moses prefigured. Flesh, he said, is offered for your body, blood for the soul, but yet what is good for both is consumed in each food, because the complete Christ is consumed under each species.]

---

[181] Lambot, "L'Office de la Fête-Dieu," 117, line 604.

[182] Scribe at first wrote *hominis,* then crossed it out.

[183] Scribe wrote *assupmsisse,* which he did not correct.

[184] *Presignavit* in Lambot.

[185] *Vestro* in KB 70.E.4.

129.   Lectio[186]

[Peter Lombard, Sententiae, *Bk. IV, Dist. VIII, ch. 54 (7)]*

Porro illa species visibilis sacramentum est gemine rei, quia utramque rem significat, et utriusque rei similitudinem gerit expressam. Nam sicut panis pre ceteris cibis corpus reficit et sustentat, et vinum hominem letificat atque inebriat, sic caro Christi interiorem hominem plus ceteris gratiis spiritualiter reficit et saginat.

[Peter Lombard, Sententiae, *Bk. IV, Dist. VIII, ch. 48 (1)]*

Unde excellenter eucharistia dicitur id est bona gratia, quia in hoc sacramento, non modo est augmentum virtutis et gratie. Sed ille totus sumitur qui est fons et origo totius gratie.

[Peter Lombard, Sententiae, *Bk. IV, Dist. VIII, ch. 54 (7)]*

Habet etiam similitudinem cum re mistyca, quod est unitas fidelium, quia sicut ex multis granis conficitur unus panis, et ex plurimis azinis[187] vinum in unum confluit, sic ex multis fidelium personis unitas ecclesiastica constat. Unde apostolus: Unus panis et unum corpus multi sumus. Unus panis et unum corpus ecclesia dicitur pro eo quod sicut unus panis ex multis granis et unum corpus ex multis menbris conponitur, sic ecclesia ex multis fidelibus caritate copulante connectitur.

[Furthermore that visible species is a sacrament of two natures, because it represents each one, and it bears each one's stamped out likeness. For just as bread above all other foods refreshes and sustains the body, and wine elates and inebriates man, so the flesh of Christ more than other gifts spiritually refreshes and satiates the inner man.

Hence it is excellently called "Eucharist," that is "good grace," because in this sacrament there is not only an increase of virtue and grace, but he, who is the font and origin of all grace, is wholly consumed.

That which is the unity of the faithful has a similarity with the sacred event, because just as one bread is made from many grains, and wine flows from many grapes into one, so the ecclesiastical unity exists from many faithful people. Hence the Apostle: We many are one bread and one body. One bread and one body is called the church, for the reason that, just as bread is composed of many grains, and one body is composed of many members, so the church is composed of many faithful people, love uniting it.]

130.   Lectio:[188]

[Gratian, De consecratione, *Dist. II, can. 59]*

Credere in Iesum Christum, hoc est manducare panem vivum. Qui credit manducat invisibiliter saginatur, quia invisibiliter renascitur. Et qui manducat carnem Christi, et bibit sanguinem illius, vitam habet eternam. Participatione enim filii, quod est per

---

[186] Lambot, "L'Office de la Fête-Dieu," 117, [48].

[187] *Multis acinis* in Lambot.

[188] Lambot, "L'Office de la Fête-Dieu," 118, [51].

unitatem corporis et sanguinis eius homo manducans vivit, non sumens tantum in sacramento quod et mali faciunt, sed usque ad spiritus participationem, ut in corpore domini tamquam menbrum maneat et eius spiritu vegetetur quo est dum eius mandata[189] servat. Ad altare dei invisibile quo non accedit iniustus ille pervenit, qui ad hoc presens iustificatus accedit. Invenit illic vitam qui illic discernit causam suam.

Jeronimus; [Gratian,] De con[secratione,] *Dist. II, [can. 77]*

Singuli autem accipiunt Christum dominum et in singulis portionibus totus est, nec per singulos minuitur, sed integrum se prebet in singulis.

Hyllarius; [Gratian] De con[secratione,] *Dist. II, [can. 78]*

Ubi pars est corporis, est et totum. Eadem ratio est in corpore domini que in manna que[190] in eius figura precessit de quo dicitur qui plus collegerat, non habuit amplius neque qui minus paraverat habuit minus.

Quarto sententiarum *[Peter Lombard,* Sententiae, *Bk. IV, Dist. VIII, ch. 49 (2)]*

Illud datum fuit antiquis post transitum Maris Rubri, ubi submersis Egyptiis liberati sunt Hebrei. Ita hoc celeste manna, non nisi regeneratis prestari debet. Corporalis panis ille, populum antiquum ad terram promissionis per desertum eduxit. Hic celestis fideles huius seculi desertum transeuntes in celum subvehit. Unde recte viaticum appellatur, quia in via nos reficiens usque in patriam deducit.

[To believe in Jesus Christ is to eat the bread, wine. He who believes, consumes invisibly, is satiated, because he is reborn invisibly. And whoever eats the flesh of Christ, and drinks his blood, has eternal life. Man eating lives through participation with the Son, that is through the unity of his body and blood, not just consuming the sacrament, just as evil ones do, but to the extent of participation with the spirit, so that he may abide as a member in the body of the Lord, and he may be invigorated by His spirit, that is as long as he follows His mandates. He, who at this time comes justified, arrives invisibly at the altar of God, whither the unjust does not come. He finds there life, who here understands its source.

Individuals receive Christ the Lord, and the whole is in the single portions, nor is he diminished in the single parts, but he offers himself whole in the individual pieces.

Where there is a part of the body, there the whole is. The same circumstance exists in the body of the Lord as in manna, which preceded it as a symbol, about which it is said: He who gathered more, did not have a greater amount, nor did the one who had acquired less, have less.

That had been given long ago after the crossing of the Red Sea, where the Hebrews were freed from the drowned Egyptians. Thus, this heavenly manna ought to be furnished to none except the reborn (baptized). That actual bread led the ancient people through the desert to the promised land. This celestial bread conducts the faithful crossing the desert of this era into heaven. Hence it is rightly called "viaticum," because, refreshing us on the way, it leads into the homeland.]

---

[189] *Mandatum* in Lambot.

[190] *Quod* in KB 70.E.4.

[CORPUS CHRISTI]
GRAZ. UNIVERSITÄTSBIBLIOTHEK, MS 134

Officium Nove sollempnitatis Corporis Christi
Graz: Universitätsbibliothek, MS 134, fols. 241–246v

Ad vesperos
Super psalmos antiphona
1. Sacerdos in eternum/Ps Dixit Dominus (=BNF 1143 #1)
Sacerdos in eternum Christus Dominus secundum ordinem Melchisedech panem et vinum obtulit. Ps Dixit Dominus.

[Christ the Lord, a priest forever after the order of Melchisedech, brought bread and wine.]

2. Miserator Dominus/Ps Confitebor (=BNF 1143 #2)
Miserator Dominus escam dedit timentibus se in memoriam suorum mirabilium. Ps Confitebor.

[The merciful Lord gave food to those who fear him in memory of his wonderful works.]

3. Calicem salutaris/Ps Credidi propter (=BNF 1143 #3)
Calicem salutaris accipiam et sacrificabo hostiam laudis. Ps Credidi propter.

[I will take up the chalice of salvation and I will offer up a sacrifice of praise.]

4. Sicut novelle/Ps Beati omnes (=BNF 1143 #4)
Sicut novelle olivarum ecclesie filii sint in circuitu mense Domini. Ps Beati omnes.

[Let the sons of the church be like olive shoots around the table of the Lord.]

5. Qui pacem ponit/Ps Lauda Iherusalem (=BNF 1143 #5)
Qui pacem ponit fines ecclesie; frumenti adype saciat nos Dominus. Ps Lauda Iherusalem.

[He imposes peace in the territory of the church; the Lord fills us with the finest grain.]

6. Capitulum
Dominus Ihesus in qua nocte tradebatur accepit panem et gratias agens fregit et dixit: Accipite et manducate. Hoc est corpus meum, quod pro vobis tradetur. Hoc facite in meam commemorationem.

[The Lord Jesus, on the night he was betrayed, took bread and, giving thanks, broke it and said: Take and eat. This is my body, which will be given up for you. Do this in my memory.]

7. Responsory: Homo quidam/Venite comedite/Gloria patri (=BNF 1143 #7)
    Homo quidam fecit cenam magnam et misit servum suum hora cene dicere invitatis ut
    venirent. Quia parata sunt omnia. V. Venite comedite panem meum et bibite vinum
    quod miscui vobis. R. Quia. D. Gloria patri et filio et spiritui sancto. R. Quia parata.

    [A man once gave a great feast and sent his servant at the hour of the feast to tell
    those invited to come, because all was prepared. V. Come and eat my bread and
    drink the wine which I have mixed for you.]

8. Hymn: Pange lingua
    Pange lingua gloriosi
    Corporis mysterium,
    Sanguinisque preciosi,
    Quem in mundi precium
    Fructus ventris generosi
    Rex effudit gentium.

    Nobis datus, nobis natus
    Ex intacta virgine,
    Et in mundo conversatus,
    Sparso verbi semine,
    Sui moras incolatus
    Miro clausit ordine.

    In supreme nocte cene
    Recumbens cum fratribus,
    Observata lege plene
    Cibis in legalibus,
    Cibum turbe duodene
    Se dat suis manibus.

    Verbum caro, panem verum
    Verbo carnem efficit:
    Fitque sanguis Christi merum,
    Et si sensus deficit,
    Ad firmandum cor sincerum
    Sola fides sufficit.

    Tantum ergo sacramentum
    Veneremur cernui:
    Et antiquum documentum
    Novo cedat ritui:
    Prestet fides supplementum
    Sensuum defectui.

    Genitori, genitoque
    Laus et iubilatio,
    Salus, honor, virtus quoque
    Sit et benedictio:
    Procedentis ab utroque
    Compar sit laudatio. Amen.

[1. Praise, my tongue, the mystery of the glorious body and of the precious blood, which the king of nations, fruit of a noble womb, poured out in ransom of the world.
2. Given to us, born to us from a pure virgin, and having lived in the world, the seed of his word having been scattered, he closed in a wondrous way his span of life.
3. At the night of the last supper, reclining with his brothers, the law of permitted foods having been fully observed, he gives himself as food with his own hands to the group of twelve.
4. The Word made flesh changes true bread into flesh by a word. And pure wine becomes Christ's blood. And if the sense fails, only faith suffices to convince the sincere heart.
5. Therefore let us eagerly venerate such a great sacrament. Let the old example cede to the new rite. Let faith render assistance to the limitations of the senses.
6. To the Father, and to the Son be praise and jubilation, salvation, honor, strength, and blessing. To the One who proceeds from them both be equal praise. Amen.]

9. Versiculus (cf. #62)
Panem de celo prestitisti eis. R. Omne delectamentum in se habentem, alleluia.

[You have furnished them with the bread of heaven. R. Having in it every delight, alleluia.]

10. In Evangelio antiphona: O quam suavis/[Magnificat] (=BNF 1143 #10)
O quam suavis est domine spiritus tuus qui ut dulcedinem tuam in filios demons-trares pane suavissimo de celo prestito esurientes replens bonis fastidiosos divites dimittens inanes. [Ps Magnificat.]

[O how kind is your spirit Lord, who, to show your sweetness towards your chil-dren, provides the sweetest bread from heaven, filling the hungry with good things, sending the haughty rich away empty.]

11. Oratio
Deus qui nobis sub sacramento mirabili passionis tue memoriam reliquisti; tribue quesumus ita nos corporis et sanguinis tui sacra mysteria venerari; ut tue redemp-tionis fructum in nobis iugiter sentiamus. Qui vivis [et regnas cum deo patre in uni-tate spiritu sancti deus per omnia secula seculorum. Amen.]

[Lord, who has left us, in a wonderful sacrament, a memorial of your passion, grant, we pray, that we may venerate the mystery of your body and blood, so that we may always feel within ourselves the fruit of your redemption. Who lives and reigns with God the father in unity with the holy spirit, God, world without end. Amen.]

Ad matutinas
12. Invitatory: Christum regem (=BNF 1143 #12)
Christum regem adoremus dominantem gentibus Qui se manducantibus dat spiri-tus pinguedinem. Ps Venite.

[Let us adore Christ the king, the Lord of all peoples, who gives nourishment of the spirit to those who eat.]

13. Hymn: Sacris sollempniis (Seems to =Strahov #13, not BNF 1143 #13)

Sacris sollempniis iuncta sint gaudia
Et ex precordiis sonent preconia
Recedant vetera nova sint omnia
Corda voces et opera.

Noctis recolitur cena novissima
Qua Christus creditur agnum et azima
Dedisse fratribus iuxta legitima
Priscis indulta patribus.

Post agnum typicum expletis epulis
Corpus dominicum datum discipulis
Sic totum omnibus quod totum singulis
Eius fatemur manibus.

Dedit fragilibus corporis ferculum
Dedit et tristibus sanguinis poculum
Dicens accipite quod trado vasculum
Omnes ex eo bibite.

Hic sacrificium istud instituit
Cuius officium committi voluit
Solis prespiteris quibus sic congruit
Ut sumant et dent ceteris.

Panis angelicus fit panis hominum
Dat panis celicus figuris terminum
O res mirabilis manducat dominum
Pauper servus et humilis.

Te trina deitas unaque poscimus
Sicut nos visitas sicut te colimus
Per tuas semitas duc nos quo tendimus
Ad lucem quam inhabitas. Amen.

[1. Let joys be joined with the sacred solemnities, and let prayers sound from our hearts. Let the old depart, let all things be new, hearts, voices, and works.
2. The night of last supper is recalled, in which Christ is believed to have given to his brethren lamb and unleavened bread, according to the rights granted to the forefathers.
3. The meal completed, after the symbolic lamb, the divine body was given to his disciples, entirely to all, entirely to each, by his own hands, this we proclaim.
4. He gave to the weak the meal of his body, and he gave to the sorrowful the drink of his blood, saying: Take the vessel which I give; all of you drink from it.
5. Thus he established this sacrifice, whose ceremony he wished to be entrusted only to those elders who were fit to consume it and give to others.
6. The bread of the angels becomes the bread of mankind, the celestial bread gives an end to symbols. O wondrous thing! the poor, the slave, the humble consumes the Lord.
7. We implore you, God three and one, just as you visit us, so do we honor you. Lead us on your pathway, by which we strive to the light which you inhabit. Amen.]

In primo nocturno
Antiphona

14. Fructum salutiferum/Ps Beatus vir (=BNF 1143 #14, Ed, 2v)
    Fructum salutiferum gustandum dedit dominus mortis sue tempore. Ps Beatus vir.
    [The Lord gave a saving fruit to taste at the time of his death.]

15. A fructu frumenti/Ps Cum invocarem (=BNF 1143 #15, Ed, fol. 2v)
    A fructu frumenti et vini multiplicati, fideles in pace Christi requiescunt. Ps Cum invocarem.
    [Having increased by the fruit of grain and wine, the faithful rest in the peace of Christ.]

16. Communione calicis/Ps Conserva me (=BNF 1143 #16; Ed, fol. 2v)
    Communione calicis quo deus ipse sumitur, non vitulorum sanguine, congregavit nos dominus. Ps Conserva me.
    [The Lord has assembled us by the communion of the chalice in which God himself is consumed, not by the blood of calves.]

17. Memor sit Dominus/ Ps Exaudiat te Dominus (=EU fol. 4r; not BNF 1143 #24)
    Memor sit dominus sacrificii nostri et holocaustum nostrum pingue fiat. Ps Exaudiat te dominus.
    [May the Lord remember our sacrifices and may he accept our burnt offering.]

18. Paratur nobis/Ps Dominus regit (EU fol. 4r; not BNF 1143)
    Paratur nobis mensa domini adversus omnes qui tribulant me. Ps Dominus regit.
    [The table of the Lord is prepared for us against those who oppress me.]

19. In voce exultationis/Ps Quemadmodum (=BNF 1143 #26; EU fol. 4r)
    In voce exultacionis resonant epulantes in mensa domini. Ps Quemadmodum.
    [The banqueters resound in a voice of exultation at the table of the Lord.]

20. Versiculus
    Panem celi dedit eis. R. Panem angelorum manducavit homo.
    [He gave them the bread of heaven. R. Mankind ate the bread of the angels.]

21. Lectio prima
    Immensa divina largitatis beneficia exhibita populo christiano inestimabilem ei conferunt dignitatem. Neque enim est aut fuit aliquando tam grandis nacio que habeat deos appropinquantes sibi sicut adest nobis deus noster. Unigenitus siquidem dei filius sue divinitatis volens nos esse participes, nostram naturam assumpsit, ut homines deos faceret factus homo. Et hoc insuper quod de nostro assumpsit totum nobis contulit ad salutem.

    [The boundless favors of divine generosity, shown to the Christian people, bestow an inestimable dignity on them. There neither is nor ever was so great a nation having gods so near to itself as our God is to us. The only-begotten Son of God, desiring that we be participants in his divinity, took on our nature, so that, having become man, he might make men gods. Whatever he assumed of our nature he made instrumental in the work of our salvation.]

23. Responsory: Immolabit hedum/Pascha nostrum (=BNF 1143 #19)
Immolabit hedum multitudo filiorum Israhel ad verperam pasche. Et edent carnes et azimos panes. V. Pascha nostrum immolatus est Christus itaque epulemur in azimis sinceri[ta]tis et veritatis. R. Et edent.

[R. The multitude of the sons of Israel shall kill the lamb on the Passover evening, and they shall eat meat and unleavened bread. V. Christ our Paschal lamb has been sacrificed. Therefore let us feast on the unleavened bread of sincerity and truth.]

24. [Lectio secunda]
Corpus namque suum pro nostra reconciliacione in ara crucis hostiam optulit deo patri, sanguinem suum fudit in precium simul et lavacrum, ut redempti a miserabili servitute a peccatis omnibus mundaremur. Et ut tanti beneficii iugis in nobis maneret memoria, corpus suum in cibum et sanguinem suum in potum sub specie panis et vini sumendum fidelibus dereliquid. O preciosum convivium salutiferum et omni suavitate repletum. Quid enim hoc convivio preciosius esse potest, in quo non carnes vitulorum et yrcorum ut olim in lege, sed nobis Christus sumendus proponitur verus deus? Quid hoc sacramento mirabilius? In ipso namque panis et vinum in corpus Christi et sanguinem substancialiter convertuntur. Ideoque Christus deus et homo perfectus sub modici panis specie continetur.

[He offered to God the Father his own body as sacrifice for our reconciliation on the altar of the cross, shed his own blood for our ransom and rebirth, so that, having been redeemed from wretched servitude, we might be washed clean of all sins. And, so that a memory of such great kindnesses might remain always in us, he left behind his body as food and his blood as drink, to be consumed by the faithful in the form of bread and wine. O most precious and wondrous banquet, full of health and filled with every delicacy! What can be more precious than this banquet, in which not the flesh of goats and calves, as once was the rule, but Christ the true God, is given to us as nourishment? What is more wondrous than this sacrament? For in it, bread and wine are changed substantially into the body and blood of Christ. Indeed Christ, the perfect God and man, is contained under the appearance of a little bread.]

25. Responsory: Panis quem ego dabo/Locutus est populus (=BNF 1143 #29)
Panis quem ego dabo caro mea est pro mundi vita. Litigabant ergo Iudei dicentes: Quomodo potest hic nobis dare carnem suam ad manducandum. V. Locutus est populus contra Dominum: Anima nostra nauseat super cibo isto levissimo. R. Quom[odo].

[The bread which I give is my flesh for the life of the world. The Jews disputed saying: How can this man give us his own flesh as food? V. The people spoke against the Lord: Our spirit is sickened by this most trifling food.]

26. [Lectio tertia]
Manducatur utique a fidelibus, sed minime laceratur, quinimmo diviso sacramento integer sub qualibet divisionis particula perseveret. Accidencia etiam sine subiecto in eodem existund, ut fides locum hebeat, dum visibile invisibiliter sumitur aliena specie occultatum, et sensus a deceptione immunes reddantur qui de accidentibus iudicant sibi notis. Nullum etiam sacramentum est isto salubrius, quo purgantur peccata, virtutes augentur, et mens omnium spritualium carismatum habundancia inpinguatur. Offertur in ecclesia pro vivis et mortuis, ut omnibus prosit quod est pro salute omnium institutum.

[He is consumed entirely by the faithful, but he is in no way broken up, but rather, even though the sacramental sign is divided, he remains entire in each particle of division. For the accidents exist in it without material form in order that faith may have its place, when the visible is invisibly consumed, hidden in the form of another thing, and our senses, which judge events that happen to them, are restored safely from deception. For no sacrament is more salubrious than this, through which sins are purged, virtues are increased, and the soul is filled with an abundance of every spiritual gift. It is offered in the Church for the living and the dead, so that what was instituted for the salvation of all may benefit all.]

27. Responsory: Comedetis carnes/Non moÿses (=BNF 1143 #21)
Comedetis carnes et saturabimini panibus. Iste est panis quem dedit vobis dominus ad vescendum. V. Non Moyses dedit vobis panem de celo sed pater meus dat vobis panem de celo verum. R. Iste est panis.

[You will eat meats, and you will be satiated with breads. This is the bread the Lord has given to you to be eaten. V. Moses did not give you bread from heaven but my father gives you true bread from heaven.]

28. [Lectio quarta]
Suavitatem denique huius sacramenti nullus exprimere sufficit, per quod spirit[u]alis dulcedo in suo fonte gustatur et recolitur memoria illius quam in sua passione Christus monstravit, excellentissime caritatis. Unde ut huiusmodi caritatis inmensitas cordibus infigeretur fidelium, in ultima cena quando pascha cum discipulis celebrato transiturus erat ex hoc mundo ad patrem, hoc sacramentum instituit, tamquam passionis sue memoriale perhenne, figurarum veterum impletivum, miraculorum omnium ab ipso factorum maximum, et discipulis omnibus de sua contristis absentia solatium singulare.

[No one suffices to express the delicacy of this kind of sacrament, through which spiritual sweetness is tasted in its source, and the memory of the most excellent charity, which Christ showed in his passion, is recalled. Whereby, so that the immensity of this kind of charity might be impressed more profoundly on the hearts of the faithful, at the last supper, when, having celebrated the passover with his disciples, he was about to leave this world and return to the father, he instituted this sacrament as an eternal remembrance of his passion, the fulfillment of ancient precursors, the greatest of the miracles performed by him, and sole solace to those saddened by his absence.]

29. Responsory: Respexit Helyas/Si quis manducaverit/Gloria patri (=BNF 1143 #23)
Respexit Helyas ad caput suum subcinericium panem qui surgens comedit et bibit. Et ambulavit in fortitudine cibi illius usque ad montem dei. V. Si quis manducaverit ex hoc pane vivet in eternum. R. Et a. D. Gloria patri et filio et spiritui sancto. R. Et amb.

[Elias saw a hearth bread by his head and arising he ate and drank. And he walked in the strength of this food up to the mountain of God. V. If anyone eats this bread, he will live forever.]

In secundo nocturno
Antiphona
30. Introibo ad altare Dei/Ps Iudica me Deus (=BNF 1143 #34)
Introibo ad altare Dei; sumam Christum qui renovat iuventutem meam. Ps Iudica me Deus.

[I will go into the altar of God, I will take on Christ who renews my youth.]

31. Cibavit nos Dominus/Ps Exultate Deo adiutori (=BNF 1143 #35)
Cibavit nos Dominus ex adype frumenti et de petra melle saturavit nos. Ps Exultate Deo.

[The Lord has fed us from the finest grain, and he has filled us with honey from a rock.]

32. Ex altari tuo Domine/Ps Quam dilecta (=BNF 1143 #36)
Ex altari tuo domine Christum sumimus in quem cor et caro nostra exultat. Ps Quam dilecta.

[From your altar, Lord, we receive Christ, in whom our soul and body rejoices.]

33. Memoriam fecit/Ps Domine exaudi (=BNF 1143 #91)
Memoriam fecit mirabilium suorum, misericors et miserator Dominus. Escam [se][191] dedit timentibus se, a[ll]e[l]uia. Ps Domine exaudi.

[He has made a memorial of his wonderful works, the gracious and merciful Lord. He has given food to those who fear him, alleluia.]

34. Memoria mea/Ps Benedic ii. (=BNF 1143 #92)
Memoria mea in generaciones populorum. Qui edunt me, adhuc esurient; et qui bibunt me, adhuc sicient, a[ll]e[l]uia. Ps Benedic ii.

[My memory will be in the generations of peoples. Those who eat me will hunger for more; and those who drink me will thirst for more, alleluia.]

---

[191] Written in the margin and carrying a 2-note descending ligature.

35. Qui habet aures/Ps Confitemini Domino et invocate (=BNF 1143 #93)
    Qui habet aures audiendi, audiat quid spiritus dicat ecclesiis. Vincenti dabo manna absconditum, a[ll]e[l]uia. Ps Confitemini Domino et invocate.

    [Let the one who has ears for hearing, hear what the Spirit says to the churches. To him who conquers I will give hidden manna, alleluia.]

36. Versiculus
    Petierunt et venit coturnix. R. Et pane celi saturavit eos.[192]

    [They asked and quail came. R. And he filled them with bread from heaven.]

37. [Lectio quinta]
    Convenit itaque devotioni fidelium, sollempniter recolere institucionem tam salutiferi tamque mirabilis sacramenti, ut ineffabilem modum divine presencie in sacramento visibili veneremur, et laudetur Dei potentia que in sacramento eodem, tot mirabilia operatur, nec non et de tam salubri tamquam suavi beneficio exsolvantur Deo gratiarum debite actiones. Verum et si in die cene, quando sacramentum predictum noscitur institutum, inter missarum sollempnia de institutione ipsius specialis mentio habeatur, totum tamen residuum eiusdem diei officium ad Christi passionem pertinet, circa cuius venerationem ecclesio illo tempore occupatur.

    [It is fitting therefore for the devotion of the faithful, solemnly to honor again the institution of such a salubrious and miraculous sacrament, so that we may venerate the ineffable mode of the divine presence in a visible sacrament, and so that the power of God may be praised, which, in the same sacrament, works so many miracles, and indeed so that the thanks owed to God for such a salubrious and sweet kindness may be discharged. But, although on the day of the last supper, when the aforesaid sacrament is known to have been instituted, special mention is made of its institution within the solemnities of the mass, nevertheless all the remaining worship of this same day is concerned with Christ's suffering, around whose veneration the church at that time is occupied.]

38. Responsory: Misit me pater/Cibavit eum (=BNF 1143 #41)
    Misit me pater vivens et ego vivo propter patrem. Et qui manducat me vivet propter me. V. Cibavit eum Dominus pane vite et intellectus. Et qui.

    [The living Father sent me and I live because of the Father. And he who eats me will live because of me. V. The Lord fed him with the bread of life and understanding.]

39. [Lectio sexta]
    Unde ut integro celebritatis officio institucionem tanti sacramenti coleret plebs fidelis, romanus pontifex Urbanus quartus huius sacramenti devocione affectus, pie statuit prefate institucionis memoriam, prima feria quinta post octavas penthecostes

---

[192] This versiculus is not part of the standard service in BNF 1143, but is found in Strahov, #17.

a cunctis fidelibus celebrari, ut qui per totum anni circulum hoc sacramentuo utimur ad salutem, eius institutionem illo specialiter tempore recolamus, quo spiritus sanctus discipulorum corda edocuit ad plene cognoscenda huius mysteria sacramenti. Nam et in eodem tempore cepit hoc sacramentum a fidelibus frequentari. Legitur enim in actibus apostolorum quod erant perseverantes in doctrina apostolorum et communicatione fractionis panis et orationibus, statim post sancti spiritus missionem.

[Hence, so that the faithful may solemnly honor again the institution of such a great sacrament by a complete office of celebration, the Roman Pope Urban IV, influenced by the devotion of this sacrament, piously decreed commemoration of the aforementioned institution on feria five after the octave of Pentecost, to be celebrated by all the faithful, so that we, who use this sacrament throughout the year for salvation, may honor again, at that time especially, its institution, by which the Holy Spirit taught the hearts of the disciples to understand fully the mysteries of this sacrament. For at the same time this sacrament began to be frequented by the faithful. It is indeed read in the Acts of the Apostles that they were persevering in the apostolic doctrine by sharing in the breaking of bread, and by prayers, immediately after the departure of the Holy Spirit.]

40. Responsory: Cenantibus illis/Dixerunt viri (=BNF 1143 #31)
Cenantibus illis accepit Ihesus panem et benedixit ac fregit deditque discipulis suis et ait: Accipite et comedite. Hoc est corpus meum. V. Dixerunt viri tabernaculi mei: quis det de carnibus eius ut saturemur? R. Accipite.

[While they were eating, Jesus took bread and blessed and broke it, and gave it to his disciples and said: Take and eat. This is my body. V. The men of my tent said: Who will give of his flesh that we may be satisfied?]

41. [Lectio septima]
Ut autem hec predicta feria quinta, et per octavas sequentes eiusdem salutaris institucionis honorificencius agatur memoria, et sollempnitas de hoc celebrior habeatur loco distributionum materialium que in ecclesiis kathedralibus largiuntur, existentibus canonicis horis nocturnis pariterque diurnis, prefatus romanus pontifex, qui huiusmodi horis in hac sollempnitate personaliter in ecclesiis interessent stipendia spiritualia apostolica largitione concessit, quatenus per hec fideles animati ad tanti festi celebritatem avidius et copiosius convenirent.

[So that, on the the aforesaid feria five and the following octave, remembrance of this same saving institution may be performed more honorably and its ceremony have greater participation, in place of the distributions of material goods that are bestowed in cathedral churches, during current established times, night as well as day, the aforesaid Roman pope grants to those who, during its times, personally take part in this ceremony at church spiritual stipends through apostolic generosity, so that by them the faithful more eagerly and more numerously may come together for the celebration of so great a feast.]

42. Responsory: Qui manducat/Non est alia (=BNF 1143 #39)
Qui manducat meam carnem et bibit meum sanguinem in me manet et ego in illo.
V. Non est alia natio tam grandis [que][193] habeat deos appropinquantes sibi sicut
Deus noster adest nobis.

[He who eats my flesh and drinks my blood remains in me and I in him. V. There is
not another nation so great who has gods so near to itself as our God is to us.]

43. [Lectio octava]
Unde omnibus vere penitentibus et confessis, qui matutinali officio huius festi pre-
sentcialiter in ecclesia ubi celebraretur adessent centum, qui vero misse totidem. Illis autem qui interessent in primis ipsius festi vesperis similiter centum, qui vero in
secundis totidem. Eis quoque qui prime, tercie, sexte, none, ac completorii adessent
officiis, pro qualibet horarum ipsarum quadraginta. Illis vero qui per ipsius festi octavas in matutinalibus, vespertinis, ac predictarum horarum officiis presentes existerent, singulis octavarum ipsarum diebus, centum, dierum indulgentiam misericorditer tribuit perpetuis temporibus duraturam.

[Hence, to all the truly penitent and to those having confessed, who are present at the
office of matins of this feast in person in the church where it is celebrated, one hundred [days' indulgence]. To those who attend mass, the same number. To those who
take part in first vespers of the feast, similarly one hundred. The same number to
those in second vespers. To those who attend the offices of prime, terce, sext, none,
and compline, forty for any of those hours. To those who personally appear through
the octave of this feast at matins, vespers, mass, and the aforesaid office hours, for
each of the days of the octave he mercifully allots one hundred days in perpetuity.]

44. Responsory: Accepit Ihesus/Memoria memor/Gloria patri (=BNF 1143 #33)
Accepit Iesus calicem postquam cenavit dicens: Hic calix novum testamentum est in
meo sanguine. Hoc facite in meam commemoracionem. V. Memoria memor ero et
tabescet in me anima mea. R. Hoc fa[cite]. D. Gloria patri et filio et spiritui sancto. R.
Hoc facite.

[After he had eaten, Jesus took the cup, saying: This cup is a new testament in my
blood. Do this in my memory. V. I shall recall this memory, and my soul will be sorrowful within me.]

45. Ad canticum: Comedi favum (Unique to Graz; WA 355?)
Comedi favum cum melle meo, bibi vinum meum cum lacte meo.

[Eat the honeycomb with my honey, drink my wine with my milk.]

46. Domine miserere nostri.

[Lord have mercy on us.]

---

[193] Written in the margin and carrying a single note.

47. Versiculus

Educas panem de terra. R. Et vinum letificet cor hominis.

[May you produce bread from the earth. R. And may wine gladden the heart of man.]

48. [Gospel] Iohannem [Jo 6: 55].

Caro mea vere est cibus, et sanguis meus vere est potus.

[My flesh truly is food and my blood truly is drink.]

Augustini episcopi de eadem lectione [Lectio nona]

Cum enim cibo et potu id appetant homines, ut non esuriant, necque siciant, hoc vere non prestat nisi iste cibus et potus, qui eos a quibus sumitur inmortales, et incorruptibiles facit, id est societas ipsorum sanctorum, ubi pax erit et unitas plena atque perfecta. Propterea quippe sicut eciam ante nos intellexerunt homines dei, dominus noster Ihesus Christus, corpus et sanguinem suum in eis rebus humanis comendavit, que ad unum aliquid rediguntur. Ex multis namque granis unus panis conficitur, et ex multis racemis vinum confluit.

[Although men desire from food and drink, that they neither hunger nor thirst, this is not assured, unless it is that food and drink which makes those, by whom it is consumed, immortal and incorruptible, that is, a community of the saints themselves, where there will be peace and full and perfect unity. Therefore, indeed, as men of God understood before us, our Lord Jesus Christ put his body and blood into these things, which are made into some one thing. Now, one bread is made from many grains, and wine flows together from many clusters of grapes.]

49. Responsory: Unus panis/Parasti in dulcedine/Gloria patri (=BNF 1143 #43)

Unus panis et unum corpus multi sumus, omnes qui de uno pane et de uno calice participamur. V. Parasti in dulcedine tua pauperi Deus qui habitare facis unanimes in domo. Omnes.

[We many are one bread and one body, we all who are made participants in one bread and one cup. V. You have prepared in your goodness for the needy, O God, You who cause us to live of one mind in your house.]

50. [Lectio decima]

Denique iam exponit, quomodo id fiat quod loquitur, et quid sit manducare corpus eius et sanguinem bibere. Et qui manducat meam carnem, et bibit meum sanguinem, in me manet, et ego in eo. Hoc est ergo manducare illam escam, et illum bibere potum, in Christo manere infinem et illum manentem in se habere, ac per hoc qui non manet in Christo, et in quo non manet Christus, proculdubio non manducat spiritualiter eius carnem, licet carnaliter et visibiliter premat dentibus sacramenta corporis et sanguinis Christi, sed magis ad iudicium sibi manducat et bibit qui inmundus presumit ad Christi sacramenta accedere, que alius non digne sumit non qui mundus est. De quibus dicitur: Beati mundo corde quoniam ipsi Deum videbunt.

[Finally he now explains how what he has spoken happens, and what it is to eat his body and drink his blood. "He who eats my body and drinks my blood abides in me and I in him." To eat that food and to drink that drink is, therefore, to abide in Christ, and to have him abiding in oneself, and thus the person who does not abide in Christ, and in whom Christ does not abide, without doubt does not eat spiritually his flesh, although physically and visibly he chews with his teeth the sacraments of the body and blood of Christ, but rather he eats and drinks the sacrament of such great importance to his own condemnation, who, impure, presumes to approach the sacraments of Christ, which no one rightly takes except the one who is pure. About whom it is said: Blessed are the pure of heart, because they shall see God.]

51. Responsory: Melchisedech vero/Benedictus Abraham (=BNF 1143 #96; Strahov #49)
Melchisedech vero rex Salem proferens panem et vinum–erat autem sacerdos Dei altissimi–benedixit Abrahe et ait. V. Benedictus Abraham Deo excelso, qui creavit celum et terram. R. Benedixit.

[Melchisedech king of Salem offered bread and wine; he was the priest of the highest God. He blessed Abraham and said. V. Blessed be Abraham by the most high God, who created heaven and earth.]

52. [Lectio undecima]
Sicut me misit inquid pater vivens, et ego vivo propter patrem. Et qui manducat me, et vivet propter me. Non enim filius participatione patris fit melior qui est natu equalis, sicut participacione filii per unitatem corporis et sanguinis, quam illa manducatio potatioque significat, efficit nos meliores. Vivimus ergo nos propter ipsum manducantes eum, id est ipsum accipientes vitam eternum quam non habemus ex nobis. Vivit autem ipse propter patrem missus ab eo, quia semetipsum exinanivit factus obediens usque ad signum crucis.

[As the living father, he said, sent me, I live because of the father. And he who eats me, will live because of me. Certainly the son, who was born equal, is not made better through the participation of the father, as he makes us better through the participation of the son through the unity of the body and blood which that food and drink signifies. We live on behalf of him, by eating him, that is, receiving him as eternal life, which we do not have by ourselves. He himself lives on behalf of the father, sent by him, because he emptied himself, made obedient up to the sign of the cross.]

53. Responsory: Calix benedictionis/Quoniam unus panis (=BNF 1143 #98)
Calix benedictionis cui benedicimus, nonne communicatio sanguinis Christi est, et panis quem frangimus, nonne participatio corporis Domini est? V. Quoniam unus panis et unum corpus multi sumus, nam omnes de uno pane et de uno calice participamus. R. Et.

[The cup of blessing which we bless, is it not a participation in the blood of Christ, and the bread which we break, is it not a participation in the body of the Lord? V. Because we many are one bread and one body, for we all partake of one bread and one cup.]

54. [Lectio duodecima]

Sicut misit me inquid pater vivens, et ego vivo propter patrem. Et qui manducat me, et ipse vivet propter me. Ac si diceret: Et ego vivo propter patrem, id est ut ad illum tanquam ad maiorem referam vitam meam exinanitio mea fecit in qua me misit. Ut autem quisque vivat propter me, participatio facit qui manducat me. Ego itaque humiliatatus vivo propter patrem, ille rectus vivit propter me.

[As the living father sent me, I live on behalf of the father. And he who eats me, he himself will live on behalf of me. This is as if to say: I live on behalf of the father, that is, I direct my life to him as to one greater, he brought about my emptying, in which form he sent me. Participation brings about for the one who eats me, that each one lives on behalf of me. Thus, I, humbled, live on behalf of the father, this man, uplifted, lives on behalf of me.]

55. Responsory: Ego sum/Ego sum/Gloria patri (=BNF 1143 #100)

Ego sum panis vite. Patres vestri manducaverunt manna in deserto et mortui sunt. Hic [est][194] panis de celo descendens. Si quis ex ipso manducaverit non morietur. V. Ego sum panis vivus qui de celo descendi. Si quis manducaverit ex hoc pane vivet in eternum. D. Gloria patri et filio et spiritui sancto. R. Hic est panis.

[I am the bread of life. Your fathers ate manna in the desert and they died. This is the bread which comes down from heaven. If anyone shall eat of it, he will not die. V. I am the living bread who came down from heaven. If anyone shall eat of this bread he will live forever.]

In matutinis laudibus

[Antiphona]

56. Sapiencia edificavit (=BNF 1143 #46)

Sapiencia edificavit sibi domum miscuit vinum et posuit mensam, a[ll[e[l]uia.

[Wisdom has built herself a house, she has prepared her wine, she has laid her table, alleluia.]

57. Angelorum esca (=BNF 1143 #47)

Angelorum esca nutrivisti populum tuum et panem de celo prestitisti illis a[ll]e[l]uya.

[You have nourished your people with the food of the angels, and you have provided them bread from heaven, alleluia.]

58. Pinguis est panis (=BNF 1143 #48)

Pinguis est panis Christi et prebebit delicias regibus a[ll]e[l]uia.

[Rich is the bread of Christ and he will offer delicacies to kings, alleluia.]

---

[194] Written in the margin and carrying a single note.

59. Sacerdotes sancti (=BNF 1143 #49)
    Sacerdotes sancti incensum et panes offerunt Deo a[ll]e[l]uia.

    [The holy priests offered incense and breads to God, alleluia.]

60. Vincenti dabo (=BNF 1143 #50)
    Vincenti dabo manna absconditum et nomen novum a[ll]e[l]uia.

    [To him who conquers I will give hidden manna and a new name, alleluia.]

61. Capitulum: Dominus Ihesus in qua nocte (See #6)

62. Short Responsory (cf. #9)
    Panem de celo prestitisti eis. R. Omne delectamentum in se habentem.

    [You have furnished them with the bread of heaven. R. Having in it every delight.]

64. Hymn: Verbum supernum prodiens
    Verbum supernum prodiens
    Nec patris linquens dexteram
    Ad opus suum exiens
    Venit ad vite vesperam.

    In mortem a discipulo
    Suis tradendus emulis
    Prius in vite ferculo
    Se tradidit discipulis.

    Quibus sub bina specie
    Carnem dedit et sanguinem
    Ut duplici substancie
    Deus cibaret hominem.

    Se nascens dedit socium
    Convescens in edulium
    Se moriens in precium
    Se regnans dat in premium.

    O salutaris hostia
    Que celi pandis hostium
    Bela[195] premunt hostilia
    Da robur fer auxilium.

    Uni trinoque Domino
    Sit sempiterna gloria
    Qui vitam sine termino
    Nobis donet in patria. Amen

---

[195] Looks like *cela* in MS.

[1. The celestial word coming forth, not leaving the right hand of the father, going out to its work, comes to the evening of life.

2. Handed over by a disciple to his enemies for his death, he first gave himself to his disciples on a plate of life.

3. He gave them his flesh and blood under two species, so that he might feed all men of twofold substance.

4. Being born he gave himself as a companion, dining he gave himself as nourishment, dying he gave himself as a ransom, reigning he gives himself as a reward.

5. O saving victim, you who opens the door of heaven, wars and enemies press us, give us strength, bring us help.

6. To the Lord, one and three, be eternal praise, may he give us eternal life in the homeland. Amen.]

65. Versiculus
Posuit fines tuos pacem. R. Et adype frumenti saciat te.

[He has established peace in your borders. R. And with the finest grain he has filled you.]

66. In Evangelio antiphona: Ego sum panis [/Benedictus] (=BNF 1143 #54)
Ego sum panis vivus qui de celo descendi. Si quis manducaverit ex hoc pane vivet in eternum, a[ll]e[l]uia. [Ps Benedictus.]

[I am the living bread who descended from heaven. If anyone eats of this bread, he will live forever, alleluia.]

67. Oratio (See #11)
Deus qui nobis sub sacra[mento . . .]

[Day Hours[
Ad i
68. Antiphon: Sapientia (incipit only)

Ad iii
69. Antiphon: Angelorum esca

70. Capitulum: Dominus Ihesus in qua.

71. Responsory
Panem celi dedit eis. [V.] Panem an[gelorum] m[anducavit] ho[mo.]

[He gave them the bread of heaven. V. Mankind ate the bread of the angels.]

72. Oratio: Deus qui nobis

Ad vi
73. Antiphon: Pinguis est

74. Capitulum

Quociens cumque manducabitis panem hunc et calicem bibetis, mortem domini annunciabitis donec veniat.

[As often as you shall eat this bread and drink this chalice, you will proclaim the
death of the Lord until he comes.]

75. Responsory

Cibavit eos ex ad[ipe] f[rumenti.]

[He fed them from the finest grain.]

76. Oratio[196]

Deus qui in deserti regione multitudinem populi tua virtute saciasti, in huius quoque seculi transeuntis excursu, victum spiritalem ne deficiamus impende.

[God who satisfied the multitude of the people in the region of the desert by your
power, apply spiritual nourishment in the course of this passing age, that we may
not be disheartened.]

Ad ix

77. Antiphon: Vincent[i]

78. Capitulum

Quicumque manducaverit panem hunc vel biberit calicem domini indigne, reus erit
corporis et sanguinis domini.

[Whoever shall eat this bread and drink the chalice of the Lord unworthily, will be
answerable for the body and blood of the Lord.]

79. Responsory

Educas panem de terra. [V.] Et vi[num] le[tificet cor hominis.] Educas.

[May you produce bread from the earth. V. And may wine gladden the heart of man.]

80. Oratio

Omnipotens sempiterne Deus qui in Christi filii tui beata passione nos reparas, conserva in nobis opera memorie tue, ut in huius celebritate mysterii perpetua devo-
cione vivamus. Per eundem [Dominum nostrum Jesum Christum Filium tuum: qui
tecum vivit et regnat in unitate Spiritus Sancti Deus, per omnia saecula saeculorum.
R. Amen.]

[All powerful and eternal God, who restores us in the blessed passion of your son
Christ, keep safe in us by the agency of your memory, so that, in the solemnity of
this mystery, we may have life through perpetual devotion.]

---

196 This prayer seems to be unique to Graz.

In secunda Vesperis

Super psalmos antiphona Sacerdos in eternum Cum R[eliqua]

81. Responsory: Accepit Ihesus Vel Responsory: Respexit Helyas

82. Versiculus

Posuit fines tuos pacem. R. Et adype fru[menti saciat te.]

[He has established peace in your borders. R. And with the finest grain he has filled you.]

83. In Evangelio antiphona: O sacrum convivium/[Magnificat] (=BNF 1143 #74 but with interesting differences)

O sacrum convivium in quo Christus sumitur recolitur memoria passionis eius mens impletur gracia et future glorie nobis pignus datur a[ll]e[l]uia.

[O sacred banquet in which Christ is received, the memory of his passion renewed, the soul is filled with grace, and a pledge of future glory is given to us, alleluia.]

Ad completorium

84. O gustu mirabilis[/Nunc dimittis]

O gustu mirabilis o panis summe dulcedinis tu nostre mesticie sanum relevamen, singulis fidelibus dans sanitatem spiritus, in antiqui specie cibi designaris, signatum signum terminans in quo patris Helye cessat cineris panis, a[ll]e[l]uia.

[O miraculis meal, O bread of greatest sweetness, you the sound relief of our sadness, giving to each of the faithful health of the spirit, you are represented in the old species of food, a designated sign defining that on which the patriarch Elias rests, a hearth bread, alleluia.]

Infra octava lectiones

Huius sacramenti figura precessit, quando manna pluit Deus [patribus] in deserto, qui cotidiano celi pascebantur alimento. Unde dictum est: Panem angelorum manducavit homo. Sed tamen panem illum qui manducaverunt omnes in deserto mortui sunt.   II.   II.[197]

Iste autem esca quam accipitis iste panis vivus, qui de celo descendit vite eterne substanciam ministrat. Et quicumque hunc panem manducaverit, non morietur in eternum, quia corpus Christi est.   III.

Considera utrum nunc prestancior sit panis angelorum an caro Christi, que III. utique est corpus vite.[198] Manna illud de celo, hoc super celum. Illud celi, hoc domini celorum. Illud corruptioni obnoxium si in diem alterum servaretur hoc alienum ab omni corrupcione.

---

[197] This is the way the Roman numerals appear in the manuscript. The first two, not in the margin, seem to indicate second and third readings for the first day, and they appear only for the first day. The capital letters beginning the second and third sentences within the texts show second and third readings in the other days. I have tried to indicate this by beginning these text portions on a new line. The Roman numerals in the margins seem to be someone's later disposition of the readings across the days of the octave.

[198] *Tu autem* inserted at this point by a different hand.

[A precursor of this sacrament occurred earlier, when God rained manna on the fathers in the desert, who daily ate the food of heaven. Wherefore it is said: Man ate the bread of the angels. But yet those who ate that bread all died in the desert.

However, this bread which you take, this living bread which descended from heaven, provides the substance of eternal life. And whoever shall eat this bread, will not die forever, because it is the body of Christ.

Consider which now is more precious, the bread of angels, or Christ's flesh, which is wholly the body of life. That manna is from heaven, this above heaven. That is of heaven, this, of the Lord of heavens. That, subject to corruption, if kept for another day, this free from all corruption.]

Die secunda

Quicumque religiose gustaverit, corruptionem sentire non poterit. Illis aqua de petra fluxit, tibi sanguis ex Christo. Illos ad horam saciavit aqua, te sanguis diluit in eternum. II. IIII.

Iudeus bibit et sitit, tu cum biberis sitire non poteris. Et illud in umbra, hoc in veritate. Si illud quod miraris umbra est, quantum istud est cuius umbram miraris? Audi quia umbra est, que apud patres facta est.

Bibebant inquit de spirituali consequente eos petra. Petra autem erat Christus. Set non in pluribus eorum complacitum est Deo. Nam prostrati sunt in deserto. Hec autem facta sunt in figura nostri.

[Whoever religiously eats, will not experience corruption. To them water flowed from the rock, to you the blood [flows] from Christ. The water satisfied them for a time, the blood cleanses you for eternity.

The Jews drank and thirsted, you, when you drink, cannot thirst. That [happened] in a shadow, this in truth. If that at which you marvel is a shadow, how much more is this whose shadow you admire. Hear why this is a shadow, which was done in the time of the forefathers.

They drank, he said, from the spiritual rock which followed them. The rock, however, was Christ. But God was not well pleased with many of them. Thus they were cast down in the desert. This was done as a symbol to us.]

Die tercia

Lectio Ia

V   Cognovisti pociora. Pocior est enim lux quam umbra, veritas quam figura, corpus auctoris quam manna de celo. Forte dicis, aliud video. Quomodo tu mihi asseris quod corpus Christi accipiam? Et hoc nobis super est ut probemus.

VI   Quantis igitur utimur exemplis, ut probemus hoc non esse quod natura formavit, sed quod benedictio conse[c]ravit, maioremque vim esse benedictionis quam nature, quia ipsa benedictione etiam natura ipsa mutatur?

Unde virgam tenebat Moyses, proiecit eam et facta est serpens. Rursus apprehendit caudam serpentis et in virge naturam revertitur. Vides ergo prophetica gratia bis mutatam esse naturam, et serpentis et virge.

[You know which is better. Light is better that shadow, truth better than a symbol, the body of the creator better than manna from heaven. Perhaps you say: I see something different. How can you claim to me that I am receiving the body of Christ? And this is what we must show.

How many examples, therefore, do we use, to show that this is not what nature has formed, but what blessing has consecrated, and that there is greater power in blessing than in nature, because by blessing even nature itself can be changed.

Hence, Moses held a rod, threw it, and it became a serpent. Again, he grasped the serpent's tail, and it reverted into its nature as a rod. You see therefore, by prophetic will, its nature is twice changed, both of a serpent and a rod.]

Die quarta

Lectio I

VII Currebant Egypti flumina, puro meatu aquarum subito de fontium venis sanguis cepit erumpere. Non erat potus in fluviis. Rursus ad prophete preces cruor fluminum cessavit, aquarum natura remeavit.

Circumclusus undique erat populus Hebreorum hinc Egyptiis vallatis, inde mari conclusus. Virgam levavit Moyses, separavit se aqua, et in murorum speciem se congelavit, adque inter undas via pedestris apparuit.

Iordanis retrosum conversus, contra naturam in sui fontis revertitur exordium. Nonne claret naturam, vel maritimorum fluctuum vel cursus fluvialis esse mutatam?

[The rivers of Egypt flowed with a pure course of waters, suddenly from the source of the waters blood began to burst forth, there was no drinkable water in the rivers. Conversely, at the prayers of the prophet, the blood of the rivers ceased, the nature of waters returned.

The Hebrew nation was surrounded on all sides, on one side blocked by the Egyptians, on the other side cut off by the sea. Moses raised a rod, the water parted and solidified itself into a kind of wall, and between the waves a foot path appeared.

The Jordan reversed course, and it returned, against nature, to the beginning of its source. Is it not clear that the nature of the ocean's waves or of the river's course was changed?]

Die Va

Lectio Ia

VIII Siciebat populus patrum, tetigit Moyses petram, et aqua de petra fluxit. Numquid non preter naturam operata est gratia, ut aquam moveret petra, quam non habebat natura?

Marath fluvius amarissimus erat, ut siciens populus bibere non posset. Moyses misit lignum in aquam, et amari . . . [199]

[The people of the forefathers thirsted, Moses touched the rock, and water flowed from the rock. Has not grace acted contrary to nature, so that a rock might spew forth water, which it did not have by nature?

The Marath River was very bitter, so that the thirsting people were not able to drink. Moses threw a branch into the water, and nature eliminated the bitterness of its waters.]

---

[199] The service breaks off at this point. See Kern, "Das Offizium *De Corpore Christi*," 46–67.

[CORPUS CHRISTI]
BRUSSELS, BIBLIOTHÈQUE ROYALE, 139, FOLS. 107–108V

1. Immolabit/Pascha nostrum =BNF 1143 #20

2. Comede/Non Moyses =BNF 1143 #21

3. Melchisedech/Benedictus/Gloria =BNF 1143 #96

4. Cenantibus/Dixerunt =BNF 1143 #31

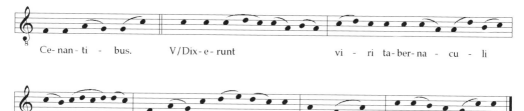

Ce- nan - ti - bus.   V/Dix- e - runt   vi - ri ta- ber- na - cu - li

me - i   quis det   de car - ni - bus   e - ius   ut sa - tu - re - mur.

5. Qui manducat/Non est alia =BNF 1143 #39

Qui   man - du - cat.   V/Non   est   a - li - a   na - ti - o

tam   gran - dis   que ha - be - at   de - os   ap- pro- pin- quan - tes   si - bi

sic - ut   De - us   no - ster   ad - est   no - bis.

6. Accepit/Memoria/Gloria =BNF 1143 #33

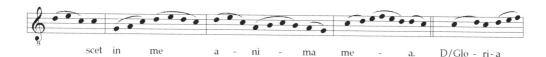

Ac - ce - pit. V/Me- mo - ri - a   me - mor e - ro et ta - be -

scet in   me   a - ni - ma   me - a.   D/Glo - ri - a

pa - tri et fi - li - o et spi - ri - tu - i   san - cto.

7. Calix/Quoniam =BNF 1143 #98[200]

Ca - lix.   V/Quo - ni - am   u-nus pa - nis et u-num   cor - pus

mul - ti su - mus   nam o-mnes de u-no   pa-ne et de u-no ca-li-ce   par-ti-ci - pa - mus.

8. Ego sum/Ego sum =BNF 1143 #99

E-go   sum. V/E - go   sum pa - nis   vi - vus   qui de ce - lo   de - scen - di.

Si quis man-du-ca - ve - rit   ex hoc   pa-ne   vi - vet   in e - ter - num.

9. Unus/Parasti/Gloria =BNF 1143 #43

U - nus.   V/Pa - ra - sti   in   dul - ce - di - ne   tu - a

pau - pe - ri   De - us   qui   ha - bi - ta - re   fa - cis

u - na - ni - mes   in   do - mo. O - mnes. D/Glo - ri - a

pa - tri   et   fi - li - o   et spi - ri - tu - i   san - cto. Et   de.

---

[200] This version is more ornate and closer to *Solem iusticie*, its source chant, than the one in BNF 1143.

10. Homo/Venite/Gloria =BNF 1143 #7 (2 Vespers responsory)

Ho - mo. V/Ve - ni - te co - me - di - te pa - nem me - um
et bi - bi - te vi - num quod mi - scu - i vo - bis, qui a pa - ra - ta.
D/Glo - ri - a pa - tri et fi - li - o et spi - ri - tu - i
san - cto. Qui - a pa - ra - ta sunt.

De sacramento ad matutinas Invit.

Brussels, Bibliothèque royale, 139, fols. 109–110[201]

11. Invitatory: Carnis/Venite

Car - nis Ps/Ve - ni - te

12. Mundum/Ad hoc continuum

Mun - dum. V/Ad hoc con - vi - vi - um tam per - ma - gni-fi - cum
vo - cat per fi - li - um ce-tum ca - tho - li - cum.

---

[201] Texts from AH 5: 32 ff.

13. Mundo/Pater namque

Mun - do. V/Pa - ter nam - que pro - pri - um fi - li - um

vi - a - to - ri dat in so - la - ci - um.

14. Verbum/Sole panis/Gloria

Ver - bum. V/So - le pa - nis re - ma-nent spe-ci - es,

in quas sen - sus in-ten-dit a - ci - es. D/Glo - ri - a

pa - tri et fi-li - o et spi-ri - tu - i san - cto.

15. Pauperibus/Apostolos

Pau-pe - ri-bus. V/A-po - sto - los si - gnat ca - ra-cte - re,

ut de - in - ceps pos-sent con - fi - ce - re.

16. Panis/Confortantem

Pa - nis. V/Con - for-tan - tem cor pa - nem su - mi - te

et pro vi - no san - gui - nem bi - bi - te.

17. Granum/Nisi locus/Gloria

Gra — num. V/Ni - si lo-tus ab o- mni sce - le- re

non pre - su — mat pa — nem hunc e - de-re. D/Glo — ri — a

pa — tri et fi - li — o et spi- ri — tu- i san — cto.

18. Felix vitis/Omnes in fide

Fe - lix vi - tis. V/O - mnes in fi - de di - vi - tes

sunt hu - ius vi - tis pal — mi — tes.

19. Discedentem/Quicumque digne

Di- sce — den - tem. V/Quicum-que di-gne se re fi — cit

i — ter ce - li se - cu - rus per — fi - cit.

20. Terminatis/Presens in mentis/Gloria

Ter - mi - na - tis. V/Pre - sens in men - tis

o - cu lis sub sa - cra - men - ti spe-ci - e sem-per est cum di-sci - pu - lis

pre-bens flu-en- ta gra - ci - e. D/Glo - ri - a pa - tri

et fi - li - o et spi-ri - tu - i san - cto.

In festo sacramenti
Brussels, Bibliothèque royale, 139, fols. 162–163

21. Gradual: Oculi/Aperis

O - cu - li. V/A- pe -

ris tu ma - num tu - am

et im - ples o - mne

a-ni - mal be - ne - di - cti-o - ne.

22. Alleluia/Caro mea

Al- le - lu - ia.

V/ Ca - ro   me - a ve-re est ci - bus et san - guis me - us

ve- re est po - tus. Qui mandu - cat me - am

car - nem et bi - bit me - um san - gui - nem in me

ma - net et e - go in e - o.

BRIGHAM YOUNG UNIVERSITY. HAROLD B. LEE LIBRARY, SPECIAL COLLECTIONS, VAULT 091 R263 1343 FOLS. 1V–4V

Incipit officium nove sollempnitatis corporis comini nostri Ihesu Christi
quam constituit dominus Urbanus papa quartus celebrari singulis annis
cum propriis octavis: prima quinta feria post octavas pentecostes

In vigilia ad vesperos super psalmos antiphona
1. Sacerdos in eternum//Ps Dixit Dominus

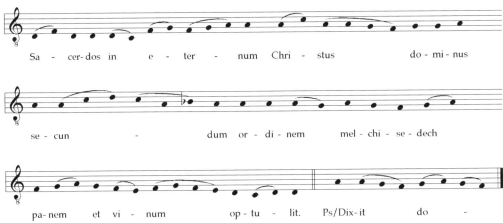

[Christ the Lord, a priest forever after the order of Melchisedech, offered bread and
wine.]

2. Miserator Dominus/Ps Confitebor

[The merciful Lord gave food to those who fear him in memory of his wonderful
works.]

3. Calicem salutaris/Ps Credidi propter

Ca - li-cem   sa - lu - ta-ris   ac - ci - pi - am   et   sa-cri-fi-ca - bo

ho   -   sti-am   lau - dis.   Ps/Cre-di - di.

[I will take up the chalice of salvation and I will offer up a sacrifice of praise.]

4. Sicut novelle/Ps Beati omnes

Si   -   cut no-vel - le   o - li - va-rum   ec-cle - si - e   fi   -   li - i

sint   in   cir - cu - i - tu   men - se   Do - mi - ni.   Ps/Be-a-ti o - mnes.

[Let the sons of the church be like olive shoots around the table of the Lord.]

5. Qui pacem ponit/Ps Lauda Iherusalem

Qui   pa-cem   po - nit fi - nes   ec-cle   -   si - e   fru - men ti a-di-pe

sa   -   ci - at   nos Do - mi-nus.   Ps/Lau - da   Ihe - ru.

[He imposes peace in the territory of the church; the Lord fills us with the finest grain.]

6. Capitulum

Dominus Ihesus in qua nocte tradebatur accepit panem et gratias agens fregit et dixit: Accipite et manducate. Hoc est corpus meum, quod pro vobis tradetur.

[The Lord Jesus, on the night he was betrayed, took bread and, giving thanks, broke it and said: Take and eat. This is my body, which will be given up for you.]

7.   Responsory: Homo quidam/Venite comedite/Gloria patri

Ho - mo qui-dam fe - cit   ce - nam ma-gnam et mi - sit   -ser-vum su - um

ho - ra   ce - ne di - ce - re   in - vi-ta-tis ut ve - ni - rent   qui - a pa - ra - ta   sunt

o   mni - a.

V/Ve- ni- te com- me- di- te   pa-nem me-um et bi- bi-te vi-num   quod mis- su- i vo - bis.   Qui - a.

Glo- ri - a   pa- tri et fi - li - o   et   spi - ri - tu - i   san - cto.   Qui - a.

[R. A man once gave a great feast and sent his servant at the hour of the feast to tell those invited to come, because all was prepared. V. Come and eat my bread and drink the wine which I have mixed for you.]

8. Hymn: Sacris sollemniis

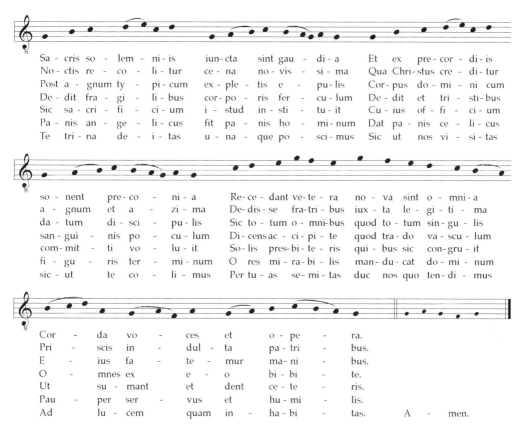

Sa - cris so - lem - ni - is   iun - cta   sint gau - di - a   Et ex pre - cor - di - is
No - ctis re - co - li - tur   ce - na   no - vis - si - ma   Qua Chri - stus cre - di - tur
Post a - gnum ty - pi - cum   ex - ple - tis e - pu - lis   Cor - pus do - mi - ni cum
De - dit fra - gi - li - bus   cor - po - ris fer - cu - lum   De - dit et tri - sti - bus
Sic sa - cri - fi - ci - um   i - stud in - sti - tu - it   Cu - ius of - fi - ci - um
Pa - nis an - ge - li - cus   fit pa - nis ho - mi - num   Dat pa - nis ce - li - cus
Te tri - na de - i - tas   u - na - que po - sci - mus   Sic ut nos vi - si - tas

so - nent   pre - co - ni - a   Re - ce - dant ve - te - ra   no - va sint o - mni - a
a - gnum   et a - zi - ma   De - dis - se fra - tri - bus   iux - ta le - gi - ti - ma
da - tum   di - sci - pu - lis   Sic to - tum o - mni - bus   quod to - tum sin - gu - lis
san - gui - nis po - cu - lum   Di - cens ac - ci - pi - te   quod tra - do va - scu - lum
com - mit - ti vo - lu - it   So - lis pres - bi - te - ris   qui - bus sic con - gru - it
fi - gu - ris ter - mi - num   O res mi - ra - bi - lis   man - du - cat do - mi - num
sic - ut   te co - li - mus   Per tu - as se - mi - tas   duc nos quo ten - di - mus

Cor - da vo - ces   et   o - pe - ra.
Pri - scis in - dul - ta   pa - tri - bus.
E - ius fa - te - mur   ma - ni - bus.
O - mnes ex e - o   bi - bi - te.
Ut su - mant et dent ce - te - ris.
Pau - per ser - vus et hu - mi - lis.
Ad lu - cem   quam in - ha - bi - tas. A - men.

[1. Let joys be joined with the sacred solemnities, and let prayers sound from our hearts. Let the old depart, let all things be new, hearts, voices, and works.

2. The night of last supper is recalled, in which Christ is believed to have given to his brethren lamb and unleavened bread, according to the rights granted to the forefathers.

3. The meal completed, after the symbolic lamb, the divine body was given to his disciples, entirely to all, entirely to each, by his own hands, this we proclaim.

4. He gave to the weak the meal of his body, and he gave to the sorrowful the drink of his blood, saying: Take the vessel which I give; all of you drink from it.

5. Thus he established this sacrifice, whose ceremony he wished to be entrusted only to those elders who were fit to consume it and give to others.

6. The bread of the angels becomes the bread of mankind, the celestial bread gives an end to symbols. O wondrous thing! the poor, the slave, the humble consumes the Lord.

7. We implore you, God three and one, just as you visit us, so do we honor you. Lead us on your pathway, by which we strive to the light which you inhabit. Amen.]

9. Versiculus

Panem de celo prestitisti eis. R. Omne delectamentum in se habentem.

[You have furnished them with the bread of heaven. R. Having in it every delight.]

10. In Evangelio antiphona: O quam suavis/[Magnificat]

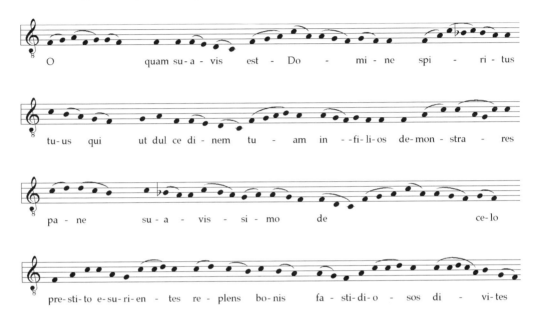

[O how kind is your spirit Lord, who, to show your sweetness towards your children, provides the sweetest bread from heaven, filling the hungry with good things, sending the haughty rich away empty.]

11. Oratio

Deus qui nobis sub sacramento mirabili passionis tue memoriam reliquisti; tribue quesumus ita nos corporis et sanguinis tui sacra mysteria venerari; ut tue redemptionis fructum in nobis iugiter sentiamus. Qui vivis et regnas cum deo patre in unitate spiritu sancti deus per o[mnia] s[ecula] seculorum. Amen.]

[God, who has left us, in a wonderful sacrament, a memorial of your passion, grant, we pray, that we may venerate the mystery of your body and blood, so that we may always feel within ourselves the fruit of your redemption. Who lives and reigns with God the father in unity with the holy spirit, God, world without end. Amen.]

Ad matutinas

12. Invitatory: Christum regem

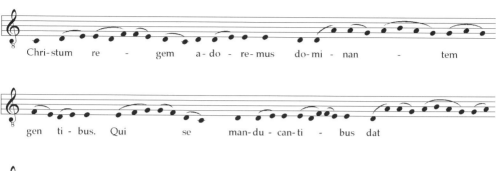

[Let us adore Christ the king, the Lord of all peoples, who give nourishment of the spirit to those who eat.]

13. Hymn: Pange lingua

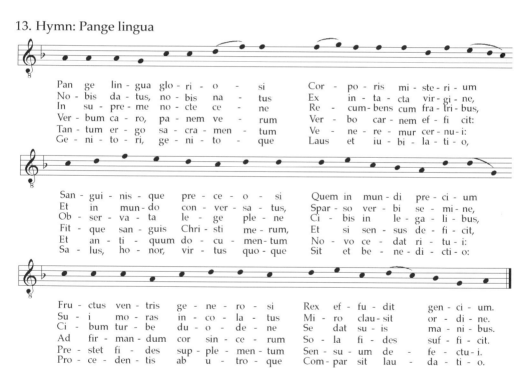

[1. Praise, my tongue, the mystery of the glorious body and of the precious blood, which the king of nations, fruit of a noble womb, poured out in ransom of the world.

2. Given to us, born to us from a pure virgin, and having lived in the world, the seed of his word having been scattered, he closed in a wondrous way his span of life.

3. At the night of the last supper, reclining with his brothers, the law of permitted foods having been fully observed, he gives himself as food with his own hands to the group of twelve.

4. The Word made flesh changes true bread into flesh by a word. And pure wine becomes Christ's blood. And if the sense fails, only faith suffices to convince the sincere heart.

5. Therefore let us eagerly venerate such a great sacrament. Let the old example cede to the new rite. Let faith render assistance to the limitations of the senses.

6. To the Father, and to the Son be praise and jubilation, salvation, honor, strength, and blessing. To the One who proceeds from them both be equal praise. Amen.]

In primo nocturno
Antiphona
14. Fructum salutiferum/Ps Beatus vir

[The Lord gave a saving fruit to taste at the time of his death.]

15. A fructu frumenti/Ps Cum invocarem

[Having increased by the fruit of grain and wine, the faithful rest in the peace of Christ.]

16. Communione calicis/Ps Conserva

Com - mu - ni - o - ne ca - li - cis quo de - us i - pse su - mi - tur,

non vi - tu - lo - rum san - gui- ne, con - gre - ga- vit nos do - mi- nus.

Ps/Con- ser - va

[The Lord has assembled us by the communion of the chalice in which God himself is consumed, not by the blood of calves.]

17. Versiculus

Panem celi dedit eis. R. Panem angelorum manducavit homo.

[He gave them the bread of heaven. R. Mankind ate the bread of the angels.]

18. Lectio prima

Immensa divina

19. Responsory i: Immolabit hedum/Pascha nostrum

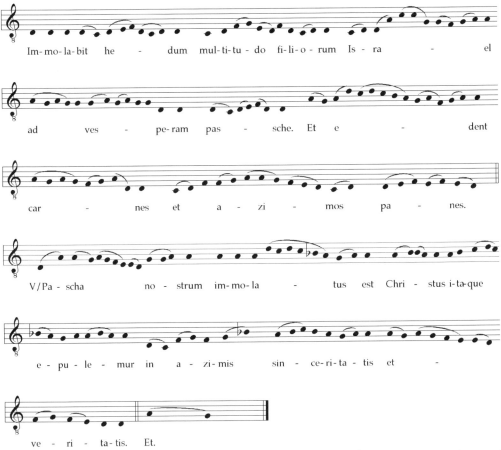

Im- mo- la- bit he - dum mul- ti- tu - do fi- li- o - rum Is - ra - el

ad ves - pe- ram pas - sche. Et e - dent

car - nes et a - zi - mos pa - nes.

V/Pa - scha no - strum im- mo- la - tus est Chri - stus i- ta- que

e - pu - le - mur in a - zi- mis sin - ce- ri- ta - tis et -

ve - ri - ta- tis. Et.

[R. The multitude of the sons of Israel shall kill the lamb on the Passover evening, and they shall eat meat and unleavened bread. V. Christ our Paschal lamb has been sacrificed. Therefore let us feast on the unleavened bread of sincerity and truth.]

20. Responsory ii: Comedetis carnes/Non moyses

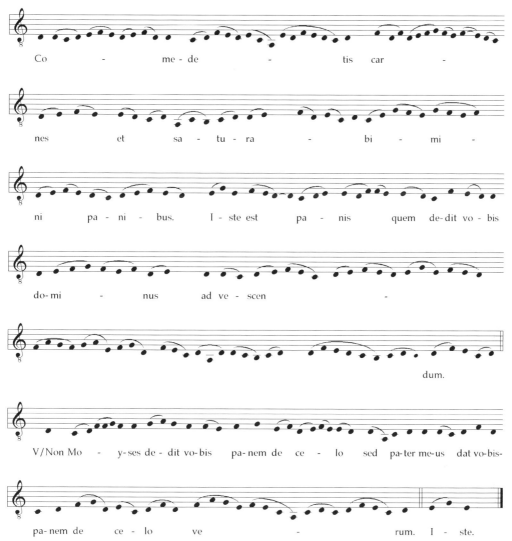

[You will eat meats, and you will be satiated with breads. This is the bread the Lord has given to you to be eaten. V. Moses did not give you bread from heaven but my father gives you true bread from heaven.]

21. Responsory iii: Respexit Helyas/Si quis manducaverit/Gloria patri

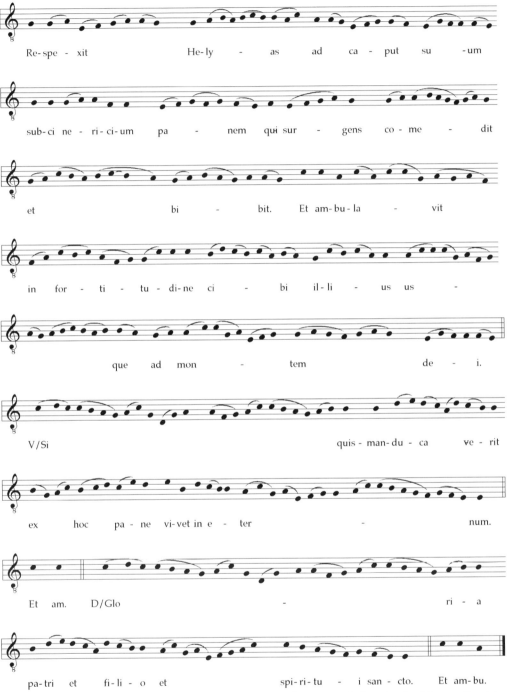

Re-spe - xit   He-ly - as   ad   ca - put   su - um

sub-ci ne - ri- ci- um   pa - nem   qui sur - gens   co - me - dit

et   bi - bit.   Et am-bu- la - vit

in   for - ti - tu - di-ne   ci - bi   il - li - us   us -

que   ad   mon - tem   de - i.

V/Si   quis - man - du - ca   ve - rit

ex   hoc   pa - ne   vi- vet in e - ter - num.

Et   am.   D/Glo - ri - a

pa-tri   et   fi- li - o   et   spi- ri - tu - i   san - cto.   Et am-bu.

[Elias saw a hearth bread by his head and arising he ate and drank. And he walked in the strength of this food up to the mountain of God. V. If anyone eats this bread, he will live forever.]

In secundo nocturno
Antiphona
22. Memor sit Dominus/Ps Exaudiat

Me- mor   sit do - mi nus   sa- cri- fi- ci - i no - stri   et ho- lo- cau - stum no - strum

pin - gue   fi - at.   Ps/ Ex- au - di - at.

[May the Lord remember our sacrifices and may he make our burnt offering rich.]

23. Paratur nobis/Ps Dominus regit

Pa- ra - tur   no - bis   men- sa do   -   mi- ni ad - ver- sus o   -   mnes

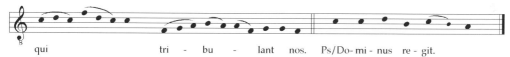

qui   tri - bu - lant nos. Ps/Do- mi - nus re - git.

[The table of the Lord is prepared for us against those who oppress us.]

24. In voce exultationis/Ps Quemadmodum

In   vo - ce   ex- ul - ta- ti - o- nis re - so- nant   e   - pu - lan - tes in

men   -   sa do- mi- ni.   Ps/Quem- ad - mo - dum.

[The banqueters resound in a voice of exultation at the table of the Lord.]

25. Versiculus
Cibavit eos ex adipe frumenti. R. Et de petra melle saturavit eos.

[He fed them from the finest grain. R. And he filled them with honey from a rock.]

26. Responsory iiii: Panis quem ego dabo/Locutus est populus

Pa-nis quem e - go da-bo ca - ro me - a

est pro mun - di vi-ta li - ti-ga - bant er - go -

iu - de i di - cen - tes. Quo-mo-do po-test hic

no-bis da-re re car-nem su - am ad man - du-can - dum?

V/Lo-cu-tus est po-pu-lus con - tra do-mi - num:

A-ni - ma no-stra nau - se-at su-per ci - bo i-sto le-vis - si - mo.

Quo-mo- do.

[The bread which I give is my flesh for the life of the world. The Jews disputed saying: How can this man give us his own flesh as food? V. The people spoke against the Lord: Our spirit is sickened by this most trifling food.]

27. Responsory v: Cenantibus illis/Dixerunt viri

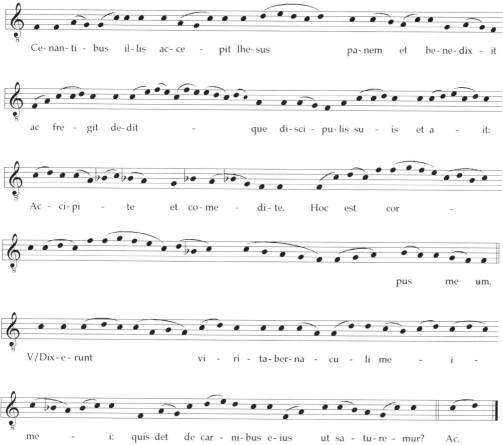

Cenantibus illis accepit Ihesus panem et benedixit ac fregit dedit que discipulis suis et ait: Accipite et comedite. Hoc est corpus meum. V/Dixerunt viri tabernaculi mei: quis det de carnibus eius ut saturemur? Ac.

[While they were eating, Jesus took bread and blessed and broke it, and gave it to his disciples and said: Take and eat. This is my body. V. The men of my tent said: Who will give of his flesh that we may be satisfied?]

28. Responsory vi: Accepit Ihesus/Memoria memor/Gloria patri

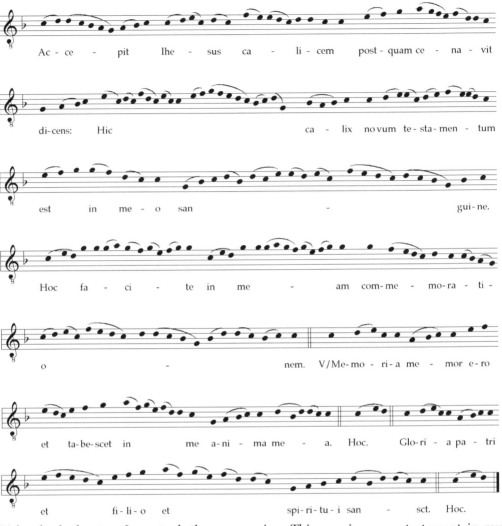

Ac - ce - pit Ihe - sus ca - li - cem post - quam ce - na - vit

di - cens: Hic   ca - lix no vum te - sta - men - tum

est   in   me - o   san   -   gui - ne.

Hoc   fa - ci - te   in   me - am com - me - mo - ra - ti -

o   -   nem. V/Me - mo - ri - a me - mor e - ro

et   ta - be - scet in   me a - ni - ma me - a. Hoc. Glo - ri - a pa - tri

et   fi - li - o   et   spi - ri - tu - i san - sct. Hoc.

[After he had eaten, Jesus took the cup, saying: This cup is a new testament in my blood. Do this in my memory. V. I shall recall this memory, and my soul will be sorrowful within me.]

In tertio nocturno
Antiphona
29. Introibo ad altare Dei/Ps Iudica me Deus

In - tro - i - bo ad al - ta - re de - i su-mam Chri-stum qui re - no-vat

iu - ven - tu-tem me-am. Ps/Iu-di-ca me.

[I go will into the altar of God, I will take on Christ who renews my youth.]

30. Cibavit nos Dominus/Ps Exultate Deo adiutori

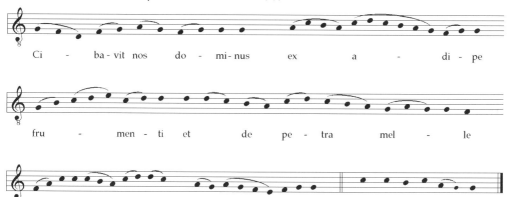

Ci - ba-vit nos do - mi-nus ex a - di - pe

fru - men - ti et de pe - tra mel - le

sa - tu - ra - vit nos. Ps/Ex-ul - ta -

[The Lord has fed us from the finest grain, and he has filled us with honey from a rock.]

31. Ex altari tuo Domine/Ps Quam dilecta

Ex al - ta-ri tu - o do - mi-ne Chri - stum su - mi - mus

in quem cor et ca - ro no - stra ex - ul - tant.

Ps/Quam di - lect.

[From your altar, Lord, we receive Christ, in whom our soul and body rejoice.]

32. Versiculus

Educas panem de terra. R. Et vinum letificet cor hominis.

[May you produce bread from the earth. R. And may wine gladden the heart of man.]

33. Responsory vii: Qui manducat/Non est alia

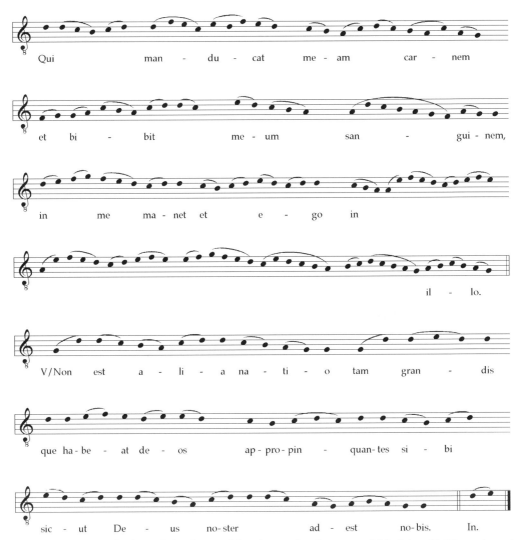

[He who eats my flesh and drinks my blood remains in me and I in him. V. There is not another nation so great who has gods so near to itself as our God is to us.]

34. Responsorium viii: Misit me pater/Cibavit eum

Mi - sit me pa- ter vi- vens et e - go vi - vo

pro - pter pa - trem. Et qui man-du - cat

me vi - vit pro- pter me.

V/Ci - ba - vit e - um do mi nus pa - ne vi - te -

et in - tel - le - ctus. Et qui.

[The living Father sent me and I live because of the Father. And he who eats me lives because of me. V. The Lord fed him with the bread of life and understanding.]

35. Responsorium nonum: Unus panis/Parasti in dulcedine/Gloria patri

U-nus pa-nis et u - num cor - pus
mul - ti su - mus. O-mnes qui de u - no
pa - ne et de u - no ca - li-ce
par -
ti - ci pa - mus. V/Pa-ra-sti - in dul-ce-di - ne
tu - a pau-pe-ri de - us qui ha - bi-ta-re fa - cis
u-na-ni - mes in do - mo. O-mnes. D/Glo-ri-a pa - tri
et fi-li - o et spi-ri - tu - i san - cto. O-mnes.

[We many are one bread and one body, we all who are made participants in one bread and one cup. V. You have prepared in your goodness for the needy, O God, You who cause us to live of one mind in your house.]

36. Versiculus

Panem de celo prestitisti eis. R. Omne delectamentum in se habentem.

[You have furnished them with the bread of heaven. R. Having in it every delight.]

Lauds
Antiphona
37. Sapiencia edificavit/Ps Dominus regnavit

Sa - pi - en - ti - a   e - di - fi - ca - vit   si - bi do-mum,

mi - scu - it vi - num,   et po - su - it men - sam,   al - le - lu - ia.

Ps/Domi- mi - nus re - gna - vit.

[Wisdom has built herself a house, she has prepared her wine, she has laid her table, alleluia.]

[CORPUS CHRISTI]
EDINBURGH UNIVERSITY LIBRARY, MS MS 211.IV.
(INCHCOLM ANTIPHONARY)

[In primis vesperis]
1. Hymn: Pange lingua (end only)
    . . . virtus quoque
    Sit et benedictio;
    Procedenti ab utroque
    Compar sit laudatio. Amen.

    [. . . strength, and blessing. To the One who proceeds from them both be equal praise. Amen.]

2. Versiculus
    [Text Source: Sap 16: 20–21]
    Panem de celo prestitisti eis, alleluia. R. Omne delectamentum in se habentem, alleluia.

    [You have furnished them with the bread of heaven, alleluia. R. Having in it every delight, alleluia.]

3. Ad Magnificat antiphona: O quam suavis/Magnificat
    [Text Source: Cf. Wisdom 12: 1, 16: 21; Luke 1: 53]

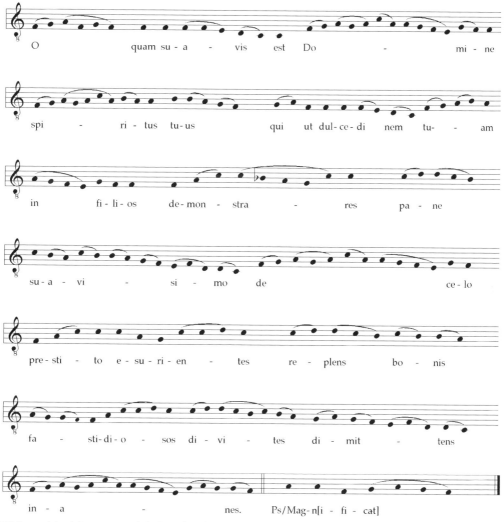

[O how kind is your spirit Lord, who, to show your sweetness towards your children, provides the sweetest bread from heaven, filling the hungry with good things, sending the haughty rich away empty.]

4. Oratio

Deus qui nobis sub sacramento mirabili passionis tue memoriam reliquisti; tribue quesumus ita nos corporis et sanguinis tui sacra misteria venerari; ut redemptionis tue fructum in nobis iugiter senciamus. [Qui vivis et regnas cum deo patre in unitate spiritu sancti deus per omnia secula seculorum. Amen.]

[Lord, who has left us, in a wonderful sacrament, a memorial of your passion, grant, we pray, that we may venerate the mystery of your body and blood, so that we may always feel within ourselves the fruit of your redemption. Who lives and reigns with God the father in unity with the holy spirit, God, world without end. Amen.]

Ad completorium

5. Antiphona: Salvator miserere

[Savior, have mercy on those singing the salubrious mystery of holy Zion, and to those standing by; give favor to your devoted ones and grant that it may profit the souls of all people.]

6. Capitulum

Tu in nobis [es, Domine, et nomen sanctum tuum invocatum est super nos: ne derelinquas nos, Domine Deus noster. R. Deo gratias.]

[You are in our midst, Lord, and your holy name has been invoked over us; do not desert us, Lord our God. R. Thanks be to God.]

7. Hymn: Te lucis ante t[erminum]

8. Versiculus

[Text Source: Ps 16 (Latin), 17 (Hebrew): 8]

V. Custodi nos D[omine ut pupillam oculi.

R. Sub umbra alarum tuarum protégé nos.]

[V. Keep us Lord as the pupil of your eye.

R. Protect us under the shadow of your wings.]

9. [Ad Nunc dimittis antiphona] O admirabile misterium/Nunc dimittis

[O wonderful mystery, one consumes the Lord. The highest meal of eternal salvation has been obtained. Through it the poor man becomes rich in all good things. Holy Jesus, sweet Jesus Christ, strong and good shepherd, you who know all things and prevail, who thus nourishes mortals here, make us live with you, alleluia.]

10. Oratio

Deus qui nos in hac mortali vita celesti pane reficis, tribue nobis quesumus, de eius visione in eterna gloria semper gaudere. Qui vivis et regnas [cum deo patre in unitate spiritu sancti deus per omnia secula seculorum. Amen.]

[God, who refreshes us in this mortal life with celestial bread, grant, we ask, that we may always praise the vision of him in eternal glory. Who lives and reigns with God the father in he unity of the Holy Spirit, God, world without end. Amen.]

Ad matutinas

11. Invitatory: Christum regem (beginning only)

Chri- stum   re   -   gem   a - do - re- mus   do - mi - nan   - tem

[gentibus Qui se manducantibus dat spiritus pinguedinem. Ps Venite.][202]

[Let us adore Christ the king, the Lord of all peoples, who give nourishment of the spirit to those who eat.]

---

[202] This portion of text and music has been cut off the top of fol. 2v.

12. Hymn: Sacris sollempniis

[Text Source: Cf. Ps 21 (Latin), 22 (Hebrew): 29 (LU 750, line 32)]

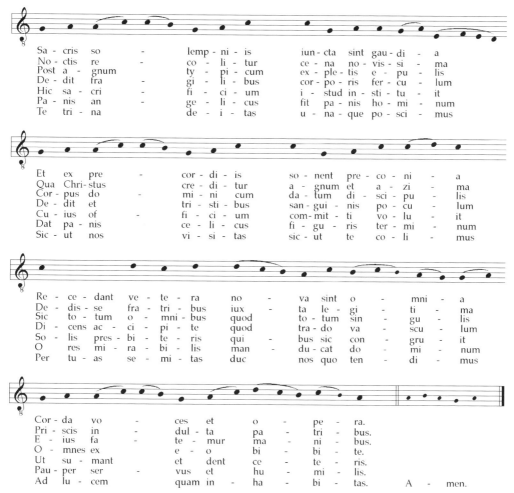

Sa - cris so - lemp - ni - is   iun - cta sint gau - di - a
No - ctis re - co - li - tur   ce - na   no - vis - si - ma
Post a - gnum ty - pi - cum   ex - ple - tis e - pu - lis
De - dit fra - gi - li - bus   cor - po - ris fer - cu - lum
Hic sa - cri fi - ci - um   i - stud in - sti - tu - it
Pa - nis an - ge - li - cus   fit pa - nis ho - mi - num
Te   tri - na de - i - tas   u - na - que po - sci - mus

Et   ex pre - cor - di - is   so - nent pre - co - ni - a
Qua Chri-stus cre - di - tur   a - gnum et   a - zi - ma
Cor - pus do - mi - ni cum   da - tum di - sci - pu - lis
De - dit et tri - sti - bus   san - gui - nis po - cu - lum
Cu - ius of fi - ci - um   com-mit - ti vo - lu - it
Dat pa - nis ce - li - cus   fi - gu - ris ter - mi - num
Sic - ut nos vi - si - tas   sic - ut te co - li - mus

Re - ce - dant ve - te - ra no - va sint o - mni - a
De - dis - se fra - tri - bus iux - ta le - gi - ti - ma
Sic to - tum o - mni - bus quod to - tum sin - gu - lis
Di - cens ac - ci - pi - te quod tra - do va - scu - lum
So - lis pres - bi - te - ris qui bus sic con - gru - it
O   res mi - ra - bi - lis man du - cat do - mi - num
Per tu - as se - mi - tas duc nos quo ten - di - mus

Cor - da vo - ces et   o - pe - ra.
Pri - scis in - dul - ta pa - tri - bus.
E - ius fa - te - mur ma - ni - bus.
O - mnes ex e - o bi - bi - te.
Ut su - mant et dent ce - te - ris.
Pau - per ser - vus et hu - mi - lis.
Ad lu - cem quam in - ha - bi - tas.   A - men.

[1. Let joys be joined with the sacred solemnities, and let prayers sound from our hearts.

Let the old depart, let all things be new, hearts, voices, and works.

2. The night of last supper is recalled, in which Christ is believed to have given to his brethren lamb and unleavened bread, according to the rights granted to the forefathers.

3. The meal completed, after the symbolic lamb, the divine body was given to his disciples, entirely to all, entirely to each, by his own hands, this we proclaim.

4. He gave to the weak the meal of his body, and he gave to the sorrowful the drink of his blood, saying: Take the vessel which I give; all of you drink from it.

5. Thus he established this sacrifice, whose ceremony he wished to be entrusted only to those elders who were fit to consume it and give to others.

6. The bread of the angels becomes the bread of mankind, the celestial bread gives an end to symbols. O wondrous thing! the poor, the slave, the humble consumes the Lord.

7. We implore you, God three and one, just as you visit us, so do we honor you. Lead us on your pathway, by which we strive to the light which you inhabit. Amen.]

In primo nocturno

Antiphona

13. Fructrum salutiferum/Ps Beatus vir

[Text Source: Cf. Ps 1: 3]

Fru - ctum sa - lu - ti - fe - rum gu   stan-dum - de - dit

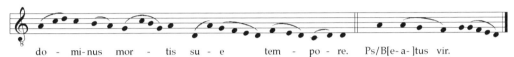

do - mi-nus mor - tis su - e   tem - po - re. Ps/B[e-a-]tus vir.

[The Lord gave a saving fruit to taste at the time of his death.]

14. A fructu frumenti/Ps Cum invocarem

[Text Source: Cf. Ps 4: 8–9]

A   fru - ctu fru-men - ti   et vi - ni mul-ti-pli - ca - ti

fi-de-les in   pa-ce   Chri-sti re-qui - es-cunt. Ps/Cum in-vo-ca-rem.

[Having increased by the fruit of grain and wine, the faithful rest in the peace of Christ]

15. Communione calicis/Ps Conserva me

[Text Source: Cf. Ps 15 (Latin), 16 (Hebrew): 5, 4]

Com-mu-ni - o-ne ca - li - cis quo de-us ip - se su - mi - tur non vi-tu-lo-rum san - gui - ne

con-gre - ga - vit nos   do - mi - nus.   Ps/Con-ser - va.

[The Lord has assembled us by the communion of the chalice in which God himself is consumed, not by the blood of calves.]

16. Versiculus

[Text Source: Ps 77 (Latin), 78 (Hebrew): 24–25]

Panem celi dedit eis, alleluia. R. Panem angelorum [manducavit homo, alleluia.]

[He gave them the bread of heaven, alleluia. R. Mankind ate the bread of the angels, alleluia.]

17. Responsory: Immolabit hedum/Pascha nostrum
    [Text Sources: R. Ex 12: 6, 8; V. 1 Cor 5: 7–8]

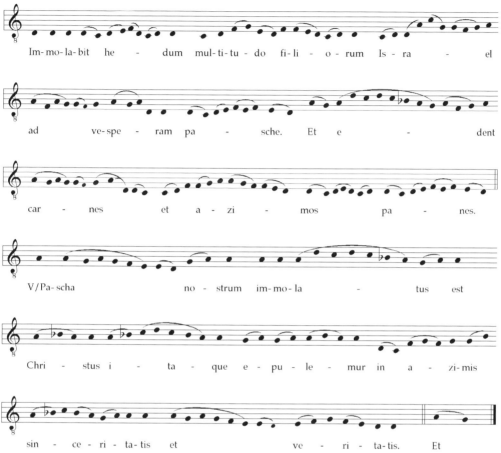

Im-mo-la-bit he - dum mul-ti-tu - do fi-li - o - rum Is - ra - el

ad   ve-spe - ram pa - sche. Et e - dent

car - nes   et a - zi - mos   pa - nes.

V/Pa-scha   no - strum im-mo-la - tus est

Chri - stus i - ta - que e - pu - le - mur in a - zi-mis

sin - ce - ri - ta-tis et   ve - ri - ta-tis. Et

[R. The multitude of the sons of Israel shall kill the lamb on the Passover evening, and they shall eat meat and unleavened bread. V. Christ our Paschal lamb has been sacrificed. Therefore let us feast on the unleavened bread of sincerity and truth.]

18. Responsory: Comedetis carnes/Non moÿses
[Text Source: R. Cf. Ex 16: 12, 15; V. John 6: 32]

[You will eat meats, and you will be satiated with breads. This is the bread [the Lord has given to you to be eaten. V. Moses did not give you bread from heaven but my father][203] gives you true bread from heaven.]

---

[203] Only a portion of this part of the text is visible at the top of fol. 4r. The music has been cut off entirely.

19. Responsory: Respexit Helyas/Si quis manducaverit/Gloria patri
    [Text Source: R. 1 Reg 19: 6–8; V. Jo 6: 53–58]

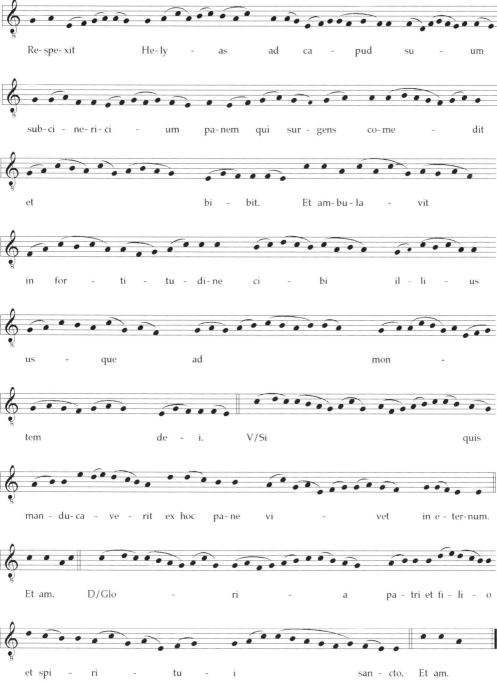

[Elias saw a hearth bread by his head and arising he ate and drank. And he walked in the strength of this food up to the mountain of God. V. If anyone eats this bread, he will live forever.]

In secundo nocturno

Antiphona

20. Memor sit Dominus/Ps Exaudiat te Dominus
     [Text Source: Cf. Ps 19: 3 (Latin), 20: 4 (Hebrew)]

Me   -   mor sit do   mi-nus   sa - cri - fi - ci - i no   -   stri

et   ho - lo - cau-stum no   -   strum   pin   -   gue   fi - at.

Ps/Ex-au - di - at.

[May the Lord remember our sacrifices and may he make our burnt offering rich.]

21. Paratur nobis/Ps Dominus regit me
     [Text Source: Cf. Ps 22: 6 (Latin), 23: 5 (Hebrew)]

Pa - ra- tur   no- bis men   -   sa do- mi   -   ni   ad   -   ver - sus   o   -   mnes

qui   tri-bu - lant   nos.   Ps/Do- mi - nus   re - git.

[The table of the Lord is prepared for us against those who oppress us.]

22. In voce exultationis/Ps Quemadmodum
     [Text Source: Cf. Ps 41 (Latin), 42 (Hebrew): 5]

In   vo - ce   ex - ul - ta - ci   -   o - nis   re   -   so - nant

e-pu - lan - tes   in   men-sa   do - mi - ni.   Ps/Quem-ad - mo- dum.

[The banqueters resound in a voice of exultation at the table of the Lord.]

23. Versiculus

[Text Source: Ps 80 (Latin), 81 (Hebrew): 17]

Cibavit illos ex adype frumenti, alleluia. R. Et de petra melle saturavit eos, alleluia.

[He fed them from the finest grain, alleluia. R. And he filled them with honey from a rock, alleluia.]

24. Responsory: Panis quem ego dabo/Locutus est populus

[Text Source: Jo 6: 51–53; V. Cf. Nm 21: 5]

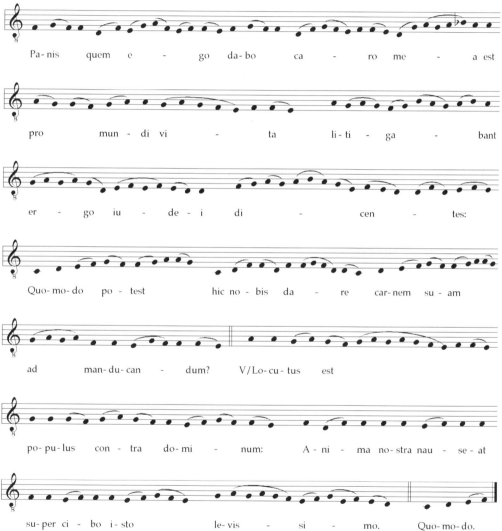

[The bread which I give is my flesh for the life of the world. The Jews disputed saying: How can this man give us his own flesh as food? V. The people spoke against the Lord: Our spirit is sickened by this most trifling food.]

25. Responsory: Cenantibus illis/Dixerunt viri
[Text Source: Mt 26: 26; V. Cf. Job 31: 31]

[While they were eating, Jesus took bread and blessed and broke it, and gave it to his disciples[204] and said: Take and eat. This is my body. V. [The men][205] of my tent said: Who will give of his flesh that we may be satisfied?]

---

[204] The first eleven words are on the first staff of fol. 4v. Half of the text has been cut off, and the music has been lost entirely.

[205] *Viri* is lost in the binding of the manuscript.

26. Responsory: Accepit Ihesus/Memoria memor/Gloria patri
    [Text Source: Luke 22: 20, 19; V. Lamentations 3: 20]

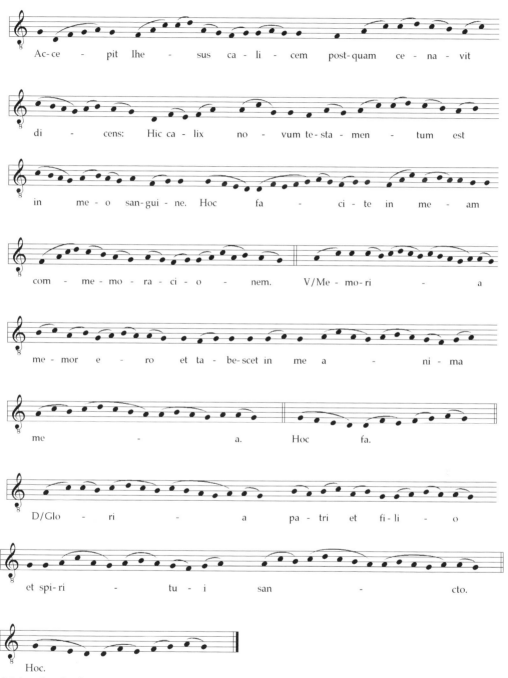

[After he had eaten, Jesus took the cup, saying: This cup is a new testament in my blood. Do this in my memory. V. I shall recall this memory, and my soul will be sorrowful within me.]

In tertio nocturno

Antiphona

27. Introibo ad altare Dei/Ps Iudica me Deus

[Text Source: Cf. Ps 42 (Latin), 43 (Hebrew): 4]

In- tro - i- bo ad al-ta - re de - i su - mamChristum qui   re - no-vat

iu - ven - tu- tem me- am.   Ps/Iu- di - ca me de-us.

[I go will into the altar of God, I will take on Christ who renews my youth.]

28. Cibavit nos Dominus/Ps Exultate Deo adiutori

[Text Source: Cf. Ps 80 (Latin), 81 (Hebrew): 17 (15 in LU 936)]

Ci - ba-vit nos do - mi-nus ex   a - di - pe fru - men - ti

et de pe - tra mel - le sa - tu - ra - vit - nos. Ps/Ex ul-ta-te de-o.

[The Lord has fed us from the finest grain, and he has filled us with honey from a rock.]

29. Ex altari tuo Domine/Ps Quam dilecta

[Text Source: Cf. Ps 83 (Latin), 84 (Hebrew): 3–4]

Ex al - ta - ri tu- o do - mi-ne Chri - stum   su - mi - mus

in quem cor et ca - ro no - stra ex - ul - tant. Ps/Quam di - le - cta.

[From your altar, Lord, we receive Christ, in whom our soul and body rejoice.]

30. Versiculus

[Text Source: Ps 103 (Latin), 104 (Hebrew): 14–15]

Educas panem de terra, alleluia. R. Et vinum letificet cor hominis, alleluia.

[May you produce bread from the earth, alleluia. R. And may wine gladden the heart of man, alleluia.]

31. Responsory: Qui manducat/Non est alia (R. and 2/3 of V. only)[206]
    [Text Source: R. Jo 6: 57; V. Dt 4: 7]

Qui man-du - cat me-am car - nem et bi - bit

me-um san-gui - nem in me ma - net

et e - go in il - lo.

V/Non est a - li-a na - ci-o tam gran - dis que ha-be-at de - os

ap-pro-pin - quan - tes si - bi sic-ut

[He who eats my flesh and drinks my blood remains in me and I in him. V. There is not another nation so great who has gods so near to itself as our God is to us.]

---

[206] The Corpus Christi service breaks off here.

PART III

POEMS OF THE MOSAN PSALTERS

INTRODUCTION TO THE MOSAN PSALTERS

Barbara R. Walters

The liturgical scholar Gy[1] noted that people of the Middle Ages had a more relaxed view of the connection between intellectual theology and popular piety than do people in the modern or postmodern world. The Miracle of Bolsena[2] provides an important exemplar of the seriousness with which popular pietistic imagery was taken. That distinctions were made is nonetheless obvious, perhaps most clearly manifest in the close surveillance of new urban preaching groups and in the interest taken by both Hugh of Saint-Cher and Urban IV in the development of liturgy and a set of rules for women living within and outside of established religious orders. Particularly relevant in this context are a group of thirteenth-century psalters from the diocese of Liège, which provide evidence for the groundswell of religious piety and eucharistic fervor among women that surrounded the inception of the feast of Corpus Christi. The psalters functioned largely as lay breviaries, and to the extent that they include prayers to be said by communicants at Mass, as lay missals.[3] They were intended specifically for the béguines

---

[1] Pierre-Marie Gy, "Office liégeois et office romain de la Fête-Dieu," in *Fête-Dieu (1246–1996)*, vol. 1, *Actes du Colloque de Liège*, ed. André Haquin (Louvain-la-Neuve: Institut d'Études Médiévales de l'Université Catholique de Louvain, 1999), 117.

[2] James Weisheipl, *Friar Thomas D'Aquino: His Life, Thought and Work* (Garden City, NY: Doubleday & Co., 1974), 179, describes The Miracle of Bolsena and its legendary role in the initiation of the feast of Corpus Christi. A fifteenth-century chronicle of St. Antoninus of Florence reports that a German priest celebrated Mass at the Church of St. Christina in the small town of Bolsena while en route to Rome. His doubts about transubstantiation were resolved when he saw the corporal drenched with blood. As rumors of this miracle spread through the town, a procession was formed, which took the blood-stained corporal to Pope Urban IV at Orvieto. According to the legend, the pope was so moved by the event that he decided to extend the celebration of the feast throughout the universal Church. The legend was immortalized by Raphael in 1512 in a fresco, *The Mass at Bolsena*, which now hangs in the *Stanza di Eliodoro* at the Vatican. Miri Rubin, *Corpus Christi: The Eucharist in Late Medieval Culture* (Cambridge: Cambridge University Press, 1991), notes that efforts to create a direct link between this miracle, with its tradition that began in the fourteenth century, and the interest of Pope Urban IV, which began in Liège in the 1240s, seem perhaps "misplaced." The Miracle of Bolsena is described on p. 32 of Part I.

[3] Judith Oliver, *Gothic Manuscript Illumination in the Diocese of Liège (c.1250–c.1330)*, 2 vols. (Leuven: Uitgeverij Peeters, 1988), 1: 35, cites eight psalters with Mass prayers.

and represent efforts on the part of the laity to imitate or participate in the Divine Office. The psalter contents corroborate conclusions by Mulder-Bakker: the new feast of Corpus Christi emerged in the context of a community with a shared spirituality, one which was deeply tied to visual images and physical objects. This was a form of religiosity that was "highly place-bound"; experienced within a physical church setting; directed toward the Trinity and Mary, who were believed to be present within the physical setting; shaped by the Church calendar; and part of a community experience.[4] The psalters therefore formed a bridge between lay vernacular religious practices and the intellectual theology exalted by priests in the Latin liturgy.[5]

Oliver, who has executed a comprehensive analysis of all known extant Mosan Psalters, succinctly describes the psalters in the opening of her two-volume study of their characteristic illuminations:

> Mosan psalters, most of which are more accurately described as psalter-hours, are very elaborate examples of this typical thirteenth-century book. They include not only the core texts usually found in books of their type—a calendar, psalter, canticles, litany and prayers, hours of the Virgin, and office of the dead—but a wealth of others as well, so that they truly function as lay breviaries. Easter tables, a calendar of health rules, and a cycle of full-page illuminations with vernacular poems of Latin prayers on the facing pages are inserted before or after the calendar. Mass devotions may appear at either the beginning or the end of the book. The core texts are followed by abbreviated offices of the Annunciation, Purification, and Assumption or other breviary offices, and by the psalter of the Virgin (a poem of one hundred and fifty Aves).[6]

The critical edition of a set of vernacular poems from the Mosan Psalters by Peter T. Ricketts which follows therefore comprises a second central component of this study dedicated to the feast of Corpus Christi. The Ricketts edition is the first critical edition of the poems and the first translation into English. With his critical apparatus and annotations, it offers to scholars invaluable evidence and insights regarding popular piety in the community of women which initiated the new feast.

The psalters and the poems are central to the study of the feast of Corpus Christi for a number of reasons. First, the psalters and the poems were clearly intended for Liège women. Second, artistically the psalters provide evidence for the break between Liège and the Rhineland after the mid-thirteenth century, when they became increasingly influenced by French traditions fortifying the existing evidence for political fault lines.[7] Third, there are direct links between themes taken up in the psalters and themes relevant to the feast of Corpus Christi, such as the *historia* of the humanity of Christ, frequent illuminations of the Elevation of the Host,[8] shared biblical references and reli-

---

[4] Anneke B. Mulder-Bakker, *Lives of the Anchoresses: The Rise of the Urban Recluse in Medieval Europe*, trans. Myra Heerspink Scholz (Philadelphia: University of Pennsylvania Press, 2005), 111.

[5] Ibid., 112.

[6] Oliver, *Gothic Manuscript Illumination*, 1: 25.

[7] Ibid., 141.

[8] See Peter Browe, *Textus antiqui de festo Corporis Christi*, Opuscula et textus, series liturgica IV (Münster: Aschendorff, 1934); Ronald Zawilla, *The Biblical Sources of the Historia Corporis Christi Attributed to Thomas Aquinas: A Theo-*

gious themes, and shared symbolic referents to the Eucharist. Fourth, both the new feast and the psalters were heavily influenced by the newer mendicant orders, especially the Premonstratensians, Franciscans, and Dominicans. And finally, one psalter makes specific reference to Juliana of Mont Cornillon;[9] another from an adjacent geographical area contains an office for the feast of Corpus Christi that was added in the early fourteenth century.[10]

The Romance philologist Paul Meyer first identified the manuscripts called Mosan Psalters as from the diocese of Liège in 1873[11] in an article on the *Grosbois Psalter.*[12] His initial article transcribed eight Old French poems in Liège dialect, which precede the Psalms in the psalter. Meyer noted that the eight poems in the *Grosbois Psalter* overlap with vernacular poems found in another psalter, Bibliothèque nationale de France, lat. 1077 (BNF 1077), and that both psalters share features with a third psalter sold in Paris in 1867, a manuscript later identified by Sinclair as Melbourne, State Library of Victoria MS *096/R66.[13] Meyer discovered five psalters that share the distinctive features of the Mosan group: special devotionals to Liège saints, including the patron saint of the diocese, Saint Lambert (635–700); a calendar naming Liège saints; and an Easter Table composed by Lambert le Bègue.[14]

Sinclair,[15] working in the tradition of Meyer, and, subsequently, Valkhoff and Långfors, identified eleven such psalters. More recently, Oliver has established a complete description and provenance for forty-one geographically dispersed manuscripts, which she catalogued as Mosan Psalters, meaning psalters from the diocese of Liège.[16] Oliver dates these psalters as from approximately 1250 to 1330,[17] a historical time roughly contemporaneous with the period of inception of the feast of Corpus Christi. In her two-volume work, she published Sinclair's complete list of twenty vernacular poems that connect fourteen of the forty-one manuscripts.[18]

---

logical Study to Determine Their Authenticity (Ph.D. diss. University of Toronto, 1985), 8–9; Oliver, *Gothic Manuscript Illumination*, 1: 153; Rubin, *Corpus Christi*; François Avril, "Une curieuse illustration de la Fête-Dieu: l'iconographie de Christ Prêtre élevant hostie et sa diffusion," in *Rituels: Mélanges offerts à Pierre-Marie Gy, o.p.*, ed. Paul De Clerck and E. Pallazzo (Paris: Les Éditions du Cerf, 1990).

[9] BR IV–1013; see also Ricketts, Poem IX n 17.

[10] New York, Pierpont Morgan Library, MS 754.

[11] Paul Meyer, "Rapport sur d'anciennes poésies religieuses en dialecte liégeois," *Revue des Sociétés Savantes des Départements*, 5e ser. 6 (1873), 236–49; see also Keith Sinclair, "Les manuscrits du Psautier de Lambert le Bègue," *Romania* 86 (1965), 22–47.

[12] New York, Pierpont Morgan Library MS 440.

[13] Sinclair, "Les manuscrits du Psautier," 22–47, and "Un Psautier de Lambert le Bègue à Melbourne," *Australian Journal of French Studies* 1 (1964), 5–10.

[14] Paul Meyer, "Le Psautier de Lambert le Bègue," *Romania* 29 (1900), 536–40.

[15] Sinclair, "Un Psautier de Lambert le Bègue," 5–10; Sinclair, "Les manuscrits du Psautier," 22–47.

[16] Oliver, *Gothic Manuscript Illumination*, 1: 109–10.

[17] The dates could be as early as 1225.

[18] New York, Pierpont Morgan Library, 440; Paris, Bibliothèque nationale de France, latin 1077; Liège, Bibliothèque de l'Université, 431; The Hague, National Library of the Netherlands 76.G.17; Melbourne, State Library of Victoria, *096/R66; London, British Library, Add. 21114; 's-Heerenberg, Stichting Huis Bergh, 35 (225); New

Table 14, adapted from Oliver,[19] lists all of the poems in the order established by Sinclair,[20] based on the order in which he discovered them.

Table 14
Vernacular Poetry in Sinclair's Order

Incipit	Manuscript
I. *O verge de droiture, qui de Jessé eissis*	M440; BNF 1077; BR IV–1066; Liège 431
II. *Sire Deus cui naisence li prophete annunczarent*	M440
III. *Beau sire, Deus, ki après vo naiscence*	M440; BNF 1077
IV. *Deus, sire, en Jerusalem venis a passion*	M440; BNF 1077; BR IV–1066; BR IV–1013
V. *Aiue, Deus, bea sire, qui le monde formas*	M440; BNF 1077
VI. *Uns faisseles de myrre est mes amis a moi*	M440; BNF 1077; Melbourne; Liège 431
VII. *Ave, Deus, beas sire, qui en la crois montas*	M440; M183
VIII. *Deus, qui a tier jor de mor resuscitastes*	M440
IX. *Pius Deus omnipotens, qui haus sies et lonc vois*	BL Add. 21114; BNF 1077; BR IV–1066; Morgan 183; Liège 431; KB 76.G.17
X. *Ave, qui ains ne commenchas*	BR IV–36; 's-Heerenberg, S. H. B. 35; Rochester; Fitzwilliam 288; BR IV–1013; Liège 431; BL Stowe 17; KB 76.G.17
XI. *Ave, rose florie*	BR IV–36; 's-Heerenberg, S. H. B. 35; Rochester; Fitzwilliam 288; BR IV–1013; BL Stowe 17; KB 76.G.17
XII. *Ave, Marie, flors de lis*	KB 76.G.17
XIII. *Sire, ki pur nos fustes traveilhés et penet*	BL Add. 21114
XIV. *Dues Jesu Christ, ki, por no savemen*	BNF 1077
XV. *Vrais Deus, qui toi dengnas en la virgene aumbrer*	Morgan 183
XVI. *Sire, donez nostre orisons*	Fitzwilliam 288
XVII. *Ave, ree de grant dulchor*	Fitzwilliam 288
XVIII. *Bea sire Deus, peres omnipotens*	BR IV–1066
XIX. *Duez Jesu Crist, ki, por nos delivreir*	BR IV–1066
XX. *Oi Pius anheas cui sain Jehans a doi*	BR IV–1066

The psalters clearly were intended for an audience of women. Oliver[21] concluded from the "ton ancelle" petitions and frequent feminine noun endings in the poetic texts that the psalters were owned by lay religious women, most probably béguines. Women artisans within the community even may have produced the psalters. Other sources corroborate Oliver's conclusions: psalter reading shaped a regular part of the religious devotion of the Liège women. Jacques de Vitry observed the devotion with which the women, including Marie D'Oignes, read from the Psalms. Juliana had memorized her psalter at a very young age. Lambert le Bègue, or Lambert of Liège (d. 1177), who preached to women in Liège during the third quarter of the twelfth century, owned a psalter. Roisin, in his analysis of the Cistercian hagiographic *vitae*, comments: "Béatrice, Lutgarde, Élisabeth recourent souvent à Marie, elles aiment réciter le 'psautier de Vierge,' précurseur de notre rosaire, chanter son office, parler d'elle avec une affection

York, Pierpont Morgan Library, 183; Cambridge, Fitzwilliam Museum, 288; Brussels, Bibliothèque royale (BR), IV–1066; BR IV–1013; BR IV–36; London, British Library, Stowe 17; Rochester, Memorial Art Gallery, 53.6.

[19] Oliver, *Gothic Manuscript Illumination*, 1: 38.

[20] Sinclair, "Les manuscrits du Psautier."

[21] Oliver, *Gothic Manuscript Illumination*, vol. 1.

qui les emporte parfois dans un ravissement"[22] [Beatrice, Lutgarde, Elisabeth often turned to Mary, they loved to recite the psalter of the Virgin, to sing her office, to speak of her with an affection that sometimes carried them away in delight].

The Old French poems in the Mosan Psalters divide into four groups. Poems I to VIII are found in the *Grosbois Psalter* (M440) as an ordered unit and constitute a closely related group that narrates events from the life of Jesus, a *historia*. The *Grosbois Psalter* was produced in Brabant in ca. 1261 for lay cathedral use, and while not chronologically first, inspired other Brabantine Psalters and Hainault artists.[23] Poems X, XI, and XII constitute three sets with fifty quatrains each of *Ave* prayers, one for each of the 150 Psalms. The *Ave* prayers appear in some psalters, such as M440, in Latin, after the Office of the Dead. Poems IX, XIII, XIV, XV, XVIII, XIX, and XX are similar in structure to Poems I to VIII and also relate events from the life of Jesus. Poems XVI and XVII are found in Fitzwilliam 288 only and depart from both the *historia* form of Jesus narrations and from the fifty-quatrain form of the *Ave* prayers found in X, XI, and XII. Thus there are two basic types of poems: the narrative or *historia* of Jesus and the *Ave* prayers, plus the poems from Fitzwilliam 288.

In the Grosbois Psalter, folios 7v–15r follow immediately after the calendar and contain eight poems that narrate scenes from the life of Jesus. The narrated scenes follow the chronological order of the biblical narrative. A full-page miniature accompanies each poem. The substance of each poem and its miniature frame a specific event in the life of Jesus; some anticipate scenes that later became part of the Rosary meditations: the Tree of Jesse, the Nativity, the Presentation, the Entrance to Jerusalem, the Washing of the Feet, the Scourging, the Crucifixion, and the Resurrection. In form, each poem consists of rhyming couplets of twelve-syllable lines that vary in metrical pattern, larger-scale rhyme scheme, and length. All of the poems are twenty-five lines, except Poems I and VI, which contain thirty lines. The form suggests stylistic borrowing between liturgical and secular genres and, perhaps, a precedent in oral tradition.

Each of the *historia* poems in the other manuscripts (i.e., Poems IX, XIII, XIV, XV, XVIII, XIX, and XX) represents a variation on the theme of one of the poems in the Grosbois Psalter, or the narration of a biblical event pertaining to the life of Jesus not found in M440. The narrative ordering of the poems in the remaining manuscripts is often disturbed.[24] Moreover, the illuminations do not always correspond to the poetic text. In the Gillet Psalter, Brussels, Bibliothèque royale, IV–1066 (BR IV–1066), miniatures illustrating the Presentation and Flight into Egypt on folio 12v accompany *Deus, sire, en Jerusalem venis a passion*, a poem describing the entrance to Jerusalem. And in BNF 1077 the cycle "is in total chaos" as a result of faithful transmission of the scribal

---

[22] Simone Roisin, I.E.J., *L'Hagiographie cistercienne dans le diocèse de Liège* (Louvain: Bibliothèque de L'Université, 1947), 114.

[23] Scholars regard the Lambert-le-Bègue Psalter (BL Add. 2114) as a copy of a 12th-c. psalter that belonged to Lambert and served as the model for the later psalters. Artists from northern France and the Hainault-Brabant region challenged artists trained in its tradition and produced changes that affected the period of psalter production between 1260 and 1280, the most prolific period. See Oliver, *Gothic Manuscript Illumination*, 1: 123–58.

[24] Oliver, *Gothic Manuscript Illumination*, 1: 47–49.

error in the Gillet Psalter, which transposed Poems IV and III, and VI and V.[25] Table 15 lists all sixteen *historia* poems and their accompanying illuminations by manuscript in the order in which the events portrayed occurred in the biblical narration of the life of Jesus. The ordering projects the biblical narrative order onto the poems and miniatures and is not found in any known manuscript; it is based on the narrative order of events eulogized as they occurred in the life of Jesus. This highlights the ordering of the Grosbois Psalter as an exemplar, which underscores the *historia* function of the poems and the unity of the psalters that contain vernacular poems. This is the order of the poems as they appear in the critical edition by Peter Ricketts.

The narrative poems invite comparison to the Latin liturgical *historia* of the late Middle Ages, such as the multiple versions of the office for the feast of Corpus Christi. The term *historia* in general refers to a biblical narrative or musical setting of such a narrative as part of an office.[26] However, the term *historia* has been employed more precisely to identify a genre consisting of newly composed, rhymed musical offices in Latin characteristic of the Franks, which emerged in the ninth century and depicted the life of a saint.[27] Jonsson used the term to refer specifically to Latin liturgical offices in which responsories and antiphons conforming to rules of versification and meter relate a narrative pertaining to celebrated events in the lives of exemplary individuals as part of the cult in formation.

In the later medieval period, there was a proliferation of such office compositions, most often with antiphons and responsories set in modal order, and these were used to relate the narratives of exemplary contemporaries. This stylistic fashion in liturgy occurred in tandem with a trend of popular religious exemplars and the canonization of individuals more recently deceased as part of the cult formation.[28] One might think of these as liturgical-musical versions of saints' *vitae*.

The *historia* style in the Mosan group highlights the connection between the earlier Marian offices and the new office for the feast of Corpus Christi. Like the new liturgical office for the new feast, which filled the void for a missing feast day honoring the sacrament, the poems offer a new vernacular *historia* celebrating the life of Jesus, which filled a lacuna in the popular devotions of the *Sanctorale*. The full-page miniatures that accompany each poem text suggest a performance tradition for the vernacular poems, one which parallels or imitates liturgical or sacerdotal practice. Each coupling of text and miniature frames or stages a crucial scene in the Gospel narrative, such as the annunciation, birth, life, and death of Jesus—perhaps as a mnemonic device in the tradition of the Prophet drama.[29]

---

[25] Ibid., 48.

[26] Zawilla, *Biblical Sources of the Historia Corporis Christi*, 82–84; see also Margot E. Fassler and Rebecca A. Baltzer, *The Divine Office in the Latin Middle Ages: Methodology and Source Studies, Regional Developments, Hagiography* (New York: Oxford University Press, 2000), 170, 430–62.

[27] Ritva Jonsson, *Historia: Études sur la genèse des offices versifiés* (Stockholm: Almqvist and Wiksell, 1968).

[28] André Vauchez, *Sainthood in the Later Middle Ages*, trans. Jean Birrell (Cambridge: Cambridge University Press, 1997).

[29] See Arthur Watson, *The Early Iconography of the Tree of Jesse* (London: Oxford University Press, 1934).

Table 15
Vernacular Poetry in Narrative Order

Incipit	Manuscript	Number in Sinclair's Ordering	Miniature
I. *Beau sire Deus peres omnipotens*	BR IV–1066	XVIII	Temptation of Adam/Murder of Abel
II.*O verge de droiture, qui de Jessé eissis*	M 440; BNF 1077; BR IV–1066; Liege 431	I	Tree of Jesse/Annunciation
III. *Vrais Deus, qui toi dengnas en la virgene aumbrer*	Morgan 183	XV	Tree of Jesse/Annunciation
IV. *Pius Deus omnipotens qui haus sies et lonc vois*	BL Add. 21114; BNF 1077; BR IV–1066; M 183 Liege 431	IX	Tree of Jesse/ Annunciation + Roundels Nativity/Adoration of the Magi Nativity/Adoration of the Magi Annunciation to the Shepherds/ Adoration of the Magi + Roundels Adoration of the Magi/ Presentation/ Christ among doctors/Entry into Jerusalem
V. *Sire Deus cui naiscence li prophete anunczarent/*	M 440	II	Nativity/Adoration of the Magi
VI. *Beau sire, Deus, ki apres vo naiscence*	M 440 BNF 1077	III	Presentation/Christ among the Doctors Presentation/Holy Family's journey to Jerusalem
VII. *Duez Jesu Crist, ki, por nos delivreir*	BR IV–1066	XIX	Holy Family's Journey to Jerusalem/Christ teaching in the Temple
VIII. *Oi! Pius anheas, cui sain Jehans a doi*	BR IV–1066	XX/	Baptism/Raising of Lazarus
IX. *Deus, sire, en Jerusalem venis a passion*	M440 BNF 1077 BR IV–1066 BR IV–1013	IV	Baptism/Entry into Jerusalem Deposition/Entombment + Roundels Presentation/Flight into Egypt No miniature
X. *Aiue, Deus, bea sire, qui le monde formas*	M440 BNF 1077	V	Last Supper/Washing Feet Last Supper/Flagellation + Roundels
XI. *Uns faisseles de myrre est mes amis a moi*	M440 BNF 1077 Liege 431 Melbourne	VI	Arrest/Flagellation Deposition/Entombment + Roundels Washing Feet, Last Supper/Gethsemene, Crucifixion, Adoration of the Magi/Presentation
XII. *Ave, Deus, beas sire, qui en la crois montas*	M440 M183	VII	Crucifixion/Three Maries at Tomb Presentation/ Baptism/Christ Among Doctors/Supper at Bethany
XIII. *Sire, ki pur nos fustes traveilhés et penet*	BL Add 2114	XIII	Presentation/Parents find Christ Preaching in the Temple + Roundels
XIV. *Dues Jesu Christ, ki, por no savemen*	BNF 1077	XIV	Three Maries/*Noli Me Tangere* + Roundels
XV. *Deus, qui a tier jor de mor resuscitastes*	M440	VIII	Limbo/*Noli Me Tangere*
XVI. *Sire, donez nostre orisons*	Fitzwilliam 288	XVI	Virgin and Child

The similarities among the poems, the liturgy, and the earlier Prophet drama, as well as their placement in the psalters, indicate that the poems were performed and possibly sung. Treitler remarks about oral traditions in liturgical music: "In the absence of scores the medium of transmission was performance."[30] And Huot provides numerous examples in her study of secular Old French lyric and lyrical narrative poetry which show the way in which books of secular verse are "arranged and decorated as if in the attempt to reproduce a performance event."[31] Each poem in the Mosan group lends itself to adaptation as *contrafacta* to an existing melody, much like the musical genre of the *sirventes* in the secular style of the troubadours,[32] or the practice that occurs so frequently in the liturgical offices. Since Liège was a musical and liturgical center associated with the production of new offices, an oral tradition of melody transmission is all the more likely.[33] Moreover, the popularity of the Victorine sequence and other oral musical forms among the urban Dominicans, Franciscans, and Premonstratensians,[34] prominent mendicant groups in Liège, provides additional support for the idea of text adaptation to existing music as an established performance practice in the historical context of psalter production. Variations on two of the Ave prayers, for example, can be found even among the source chants in BNF 1143.

A number of themes in the *historia* poems and the accompanying miniatures reveal the eucharistic fervor among the community of women associated with the initiation of the feast of Corpus Christi and complement themes in the Latin liturgical versions of the office. Especially significant are visual and textual images of the Eucharist as the fruit from the tree of life. In his Maundy Thursday sermon, Jacques de Vitry, author of the *vita* of Marie D'Oignes and protector of the Liège women, specifically connected the *lignum vite* and *medio Paradisi* to the Eucharist:

> Unde in fronte fit signum cruces, ut non erubescamus, sed magis veneremur signum redemptionis nostrae, arborem ligni vitae in medio Paradisi, per quam operatus est Dominus salutem in medio terrae. . . . Hoc ligno cum igne passionis decoctus est panis Eucharistiae, ut esset esui aptus.[35]

> [Whence in front is made the sign of the cross, so we are not ashamed but to a greater extent we worship the sign of our redemption, the tree that is the tree of life in the center of paradise, through which the Lord works for our salvation in the center of the

---

[30] Leo Treitler, "Homer and Gregory: The Transmission of Epic Poetry and Plainchant," *The Musical Quarterly* 60/3 (1974), 333–72.

[31] Sylvia Huot, *From Song to Book: The Poetics of Writing in Old French Lyric and Lyrical Narrative Poetry* (Ithaca, NY: Cornell University Press, 1987), 328.

[32] Elizabeth Aubrey, *The Music of the Troubadours* (Bloomington and Indianapolis: Indiana University Press, 1996), 109–23.

[33] A. Auda, *L'École musicale liégeoise au Xe siècle: Étienne de Liège* (Brussels: Académie royale de Belgique; Paris: H. Welter, 1923).

[34] Margot Fassler, *Gothic Song: Victorine Sequences and Augustianian Reform in Twelfth-Century Paris* (Cambridge: Cambridge University Press, 1993).

[35] Jacques de Vitry, "Feria Quinta in Coena Domini," (c. 1220; repr. *Sermones in Epistolas et Evangelia Dominicalia totius anni*. Venetiis: Apud Giordanum Zilettum, 1578), 328.

earth. . . . This tree ignited with passion cooks the bread of the Eucharist so that it might be suitably consumed.]

The literal fruit of the tree most often employed as a metaphor for the Eucharist was the apple: just as Eve represented the fall, Mary—the flower of the tree—and Jesus—her fruit—represented the Eucharist and redemption. Specific references to the apple, fruit of the tree of life, as a metaphor for the Eucharist disclose the complex tapestry of medieval concatenations in popular piety and thought. Bernard's commentary on the Song of Songs constitutes one likely source for these interpretations:

> As an apple tree among the trees of the orchard,
> so is my Beloved among the young men.
> In his longed-for shade I am seated
> and his fruit is sweet to my taste.
> For he has taken me to his banquet hall,
> and the banner he raises over me is love.
> Feed me with raisin cakes,
> restore me with apples,
> for I am sick with love. [Song of Songs 2: 3–5]

Bernard writes about this verse:

> The figure of the apple-tree, which gives both grateful shade and pleasant food, befits Him too; for He, and He alone, is verily the Tree of Life to them that lay hold upon Him; He only is the Living Bread that came down from heaven and gives life to the world. The Bride, therefore, goes on to say, 'I sat down under the shadow of Him for Whom I had longed, and His fruit was sweet to my taste.'[36]

Juliana of Mont Cornillon had memorized both the Song of Songs and many of Saint Bernard's sermons at an early age. Her *vita* reports that Juliana gave an apple to her friend, which thereafter became sweeter. And, she was certainly familiar with Guiard of Laon's texts about the *Fruits of the Eucharist*.[37]

The theme of the apple as a metaphor for the Eucharistic is central in the narrative poems in the psalters. The focus of Poem I is Eve who, counseled by the evil one disguised as a serpent, ate the forbidden apple from the Tree of Paradise in the Garden of Eden. Here, as characteristic of the medieval popular *mentalité*, Mary represented the flower of the Tree of Jesse, and Jesus, as the Eucharist, its fruit. The first poem on folio 8r in the Grosbois Psalter (Poem II in Table 15), *O verge de droiture, qui de Jessé eissis* [O virgin of righteousness who descended from Jesse], is also clearly centered on this high medieval metaphor.

The Tree of Jesse was among the most popular Gothic images in the burgeoning Marian devotion of the late-twelfth and thirteenth centuries;[38] it appears in the prefa-

---

[36] Saint Bernard, *On the Song of Songs: Sermones in Cantica Canticorum* (1135–53; repr., trans., and ed. by a religious of C.S.M.V, 1952; London: A. R. Mowbray & Co, 1952), 151–52.

[37] Mulder-Bakker, *Lives of the Anchoresses*, 94.

[38] Watson, *Early Iconography of the Tree of Jesse*.

tory miniatures of nine other Mosan Psalters.[39] In its more elaborated versions, such as the cathedral at Chartres, the image includes one column linking Jesse to the genealogical line of kings describing the royal heritage of Jesus, and a second linking the line of prophets. The two lines culminate in an image of the Virgin, mother of Jesus.[40] The Tree of Jesse in the first poem in the Grosbois Psalter complements the appearance of the genealogical verses from Matthew 1: 2–17 at the end of the manuscript (fols. 247r–248r). The poetic text develops the theme of Mary as Mother of Jesus and her royal lineage through Jesse, the father of David, as prophesied in Isaiah 11: 1. The accompanying miniature depicts Mary, the mother of Jesus, seated on a throne holding a book in her hand. Jesse, the father of David, lies asleep below. A female figure on the Virgin's right holds a scroll that reads "*Egredietur uirga de radice Iesse*" (Is 11: 1). A male figure to the Virgin's left in parallel holds a scroll that reads "*Novum faciet dominus super terram*" (Jer 31: 22).

> O verge de droiture, qui de Jessé eissis,
> ki la flur engendras sor cui li Sains Espirs
> reposat plainemen, si com dist Ysaies,
> et en toi s'enspandi par don dé set parties;
> racine de Jessé, ensprendemen d'amur,
> flur et liz de casté, dame digne d'onor,
> otroi' a ton ancelle savorer le savur
> de cel saintisme fruit dont tu portas le flur.

> [O, virgin of righteousness, who descended from Jesse,
> who gave birth to the flower in whom the Holy Spirit
> finds true rest, as Isaiah said,
> and bloomed in you through the gift of the seven parts;
> root of Jesse, fire of love,
> flower and lily of chastity, lady worthy of honor,
> grant to your servant to savor the taste
> of the holiest fruit of whom you bore the flower.][41]

The first six lines of Poem II hail the noble birth of Mary and the genealogical linkages between her son Jesus and Jesse, the father of David. They cite the Isaiah verse referred to in the illumination and make specific mention of the seven gifts of the Holy Spirit, each of which is specifically mentioned in lines 13–26. These lines form seven couplets, one for each of the seven gifts: wisdom, piety, counsel, fortitude, knowledge, understanding, and fear of the Lord. It is noteworthy that Book 2 of the *vita* of Marie D'Oignies by Jacques de Vitry organizes Marie's biographical information around these

---

[39] See Oliver, *Gothic Manuscript Illumination*, 1: 43–46; manuscripts in which the Tree of Jesse appears as part of the prefatory miniatures: London, BL Add. 21114; Oxford, Keble College 17; New York, Morgan 440; Paris, BNF lat. 1077; BR IV–1066; London, Abbey 7122; Paris, Lardanchet 53 no. 252; New York, Morgan 183; Liège, BU 431; London, BL Add. 28784B.

[40] Watson, *Early Iconography of the Tree of Jesse*.

[41] See Poem II in the Mosan Psalters.

seven gifts.[42] Lines 27–30 highlight the feminine status of the petitioner through the "ton ancelle" petitions and that petitioner's wish to partake in the Eucharist as a daughter and "amie," in line 30.

> 27   Flor de totes vertus, maison del Saint Enspir,
>   del arbre de tes grasces moi denges repartir
>   k'en cest siecle present si florisse ma vie
>   ke tes fiz moi conoisse a filhe et a amie.
>
> [Flower of virtues, mansion of the Holy Spirit,
> deign to share with me of the tree of your graces
> so that, in this world of today, my life may so flourish
> that your son may know me as daughter and friend.]

A second important component of the popular theology among the Liège women for whom Poem II serves as an exemplar is the reverence for *sapientia,* "the highest form of knowledge obtainable by a human being."[43] Whereas men achieved knowledge through education, women achieved wisdom through the gifts of the Holy Spirit. The wisdom of Mary was esteemed most highly. The premium placed on *sapientia,* wisdom, and the gifts of the Holy Spirit are emphasized in the poems, in the Latin liturgy for the feast of Corpus Christi, and in Juliana of Mont Cornillon's *vita.* The first vespers antiphon from The Hague, National Library of the Netherlands 70.E.4 (KB 70.E.4) with the title incipit *Animarum cibus,* paraphrased from *De sacramentis* by Hugh of Saint-Victor, for example, makes specific reference to *sapientia.* This emphasis is carried forward into the first official version of the office in Strahov: MS D.E.I.7 and title incipit of SAS, *Sapientia aedificavit sibi,* a quotation from Proverbs 9: 1–2.

KB 70.E.4

> *Animarum cibus dei sapientia nobis carnem assumptam proposuit in edullium ut per cibum humanitatis invitaret ad gustum divinitatis.*
>
> [Food for souls, the wisdom of God has offered to us for the flesh that he has assumed, so that through the food of humanity he might invite us to taste of divinity.]

SAS (STRAHOV: MS D.E.I.7)

> *Sapiencia edificavit sibi domum excidit columpnas septem; immolavit victimas suas miscuit vinum et posuit mensam suam.*
>
> [Wisdom has built herself a house, she has erected her seven pillars, she has slaughtered her beasts, prepared her wine, she has laid her table.]

The *Animarum cibus* antiphon has its source in Hugh of Saint-Victor's *De sacramentis* and therefore is not directly biblical. The antiphon from SAS, however, is a direct quote

---

[42] Jacques de Vitry, *The Life,* trans. Margot H. King, in *Two Lives of Marie D'Oignies,* 4th ed. (Toronto: Peregrina Publishing, 1998), 79–123.

[43] Mulder-Bakker, *Lives of the Anchoresses,* 41.

from Proverbs 9. This represents the first use of Proverbs 9 in reference to the Eucharist, an interpretation initiated by Hugh of Saint-Cher:

> *Sapientia* is the Word of God, the *domum* is his flesh, the *columnas septem* are the churches illuminated by the seven gifts of the Holy Spirit; *immolavit* refers to the passion of Christ by which he consecrated the church and *miscuit* refers to the divinity concealed in his humanity and in his word.[44]

This opening theme in the two earliest versions of the liturgy, wisdom as the source of the seven gifts of the Holy Spirit, is echoed in the opening theme of Poem II, in which the poet-narrator also links the theme of the Isaiah verses and the seven gifts of the Holy Spirit to the Eucharist, in this instance through Mary.[45] The reverence for Mary as the "house" of the Holy Spirit and the seven gifts is coupled in the poem with a desire to share these in a community format in which the Scriptures were read. Also noteworthy is the fact that Sapientia was the name of Juliana's teacher.

Anna of the tribe of Asher, which is the focus of Poem VI, is a third common theme directly linking the contents of the poems to the origins of the feast of Corpus Christi. The poem celebrates the Presentation of Jesus at the Temple, which figured prominently in the visions of Marie d'Oignies and other women religious in Liège during the late-twelfth and thirteenth centuries. The feast of the Presentation had special appeal to women; it highlights the purification of the Virgin forty days after the birth and enshrines the encounter between the baby Jesus and the aged Simeon who had long awaited the Lord. Simeon's song was recorded by the prophetess Anna and given the name *Nunc dimittis*. "The distinguishing feature" of the feast of the Presentation, also known as the Candlemas, "was the procession of the whole congregation bearing their lighted candles."[46] The earliest medieval occurrences of Candlemas visions can be found in Jacques de Vitry's biography of Marie.

The Presentation scene and related scriptural verses are referred to three times in Juliana's *vita*. When Jesus relates to Juliana that she should be the one to initiate the new feast, she remarks: "Dimitte me in pace" [let me depart in peace].[47] When she related her vision to her friend Isabella and it was clear that this secret had not been revealed to Isabella, her response paraphrased Simeon's prophecy:

---

[44] *Glossa ordinaria* in Prov 9 (3.318ra), quoted in Zawilla, *Biblical Sources of the Historia Corporis Christi*, 128.

[45] See Barbara R. Walters, "O verge de droiture ki de Jessé issis from the Mosan Psalters," in *Études de langue et de litterature médiévales offertes à Peter T. Ricketts à l'occasion de son 70ème anniversaire*, ed. A. Buckley and D. Billy (Turnhout: Brepols, 2005).

[46] Carolyne Larrington, "The Candlemas Vision and Marie D'Oignie's Role in Its Dissemination," in *New Trends in Feminine Spirituality: The Holy Women of Liège and Their Impact*, ed. Juliette Dor, Lesley Johnson, and Jocelyn Wogan-Browne (Turnhout: Brepols, 1999), 208.

[47] *Vie de Sainte Julienne de Cornillon*, Critical Edition, vol. 2 of *Fête-Dieu (1246–1996)*, ed. Jean-Pierre Delville (Louvain la Neuve: Institut d'Études Médiévales de l'Université Catholique de Louvain, 1999), 124.

You see this child: he is destined for the fall and for the rising of many in Israel, destined to be a sign that is rejected—and a sword will pierce your own soul too—so that the thoughts of many may be laid bare.[48]

When people in Liège opposed the feast of Corpus Christi, the author of the *vita* used the prophecy of Simeon as a metaphor:

> Profecto sicut olim senex iustus symeonem loquor cuius senectus in misericordia uberi cum christum infantem accepisset in ulnas suas de ipso predixit sic et de presenti festivitate potuit dici quod posita esset in ruinam et resurrectionem multorum, et in signum cui contradiceretur.[49]

> [It was just as it once was with the righteous elder Simeon, whose old age was rich in mercy, when he received the Christ Child in his arms and prophesied of him. So too it could be said of the present feast that it was set for the fall and rising of many, and for a sign that would be spoken against.][50]

The *Nunc dimittis* theme is echoed by Pope Urban IV in his letter to Eve, sent on 8 September along with the *Transiturus*: "Therefore let your soul magnify the Lord and your spirit rejoice in God your savior, for now your eyes have seen your salvation, which we have prepared before the face of all peoples."[51] Zawilla notes that Urban IV here pays Eve a double tribute. He praises her for her role in establishing the feast and her long-suffering patience in seeing it established.[52]

A fourth theme connecting the poems to the new feast can be found in lines 53–56 of Poem XX, which reflect on a prominent theme in both the *vita* of Juliana of Mont Cornillon and in thirteenth-century interpretations of the Eucharist. The poem recaptures the exact language of the *vita* when the abbess urged Juliana "to proclaim on some of that honeyed sweetness she perceived" in the *Magnificat*. In the scene in the *vita*, Juliana behaved as if "intoxicated," although not from wine. The duplication of language in the poems and the *vita* corroborates the thesis of interrelated communities with shared beliefs for both. The thesis is further substantiated in the replacement of the words *Susanne* and *perdition* with *Juliana* and *predication* in Poem IX:

> Ave, li plus douce enmiliee,
> li plus ardenment enivree
> de redes jus de paradis,
> ou est amors, u est amis.

> [Hail, most gentle honeyed one
> most ardently intoxicated
> with proclamations outside of paradise,
> where there is love, where there is a friend.]

---

48 Lk 2: 33–35.

49 Delville, *Vie de Sainte Julienne de Cornillon*, 142.

50 *The Life of Juliana of Mont Cornillon*, trans. Barbara Newman (Toronto: Peregrina, 1988), 90.

51 Ibid., 147.

52 Zawilla, *Biblical Sources of the Historia Corporis Christi*, 52.

The second group of vernacular poems—Poems X, XI, and XII in Sinclair's initial ordering (Poems XVII, XVIII, and XIX here)—consists of *Ave* prayers in three sets of fifty quatrains, one quatrain for each of the 150 Psalms. Poem XVII in Sinclair's ordering (Poem XX here) from Fitzwilliam 288 is also a set of *Ave* prayers, but this set contains seventy-seven *Ave* prayers that are slightly more irregular in form; several meditations deviate from the quatrain form. *Ave porta paradysi*[53] is the title given to the Latin *Ave* prayers, based on the incipit of the first set of fifty prayers. It can be found in a Latin psalter of French Cistercian origin in which each of the *Ave* prayers reflects or paraphrases a verse from one of the one hundred and fifty Psalms.[54] As part of the earliest and most widespread of the Marian Psalters,[55] the *Ave porta paradysi* may be dated at ca. 1130.[56] Numerous *Ave* prayers were composed later, following this tradition of interpreting the Psalms with reference to Christ or Mary. Winston-Allen suggests that the *Ave* form of devotion eventually was shortened by eliminating recitation of the Psalms and coupled with prayer counters or beads to form the Rosary meditation.

Table 16 lists all of the manuscripts of Mosan Psalters that contain the Latin version of *Ave porta paradysi* and all of the manuscripts that contain Poems X, XI, and XII in Sinclair's ordering (Poems XVII, XVIII, and XIX here), the *Ave* reflections in Old French.

Table 16
Ave Prayers by Manuscript

Manuscript	Latin	French
BR 19095	X	
BR IV–36		X
BR IV–1013		X
Fitzwilliam 288		X
Fitzwilliam, McLean 43	X	
Darmstadt H.L.B.	X	
Dublin, Trinity College 90	X	
KB 76.G.17		X
Ex-Heidelberg, T.A. 130, MS 448	X	
Liège 431		X
London BL 21114		X
London BL Harley 2930	X	
London BL Stowe 17		X
Melbourne 096/R66	X	
M183	X	
M440	X	
Oxford Bodleian	X	
BNF 1077	X	
Rochester		X
's-Heerenberg S. H. B. 35		X

---

[53] Published in Guido M. Dreves and Clemens Blume, eds., AH 35, *Psalteria Rhythmica: Gereimte Psalterien des Mittelalters* (Leipzig, 1900; New York: Johnson Reprint Corporation, 1961), 189–99.

[54] See Oliver, *Gothic Manuscript Illumination*, 1: 41–42.

[55] Ibid., 42.

[56] Anne Winston-Allen, *Stories of the Rose: The Making of the Rosary in the Middle Ages* (University Park: Pennsylvania State University Press, 1997), 15.

The Latin version typically appears after the Office of the Dead, as is the case in the *Grosbois Psalter* as well as ten other psalters in the Mosan group. An interesting relationship exists between the Old French vernacular *Ave* meditations and the Latin version. The Ave prayers in vernacular French do not correspond exactly to the *Ave porta paradysi* in Latin. Sinclair's Poem XII (here Poem XIX) adapts the first forty-six stanzas and then skips to the last four stanzas. Moreover, stanzas 11, 16, 21, 25, 26, 38, and 46 do not correspond with their equivalent Latin stanza. Equally interesting is the odd singular appearance in Old French of the venerable *Ave, mater, stella maris*, found in stanza 5 of Poem XVII [now Poem XX]. In both instances of translation into the vernacular, the forty-six quatrains of Poem XIX and stanza 5 of XX, the Old French adapts to a more complex and artistic statement in Latin.

An example of the reflexive relationship between the Old French and Latin stanzas and of thematic content can be examined by comparing the Latin *Ave porta paradysi* and its reflection in French, as it appears in M440, folio 240r. The theme reiterates the theme of Poem II and of lines 5–8 in Poem VIII. The reference to Ezekiel 44: 2 in the opening stanza of the *Ave porta paradysi* uses the image of the gate that is shut: "This gate shall be shut, it shall not be opened, and no man shall enter in by it; because the Lord, the God of Israel, hath entered in by it, therefore it shall be shut." The theme again echoes the theme of Mary as the flower of the tree of life, who sweetens the fruit of redemption.

Ave, porta paradysi,	Ave, Marie, flors de lis,
lignum vite quod amisi,	haute porte de paradis,
per te michi iam dulcessit	par toi nos est li fruis rendus
et salutis fructus crescit.	ki par est vrai, a tort perdus.
[Hail, gate of paradise,	[Hail Mary, flower of the lily,
the tree of life, which was lost,	high gate of paradise,
through you is sweetened for me	through you is returned to us the fruit
and becomes healthy fruit.]	which is indeed real, wrongly lost.]

Ricketts earlier noted that in the Latin version of the psalter poems, the reference to Mary as the *porta paradysi* or *lignum vite* is oblique.[57] The reference is part of an ancient and venerable Church tradition dating back to at least Saints Augustine and Ambrose. In the Latin *Ave* prayer as found in the psalters, only the accompanying miniature of the Annunciation on folio 240r specifically links the passage to Mary and her redemptive role in giving birth to Christ. However, in the passage in Old French, *haute porte de paradis* refers not obliquely but rather directly to Mary, who is named in the first line of the quatrain as the *flors de lis*, also the emblem of the French kings. This emphasizes the reformulation or recasting of the poems for a feminine audience.

The redemptive role of Mary as the Gate of Paradise is a sub-textual theme of the fourth nocturn for monastic use in the office of the feast of Corpus Christi attributed to Thomas Aquinas, as found in BNF 1143, *Sacerdos in [a]eternum*. Especially the first anti-

---

[57] See Peter T. Ricketts, "A Woman's Poem: The *Priere de Theophile* in Occitan," in *L'Offrande du Cœur: Medieval and Early Modern Studies in Honour of Glynnis Cropp*, ed. Margaret Burrell and Judith Grant (Christchurch, N.Z.: Canterbury University Press in association with Massey University, 2004), 87–95.

phon of this nocturn, which is shared with the earlier version, *Sapiencia [a]edificavit sibi* and is drawn from Psalms 110, is set to the music of a Marian antiphon: "Paradisi porta per Evam cunctis clausa est et per Mariam virginem hodie patefacta est" [Through Eve the gate of Paradise has been closed, and through the Virgin Mary it has been opened again]. A responsory dedicated to Mary, Star of the Sea, provides the music for the second responsory of the fourth nocturn in BNF 1143: "Solem iustitie regem paritura supremem Stella Maria maris hodie processit ad ortum" [About to give birth to the highest sun, the King of justice, Mary, the Star of the Sea today proceded to the east]. *Ave Maria Stella maris* is the theme of another extremely popular *Ave* prayer found in the psalters.

This brief discussion provides only a small sample of the many potential thematic connections linking the audience for the psalters to the congregation which formed in churches around the sacrament and the institution of the new feast of Corpus Christi amidst the political tumult of the thirteenth century. The critical edition of the poems in the Mosan Psalters by Peter T. Ricketts fills a lacuna between the popular piety of women and the intellectual theology of the Eucharist in the movement to establish the new feast. It thus provides an invaluable resource to scholars and forges the path for a new generation with perhaps different goals and aims from those of the past.

CRITICAL EDITION OF
THE POEMS OF THE MOSAN PSALTERS

Peter T. Ricketts

Each poem is edited from all manuscripts available in a critical edition based on a comparison (where applicable), from which one is then chosen on the principle that it is most respected by the others. Certain groupings will become apparent, superficially, from the presence of certain poems in particular manuscripts, but only after an analysis of common readings, peculiar to groups of manuscripts, can the validity of a particular base manuscript be substantiated fully.

The form of presentation adopted here is an edition of each poem with expansion of abbreviations, capitalization, where required, according to modern punctuation and in respect of proper names, but ignoring the practice of introducing each new line by capitals unless a new sentence is involved. The critical apparatus of rejected readings does not privilege those of the base manuscript, in the few cases that they occur, but sets these too in the context of relationships with the other manuscripts. The form of the rejected readings follows exactly the spelling in the manuscript except that abbreviations are not shown unless they are of significance to the reasons for rejection, and consonantal *u* is shown as *v*. However, those which are purely orthographic are not included, unless they appear at the rhyme and reveal links between grapheme and phoneme or are of particular morphological interest. The identification of the segment of the text being considered in comparison with the reading in the other manuscripts is achieved by the reading of the critical text being given in italics followed by a bracket, after which the readings from the other manuscript(s) are presented, identified by their *siglum*, in alphabetical order, where the spelling of the first manuscript is privileged. Notes on points of linguistic and textual interest follow the critical apparatus, along with comments on the substance of poems.

Throughout the notes, references to the Bible are to the Vulgate edition: *Biblia sacra*, vulgatae editionis Sixti V Pont. Max. iussu recognita et Clementis VIII auctoritate edita; editio emendatissima apparatu critico instructa cura et studio Monachorum Abbatiae Pontificiae Sancti Hieronymi in Urbe Ordinis Sancti Benedicti. Rome: Marietti, S. Sedis Apostolicae Typographiae Editores, 1965).

The manuscripts are identified in the list which follows, using the *sigla* that have been assigned in this edition to reflect the narrative order of the first sixteen poems, and then the group of *Aves* (XVII, XVIII and XIX), arranged according to the order adopted, for those deriving from the *Ave, porta paradisi*, in MS *D* (The Hague, National Library of the Netherlands, 76.G.17 [KB 76.G.17]), the only manuscript to contain all three. These are followed by an innovative *Ave* in last place, Poem XX: the quatrain is not respected in all stanzas and the content, while it relates to Mary, is different in style and emphasis. It is clear that Sinclair,[1] following Valkhoff and Långfors, numbered the poems on the basis of the order in which he discovered them. Further, he had not been able to consult the manuscripts designated *G* and *L* and was not aware of the poems contained therein. In addition, three manuscripts not listed in his article have been added here, to which the *sigla M, N* and *O* have been given. Sinclair refers to the work of Meyer, who had discovered and studied five of the manuscripts.[2] Later, Valkhoff and Långfors pointed to the existence of two further manuscripts,[3] with comments and corrections added in 1948 by Legros.[4]

In 1964, Sinclair identified MS *E* as an example of the same psalter.[5] Since then, Oliver has given the authoritative list of manuscripts,[6] from which the following is taken:

A New York, Pierpont Morgan Library, 440

B Paris, Bibliothèque nationale de France, latin 1077

C Liège, Bibliothèque de l'Université, 431

D The Hague, National Library of the Netherlands, 76.G.17 (KB 76.G.17)

E Melbourne, State Library of Victoria, *096/R66

F London, British Library, Add. 21114

G 's-Heerenberg, Stichting Huis Bergh, 35 (225)

H New York, Pierpont Morgan Library, 183

I Cambridge, Fitzwilliam Museum, 288

K Brussels, Bibliothèque royale, IV–1066 (BR IV–1066)

L Brussels, Bibliothèque royale, IV–1013 (BR IV–1013)

M Brussels, Bibliothèque royale, IV–36 (BR IV–36)

N London, British Library, Stowe 17

O Rochester, Memorial Art Gallery, 53.68

The distribution of the twenty poems is shown in Table 1.

---

[1] Keith V. Sinclair, "Les manuscrits du Psautier de Lambert le Bègue," *Romania* 86 (1965), 22–47 (hereafter Sinclair, *Manuscrits*).

[2] Paul Meyer, "Rapport sur d'anciennes poésies religieuses en dialecte liégeois," *Revue des Sociétés Savantes des Départements*, 5e ser. 6 (1873), 236–49 (hereafter Meyer, "Rapport"), and "Le Psautier de Lambert le Bègue," *Romania* 29 (1900), 528–45.

[3] M. Valkhoff, "Le manusrit 76 G 17 de la Haye et l'ancienne hymne wallonne," *Romania* 62 (1936), 17–26; A. Långfors, "Le manusrit 76 G 17 de la Haye et le psautier de Lambert le Bègue," *Romania* 62 (1936), 541–43.

[4] E. Legros, "Note bibliographique sur les hymnes liégeoises du moyen âge," *Les dialectes belgo-romans* 7 (1948), 171–74.

[5] Sinclair, "Un psautier de Lambert le Bègue à Melbourne," *Australian Journal of French Studies* 1 (1964), 5–10 (hereafter Sinclair, *Psautier*).

[6] Judith Oliver, *Gothic Manuscript Illumination in the Diocese of Liège (c.1250–c. 1330)*, 2 vols. (Leuven: Peeters, 1988), 1: 38–39 and 2: 239–311.

Table 1
Distribution of the Twenty Poems

	A	B	C	D	E	F	G	H	I	K	L	M	N	O
I										+				
II	+	+	+							+				
III								+						
IV		+	+			+		+		+				
V	+													
VI	+	+												
VII										+				
VIII										+				
IX	+	+								+	+			
X	+	+												
XI	+	+	+		+									
XII	+							+						
XIII						+								
XIV		+												
XV	+													
XVI									+					
XVII			+	+			+		+		+	+	+	+
XVIII				+			+		+		+	+	+	+
XIX				+										
XX									+					

I

BEA SIRE DEUS, PERES OMNIPOTENS

MS: *K* fol. 10 rᵒ.

Versification: decasyllabic lines in rhyming couplets. The rhyme scheme is as follows:

a a b b b b c c d d e e f f g g h h i i j j k k l l m m

        Bea sire Deus, peres omnipotens,
        ki todis fus et ki seras totens,
        ki sire Adam le promu hom creastes
        et dame Evain de sa coste formastes.
5   De paradis le fruit lor otriastes,
        for ke d'un seul; celui li deveastes.
        Mais mut petit furent obedien
        par le conselh et par l'enortemen
        del fel mavais, ki par son grant orguelh
10   chaï del ciel, non pas por le sien vuelh.
        Par che k'ilh sot ke restoreir devoit
        Adans le siege dont ilh cheus astoit,
        envie en ot; envers Evain se traist,
        se li a dit ke le pome manjaist.
15   Elle si fist et son marit en done,
        et li chaitis a mangir s'abandone.
        Andui tantost de lor mesaventure

sont aparchuet et ont mise lor cure
d'eas absconseir de fuelhe de figuir.
20 Mut chierement achetent teil mangir;
de paradis sunt andui for buteit.
Apres ce, sunt Cain et Abel neit,
et vit Cain ke li offrande Abeal
plaisoit a Deu, ne li astoiet mie beal.
25 Son frere ocist; mut fut gran felonie
par mavastié et par trop grant envie.
Je te pri, sire, ke por la tiene aie
soie gardee de tos maz et d'envie.

Translation

Fine Lord God, almighty father,
who was for all time and who will be forever,
you who created Sir Adam, the first man
and formed Lady Eve from his rib.
5   You granted to them the fruits of paradise
except for one; this one you forbade to them.
But they were scarcely obedient
because of the counsel and the exhortation
of the evil wicked one, who, through his great pride
10   fell from heaven, not according to his own wishes.
Because he knew that Adam might restore
the seat from which he had fallen,
he wanted it; he went to Eve
and told her to eat the apple.
15   She did so and gave of it to her husband,
and the wretched one let himself eat.
Both straightway became aware
of their mistake and were intent
on covering themselves with fig leaves.
20   They pay dearly for the food they eat;
they are both driven out from the paradise.
After this, Cain and Abel were born,
and Cain saw that Abel's offering
was pleasing to God, but his was not.
25   He killed his brother: it was a very great crime
out of wickedness and extreme enviousness.
I pray to you, Lord, that, through your help,
I may be guarded from all evils and from envy.

Critical Apparatus

3. *ki sire*] ki.—21, *sunt*] se sunt.—24, *a Deu*] adam.—

Notes

3. *sire*. Sinclair (*Manuscrits*, 44) correctly adds this word to rectify the metric balance. *sire Adam* is rightly given as a title to Adam to match *dame Evain*.

28. *tos maz*. Sinclair incorrectly reads *ces mas*.

II
O VERGE DE DROITURE, QUI DE JESSÉ EISSIS

MSS: *A* fol. 8 rᵒ, *B* fol. 9 rᵒ, *C* fol. 9 rᵒ, *K* fol. 11 rᵒ.

Base: *K*.

Versification: twelve syllable lines in rhyming couplets, according to the following rhyme scheme:

a a b b c c c c c c d d e e f f g′ g′ h h i i c c j j d d g′ g′

Earlier edition: Meyer, "Rapport," 241–42 (following MS *A* and with the text of MS *B*).

O verge de droiture, qui de Jessé eissis,
ki la flur engendras sor cui li Sains Espirs
reposat plainemen, si com dist Ysaies,
et en toi s'enspandi par don dé set parties;

5   racine de Jessé, ensprendemen d'amur,
flur et liz de casté, dame digne d'onor,
otroi' a ton ancelle savorer le savur
de cel saintisme fruit dont tu portas le flur.
Le cuer de ton ancelle enspren de la chalur

10   ki desent par set grasces et de par son ardur
ke li flur de casté ne puist en moi marchir
ne la flame d'amur caritable alentir.
Mon estre et mon penser, mon vivre et mon parler
puist l'ispirs de science ensenher et donter,

15   et cilh de pieté raemplisse mon cuer
por membrer té vertus et de nuit et de jor.
Spiritus consilii ne moi defalhe mie
c'al conselh d'Enscriture puisse aturneir ma vie.
Force enapres m'otroie d'ester al detement,

20   ke dire et lire orai prestes et sages gent.
El palais de mon cuer, par l'espir de savoir
fai sentir com est duz li savoir toi savoir,
si moi garde partot li enspirs d'entendor
ke mi arme et mé cors ne chaet en error.

25   Le cremor alsiment si loal ferme en moi
ki enchacet l'orguelh et de pechié le loi.
Flor de totes vertus, maison del Saint Enspir,
del arbre de tes grasces moi denges repartir
k'en cest siecle present si florisse ma vie

30   ke tes fiz moi conoisse a filhe et a amie.

Translation

    O, virgin of righteousness, who descended from Jesse,
    who gave birth to the flower in whom the Holy Spirit
    finds true rest, as Isaiah said,
    and bloomed in you through the gift of the seven parts;
5   root of Jesse, fire of love,
    flower and lily of chastity, lady worthy of honor,
    grant to your servant to savor the taste
    of the holiest fruit of whom you bore the flower.
    Enflame the heart of your servant by the heat
10   which comes down through the seven graces and by its ardor
    so that the flower of chastity may not wither in me
    nor the flame of beneficent love die down.
    May my being and my thoughts, my existence and my words
    be guided and directed by the spirit of knowledge,
15   and my heart be filled by the spirit of piety
    so that I may remember your virtues both night and day.
    May the *spiritus consilii* never fail me
    so that I may regulate my life according to the counsel of the
       Scriptures.
    Give me strength to be present at the exegesis
20   so that I shall hear priests and wise people speaking and reading.
    In the palace of my heart, through the spirit of knowledge,
    make me feel how gentle is the knowledge of knowing you,
    and everywhere keep in me the spirit of understanding
    so that my soul and my body may not fall into sin.
25   Place in me, too, that legitimate fear
    which drives out pride and the law of sin.
    Flower of all virtues, mansion of the Holy Spirit,
    deign to share with me of the tree of your graces
    so that, in this world of today, my life may so flourish
30   that your son may know me as daughter and friend.

Critical Apparatus

4, *s'enspandi*] *A* sensparti.—5, *d'amur*] *ABC* damors.—6, *d'onor*] *B* damur.—7, *ton*] *A* tue, *B* tiue, *C* tu.—9, *de ton*] *A* a tue.—11, *moi*] *C* moie.—13, *estre*] *K* cuer.—15, *cilh*] *A* cis.—16, *por*] *C* par; *membrer*] *A* ramenbrer; *nuit et de jor*] *B* ior e de nuit.—17, *Spiritus consilii*] *A* li espirs de conselh; *defalhe*] *C* defalh.—18, *c'al*] *K* ca; *conselh*] *C* conseilhe.—19, *m'otroie*] *AB* motroi, *K* motroit.—20, *prestes*] *C* pecheors.—21, *El*] *C* li.—22, *li savoir*] *C* li savoi-res.—23, *d'entendor*] *A* dentendemen, *B* mon senhor, *CK* denteilhor.—24, *A* ke ne chai en error par dis de male gen; *chaet*] *B* chai, *C* chaie.—25, the remainder of the text is missing from *C*; *alsiment*] *B* al siruen.

Notes

1–3. The ancestry of the Virgin as a descendant of the family of David is traced back to Jesse, the son of Obed and the father of David, and to the prophetic words of Isaiah, "Et egredietur virga de radice Iesse, et flos de radice eius ascendet, et requiescet super eum spiritus Domini" (*Isaias* 11: 1–2). Here (2), the traditional refer-ence is to Christ as the flower in which the Holy Spirit dwells. The theme of the line of Jesse is to be found also in the *Dulce lignum* and is used by Jacques de Vitry in his Good Friday sermon.

4. *don dé set parties*: the progeniture of Mary is related further by reference to the division of the land in Canaan among the seven tribes of the Israelites who had not yet received their inheritance, decided initially by Joshua and then on the basis of drawing lots (*Iosue* 18: 5).

6. *flur et liz de casté*: the notion of chastity and purity is permanently linked to the Virgin, and the image of the lily is widespread in both devotional literature and in the extension of the image in lyric verse which takes Mary as its subject.

7. *otroi' a ton ancelle*: many prayers written for and by women will cite biblical authority and then, describing themselves as a handmaiden or faithful servant, beg to be granted, as here, the right to taste the fruit (8). This participation is fundamental to the process of inclusiveness that marks such poetry as the Mosan Psalters.

10. *set grasces*: these are the seven gifts of the Holy Spirit, which, in the Middle Ages, were probably codified by Thomas Aquinas: wisdom (*savoir*, 21), understanding (*enspirs d'entendor* 23), counsel (*spiritus consilii*, 17 and *conselh*, 18), strength (*force*, 19), knowledge (*science*, 14), piety (*pieté*, 15) and fear (*cremor* 25); cf. *Isaias* 11: 2–3: "spiritus sapientiae et intellectus, spiritus consilii et fortitudinis, spiritus scientiae et pietatis, et replebit eum spritus timoris Domini." It is intriguing to speculate on the reason for calling them *graces*: in the Old Testament, they are referred to as different manifestations of the *spiritus* (*espir* or *enspir* in the poem). In the New Testament, especially *Ad Romanos* 12: 6: "Habentes autem donationes secundum gratiam quae data est nobis differentes . . .," the link may have been made between these *donationes* and the seven gifts of the Holy Spirit, and confused with the *charismata*, of which there are nine, but which include wisdom and knowledge; see especially *I Ad Corinthios* 12: 4–11.

23. *enspirs d'entendor*. While the reading of *A*, *dentendemen*, destroys the rhyme sequence and that of *B*, *mon senhor*, is a *lectio facilior*, the reading in *CK* seems unlikely and probably is based on an error that goes back to their common archetype. The notion of "enspirs d'entelhor," 'spirit of the sculptor' does not sit well here, whereas that of *entendor*, which is graphemically similar, is more reasonable and is a match with *spiritus intellectus* (see note 10).

III
VRAIS DEUS, QUI TOI DENGNAS EN LA VIRGENE AUMBRER

MS: *H* fol. 10 rº.

Versification: decasyllabic lines in rhyming couplets. Lines 5 and 22 are hypometric. The rhyme scheme is as follows:

a a b b c c d d e e c c f f g g h h i i j j k k k

Earlier Edition: Sinclair, *Manuscrits*, 33.

> Vrais Deus, qui toi dengnas en la virgene aumbrer,
> por Gabriel volsistes le message mandeir.
> Ce fut voirs, sires, le message portat,
> et ta venue en la virgene anonchas
> 5   cant ilh li dist: "Deus toi salue, Marie!
> De la Deu grasce seras tu raemplie."
> La pucelle forment s'en embahit
> cant la parolle de Gabriel oit;
> puis demandat comment estre poroit
> 10   qu'en teil maniere virgene enfant averoit.
> "Car ains encor en trestote ma vie
> avuec home n'out part ne compangnie."
> L'angles respont maintenant en riant:
> "Virgene pucelle, ne t'enmaies niant;

15 li Sains Espirs en toi descenderat
    et ton saint cors de lui raemplirat,
    si enfanteras Jesu Crist, le tien pere,
    a cui es filhe, et puis seras sa mere;
    raemplie seras de trestotes vertus.
20 L'emfes que porteras avrat a nom Jesus."
    Virgene pucelle, Marie, cui Deus aime,
    la toie ancelle hui cest jor toi reclaime
    de tes proieres que moi vuelhes aidier
    . . . .
25 envers ton filh, qui nos doit justechier,
    que ilh moi vuelhe paradys otroier.

Translation

    True God, who deigned to become flesh in the virgin,
    you decided to send the message through Gabriel.
    It was true, Lord, that he carried the message,
    and you announced your coming to the virgin
5   when he said to her: "God salutes you, Mary!
    You will be filled with the grace of God."
    The maiden was sorely troubled
    when she heard the word of Gabriel;
    then she asked how it could be
10 that, in such a way, a virgin could be with child;
    "for never yet in all my life
    was there a relationship with a man."
    The angel now replies, laughing:
    "Virgin maid, have no fear whatsoever;
15 the Holy Spirit will come down into you
    and will fill your holy body with himself,
    and you will give birth to Jesus Christ, your father,
    whose daughter you are, and then you will be his mother;
    you will be filled with every virtue.
20 The child whom you will bear shall be called Jesus."
    Virgin maid, Mary, whom God loves,
    your handmaid this very day calls on you
    that, with your prayers, you may wish to intercede for me
    . . . .
25 with your son, who is to judge us,
    that he may wish to grant me paradise.

Critical Apparatus

5, *li*] toi.

Notes

5. Sinclair (ibid.) rightly suggests the emendation of *toi* to *li*.

20. *porteras*. Sinclair (*Manuscrits*, 33) erroneously reads this verb as *portera*.

24. It must be assumed that this line is lacking in the MS because of the rhyme scheme. Sinclair (ibid.) does not give any indication of the lacuna.

IV

PIUS DEUS OMNIPOTENS, QUI HAUS SIES ET LONC VOIS

MSS: *B* fol. 10 r°, *C* fol. 10 r°, *F* fol. 9 r°, *H* fol. 11 r°, *K* fol. 12 r°.
Base: *C*.
Versification: twelve syllable lines in rhyming couplets. The rhyme scheme is as follows:

a a a a a a a a a a a a b b b b b b b b a a a

        Pius Deus omnipotens, qui haus sies et lonc vois,
        ki juske as fins dé terres apparustes as rois,
        kant cele estoile virent en Orien to droit
        ki la vostre naiscence finement demostroit.
5   Et nez astoit en terre, qui tos nos saveroit
        de son precious sanc, s'en nos ne remanoit.
        En Jerusalem vindrent a Herode le roi,
        ki de vostre naiscence astoit en grant effroit.
        Il mandat tos les sages et si lor demandoit
10   ke disoit l'Escriture u Jesus nasteroit,
        et ilh li respondirent: "En Bethleem," to droit,
        "ce dient li prophete ke ilh la nasteroit."
        Atant li troi roi d'Erode soi turnarent
        et droit vers Bethleem lor chemin arotarent.
15   Et vos, beas sire Deus, illuc si vos trovarent,
        et vos et vostre mere bonement aorarent.
        Offrande de hau pris avuec eas aportarent,
        or et encens et myrre bonement vos donarent.
        Lé roi la deiteit la mort signifiarent,
20   de celle amere mort ke Giu vos donarent
        kant, en la sainte crois, vo cors afficharent.
        Si, voirement, bea Deus, com c'est voirs et je·l croi,
        mon cors et la moie arme gardeis en droite foi
        k'enapres ceste vie puisse venir a toi.

Translation

        Holy almighty God, you who sit on high and see far,
        who appeared to the kings as far as the ends of the earth,
        when they saw that star in the East straight before them
        which gave telling proof of your birth.
5   And he was born on earth, the one who was to save us
        with his precious blood, and it was no longer in us.
        They came into Jerusalem to Herod the king,
        who was in great fear of your birth.
        He called before him all the wise men and asked them
10   what the Scriptures said of where Jesus would be born,
        and they replied: "In Bethlehem," directly;
        "the prophets say that he would be born there."
        Then the three kings departed from Herod
        and went on their way straight to Bethlehem.

15   And you, fine Lord God, they found you there,
      and devoutly adored you and your mother.
      They brought with them offerings of great price,
      gold, incense and myrrh they freely gave you.
      The kings predicted the death of the deity,
20   that bitter death which the Jews dealt you
      when they raised your body on the holy cross.
      Thus, indeed, fine God, as it is true and I believe it,
      keep my body and my soul on the path of true faith
      so that, after this life, I may come to you.

Critical Apparatus

1, *vois*] K voit.—2, *juske as*] BK ius ka, H ius quauz; *fins*] BK fin, F sieus; *dé terres*] B de terre, FH des terres; *apparustes*] F apparuis; *as*] B a.—3, *virent*] H vint; *Orien*] K belleen.—5, *nos*] BK nos.—8, *naiscence*] BK venue.—10, *Jesus*] BCFH ihesu crist.—11, *et ilh*] B et cilh, HK ilh.—13, *d'Erode soi*] F de herode se.—14, *chemin*] C chemine.—15, missing in B; *illuc si*] C illos si, H illuques.—16, missing in H; *et vos*] K vos.—17, *hau*] K ha; *aportarent*] K portarent.—19, *deiteit la mort*] B la deite, K deite le mor.—20, *amere mort*] B mor; *vos*] B moi, F nos i.—21, *vo*] CFH vostre; *afficharent*] H travilharent.—22, *bea Deus*] H biaus; *com*] BHK que; *voirs*] C voires.—23, *mon*] F et mon; *la moie*] F mi; *arme*] FH anrme; *droite*] BK bone.—24, *ceste*] C cest; C adds *amen* at the end of the line; H adds two further lines: et trestuit mi amis biaus sire ie te proi / et trestos pecheors ramoine a droite foi.

V

SIRE DIEUS, CUI NAISCENCE LI PROPHETE ANUNCZARENT

MS: *A* fol. 9 rº.

Versification: twelve syllable lines in rhyming couplets. The rhyme scheme is as follows:

a a b b c c c c e e e e f f f f f f f f f f f f

Earlier edition: Meyer, "Rapport," 242–43 (following MS *A* and with the text of MS *B*).

      Sire Dieus, cui naiscence li prophete anunczarent
      et li angle a pastors joaument la nunczarent,
      to droit en Bethleem maintenant en alerent,
      gisant enz en la crepe humlement toi trovarent,
5   entre lé mues bestes toi trovarent gisant,
      envelopeit en dras en guise d'un enfant;
      les ensenges del angle trovarent maintenant,
      lors s'en tornarent baut et liet et joant;
      la vostre duce mere humlement i gisoit
10   et Joseph li vilhas bonement la gardoit;
      de vostre povreteit forment soi complaindoit,
      ke Deus estiez et hom nekedent bien savoit.
      Hautisme Deus, beas sire, par vo saintisme nom,
      ki en la sainte virgene presis carnation
15   por nos a rachater de la main a felons
      ke n'aleisiens, beas sire, en ifer le parfon,
      si, voirement, pius sires, ke nos ici creons
      k'al tier jor suscitastes de mor sain Lazaron,
      Marie Magdalene fesistes vrai pardon,

20   cant lavat les vos piez en la maison Simon,
     defen moi et les miens de honte et de prison
     ke ne puissent gaber nostre anemi felon;
     je meimes aie, sire, vraie confession
     anchois ke m'arme parte de cest sicle u nos soms.

Translation

Lord God, whose birth the prophets announced
and the angels joyously told to the shepherds,
straightway they set out for Bethlehem,
and found you lying humbly in the manger,
5   among the dumb beasts they found you lying,
wrapped in clothes like a child;
thereupon, they discovered the proof of what the angel said
and then returned from there, happy, joyous and rejoicing;
your gentle mother humbly lay there
10   and Joseph, the simple man, loyally tended to her;
your poverty greatly distressed her
for she knew well you were God and yet also man.
Supreme God, fine Lord, by your most holy name,
you who became flesh in the holy virgin
15   to redeem us out of the hands of the wicked
in order that we might not, fine Lord, go down to deepest hell,
so that we truly believe here, holy Lord,
that on the third day you raised Saint Lazarus from the dead,
gave true pardon to Mary Magdalene,
20   when she washed your feet in the house of Simon,
protect me and my kin from shame and captivity
so that our wicked enemies may not boast;
may I, myself, Lord, have true confession
before my soul leaves this world in which we live.

Critical Apparatus

15, *main*] mains.

Notes

4. *crepe*—'manger.' This seems to be a N.-E. form, deriving from Frankish *krepja* (cf. Germ. *krippe* aand Old Walloon *grebe*), according to *Romanisches Etymologisches Wörterbuch* 4773.

14. *presis carnation*: this is clearly a learned form taken from Late Latin CARNATIONEM, with the sense of taking on physical form.

15. *felons*: the word here is an epithet for 'devils,' after the sin of Adam and Eve, which condemned humanity to damnation until the coming of Christ.

19. *Marie Magdalene.* According to *Luc* 7: 38, which is the source of this line, it was merely a sinner, not necessarily Mary Magdalene.

22. *anemi felon*: another epithet, but this time for the Devil, the old adversary of God.

23–24. The emphasis on personal confession is not unusual in this type of poetry, in which the writer is making a plea for a special place in heaven, especially in the light of the earlier remarks about the consignment to hell of mankind without the intervention of Christ; cf. Poem III, 23.

VI
BEA SIRE, DEUS, KI, APRES VO NAISCENCE

MSS: *A* fol. 10 r°, *B* fol. 12 r°.

Base: *A*.

Versification: ten syllable lines in rhyming couplets. Where atonic *e* occurs at the hemistich, the syllable containing it is discounted. The rhyme scheme is as follows:

a´ a´ b b c c b b c c e e f f g g h h i i j j k k

Earlier edition: Meyer, "Rapport," 243–44 (following MS *A* and with the text of MS *B*).

Bea sire, Deus, ki, apres vo naiscence,
quarante jors, fustes offers el temple,
es mains de Symeon, prodome chenu,
ki, en vilhece, main jor t'out atendu,
5   car le respons, de tue part, avoit
ke ilh la mort a nul jor ne voroit
jusk'a cele ore ke t'averoit tenut
et en sé bras acolé et sentut;
Anne meisme, la prophete, i astoit
10 k'en continence par main jor t'atendoit.
Offrande, sire, vostre mere i portat—
ke vos del temple, car c'est droit, rachata—
dous turtereles u dous columbeal;
don fu de povre, car n'avoit angeal.
15 La chanta, sire, Symeon la chanczon,
ki mut ert bele et si avoit bel son;
ilh le chanta, li prodome, si l'escrit,
si le savons parmi lui, car il dist:
'Or laisses tu, sire, ton serf en pais;
20 je t'ai veu, vivre ne quier jamais.'
Or te prie je, par ta misericorde,
ke enver toi n'aie nule descorde
a icel jor kant deverai finer;
ce nos otroie, ki sen fin deis regner.

Translation

Beautiful Lord God, who, forty days
after your birth, were offered up in the temple
into the hands of Simeon, a white-haired man of worth,
who, in his old age, had waited for you many days,
5   for he had from you the answer
that he would never see death
until such time as he had held you
and embraced and felt you in his arms;
Anna herself, the prophetess, was there

10   who, abstemiously for many days had waited for you.
     Your mother brought there an offering, Lord,—
     for, as it is right in respect of the temple, she redeemed you—
     two turtledoves or two young pigeons;
     it was the gift of a poor woman, for she had no lamb.
15   Symeon sang the song, Lord,
     which was very beautiful and had a fine sound;
     this man of worth sang and wrote it,
     and we know it through him, for he said:
     'Now leave your servant, Lord, in peace.
20   I have seen you; I wish to live no longer.'
     Now I pray to you that, through your forgiveness,
     I may have no dispute with you
     on the day when I come to my end;
     grant us this, you who shall reign eternally.

Critical Apparatus

1. *vo*] *B* ta.—2, *el*] *B* a.—3, *es mains*] *B* el main; *prodome*] *AB* le prodome.—4, *en*] *B* en sa.—7, *t'averoit*] *B* taroit.—8, *sentut*] *A* sentuu.—9, in *A*, after *meisme*, *iasto* expunctuated.—10, *k'en*] *A* ki en; *par*] *B* en.—11, *portat*] *B* porta.—12, *vos*] *A* nos; *c'est*] *B* cert; *rachata*] *A* rachaa.—13, *dous*] *B* dois; *dous*] *B* de dois; *columbeal*] *B* columbeas.—14, *don fu de povre*] *A* dont si fu poures; *angeal*] *A* nul angeal, *B* nul anheal.—15, *chanczon*] *A* chaczon, *B* chanchon.—19, *laisses*] *A* laissies, *B* lais.—22, *ke*] *A* ki; *n'aie*] *AB* nai.—24, *otroie*] *B* otroi; *sen*] *A* saint; *deis*] *A* doit; *regner*] *B* regneir.

Notes

* The poem is based on the presentation of Jesus in the temple taken from *Luc* 2: 21–38. The details of the Law are to be found in *Lev* 2. The custom of the Church is to readmit the mother of the newly born child forty days after the birth for a service of cleansing in accord with the medieval belief that woman is tainted and must be purified.

3. *prodome*—*AB* le prodome, which makes the line hypermetric.

9. *Anne*. Anna, the daughter of Phanuel, and a descendant of Asher (*Luc* 2: 36). Her title, prophetess, came in old age. She was a wife for seven years and a widow for eighty-four, and had devoted herself to worshipping and supplications (1 *Tit* 5: 5). When she heard Simeon's benediction and prophecy, she transmitted the refrain of praise to her intimates, in preparation for the coming of the child Jesus.

10. *k'en*. The reading from *B* is preferred to maintain the metrics of the line.

14. The sense demands the reading from *B*: Mary was poor and could not afford a lamb. MS *A* has misunderstood *don* (*dont*) and inserts *si* to support *car*. To preserve the correct length, *nul* has been suppressed.

15–20. Simeon's song (*Symeon la chanczon*), "Or laisses tu, . . ." is the name which is popularly given to the *Nunc dimittis*, which is sung at the service of evening prayer. It also is given this name in the life of Juliana. Simeon, a pious man of Jerusalem, who was favored with the intimation that he would live to see the Redeemer (*Luc* 2: 29). When Jesus was brought to the temple, Simeon took him in his arms and gave thanks. His words are an affirmation that God had prepared him for a happy death by thus seeing the Christ in accord with the promise of God. Hence *laisses tu*: the reading of *A*, *laissies*, could be justified if the verb were 2nd plural. The presence of *tu* suggests that this is not an imperative, however, and demands the correction adopted.

22. *aie*. Both manuscripts have *ai*, which makes the line hypometric and does not reflect the need for a subjunctive here.

VII
DUEZ JESU CRIST, KI, POR NOS DELIVREIR

MS: *K* fol. 14 r°.

Versification: decasyllabic lines in rhyming couplets. The rhyme scheme is as follows:

a a b b c c d d e e f f g g h h i i j j k k l l

Duez Jesu Crist, ki, por nos delivreir
del poor a deable u astimes livreit
par le pechié Adan, no promier pere
et dame Evain nostre promiere mere,
5   denhas descendre del ciel cha jus aval,
de si duz mont en si amere val.
En komon liu et vilh vasistes naistre
par humelité, et vo sofristes a paistre
et alaitier et culchier et lever,
10   si con enfan meneir et rameneir,
dont ilh avint, cant om vos ot mené
a la gran feste en le sainte cité,
on vo perdi; et desputer alastes
en scole a Gius et si vos i provastes.
15   Encore fuissiés petis et jovenes enfés;
par vo respons lé mistes en gran pensés.
Illuc vos ont trové vostre paren
ki par vos astoent et triste et dolen.
Et avueke eaz en lor subjection
20   vos en ralastez sen contradiction.
Si voiremen ke ge ce, sire, croi,
te prie ge, ki moi venhe de toi
parmi le grasce del Saint Ensperite,
ke m'arme soit de tos sé pechies quite.

Translation

Gentle Jesus Christ, who, to deliver us
from the power of the Devil, into which we were delivered
through the sin of Adam, our first father
and Lady Eve, our first mother,
5   deigned to come down from heaven here below,
from such a gentle mountain into such a bitter vale.
In a common, low place you wished to be born
humbly, you suffered being fed
and suckled and put to bed and got up
10   and, like a child, taken and brought back,
because of which it happened, when you had been taken
to the great feast in the holy city,
that they lost you; and you went to debate
in school with the Jews and thus proved yourself there.

15   You were still little and a young child;
        by your responses you gave them much to think about.
        Your parents found you there
        and they were sad and grieving because of you,
        and, in their submissiveness, you went back
20   with them without argument.
        As I truly believe, Lord,
        I pray to you, I who come from you
        by the grace of the Holy Spirit,
        that my soul may be free of all its sins.

Critical Apparatus

6, *duz*] duz with *z* expunctuated and *ce* added in superscript.—7, *komon*] kemon.—16, *mistes*] metis.—18, *astoent*] astoen.—21, *voiremen*] voireme.—

Notes

8. Sinclair (*Manuscrits*, 45) suggests that the line is hypermetric and proposes to emend *humelité* to *umbleté* (or the like). However, the hemistich regularly occurs after the fourth foot, and this is no doubt the semi-learned form where the *schwa* does not count (as in the extra syllable in *virgene*).—Sinclair (ibid.) emends the MS reading *et vos sofris* to *et toi sofris* in order to avoid a further foot. However, since the *-es* of *sofristes* elides with the following *a*, the line is not made longer.

12. *gran*: Sinclair (ibid.) reads *grand*.—*en le*: Sinclair retains the MS reading, *elle*. This is more likely to be the clitic form for *en le*, with the typical Northern use of *le* for the fem. def. art. (indeed, such an example occurs in line 23: *le grasce*); *en* has been used for the sake of clarity.

16. *lé mistes*. Since the object (= *Jews*) is plural, it is necessary to read *lé* where Sinclair has *le* (ibid.) Sinclair recognizes that the line is hypermetric and suggests a reading of *mis* in place of *metis* of the MS. The form *mistes*, which goes with the majority use of *vos* in this poem, does not add to the length of the line, given following *en*.

VIII
OI!, PIUS ANHEAS CUI SAIN JEHANS A DOI

MS: *K* fol. 15 r°.

Versification: decasyllabic lines in rhyming couplets. The rhyme scheme is as follows:

a a b b c c d d e e f f g g h h i i j j

        Oi!, pius anheas, cui sain Jehans a doi
        mostrat a ceas qui erent entor soi,
        et puis a lui te fesis batesier,
        non pas par ce ke tu n'ausses mestier
5   . . . .
        mais, par les ondes del flon saintefiier,
        i fesistes vostre sain cors plonkier,
        et ilh n'osoit ton sen chief atochier.
        Tu li desis ke ilh tei batisaist,

10 et ilh le fist, car laissir ne l'osaist.
     Oïe fut la vois le pere, si dist:
     "Oiés cestui! C'est me fiz." Et si fist
     venir tantost en spese de colon
     le Sent Enspir sor ton chief a bandon.
15 Si con c'est voirs et ke j'ensi le tien
     si vraimen ke je n'en dote de rien,
     si moi fai estre de mé pechies mundee
     k'en paradis soit mi arme menee
     avués les angeles en la sovraine pais
20 ki a nul jour ne farat a jamais.

Translation

Ah!, holy lamb, whom Saint John
pointed out to those who were around him,
and then by him you had yourself baptized
not because you needed to
5 . . . .
but, sanctified by the water of the river,
you had your holy body immersed there,
and he dared not touch your holy head.
You told him that he should baptize you,
10 and he did so, for he dared not forego it.
The voice of the father was heard and he said:
"Hear him! This is my son." And straightway
he had come down, the Holy Spirit,
in the form of a dove, on your head freely.
15 As it is true and I hold it to be so
so truly that I have no fears whatever,
cleanse me of my sins
so that my soul may be taken to paradise
with the angels in that sovereign country,
20 which will never fail for all time.

Critical Apparatus

2, *entor*] entire.—4, *ke tu*] ke.—9, *desis*] desist.—11, *si*] et si.—14, *Sent*] sente.—16, *ke je*] ke.—18, *mi arme*] marme.

Notes

*The main emphasis of the poem is baptism, reflecting the change of perception of the sacraments.

8. *atochier*. Sinclair erroneously reads *atechier* (*Manuscrits*, 45 and 46).

11. With Sinclair (ibid., 45), the *et* of the MS is suppressed to balance the line.

16. Sinclair (ibid.) corrects *vraimen* to *voiremen* to balance the line, which is hypometric. A preferable solution (since *voirs* occurs in line 15) is to add *je*.

18. *mi arme*: this correction brings about the requisite balance to this hypometric line (as noted by Sinclair, ibid.).

IX

DEUS, SIRE, EN JERUSALEM VENIS A PASSION

MSS: *A* fol. 11 r°, *B* fol. 11 r°, *K* fol. 13 r°, *L* fol. 8 r°.

Base: *A*.

Versification: twelve syllable lines in rhyming couplets. Final atonic *e* occurring at the hemistich (6 + 1) does not count. The rhyme scheme is as follows:

a a b b b b b b b b b b b b a a a a a a a a a a

Earlier edition: Meyer, "Rapport," 244–45 (following MS *A* and with the text of MS *B*).

> Deus, sire, en Jerusalem venis a passion
> et chevauchastes l'asne, ice nos aprent on;
> vos i venistes, sire, ce fut voirs, humlement
> et si fustes loés de trestote la gent:
> 5 'Osanna! li nos rois, bin soies vos venans!'
> Et ensi fu parfaite la loange as enfans:
> li un jetarent flor, li autre vestimens,
> et li alcant sternirent tresto le pavement
> la u deviés venir, fors rois omnipotenz.
> 10 Joaument vos receurent can venistes laenz,
> et li vostre disciple vos i vinrent siuvant;
> sor la beste u seistes misent lor vestimens,
> et li atre aloent et derire et devant.
> 'Osanna! fiz David,' i aloent criant.
> 15 Duz Deus, si com c'est voirs ke nos ici disons,
> sain Daniel jetastes de la fosse a lions,
> sainte Susanne ostastes de la perdition
> et Jonas delivrastes del ventre del peisson,
> et ceste vostre ymagene, ke nos ici veons,
> 20 ramenbre les vos fais, si com nos le creons.
> Doneis moi, vostre ancelle, pive confession
> et de tos mé pechiés vraie remission,
> ki saint Piere l'apostles donastes le pardon
> de ce k'ilh vos renoat por paur des felons.

Translation

> Lord God, you came to Jerusalem to suffer death
> and rode on the ass, as we are taught;
> you came there, Lord, humbly, in truth
> and you were praised by all the people:
> 5 'Hosanna! our king, you are most welcome!'
> And thus was praise made complete by the children:
> some threw flowers, others clothes,
> and some strewed branches along all of the path
> where you would be coming, powerful, omnipotent king.

10   They received you joyfully when you came therein,
     and your disciples came there following you;
     they put their garments on the beast on which you sat,
     and the others went along before and behind.
     'Hosanna! son of David,' they cried as they went.
15   Sweet God, as what we say here is true,
     you released saint Daniel from the lions' den,
     you saved saint Susanna from perdition
     and delivered Jonah from the belly of the whale,
     and the image of you, which we see here,
20   brings to mind your acts, as we believe.
     Give me, your handmaid, holy confession
     and true forgiveness for all my sins,
     you who pardoned saint Peter the apostle
     for having denied you through fear of the perfidious.

Critical Apparatus

1, *Deus, sire*] L sires deus; *en*] ABKL ki en.—2, *chevauchastes*] A chevauste; *l'asne*] KL laine; *ice*] B ce, L et che; *nos*] L uos.—3, *i venistes*] B revenistes; *ce fut*] B cest, K chu est.—4, *gent*] K gens.—5, *soies vos*] AK sois tu, B soi tu.—6, *Et ensi*] ABK ensi.—7, *li un*] A li.—8, *et li*] K li; *alcant*] B acan.—10, *Joaument*] AK ioanment, B ioamen.—11, *vos i vinrent*] L i uinrent tuit.—13, *et li atre*] A et le gens, L li altre gent.—14, *fiz*] L filh; *i aloent criant*] A bien sois tu venans, B li aloent criant, L aloient tuit criant.—15, *ke*] L et; *ici*] L iche.—16, *jetastes*] L getas.—17, *Susanne*] L iuliane; *perdition*] B perditicion, L predication.—18, *Jonas delivrastes*] AK ionas ietastes, B si getas ionas.—20, *ramenbre*] AL ramenbrer; *les vos*] B le vos, K le nos, L de nos; *fais*] BL fait; *com*] B ke; *nos le*] AK nos, L ce nos.—21, *pive*] KL pure.—22, manque à L; *mé*] B no; *vraie*] AB vrai.—23, *ki*] L que; *donastes*] K fesistes.—24, *de ce k'ilh*] B cant ilh, K de ce ke; *renoat*] L renoait; *des*] BK de.

Notes

1. The four MSS present a reading, *ki en*, which renders the line hypermetric. The change from 2nd singular (*venis*) to 2nd plural (*chevauchastes*) in line 2 might seem to justify the presence of a relative clause. However, the freedom to change from *tu* to *vos* is general and is usually based on affectivity. Examples of the change between MSS can be found in lines 5, 16, and 18.

5. *soies vos*. It is necessary to accept the reading of L, *soies vos*, from a metrical standpoint, in spite of the presence of the 2nd singular in the other MSS. —*venans*. It must be taken as a present participle but, given the presence of *bin*, with the same force as 'bienvenu' in modern French.

14. *i aloent criant*. The readings from the other MSS confirm that A has merely repeated the formula from line 5.

17. *sainte Susanne*. See the story of Susanna, which appears in some versions of the books of the *Apocrypha*. It is interesting to note the intervention of the scribe of L, who replaces the name Susanna with that of Juliana herself and the reading *perdition* with *predication*.

18. *delivrastes*. Not only does the reading of L avoid repetition of *jeter* (line 16) but also it prevents the line from being hypometric.

19. *ymagene*. This element is trisyllabic, the written form deriving from the Latin original, which is here respected in its semi-learned state, like *angele* (as against *angle*) elsewhere.

20. *ramenbre* against *ramenbrer/eir* in AL. There may have been confusion about the meaning, if *fais* were regarded as a verb in a causative construction, thus justifying an infinitive. However, apart from the sense of the line, it would be hypermetric if the infinitive were maintained.

21–22. See note to Poem II, 7.

22. *vraie*. The reading of KL is indicated both for agreement and for the metrics of the line.

X
AIUE, DEUS, BEA SIRE, QUI LE MONDE FORMAS

MSS: *A* fol. 12 r°, *B* fol. 14 r°.

Base: *A*.

Versification: twelve syllable lines in rhyming couplets. The rhyme scheme is as follows:

a a a a a a a a a a a a a a a a a b b c′ c′ c′ c′ c′ c′

Earlier edition: Meyer, "Rapport," 245–46 (following MS *A* and with the text of MS *B*).

> Aiue, Deus, bea sire, qui le monde formas,
> Adam, le promier pere, de la terre creas.
> Cant sesis a la cene, tes apostles apelas;
> k'ert a venir de toi, bonement lor nunczas,
> 5   et ke tuit vo i laissent sovent lor chastias.
> Et sain Johan l'apostle sor ton piz reposas;
> ce fut voirs, bea duz sire: plus des autres l'amas.
> Don si presis le pain, si lo saintefias,
> puis le brisas en pieces et si lor devisas.
> 10   Judas le traitor meimes en donas;
> ke ch' astoit li tiens cors, tres bien le demostras,
> ki por nos fu vendus a la gens Kaifas.
> Puis presis le tuaile, entor toi le fermas,
> presis l'aiwe el bacin, tos lor piez les lavas;
> 15   signe fu d'umlité, ke tu la demostras.
> Apres a l'autre mot forment le contristas,
> cant tu desis, bea sire: 'Li uns moi trairat
> de vos por crucefier; a felons moi donrat.'
> De ce furent dolant, si prist chascuns a dire:
> 20   'Sui je donkes icilh? Dite le moi, bea sire.'
> Si com ice fut voirs, bien l'avons oi dire
> ke por nos pecheors soffristes grief martyre.
> Defen moi en cest sicle et de honte et d'ire,
> k'enapres ceste vie regne o toi, bea du sire.

Translation

> Give help, fine Lord, you who created the world,
> and formed Adam, the first father, from the earth.
> When you sat at the last supper, you summoned your apostles;
> you gently announced to them what was to become of you,
> 5   and you frequently advised them that they should leave you there.
> And you gave repose to Saint John the apostle on your bosom;
> it was true, fine, gentle Lord: you loved him more than the others.
> Then you took the bread and blessed it,
> then broke it into pieces and divided it among them.

10   You gave some even to Judas the traitor.
     You freely showed that your body was there,
     which was sold for us to the people of Caiaphas.
     Then you took the towel, wrapped it around you,
     took the water in the basin and washed all their feet;
15   it was a mark of humility that you showed there.
     Afterwards you gave very great sorrow to the other one
     when you said, fine Lord: 'One of you will betray me
     so that I am crucified; he will hand me over to felons.'
     They were saddened by this, and each one began to say:
     'Am I the one? Tell me, fine Lord.'
20   As it was true, we have indeed heard said
     that for us sinners you suffered cruel martyrdom.
     Protect me in this world from shame and grief,
     so that, after this life, I may reign with you, fine, gentle Lord.

Critical Apparatus

8, *presis*] *A* presipersi.—8, *si lo saintefias*] *B* et si lor devisas.—9, *si lor devisas*] *B* et le saintefias.—10, *meimes*] *B* menries.—11, *le*] *B* lor.—14, *piez les*] *B* puis lor.—15, *fu*] *B* fict.—20, *Dite le moi, bea sire*] *B* si prist chascuns a dire.—21, *bien*] *B* et.—22, *grief*] *B* gran.—24, *k'enapres ceste*] *B* capres iceste; *toi*] *A* vos.

Notes

11. *ch[i]* - 'there.' This is a typical spelling in the N.-E. dialect.

12. *gens Kaifas*. Caiaphas was the high priest who presided at the trial of Jesus. The reference to his people relates to the Jews and especially those who brought Jesus to him; see *Ioannes* 18: 14 and 28.

17–18. Typically, see *Matt* 26: 21 and 45. The reference to *felons* is not part of the biblical tradition, but here refers specifically to the Jews, whose name was often accompanied by the epithet *felon* in medieval writings.

XI

UNS FAISSELES DE MYRRE EST MES AMIS A MOI

MSS: *A* fol. 13 rᵒ, *B* fol. 13 rᵒ, *C* fol. 11 rᵒ, *E* fol. 19 rᵒ.

Base: *C*.

Versification: twelve syllable lines in rhyming couplets. The rhyme scheme is as follows:

a a b' b' c c d d e e f f e e f f c c c c e e f f f f f f g' g'

Earlier edition: Meyer, "Rapport," 246–47 (following MS *A* and with the text of MS *B*), Sinclair, *Psautier*, 9–10 (text of *E* with variants from *A* and *B*).

     Uns faisseles de myrre est mes amis a moi
     cui semblance en dolur traitier en presen voi;
     done moi, pius saveres, tel myrre en moi comprendre
     ke puisse dignement et plorer et complaindre
5   sor tes aigres batures ke toi, sens okison,
     flaelerent a l'astache, menteor et felon.
     Mes amis, done moi tel myrre conquelhir
     k'amertume a to jors en puisse mais sentir.
     Amere fu ta mors mais mult de bone odor

10 car le honte en soffris dont nos portons l'onor.
    Oi! Cum [est] doce myrre, qui metroit son penser
    d'esgarder itel home qui l'ome avoit formeit.
    Le creator del monde et del ciel le saignor
    traitier et demener a tele desonor!
15 Es bras de mon desir fai moi, sire, assembler
    cest faisselet de myrre ke je puisse porter
    legierement le fais de tribulation,
    ke moi font anemi et la chars et li mons,
    et tote ma grevance en ta subjection
20 torner par la vertu de ta compassion
    si ensiuvre ta vie et curre aprés t'odor
    et amender ma vie et servir a t'onor.
    Et de la pureture de la mortaliteit,
    ke venins de pechiet at en nos ameneit,
25 la myrre de ta mort, qui le monde at salveit,
    garir en puist mi arme el fin de mon eet
    par la confession de ta grande piteit,
    et si l'atrai a toi a ta bieneurteit,
    u la vie serat et la santeis durable,
30 en cui li amis Deu joie aront permanable.

Translation

    A bundle of myrrh is my beloved
    whose semblance I now see as a source of pain;
    give me, holy savior, such myrrh to take into myself
    so that I may be worthy to weep and lament
5   over your cruel beatings, for, without reason,
    liars and criminals whipped you at the stake.
    My beloved, give me such myrrh to collect
    that I may experience more bitterness forever.
    Your death was bitter but the odor was beautiful
10 for you suffered the shame from which we derive honor.
    Ah! How sweet is this myrrh, for anyone who would concentrate
    on contemplating that man who formed mankind.
    To treat thus and bring to such dishonor
    the creator of the world and the lord of heaven!
15 In the arms of my desire have me, Lord, put together
    this bundle of myrrh so that I may easily bear
    the burden of tribulation,
    for the flesh and the world are hostile to me,
    and have me turn my pain towards your submission
20 through the strength of your compassion
    so as to follow your life and run towards your odor
    and improve my life and give service in your honor.
    And may the myrrh of your death, which saved the world,
    protect my soul from the putrefaction of mortality,

25　which the poison of sin brought upon us,
　　at the end of my life
　　through confession of your great mercy,
　　and thus draws it to you in your happiness,
　　where life and health will be everlasting,
　　in which the beloved of God will have eternal joy.

Critical Apparatus

1. *faisseles*] *E* faisselet.—2, *voi*] *C* vos.—3, *done moi, pius saveres*] *B* done moi du savere, *E* mes anemis done moi (*ne* expunctuated); *tel*] *C* del; *comprendre*] *E* comprende.—5, *toi*] *A* to; *okison*] *E* okisons.—6, *a l'astache*] *B* astache.—7, *moi*] *C* moie.—8, *A* ke ie puisse amertume a to iors mais sentir; *E* kameretoigne en pui a to iors mais sentir; *k'amertume*] *C* kamertoigne; *puisse*] *B* puis.—9, *odor*] *B* odur.—10, *en soffris*] *AB* soffris; *l'onor*] *B* lonur.—11, *metroit*] *E* meteroit.—12, *d'esgarder*] *B* dengardeir; *itel*] *B* icel; *home*] *E* homo.—14, *demener*] *C* demenere; *tele*] *E* tel.—15, *Es*] *A* el, *B* e; *desir*] *C* desire.—16, *porter*] *BE* porteir.—18, *et la chars et li mons*] *ACE* diable la chars li mons.—19, *tote ma grevance*] *A* totes mes grevances, *B* totes ma gravance; in *E*, second hemistich is faded.—20, *torner*] *CE* torne.—21, *vie*] *A* mor; *et*] *AB* si; *curre*] *CE* cure; *t'odor*] *B* todur.—22, *t'onor*] *B* tunur.—23, *pureture*] *A* poureture.—24, *ameneit*] *E* amenet.—25, *ta*] *A* la; *salveit*] *E* saveit; *A* unreadable from here to the end.—26, *arme*] *C* anrme; *el*] *BE* al; *eet*] *E* aeit.—27, *grande*] *E* grand.—30, *E* adds *Amen* at the end of the line.

Notes

See *Canticum Canticorum* 1: 13.

5. *Cum est doce.* . . . The line is hypometric, and Meyer ("Rapport," 246), working from MS *A*, amends *com* to *com[e]*, an alternative solution.

11/12. *penser* / *formeit*. The graphemic differentiation between this pair of rhymes masks the phonetic alignment which the language is undergoing, so that the situation is, in fact, that of modern French, with the sound [e].

15. See *Canticum Canticorum* 7: 10.

27. See note to Poem II, 7.

XII
AVE, DEUS, BEAS SIRE, QUI EN LA CROIS MONTAS

MSS: *A* fol. 14 r°, *H* fol. 12 r°.
Base: *A*.
Versification: twelve syllable lines in rhyming couplets. The rhyme scheme is as follows:

a a a a a a a a b b b b b a a a a c′ c′ c′ c′ e e e e

Earlier edition: Meyer, "Rapport," 247–48 (following MS *A*).

　　Ave, Deus, beas sire, qui en la crois montas;
　　de ton prescios sanc trestos nos rachatas,
　　estendus en la crois por nos et piez et bras;
　　por nos soffris la mor, car forment nos amas.
5　Longis li chevaliers le costé vos percha,
　　vostre prescios sanc juske a puins li cola;
　　ilh le mist a ses iez, dont si vos regarda
　　de ce ke forfait ot merci vos en priat.
　　Cant issi fustes, sire, en la crois deviez,

10 Joseph rova vo cors et ilh li fu donez;
    d'un sidone mut bel fustes envolepez,
    en mirre et aloez el sepulchre posez.
    Sains Johans li apostles, ce creons, i fu la,
    et vostre duce mere, qui forment vos ama,
15 l'enspee de dolor, ce fut voirs, senti la,
    ko Symeons li justes devant li propheta.
    Gran joie, a premerains, ce fut voirs, en ot ele
    cant ele sout de fi ke vos porta, pucelle,
    car Deus estiez et hom, de fit savoit la belle,
20 et si vos alaita a sa tenre mamelle.
    Or vos prions nos, sire, par vo saintisme nom,
    par ce vostre ymagene ke nos ici veons,
    ki de la crois recorde vo deposition,
    de trestos nos forfais nos faites vrai pardon.

Translation

    Hail, God, fine Lord, who underwent crucifixion,
    you redeemed us all by your precious blood,
    your feet and arms stretched out on the cross;
    for us you suffered death, for you loved us greatly.
5   Longinus the soldier pierced your side
    and your precious blood ran down right to the hilt;
    he put it in his eyes, because of which he looked at you such
    that he begged you for mercy for his misdeeds.
    When you had thus died, Lord, on the cross,
10 Joseph asked for your body and it was given to him;
    you were wrapped in a very fine shroud
    in myrrh and aloe and placed in the tomb.
    Saint John, the apostle, as we believe, was there,
    and your gentle mother, who loved you greatly,
15 experienced there, it was true, the sword of pain,
    like Simeon, the just, before the prophets.
    She felt great joy, it was true, at first
    when she knew by faith that she, a virgin, bore you,
    for you were God and man, this the comely one knew in truth,
20 and she suckled you at her tender breast.
    Now we pray you, Lord, by your most holy name.
    by this picture of you which we see here,
    which records your descent from the cross,
    that you give us true pardon for all our sins.

Critical Apparatus

1, *Ave*] *A* aiue; *beas sire*] *H* haus rois.—3, *en*] *AH* enz en.—4, *por*] *H* par.—6, *vostre*] *H* et vos; *juske a puins li cola*] *H* ius quaitz puins lescola.—7, *le*] *H* en; *dont si vos*] *H* et puis vos.—11, *d'un*] *A* don.—12, *et*] *H* en.—16, *ko*] *H* ke.—17, *ele*] *H* la.—21, *saintisme*] *H* saintim.—22, *ce*] *H* ceste.—23, *vo deposition*] *H* la vostre passion.—24, *nos forfais*] *A* no forfais. After this line, *H* adds: en la fin de nos vies vraie confession.

Notes

3. *en.* The MSS have *enz en*, which renders the line hypermetric, no doubt through an original hesitation about which form of *en* to use.

5. *Longis*—the centurion Longinus. His name may have derived from Λόγχη, 'lance.' The name does not appear in the *Acts* of the apostles, but occurs in the apocryphal *Acts of Pilate*, one version of which also lends the name to the centurion standing by the cross who confessed Christ to be the son of God.

13. *i fu la*: *i* appears to be a reinforcement of *la*.

19. *fit*—'truth, fact.' This is a normal reduction of the diphthong *-ei-* in the North-East.

21–24. The emphasis on penance is consistent with the overall tone of this set of poems. See Poems II, 7 and XIII, 22–23.

XIII
SIRE, KI PUR NOS FUSTES TRAVEILHÉS ET PENET

MS: *F* fol. 10 rᵒ.

Versification: twelve syllable lines in rhyming couplets. The rhyme scheme is as follows:

a a b b c c c c b b b b a a a a d d d d b b b b

Sire, ki pur nos fustes traveilhés et penet,
par la main de Joseph el sepulcre poset,
ki rova vostre cors et ilh li fu donez,
et en un nuef sepulcre la fustes vos posez.
5   Chevalier nus i furent pur vostre cors garder;
les trois Maries vinrent pur nos a visiter,
pur oindre les vos plaies ke quiderent saner.
Mult tres bon ungement i ont fait aporter.
En enfer en alastes, c'est fine veritez,
10   et si engenrastes les vos amis privez.
Adans i astoit mis et toz ses parentez,
ki .v. mil ans u plus i astoit tormentez;
cant vos virent venir, forment en furent liet,
car en vostre venue furent tuit desloiet.
15   Les en jetastes fors cant eustes briesiet
enfer, u ilh estoient maintes fois traveilhiet.
Cant ce eustes fait, si vos en revenistes;
Marie Magdalene premerain apparistes;
ele ne vos conut mais vos le conuistes.
20   Puys apres vos conut cant arainié l'eustes.
Si voirement, biaus sire, k'el sepulcre fus chociés,
si me faites pardon de trestoz mes pechiés
ke ne me puist grever li malois aversiers,
mais m'aie et ma garde en trestoz lieus soiés.

Translation

      Lord, you who for us were tormented and suffered,
      and placed in the tomb by the hand of Joseph,
      who asked for your body and it was given to him,
      and in a new sepulchre there were you placed.
5   There were knights there for us to guard your body;
      the three Marys came to visit you for us,
      to put ointment on your wounds, which they thought they could heal.
      They had the finest ointment brought there.
      You went down into hell, it is the absolute truth,
10   and thus you created your special friends.
      Adam was put there and all his folk,
      who was tortured there for five thousand years or more;
      when they saw you come, they were most gladdened,
      for in your coming they were all released.
15   You expelled them from there when you had destroyed
      hell, where they were continually tormented.
      When you had done this, you returned from there;
      you first appeared to Mary Magdalene;
      she did not recognize you, but you knew her.
20   Then she recognized you when you had addressed her.
      As it is true, fine Lord, that you were laid in the sepulchre,
      grant me forgiveness for all my sins
      so that the evil adversary may not burden me,
      but that you may be my help and protector in all places.

Critical Apparatus

15, *Les en jetastes*] ses en ierastes.—17, *revenistes*] resistes.—20, *l'eustes*] lo uistes.

XIV
DUES JESU CHRIST, KI, POR NO SAVEMEN

MS: *B* fol. 15 rº.

Versification: decasyllabic lines in rhyming couplets. Lines 5 and 22 are hypometric. The rhyme scheme is as follows:

a a a a a a b b c c b b d d e e f f g g h h a a

      Dues Jesu Christ, ki, por no savemen,
      venistes en terre morir destroitemen,
      puis vos amis, Joseph, el monument
      k'ilh avoit fait a son ues proprement,
5   envolepeit mut onestement   (-1)
      d'un blan sydone, ki fut fais subtilment.
      Lé trois Maries, a point de la jornee,
      vos i requient sen nulle demoree,
      et ungemen portaren precios

10   por en uindre vostre cors glorios.
     L'angele ont trové seant ki lor at demostreit
     le liu u poseis fuistes et astiés releveis,
     et si lor dist c'a desciple alaissent
     et a Piron et a eas denunchaisent
15   ke relevez astiés de mort a vie.
     Et apres ce, vo mostras a Marie
     le Magdalene, ki tan for vos amat
     et a vo pies si tenremen plorat
     ke sé pechies trestos li pardonastes:
20   por ce prouver a lui vo demostrastes.
     Dues Jesu Christ, ke c'est voirs et je·l croi,
     mon deseir et m'amor trai a toi   (-1)
     si purement et si entieremen
     ke ge veoir te puisse seure al jugement.

Translation

     Gentle Jesus Christ, who, for our salvation,
     came on earth to die a harsh death,
     then your friend, Joseph, in the tomb
     which he had made for himself entirely,
5   wrapped you very carefully
     in a white shroud, which was skillfully crafted.
     The three Marys, as the dawn broke,
     asked for you there without delay
     and brought a precious ointment
10   to spread on your glorious body.
     They found the angel sitting there, who showed them
     the place where you had been laid and you had risen,
     and you told them to go to the disciples
     and to announce to Peter and to them
15   that you had risen from death to life.
     And after, you showed yourself to Mary
     Magdalene, who loved you so much
     and at your feet wept so tenderly
     that you forgave her all her sins:
20   to prove this, you showed yourself to her.
     Gentle Jesus Christ, as it is true and I believe it,
     my desire and my love I bring to you
     so purely and so completely
     that I may see you on high on the day of judgment.

Critical Apparatus

2, *venistes*] venis.—4, *son*] sin.—6, *d'un*] don.—9, *portaren*] portoen.—20, *prouver*] prourir; *demostrastes*] demostraste.

Notes

*As in Poem XIII, the particular references to Mary Magdalene speak for a doctrine of forgiveness and redemption.

2. *venistes*. Consistent with the use of the second plural, *venis* in the MS has been emended. The additional syllable does not change the metric balance.

14. *Piron*—the oblique form of *Pierre*.

XV
DEUS, QUI A TIER JOR DE MOR RESUSCITASTES

MS: *A* fol. 15 rº.

Versification: twelve syllable lines in rhyming couplets. The rhyme scheme is as follows:

a a b′ b′ c c c c d d e e f f g g f f d d h′ h′ d d

Earlier edition: Meyer, "Rapport," 248–49.

Deus, qui a tier jor de mor resuscitastes,
quarante jors en terre puissedi conversastes;
a pluisors aparustes, si com dist l'Escriture,
et a tes sains apostles ce fu bone aventure.
5   Et puis si lor desis ke un pau demorroit
ke nus de tes disciples veor ne te poroit,
et puis un pau apres a ceas si revenrois
et a tes bons amis si toi demosterois,
et puis, voanz auz tos, el ciel, sire, montas.
10   Ton Saint Espir apres, sire, lor envoas
en icel liu u ilh asembleit astoent,
u la tue promesse fiement atendoent.
Lor furent ilh apris tot subitainement
ke de tos les lenguages orent entendement,
15   et puis en totes terres les fesis departir
por miserins pechors enver toi convertir.
Et ilh i alerent mut debonairement
et si baptizarent en ton nom mut de gent;
et puis, tantost, el ciel, peres, sire, montas,
20   et puis, al fin del sicle, jugier nos revenras.
Or te vulh proier, Jesus, li fis Marie,
ke la moi' arme de toi ne soit partie,
mais, al jor del juvuise, cant veor nos venras,
mon cors et la moi' arme avuec toi enportras.

Translation

God, who rose from the dead on the third day,
you from then on spent forty days on earth;
you appeared to several, as the Scripture told,
and for your disciples it was a good experience.

5   And then you told them that there would be a little while
     when none of your disciples could see you,
     and then after a while you would come back to these
     and you would show yourself to your good friends
     and then, with all looking on, Lord, you went up to heaven.
10   After, you sent your Holy Spirit, Lord, to them
     to that place where they were all assembled,
     where they faithfully awaited you, as promised.
     Then they were instructed in an instant
     so that they had an understanding of all languages,
15   and then you had them leave for all lands
     to convert miserable sinners to you.
     And they went there very willingly
     and in your name baptized many people.
     And then, straightway, Lord, Father, you went up to heaven,
20   and then, with the end of the world, you will come back to us.
     Now I wish to pray you, Jesus, son of Mary,
     that my soul be not separated from you,
     but, on the day of judgment, when you come to see us,
     you will take away with you my body and my soul.

Critical Apparatus

2, *jors*] jor.—5, *desis*] desistes.—7, *revenrois*] revenroit.—8, *demosterois*] demosteroit.—9, *sire, montas*] si remonta.—11, *icel*] ciel icel (*ciel* expunctuated).—14, *languages*] lenvuages; *entendement*] entemens.

Notes

5. *desis*—MS *desistes*. Given that God is addressed in the 2nd person singular throughout the poem, it seems reasonable to correct here. But it is also the case that in other poems, the form of address swings between *tu* and *vos*.

7–8. *revenrois, demosterois*. The MS has a rhyme in *-oit* for these two verb forms. It is clear that they apply to God and the error comes from the presence of *-oit* in the two preceding lines.

11. Meyer ("Rapport," 249) suggests a corrected reading: *De ciel en icel liu u asembleit*. However, the expunctuated *ciel* makes the reading clear.

XVI
SIRE, DONEZ NOSTRE ORISONS

MS: *I* fol. 14 r°.
Versification: octosyllabic lines, of which line 5 is hypermetric, with the following rhyme scheme:

a b a b c b c b d b d b e f e f g f g f h j h j k f k f

It is assumed that lines 29 and 30, while conforming to the metric length, constitute a *coda* that does not follow the rhyming pattern of the body of the poem.

Earlier Edition: Sinclair, *Manuscrits*, 33–34.

Sire, donez nostre orisons
a vos proier soit acceptable
k'il ne nos poit grever nus hom
ne nus angins a vi dyable.
5   Ki por nos fut el sepulchre mis,
sire, donez ke si metable
soiens ke nos ne soiens mie
al jugement avuec le dyable.
Ainz nos donez toz jors si vivre
10   ke vos troviens si merciable
ke nos poissons tout a delivre
avoir la joie parmenable.
Biax sire Dex, nos, povres gent,
ki ne poons vo sepulture
15   por fleveteit u por argent
requerre, sire, nostre faiture
pas n'obliez, ainz nos livreiz
kant vos plaira a teil mesure
ke nos aiens tant ke durreiz
20   icele joie qui tout jors dure.
Sire, Joseph et les Maries
aidier nos puissent en teil tiere
k'eles qui pas ne sunt maries
nos aünent de joie entiere.
25   Tuit li apostle et li perrin,
ki ont requiz vo sepulture,
garder nos puissent en la fin
de la parole qui tant iert dure.

Sire, metez a bone fin
30   ki ci ditat et ce escrit.

Translation

Lord, grant that our prayers
be acceptable to pray to you
so that no man nor trickery
of a vile devil can harm us.
5   Grant, Lord, that we may be so worthy
of him who was laid in the tomb
that we may not be with the Devil
on the day of judgment.
Rather grant that we may always so live
10   as to find you so merciful
that we may immediately
find eternal joy.
Fine Lord God, to us, poor folk,
who may not seek your burial-place

15 through weakness or lack of money,
    Lord, do not forget our physical make-up
    but rather permit us,
    when it pleases you and in such measure,
    to have, for as long as we live,
20 that joy which is all-enduring.
    Lord, may Joseph and the three Marys
    help us in such a way
    that these three, who are not saddened,
    bring us together with perfect joy.
25 May all the apostles and pilgrims
    who sought your burial-place
    protect us at the end
    from the word which will be so hard.

    Lord, give a good end
30 to the one who spoke and wrote this.

Critical Apparatus

2, *vos*] nos. —24, *aünent*] aunent (*n* expunctuated).

Notes

2. *vos*. With Sinclair (*Manuscrits*, 33) read *vos* instead of *nos* of the MS.

13–20. The humble status alluded to here suggests that the poem may have been written specifically for the use of ordinary folk in their worship. See *Prier au Moyen Age: Pratiques et expériences (Ve–XVe siècles)*, trans. and commentary by Nicole Bériou, Jacques Berlioz, and Jean Longère, intro. by Nicole Bériou (Turnhout: Brepols, 1991), chap. 6, "La prière des 'simples gens,'" 201–52.

19. *aiens*. Sinclair (*Manuscrits*, 33) reads *aviens*, wrongly.

21. The repetition of the theme of Joseph of Arimathaea and the three Marys (cf. Poem XIII, 2 and 6) is hardly surprising, given its presence in *Matt* 27: 56–57 and *Marc* 15: 40 and 43. The three Marys is a concept fostered in the Middle Ages and might suggest an alliance conceived of within that tradition.

24. *aünent*. Sinclair reads *aüent* since the first *n* is expunctuated in the MS. The base form is from *aüner, aduner* and it is justifiable to reinstate the *n*.

XVII
AVE, QUI AINS NE COMMENCHAS

MSS: *C* fols. 222 v°–223 v°, *D* fols. 213 r°–216 v°, *G* fols. 147 v°–150 r°, *I* fols. 210 r°–213 r°, *L* fols. 242 r°–245 v°, *M* fols. 194 v°–197 v°, *N* fols. 256 r°–265 r°, *O* fols. 232 r°–235 v°.
Base: *M*.
Versification: octosyllabic quatrains in rhyming couplets with random rhyme patterns.

        Ave, qui ains ne commenchas
        ne qui ja fin ne prainderas;
        de totes creatures rois
        et jugieres de totes lois.

5   Ave, ki, por ta creature
delivrer de la grant ardure,
desçaindis, sires, de hautece
en grant dolur et en tristece.

Ave, qui la flur convoitas
10 et qui ta mansion posas
el cors de la virgene Marie,
de totes vertus aemplie.

Ave, dont eissit la funtaine
qui tot dis est de grasce plainne,
15 qui, ki par toi en beverat,
a toz jors sain fin viverat.

Ave, qui rescossis la proie
que cil qui sovent nos desvoie
avoit par li obedience
20 toloit Adam et sa semence.

Ave, qui entras en Marie,
la gloriose flurs florie,
et en reissis a porte close;
tu es la flurs, elle la rose.

25 Ave, tu qui nos deslivras
des granz tenebres et des chauz
u Adans nos ot enbatus,
qui par Evain fut decheuz.

Ave, filz de franke pucelle,
30 sain mere en ciel, sain pere en terre,
rois qui justices les parvers,
rechoiz proieres de tes sers.

Ave, qui por nos combatis
et qui az tenebres raindis
35 lumiere, lor droit hyretage,
et delivras del grant servage.

Ave, tu qui es filz et pere
ta gloriouse dulce mere,
saveres par ton saint merite,

40   conduiz a toi mon esperite.

Ave, tu qui es vie et voie
de paradis et de la joie
qui par tot tens serrat durable
devant le pere esperitable.

45   Ave, tu qui soffris pesance
por de nos pechiez aligance,
otroie nos ta compangnie,
tu qui es pais et voie et vie.

Ave, par cui David lingnie
50   florit solonc la prophecie
et porta fruit; qui en atoche
n'en puet asaziier sa boche.

Ave, tu qui devenis sers
por traire des morteiz infers
55   ceaz qui avoient longement
esteit en poinne et en torment.

Ave, qui tant amas les tiens
que tu en toi et de toz biens
lor as donnee mansion;
60   dulz pieuz, otroie nos pardon.

Ave, *Criste*, salue, Marie,
en cui tu presis mortel vie
et cors, qui raemplit les places
de paradis, qui erent gastes.

65   Ave, glorious pains de vie
en cui l'arme se glorifie
cant elle se sent repoue,
pieuz saveres, par ta veue.

Ave, posteis, rois de glore,
70   otroie nos, sire, en memore
que si te puissons desireir
qu'en toi puissomes habiteir.

Ave, tu ki venquis la guerre
qui tant jors ot esteit en terre,

75   et derobas le boiseur,
       sire, par ton sanc preciuz.

       Ave, tu qui n'es pas faiture
       mais tote riens ta creature;
       sire, a ta merci nos acorde,
80   qui ja n'iert sainz misericorde.

       Ave, *mirabilis Deus,*
       misericors Jhesus Criste,
       qui rachatas nostre lignie
       par la virginiteit Marie.

85   Ave, cui la meirs obeit
       cant elle encontre ceaz partit
       cui tu d'Egypte conveias
       et dont tu puis naitre dengnas.

       Ave, par cui li enfant furent
90   martirizet ultre mesure:
       ce fut oevre de ton jovent;
       a ton pere en fesis present.

       Ave, ki tant t'umilias
       ke mortelment naistre dengnas
95   por la mort occire et destruire
       et por les tiens a toi conduire.

       Ave, ki toi soffris a vendre
       et a loiens loier et prendre,
       les oez bendeir et decrachier
100 et en la croiz crucefier.

       Ave, cil cui Judas trait
       et az felons Juez vendit;
       ce fu por nos, haltismes rois,
       que tu fus penduz en la croiz.

105 Ave, qui toi laissas estendre
       ens en la croiz et dengnas pendre
       a ton saint pere amendement
       por nos delivreir de torment.

       Ave, *Criste,* salve, li croiz,

110 salve, tes plaies et li sois
    que tu soffris por tes amis
    osteir del pooir l'anemis.

    Ave, la cui mors done vie,
    qui en li vraiement s'afie,
115 en cui vivent trestot li saint
    et servent que nulz ne s'en faint.

    Ave, qui la parution
    fesis, puis la surrection,
    a ceaz cui tenebres tenoient
120 et tant jors desireit t'avoient.

    Ave, *Criste*, ki en Marie
    presis cors, dont tu n'avoiz mie,
    por osteir l'uevre de ta main
    del pechiet Adam et Evain.

125 Ave, temples qui abatus
    fut cant tu fus en crois pendus;
    en trois jors le redefias
    cant tu de mort resuscitas.

    Ave, Deus, tu cui li angele
130 servent en ciel et li archangele;
    sire, rechoiz ta creature
    par ta pieteit, qui tot tens dure.

    Ave, qui de virgene fuz neiz,
    ne pas ne fuz faiz ne creetz,
135 mais la parolle de ton pere
    devint char el ventre ta mere.

    Ave, Deus, princes et rois
    et ensanchiez de maintes lois;
    pieuz sire, en toi habiterat
140 qui ta croiz porteir t'aiderat.

    Ave, qui Lucifer loias
    et, par humiliteit, matas,
    qui mainte arme avoit travilhié
    puis ke la pome fu mangié.

145 Ave, qui tot dis es loeiz;
    cil de trestotes posteeiz
    tot tens regardent en ta face
    et servent que nulz ne s'en lasse.

    Ave, qui tant comparas chier
150 la pome et le petit mangier,
    dont tu, puis, por ta creature,
    soffris laidenge ultre mesure.

    Ave, gloriouz pains de vie,
    qui la celeste compangnie
155 tot dis de ta veue paist;
    tant bor fu neiz qui en toi naist.

    Ave, boens pastres et hardis,
    qui ton saint cors, por tes amis,
    posas ens en la sainte crois
160 et soffris de mort les destrois.

    Ave, Deus Emmanuel,
    qui par ton angele Gabriel
    nunchas l'anuntiation
    de ta sainte incarnation.

165 Ave, ki povres devenis
    por faire riches tes amis,
    et, por les tiens frans a faire,
    devenis sers a grant contraire.

    Ave, li preciouz hostages,
170 qui por nos toz soi mist en gages
    et delivrat sa creature,
    par soi, del fou qui tot tens dure.

    Ave, qui sor le throne siez
    et tot le mont en ta main tiens,
175 en cui prist tot commenchement;
    rechoiz ma proiere et entens.

    Ave, rois de bone maniere,
    pieuz sires, rechoiz ma proiere,
    et celui mez en tes bonteiz

180 qui scrit et trovat cez aveiz.

Ave, ki le mont jugeras
ansi com tu commanderas
et donras chascun sa deserte;
dulz pieuz, otroie nos ta destre.

185 Ave, qui es confors des armes,
solaz et lumiere des angeles,
mirabilis en majesteit
et az tiens plains d'umiliteit.

Ave, *pater,* salue, li filz,
190 salue, Deus, Sainz Esperiz;
sire, a toi grasce et a ton pere
et a ta gloriouse mere.

Ave, Deus en Triniteit
et *Trinitas* en uniteit;
195 otroie nos vraie esperance,
qui tot dis es une substance.

Ave, Deus, princes en glore,
solaz, saluz, rois de victore;
grasce et loenge soit a toi
200 et li Sainz Esperiz en moi. Amen.

Translation

Hail, you who had no beginning
and who will never have an end,
king of all creatures
and judge of all laws.

5   Hail, you who, in order to deliver
your creature from the great conflagration,
descended, Lord, from on high
into great pain and into sadness.

Hail, you who desired the flower
10 and who made your home there
in the body of the virgin Mary,
filled with every virtue.

Hail, you from whom came forth the spring
which is forever full of grace,

15   which, if anyone shall drink of it through you,
     will live to all days without end.

     Hail, you who recovered the possessions
     which the one who often leads us astray
     had, by obedience to him,
20   seduced Adam and his seed.

     Hail, you who entered Mary,
     the glorious flower in full bloom,
     and came out again through a closed door;
     you are the flower, she is the rose.

25   Hail, you who freed us
     from the deep shadows and the quicklime
     into which Adam had driven us,
     who was deceived by Eve.

     Hail, son of the noble maid,
30   holy mother of heaven, holy father on earth,
     you, the king who punishes the wrongdoers,
     receive the prayers of your servants.

     Hail, you who fought for us
     and brought back to the shadows
35   light, their rightful heritage,
     and delivered us from that great enslavement.

     Hail, you who are son and father
     of your glorious, gentle mother,
     saviour through your holy worth,
40   lead my spirit to you.

     Hail, you who are the life and the way
     of paradise and of the joy
     which will last for all time
     before God spiritual.

45   Hail, you who suffered affliction
     for relief of our sins,
     grant us your company,
     you who are peace and way and life.

     Hail, you through whom the line of David

50   flourished, according to the prophecy
      and bore fruit; anyone who touches it
      cannot satisfy his hunger.

      Hail, you who became a servant
      to bring from deadly hell
55   those who had long been
      in pain and in torment.

      Hail, you who so loved your own
      that you in yourself and by your gifts
      gave them a dwelling;
60   gentle, holy one, grant us pardon.

      Hail, Christ, greetings, Mary,
      in whom you took on mortal life
      and a body, which fills the rooms
      of paradise, which were empty.

65   Hail, glorious bread of life
      in whom the soul is glorified
      when it feels itself to be sated,
      holy saviour, by the sight of you.

      Hail, pillar, king of glory,
70   grant us, Lord, to recall
      that we may so desire you
      that we may live in you.

      Hail, you who won the war
      which had for so long been waged on earth,
75   and deprived the deceiver,
      Lord, by your precious blood.

      Hail, you who are not a creation
      but every being is your creature;
      Lord, bring us to your mercy,
80   which was ever merciful.

      Hail, wondrous God,
      pity of Jesus Christ,
      you who redeemed our line
      through the virginity of Mary.

85   Hail, you whom the sea obeys
      when it parted before those
      whom you took out of Egypt
      and from whom you deigned to be born.

      Hail, you through whom the children
90   were martyred beyond measure:
      it was the work of your childhood;
      you gave it to your father as a gift.

      Hail, you who abased yourself so much
      that you deigned to be born as man
95   in order to kill and destroy death
      and to bring your people to you.

      Hail, you who allowed yourself to be sold
      and be tied and held with bonds,
      blindfolded and spat on
100 and crucified on the cross.

      Hail, you whom Judas betrayed
      and sold to the wicked Jews;
      it was for us, supreme king,
      that you were hung on the cross.

105 Hail, you who allowed yourself to be stretched out
      on the cross and deigned to hang there
      to make reparation to your holy father
      in order to deliver us from torment.

      Hail, Christ, hail to the cross,
110 hail to your wounds and the thirst
      you suffered to remove your friends
      from the power of the enemy.

      Hail, him whose death gives life
      to those who truly believe in him,
115 in whom all the saints live on
      and make certain that no one loses heart.

      Hail, you who appeared
      then was resurrected
      for those who were in darkness

120 and had longed for you so long.

Hail, Christ, who, in Mary, took human form,
you who had none,
to remove the work of your hands
from the sin of Adam and Eve.

125 Hail, temple which was demolished
when you were hung on the cross;
in three days you rebuilt it
when you came back from the dead.

Hail, God, you whom the angels
130 serve in heaven with the archangels;
Lord, receive your creature
through your pity, which is everlasting.

Hail, you who were born from a virgin,
you were not made nor created,
135 but the word of your father
became flesh in the womb of your mother.

Hail, God, prince and king
and supreme in many laws;
holy Lord, in you will dwell
140 the one who will help you carry the cross.

Hail, you who bound
and, in humility, killed Lucifer,
who had tormented many a soul
after the apple was eaten.

145 Hail, you who is ever praised;
those of many realms
forever look on your face
and make certain that no one tires of this.

Hail, you who bought so dearly
150 the apple and the meagre food,
because of which you, then, for your creature,
suffered extreme abuse.

Hail, glorious bread of life,
which feeds the celestial company

155 every day with the sight of you;
   the one who is born in you was so happily born.

   Hail, good and daring shepherd,
   who placed your holy body
   for your friends on the holy cross
160 and underwent the sufferings of death.

   Hail God Emmanuel,
   you who, through your angel Gabriel,
   declared the annunciation
   of your holy incarnation.

165 Hail, you who became poor
   to make your friends rich
   and to make your people free,
   you became a servant, to your loss.

   Hail, precious hostage,
170 who, for us all, put himself in pledge
   and freed his creature,
   of himself, from the fire which is everlasting.

   Hail, you who sit on the throne
   and hold all the world in your hand,
175 in whom was the beginning of all;
   receive and hear my prayer.

   Hail, excellent king,
   holy Lord, receive my prayer,
   and accord your kindness to the one
180 who wrote and composed these *aves*.

   Hail, you who will judge the world
   as you will command
   and will give each his deserts;
   gentle, holy one, give us your right hand.

185 Hail, you who are the comfort of souls,
   solace and light of angels,
   wonderful in majesty
   and full of humility towards your own.

   Hail, father, greetings to the son,

190 hail, God, Holy Spirit;
    Lord, grace to you and to your father
    and to your glorious mother.

    Hail, God in the Trinity
    and three in one;
195 grant us true hope,
    you who are forever a substance.

    Hail, God, prince in glory,
    solace, salvation, king of glory;
    may grace and praise be yours
200 and the Holy Spirit in me. Amen.

Critical Apparatus

The poem in *I* is preceded by the Latin prologue *Suscipe regina, MO* are preceded by: "Ci commenchent uns aveiz de nostre saignor jesu crist. Puis si redirons apres uns altres de nostre damme le bien euuirouse virgene marie" (following the spelling of *M*).

GMO add at the end of the poem: "ci definent li ave solonc nostre saingnor" (following the spelling of *M*). In *C*, the poem is curtailed after the first 92 lines. *I* lacks vv. 177–80.

4, *jugieres*] *N* iugiers.—5, *por*] *CL* par.—6, *delivrer*] *M* deliures, *N* deliure.—8, *dolur*] *L* dalur.—10, *et qui*] *N* et; *posas*] *I* i posas.—12, *aemplie*] *I* raemplie.—14, *grasce*] *D* grausce.—15, *qui, ki par toi*] *D* ki par vos sire, *I* ki ui par es, *N* qui ki por toi; *beverat*] *N* bevera.—16, *viverat*] *N* vivera.—17, *qui*] *C* cil ki, *L* chis.—18, *nos*] *M* no.—19, *par li*] *C* per luie, *D* par lin, *L* par li ue.—22, *flurs*] *C* flure.—23, *porte close*] *I* portes clauses.—24, *elle*] *CL* el est, *MO* elle est.—25, *Ave, tu*] *N* ave; *deslivras*] *D* delivas.—26, *des chauz*] *I* jetas, *N* de haus.—28, *fut*] *O* fui.—29, *filz*] *I* rois.—30, *mere*] *C* pere; *sain pere*] *N* sa pere.—31, *parvers*] *C* pavers.—32, *proieres*] *C* priier, *D* proiere, *I* les proieres; *tes*] *N* ces.—33, *por*] *C* par.—35, *lumiere, lor*] *CL* lor, *I* lumiere le.—36, *delivras*] *D* delivraus; *del*] *I* de, *N* delle.—37, *pere*] *O* peres.—39, *ton saint*] *DI* le sieu, *N* la siu.—41, *qui es*] *I* ies.—45, *pesance*] *C* pensance.—46, *por de*] *D* por tos, *CILO* por; *aligance*] *CI* aaligance.—47, *otroie*] *L* otroi.—48, *pais*] *L* pains.—50, *florit*] *IN* florist.—52, *n'en*] *I* ne.—54, *des morteiz infers*] *I* de mortel infer.—56, *poinne*] *I* paur.—58, *que tu*] *CL* ki tu, *N* tu.—60, *dulz pieuz*] *C* dues pies, *D* dulz pius sire, *GO* dulz piez, *L* dus pies, *N* pius; *otroie*] *M* otroiez, *N* otroiet, *O* otroies.—61, *O criste qui en marie presis cors dont tu navois mie salue marie; salue*] *G* save.—64, *erent*] *I* ieres, *M* errent; *gastes*] *N* gastees.—66, *I* ki la celeste compaignie; *l'arme*] *CLM* lanrme.—67, *se*] *D* soi; *repoue*] *L* repouz.—68, *pieuz*] *CLO* pies, *G* piez, *I* pus; *par*] *C* de, *GIMNO* por.—69, *rois*] *C* du rois, *L* dus rois.—70, *D* sire ades nos tiens em memoire; *sire*] *L* dussi; *en memore*] *C* en ta memoire, *I* memoire, *L* en te memore.—71, *que si*] *D* ken si, *L* que; *te*] *N* tu.—72, *qu'en*] *L* et en; *habiteir*] *D* habiteit.—74, *ot*] *N* at.—75, *derobas*] *I* deroubaz; *boiseur*] *C* boiseure.—76, *D* tes amis getas de dolur; *par*] *C* per.—77, *n'es pas*] *I* niez par.—78, *mais*] *C* main, *L* mains.—79, *nos acorde*] *CILN* nos acordes, *D* macorde.—84, *par*] *D* por.—85, *cui*] *C* a cui (*a* inserted above the line) *L* a cui, *N* cui a.—86, *ceaz*] *N* eaus; *partit*] *I* parut.—87, *d'Egypte*] *IN* de egypte.—89, *par*] *C* per.—90, *D* mort et tueit a grant lardure; *ultre*] *L* et ultre; *mesure*] *C* mesure detrenchiet.—91, *jovent*] *I* iovant, *N* iovente.—93, *t'umilias*] *L* te humilias, *N* tu umilias.—94, *mortelment*] *DILMO* mortement, *N* mortent; *naistre*] *N* nastret.—95, *por*] *O* par.—97, lacking in *N*; *ki toi*] *DI* ki te, *L* ki to, *N* ki.—98, *a*] *D* de, *L* as; *prendre*] *L* pendre.—99, *decrachier*] *GILMNO* derachier.—101, *cil cui*] *O* cui; *trait*] *D* vendit.—102, *Juez vendit*] *D* iuieres rendit.—103, *ce fu*] *N* fut; *por nos*] *D* par vos.—106, *ens en*] *I* en ens.—109, *croiz*] *I* croiez.—110, *sois*] *I* soiez, *N* soies.—112, *del pooir*] *N* del; *l'anemis*] *I* lanemi.—113, *la cui*] *I* cui.—116, *ne s'en*] *I* ne.—118, *surrection*] *LN* ressurection.—119, *tenebres*] *N* tenebre.—120, *tant*] *I* tou; *jors*] *N* iour.—122, *dont*] *I* ke; *mie*] *GL* mies.—126, *fut*] *GI* fuz.—127, *en trois jors*] *I* au tier ior.—129, *Deus*] *D* duz ihesus, *L* tu deus; *tu cui li*] *N* cui tuit li; *angele*] *N* angele, *O* angle.—130, *li archangele*] *I* li archangle, *N* archangele.—132, *par*] *G* por; *tot tens*] *I* tou tant.—133, *fuz*] *I* fu.—134, *D* ne ne fustes fais ne creeis.—135, *mais*] *L* main.—136, *devint*] *L* devient; *el*] *IN* en.—138, *C* ensancieres de totes lois; *ensanchiez*] *O* ensanchies.—139, *pieuz*] *D* cilh, *L* pies; *en toi habiterat*] *I* ki en toi abitra.—140, *qui ta*] *I* et ki ta, *N* ta.—142, *par humiliteit*] *N* humiliteit.—143, *arme*] *DM* anrme.—144, *pome*] *I* poine.—145, *tot dis*] *GINO* semper.—146, *D* de trestotes les posteez del ciel; *I* cilh ki trestote posteiet; *trestotes*] *N* trestot.—147, *regardent*] *D* ki gardent, *N* regardet.—148, *lasse*] *I* lassent.—150, *pome*] *I* poine.—151, *puis*] *D* deus; *por*] *L* par.—152, *ultre*] *D* sens.—153, *Ave*] *I* A.—155, *I* semper de paire ne paist; *N* semper de sa veue paist.—156, *bor*] *G* borc.—159, *sainte*] *O* saint.—160, *les destrois*] *L* le destroit.—162, *angele*] *IN* angle.—163, *l'anuntiation*] *L* la nuntion, *N* la nutination.—167, *tiens*] *D* tiens amis; *frans*] *I* a frans.—168, *a grant contraire*] *D* tres debunaire, *I* por grant contraire.—170, *soi*] *N* so; *gages*] *I* gage.—172, *soi*] *L* foi; *fou*] *I* foul; *tot*] *N* tan.—174, *mont*] *N* monde; *main*] *O* mains.—175, *D* tote riens fesis de nient; *tot*] *L* ton.—176, *ma proiere*] *L* nos proires, *MO* no proiere; *et entens*] *I* enceluiment.—178, *pieuz*] *D* grans, *L* pies; *ma*] *MO* no; *proiere*] *L* proires, *N* proier.—180, *scrit et trovat*] *D* fist et escrit, *N* scrist et trovat, *O* fist et trovat.—182, *ansi*] *I* ausi, *N* assi.—184, *D* sire or nos maines vers ta destre; *pieuz*] *O* pieitz; *otroie*] *M* otroiez, *N* otroies; *nos ta*] *G* moi de, *M* nos de.—185, *armes*] *DM* anrmes, *N* aur mes.— 186, *solaz et*] *IL* solaz; *angeles*] *IN* angles.—187, *majesteit*] *I* maiestate.—188, *az tiens*] *IL* a tiens, *N* ades.—190, *Sainz Esperiz*] *D* li sains espirs.—191, *grasce*] *D* grasces; *a ton*] *N* ton.—193, *Triniteit*] *I* trinitez.—195, *otroie nos*] *G* otroie moi.—196, *tot dis*] *N* semper.—197, *princes*] *N* princeps.—198, *solaz, saluz*] *D* salus solas.—200, *en*] *D* soit em; *ILN* lacking *amen.*

Notes

*This poem, along with XVIII and XIX, constitutes a second group of *Ave* poems, which are based in part on the *Ave Porta Paradysi*, which occurs in some of the MSS.

9–12. These lines are reflected in the opening of Poem II.

65. *pains de vie*: Christ is often thus referred to, and recalls the Eucharist. See also 153–56.

94. *mortelment*. Although the form *mortement* for *mortelment*, with loss of *l* before *m*, is almost certainly justifiable, the *l* has been reinstated to remove any ambiguity.

99. *decrachier*— reading from *D*, whereas the other MSS have *derachier*. The sense of the latter scarcely fits the context with its meaning of 'to raise from the quagmire, the pit.'

149–150. The sacrifice of Christ and his death are related here to the apple of Eden (*la pome*) and perhaps to the betrayal at the time of the Last Supper (*petit mangier*).

153–156. The *pains de vie* is again invoked, here in terms of sustenance of the company of saints.

XVIII
AVE, ROSE FLORIE

MSS: *D* fols. 216 v°–219 r°, *G* fols. 150 v°–151 v°, *I* fols. 213 r°–215 r°, *L* fols. 246 r°–248 v°, *M* fols. 198 r°–200 r°, *N* fols. 265 v°–273 r°, *O* fols. 235 v°–238 v°.
Base: *M.*
Versification: hexasyllabic quatrains in rhyming couplets with random rhyme patterns.

> Ave, rose florie
> et de roial lignie
> en cui prist reposance
> li rois de grant poissance.
>
> 5   Ave, fermee porte,
> portas lui qui tot porte;
> virgene et caste pucelle,
> donat lait ta mamelle.
>
> Ave, qui enfantas,

10   qu'a homme n'atochas,
     par la vertu ton pere,
     ki de toi fist sa mere.

     Ave, de grasce plainne
     et de vertuz funtainne
15   par cui est redrechié
     la cheue lingnié.

     Ave, qui par message
     et par icel lainguage
     que l'angele dist a toi,
20   conceis Deu le roi.

     Ave, tu de cui cors
     li sires eissit fors,
     par cui tu es servie
     en la celeste vie.

25   Ave, rose et racine
     cui biateiz enlumine
     la celeste clarteit
     devant la deiteit.

     Ave, li vrais osteiz
30   en cui la deiteiz
     prist incarnation,
     cresme et devotion.

     Ave, la flur de pris
     par cui nos raconquis
35   l'entree de la porte
     cil qui la mort at morte.

     Ave, qui es az liens
     confors et de tos biens
     vraie habundantion
40   et temples d'orison.

     Ave, virgene pucelle,
     tu es la flurs novelle
     qui ne pert sa valur,
     funtainne de dulçur.

45   Ave, qui el salut
    conceistes Jesu,
    que l'angele dist a toi
    de par le sovrain roi.

    Ave, tu, la ferteiz
50   en cui la deiteiz
    prist conseilh et confort
    por destruire la mort.

    Ave, qui sains dotance
    portas tote creance;
55   par toi fust solaciee
    la dolante ligniee.

    Ave, stoile de meir
    et temples por oreir;
    damme, conseilhe moi
60   par la pieteit de toi.

    Ave, par cui bonteiz
    fut enfers derobeiz
    et Lucifer loiez,
    qui sire est de pechiez.

65   Ave, li cleirs ovroirs
    u bonteiz et savoirs
    ovrat de son mestier
    por les povres aidier.

    Ave, li sainz alteiz
70   u li cors fut sacreiz,
    qui entrat en loie
    par ton temple, Marie.

    Ave, cui li filz fut
    qui crucefiiez fut
75   et vendus Cayphas
    del traite Judas.

    Ave, qui es santeiz
    de totes enferteiz;
    par ta misericorde

80   a ton fil nos acorde.

    Ave, *Christi* chapelle,
    tres loiaz turturelle
    sens sur et sens ameir,
    dengne nos esgardeir.

85   Ave, cui orison
    fut exaltation
    et confors a torment
    de vain tresbuchement.

    Ave, li sains sacraires
90   et li chiers laituaires,
    qui de mort suscitat
    ceaz cui Adans tuat.

    Ave, parfaite joie
    ceaz qui lor tens emploient
95   engrasciier le roi
    qui s'aumbrit en toi.

    Ave, cui biateiz
    sormonte les clarteiz
    devant le creator,
100 roine de valor.

    Ave, li tabernacles
    u Deus fit telz miracles
    ke, vraiz hom et vrais roiz,
    i sorjorna .ix. moiz.

105 Ave, tant preciouse
    roine vertuose,
    qui occit le serpens
    de maleoit porpens.

    Ave, roial Marie,
110 novelle ente florie;
    tes fruis, ce est li cors
    qui por nos toz fut mors.

    Ave, loial espouse
    cui toz lo mons golouse,

115 tres pieuve en ramembrance,
      faiz droite no sperance.

      Ave, liz de valeie
      blanche et gent coloreie,
      solaz et vie et voie
120 de la celeste joie.

      Ave, blance que liz,
      nobile empereris,
      rose tot tens novelle,
      qui ain nuit s'apareilhe.

125 Ave, roiaz palaiz,
      vergiers emperiauz
      en cui Dieus herbegier
      dengnat por nos aidier.

      Ave, li segurs pors
130 et li saintisme cors
      en cui Dieus s'aumbrat
      cant il nos visentat.

      Ave, flurs de beateiz
      qui, en tes franz costeiz,
135 conceis le sovrain,
      qui tot tient en sa main.

      Ave, li vrais refus,
      par cui Theophylus
      a Dieu soi racordat
140 cant il le renoiat.

      Ave, li sainz soliaz,
      tot dis cleirs et noviaz,
      funtaine gratiose,
      estoile gloriouse.

145 Ave, caste Marie,
      car en toi est flurie
      la verge de Jessé;
      tu as virgene enfanté.

      Ave, qui, par ton sens,

150 sormontas le serpent,
    qui Adam venimat;
    ta bonteit le sanat.

    Ave, la posteeiz
    en cui humiliteiz
155 herbergat par science
    et tote sapience.

    Ave, sale paveie,
    de toz biens aornee,
    en cui Dieus prist faiture,
160 corporele figure.

    Ave, Saint Esperiz
    fist de toi ses deliz;
    en toi format le roi
    de la novelle loi.

165 Ave, sainte Marie,
    tres dulce melodie;
    la gloire de tes lais
    n'alentirat ja mais.

    Ave, li vraiz recuers,
170 aparilhiez soccuers
    ceaz qui en la batailhe
    de la char se travailhent.

    Ave, par cui li fer
    furent brisiet d'enfer,
175 et delivras la proie
    de ceaz qui nos guerroient.

    Ave, dulce roscie,
    tu es del ciel entreie;
    entens nos et conforte,
180 par cui la mors est morte.

    Ave, la forterece
    u toz li biens s'adrece,
    qui, par ta grande foi,
    estainsis nostre soif.

185 Ave, franke roine
     qui, par grasce divine,
     aportas le vif pain
     a la nostre grant faim.

     Ave, virginiteiz
190 en cui la Triniteiz
     si grant clarteit trovat
     que regneir i dengnat.

     Ave, mere ton pere
     et de toz biens mistere,
195 virgene et caste pucelle,
     spouse Deu et ancelle.

     Ave, purpre roiauz,
     li rois angelicauz
     prist vesteure en toi;
200 dulce virgene, oiez moi. Amen.

Translation

     Hail, rose in full bloom
     and of royal line
     in whom the most powerful
     king took his rest.

5   Hail, closed door,
     you bore him who bears all;
     virgin and chaste maid,
     your breast gave milk.

     Hail, you who touched no man,
10   who gave birth
     by the virtue of your father,
     who made you his mother.

     Hail you, full of grace
     and fountain of virtues,
15   through whom the fallen line
     is restored.

     Hail, you who, through the messenger
     and through that speech
     which the angel spoke to you,

20   conceived God the king.

Hail, you from whose body
the Lord came forth,
by whom you are served
in the heavenly life.

25   Hail, rose and root
whose beauty illuminates
the heavenly brightness
before the deity.

Hail, true host,
30   in which the deity
became flesh,
holy oil and devotion.

Hail, prized flower,
by whom the one
35   who killed death conquered
for us the entrance to the gate.

Hail you who are to your own
confort and true abundance
of your gifts,
40   and temple of prayer.

Hail, virgin maid,
you are the new flower
which loses not its worth,
fountain of sweetness.

45   Hail, you who in salvation
conceived Jesus,
which the angel told you
on behalf of the sovereign king.

Hail, you, the pride
50   in which the deity
took counsel and comfort
in order to destroy death.

Hail, you who, without fear,
bore the weight of trust;

55   by you the grieving family
     was comforted.

     Hail, star of the sea
     and temple for prayer;
     lady, counsel me
60   through your piety.

     Hail, you by whose goodness
     hell was plundered
     and Lucifer put in bonds,
     who is the lord of sins.

65   Hail, bright workshop
     in which goodness and knowledge
     worked as their trade
     to help the poor.

     Hail, holy altar
70   on which the body was consecrated,
     which entered into dominion
     by your temple, Mary.

     Hail, whose son it was
     who was crucified
75   and sold to Caiaphas
     by the traitor Judas.

     Hail, you who are the health
     of all illnesses;
     by your pity
80   reconcile us with your son.

     Hail, chapel of Christ,
     most beautiful turtledove
     without sourness, without bitterness,
     deign to look on us.

85   Hail, you whose prayer
     was exaltation
     and comfort from torment
     because of the worthless stumbling-block.

     Hail, holy sanctuary

90   and the dear electuary,
      who raised from death
      those whom Adam killed.

      Hail, perfect joy
      of those who devote themselves
95   to anointing the king,
      who became flesh in you.

      Hail, you whose beauty
      surpasses the brightness
      before the creator,
100   worthy queen.

      Hail, tabernacle
      where God performed such miracles
      that, true man and true king,
      he dwelt there for nine months

105   Hail, most precious
      queen of virtue,
      who killed the serpent
      evil in thought.

      Hail, royal Mary,
110   new shoot in flower;
      your fruit is the body
      which was killed for us all.

      Hail, loyal spouse
      whom all the world covets,
115   most holy in memory,
      you make our hope just.

      Hail, lily of the valley,
      white and delicately colored,
      solace and life and way
120   of the celestial joy.

      Hail, you, white as a lily,
      noble empress,
      forever new rose
      which is formed before night falls.

125 Hail, royal palace,
     imperial orchard
     in which God deigned to live
     to help us.

     Hail, safe port
130 and the most holy body,
     in which God became flesh
     when he visited us.

     Hail, flower of beauty
     who in your noble flanks
135 conceived the sovereign
     who holds all in his hand.

     Hail, true refuge
     by which Theophile
     reconciled himself with God,
140 when he denied him.

     Hail, holy sun,
     always bright and new,
     comely fountain,
     glorious star.

145 Hail, chaste Mary,
     for in you bloomed
     the rod of Jesse:
     you, a virgin, gave birth.

     Hail, you who, by your good sense
150 overcame the serpent
     which poisoned Adam;
     your goodness cured him.

     Hail, the power
     in which humility lodged
155 through knowledge
     and all wisdom.

     Hail, paved room
     adorned with all gifts,
     in which God took form,

160 a symbol made flesh.

Hail; the Holy Spirit
took his pleasure in you;
in you he formed the king
of the new law.

165 Hail, holy Mary,
most sweet melody;
the glory of your lays
will never cease.

Hail, true rescue,
170 ever ready help
of those who struggle
in the battle of the flesh.

Hail, you by whom the shackles
of hell were broken,
175 and you delivered the booty
of those who wage war on us.

Hail, sweet dew,
you came down from heaven;
hear and comfort us,
180 you by whom death was killed.

Hail, fortress
where all good is made ready,
you who, by your great faith,
quenched our thirst.

185 Hail, noble queen,
you who by divine grace
brought the living bread
to satisfy our great hunger.

Hail, virginity
190 in which the Trinity
found such great brightness
that it deigned to reign therein.

Hail, mother of your father
and mystery of all blessings,

195   virgin and chaste maid,
       spouse of God and maidservant.

       Hail, royal purple,
       the angelic king
       was clothed in you;
200   gentle virgin, hear me. Amen.

Critical Apparatus

The poem in *D* is preceded by: "ci comencent li ave de nostre damme," in *G* by: "ci recommenchent li altre aveiz solonc nostre damme," in *MO* by: "ci recommencent li atre de (*O* solonc) nostre damme."

Lines 101–04 are found only in *DIN*, but there seems no reason to not include them, especially as the common opening word, *Ave*, can lead to haplology. Text follows *I*.

After line 192 and only in *LM*, the following is inserted (text following *M*), which is clearly not part of the poem, with its octosyllabic lines.

    Ave, en cui cors Dieus torna (*L* turnat),
    ki del (*L* de) grief fais no (*L* nos) destorna (*L* destornat),
    dont il nos covint (*L* covient) a servir
    et en vilh maniere fenir (*LM* servir).

The poem in *O* ends at the foot of fol. 238 rᵒ with *Ave li vrais* of line 169.

5, *fermee*] *I* ferme.—6, *portas*] *L* ce portas, *N* portans; *lui*] *I* liue; *tot*] *N* tote; *porte*] *I* portet.—7, *virgene et*] *I* virgine.—8, *donat*] *L* denat; *lait*] *I* lau, *L* lait de.—11, *par*] *D* por.—14, *vertuz*] *IN* vertu.—15, *redrechié*] *N* redechie.—16, *cheue*] *D* chative.—18, *par icel*] *I* ki par cest, *N* par icelle.—19, *dist*] *GM* dest.—20, *conceis*] *D* conchuis, *IO* conceuz, *LN* conceuuis.—22, *eissit*] *I* eisist.—30, *deiteiz*] *O* detreiz.—32, *cresme et*] *D* creis ma, *G* crensme et, *IN* cresma.—34, *raconquis*] *I* raconquist, *L* at conquis, *M* rat conquis.—36, *cil qui*] *IN* par cui.—37, *es*] *G* ez; *az*] *IL* a.—38, *confors et de*] *I* et confors de.—39, *vraie*] *N* vrai; *habundation*] *DI* habundations, *M* habundantion.—40, *d'orison*] *D* dorisons.—46, *conceistes*] *D* conchuistes, *I* conceuste, *L* conceuuistes, *N* conchiuuistes.—47, *dist*] *GMO* dest.—48, *I* conceustes le roi; *par*] *NO* part.—49, *la ferteiz*] *N* la sexte, *O* lenferteiz.—55, *par*] *IN* por.—57, *meir*] *N* mere.—59, *damme*] *I* dama; *conseilhe*] *GIO* consilhiez, *MN* conseilhes.—64, *qui sire est*] *I* li sires, *L* ki sires; *pechiez*] *O* pechiet.—65, *ovroirs*] *NO* ovrois.—66, *et*] *I* ou.—67, *ovrat*] *L* cuirat (?).—68, *les povres*] *I* le povre.—71, *en*] *D* par.—72, *par*] *D* en.—73, *filz*] *I* fuizz, *N* fius.—76, *traite*] *D* traitor.—80, *acorde*] *I* racorde, *L* racordes.—83, *sur*] *I* fiel.—84, *GLMNO* dengnons en li gardeir; *esgardeir*] *I* regarder.—88, *de vain*] *I* dievaint.—90, *laituaires*] *L* lentuaires.—91, *suscitat*] *INO* suscitas.—92, *Adans*] *I* iudas.—94, *emploient*] *LMN* emploie.—95, *engrasciier*] *I* e gracier, *N* grasire.—96, *qui s'aumbrit en toi*] *I* ki soumbrat en toi, *L* ki saombrit (for a second reading of this line, see variant reading in *L* for line 112) , *N* sa umbra en toi.—97, *cui*] *DIL* la cui; *biateiz*] *O* biatete.—98, *sormonte*] *DIN* sormontat; *les clarteiz*] *L* le clarte.—99, *creator*] *N* creatur.—100, *valor*] *DLO* valur, *N* valour.—101, *li*] *N* ki.—104, *.ix.*] *D* nuef.—107, *le serpens*] *M* les serpens.—109, *roial*] *L* loias.—110, *ente*] *GN* oerte.—111, *tes*] *I* li tienz; *ce*] *D* chu.—112, *L* ki saombrit en toi.—113, *loial*] *I* roias.—115, *ramembrance*] *I* ta manbrance.—116, *faiz*] *DIL* fai.—118, *gent*] *D* bien.—121, *que*] *I* cum.—122, *nobile*] *N* noble.—123, *novelle*] *D* vermelhe.—124, *D* nus ne vit ta parelhe; *I* ki a nos saparoilhle; *nuit*] *L* not, *N* no; *s'apareilhe*] *L* sa parelh.—126, *D* tres dignes cors et vrais.—133, *de*] *D* et; *beateiz*] *I* bonte.—135, *conceis*] *D* conchuis, *GLN* concevvis, *I* conceuz; *le*] *I* li, *L* deu le.—139, *soi*] *I* se, *N* sa.—140, *D* ki ihesum renoia; *renoiat*] *IN* denoiat.—146, *car*] *I* cant.—148, *tu as*] *D* mas, *GM* tu es; *enfanté*] *IM* enfance.—150, *le serpent*] *D* le serpens, *N* les serpens.—151, *venimat*] *I* eniurat.—156, *sapience*] *I* pacience.—160, *corporele*] *DI* et corporeil.—161, *Saint*] *I* li sainz.—162, *ses deliz*] *I* son delit.—163, *format*] *I* formas, *O* forment; *le*] *N* li.—164, *novelle*] *N* nolle.—167, *tes*] *I* ces.—168, *n'alentirat*] *I* valantira, *L* naleterat.—169, *vraiz recuers*] *I* veraiz cors.—170, *aparilhiez*] *I* et aparlhiez.—171, *batailhe*] *N* batailh.—172, *I* soi travailhent; *travailhent*] *N* travailhe.—173, *fer*] *N* enfer.—174, *d'enfer*] *N* de fier.—175, *delivras*] *DN* delivre.—176, *nos*] *I* vos; *guerroient*] *N* garoie.—178, *del*] *L* en; *entreie*] *D* lentreie.—179, *entens*] *I* entre; *conforte*] *GL* confortes.—180, *D* par toi est la mors morte.—181, *forterece*] *N* fortece.—182, *s'adrece*] *GM* sadrechent.—183, *grande*] *I* tres grant; *foi*] *DGLN* foit, *M* foie.—184, *estainsis*] *D* estaindis; *soif*] *GLMN* soit.—186, *par*] *N* de.—188, *la*] *L* le.—191, *si*] *I* li.—193, *mere*] *N* mater.—194, *toz biens*] *DIN* tot bien—195, *et caste*] *L* caste.—196, *IN* donat lait ta mamele; *spouse Deu*] *D* deu espouse, *L* mere deu.—200, *oiez*] *L* aidies. (Amen is lacking in *D* only).

Notes

1–4. These lines echo the opening of Poem II and lines 9–12 of Poem XVII.

5. *fermee porte*. It was sufficient, in what was no doubt a clerical context, to refer to the Virgin through one of the many references as the means of man's salvation in giving birth to Jesus. The prophecy in *Ezechiel* 44 uses the image of the gate which is shut. In verse 2, which is the one frequently quoted, we read: "This gate shall be shut, it shall not be opened, and no man shall enter in by it; because the Lord, the God of Israel, hath entered in by it, therefore it shall be shut." There is certainly also a relationship with the Garden of Eden as the earthly paradise from which Adam and Eve were excluded, so that man could not find that paradise on earth until the coming of Christ and his birth. Verse 3 makes this explicit: Jesus, referred to as the prince, "shall enter by the way of the porch of that gate, and shall go out by the way of the same" (see lines 33–36).

15–6. *redrechié, lingnié*. The practice in this and other MSS is to not observe the agreement with a feminine noun, except on a few occasions.

29–30. *osteiz, deiteiz*. The underlying form which is most likely is *hostie* and *deitie* (which is a variant form for *deité*, found in Anglo-Norman).

33–36. The reference here is to Christ, who allowed the door of salvation to be opened to mankind. See note to line 5.

57–60. These lines echo the famous hymn, *Ave maris stella*, and the entire poem goes on to develop this theme.

84. In spite of the group of manuscripts supporting the rejected reading, *dengnons en li gardeir*, that of DI is preferred because it is consistent with the supplications to the Virgin rather than a reading that shifts the subject to the supplicants, as well as offering a confused and arrogant message.

116. *faiz*. This reading, supported by *GMNO*, is preferable to that of *DIL*, *fai*, imperative: the existence of Mary gives hope.

129–132. *li segurs pors*. The theme of arrival at the safe port is a long-established one. See Campbell Bonner, "Desired Haven," *Harvard Theological Review* 34 (1941), 49–63, and Hugo Rahner, *Symbole der Kirche. Die Ekklesiologie der Väter* (Salzburg: Otto Müller Verlag, 1964), esp. 548–64, "Die Ankunft im Hafen."

Theophylus. Not the Theophile of *Luc* 1: 3, but a reference to the miracle of Theophilus, who is saved from the devil by the Virgin, after his prayer to her, as in the poem of Gautier de Coincy (*Les Miracles de Nostre Dame par Gautier de Coinci, publiés par* V. Frédéric Koenig, vol. 4 [Geneva: Droz, 1970], 580–84).

145–148. The image of the rod of Jesse as referred to by Isaiah in chap. 11: "And there shall come forth a rod out of the stem of Jesse, and a Branch shall grow out of his roots." It is interesting that the Vulgate uses "flos" for "branch," which strengthens the prophetic account: Mary bearing a flower (cf. *flurie*).

182. *s'adrece*. Two MSS, G and M have the plural following *toz li biens*; however, *biens* is a non-count noun and is the equivalent in modern French of *tout le bien*. The breakdown of the case system means that *-s* is associated with the notion of plurality. It would be possible for the rhyme to be *forterece / s'adrecent*, as above in lines 171 and 172.

187. *le vif pain*. Yet another eucharistic reference to Christ.

196. *(LM)*. *fenir / servir*. Given that this stanza is found only in MSS *LM* and they are close, it is not surprising that they both make the same error by repeating *servir* at the end of this line. The substitution is based on the overall sense of the stanza and on the similar overall graphemic profile.

XIX
AVE, MARIE, FLORS DE LIS

MS: *D* fols. 219 rº–223 rº.

Versification: octosyllabic quatrains in rhyming couplets with random rhyme patterns.

Ave, Marie, flors de lis,
haute porte de paradis,
par toi nos est li fruis rendus
ki par est vrai, a tort perdus.

5   Ave, damme hautime et gente,
voie et vie estes et ente;
l'iror de Deu apaisentas,
quant ton chier filh nos aportas.

Ave, virgene, cui piuve amurs
10   sormontat trestotes dolurs
cant la parole en char muat,
lorske li angeles t'anunchat.

Ave, cui la splendors del pere
fist la pense devenir cleire;
15   de la splendor de ton semblant
sunt enclarcit tuit ti serjant.

Ave, temples de Jesu Crist,
a tun aide curent tuit cist
ki sunt el las del anemis,
20   ki de pechiés les at sorpris.

Ave, garisons des languis,
tu, ki es solas des chaitis,
defen nos de la grant iror
ki iert el siecle al derain jor.

25   Ave, cui cors e cui semblans
nostre sires sor tos vivans
convoitat et trovat le cuer
net et pur sens nule laidur.

Ave, de cui li fis fut neis,
30   par cui li mons fut rachateis,
a cui li peres tos poissans
donat roiame parmanans.

Ave, virgine, nos te prions
ke des mains az deables felons

35   nos ostes si k'o toi aleir
     puissons et ton saint nom loier.

     Ave, del siecle la splendors,
     medecine des tenebrors,
     enlumineis nos cuers dedens
40   ke bien facent az poures gens.

     Ave, cui raisons est sonante,
     ki en paradis est manante,
     priiés por nos al roi de glore,
     envers tos maus nos doinst victore.

45   Ave, tu ki es salveie,
     cui venue fut desireie;
     Marie, virgene, entens a nos
     et si aie pieteit de nos.

     Ave, ki es Syon nomeie,
50   par cui est saveteis doneie
     a ceaz qui erent en dolur,
     en tenebres et nuit et jor.

     Ave, ki es el tabernacle,
     u ilh at joie parmanable;
55   en la maison des droituriers
     es tu apeleie vergiers.

     Ave, qui es damme des angeles,
     de cerubien et des archangeles,
     trestote riens vos doit loier
60   car vos estes stoile de meir.

     Ave, tres gloriose mere,
     moiene entre nos et ton pere;
     grant mestier nos as nuit e jor
     por racordeir al saveor.

65   Ave, cui Deus out aurneie
     cant az chius fist sa remonteie;
     en toi descendit la parolle,
     ki combrisat la beste folle.

     Ave, de cui ventre naskit

70   Jesus, qui por nos mort soffrit;
en ton ventre fist mansion
cilh ki governe tot le mont.

Ave, damme, tres sainte chose,
par cui la porte que fust close
75   de paradis, fut desereie,
la gent d'infer deprisoneie.

Ave, roine de dulchor,
el siecle fust sens error;
de Jesu Crist, le roi del ciel,
80   aveis coroneit vostre chief.

Ave, de cui li rois naski,
ki, sens pechiet, dame veski;
d'infer ses amis tos getat
et paradis lor delivrat.

85   Ave, virgene tres droituriere,
az desolus humle et entiere,
vos portastes le buen des boens,
dont fust rachateis tos li mons.

Ave, bienavoirouse femme,
90   des vertus del ciel estes gemme;
fai a Deu por nos orison
qu'ilh ne nos mete en sa prison.

Ave, virgine, qui es saintisme,
l'arme de toi fut cleire et fine;
95   or es el ciel damme honoreie,
del pain des angeles saoleie.

Ave, virgine, qui es ameie
et de boens crestiens reclameie,
a toi prions, virgene honoreie,
100 ke droite fais nostre penseie.

Ave, de lumiere plaintive,
car tu es mere al tres hatime;
par toi fut infers derobeis
et li fel Lucifers mateis.

105 Ave, de cui confession
   li cuers out grant devotion;
   ta chars fut moult bien reflorie
   quant li fis Deu prist en toi vie.

   Ave, la cui vois est sonante,
110 plus ke d'orguene la concordance,
   mere Jesu, qui fut ocis
   por les pechiés de nos, chaitis.

   Ave, ki mere devenis
   al saveor de paradis
115 quant li sains angeles dist a toi:
   "Nostre sires soit avuec toi."

   Ave, li cui entendemens
   fut plains de grant bien et de sens;
   quant la parole deven char,
120 turnat en toi ne fut par char.

   Ave, cui, devant sa naiscence,
   Deus li duz rois, par sa poissance,
   enliut sa mansion en toi
   sens vilonie et sens anoi.

125 Ave, virgene, ki savoras
   ke duz est cilh ke tu portas;
   sor totes autres meadre fus
   quant tel signor porteir pous.

   Ave, mere de grant casteit,
130 moult fus plaine de grant bonteit,
   ki t'en jois en teil sangnor
   u ilh at joie sens tristor.

   Ave, la maisons habundable,
   de grasce plaine et delitable,
135 la fontaine de vie fus,
   tote remplie de vertus.

   Ave, virge, cui la porture
   vequist del siecle la pasture;
   mais le pain des angeles donat

140 habudantment ceaz cui salvat.

Ave, de cui li desiers fut
remplis de bien e de vertut
et dont li saint gemissement
sunt devant Deu ades present.

145 Ave, de cui substance fut
ke Deus char humaine conchut,
ke tant avoient desireit
li ancien pere et agardeit.

Ave, Marie, ave, tes fis,
150 ki por le pople fut ocis;
le viel sacrefice cassat
quant en la crois son cors posat.

Ave, virgene, par la cui grasce
li fis Deu nos remist en grasce
155 et delivrat manoir moult gent
avuec les sains el firmament.

Ave, virgene, ki soif avuis
et l'aigue de vie bevuis
quant tu conchuis le soverain,
160 ki tote riens tient en sa main.

Ave, mere de grant clarteit
car Jesu Crist t'a alumeit;
ilh t'amat, damme sens mesure:
sor totes out ilh de toi cure.

165 Ave, par cui sumes salveit
et nostre anemis sunt mateit;
quant toi loions, ton filh loons,
quant toi servons, a Deu servons.

Ave, roine noble et gente,
170 caste pucele de jovente,
tu sies a la destre ton pere,
ki de toi fist sa digne mere.

Ave, sainte virginiteis,
al parmanable roi citeis,

175 tu es fontaine de vertut,
     par la sainteit del haut, salut.

     Ave, par cui done li fis
     rovat et priat ses amis
     qu'ilh te servent de cuer, de cors,
180 car de pecheors es confors.

     Ave, salve, tres duce gemme
     preciose, k'ain ne fuist femme;
     son cors nos donne al derain jor
     de nostre fin par vostre amur.

185 Ave, de cui fut la loquence
     et [en] ton cuer la vraie pense,
     qu'ensegnat li vrais Salemons,
     ki fut de science li dons.

     Ave, mere al rachateor
190 et al tot poissant creator,
     a cui [est] terre et meirs et ciel
     et tote riens doit adengnier.

     Ave, Marie, ave, tes fis,
     qu'en joie si es em paradis,
195 o Deu le roi estes en glore;
     ke nos doinst, se li plaist, victore.

     Ave, *Christe*, salue, ta mere,
     salveiz soit Deus, li tiens pere,
     tote la sainte triniteis,
200 qu'est une soule deiteis. Amen.

                    Translation

     Hail, Mary, flower of the lily,
     high gate of paradise,
     through you is returned to us the fruit
     which is indeed real, wrongly lost.

5   Hail, most high and courtly lady,
     you are the way and the life and the shoot;
     you calmed the pain of God,
     when you brought us your dear son.

     Hail, virgin, whose pious love

10 overcame all manner of grief
    when the word became flesh,
    when the angel made the announcement to you.

    Hail, you for whom the splendor of the father
    made thinking become clear;
15 by the splendor of your countenance
    all your servants are enlightened.

    Hail, temple of Jesus Christ,
    to seek your help all those hurry,
    who are in the snare of the enemy,
20 who has tricked them into sinning.

    Hail, defense of the weak,
    you, who are solace of the poor,
    defend us from the great anger
    there will be in the world on the last day.

25 Hail, to you whose body and countenance
    our Lord desired above those of all living beings
    and whose body he found
    clean and pure without any ugliness.

    Hail, you from whom the son was born,
30 through whom the world was redeemed,
    and to whom the all-powerful father
    gave an everlasting kingdom.

    Hail, virgin, we pray you
    that, from the hands of evil devils
35 you deliver us so that we may
    accompany you and praise your holy name.

    Hail, splendor of the world,
    healing power over darkness,
    light up our hearts within us
40 so that they may do good to the poor.

    Hail, you whose word rings out,
    who resides in paradise;
    pray for us to the king of glory
    that he may give us victory over all evil.

45 Hail, you who are saved,
    whose coming was desired;
    Mary, virgin, hear us
    and have pity on us.

    Hail, you who are daughter of Zion
50 through whom salvation is given
    to those who were in distress,
    in darkness, night and day.

    Hail, you who are in the tabernacle,
    where there is everlasting joy;
55 in the house of the just
    you are called garden.

    Hail, you who are mistress of the angels,
    of cherubim and the archangels;
    every being must praise you
60 for you are star of the sea.

    Hail, most glorious mother,
    intercede between us and your father;
    we need you greatly, night and day,
    to reconcile us with the savior.

65 Hail, you whom God adorned
    when he went back up into heaven;
    in you the word descended,
    which destroyed the mad beast.

    Hail, you from whose womb was born
70 Jesus, who suffered death for us;
    in your womb took residence
    he who rules over all the world.

    Hail, lady, most holy person,
    by whom the door of paradise
75 which was closed was unlocked,
    and the people released from hell.

    Hail, queen of gentleness,
    in the world you lived without fault;
    you crowned your head

80   with Jesus Christ, the king of heaven.

Hail, you from whom the king was born,
who lived, as a lady, without sin;
he took all his friends out of hell
and delivered paradise to them.

85   Hail, most just virgin,
humble and sincere to the abandoned,
you bore the good of the good,
through whom all the world was redeemed.

Hail, blessed woman,
90   you are the jewel of heavenly virtues;
offer your prayer to God for us
that he should not consign us to his prison.

Hail, virgin, you who are most holy,
your soul was bright and noble;
95   now you are the honored lady in heaven,
your hunger satisfied by the bread of the angels.

Hail, virgin, who are loved
and invoked by good Christians,
to you we pray, honored virgin,
100 that you make our thinking just.

Hail, you, who intercede for light,
for you are the mother of the supreme one;
through you hell was pillaged
and perfidious Lucifer overcome.

105 Hail, you, by whose confession
your heart received great piety,
your flesh truly blossomed again
when the son of God took life in you.

Hail, you, whose voice resounds
110 more than the harmonies of the organ,
mother of Jesus, who was killed
by the sins of us, the poor.

Hail, you, who became mother
to the savior of paradise

115 when the holy angel said to you:
     'Our Lord be with you.'

     Hail, you whose understanding
     was full of great good and sense;
     when the word becomes flesh,
120 it was not directed into you by the flesh.

     Hail, you, whom, before his birth,
     God, the gentle king, by his power,
     elected as his dwelling in you
     without baseness or pain.

125 Hail, virgin, who took delight
     in the gentleness of the one you bore;
     you were the best over all other women
     since you were able to bear such a Lord.

     Hail, mother of great purity,
130 you were filled with great goodness,
     who, for that reason, delighted in such a Lord
     in whom there is joy without sadness.

     Hail, munificent dwelling,
     full of grace and agreeable,
135 you were the fountain of life,
     fully endowed with virtues.

     Hail, virgin, whose pregnancy
     experienced the shackles of the world;
     but she gave the bread of the angels
140 in abundance to those whom she saved.

     Hail, you whose desire
     was filled with goodness and virtue
     and whose holy sighs
     are always present before God.

145 Hail, you from whose existence it was
     that God took on human flesh,
     which the fathers of old
     had desired and awaited.

     Hail, Mary, hail, your son,

150 who was killed for the people;
    he destroyed the old sacrifice
    when he placed his body on the cross.

    Hail, virgin, by whose grace
    the son of God brought us back to grace
155 and offered a most fine dwelling
    with the saints in heaven.

    Hail, virgin, who was thirsty
    and drank the water of life
    when you conceived the sovereign king,
160 who holds every being in his hand.

    Hail, mother of great brightness
    since Jesus Christ gave you light;
    he loved you, bountiful lady:
    above all other women he took care of you.

165 Hail, you, by whom we are saved
    and our enemies are overcome;
    when we praise you, we praise your son,
    when we serve you, we serve God.

    Hail, noble and courtly queen,
170 pure maiden of youth,
    you sit on the right hand of the father,
    who made you his worthy mother.

    Hail, holy virginity,
    citadel of the everlasting king,
175 you are the fount of virtue,
    by the sanctity of the one on high, salvation.

    Hail, by this gift the son
    calls on and exhorts his friends
    to serve you with heart and with body,
180 for you are the comfort of sinners.

    Hail, greetings, most gentle
    precious jewel, which no woman might ever be;
    give us his body on the last day
    of our end by your love.

185 Hail, you, whose was the word
    and in your heart true thought,
    which the true Solomon taught,
    who was the master of knowledge.

    Hail, mother of the redeemer
190 and the all-powerful creator,
    whose is earth and sea and sky
    and all beings must consider worthy of love.

    Hail, Mary, hail, your son,
    who lives in joy in paradise,
195 with God the king you are both in glory;
    may he accord us, if it please you, victory.

    Hail, Christ, hail, your mother,
    may God, your father, be protected,
    all the holy Trinity,
200 which is one God. Amen.

Critical Apparatus

4, *a*] as.—36, *loier*] loier puisons.—38, *tenebrors*] tenebros.—66, *chius*] chiys.—74, *que fust*] queix.—84, *lor*] les.—159, *soverain*] sovrain.—183, *donne*] damme.

Notes

* This poem presents an adaptation of the first 46 stanzas of the *Ave Porta Paradysi*, in which the order of presentation is respected, and then uses the last 4 to round off the poem. Some stanzas do not correspond in their content to the equivalent stanza in Latin: these are nos. 11, 16, 21, 25, 26, 38, and 46. In one case, there is a stanza in the Latin, placed between the equivalent of French stanzas 29 and 30, and which is, therefore, not part of the French sequence.

1. *haute porte de paradis*: see note to XVIII, 5.

76. Cf. Poem XIII, 11–16.

XX
AVE, REE DE GRANT DULCHOR

MS: *I* fol. 215 r⁰–219 v⁰.
Versification: octosyllabic quatrains (but with a few stanzas of two and six lines) in rhyming couplets with random rhyme patterns.
Earlier Edition: Sinclair, *Manuscrits*, 34–43.

    Ave, ree de grant dulchor,
    virgine plainne de bone amor,
    douce dame sainte Marie,
    Deu filhe, mere et amie.

5   Ave, virgine bieneuree,
flors, Marie haut mariee
a Deu amont spiritaument
en sainte amor virginaument.

Ave, espouse bien doee,
10   de bon doaire aseguree,
c'est del regne Deu pardurable,
liee et joiouse et delitable.

Ave, rose tout tans novelle,
caste amorouse torterele,
15   colons d'amors, sen fiel,
gloriouse porte del ciel.

Ave, clere estoile Marie:
ciz nons lumiere senefie;
cest non doit om ensi gloser:
20   Marie est estoile de mer.

Ave, forme d'umiliteit,
embrasemens de chariteit,
de droiture granz exemplaires,
de virginiteit luminaires.

25   Ave, virgine de grace plaine,
apres Deu el ciel premeraine,
desur les angles gloriouse,
sor les archangles bieneurouse.

Ave, sainte douce provee,
30   sovant bone amie trovee,
de pecheors deliveresse,
de piues, de justes amaresse.

Ave, cui beatet mut amat,
cui humilitet essauchat,
35   et de cui prist humaniteit
Deus, cant se traist par chariteit.

Ave, virgine de cui eissit
li douz resins, *botrus cypri*,
dont li vinz vermouz decorut,

40   par cui les genz truevent salut.

Ave, enspesces ardens et douce,
ki faiz bon cuer et bone boche
cealz ki de tes biens s'aemplissent
et en tue amor s'enjoissent.

45   Ave, tote plaine de vie,
tu ki nen az besoing d'aie.
Par toi es rumpus li durs mers
dont Eve avoiet le mont fineit.

Ave, fusions de grant douçor,
50   dont sunt angoissouz en amor
li haut baron de la citet,
ou regnes, cort de chariteit.

Ave, li plus douce enmiliee,
li plus ardenment enivree
55   de redes jus de paradis,
ou est amors, u est amis.

Ave cui beatez est mervelhe.
Li cors ki n'i voiet sa paralhe,
cui clartez passe cherubin,
60   cui amor la rent seraphin.

Ave, roine debonaire,
de cui loier nus se doit taire,
cuers ki sovent est abevrez
de vin d'Ausaiz, de bon clareit.

65   Ave li plus douce des autres
. . . .
cui vins enivre myrre et balsame
. . . .

Ave, li plus amee amie
70   del haus amis, le roi de vie,
ki, par la sue grant amor,
nos vint atraire a sa douçor.

Ave, li plus parfont navree
de la sue tranchans espee,

75 ki chariteiz est apelee,
    dont li plaie n'iert ja sanee.

    Ave, li plus ambausemee,
    li plus soef empimentee
    de la terre celestiel,
80 ki decort de lait et de miel.

    Ave, li plus enluminee,
    de vroi solheil li mieus tostee,
    ki le monde ait enlumineit
    et de sainte amor enchaufeit.

85 Ave, virgine, filhe Jessé,
    filhe David, filhe Abrahé,
    mere Deu nostre salveor,
    ki nos racheta por s'amor.

    Ave, enliz vaisiauz d'onor,
90 mere le grammere de douçour,
    le duel amis, le duel senior,
    ki soi laissat vaincre d'amor.

    Ore se je disoie avant
    de cele doçor enflamant,
95 Deus, ki le porroit sostenir
    u sens pasmer u sens morir!

    Ave, mere et mielx que mere,
    Adonai, c'est nostre deu frere. Amen.

    Ave, boiste de blanc ivoire
100 u herbegat li rois de gloire,
    li sauverez, li douz provez;
    miaudres amis n'iert mais trovez.

    Ave, de vertus acesmee,
    roine de vesture adoree,
105 de diverse grasce paree,
    a destre le roi coronee.

    Ave, aleine afilee,
    el feu del Saint Espir tempree,
    a cele mole aguisie

110 ki parfaite amor signifie.

Ave, vaisauz d'or a l'amande,
virge Aaron dont vint l'amande,
viaures arosez Gedeon,
yvoriens thrones Salemon.

115 Ave, mere del douz agnel,
le saverouz, le bon, le bel,
ki vat paissant fines amors
ens en vert pré entre les flors.

Ave, douce dame honoree,
120 en la citet estes entree
ki est plainne de grant douçor;
vos estes mere au creator.

Ave, jardins d'umilitet
u li douz arbres est plantez
125 ki porte fruit de chariteit
et si an mangiens a planté.
Li dous Deus at l'uiz defermet
a ceaz qui ont humiliteit.

Ave, virgine ki entrat
130 en orison et si trovat
son tres chier filh si l'embrachat
. . . .
sachiez ke pas ne refusat
et trestout son cuer li donat.

135 Ave, par cui Deus reformat
l'ome kant Gabriel format
del non Deu a cest dulce avé
dont li fil en sunt tuit laveit.

Ave, tres gloriouse dame,
140 virgine de cors, de cuer, d'arme,
en cui Deus vout char et sanc prendre
cui touz li mons ne puet comprandre.

Ave, virge Jessé florie
ki aportas le fruit de vie,

145 sor cui Sains Espirs se repose,
    en cui nostre vie est enclouse.

    Ave, sainz tresorierz et fors
    en cui fut gardez li tresors
    par cui nos somes rachetet
150 de l'infernal captiviteit.

    Ave, dame qui alaitas
    et ki em bersuel afaitas
    d'angles et d'omes la pasture,
    ki en croiz prist tue nature.

155 Ave, mere de cel filh meimes
    dont peres est Deus li hautisme,
    qui el ciel at pere sens mere,
    et de toi, dame, eisist sens pere.

    Ave, tres povre berbisete
160 ki la lainne portas blanchete,
    dont li filx Deu se vout vestir
    parmi l'ovre del Saint Espir.

    Ave, tres glorious mestiers
    u Deus vestit ses dras premiers;
165 la vie prist, dame, en ton cloistre,
    par cui i puist l'ome conoistre.

    Ave, sainte arche qui aporte
    le dul mane qui nos conforte
    en cest desert, la gens elite,
170 cealz qui vuelent eissir d'Egypte.

    Ave, jardins plains de floretes,
    de roses, de liz, de violetes.
    Roses d'amors, liz de chastez,
    violete d'umiliteit.

175 Ave, merveillouse merveile
    ki conceus Deu par oreille;
    li verbes Deu en char muat
    kant Gabriel toi saluat.

    Ave, palaiz de haut afaire

180 en cui Deus vuolt ses noces faire
kant il Sainte Eglise espousat
et Synagoge refusat.

Ave, trone de nouvel roi,
arche de la nouvelle loi.
185 En toi fut Damedex .ix. moiz;
par toi done decrez et loiz.

Ave, qui ja n'auras pareille,
de cui nature se merveille
de ce ke tu portas ton pere
190 et ke tu fuz et virge et mere.

Ave, la porte u Dex passat,
ki nen ovrit ne ne quassa.
Par toi vint Deus en tel maniere
ke remainsiz clouse et entiere.

195 Ave, par cui Deus avalat,
par cui li hom haut remontat.
Par toi vint Dex, dame, sa jus;
par toi no[s] stuet monster lai ssus.

Ave, saintismes saintuaires
200 de cui eisit li sains triacles
dont li hom fut rasoagiez,
ki touz astoit a mort jugiez.

Ave, debonaire mecine
ki aportas vraie mesine
205 au chaitif home despoilliet,
cui dyables out a mort plaiet.

Ave, glorious tabernacles
u fut gardez li duz triacles
ki le mortel venin destruit
210 k'Adans nos peres avoit buit.

Ave, lampe bele et entiere
u Deus absconsat sa lumiere
kant le malade vint saner
ki sa clarteit ne pout porter.

215 Ave, gloriouse voiriere
 par cui vint el mont la lumiere
 dont li hom fut renluminés,
 ki en la chartre iert avoiglez.

 Ave, chambre belle et parfite
220 en cui la prisons fut confite
 dont li hom fut raceurez,
 ki de sa vie iert desperez.

 Ave, vaisaux en cui pendit
 li pains ki del ciel descendit,
225 par cui li hom fut resoulés,
 ki iert de fain touz afolez.

 Ave, par cui furent destroites
 de peaz de bestes les deçoites
 c'umilitez at revestut,
230 ceaz ke orguelz laissat tous nuz.

 Ave, sainte color et pure
 u li filz Deu tint sa vesture.
 Benoite soit ceste colors
 ki sanat toutes nos dolors.

235 Ave, gentilz pupres roialz,
 tu es la thache emperiaus.
 L'empereres en toi format
 ki d'enfer les portes brisat.

 Ave, ki purgast l'amertume
240 k'Adans trovat ens en la pome
 par la douce reie de miel
 ki descendit en toi del ciel.

 Ave, virgine bien arosee
 de la celestial rosee,
245 car tu portas cel tres douz fruit
 ki done as siens joie et deduit.

 Ave, pucelle Maria
 a cui Deus son filh maria.
 C'est mariages glorious,

250 car tes filz est et tes espous.

Ave, gloriouse enjornee
par cui la nuis fut terminee
kant li solaus en toi levat,
ki tout le mont enluminat.

255 Ave, flors qui ne desflorist
kant li dous fruiz de toi eisist,
mais ta flors se tient ades,
virgine devant et virge aprez.

Ave, gloriouse citez,
260 nunques ne fut ne mes n'iert telz.
En toi meismes se format
l'empereres qui tout format.

Ave, dame ki recordas
l'ovre a douz Deu ke tu portas.
265 Par toi out pais, joie et planté
cilh qui out bone volentet.

Ave, armaires honorez
ou li bons livres fut gardez,
en cui sunt mis tuit li tresor
270 et de science et de savoir.

Ave, de totes virgines flors
a cui Deus requesist d'amors.
Dame, par toi est alegié
toute li humaine lignié.

275 Ave, par cui nos fut randue
l'anors k'Adans avoit perdue.
La terre nos at desegié
ki a cort nos iert forjugié.

Ave, conduiz de la fontaine
280 ki del ciel vint, de pitiet plaine,
par cui li mons est arosez
ki de vechiez astoit brulez.

Ave, ki si tres haut volas,
ki a la Trinitet montas

285 et asportas del sain del pere
     a nos *Jhesum*, nostre dul frere.

     Ave, ki nos asportas joie
     k'en paradis nos trovas voie.
     Li filz Deu le te renseignat
290 kant il descendre en toi daignat.

     Ave, par cui Deus nos rendit
     sa samblance, k'Adans perdit.
     En toi, dame, fut reformee
     la loiz Deu, ki astoit faucee.

295 Ave, doulitous paradis
     ou li noveaz Adans fu mis,
     ki Sainte Eglise ait bin plantee
     et de bons arbres aornee.

     Ave, par cui Adans li viez
300 del viel home fut despoilliez,
     et del novel fut revestuz
     kant il, deschalz, fut devestuz.

     Ave, arbres dignes d'amor
     k'aportas fruit sens nul labor,
305 dont ja Adans n'iert deceus,
     car sens cest fruit ne vivra nus.

     Ave, par cui cil fut vencuz
     ki fit le prothoplaste nut.
     Dame, le serpent as foleit,
310 ky paradyz nos out embleit. Amen.

Translation

     Hail, creature of great gentleness,
     virgin full of good love,
     gentle lady, holy Mary,
     daughter of God, mother and friend.

5   Hail, blessed virgin,
     flower, Mary married on high
     to God above spiritually,
     in holy love, in virginity.

     Hail, well-favored bride,

10   assured of a good dowry,
      which is the everlasting kingdom of God,
      happy and joyous and delightful.

      Hail, rose forever new,
      chaste, loving turtledove,
15   dove of love, dove without gall,
      glorious gate of heaven.

      Hail, bright star Mary:
      this name means light;
      thus should one gloss this name:
20   Mary is star of the sea.

      Hail, embodiment of humility,
      fire of charity,
      perfect model of uprightness,
      light of virginity.

25   Hail, virgin full of grace,
      supreme in heaven after God,
      glorious above the angels,
      blessed above the archangels.

      Hail, proven gentle saint,
30   often an appropriate friend,
      deliverer of sinners,
      lover of the holy and the just.

      Hail, you, whose beauty he loved greatly,
      whose humility he exalted
35   and from whom God accepted humanity
      when he was born through charity.

      Hail, virgin from whom issued forth
      the gentle resin, *botrus cypri*,
      from which the red wine came,
40   through which the people find salvation.

      Hail, ardent and gentle spice,
      who give a good heart and mouth
      to those who are replete with your bounties
      and rejoice in your love.

45   Hail, you who are full of life,
     you who have no need of help.
     Through you is broken the hard transaction
     with which Eve had paid for the world.

     Hail, spindle of great gentleness
50   which brings anguish in love
     to the powerful barons of the city,
     where you reign, court of charity.

     Hail, most gentle honeyed one,
     most ardently intoxicated
55   with proclamations outside of paradise,
     where there is love, where there is a friend.

     Hail, you whose beauty is a marvel,
     whose body which cannot see its equal,
     whose brightness outstrips the cherubim,
60   whose love makes it seraphim.

     Hail, splendid queen;
     praise of you no one can conceal,
     heart which is often sated
     with wine of Alsace, with good claret.

65   Hail, gentlest of the others
     . . . .
     whose wine intoxicates myrrh and balsam
     . . . .

     Hail, most beloved lady
70   of the supreme friend, the king of life,
     who, by his great love,
     came to bring us to his gentleness.

     Hail, most deeply wounded one
     with his sharp sword
75   which is called charity,
     whose wound will never be healed.

     Hail, most anointed one,
     most pleasantly perfumed
     of the soil of heaven,

80   which flows with milk and honey.

Hail, most radiant one,
most warmed by the true sun
to have given light to the world
and warmed it by holy love.

85   Hail, virgin, daughter of Jesse,
daughter of David, daughter of Abraham,
mother of God our savior,
who redeemed us through his love.

Hail, chosen vessel of honor,
90   mother of the scholar of gentleness,
of the gentle friend, of the gentle Lord,
who let himself be overcome through love.

Now, were I to speak before
of this burning gentleness,
95   God, who could bear it
without fainting or dying!

Hail, mother and better than mother,
Adonai, he is our gentle brother. Amen.

Hail, box of white ivory
100   where the king of glory resided,
the savior, the gentle one revealed;
a better friend will never more be found.

Hail, you adorned with virtues,
queen of an adored harvest,
105   endowed with different graces,
crowned on the right hand of the king.

Hail, sharp awl,
tempered in the fire of the Holy Spirit,
sharpened on that stone
110   which means perfect love.

Hail, vessel of gold with diamonds,
rod of Aaron from which came the almonds,
Gideon's fleece wet with dew,
ivory throne of Solomon.

115 Hail, mother of the gentle lamb,
       the delicate, the good, the beautiful,
       who feeds on perfect loves
       in a green meadow among the flowers.

       Hail, gentle honored lady,
120 you entered the city
       which is full of great gentleness;
       you are the mother of the creator.

       Hail, garden of humility
       where the gentle tree is planted
125 which bears the fruit of charity
       and we eat of it in abundance.
       The gentle God has unlocked the door
       to those who have humility.

       Hail, virgin who began
130 to pray and found
       her very dear son and kissed him.
       . . . .
       know that he did not refuse
       and gave her all his heart.

135 Hail, you through whom God reformed
       man when he created Gabriel
       from the name of God to this gentle *Hail Mary*
       by which the children are all washed clean.

       Hail, most glorious lady,
140 virgin in body, heart and soul,
       in whom God wished to take on flesh and blood,
       which all people may not understand.

       Hail, rod of Jesse in bloom,
       you who brought the fruit of life,
145 in whom the Holy Spirit takes rest,
       in whom our lives are contained.

       Hail, holy, strong treasury
       in whom the treasure was kept
       by which we are redeemed
150 from the captivity of hell.

       Hail, lady, who suckled
       and in a little cradle raised
       the food of angels and mankind,
       who took on your nature on the cross.

155 Hail, mother of the very son
    whose father is the supreme God,
    who in heaven has father without mother,
    and from you, lady, came forth without father.

    Hail, poorest of little ewes,
160 you who wore the white wool
    with which the son of God wished to clothe himself
    through the work of the Holy Spirit.

    Hail, most glorious office
    where God put on his first garments;
165 he took life, lady, in your cloister,
    through which one may recognize him.

    Hail, holy ark which brings
    the sweet manna which comforts us
    in this desert, the chosen people,
170 those who wished to go out of Egypt.

    Hail, garden full of little flowers,
    of roses, lilies and violets,
    rose of love, lily of chastity,
    violet of humility.

175 Hail, marvelous miracle
    who conceived God through your ears;
    the word of God became flesh
    when Gabriel hailed you.

    Hail, palace of great authority
180 in which God wished to wed
    when he took in marriage Holy Church
    and refused the Synagogue.

    Hail, throne of the new king,
    ark of the new law.
185 In you was the Lord God for nine months;
    through you he proclaims decrees and laws.

    Hail, you who will never have an equal,
    whose nature is marveled at
    because you bore your father

190 and you were virgin and mother.

Hail, gate through which God passed
which never opened nor broke.
Through you God came in such manner
that it remained closed and whole.

195 Hail, you through whom God came down,
through whom mankind rose on high.
Through you, lady, God came down here;
through you, it behooves us to rise up there.

Hail, most holy sanctuary
200 from whom came forth the holy antidote
by which mankind was refreshed
when all were condemned to death.

Hail, kindly medicine,
you who brought the true remedy
205 to wretched man, stripped bare,
whom the Devil had sentenced to death.

Hail, glorious tabernacle
in which was kept the sweet antidote
which destroyed the deadly poison
210 which Adam our father had drunk.

Hail, beautiful and unsullied lamp
where God hid his light
when he came to heal the sick man
who could not bear his light.

215 Hail, glorious window
through which the light came into the world
by which mankind was given new light
when it had been blinded in the prison.

Hail, beautiful and perfect bedchamber
220 in which the prison was defeated,
because of which mankind was reassured
when it despaired of life.

Hail, vessel which contained
the bread which came down from heaven,

225 through which mankind was satisfied,
     who was driven mad by hunger.

     Hail, you through whom were destroyed
     under the feet of animals the deceits
     which humility took on,
230 those which pride left quite naked.

     Hail, holy, pure color
     in which the son of God dyed his garments.
     Blessed be this color,
     which heals all pain.

235 Hail, noble royal purple,
     you are the imperial mark.
     In you, the emperor formed
     the one who broke down the doors of hell.

     Hail, you eradicated the bitterness
240 which Adam found in the apple
     through the sweet stream of honey
     which came down into you from heaven.

     Hail, virgin wet
     with the celestial dew,
245 for you bore that most sweet fruit,
     which gives to his people joy and delight.

     Hail, maid Mary,
     to whom God married his son.
     It is a glorious marriage,
250 for he is your son and your husband.

     Hail, glorious dawn
     by which the night was ended
     when the sun rose in you
     which gave light to the whole world.

255 Hail, flower, which did not wane
     when the sweet fruit came out of you;
     but your flower remains now,
     virgin before and virgin after.

     Hail, glorious city,

260 never was there nor will there be such.
      In you yourself was created
      the emperor who created all.

      Hail, lady who recalled the handiwork
      to gentle God, whom you bore.
265 Through you the one who had good will
      had peace, joy and plenty.

      Hail, honored cabinet
      where the good book was kept,
      in which are placed all the treasures
270 of knowledge and wisdom.

      Hail, flower of all virgins
      in whom God sought love.
      Lady, through you all the human race
      is given relief.

275 Hail, you by whom the love which Adam had lost
      was given back to us.
      The earth was delivered up to us
      which was taken away from us in the court.

      Hail, channel of the fountain
280 which came from heaven, full of pity,
      with which all the world is watered,
      which was burned by the deceitful.

      Hail, you who flew so very high,
      who rose up to the Trinity
285 and brought us from the bosom of the father
      Jesus, our gentle brother.

      Hail, you who brought us joy
      so that you found for us the way to paradise.
      The son of God told you this
290 when he deigned to come down into you.

      Hail, you by whom God gave us back
      his semblance, which Adam lost.
      In you, lady, was reformed
      the law of God, which had been falsified.

295 Hail, delightful paradise
in which the new Adam was placed,
who planted Holy Church there
and adorned it with good trees.

Hail, you through whom the old Adam
300 was stripped of the old man
and was clothed in the new one
when he, barefoot, was unclothed.

Hail, tree worthy of love,
you who brought forth fruit without travail,
305 because of which never was Adam disappointed,
for without this fruit no one will live.

Hail, you through whom the one who made
the first man naked was conquered.
Lady, you trod underfoot the serpent,
310 who had stolen paradise from us. Amen.

Critical Apparatus

13, *tout*] tou.—15. *fiel*] fiez.—24, *de*] et de; *luminaires*] luminaire.—43, *aemplissent*] caemplissent.—45, *de*] da.—47, *toi*] toie.—53, *enmiliee*] enmilie.—54, *ardenment*] ardentement.—71, *la*] le.—82, *solheil*] solh.—95, *ki le*] ki.—112, *l'amande*] lamandre.—113, *viaures*] veaices.—114, *yvoriens*] ys yvoriens.—126, *et si*] si.—138, *en sunt*] sunt.—158, *sens*] se.—167, *aporte*] aporteit.—192, *ovrit*] orit.—198, *nos stuet*] nostuet.—225, *resoulés*] resolues.—228, *deçoites*] cecostes (?).—233, *colors*] color.—239, *amertume*] armertume.—246, *as*] a.—254, *enluminat*] enluminumat.—255, *desflorist*] desfloris.—260, *ne mes*] mes.—295, *doulitous*] doulirous.—302, *deschalz*] dechal.

Notes

5. Sinclair (*Manuscrits*, 34) considers that this line is hypermetric. However, here and elsewhere the semi-learned form *virgine* counts for only two feet.

13. *novelle*—Sinclair (ibid., 35) wrongly transcribes as *nouvelle*.

17–20. Another reference to the *stella maris*; see also Poem XVIII, 57–60.

21–24. Note the similarity between this image and that of Poem II, 5–6.

32. Sinclair (*Manuscrits*, 35): "Vers hypermétrique. On peut supposer que l's final de justes ne compte pas pour la scansion."

38. *botrus cypri*: cf. *Canticum Canticorum* I, 13: "Botrus cypri dilectus mihi / in vineis Engaddi."

39–40: a reference to the Eucharist.

49. *fusions*. Sinclair (*Manuscrits*, 36) mistakenly reads as *fusious*.

52. *regnes*: 2 p.s. pres. ind. Sinclair suggests a possible correction to *regne*, which would give the meaning 'where a court of charity reigns.'

53. *enmiliee*. Sinclair (*Manuscrits*, 36) preserves the reading of the MS, *enmilie*, amended here for the visual rhyme. The form is unusual, given the presence of a yod after the *l*, but it is also found in the variant reading for the form in Gautier de Coincy (ed. V. Frédéric Koenig, *Les Miracles de Nostre Dame*, vol. 1[Geneva: Droz, 1955], 158–59): "Mais tant est dous et enmielez / Li noms de la douce Marie" and the spelling in MS B (Brussels, Bibliothèque royale): *enmiliez*. Further examples of the association of *enmielee* with Mary can be found in Gautier de Coincy. Juliana's *vita* uses the same image: "sentiebat mellitam dulcedinem," and, further, in the following line, picks up the image of intoxication: "inebriata non tamen vino sed spiritu."

55. *redes*: it occurs infrequently in French, but is listed by W. von Wartburg (*Französisches etymologisches Wörterbuch, q.v.* RECITARE) in one example taken from the *Mistere de Saint Quentin, suivi des Inventions de Saint Quentin* (p. p. H. Chatelain, Saint Quentin, 1908), with, however, the meaning 'rêve extravagant.' This is difficult to square with the etymology of *rede*, especially as in Old Spanish *rezar* means 'to relate, to proclaim.' The likely reference here is to the annunciation, the proclamation by the angel Gabriel to Mary.

71. *la . . . amor.* The MS has *le*, but this use of the definite article with feminine nouns is not typical of MS *I*.

90. As Sinclair (*Manuscrits*, 37) points out, the line is hypermetric.

95. *ki le*: Sinclair has *ki [se]* to complete the sense.

98. *Adonai*: there are links with the Babylonian god, Tammuz, who was a form of Sun-god and bridegroom of Ishtar, and who was cut off in early life. The name Adonai has been thought to be Canaanite, but in Hebrew it means 'my lord' and therefore can be linked directly to the tradition of the Old Testament and later association with Jesus. The mourning related to the passing of Tammuz may well find an echo in the reference to the "quasi luctum unigeniti" (*Amos* 8: 10) and the "planctu quasi super unigenitum" (*Zach.*12: 10). The use of "sweet brother" and the suffering of Christ in the preceding stanzas makes the connection clear and would have been understood by believers of the 13th c.

111. *amande*—'diamond,' *viz. Anglo-Norman Dictionary*, ed. Louise W. Stone and William Rothwell (London: MHRA, 1977), fasc. 1, 9 under *adamant*.

112. *l'amande.* The reading of the MS, *mandre*, is retained by Sinclair (*Manuscrits*, 38) with the meaning 'manne' (47). But, apart from the question of the rhyme, the reference to Aaron is clear: "in amygdalas deformati sunt" (*Num.* 17: 8).

113. *viaures.* Sinclair (*ibid.*) considers that the reading of the MS, *veaices*, "paraît être une bévue de copiste." However, he proposes *veaires* as a replacement, but with a question mark against it in the glossary (47). The reference to *Iud.* 6: 36–39 is clear, as Sinclair says.

123–128. The accumulation of metaphors here is reflected in the writings / *vita* of Juliana.

127. *defermet*—Sinclair (*Manuscrits*, 47) *defermez*, which is not in the MS and falsifies the rhyme pattern.

159–163. Mary, the ewe, as mother of the Lamb of God, gives corporeal form to Christ, here, in the wool of her coat. The metaphor is well known and is picked up in hymns.

167–168. This allusion to the ark is taken from *Ad Hebr.* 9: 4.

176. See *Luc.* 1: 44.

183–184. The theme of the old and the new, used in office of Corpus Christi, and the new law or covenant, finds its reflection in *Ezech* 36: 26–27 and further in *Ad Hebraeos* 8: 8–10.

198. *no[s] stuet.* Sinclair (*Manuscrits*, 40) comments: "vostuet *lecture incertaine; le sens paraît être* voulut, *ou peut-être* no[s] stuet: 'il nous faut.'" The reading is, indeed, *nostuet* with the meaning suggested.

203–206. In the Victorine doctrine, the Eucharist is understood as a remedy or medicine.

207–208. Mary is the receptacle which contains the antidote to sin of Adam, in the form of the body and blood of Christ.

223–224. Mary carries Christ, seen as manna from heaven, which becomes the wafer of the Eucharist.

228. *deçoites*—a tentative solution to the problem of this line. Sinclair (*Manuscrits*, 40) reads *derostes* and analyses it as the past part. of *derompre* (ibid., 47).

239–242. The bitterness of the apple is countered by the sweetness of honey. See above lines 53–54.

253, *en toi.* Sinclair (*Manuscrits*, 42) misreads as *encor.*

273–274. *alegié / lignié.* Sinclair (*ibid.*) has *alegie* and *lignie.* The verb is certainly a past part. and *lignié* is a feminine noun with the typical shortening from -*ee* in the N.-E. dialect.

277–278. *desegié / forjugié.* The same phenomenon as in the previous note.

295–298. The new Adam, saved by Christ is contrasted with the old Adam. The allusion to trees is pertinent in that those of the Garden of Eden were the cause of his downfall. The metaphor, related to the Eucharist, is continued in the succeeding stanzas.

BIBLIOGRAPHY

MANUSCRIPTS

Brigham Young University, Harold B. Lee Library, Special Collections, Vault 091 263 1343

Brussels, Bibliothèque royale, 139

Brussels, Bibliothèque royale, IV–36

Brussels, Bibliothèque royale, IV–1013

Brussels, Bibliothèque royale, IV–1066

Cambridge, Fitwilliam Museum, 288

Edinburgh, University Library MS 211.iv

Graz, Universitätsbibliothek, MS 134

Liège, Bibliothèque de l'Université, 431

London, British Library, Add. 21114

London, British Library, Stowe 17

Melbourne, State Library of Victoria, *096/R66

New York, Pierpont Morgan Library, 183

New York, Pierpont Morgan Library, 440

Paris, Bibliothèque nationale de France, latin 755

Paris, Bibliothèque nationale de France, latin 1051

Paris, Bibliothèque nationale de France, latin 1077

Paris, Bibliothèque nationale de France, latin 1143

Paris, Bibliothèque nationale de France n.a., latin 1235

Prague, Abbey of Strahov, MS D.E.I.7

Rochester, Memorial Art Gallery, 53.68

Rome, Biblioteca Apostolica Vaticana, Vat. lat. 10770

Rome, Biblioteca Apostolica Vaticana, Vat. lat. 10772

Rome, Biblioteca Apostolica Vaticana, Barb. BBB. 1 1 [Dominican breviary, 1481]

Rome, Biblioteca Apostolica Vaticana, Chigi C V 138

Rome, Biblioteca Apostolica Vaticana, Codex Reg. Lat. V1–133 [Dominican breviary, 1480s] [Thomas of Cant. uses Common of One Martyr. St. James' service has *Apostolus Christi Iac per syn* as first antiphon of matins and as responsory 1 text. This is the old Spanish service Hohler talks about. The last responsory at matins is *O speciale decus*, one of the texts Calixtus mentions in conjunction with St. John the Baptist.]

's-Heerenberg, Stichting Huis Bergh, 35 (225)

The Hague, National Library of the Netherlands, MS 70.E.4

The Hague, National Library of the Netherlands, 76.G.17

PUBLISHED SOURCES

Abulafia, D. 1999. The Kingdom of Sicily under the Hohenstaufen and Angevins. *The New Cambridge Medieval History V: c.1198–c.1300.* Ed. David Abulafia. Cambridge: Cambridge University Press, 497–521.

Acta Capitulorum Generalium Ordinis Praedicatorum. 1898 and 1899. Ed. B. M. Reichert. Vol. 1 (1220–1303); Vol. 2 (1304–78). *Monumenta Ordinis Fratrum Praedicatorum historica* 3–4. Rome.

Alcuin. *Commentaria in S. Joannis evangelium.* PL 100, cols. 835–40.

Alexander, J. 2004. Cultural Pragmatics: Social Performance Between Ritual and Strategy. *Sociological Theory* 22 (4), 527–73.

Alger of Liège. *De sacramentis corporis et sanguinis Dominici.* PL 180, cols. 743–854.

Ambrosius. *De sacramentis.* 1990. Ed. Josef Schmitz. Freiburg and New York: Herder.

———. *De officiis.* 2000. Ed. Maurice Testard. Corpus Christianorum Series latina, 15. Turnhout: Brepols.

———. *De mysteriis.* PL 16, cols. 404 ff.

Anglo-Norman Dictionary. 1977. Ed. Louise W. Stone and William Rothwell. London: MHRA.

Antiphonaire monastique XIIIe siècle: Codex F. 160 de la Bibliothèque de la Cathédrale de Worcester. Paléographie musicale XII. Berne: Editions Herbert Lang et Cie, 1971.

Antiphonale Pataviense (Wien 1519). Ed. Karlheinz Schlager. *Das Erbe deutscher Musik.* Vol. 88. Kassel: Bärenreiter, 1985.
[In BNF 1143, #16 is cited as a reworking of *Crescente etate* from feast of St. Bernard. Pat uses the same text and music for St. Rubberto.]

Apel, W. 1990. *Gregorian Chant.* Bloomington: Indiana University Press.

Arjomand, Said. 1996. The Consolation of Theology: Absence of Iman and Transition From Chiliasm to Law in Shi'ism. *The Journal of Religion*, 548–71.

Aubrey, Elizabeth. 1996. *The Music of the Troubadours.* Bloomington and Indianapolis: Indiana University Press.

Aubry, Pierre. 1900. *Les Proses d'Adam de Saint-Victor: texte et musique précédé d'une étude critique.* Paris: H. Welter, 1900. Repr. *Melanges de musicologie critique.* Geneva: Minkoff Reprint, 1980.

Auda, A. 1923. *L'École musicale liégeoise au Xe siècle: Étienne de Liège.* Brussels: Académie royale de Belgique; Paris: H. Welter.

———. 1930. *La musique et les musiciens de l'Ancien Pays de Liège.* Brussels: Van Damme & Duquesne.

Augustinus. *In Iohannis Evangelium tractatus CXXIV.* Ed. Radbotus Willems. 1954. Corpus Christianorum, Series latina, 36. Turnholt: Brepols.

———. 1963. *The Trinity [De trinitate].* Trans. Stephen McKenna. Washington, Catholic University of America Press.

———. 1966. *Enarrationes in Psalmos.* Corpus Christianorum, Series latina, 38–40. Turnholt: Brepols.

Avril, F. 1990. Une curieuse illustration de la Fête-Dieu: l'iconographie de Christ Prêtre élevant hostie et sa diffusion. *Rituels: mélanges offerts à Pierre-Marie Gy, O.P.* Ed. Paul De Clerck and E. Pallazzo. Paris: Les Éditions du Cerf.

Baix, F., and Lambot, C. 1946. *La dévotion à l'eucharistie et le VIIe centenaire de la Fête-Dieu.* Gembloux-Namur: J. Ducolot.

Bartoli, M. 1999. Les femmes et l'Église au 13e siècle. *Actes du Colloque de Liège.* Vol. 1 of *Fête-Dieu (1246–1996).* Ed. André Haquin. Louvain-la-Neuve: Institut d'Études Médiévales de l'Université Catholique de Louvain, 55–79.

Bataillon, L-J. 1983. Le sermon inédit de saint Thomas "Homo quidam fecit cenam magnam": introduction et édition. *Revue des sciences philosophiques et théologiques* 67, 353–69. (also available at: http://www.corpusthomisticum.org/hhf.html.

Bériou, N. , J. Berlioz, and J. Longère (Trans.). 1991. *Prier au Moyen Age: pratiques et Expériences (Ve–XV siècles).* Turnhout: Brepols.

Berman, C. H. 2000. *The Cistercian Evolution: The Invention of Religious Order in Twelfth-Century Europe.* Philadelphia: University of Pennsylvania Press.

Bertamini, T. 1968. La bolla "Transiturus" di papa Urbano IV e l'uffizio del "Corpus Christi" secondo il codice di S. Lorenzo di bognanco. *Aevum* 42, 29–58.

Bertholet, J. 1846. *Histoire de l'Institution de la Fête-Dieu: avec la Vie des Bienheureuses Julienne et Eve qui en furent les premières promulgatrices.* Liège: Jacques-Antoine Gerlachm, 1746; 3rd ed. Liège: F. Oudart.

Biblia sacra, vulgatae editionis Sixti V Pont. Max. iussu recognita et Clementis VIII auctoritate edita; editio emendatissima apparatu critico instructa cura et studio Monachorum Abbatiae Pontificiae Sancti Hieronymi in Urbe Ordinis Sancti Benedicti. 1965. Rome.

Blockmans, W. 1999. Flanders. *The New Cambridge Medieval History V: c.1198–c.1300.* Ed. David Abulafia. Cambridge: Cambridge University Press, 405–16.

Blume, C. 1909. Das Fronleich-nams-Fest. Seine erten Urkunden und Offizien. *Theologie und Glaube* 3, 337–49.

———. 1911. Thomas von Aquin und das Fronleichnamsoffizium, inbesondere der Hymnus "Verbum supernum." *Theologie und Glaube* 3, 358–72.

Bolton, B. 1999. Thirteenth-Century Religious Women: Further Reflections on the Low Countries as a "Special Case." *New Trends in Feminine Spirituality: The Holy Women of Liège and TheirImpact.* Ed. Juliette Dor, Lesley Johnson, and Jocelyn Wogan-Browne. Turnhout: Brepols, 129–57.

Bonner, C. 1941. Desired Haven. *Harvard Theological Review* 34, 49–63.

Bourdieu, P. 1984. *Distinction: A Social Critique of the Judgment of Taste.* Trans. Richard Nice. Cambridge, MA: Harvard University Press.

———. 1994. *Language and Symbolic Power.* Cambridge, MA: Harvard University Press

Bourlet, I., and Devaux, J. 1990. Le Mal Saint-Martin. *Saint-Martin, Mémoire de Liège.* Liège: Éditions du Perron, 73–79.

Brentano, R. 1974. *Rome before Avignon: A Social History of Thirteenth-Century Rome.* New York: Basic Books.

Breviarium juxta ritum sacri ordinis Praedicatorum. 1856. Manila: Typis Collegii S. Thomae.

Browe, P. 1928. Die Ausbreitung des Fronleichnamsfestes. *Jahrbuch für Liturgiewissenschaft* 8, 107–43.

———. 1934. *Textus antiqui de festo Corporis Christi.* Opuscula et textus, series liturgica IV. Münster: Aschendorff.

Brussels, Bibliothèque royale de Belgique. Section des manuscrits. *Catalogue des manuscrits de la Bibliothèque royale de Belgique.* Ed. J. Van den Gheyn. Vol. 1 (Écriture sainte et Liturgie). Brussels: Henri Lamertin, Libraire-Éditeur, 1901.

Bryden, J. R., and D. Hughes. 1969. *An Index of Gregorian Chant.* 2 vols. Cambridge, MA: Harvard University Press.

Bucchingerus, Michael. 1560. *Historia ecclesiatica nova qva brevi compendio.* Antwerp: Widow S. Sasseni.

Bynum, C. 1982. *Jesus as Mother: Studies in the Spirituality of the High Middle Ages.* Berkeley: University of California Press.

———. 1987. *Holy Feast and Holy Fast: The Religious Significance of Food to Medieval Women.* Berkeley: University of California Press.

———. 1991. *Fragmentation and Redemption: Essays on the Study of the Human Body in Medieval Religion.* New York: Zone Books.

Capellanus, A. 1960. *The Art of Courtly Love.* Trans. John Jay Parry. New York: Columbia University Press.

Carruthers, M. 1990. *The Book of Memory: A Study of Memory in Medieval Culture* Cambridge: Cambridge University Press.

Chevalier, Ulysse. 1920–21. *Repertorium hymnologicum.* Brussels: Société Bollandistes.

Coakley, J. 1991. Friars as Confidants of Holy Women in Medieval Dominican Hagiography. *Images of Sainthood in Medieval Europe.* Ed. R. Blumenfeld-Kosinski and T. Szell. Ithaca and London: Cornell University Press.

Corrigan, V. 2001. *Paris, Bibliothèque Nationale Fonds Latin 1143*. Ottawa: The Institute of Medieval Music.

———. 2001. The Music for the Corpus Christi Office. Leeds. International Medieval Congress.

———. 2003. Travel and Transformation: The Corpus Christi Office in Germany. (Paper delivered at the 23rd Annual Medieval Forum, Plymouth, NH: Plymouth State College, 19–29 April 2002)

Cottiaux, J. 1963. L'Office liégeois de la Fête-Dieu, sa valeur et son destin. *Revue d'histoire ecclésiastique* 58, 5–81, 405–59.

———. 1991. *Sainte Julienne de Cornillon, promotrice de la Fête-Dieu: Son pays, son temps, son message*. Liège: Carmel de Cornillon.

Cottiaux, J., and Delville, J.-P. 1990. La Fête-Dieu: Eve, Julienne et la Fête-Dieu à Saint-Martin. *Saint-Martin, Mémoire de Liège*. Liège: Éditions du Perron, 31–53.

Cox, E. 1999. The Kingdom of Burgundy, the Lands of the House of Savoy and Adjacent Territories. *The New Cambridge Medieval History V: c.1198–c.1300*. Ed. David Abulafia. Cambridge: Cambridge University Press, 358–74.

Crossan, D. 1991. *The Historical Jesus: The Life of a Mediterranean Jewish Peasant.* Edinburgh: T. & T. Clark.

———. 1994. *Jesus: A Revolutionary Biography*. San Francisco: HarperSanFrancisco.

Cruls, J. 1890. *The Blessed Sacrament and the Church of St. Martin at Liège*. Trans. by William S. Preston, with the permission of Monseigneur Doutreloux, Bishop of Liège. New York: Catholic Publication Society; London: Burns & Oates.

De Ganck, R. 1970. The Cistercian Nuns of Belgium in the Thirteenth Century. *Cistercian Studies* 5, 169–87.

De Voragine, J. 1993. *The Golden Legend: Readings on the Saints*. Trans. William Granger. Princeton, Princeton University Press.

Delaissé, L. M. J. 1949. Les remaniements d'un légendier témoins de l'évolution de la liturgie romaine au XIIIe s. (Paris Lat. 755). *Scriptorium* 3, 26–44.

———. 1950. A la recherche des origines de l'office du Corpus Christi dans les manuscrits liturgiques. *Scriptorium* 4, 220–39.

Delville, J.-P. 1999. *Vie de Sainte Julienne de Cornillon*, Critical Edition. Vol. 2 of *Fête-Dieu (1246–1996)*. Louvain-la-Neuve: Institut d'Études Médiévales de l'Université Catholique de Louvain.

———. 1999. Julienne de Cornillon à la lumière de son biographe. *Actes du Colloque de Liège*. Vol. 1 of *Fête-Dieu (1246–1996)*. Ed. André Haquin. Louvain-la-Neuve: Institut d'Études Médiévales de l'Université Catholique de Louvain, 27–53.

Demarteau, J. 1896. *La première auteur Wallonne: la bienheureuse Eve de Saint-Martin*. Liège: Demarteau.

Denis, E. 1927. *Sainte Julienne et Cornillon*. Liège: Printing Co.

De Vitry, Jaques. 1867. *Vita Mariae Oigniacensis*. Ed. Daniel Papebroch. *Acta Sanctorum, Jun. t. V*, 542–72.

———. 1578. Feria Quinta in Coena Domini. *Sermones in Epistolas et Evangelia Dominicalia totius anni*. Venetiis: Apud Giordanum Zilettum.

———. 1998. *The Life*. Trans. Margot H. King. *Two Lives of Marie D'Oignies*. 4th ed. Toronto: Peregrina, 3–180.

Dreves, G. M., and Blume, C. (Eds.). 1961. *Analecta Hymnica medii aevi*. 55 vols. Leipzig, 1886–1922. Repr. New York: Johnson Reprint Corporation.

Duby, G. 1978. *Medieval Marriage: Two Models from Twelfth-Century France*. Trans. Elborg Forster. Baltimore: The Johns Hopkins University Press.

———. 1993. *France in the Middle Ages: 987–1460*. Trans. Juliet Vale. Oxford: Blackwell.

Durkheim, E. [1915] 1965. *The Elementary Forms of Religious Life*. Trans. Joseph Ward Swain. New York: The Free Press.

Dyer, J. 2004. The 'Rite Way' of Studying the Old Roman and Gregorian Tradition. Kalamazoo, MI: International Congress of Medieval Studies, Kalamazoo, MI.

Edbury, P. 1999. The Crusader States. *The New Cambridge Medieval History V: c.119–c.1300*. Ed. David Abulafia. Cambridge: Cambridge University Press, 590–606.

Elias, N. 1994. *The Civilizing Process*. Trans. E. Jephcott. Oxford: Blackwell [first published in 1939: *Über den Prozess der Zivilisation*].

———. 1998. Group Charisma and Group Disgrace. Ed. J. Goudsblom and S. Mennell. *The Norbert Elias Reader*. Oxford: Blackwell.

Ehrensberger, H. 1897. *Biblioteca apostolica vaticana: Libri liturgici Bibliothecae apostolicae Vaticanae manuscripti; digessit et recensvit Hugo Ehrensberger*. Friburgi Brisgoviae: Herder.

Ehrle, F. 1890. *Historia bibliothecae romanorum pontificum tum Bonifatianae tum Avenionensis*. Rome: Typis Vaticanis.

Eisenstadt, S. N. 1963. *The Political System of Empires*. New York: Free Press.

———. 1981. Cultural Traditions and Political Dyamics: The Origins and Modes of Ideological Politics. *British Journal of Sociology* 32 (2), 155–81.

———. 1982. The Axial Age: The Emergence of Transcendental Visions and the Rise of Clerics. *European Journal of Sociology* 23 (3), 294–314.

Fassler, M. 1993. *Gothic Song: Victorine Sequences and Augustinian Reform in Twelfth-Century Paris*. Cambridge: Cambridge University Press.

Fassler, M., and Baltzer, R. 2000. *The Divine Office in the Latin Middle Ages: Methodology and Source Studies, Regional Developments, Hagiography*. New York: Oxford University Press.

Franceschini, E. 1965. Origine e stile della bolla "Transiturus." *Aevum* 39, 218–43.

Frere, Walter Howard. 1966. *Antiphonale Sarisburiense*. London: Plainsong and Mediaeval Music Society, 1901–25. Repr. Farnborough, Hants., Eng.: Gregg Press.

————. *Graduale Sarisburiense*. 1966. London: Plainsong and Mediaeval Music Society, 1894. Repr. Farnborough, Hants., Eng.: Gregg Press.

Gallet, R. M. 1946. Bibliographie bij het Festum Corporis Christi. *Studie eucharistice*. Anvers, 415–50.

Gautier de Coinci. 1966–70. *Les miracles de Nostre Dame*. Publies par V. Frédéric Koenig. 4 vols. Geneva: Droz.

Geertz, C. 1973. *The Interpretation of Cultures*. New York: Basic Books.

Gerth, H., and Mills, C. 1946. *From Max Weber*. New York: Oxford University Press.

Giddens, A. 1984. *The Constitution of Society*. Berkeley: University of California Press.

Gierke, O. 1913. *Political Theories of the Middle Ages*. Trans. Frederic William Maitland. Cambridge: Cambridge University Press.

Gilson, E. 1940. *The Mystical Theology of Saint Bernard*. Trans. A. H. C. Downes. London: Sheed and Ward.

Girard, R. 1986. *The Scapegoat*. Trans. Yvonne Freccero. Baltimore: The Johns Hopkins University Press.

Goffman, E. 1959. *The Presentation of Self in Everyday Life*. New York: Doubleday.

————. 1967. *Interaction Ritual*. New York: Pantheon Books.

Goudsblom, J., and Mennell, S. (Eds.). 1998. *The Norbert Elias Reader*. Oxford: Blackwell.

Gratian, *Corpus iuris canonici*. Ed. E. Friedberg. 1959. Leipzig: Bernhard Tauchnitz, 1879–81. Repr. Graz: Akademische Druck- u. Verlagsanstalt.

Grundman, H. 1995. *Religious Movements in the Middle Ages*. Trans. Steven Rowan. Notre Dame: University of Notre Dame Press [first published in 1935: *Religiöse Bewegungen im Mittelalter*].

Gy, P.-M. 1980. L'Office du Corpus Christi et s. Thomas d'Aquin: état d'une recherché. *Revue des sciences philosophiques et théologiques* 64, 491–507.

————. 1982. L'office du Corpus Christi et la théologie des accidents eucharistique. *Revue des sciences philosophiques et théologiques* 66, 81–86.

————. 1999. Office liégeois et office romain de la Fête-Dieu. *Actes du Colloque de Liège*. Vol. 1 of *Fête-Dieu (1246–1996)*. Ed. André Haquin. Louvain-la-Neuve: Institut d'Études Médiévales de l'Université Catholique de Louvain, 117–26.

Hamilton, B. 1999. The Albigensian Crusade and Heresy. *The New Cambridge Medieval History V: c.1198–c.1300*. Ed. David Abulafia. Cambridge: Cambridge University Press, 164–81.

Hankart, R. 1966. L'hospice de Cornillon à Liège. *La Vie wallonne* 40, 5–49, 93–135.

————. 1967. L'hospice de Cornillon à Liège. *La vie wallonne* 41, 79–112.

Henle, R. J. (Ed.). 1993. *St. Thomas Aquinas Summa Theologiae I-II; qq. 90–97: The Treatise On Law*. Notre Dame: University of Notre Dame Press.

Henschenius, G., and Papebrochius, D. (Eds.) 1866. Vita Julianae, *Acta Sanctorum* April t. 1, 435–75.

Hesbert, Rene-Jean. 1963–75. *Corpus antiphonalium officii*. 5 vols. Rome: Herder.

Hood, J. Y. B. 1995. *Aquinas and the Jews*. Philadelphia: University of Pennsylvania Press.

Hugh of Saint-Victor. *De sacramentis corporis et sanguinis Dominici*, Book II, pt. 8, Ch. 11. PL 176, col. 467.

Hughes, A. 1983. Modal Order and Disorder in the Rhymed Office. *Musica disciplina* 37, 29–43.

———. 1988. Chants in the rhymed Office of St. Thomas of Canterbury. *Early Music* 16, 185–201.

———. 1994. *Late Medieval Liturgical Offices*. Toronto: Pontifical Institute of Mediaeval Studies.

Huglo, M. 1971. *Les tonaires: inventaire, analyse, comparaison*. Publications de la Société française de musicologie. 3 ser.;vol. 2. Paris: Société française de musicologie.

Huot, S. 1987. *From Song to Book: The Poetics of Writing in Old French Lyric and Lyrical Narrative Poetry*. Ithaca, NY: Cornell University Press.

James, W. 1982. *The Varieties of Religious Experience*. New York: Penguin.

Jeffery, P. 1992. *Re-Envisioning Past Musical Cultures: Ethnomusicology in the Study of Gregorian Chant*. Chicago: University of Chicago Press.

Johnson, B. 1963. On Church and Sect. *American Sociological Review*. 28 (4), 539–49.

Jones, C. W. 1963. *The Saint Nicholas Liturgy and its Literary Relationships*. Berkeley: University of California Press.

Jonsson, R. 1968. *Historia: Études sur la genèse des offices versifiés*. Stockholm: Almqvist and Wiksell.

Knowles, D. 1962. *The Evolution of Medieval Thought*. New York: Vintage Books.

Kaelber, L. 1998. *Schools of Asceticism: Ideology and Organization in Medieval Religious Communities*. University Park: Pennsylvania State University Press.

Kantorowicz, E. H. 1997. *The King's Two Bodies: A Study in Mediaeval Political Theology*. Princeton: Princeton University Press. [first published in 1957]

Kehrein, J. 1969. *Lateinische Sequenzen des Mittelalters*. Mainz: Florian Kupferberg. Repr. Hildesheim: Georg Olms Verlag.

Kern, A. (Ed.). 1952. Aus alten Handschriften. Die ursprüngliche Fassung des Fronleich-nams- Officiums vom hl. Thomas in der UB Graz gefunden. *Neue Chronik* 7.

———. 1954. Das Offizium *De Corpore Christi* in Österreichen Bibliotheken. *Revue bénédictine* 64, 46–67.

———. 1956. *Die Handschriften der Universitäsbibliothek Graz*. Vienna: Österreichischen Staatsdruckerei.

Kupper, J. L. 1990. Les origins de la collégiale Saint-Martin. *Saint-Martin, Mémoire de Liège*. Liège: Éditions du Perron, 15–22.

———. 1999. La cité de Liège au temps de Julienne de Cornillon. *Actes du Colloque de Liège*. Vol. 1 of *Fête-Dieu (1246–1996)*. Ed. André Haquin. Louvain-la-Neuve: Institut d'Études Médiévales de l'Université Catholique de Louvain, 19–26.

Lambert, G. 1936. Sainte Julienne de Liège dans le Brabant: Considérations sur ses Reliques. *Le Folklore Brabaçon* 16, 100–14.

Lambert, M. 2002. The Cathars. *Medieval Heresy: Popular Movements from the Gregorian Reform to the Reformation.* Ed. M. Lambert. 3rd ed. Oxford, UK, and Malden, MA: Blackwell.

Lambot, C. 1948. 1942. L'Office de la Fête-Dieu: Aperçu nouveaux sur ses origines. *Revue bénédictine* 54, 61–123.

———. La Bulle d'Urban IV à Eve de Saint-Martin sur l'institution de la Fête-Dieu. *Scriptorium* 2, 69–77; repr. in *Revue bénédictine* 79 (1969), 261–70.

Lambot, C., and Fransen, I. 1946. *L'Office de la Fête-Dieu primitive: Textes et mélodies retrouvés.* Maredsous: Editions de Maredsous.

Långfors, A. 1936. Le manusrit 76 G 17 de la Haye et le psautier de Lambert le Bègue. *Romania* 62, 541–43.

Larrington, C. 1999. The Candlemas Vision and Marie D'Oignie's Role in Its Dissemination. *New Trends in Feminine Spirituality: The Holy Women of Liège and Their Impact.* Ed. Juliette Dor, Lesley Johnson, and Jocelyn Wogan-Browne. Turnhout: Brepols, 195–214.

Le Codex 903 de la Bibliothèque Nationale de Paris (XIe siècle): Graduel de Saint-Yrieix. Paléographie musicale XIII. Berne: Editions Herbert Lang et Cie, 1971.

Leff, G. 1967. *Heresy in the Later Middle Ages: The Religion of Heterodoxy to Dissent, c. 1250–1450.* Manchester: Manchester University Press.

Le Goff, J. 1999. Contexte socio-culturel du XIIIe siècle en Europe. *Fête-Dieu (1246–1996)* 2. *Actes du Colloque de Liège.* Ed. André Haquin. Louvain-la-Neuve: Institut d'Études Médiévales de l'Université Catholique de Louvain, 11–18.

Legros, E. 1948. Note bibliographique sur les hymnes liégeoises du moyen âge. *Les dialectes belgo-romans* 7, 171–74.

Leroquais, V. 1934. *Les bréviaires manuscrits des bibliothèques publiques de France.* 6 vols. Paris: Macon, Protat frères, imprimeurs.

Liber responsorialis juxta ritum monasticum. 1895. Solesmis: Typographeo Sancti Petri.

Liber usualis, with Introduction and Rubrics in English. 1963. Tournai: Desclée.

Loader and Alexander. 1985. Max Weber on Churches and Sects in North America: An Alternate Path toward Rationalization. *Sociological Theory* 3 (1), 1–6.

Lombard, Peter. 1971–81. *Sententiarum in IV libris distinctae.* Spicilegium Bonaventurianum, 4–5. 3rd ed. Rome: Grottaferrata, Editiones Collegii S. Bonaventurae ad Claras Aquas.

Macy, G. 1984. *The Theologies of the Eucharist in the Early Scholastic Period. ASstudy of the Salvific Function of the Sacrament According to the Theologians, c. 1080–c. 1220.* Oxford: Clarendon.

———. 1999. *Treasures from the Storehouse: Medieval Religion and the Eucharist.* Collegeville, MN: The Liturgical Press.

Mandonnet, P. (Ed.). 1910. *Des écrits authentiques de saint Thomas d'Aquin.* 2nd ed. Fribourg en suisse: Imprimerie de l'œuvre de Saint-Paul.

Mathiesen, T. J.1983. "The Office of the New Feast of Corpus Christi" in the *Regimen Animarum* at Brigham Young University. *The Journal of Musicology* 2, 13–44.

McDonnell, E. 1954. *The Beguines and Beghards in Medieval Culture with Special Emphasis on the Belgian Scene.* New Brunswick, NJ: Rutgers University Press.

McGinn, B. 1998. *The Flowering of Mysticism: Men and Women in the New Mysticism– 1200–1350.* Vol. 3 of *The Presence of God: A History of Western Christian Mysticism.* New York: Crossroad.

McGrade, M. 1996. Gottschalk of Aachen, The Investiture Controversy, and Music for The Feast of the *Divisio Apostolorum. Journal of the American Musicological Society* 3, 351–408.

Meyer, P. 1873. Rapport sur d'anciennes poésies religieuses en dialecte liégeois. *Revue des Sociétés Savantes des Départements.* 5e ser. 6, 236–49.

———. 1900. Le Psautier de Lambert le Bègue. *Romania* 29, 536–40.

Molesme Breviary (The Summer Season): Troyes, Bibliothèque Municipale MS. 807. 1985. Cistercian Liturgy Series: Number 12. Trappist, KY: Gethsemani Abbey.

Mooney, C. (Ed.).1999. *Gendered Voices: Medieval Saints and their Interpreters.* Philadelphia: University of Pennsylvania Press.

Moore, R. I. 1990. *The Formation of a Persecuting Society: Power and Deviance in Western Europe, 950–1250.* Oxford: Oxford University Press.

———. 1996. Heresy, Repression, and Social Change in the Age of Gregorian Reform. *Christendom and its Discontents: Exclusion, Persecution, and Rebellion, 1000–1500.* Ed. L. Waugh and P. D. Diehl. Cambridge: Cambridge University Press

Morin, G. 1910. L'Office cistercien pour la Fête-Dieu comparé avec celui de saint Thomas D'Aquin. *Revue bénédictine* 27, 236–46.

Mulder-Bakker, A. 2005. *Lives of the Anchoresses: The Rise of the Urban Recluse in Medieval Europe.* Trans. Myra Heerspink Scholz. Philadelphia: University of Pennsylvania Press.

National Library of Wales MS 20541 E: The Penpoint Antiphonal. 1997. Intro. and indices by Owain Tudor Edwards. Ottawa: The Institute of Medieval Music.

Newman, B., (Trans.). 1988. *The Life of Juliana of Mont Cornillon.* Toronto: Peregrina.

———. 1995. *From Virile Woman to WomanChrist: Studies in Medieval Religion and Literature.* Philadelphia: University of Pennsylvania Press.

———. 2003. *God and the Goddesses: Vision, Poetry, and Belief in the Middle Ages.* Philadelphia: University of Pennsylvania Press.

Offertoriale Triplex. 1985. Solesmes: Abbaye Saint-Pierre de Solesmes.

Oliver, J. 1988. *Gothic Manuscript Illumination in the Diocese of Liège (c. 1250–c. 1330).* 2 vols. Leuven: Uitgeverij Peeters.

————. 1999. Image et devotion: le role de l'art dans l'institution de la Fête-Dieu. *Fête-Dieu (1246–1996) 2. Actes du Colloque de Liège*. Ed. André Haquin. Louvain-la-Neuve: Institut d'Études Médiévales de l'Université Catholique de Louvain, 153–72.

Ordo divini officii Beati Jacobi Apostoli Maioris, patroni ecclesie parrochialis eiusdem sancti Hacobi de Carnificeria. 1581. Paris.

Ott, C. 1935. *Offertoriale sive versus offertoriroum.* Tournai: Desclée. Paris, Bibliothèque nationale, Dept. des manuscrits. *Catalogue général des manuscrits latins.* Published under the direction of Ph. Lauer. Vol. 1 (Nos. 1–1438). Paris: Bibliothèque nationale, 1939.

Oxford: Bodleian Library MS. Lat. Liturg. B. 5. 1995. Ed. David Hiley. Publications of Mediaeval Musical Manuscripts No. 20. Ottawa: The Institute of Mediaeval Music.

Parkes, M. B. 1993. *Pause and Effect: An Introduction to the History of Punctuation in the West.* Berkeley: University of California Press.

Paschasius Radbertus, Saint. 1969. *De corpore et sanguine Domini cum appendice Epistola ad Fredugardum.* Ed. Beda Paulus. Turnholt: Brepols.

Patrilogiae cursus completus: series latina. 1841–64. Ed. J.-P. Migne. 221 vols. Paris.

Pennington, K. 1989. Gregory IX, Emperor Frederick II, and the Constitutions of Melfi. *Popes, Teachers, and Canon Law in the Middle Ages.* Ed. J. R. Sweeney and S. Chodorow. Ithaca: Cornell University Press.

Peters, Edward. 1988. *Inquisition.* New York: The Free Press.

Pirenne, H. 1963. *Early Democracies in the Low Countries: Urban Society and Political Conflict in the Middle Ages and the Renaissance.* Trans. J. V. Saunders. New York: Harper and Row [first published in 1915].

————. 1929. *Histoire de Belgique.* Vol. 1, 5th ed. Brussels: Maurice Lamertine.

Planchart, Alejandro Enrique. 1976. Guillaume Dufay's Masses: A View of the Manuscript Tradition. *Dufay Quincentenary Conference: Papers Read at the Dufay Quincentenary Conference, Brooklyn College, Dec. 6–7, 1974.* Dept. of Music, Brooklyn College, 26-53.

Principe, W. H. 1970. *Hugh of Saint-Cher's Theology of the Hypostatic Union.* Toronto: Pontifical Institute of Mediaeval Studies.

Processional monasticum. 1893. Solesmis: Typographeo Sancti Petri.

Quenardel, O. 1997. *La Communion Eucharistique dans "Le Héraut de L'Amour Divin" de Sainte Gertrude D'Helfta.* Abbaye de Bellefontaine: Brepols.

Rahner, H. 1964. *Symbole der Kirche. Die Ekklesiologie der Väter.* Salzberg: Otto Müller Verlag.

Ricketts, P. 2004. A Woman's Poem: The *Priere de Theophile* in Occitan. *L'Offrande du Cœur: Medieval and Early Modern Studies in Honour of Glynnis Cropp.* Ed. Margaret Burrell and Judith Grant. Christchurch, N.Z.: Canterbury University Press in association with Massey University.

Roisin, S. 1947. *L'Hagiographie cistercienne dans le diocèse de Liège.* Louvain: Bibliothèque de L'Université.

Rosenwein, B. 1989. *To Be the Neighbor of Saint Peter: The Social Meaning of Cluny's Property, 909–1049.* Ithaca: Cornell University Press.

Rubin, M. 1991. *Corpus Christi: The Eucharist in Late Medieval Culture.* Cambridge: Cambridge University Press.

Saint Bernard. 1135–53. *On the Song of Songs: Sermones in Cantica Canticorum.* Trans. and ed. an anonymous religious of C.S.M.V. 1952. London: A. R. Mowbray & Co.

Salmon, Pierre. 1968–72. Les manuscrits liturgiques latins de la Bibliothèque vaticane. *Studi e testi,* 251, 253, 260, 267, 270. Vatican City: Biblioteca Apostolica Vaticana:

I.   Psautiers, Antiphonaires, Hymnaires, Collectiares, Bréviaires.

II.   Sacramentaires, Épistoliers, Évangéliaires, Graduels, Missels.

III.   Ordines Romani Pontificaux Rituels, Cérémoniaux

IV.   Les Livres de Lectures de L'Office, Les Livres de L'Office du Chapitre, Les Livres D'Heures

V.   Liste Complémentaire, Tables Générales.

Sanders, J. T. 2000. *Charisma, Converts, Competitors: Societal and Sociologicval Factors in the Success of Early Christianity.* London: SCM Press.

Schoolmeesters, E. 1905. Regestes de Robert de Thourette. *Bulletin de la Societé d'art et d'histoire du diocèse de Liège* 15, 1–126.

———. 1906. Le Diplôme de Hughes de Saint-Cher instituant la Fête-Dieu. *Leodium* 5, 42–43.

———. 1907. Les actes du cardinal-légat Hughes de Saint-Cher en Belgique, durant les années de sa légation, 1251–53. *Leodium* 6, 150–66, 172–76.

Schlager, K-H. 1965. *Thematischer katalog der ältesten Alleluia-Melodien aus Handschriften des 10 und 11 Jahrhunderts.* Munich: Walter Ricke.

Schluchter, W. 1989. *Rationalism, Religion, and Domination: A Weberian Perspective.* Trans. N. Solomon. Berkeley: University of California Press.

———. 1996. *Paradoxes of Modernity: Culture and Conduct in the Theory of Max Weber.* Trans. Neil Solomon. Stanford: Stanford University Press.

Schuermans, H. 1899. *Les reliques de la B. Julienne de Cornillon.* Nivelles: Ch. Guignarde.

———. 1900. *La chasse des XXXVI saints à Anvers—Julienne de Cornillon.* Brussels: Vive de Backer.

———. 1904. *L'Église de l'abbaye de Villers.* Brussels: Van Langendonck.

Seyfarth, J. (Ed.). 1990. *Speculum Virginum* V. Corpus Christianorum, Continuatio Mediavalis V. Turnholt: Brepols.

Silber, I. F. 1995. *Virtuosity, Charisma, and Social Order: A Comparative Sociological Study of Monasticism in Theravada Buddhism and Medieval Catholicism.* Cambridge: Cambridge University Press.

Simenon, G. 1922. *Les Origines de la Fête-Dieu. Revue Ecclésiastique de Liège* 13, 345–58.

Simons, W. 2001. *Cities of Ladies: Beguine Communities in the Medieval Low Countries 1200–1565.* Philadelphia: University of Pennsylvania Press.

Sinclair, K. V. 1964. Un Psautier de Lambert le Bègue à Melbourne. *Australian Journal of French Studies* 1, 5–10.

———. 1965. Les manuscrits du Psautier de Lambert le Bègue. *Romania* 86, 22–47.

Stäblein, Bruno. 1956. *Die Hymnen. Monumenta monodica medii aevi* Bd. 1. Kassel: Bärenreiter.

[Pange lingua . . . gloriosi prelium certaminis (1 Vespers hymn) is item ST 90, but also compare with ST 286 and 336. Sanctorum meritis (Matins hymn) is item ST 43. Eterne rex altissime (Lauds hymn) ST 37, 93.]

Stark, R., and Bainbridge, W. S. 1980. Networks of Faith: Interpersonal Bonds and Recruitment to Sects and Cults. *American Journal of Sociology* 85, 1376–95.

Stevenson, H. 1886–. *Codices Palatini Latini Bibliothecae Vaticanae.* Rome: Typographeo Vaticano.

Stock, B. 1983. *The Implications of Literacy: Written Language and Models of Interpretation in the Eleventh and Twelfth Centuries.* Princeton: Princeton University Press.

———. 1996. *Listening for the Text: On the Uses of the Past.* Philadelphia: University of Pennsylvania Press. [first published Baltimore: Johns Hopkins University Press, 1990]

Swatos, W. 1975. Monopolism, Pluralism, Acceptance, and Rejection: An Integrated Model for Church-Sect Theory. *Review of Religious Research* 15.

———. 1981. Church-Sect and Cult. *Sociological Analysis* 42 (1), 17–26.

———. 1998. Church-Sect Theory. In *Encyclopedia of Religion and Society.* Ed. W. Swatos. Walnut Creek, CA: AltaMira Press, 90–93.

Sweeney, J., and Chodorow, S. (Eds.). 1989. *Popes, Teachers, and Canon Law in the Middle Ages.* Ithaca, NY: Cornell University Press.

Switten, M. 1985. *The Cansos of Raimon de Miraval: A Study of Poems and Melodies.* Cambridge, MA: The Medieval Academy of America.

Symes, C. 2002. The Appearance of Early Vernacular Plays: Forms, Functions, and the Future of Medieval Theater. *Speculum* 77 (3), 778–831.

Szendrei, J. 1998. *Breviarium notatum Strigoniense: saeculi XIII.* Musicalia Danubiana 17. Budapest: Magyar Tudományos Akadémia Zentudonáhyo Intézet.

Thompson, A. 2005. *Cities of God: The Religion of the Italian Commune, 1125–1325.* University Park: Pennsylvania State University Press.

Toch, M. 1999. Welfs, Hohenstaufen and Habsburgs. *The New Cambridge Medieval History V: c.1198–c.1300.* Ed. David Abulafia. Cambridge: Cambridge University Press, 375–403.

Torrell, J.-P. 1996. *Saint Thomas Aquinas.* Trans. Robert Royal. 2 vols. Washington, D.C.: Catholic University of America Press.

Tosti-Croce, M. R. (Ed.). 2000. *Bonifacio VIII e il suo tempo: anno 1300 il primo Giubileo.* Milan: Electa.

Treitler, L. 1974. Homer and Gregory: The Transmission of Epic Poetry and Plainchant. *The Musical Quarterly* 60 (3), 333–72.

Troeltsch, E. 1960. *The Social Teachings of the Christian Churches.* Trans. O. Wyon. New York: Macmillen. [first published in 1931]

Ullman, W. 1965. *The Growth of Papal Government in the Middle Ages.* London: Methuen & Co., Ltd.

Utrecht: Bibliotheek der Rijksuniversiteit, Ms 406 (3.J.7). Intro. Ike de Loos, index by Charles Downey, ed. Ruth Steiner. Ottawa: The Institute of Medieval Music, 1997.

Valkhoff, M. 1936. Le manuscrit 76 G 17 de la Haye et l'ancienne hymne wallonne, *Romania* 62, 17–26.

Van Dijk, S. J. P. 1952. Three Manuscripts of a Liturgical Reform by John Cajetan Orsini (Nicholas III). *Scriptorium* 6, 213–42.

Van Engen, J. (Ed. and trans.). 1988. *Devotio Moderna: Basic Writings.* New York: Paulist Press.

Vauchez, A. 1999. The Church and the Laity. *The New Cambridge Medieval History V: c.1198–c.1300.* Ed. David Abulafia. Cambridge: Cambridge University Press, 182–203.

———. 1997. *Sainthood in the Later Middle Ages.* Trans. J. Birrell. Cambridge: Cambridge University Press.

Vercauteren, F. 1946. *Luttes sociales à Liège.* Brussels: La Renaissance du Livre.

———. 1942. *Verzeichnis der Handschriften im Deutschen Reich.* Teil 2, Band 1. Leipzig: Harrassowitz.

Walters, B. 2002. Women Religious *Virtuosae* from the Middle Ages: A Case Pattern and Analytic Model of Types. *Sociology of Religion* 63 (1), 69–89.

———. 2004. Church-Sect Dynamics and the Feast of Corpus Christi. *Sociology of Religion* 65 (3), 285–301.

———. 2005. *O verge de droiture ki de Jessé eissis* from the Mosan Psalters. *Études de langue et de litterature médiévales offertes à Peter T. Ricketts à l'occasion de son 70ème anniversaire.* Ed. A. Buckley and D. Billy. Turnout: Brepols.

———. 2005. Homo quidam fecit Contra Virgo flagellautur crucianda: Text and Musical Subtext. Kalamazoo, MI: International Congress of Medieval Studies.

Watson, A. 1934. *The Early Iconography of the Tree of Jesse.* London: Oxford University Press.

Watt, J. 1965. *The Theory of Papal Monarchy in the Thirteenth Century.* London: Burns & Oates.

Weber, M. 1978. *Economy and Society.* Trans. Ephraim Fischoff, Hans Gerth, A. M. Henderson, Ferdinand Kolegar, C. Wright Mills, Talcott Parsons, Max Rheinstein, Guenther Roth, Edward Shils, Claus Wittich. Ed. Guenther Roth and Claus Wittich. 2 vols. Berkeley: University of California Press.

Weinstein, D., and Bell, R. M. 1982. *Saints and Soceity: The Two Worlds of Western Christendom, 1000–1700*. Chicago: University of Chicago Press.

Weisheipl, J. A. 1974. *Friar Thomas D'Aquino: His Life, Thought and Works*. Garden City, NY: Doubleday & Co.

Wilms, H., O.P. 1920. *Geschichte der deutschen Dominikanerinnen: 1206–1916*. Dülman, i. W.: A Laumann.

Winston-Allen, A. 1997. *Stories of the Rose: The Making of the Rosary in the Middle Ages*. University Park: Pennsylvania State University Press.

———. 2004. *Convent Chronicles: Women Writing About Women and Reform in the Late Middle Ages* (University Park: Pennsylvania State University Press).

Wogan-Browne, J., and Henneau, M. 1999. Liège, the Medieval "Woman Question," and the Question of Medieval Women. *New Trends in Feminine Spirituality: The Holy Women of Liège and Their Impact*. Ed. Juliette Dor, Lesley Johnson, and Jocelyn Wogan-Browne. Turnhout: Brepols, 1–32.

Woods, I. 1987. "Our Awin Scottis Use": Chant Usage in Medieval Scotland. *Journal of The Royal Musical Association* 112, 21–37.

Wright, N. T. 1992. *The New Testament and the People of God*. Minneapolis, MN: Fortress Press.

———. 1996. *Jesus and the Victory of God*. Minneapolis, MN: Fortress Press.

———. 2003. *The Resurrection of the Son of God*. Minneapolis, MN: Fortress Press.

Yinger, J. 1970. *The Scientific Study of Religion*. New York, NY: MacMillan.

Zawilla, R. J. 1985. *The Biblical Sources of the Historia Corporis Christi Attributed to Thomas Aquinas: A Theological Study to Determine Their Authenticity*. Ph.D. Diss., University of Toronto.

INDEX

18602240R00347

Made in the USA
Middletown, DE
12 March 2015